AN
OPEN
LANGUAGE

Selected Writing on Literacy, Learning, and Opportunity

Mike Rose
University of California, Los Angeles

BEDFORD / ST. MARTIN'S   Boston   •   New York

For Bedford / St. Martin's

Executive Editor: Leasa Burton
Editorial Assistant: Katherine Bouwkamp
Senior Production Supervisor: Dennis Conroy
Project Management: Books By Design, Inc.
Text Design: Anna Palchik
Cover Design: Donna L. Dennison
Composition: Macmillan India, Ltd.
Printing and Binding: RR Donnelley & Sons Company

President: Joan E. Feinberg
Editorial Director: Denise B. Wydra
Editor in Chief: Karen S. Henry
Director of Marketing: Karen Melton Soeltz
Director of Editing, Design, and Production: Marcia Cohen
Manager, Publishing Services: Emily Berleth

Library of Congress Control Number: 2005933169

Manufactured in the United States of America.

1 0 9 8 7 6
f e d c b a

For information, write: Bedford/St. Martin's, 75 Arlington Street, Boston, MA 02116   (617-399-4000)

ISBN: 0-312-44474-5
EAN: 978-0-312-44474-7

ACKNOWLEDGMENTS

Acknowledgments and copyrights are continued at the back of the book on pages 443–45, which constitute an extension of the copyright page.

To the memory of Constance Coiner and Steve Witte,
two fine thinkers and dear friends, and Chip Anderson, my first
boss in higher education, a good man who was full of heart

For all the people at the core of this writing

And, as always, for Tommy and Rosie, in the restaurant and
the garden

CONTENTS

Introduction: Finding the Work

A s anyone who spends an evening with a box of old photographs knows, it can be, by turns, wistful and revealing to go back through your past. For me, the collecting of these pieces of writing, published between 1979 and early 2005, was both. Rereading the early articles called up the books and the work of the time — teaching or running a program — and people, whose letters I read again, bringing back old acquaintances and the ideas that came with them. There are flaws and limits in that early writing, yes, but particular kinds of beginnings as well, and for those I feel grateful.

Selecting the more recent material and laying it alongside the old affords a new reading of the old. I think I understand it better . . . or a little more fully. And I see what carries over to the new, the long-running concerns and commitments.

There is a deep belief in people's ability, and my interest is in language use and thinking, how they are defined and assessed, and how they are opened up or shut down by social circumstances. There is a belief in the richness, the complexity and variability of human behavior, and an attempt to study and represent it through the details of the classroom, the workplace, and the run-of-the-mill events of our daily lives. Hand-in-glove, there is a distrust of abstraction about all this, a skepticism about broad claims and big theories concerning how people — either generically or by group identity — think, or use language, or make meaning of the world.

Over time, I have been driven to understand different disciplines and to forge syntheses: synthesis of practice and theory, of the cognitive and the social, of forms of writing, of research methodologies. Thus, over time, I've paid a lot of attention to methodology itself, to the process of inquiry. I'm aware, looking back over this writing, of some kind of restlessness, at the least a discomfort with the professional confines of disciplinary life — at the same time that I've struggled to learn how a particular discipline works and what it enables one to do.

Many of the pieces in this collection are critical of standard practice and the social order, but it is hope that drives the writing, hope that careful analysis and the right phrasing might in some small, small way open a space to think anew.

Rhetoric and composition was the place where the pieces of my academic life—and of my personal history, too—came together. Since I joined the Great Society program Teacher Corps at age twenty-four, I have earned my living in the classroom: in elementary school; in a range of community and developmental programs to provide job training, a high school equivalency, or preparation for college; in community college; in a university's tutoring center and writing program; and now in a graduate school of education.

My own education plays in and out of this history. The first in my family to go to college, I graduated with a degree in English; went on to graduate study in English; then in psychology; left to join the Teacher Corps, which included courses in education; left school for a long stretch; and, finally, in my early thirties, entered a doctoral program in education. Through a fair amount of this scholastic journey, I was tutoring or teaching while going to school (or in between bouts of schooling), a situation, I believe, that profoundly affected the way I would come to think about writing and research.

Early on—through college and into graduate school—I fantasized about being a public interest lawyer, then an English professor, then a clinical psychologist. It was a restless period, a searching for a disciplinary and occupational home. I liked my studies themselves, however. Reading literary and cultural history or, on quite a different front, learning about experimental psychology held my interest both for the specific knowledge (the books that Melville wrote before *Moby-Dick*; the details of visual perception) and, as I got a little older, for the way researchers went about their inquiries. To this day, I am interested in the modes of investigation and argument of various disciplines. But what spooked me was the professional side of things. The life of the academic—at least as I could see it through the limited experience of my twenties—seemed too narrow and isolating, closed down, an existential end game.

So I left graduate study altogether to work full time in a remarkable program for returning Vietnam War veterans who wanted to go to college, a twelve-week preparatory program in which I taught—learning as I did it—writing, critical reading, and literature. And because small programs like this maximize resources—you end up doing whatever is needed—I also, on a wing and a prayer, did some counseling. The Veteran's Program immersed me in literacy work, particularly with an eye toward getting people ready for college. From there, I was hired to run the Economic Opportunity Program's tutorial center at UCLA, and that job would soon include the development of a curriculum for a summer bridge program. Again, issues of college preparation were in the foreground.

I should add an important historical note here: All of the programs in which I taught or tutored emerged in the 1960s and 1970s—a time of social movements aimed at increasing opportunity and access, and various institutional responses to these demands. Though I didn't at the time know a lot about the national picture—about, for example, the open access programs in New York from which Mina Shaughnessy would do her work—the ideas were in the air, and I was lucky to be participating in some of their local manifestations in Los Angeles County. This early work, as I said, would have a lasting effect on my own teaching and learning.

It was during this tutorial center period that my boss's encouragement and my own recognition of the university's demands for certification led me back to graduate school, this time in education. I was a dutiful but reluctant student, going to class after work, not particularly happy to be back in school—reexperiencing that feeling of social and intellectual isolation, of life passing me by. In my second year, I took a required course from Merle Wittrock, a widely respected member of our faculty who had been one of the key figures in moving educational psychology away from behaviorism and—mirroring a general shift in the behavioral sciences—toward the emerging cognitive perspective. I had taken a year's worth of academic psychology ten years earlier—including courses in perception and learning theory—so I was familiar with the experimental psychologist's take on things. But Wittrock's course caught me up. In the ten years since those earlier courses, the field had changed; psychologists were venturing into the behaviorist's unknowable "black box" of cognition, positing various processes by which the mind functions.

I had been teaching for a decade, trying to help people write more effectively and in forms new to them, for new audiences, helping them read critically, raise questions, probe assumptions. So I had been thinking a lot about thinking, about how it works or seems to go awry, about how to foster particular kinds of inquiry, about how to help people develop the linguistic conventions that foster such inquiry. Wittrock's course covered topics like the mental organization of knowledge, problem solving, the effects of various kinds of instruction on memory and recall, the way we comprehend written texts, and so on. Looking back on his reading list, it's easy to see its limits—and I'll say more about such limits as we move through this book—but, at the time, it seemed as fresh as could be, and it addressed the issues I was wrestling with in my own teaching. Wittrock's course opened up a new way to think about the issues that emerged daily in the writing classroom.

I didn't know much of anything about rhetoric and composition at this point. My introduction would come in 1978 via participation in a writing research group formed by a politically savvy vice chancellor who wanted to reform freshman composition at UCLA. The group had a faculty member from psychology, two from English, and the two of us who directed campus tutorial centers. These people introduced me to the composition literature where I would discover Shaughnessy's *Errors and Expectations*, Bartholomae and Petrosky's attempts to create a rigorous curriculum for underprepared students, Elaine Maimon and her colleagues' writing-across-the curriculum program, the early composing process literature (Janet Emig, Sharon Pianko, Ann Matsuhashi [Feldman], Sondra Perl, Nancy Sommers), and Flower and Hayes's application of cognitive psychology to the study of process.[1] Here were academics who were putting student writing—and writing that was, at times, underdeveloped and error-ridden—at the center of scholarly attention.

Their work was close and detailed; they were respectful of student writing as writing, curious about how it was produced and what it meant.

The other thing that happened during this period was the connection I made with another ed school faculty member, Richard Shavelson, a statistician who was also expert in educational cognitive psychology. The two of us framed my dissertation project, one that would draw on my coursework with Merle Wittrock, the composition literature I was reading, and my years of teaching: a study of the cognitive dimension of writer's block. Shavelson and I couldn't have been more different in academic training and sensibility, but he gave me free rein to draw on my background, and he contributed his knowledge of the cognitive literature and his considerable skill as a research methodologist.

I was lucky in that the distinct strands of my postbaccalaureate life — literary study, psychology, teaching — were brought together in the year-and-a-half that I worked with Shavelson on the dissertation. My unease with single disciplinary perspectives, yet a need to create synthesis, would stay with me to this day — as would the need to ground, to test those perspectives in everyday human behavior.

My early work in composition, then, would emerge out of a mix of the experience of teaching in a range of settings, the concern with preparation and opportunity, and training in both humanities and social science, particularly educational and cognitive psychology.

~

In addition to knowing something about the era — the social climate and social movements and the composition research of the 1970s — it might be helpful to also have a sense of the local context: writing instruction at UCLA.

Freshman composition was taught out of the English Department. It had a literary orientation, and the textbooks used were traditional rhetorics and readers. Though the department had several faculty who either provided supervision for the course or occasionally taught a class in stylistics or pedagogy, and though there were certainly graduate students who worked hard at their teaching, freshman composition was a pretty marginal enterprise. Separate from composition was the remedial English course (called Subject A at the University of California), which was run out of a different building and was even more marginal. Labeled "Bonehead English" by more than a few, the Subject A curriculum was typical for the time: workbooks, grammar exercises, short essays. Again, some dedicated and skillful people worked in that program, but the curriculum that was provided to them was limited and uninspiring fare.

I don't think it's unfair to say that the teaching of freshman writing at UCLA was a fairly closed system. (There were, at the time, no expository writing courses to speak of beyond the freshman level.) Traditional curricula were in place for both the standard and remedial courses, and the administrative goal for the program was effective management more than curricular innovation. This equilibrium was reinforced by the low status of composition and by assumptions about the nature of error and the appropriate remedies for it. Thus, there were no good reasons to disturb the steady state.

That's why what change did come to UCLA—and as we move into the 1980s, there was significant change—came from outside of the formal structure of the English Department. One source, as I mentioned, was the EOP Tutorial Center, as we created a cross-disciplinary summer bridge program, and, later, a full freshman-year program. Both were built on early writing-across-the-curriculum models and on work in applied linguistics—writing for special (or academic) purposes curricula that sought to make explicit the features and conventions of disciplinary prose. A second element was the aforementioned interdisciplinary Writing Research Project, which produced several volumes of working papers that provided early theoretical and pedagogical challenges to business as usual. But the most significant administrative force for change was the creation (by another reform-minded vice chancellor) of UCLA Writing Programs, which brought together both remedial and freshman English and generated a slew of new courses as well. Writing Programs was aligned to English but originally had its own budget and reporting line. (For an account of the founding of the program, see Richard A. Lanham, *Literacy and the Survival of Humanism*, Chapter 9.) I was moved from the tutorial center to Writing Programs, and though the Writing Research Project would be disbanded, some of its participants, and many of its ideas, would transfer to Writing Programs as well.

My participation in these various programs and projects taught me a lot, and one of the big lessons was to witness up close the organizational and political dynamics that shape curriculum and instruction. The traditions, personal histories, and departmental agendas at UCLA created many obstacles but also some opportunities. It certainly made me appreciate the importance of institutional context in trying to change what goes on in the classroom. Analyzing larger institutional and social contexts would later become important to my work, and it was here that I began to understand something about those contexts.

～

With this brief history in mind, I want to add a bit more about the importance of writing-across-the-curriculum and cognitive psychology in the work I was doing.

I think it's fair to say that my teaching in the Veteran's Program had a writing-across-the-curriculum spirit to it; at the least, it was loosely cross-disciplinary. The significant challenges facing the vets—many of whom had poor academic records—as they began the move to college set me in WAC mode. I thought back over my own variety of courses in the humanities and social sciences, and I surveyed the lower-division curriculum at several local colleges. What kinds of writing might the vets have to do? What kinds of reading? What were the intellectual strategies they would need to master?

This orientation stayed with me as I moved to the EOP tutoring center. It made sense there, given our goal of improving the quality of our students' education and increasing retention. When the call came from the administrators over us to develop a summer bridge program, the director of EOP, myself, and several talented tutors set out to create a program that linked writing courses to introductory courses in psychology, political science, and history.

During this time—the mid- and late 1970s—articles were appearing in journals aimed at the teaching of subject areas (from mathematics to social studies) advocating the use of writing to aid learning.[2] Elaine Maimon and her colleagues at Beaver College had been exporting their writing-across-the-curriculum model, and several colleagues in California were attempting it. And there was a growing theoretical and methodological literature exploring the role of writing in the construction of disciplinary knowledge—Bruno Latour and Steve Woolgar's *Laboratory Life*, for example, was published in 1979. This was the emerging intellectual context in which we continued to develop our preparatory programs, applying these ideas down the curricular ladder, so to speak, finding ways to realize them in the basic writing classroom.

As many of the readers of this book know from experience, running a tutoring or learning center or a writing program is difficult work. In addition to all the administrative routines and crises, there is often the need to defend your practice, even the very purpose of your program. And you have to make these defenses in an environment shot through with assumptions about writing, learning, and students' rights and needs that you can't abide. As we heard about other programs doing something similar to what we were doing, we reached out. I have a folder of correspondence from that time, and it reminds me of both the hunger for like minds and the shot of encouragement when an idea was exchanged, or an article or outline of curriculum, or an invitation to visit. All this lent support and direction to our projects and—how to say it?—a sense of weight, of larger meaning that helped embolden our own local efforts. It's no wonder that once technology enabled it, a robust writing program administrators network would evolve.

Now to cognitive psychology.

Thinking back on my early exposure to the cognitive literature, looking through old files and books, I remember how compelling it was to me. I read everything I could find, one source leading to another, many of them not of much use, too tied to a narrow laboratory paradigm or focused on tasks too atomistic and discrete for my interests, like letter recognition. There was also fascinating stuff of historical importance—like the experiments of the German gestalt psychologists—though not directly relevant to my concerns. But while much of it didn't help in a specific way, it did provide a frame of mind, a line of sight, and—I loved this about it—it contained democratic possibilities. Student writing that was not proficient could be analyzed in ways that didn't imply things about the intelligence of the writer (recall the appellation of "bonehead" to the remedial course). Such writing, even the most flawed, made sense, was supported by explainable—if counterproductive or "buggy"—rules and strategies, and thus was open to instruction that didn't carry with it a judgment of intellectual or moral failure.

Over my ten years of teaching and tutoring—and simply reflecting on my own personal background—I certainly saw a range of social and economic reasons to account for the difficulties people were having with writing: poor education related to poverty, race, and region; norms of domesticity that restricted what girls could accomplish through schooling; inept or insensitive literacy instruction. Over the years, I had a lot of discussions with students about such issues and used these discussions to pedagogical ends. What cognitive psychology afforded me was a further set of tools with which to understand, describe, and intervene in the counterproductive beliefs, rules, and strategies that my students had, some of which emerged from their difficult school histories. The cognitive perspective provided a lens and a vocabulary, enabling me to approach some of what I saw in student papers a little more systematically and precisely. It also freed me from focusing only on the students' texts themselves, on errors on a page, and provided a means to consider the interaction of person and paper—an important move for someone with a traditional literary studies background. To be sure, others at this time *were* able to draw on literary studies to arrive at dynamic readings of students' texts. Mina Shaughnessy, trained in Milton, certainly did. And David Bartholomae and later Mariolina Salvatori at Pitt would apply newer theories of reading and discourse to powerful ends.[3] But for me, at my time and place, cognitive psychology served this function.

And it provided something else: a methodology, a systematic approach to human behavior—writing and reading in particular—that brought with it cautions, limits, a set of constraints on overgeneralization. I had been troubled by the tendency I found in some areas of the humanities and social sciences to make sweeping statements about behavior, intelligence, and language—particularly where poor people were concerned. I'm not sure exactly when all this hit me, though I have a class paper I wrote in 1978 using the work of sociolinguist William Labov to criticize Basil Bernstein's theory about the restricted linguistic codes of the working class. Now, certainly, generalizations can be made about human behavior: We make meaning, use language, classify objects and events (though in different ways), are oriented toward the social, and so on. And tendencies within groups can be identified, identified by race or ethnicity, by gender, by social class, by region. But they are *tendencies*, and they are complex in origin and manifestation.

People working in cognitive psychology are as vulnerable as anyone to the grand generalization. But for me it provided a powerful way to criticize the pronouncements about student writing and intelligence that floated like spores throughout the university. This critical perspective would carry through into later essays, "The Language of Exclusion" and "Narrowing the Mind and Page," which I'll present and discuss in Part Three.

I mentioned the "closed system" of writing instruction at UCLA. The curriculum was set, as were the assumptions about student writing. Writing across the curriculum and cognitive psychology offered a way in, a set of new arguments, fresh conceptual air in a stale classroom. They provided a vocabulary and some curricular models that could function as a wedge in administrative deliberations about curriculum, course credit, finance, and program development. No small thing circa 1980 at a place like UCLA.

~

The material I have collected in this book extends from my early work at UCLA to my current research and writing. The collection is split into six sections; they are thematic and roughly chronological. There is overlap, however, because the themes, the big passions and problems of a research and writing life, are not neatly separable. We keep revisiting the issues that matter to us, in new institutional and social settings, farther along the path of our own development, influenced, one hopes, by experience and by the fresh ideas emerging around us.

One set of topics that keeps reappearing is the duet of research methodology and written genre. I try to describe the methods and forms that I was using at a particular time and the justifications for them — given the issue I was trying to understand and render. There is a close relationship between what I wanted to know — the history behind institutional discourse about writing, for example, or the thought that enables physical work — and the methods I chose and combined to try to know it. I can see, over time, a push away from analysis of the individual and toward analysis of broader social contexts, yet the desire to not lose the individual in a flux of social forces. This tension also contributes to a mixing of methods and genres.

Part One, "The Cognition of Composing," covers my early empirical work on the composing process, which was developed out of the methods and models afforded by cognitive psychology. My contribution to the composing process literature (a literature that pretty much began with Janet Emig's 1971 monograph, *The Composing Processes of Twelfth Graders*) was to focus on writer's block and other disruptions in the composing process. But the cognitive orientation would prove useful to me beyond these studies, helping me to develop a research methodology and to examine textbooks (several articles in that vein are included here), pedagogy, program development, learning and intelligence, and institutional and social policy. I would return to these topics throughout my work.

Part Two, "Teaching Academic Writing," begins with the cross-disciplinary curriculum development I was doing in special preparatory programs, a melding of college access efforts and writing-across-the-curriculum. It then moves to a critique of the typical remedial writing courses of the day (which, unfortunately, are still with us) and, building from that critique, to the development of a freshman composition curriculum. It ends with a call to teach at the graduate level writing for scholarly and more general audiences. All of this work is built from cognitive theory, writing-across-the-curriculum, and analyses of disciplinary and institutional writing demands. Each of these provides a perspective that, to this day, informs what I do in the classroom.

The four articles collected in Part Three, "Integrating the Cognitive and the Social: Critical Perspectives on Writing Instruction," illustrate a broadening of my research methodology and a continued attempt to fuse cognitive and social modes of analysis. There are several overlapping concerns in these pieces: the institutional and professional language used to depict the teaching of writing; the effect this language can have on practice; and the misperceptions of students' abilities that can result from this language and practice. These articles, each in their way, helped me forward — and better articulate — my understanding of how embedded even the solitary tutorial session is in a matrix of much broader routines, vocabularies, beliefs, and ideas.

Part Four, "School and Society," provides excerpts from *Lives on the Boundary* and *Possible Lives*, two books that draw on my scholarly work but are written for a more general audience. In both books, I combine narrative and analysis in an attempt to foster a shift in perception about two current issues in education: underpreparation and the viability of public schooling. Genre, style, and method really do blend here in the push to not only figure something out but also to render it accurately and accessibly. Again, the problems — both of inquiry and audience — drove the solutions of method and form that I tried to fashion.

The material reprinted in Part Five, "The Mind at Work: Researching the Everyday," is informed by the cognitive and social perspectives and methods I have been acquiring since my early work. Here, though, the focus is on everyday labor, blue-collar and service occupations more so than on language and literacy. But the intention is the same in all cases: to spark through the detail of life lived in classrooms or the workplace a reconsideration of common assumptions and discourse about intelligence and ability.

Part Six, "Public Writing: Style and Persuasion," presents a selection of opinion and commentary pieces on the issues and topics represented in the previous sections: education policy, underpreparation, work and intelligence, and so on. Pieces like these provide an opportunity to bring research and practice into the public sphere, both to test and refine them and to seek broader influence. Perhaps such work also sets the stage for us to rethink the borders — partly of our own construction — between scholarship and public life, making the borders porous, defining the scholarly and the public in more generative ways.

～

There are so many people who make a book possible, from its origins in informal conversation to the nuts and bolts of production.

I am grateful to Joan Feinberg, president of Bedford/St. Martin's, for encouraging this project and for her many suggestions as to how to make it better. And I have been blessed once again with an editor of exceptional talent: Leasa Burton. Leasa was involved from the beginning, and her keen intelligence is evident throughout the book.

I benefited immensely from the reviews of six experts in rhetoric and composition: David Bartholomae, Ellen Cushman, Joseph Harris, Glynda Hull, Min-Zhan Lu, and Michael Palmquist. I thank them for their careful reading and for their support of the project.

In the winter of 2005, Julie Lindquist used an earlier version of this collection in her graduate survey of rhetoric and composition studies at Michigan State University. The feedback that she and the class provided helped a great deal as I wrote the final draft. Special thanks to Michele Fero, Jim Fredrickson, Troy Hicks, Dundee Lackey, and Kendra Matko for their thoughtful written comments.

Along the way, I sought counsel from a number of scholars who were generous with their time and gracious with their advice. Thanks to Linda Adler-Kassner, Arif Amlani, Deborah Appleman, Jennifer Beech, Linda Flower, Kris Gutierrez, Susan Jarrett, Gesa Kirsch, Andrea Lunsford, Richard Miller, Beverly Moss, Irvin Peckham, Christopher Thaiss, John Trimbur, and Terry Myers Zawacki.

Sara Jameson, a student at Oregon State University, was completing a master's thesis on my work at about the time I was beginning this book. Her thesis enabled me to read many of the pieces included here through another person's eyes. Thank you, Sara.

Octavio Estrella, Maija Burnett, Kewal Lalwani, and, at the end, Nicole Gerardi ran down sources and typed and retyped the manuscript. They saved the day. Back at Bedford/St. Martin's, Katherine Bouwkamp moved things forward with efficiency and good cheer. I also want to acknowledge Donna Dennison and Kim Cevoli for designing the terrific cover.

During production Emily Berleth coordinated the project, and Nancy Benjamin and copyeditor Debbie Prato skillfully turned this pile of paper into a book.

Finally, let me acknowledge again the hundreds and hundreds of people who contributed to the selections included in *An Open Language*. Collecting and rereading this work called up many memories of conversations and correspondence that became an integral part of the writing.

NOTES

Note to Readers: Footnotes in introductory sections refer to the bibliography at the end of the book.

[1]See, for example, Shaughnessy (1977). On Bartholomae and Petrosky, see Bartholomae (1979); Maimon (1978); Emig (1971); Pianko (1977); Matsuhashi (1979); Perl (1978); Sommers (1978); and Flower and Hayes (1979).

[2]See, for example, Beyer (1979) and Giroux (1978).

[3]See, for example, Shaughnessy (1977); Bartholomae (1980); Salvatori (1983).

PART ONE

The Cognition of Composing, 1980–1985

Introduction to Part One

My understanding and use of the cognitive perspective would change over the years, but as I noted in the Introduction, I always found in it democratic possibility and a critical vocabulary. There are many fields within cognitive psychology, and there are many cognitively oriented sciences and social sciences. The interested reader can consult Howard Gardner's *The Mind's New Science* for a somewhat dated but still useful overview and Michael Cole's *Cultural Psychology* for a discussion of cognition and culture.

I would like to do two quick things in this introduction: explain the use of cognitive psychology in my early research, and situate that use in some current conversations in composition studies.

Cognitive psychology has been criticized in our field for some time now. The essence of the criticism is that cognitive psychology, as do other modernist projects, attempts to rationalize human behavior and, through rationalization, subject it to technical control. There is also the issue that through its focus on individual cognition, it excludes from analysis history and social context. Fair enough. Both are legitimate concerns, and, in fact, over the last two decades, people within the cognitive sciences as well as those in other disciplines have attempted to respond to them. I don't intend this preface to be a defense of the whole cognitive enterprise, but I would like to briefly address several issues of importance to the composition community and explain further what I saw in cognitive psychology and why and how I used it.

First, let me address the link between rationalizing human behavior and controlling it. I'm not sure that an attempt to describe human behavior with cognitive constructs necessarily leads to the diminishment or domination of the person. In addition to the way the cognitive constructs are articulated and theorized, time, place, use, and motive are also critical variables here. Noam Chomsky's highly formalized representation of grammar, for example, could be used to argue for the universality of linguistic sophistication—an equalizing move. Conversely, a social theory of learning or writing could have embedded in it biases about the ability and behavior of particular social groups, and narrative, metaphor, or myth—often contrasted with cognitive representations—can be used to horrific ends, as evidenced in state justifications of genocide. Moral principle is not by necessity aligned with a specific model or method; context matters.

The critique of the individual focus of traditional cognitive psychology has merit, though there can be analytic or pedagogical value in focusing on the individual. That said, it is important to note that some cognitive work has developed to include, in its way, consideration of social context and history. In my own work, the attempt to move beyond the individual began soon after my first studies of writer's block, and the cognitive perspective would become matched with other disciplinary lenses in my research and writing.

Finally, let me say something about the model of mind that underlies traditional cognitive psychology. The standard analogy is that the human mind works somewhat like an information-processing computer. This comparison — and in some strong versions, it was more than a metaphor — understandably drives humanists nuts. The analogy appeared to me at the time to be interesting but, ultimately, inadequate — too mechanistic and too limited in explanatory power, a point made powerfully by Hubert Dreyfus in *What Computers Can't Do*. Yet, as I noted earlier, some of the constructs of cognitive psychology seemed to have promise as a provisional vocabulary, as a set of terms (rule, plan, strategy) that helped me specify the analysis of writing, particularly the learning and teaching of the conventions of academic writing. This issue of specificity was a big one for me, because a good deal of the writing instruction I had encountered up to that point was either focused on grammar, error, and text editing devoid of consideration of the writer's thought and intention or was a general, even vague, discussion of style. (Some of this is addressed in the two upcoming articles on composition textbooks.) Still, the question remains: Doesn't the underlying computer model of mind render bankrupt the constructs I used? I wonder, though, if there is a philosophically legitimate way out of this dilemma, one I can articulate now better than I could have then. I think it is possible to accept concepts operating at one level of analysis while remaining agnostic about ultimate causal structures and processes. That is, there can be analytic and descriptive benefit to a term like *rule* or *plan* — I certainly thought they mapped onto what I saw in the classroom — without having to commit to a particular foundational model of the computer as their source or as determining the precise structure of their operation. In fact, to the degree that a particular theorist held fast to computer-like formalisms, I found myself needing to qualify and modify the concepts, as you'll see in the upcoming articles.

In any event, the reader can decide how legitimate this line of argument is and how useful the cognitive perspective becomes.

1

Rigid Rules, Inflexible Plans, and the Stifling of Language: A Cognitivist Analysis of Writer's Block

1980

AUTHOR'S NOTE: This article presents the preliminary study I did that would lead to my dissertation: a study of ten students, five of whom reported difficulty composing and five of whom found it relatively easy. Relying on a cognitive framework, I interviewed them, looked at drafts of papers written for their classes, and later provided tutoring.

Rereading the article twenty-five years later, I certainly see its flaws. It truly is preliminary in its method, pretty informal. Also, it is dated in terms of the literature and concepts it draws on. I was trying to adapt the material I was reading, and some elements of that adaptation seem forced to me now. Furthermore, much of the literature itself—not atypical of the cognitive literature of the time—is, as I just noted, limited by its commitment to mechanical models. Finally, and I suppose this is inevitable, there is some phrasing that I wouldn't use today: phrasing that is sexist (the generic "man"), overly clinical ("dysfunctional"), of its time ("third-world students"), or unsupple—for example, the blocker/non-blocker dichotomy rather than a more fluid continuum.

But I do like the rendering of the students' writing, the way the cognitive framework aids in detailing and conceptualizing aspects of their composing processes—and with an eye toward intervention. I still find it helpful in teaching and tutoring to think out loud with students about the rules they follow and the way they're understood (e.g., as heuristic or as algorithmic), the strategies they use, the assumptions they hold about writing. For me the cognitive framework provided a way to think carefully and closely about the process of getting words onto paper.

Ruth will labor over the first paragraph of an essay for hours. She'll write a sentence, then erase it. Try another, then scratch part of it out. Finally, as the evening winds on toward ten o'clock and Ruth, anxious about tomorrow's deadline, begins to wind into herself, she'll compose that first paragraph only to sit back and level her favorite exasperated interdiction at herself and her page: "No. You can't say that. You'll bore them to death."

From *College Composition and Communication* 31.4 (December 1980): 389–401.

Ruth is one of ten UCLA undergraduates with whom I discussed writer's block, that frustrating, self-defeating inability to generate the next line, the right phrase, the sentence that will release the flow of words once again. These ten people represented a fair cross-section of the UCLA student community: lower-middle-class to upper-middle-class backgrounds and high schools, third-world and Caucasian origins, biology to fine arts majors, C+ to A– grade point averages, enthusiastic to blasé attitudes toward school. They were set off from the community by the twin facts that all ten could write competently, and all were currently enrolled in at least one course that required a significant amount of writing. They were set off among themselves by the fact that five of them wrote with relative to enviable ease while the other five experienced moderate to nearly immobilizing writer's block. This blocking usually resulted in rushed, often late papers and resultant grades that did not truly reflect these students' writing ability. And then, of course, there were other less measurable but probably more serious results: a growing distrust of their abilities and an aversion toward the composing process itself.

What separated the five students who blocked from those who didn't? It wasn't skill; that was held fairly constant. The answer could have rested in the emotional realm—anxiety, fear of evaluation, insecurity, etc. Or perhaps blocking in some way resulted from variation in cognitive style. Perhaps, too, blocking originated in and typified a melding of emotion and cognition not unlike the relationship posited by Shapiro between neurotic feeling and neurotic thinking.[1] Each of these was possible. Extended clinical interviews and testing could have teased out the answer. But there was one answer that surfaced readily in brief explorations of these students' writing processes. It was not profoundly emotional, nor was it embedded in that still unclear construct of cognitive style. It was constant, surprising, almost amusing if its results weren't so troublesome, and, in the final analysis, obvious: the five students who experienced blocking were all operating either with writing rules or with planning strategies that impeded rather than enhanced the composing process. The five students who were not hampered by writer's block also utilized rules, but they were less rigid ones, and thus more appropriate to a complex process like writing. Also, the plans these non-blockers brought to the writing process were more functional, more flexible, more open to information from the outside.

These observations are the result of one to three interviews with each student. I used recent notes, drafts, and finished compositions to direct and hone my questions. This procedure is admittedly non-experimental, certainly more clinical than scientific; still, it did lead to several inferences that lay the foundation for future, more rigorous investigation: (a) composing is a highly complex problem-solving process[2] and (b) certain disruptions of that process can be explained with cognitive psychology's problem-solving framework. Such investigation might include a study using "stimulated recall" techniques to validate or disconfirm these hunches. In such a study, blockers and non-blockers would write essays. Their activity would be videotaped and, immediately after writing, they would be shown their respective tapes and questioned about the rules, plans, and beliefs operating in their writing behavior. This procedure would bring us close to the composing process (the writers' recall is stimulated by their viewing the tape), yet would not interfere with actual composing.

In the next section I will introduce several key concepts in the problem-solving literature. In section three I will let the students speak for themselves. Fourth, I will offer a cognitivist analysis of blockers' and non-blockers' grace or torpor. I will close with a brief note on treatment.

SELECTED CONCEPTS IN PROBLEM SOLVING: RULES AND PLANS

As diverse as theories of problem solving are, they share certain basic assumptions and characteristics. Each posits an *introductory period* during which a problem is presented, and all theorists, from Behaviorist to Gestalt to Information Processing, admit that certain aspects, stimuli, or "functions" of the problem must become or be made salient and attended to in certain ways if successful problem-solving processes are to be engaged. Theorists also believe that some conflict, some stress, some gap in information in these perceived "aspects" seems to trigger problem-solving behavior. Next comes a *processing period*, and for all the variance of opinion about this critical stage, theorists recognize the necessity of its existence—recognize that man, at the least, somehow "weighs" possible solutions as they are stumbled upon and, at the most, goes through an elaborate and sophisticated information-processing routine to achieve problem solution. Furthermore, theorists believe—to varying degrees—that past learning and the particular "set," direction, or orientation that the problem solver takes in dealing with past experience and present stimuli have critical bearing on the efficacy of solution. Finally, all theorists admit to a *solution period*, an end-state of the process where "stress" and "search" terminate, an answer is attained, and a sense of completion or "closure" is experienced.

These are the gross similarities, and the framework they offer will be useful in understanding the problem-solving behavior of the students discussed in this paper. But since this paper is primarily concerned with the second stage of problem-solving operations, it would be most useful to focus this introduction on two critical constructs in the processing period: rules and plans.

Rules

Robert M. Gagné defines "rule" as "an inferred capability that enables the individual to respond to a class of stimulus situations with a class of performances."[3] Rules can be learned directly[4] or by inference through experience.[5] But, in either case, most problem-solving theorists would affirm Gagné's dictum that "rules are probably the major organizing factor, and quite possibly the primary one, in intellectual functioning."[6] As Gagné implies, we wouldn't be able to function without rules; they guide response to the myriad stimuli that confront us daily, and might even be the central element in complex problem-solving behavior.

Dunker, Polya, and Miller, Galanter, and Pribram offer a very useful distinction between two general kinds of rules: algorithms and heuristics.[7] Algorithms are precise rules that will always result in a specific answer if applied to an appropriate problem. Most mathematical rules, for example, are algorithms. Functions are constant (e.g., pi), procedures are routine (squaring the radius), and outcomes are completely predictable. However, few day-to-day situations are mathematically circumscribed enough to warrant the application of algorithms. Most often we function with the aid of fairly general heuristics or "rules of thumb," guidelines that allow varying degrees of flexibility when approaching problems. Rather than operating with algorithmic precision and certainty, we search, critically, through alternatives, using our heuristic as a divining rod—"if a math problem stumps you, try working backwards to solution"; "if the car won't start, check x, y, or z," and so forth. Heuristics won't allow the precision or the certitude afforded by algorithmic operations; heuristics can even be so "loose" as to be vague. But in a world where tasks and problems are rarely mathematically precise, heuristic rules become the most appropriate, the most functional rules available to us: "a heuristic does not guarantee the optimal solution or, indeed, any solution at all; rather, heuristics offer solutions that are good enough most of the time."[8]

Plans

People don't proceed through problem situations, in or out of a laboratory, without some set of internalized instructions to the self, some program, some course of action that, even roughly, takes goals and possible paths to that goal into consideration. Miller, Galanter, and Pribram have referred to this course of action as a plan: "A plan is any hierarchical process in the organism that can control the order in which a sequence of operations is to be performed" (p. 16). They name the fundamental plan in human problem-solving behavior the TOTE, with the initial T representing a *test* that matches a possible solution against the perceived end-goal of problem completion. O represents the clearance to *operate* if the comparison between solution and goal indicates that the solution is a sensible one. The second T represents a further, post-operation, *test* or comparison of solution with goal, and if the two mesh and problem solution is at hand the person *exits* (E) from problem-solving behavior. If the second test presents further discordance between solution and goal, a further solution is attempted in TOTE-fashion. Such plans can be both long-term and global and, as problem solving is underway, short-term and immediate.[9] Though the mechanicality of this information-processing model renders it simplistic and, possibly, unreal, the central notion of a plan and an operating procedure is an important one in problem-solving theory; it at least attempts to metaphorically explain what earlier cognitive psychologists could not—the mental procedures underlying problem-solving behavior.

Before concluding this section, a distinction between heuristic rules and plans should be attempted; it is a distinction often blurred in the literature, blurred because, after all, we are very much in the area of gestating theory and preliminary models. Heuristic rules seem to function with the flexibility of plans. Is, for example, "If the car won't start, try x, y, or z" a heuristic or a plan? It could be either, though two qualifications will mark it as heuristic rather than plan. (A) Plans subsume and sequence heuristic and algorithmic rules. Rules are usually "smaller," more discrete cognitive capabilities; plans can become quite large and complex, composed of a series of ordered algorithms, heuristics, and further planning "sub-routines." (B) Plans, as was mentioned earlier, include criteria to determine successful goal-attainment and, as well, include "feedback" processes — ways to incorporate and use information gained from "tests" of potential solutions against desired goals.

One other distinction should be made: that is, between "set" and plan. Set, also called "determining tendency" or "readiness,"[10] refers to the fact that people often approach problems with habitual ways of reacting, a predisposition, a tendency to perceive or function in one way rather than another. Set, which can be established through instructions or, consciously or unconsciously, through experience, can assist performance if it is appropriate to a specific problem,[11] but much of the literature on set has shown its rigidifying, dysfunctional effects.[12] Set differs from plan in that set represents a limiting and narrowing of response alternatives with no inherent process to shift alternatives. It is a kind of cognitive habit that can limit perception, not a course of action with multiple paths that directs and sequences response possibilities.

~

The constructs of rules and plans advance the understanding of problem solving beyond that possible with earlier, less developed formulations. Still, critical problems remain. Though mathematical and computer models move one toward more complex (and thus more real) problems than the earlier research, they are still too neat, too rigidly sequenced to approximate the stunning complexity of day-to-day (not to mention highly creative) problem-solving behavior. Also, information-processing models of problem-solving are built on logic theorems, chess strategies, and simple planning tasks. Even Gagné seems to feel more comfortable with illustrations from mathematics and science rather than with social science and humanities problems. So although these complex models and constructs tell us a good deal about problem-solving behavior, they are still laboratory simulations, still invoked from the outside rather than self-generated, and still founded on the mathematico-logical.

Two Carnegie-Mellon researchers, however, have recently extended the above into a truly real, amorphous, unmathematical problem-solving process — writing. Relying on protocol analysis (thinking aloud while solving problems), Linda Flower and John Hayes have attempted to tease out the role of heuristic rules and plans in writing behavior.[13] Their research pushes problem-solving investigations to the real and complex and pushes, from the other end, the often mysterious process of writing toward the explainable. The latter is important, for at least since Plotinus many have viewed the composing process as unexplainable, inspired, infused with the transcendent. But Flower and Hayes are beginning, anyway, to show how writing generates from a problem-solving process with rich heuristic rules and plans of its own. They show, as well, how many writing problems arise from a paucity of heuristics and suggest an intervention that provides such rules.

This paper, too, treats writing as a problem-solving process, focusing, however, on what happens when the process dead-ends in writer's block. It will further suggest that, as opposed to Flower and Hayes' students who need more rules and plans, blockers may well be stymied by possessing rigid or inappropriate rules, or inflexible or confused plans. Ironically enough, these are occasionally instilled by the composition teacher or gleaned from the writing textbook.

"Always Grab Your Audience" — The Blockers

In high school, *Ruth* was told and told again that a good essay always grabs a reader's attention immediately. Until you can make your essay do that, her teachers and textbooks putatively declaimed, there is no need to go on. For Ruth, this means that beginning bland and seeing what emerges as one generates prose is unacceptable. The beginning is everything. And what exactly is the audience seeking that reads this beginning? The rule, or Ruth's use of it, doesn't provide for such investigation. She has an edict with no determiners. Ruth operates with another rule that restricts her productions as well: if sentences aren't grammatically "correct," they aren't useful. This keeps Ruth from toying with ideas on paper, from the kind of linguistic play that often frees up the flow of prose. These two rules converge in a way that pretty effectively restricts Ruth's composing process.

The first two papers I received from *Laurel* were weeks overdue. Sections of them were well written; there were even moments of stylistic flair. But the papers were late and, overall, the prose seemed rushed. Furthermore, one paper included a paragraph on an issue that was never mentioned in the topic paragraph. This was the kind of mistake that someone with Laurel's apparent ability doesn't make. I asked her about this irrelevant passage. She knew very well that it didn't fit, but believed she had to include it to round out the paper. "You must always make three or more points in an essay. If the essay has less, then it's not strong." Laurel had been taught this rule both in high school and in her first college English class; no wonder, then, that she accepted its validity.

As opposed to Laurel, *Martha* possesses a whole arsenal of plans and rules with which to approach a humanities writing assignment, and, considering her background in biology, I wonder how many of them were formed out of the assumptions and procedures endemic to the physical sciences.[14] Martha will not put pen to first draft until she has spent up to two days generating an outline of remarkable complexity. I saw one of these outlines and it looked more like a diagram of protein synthesis or DNA structure than the time-worn pattern offered in composition textbooks. I must admit I was intrigued by the aura of process (vs. the static appearance of essay outlines) such diagrams offer, but for Martha these "outlines" only led to self-defeat: the outline would become so complex that all of its elements could never be included in a short essay. In other words, her plan locked her into the first stage of the composing process. Martha would struggle with the conversion of her outline into prose only to scrap the whole venture when deadlines passed and a paper had to be rushed together.

Martha's "rage for order" extends beyond the outlining process. She also believes that elements of a story or poem must evince a fairly linear structure and thematic clarity, or — perhaps bringing us closer to the issue — that analysis of a story or poem must provide the linearity or clarity that seems to be absent in the text. Martha, therefore, will bend the logic of her analysis to reason ambiguity out of existence. When I asked her about a strained paragraph in her paper on Camus' "The Guest," she said, "I didn't want to admit that it [the story's conclusion] was just hanging. I tried to force it into meaning."

Martha uses another rule, one that is not only problematical in itself, but one that often clashes directly with the elaborate plan and obsessive rule above. She believes that humanities papers must scintillate with insight, must present an array of images, ideas, ironies gleaned from the literature under examination. A problem arises, of course, when Martha tries to incorporate her myriad "neat little things," often inherently unrelated, into a tightly structured, carefully sequenced essay. Plans and rules that govern the construction of impressionistic, associational prose would be appropriate to Martha's desire, but her composing process is heavily constrained by the non-impressionistic and non-associational. Put another way, the plans and rules that govern her exploration of text are not at all synchronous with the plans and rules she uses to discuss her exploration. It is interesting to note here, however, that as recently as three years ago Martha was absorbed in creative writing and was publishing poetry in high school magazines. Given what we know about the complex associational, often non-neatly-sequential nature of the poet's creative process, we can infer that Martha was either free of the plans and rules discussed earlier or they were not as intense. One wonders, as well, if the exposure to three years of university physical science either established or intensified Martha's concern with structure. Whatever the case, she now is hamstrung by conflicting rules when composing papers for the humanities.

Mike's difficulties, too, are rooted in a distortion of the problem-solving process. When the time of the week for the assignment of writing topics draws near, Mike begins to prepare material, strategies, and plans that he believes will be appropriate. If the assignment matches his expectations, he has done a good job of analyzing the professor's intentions. If the assignment *doesn't* match his expectations, however, he cannot easily shift approaches. He feels trapped inside his original plans, cannot generate alternatives, and blocks. As the deadline draws near, he will write something, forcing the assignment to fit his conceptual procrustian bed. Since Mike is a smart man, he will offer a good deal of information, but only some of it ends up being appropriate to the assignment. This entire situation is made all the worse when the time between assignment of topic and generation of product is attenuated further, as in an essay examination. Mike believes (correctly) that one must have a plan, a strategy of some sort in order to solve a problem. He further believes, however, that such a plan, once formulated, becomes an exact structural and substantive blueprint that cannot be violated. The plan offers no alternatives, no "sub-routines." So, whereas Ruth's, Laurel's, and some of Martha's difficulties seem to be rule-specific ("always catch your audience," "write grammatically"), Mike's troubles are more global. He may have strategies that are appropriate for various writing situations (e.g., "for this kind of political science assignment write a compare/contrast essay"), but his entire approach to formulating plans and carrying them through to problem solution is too mechanical. It is probable that Mike's behavior is governed by an explicitly learned or inferred rule: "Always try to 'psych out' a professor." But in this case this rule initiates a problem-solving procedure that is clearly dysfunctional.

While Ruth and Laurel use rules that impede their writing process and Mike utilizes a problem-solving procedure that hamstrings him, *Sylvia* has trouble deciding which of the many rules she possesses to use. Her problem can be characterized as cognitive perplexity: some of her rules are inappropriate, others are functional; some mesh nicely with her own definitions of good writing, others don't. She has multiple rules to invoke, multiple paths to follow, and that very complexity of choice virtually paralyzes her. More so than with the previous four students, there is probably a strong emotional dimension to Sylvia's blocking, but the cognitive difficulties are clear and perhaps modifiable.

Sylvia, somewhat like Ruth and Laurel, puts tremendous weight on the crafting of her first paragraph. If it is good, she believes the rest of the essay will be good. Therefore, she will spend up to five hours on the initial paragraph: "I won't go on until I get that first paragraph down." Clearly, this rule—or the strength of it—blocks Sylvia's production. This is one problem. Another is that Sylvia has other equally potent rules that she sees as separate, uncomplementary injunctions: one achieves "flow" in one's writing through the use of adequate transitions; one achieves substance to one's writing through the use of evidence. Sylvia perceives both rules to be "true," but several times followed one to the exclusion of the other. Furthermore, as I talked to Sylvia, many other rules, guidelines, definitions were offered, but none with conviction. While she *is* committed to one rule about initial paragraphs, and that rule is dysfunctional, she seems very uncertain about the weight and hierarchy of the remaining rules in her cognitive repertoire.

"If It Won't Fit My Work, I'll Change It" — The Non-Blockers

Dale, Ellen, Debbie, Susan, and Miles all write with the aid of rules. But their rules differ from blockers' rules in significant ways. If similar in content, they are expressed less absolutely — e.g., "*Try* to keep audience in mind." If dissimilar, they are still expressed less absolutely, more heuristically — e.g., "I can use as many ideas in my thesis paragraph as I need and then develop paragraphs for each idea." Our non-blockers do express some rules with firm assurance, but these tend to be simple injunctions that free up rather than restrict the composing process, e.g., "When stuck, write!" or "I'll write what I can." And finally, at least three of the students openly shun the very textbook rules that some blockers adhere to: e.g., "Rules like 'write only what you know about' just aren't true. I ignore those." These three, in effect, have formulated a further rule that expresses something like: "If a rule conflicts with what is sensible or with experience, reject it."

On the broader level of plans and strategies, these five students also differ from at least three of the five blockers in that they all possess problem-solving plans that are quite functional. Interestingly, on first exploration these plans seem to be too broad or fluid to be useful and, in some cases, can barely be expressed with any precision. Ellen, for example, admits that she has a general "outline in [her] head about how a topic paragraph should look" but could not describe much about its structure. Susan also has a general plan to follow, but, if stymied, will quickly attempt to conceptualize the assignment in different ways: "If my original idea won't work, then I need to proceed differently." Whether or not these plans operate in TOTE-fashion, I can't say. But they do operate with the operate-test fluidity of TOTEs.

True, our non-blockers have their religiously adhered-to rules: e.g., "When stuck, write," and plans, "I couldn't imagine writing without this pattern," but as noted above, these are few and functional. Otherwise, these non-blockers operate with fluid, easily modified, even easily discarded rules and plans (Ellen: "I can throw things out") that are sometimes expressed with a vagueness that could almost be interpreted as ignorance. There lies the irony. Students that offer the least precise rules and plans have the least trouble composing. Perhaps this very lack of precision characterizes the functional composing plan. But perhaps this lack of precision simply masks habitually enacted alternatives and sub-routines. This is clearly an area that needs the illumination of further research.

And then there is feedback. At least three of the five non-blockers are an Information-Processor's dream. They get to know their audience, ask professors and T.A.s specific questions about assignments, bring half-finished products in for evaluation, etc. Like Ruth, they realize the importance of audience, but unlike her, they have specific strategies for obtaining and utilizing feedback. And this penchant for testing writing plans against the needs of the audience can lead to modification of rules and plans. Listen to Debbie:

> In high school I was given a formula that stated that you must write a
> thesis paragraph with *only* three points in it, and then develop each of

those points. When I hit college I was given longer assignments. That stuck me for a bit, but then I realized that I could use as many ideas in my thesis paragraph as I needed and then develop paragraphs for each one. I asked someone about this and then tried it. I didn't get any negative feedback, so I figured it was o.k.

Debbie's statement brings one last difference between our blockers and non-blockers into focus; it has been implied above, but needs specific formulation: the goals these people have, and the plans they generate to attain these goals, are quite mutable. Part of the mutability comes from the fluid way the goals and plans are conceived, and part of it arises from the effective impact of feedback on these goals and plans.

ANALYZING WRITER'S BLOCK

Algorithms Rather Than Heuristics

In most cases, the rules our blockers use are not "wrong" or "incorrect" — it is good practice, for example, to "grab your audience with a catchy opening" or "craft a solid first paragraph before going on." The problem is that these rules seem to be followed as though they were algorithms, absolute dicta, rather than the loose heuristics that they were intended to be. Either through instruction, or the power of the textbook, or the predilections of some of our blockers for absolutes, or all three, these useful rules of thumb have been transformed into near-algorithmic urgencies. The result, to paraphrase Karl Dunker, is that these rules do not allow a flexible penetration into the nature of the problem. It is this transformation of heuristic into algorithm that contributes to the writer's block of Ruth and Laurel.

Questionable Heuristics Made Algorithmic

Whereas "grab your audience" could be a useful heuristic, "always make three or more points in an essay" is a pretty questionable one. Any such rule, though probably taught to aid the writer who needs structure, ultimately transforms a highly fluid process like writing into a mechanical lockstep. As heuristics, such rules can be troublesome. As algorithms, they are simply incorrect.

Set

As with any problem-solving task, students approach writing assignments with a variety of orientations or sets. Some are functional, others are not. Martha and Jane (see footnote 14), coming out of the life sciences and social sciences, respectively, bring certain methodological orientations with them — certain sets or "directions" that make composing for the humanities a difficult, sometimes confusing, task. In fact, this orientation may cause them to misperceive the task. Martha has formulated a planning strategy from her predisposition to see processes in terms of linear, interrelated steps in a system. Jane doesn't realize that she can revise the statement that "committed" her to the direction her essay has taken. Both of these students are stymied because of formative experiences associated with their majors—experiences, perhaps, that nicely reinforce our very strong tendency to organize experiences temporally.

The Plan That Is Not a Plan

If fluidity and multi-directionality are central to the nature of plans, then the plans that Mike formulates are not true plans at all but, rather, inflexible and static cognitive blueprints.[15] Put another way, Mike's "plans" represent a restricted "closed system" (vs. "open system") kind of thinking, where closed system thinking is defined as focusing on "a limited number of units or items, or members, and those properties of the members which are to be used are known to begin with and do not change as the thinking proceeds," and open system thinking is characterized by an "adventurous exploration of multiple alternatives with strategies that allow redirection once 'dead ends' are encountered."[16] Composing calls for open, even adventurous thinking, not for constrained, no-exit cognition.

Feedback

The above difficulties are made all the more problematic by the fact that they seem resistant to or isolated from corrective feedback. One of the most striking things about Dale, Debbie, and Miles is the ease with which they seek out, interpret, and apply feedback on their rules, plans, and productions. They "operate" and then they "test," and the testing is not only against some internalized goal, but against the requirements of external audience as well.

Too Many Rules—"Conceptual Conflict"

According to D. E. Berlyne, one of the primary forces that motivate problem-solving behavior is a curiosity that arises from conceptual conflict—the convergence of incompatible beliefs or ideas. In *Structure and Direction in Thinking*,[17] Berlyne presents six major types of conceptual conflict, the second of which he terms "perplexity":

> This kind of conflict occurs when there are factors inclining the subject toward each of a set of mutually exclusive beliefs. (p. 257)

If one substitutes "rules" for "beliefs" in the above definition, perplexity becomes a useful notion here. Because perplexity is unpleasant, people are motivated to reduce it by problem-solving behavior that can result in "disequalization":

> Degree of conflict will be reduced if either the number of competing . . . [rules] or their nearness to equality of strength is reduced. (p. 259)

But "disequalization" is not automatic. As I have suggested, Martha and Sylvia hold to rules that conflict, but their perplexity does *not* lead to curiosity and resultant problem-solving behavior. Their perplexity, contra Berlyne, leads to immobilization. Thus "disequalization" will have to be effected from without. The importance of each of, particularly, Sylvia's rules needs an evaluation that will aid her in rejecting some rules and balancing and sequencing others.

A NOTE ON TREATMENT

Rather than get embroiled in a blocker's misery, the teacher or tutor might interview the student in order to build a writing history and profile: How much and what kind of writing was done in high school? What is the student's major? What kind of writing does it require? How does the student compose? Are there rough drafts or outlines available? By what rules does the student operate? How would he or she define "good" writing? etc. This sort of interview reveals an incredible amount of information about individual composing processes. Furthermore, it often reveals the rigid rule or the inflexible plan that may lie at the base of the student's writing problem. That was precisely what happened with the five blockers. And with Ruth, Laurel, and Martha (and Jane) what was revealed made virtually immediate remedy possible. Dysfunctional rules are easily replaced with or counter-balanced by functional ones if there is no emotional reason to hold onto that which simply doesn't work. Furthermore, students can be trained to select, to "know which rules are appropriate for which problems."[18] Mike's difficulties, perhaps because plans are more complex and pervasive than rules, took longer to correct. But inflexible plans, too, can be remedied by pointing out their dysfunctional qualities and by assisting the student in developing appropriate and flexible alternatives. Operating this way, I was successful with Mike. Sylvia's story, however, did not end as smoothly. Though I had three forty-five minute contacts with her, I was not able to appreciably alter her behavior. Berlyne's theory bore results with Martha but not with Sylvia. Her rules were in conflict, and perhaps that conflict was not exclusively cognitive. Her case keeps analyses like these honest; it reminds us that the cognitive often melds with, and can be overpowered by, the affective. So while Ruth, Laurel, Martha, and Mike could profit from tutorials that explore the rules and plans in their writing behavior, students like Sylvia may need more extended, more affectively oriented counseling sessions that blend the instructional with the psychodynamic.

NOTES

[1]David Shapiro, *Neurotic Styles* (New York: Basic Books, 1965).

[2]Barbara Hayes-Ruth, a Rand cognitive psychologist, and I are currently developing an information-processing model of the composing process. A good deal of work has already been done by Linda Flower and John Hayes. I have just received — and recommend — their "Writing as Problem Solving" (paper presented at American Educational Research Association, April, 1979).

[3]Robert M. Gagné, *The Conditions of Learning* (New York: Holt, Rinehart and Winston, 1970), p. 193.

[4]E. James Archer, "The Psychological Nature of Concepts," in H. J. Klausmeier and C. W. Harris, eds., *Analysis of Concept Learning* (New York: Academic Press, 1966), pp. 37–44; David P. Ausubel, *The Psychology of Meaningful Verbal Behavior* (New York: Grune and Stratton, 1963); Robert M. Gagné, "Problem Solving," in Arthur W. Melton, ed., *Categories of Human Learning* (New York: Academic Press, 1964), pp. 293–317; George A. Miller, *Language and Communication* (New York: McGraw-Hill, 1951).

[5]George Katona, *Organizing and Memorizing* (New York: Columbia University Press, 1940); Roger N. Shepard, Carl I. Hovland, and Herbert M. Jenkins, "Learning and Memorization of Classifications," *Psychological Monographs*, 75, No. 13 (1961) (entire No. 517); Robert S. Woodworth, *Dynamics of Behavior* (New York: Henry Holt, 1958), chs. 10–12.

[6]Gagné, *The Conditions of Learning*, pp. 190–91.

[7]Karl Dunker, "On Problem Solving," *Psychological Monographs*, 58, No. 5 (1945) (entire No. 270); George A. Polya, *How to Solve It* (Princeton: Princeton University Press, 1945); George A. Miller, Eugene Galanter, and Karl H. Pribram, *Plans and the Structure of Behavior* (New York: Henry Holt, 1960).

[8]Lyle E. Bourne, Jr., Bruce R. Ekstrand, and Roger L. Dominowski, *The Psychology of Thinking* (Englewood Cliffs, NJ: Prentice-Hall, 1971).

[9]John R. Hayes, "Problem Topology and the Solution Process," in Carl P. Duncan, ed., *Thinking: Current Experimental Studies* (Philadelphia: Lippincott, 1967), pp. 167–81.

[10]Hulda J. Rees and Harold E. Israel, "An Investigation of the Establishment and Operation of Mental Sets," *Psychological Monographs*, 46 (1925) (entire No. 210).

[11]Ibid.; Melvin H. Marx, Wilton W. Murphy, and Aaron J. Brownstein, "Recognition of Complex Visual Stimuli as a Function of Training with Abstracted Patterns," *Journal of Experimental Psychology*, 62 (1961), 456–60.

[12]James L. Adams, *Conceptual Blockbusting* (San Francisco: W. H. Freeman, 1974); Edward DeBono, *New Think* (New York: Basic Books, 1958); Ronald H. Forgus, *Perception* (New York: McGraw-Hill, 1966), ch. 13; Abraham Luchins and Edith Hirsch Luchins, *Rigidity of Behavior* (Eugene: University of Oregon Books, 1959); N. R. F. Maier, "Reasoning in Humans. I. On Direction," *Journal of Comparative Psychology*, 10 (1920), 115–43.

[13]"Plans and the Cognitive Process of Writing," paper presented at the National Institute of Education Writing Conference, June 1977; "Problem Solving Strategies and the Writing Process," *College English*, 39 (1977), 449–61. See also footnote 2.

[14]Jane, a student not discussed in this paper, was surprised to find out that a topic paragraph can be rewritten after a paper's conclusion to make that paragraph reflect what the essay truly contains. She had gotten so indoctrinated with Psychology's (her major) insistence that a hypothesis be formulated and then left untouched before an experiment begins that she thought revision of one's "major premise" was somehow illegal. She had formed a rule out of her exposure to social science methodology, and the rule was totally inappropriate for most writing situations.

[15]Cf. "A plan is flexible if the order of execution of its parts can be easily interchanged without affecting the feasibility of the plan. . . . The flexible planner might tend to think of lists of things he had to do; the inflexible planner would have his time planned like a sequence of cause-effect relations. The former could rearrange his lists to suit his opportunities, but the latter would be unable to strike while the iron was hot and would generally require considerable 'lead-time' before he could incorporate any alternative sub-plans" (Miller, Galanter, and Pribram, p. 120).

[16]Frederic Bartlett, *Thinking* (New York: Basic Books, 1958), pp. 74–76.

[17]D. E. Berlyne, *Structure and Direction in Thinking* (New York: John Wiley, 1965), p. 255.

[18]Flower and Hayes, "Plans and the Cognitive Process of Writing," p. 26.

2

Two Case Studies from Writer's Block: The Cognitive Dimension

1984

AUTHOR'S NOTE: The study described in "Rigid Rules" led to the fuller dissertation (Rose, 1981) that was later condensed, revised, and published as an early volume in the Southern Illinois University Press series Studies in Writing and Rhetoric. Here I present the two case studies from the book—one of a student who reports a fair amount of difficulty composing and one of a student who composes with relative ease. I'll begin with an overview of the dissertation research, which is further elaborated in the first few pages of the next selection, "Complexity, Rigor, Evolving Method." I utilized the cognitive framework found in "Rigid Rules," but that framework is refined here, made more precise through the dissertation study itself and played out in the analysis in a more systematic and detailed way.

During the first phase of the study, I developed a questionnaire with which to identify students experiencing writer's block. The questionnaire was the idea of my chair, Richard Shavelson. He wanted a methodical way to survey large numbers of students and get a reading—an admittedly quick one—on how they composed. The questionnaire contained items that describe blocking behaviors and items that describe cognitive and attitudinal variables related to blocking. The final version—which was given to 351 UCLA undergraduates—contained twenty-four items that could be subsumed under five subscales. Each item included an "Almost Always" to "Almost Never" Likert-type response sequence. The subscales and one item from each follow.

Blocking (this subscale provides a set of behaviors related to writer's block): "There are times when I sit at my desk for hours, unable to write a thing." *Lateness* (i.e., missing deadlines): "I run over deadlines because I get stuck while trying to write my papers." *Premature Editing* (i.e., editing too early in the composing process): "Each sentence I write has to be just right before I'll go on to the next sentence." *Strategies for Complexity* (i.e., not possessing adequate strategies for interpreting and writing on complex material): "I have trouble figuring out how to write on issues that have many interpretations." *Attitudes* (i.e., feelings and beliefs about writing and evaluation): "I think my writing is good."

The entire questionnaire is presented in Appendix A, p. 51. Readers interested in a fuller discussion of rationale, development, and limitations can consult *Writer's Block: The Cognitive Dimension* (Rose, 1984).

During the second phase of the study, I selected ten students who scored high and low on various combinations of the questionnaire's items and who had different levels of coursework that involved writing. Each of the ten students was videotaped while writing on a university-level expository topic (see Appendix B, p. 54). Immediately after composing, the videotape was replayed to the student, and he or she was questioned about all observed composing behaviors. My conversation with the student was audiotaped and later transcribed. The students were paid for their time, and I provided a follow-up tutorial once the study was completed.

Phase three involved analysis of the transcriptions, of the behaviors recorded on videotape, and of the notes and essays produced by the students. The idea was to bring together all the different kinds of information I had, to "triangulate" them, looking for places of agreement and of dissonance. More specifically, I and my assistants tallied evidence of behaviors, cognitive processes, and attitudes in the transcriptions; measured prewriting, planning, and pausing times; counted words produced and deleted on the assignment materials, scratch paper, and essays; and, finally, had the essays evaluated by two independent readers. All the resulting data were both analyzed separately and consolidated into ten case studies. (Again, fuller discussion can be found in both Rose, 1981 and 1984.)

Let me say a little more about the ten students to provide some context for the two upcoming cases.

As I noted, the ten students were chosen according to their high or low scores on the questionnaire subscales and by the level of coursework they had that involved writing. They ranged from freshmen to seniors, humanities to life science majors, 1.9 to 3.9 GPA's. Some who reported a high degree of blocking were relatively inexperienced freshmen, whereas others were upper-division English majors—and the same variation was found among those who reported little problem composing. Of the six students reporting a high level of blocking, four were female, two male; four of the students were white, one was African-American, and one was Japanese-American. Of the four students who reported few problems with blocking, three were female, one male; three were white, and one was Latina. The Studies in Writing and Rhetoric Studies series had restrictions on length, so I could only include two case studies. I opted for the two that would best illustrate the differences I was finding with blocking, premature editing, and conflict with rules and strategies. These are the upcoming cases of Liz and Glenn.

The questionnaire was statistically valid, but the big question was whether it would identify students who actually had problems composing or were fluent writers. It did. And though the setting for the study and the sixty-minute time limit were clearly artificial, all students reported that the sorts of things they did when writing the essay for the study were typical of what they did on their own with school assignments.

This was a pretty detailed and technical study, and a good deal of effort went into refining and implementing the techniques. There is the danger in such studies that the technical side of things takes over; we get lost in specifics, can't see the forest for the trees. And the studies can be reductive, reducing complex processes to individual bits and pieces. I hope the case studies integrate and animate the details.

I also want to suggest that there can be a reflective dimension to work like this. Recasting an aphorism of Claude Levi-Strauss's, numbers can be good to think with. I remember sitting down with the questionnaire results—I used to work at a big kitchen table—examining the full sweep of the data, the patterns or variability they revealed. Or, shifting to the particular, I'd reread the students' transcripts. Then, back at UCLA, I'd watch and watch again the videotapes of the students composing, and I'd puzzle over the rules about style or the assumptions about writing that the students expressed, trying to see if they followed them as they wrote, when, how it all played out. I would wonder, too, how the students acquired the rules and assumptions, and, if they were wrong or counterproductive, how a tutor might help to modify them.

I had taught for a dozen or more years by this point, and yet this study revealed a lot to me, afforded other lines of sight onto what I thought I knew.

We rarely find studies of this type in rhetoric and composition within the United States anymore. I believe this is due to the reasons I mentioned in the beginning of this section. What is done in this tradition continues, however, in education, applied linguistics, and psychology—both inside and outside of the United States. I think that some of the current questions I hear in our field about the effect of technology on the composing process, or the interplay of reading and writing, or composing in a nonnative language could be fruitfully explored by methods in this tradition—though, of course, in their new guise, revised by what we've learned over the past two decades.

O f the 10 students chosen for the stimulated-recall study, six were designated as high-blockers by the questionnaire and four were designated as low-blockers. Though the tallies of cognitive functions, composing behaviors, and essay features and the reader evaluations of the essays all suggest differences between these two groups, some students more neatly fit the study's conceptualization and hypotheses than others. The high-blockers Liz and Gary and the low-blockers Glenn and Amy most dramatically illustrated blocked vs. fluid composing and confirmed the study's cognitive orientation. Three other high-blockers (Terryl, Debbie, and Stephanie) were, surprisingly enough, impelled by the study's deadline and wrote more than they reported they usually would under less restricting circumstances. Still, their protocols illustrate the kinds of problems that are related to their blocking. Finally, one

From *Writer's Block: The Cognitive Dimension*. Carbondale: Southern Illinois University Press, 1984. 43–69, 107–10, 115–17.

high-blocker (Ruth) became anxious and frantically wrote a good deal of disconnected, erratic prose. Of the six high-blockers, only one (Stephanie) presented problems for which the study's cognitive model had markedly limited explanatory power. Her composing problems were more related to self-image and self-reliance than to cognitive interferences like rigid rules. [Stephanie will be further discussed in the next selection, "Complexity, Rigor. . . ."]

I present two of the 10 case studies found in [the dissertation] "The Cognitive Dimension of Writer's Block"; these two cases provide a vivid illustration of the study's thesis.

A word on the variety of citations presented in the case studies. Most will be student reports from the protocols, though responses to the questionnaire (e.g., "Always," "Occasionally"), my questions, passages from the essays, and readers' comments will also be presented. *Unless otherwise noted in the text, all citations will be student protocol commentary.*

One last note: Each case study is preceded by a typed verbatim copy of the student's essay. Nothing is corrected, but words the student lined out are not included.

A HIGH-BLOCKER: LIZ

Liz is a senior English major with a 610 VSAT and a 2.67 GPA. Her writing experience placed her in category 7 (1 is lowest, 8 highest). She received a score of 12.50 (on a scale of 1–39) on her essay. Her questionnaire results follow: 1.9 standard deviations above the Blocking mean (i.e., in the direction of blocking); 1.4 standard deviations above the Lateness mean; .6 of a standard deviation above the Premature Editing mean; .05 of a standard deviation above the Strategies for Complexity mean; .1 of a standard deviation above the Attitude mean.

Liz's Essay

> The depression Angelo experiences and the discontinuity Jaspers describes can both be accounted for, at least in some sense by the quality of city life; by the modern experience. Angelo's "blues" for example may result directly from breakup with his girlfriend but even if they do

Liz's Session

Overview. At the 60-minute deadline, Liz turned in a draft of 45 words—a topic sentence and part of a second, apparently qualifying, sentence. This extremely brief product, however, belied the amount of writing she actually produced. After rereading the assignment materials for 2½ minutes, Liz began underlining the Jaspers passage and the case history, glossing the former and jotting down fragments and sentences on scratch paper. Liz did not pause a great number of times while writing (62), but her pauses were relatively long (28.9 seconds on the average). During most of these pauses, Liz was weighing ideas and rehearsing sentences. She often spoke aloud and gestured with her hand while rehearsing, apparently testing the rhythm of her sentences, measuring rhythm with the waves of her hand in the air.

From the beginning, Liz "was trying to make a connection . . . between" the passages. (A sentence from the first page of her scratch paper revealed this attempt at fusion: "Jaspers attributes the personal unhappiness of people like Cacci to the noncreative nature of their jobs.") But, at the same time, Liz was wrestling with the legitimacy of the Jaspers passage itself, raising a solid argument against the romanticism inherent in the work of mass society critics: "I've heard this type of argument before, and they say, 'Farmers, oh, they grow. They have such a wonderful life.' And it's not true. They can be real, real, you know, just as unhappy and miserable and a lot worse than we are." Simultaneous with her attempts to effect a connection between Angelo's life and Jaspers' vision (mentally arguing with Jaspers' vision all the while), Liz was also making a number of lexical to phrase-level changes in her glossing and rough draft. Within the first 10 minutes of writing, Liz made the following alterations: passive constructions were changed to active ones; "to be" forms were changed to more striking verbs; certain words (e.g., "says") were rejected as being "too colloquial"; other words (e.g., "like") were rejected for being "too simple . . . too easy"; clauses were rejected or accepted by the way they sounded; clauses were also rejected for containing a preposition; and, finally, spelling was corrected. These emendations were supported with rules like: "You're not supposed to have passive verbs"; "You can't start a sentence with 'says'"; "If you can singsong it, it's not good stylistically." Sometimes Liz's decisions were based on rules and concepts she did not fully understand: "When he's [a textbook author] talking about 'to be' verbs, I don't really even understand what he's saying." Other times, her rules and resulting word choices would conflict. When she changed "is saying" to "says," she noted that the new verb "would . . . be too colloquial" and thus would not be acceptable. Further on she wrote "to the noncreative nature of their jobs" and said it "is good [because it sounds good], and it's bad because of the 'of.'" Finally, there were times when Liz's preoccupation with editing resulted in her forgetting her thought. Very early in the hour she wrote an interpretive note under the Jaspers passage: "is saying that not having creative (generative) work is the"; she stopped and changed "is saying" to "says" and "is the" to "causes." Then came a long pause. She couldn't remember the rest of her insight. "That happens a lot," she later observed.

Through the second third of her hour, Liz continued to pause, rehearse, and jot down ideas on scratch paper. The ideas of this period were expressed in strings of sentences as Liz's disagreement with Jaspers (and her attempt to work that disagreement into the assignment) was becoming more evident (e.g., "The breakup between Angelo and his girlfriend is probably the reason for his depression. Jaspers, if you accept the little that is given in this selection, might attribute the breakup to the kind of job that he is talking about"). As Liz continued to attempt new sentences and rephrase old ones, it became obvious that she was trying to form an approach to the assignment that would allow her to work with Jaspers' vision while taking issue with it. This approach would become the stuff of a topic sentence as well as a conclusion, and, for Liz, thinking of some sort of a conclusion fairly early is important: "A place to end up. I always have that." But mid-way through the hour, she had not yet found her approach. When asked if, at this point, she could have told what her paper was going to be about, she replied, "No. No way." She was experiencing "real confusion" as she continued to think of and set down one and two sentence "blocks of information," wrestling with Jaspers all the while. Then, at this mid-point, she suddenly put her scratch paper aside and began the draft she would turn in, framing a beginning sentence and part of another that gave some structure to her complex stance toward Jaspers and the case of Angelo Cacci.

After working on her introductory sentences for 5½ minutes, Liz went back to the case study and began to gloss it. (She had originally only under-lined it.) "It's from this sort of stuff that I get my best ideas." She was asked why, then, she did not begin her 60 minutes by performing this interpretive glossing. "I don't know," she answered.

As Liz moved through the last third of the hour, she continued reading the case study closely, following line by line with her finger, glossing every tenth line or so. At one point she commented, "Well, maybe he [Jaspers] is right," only to return to her original skepticism several minutes later: "All he [Jaspers] is really saying is that you don't get to see the end of your work. That means all these terrible things?" Liz was asked again if she was any closer to a thesis: "I don't know. Can't tell. Because it [is] actually only an hour. You know, you can't exactly judge . . . [You can] never really tell what it is until you're halfway done." Queried about the continual conflict be-tween her quarrel with Jaspers and the requirements of the assignment as she understood them, she replied, "I just really didn't think it out well enough."

Looking back over the 60 minutes, three things about Liz's composing behavior are evident: (1) she never truly resolved the conceptual/rhetorical problem presented by the assignment; (2) she did not map out her dis-course in advance but planned in increments as she wrote; (3) she edited prematurely.

1. Though the assignment instructions required that Cacci's case be discussed in light of Jaspers' quotation, they also gave latitude to dispute the ap-plicability of Jaspers' vision. Liz began interpreting and applying the quotation almost immediately, but was not able to come up with an approach and resulting thesis that would enable her to deal with her reservations and the assignment's broad requirements. It is possible that Liz began writing too soon; even though most of the writing she produced was glossing and notes, these could have con-stricted a free-flowing reflection on Jaspers' vision and Angelo's life. At several points in the protocol Liz reported needing a good deal of time to "boil down" her ideas — with or without pen and paper — before any sort of final draft is con-sidered. The 60-minute limit perhaps forced her to record more of that boiling

down than she normally would. According to her reports, she spends a great deal of time at home ruminating on an assignment, jotting down notes, smoking cigarettes (she smoked five during this 60 minutes), drinking coffee, and taking breaks to watch television. Only when a deadline is upon her does she force herself to churn out what has yet to be done: "What I usually do is start about 6:00 p.m. and it's due the next day. . . . Pressure helps me. . . . If I have spare time, I'll just end up thinking instead of actually writing. . . . I don't like to work continuously." The present assignment, of course, made extensive rumination impossible.

2. Liz did not plan her essay in advance. She made decisions about the direction and shape of her discourse incrementally as she proceeded. This approach led to discoveries as well as dead ends, most of which, however, were fragmented. Her inability to arrive at a satisfactory approach to the assignment led to a further problem: Liz said she needed "a place to end up," a conclusion, perhaps to provide a focus, a termination point for her incremental planning style. The fact that such a conclusion never emerged most likely worked against the success of Liz's incremental planning.

3. It is important to keep in mind that while Liz was trying to conceptualize an approach to the assignment and while she was laying out discourse in increments, in small "chunks of information," she was also scrutinizing her prose. She edited her earliest written reflections as she produced them.

THE INVOKING OR DENIAL OF FUNCTIONAL AND NONFUNCTIONAL COMPOSING-PROCESS RULES AND ASSUMPTIONS

Liz expressed a number of rules directly: "Writing has to be logical"; "You're supposed to read [what you've written] to see how it sounds"; "You're not supposed to have passive verbs"; "If you can singsong [your writing], it's not good stylistically"; "You can't start a sentence with 'says.'" Several more rules could be implied from specific composing behaviors and Liz's comments on them: Writing is not good if "it's not clear, vibrant prose"; School writing should not "be too colloquial"; Word choices should not be "too simple . . . too easy"; Writing is not good if it contains too many prepositional phrases.

Many of the above rules apparently came from an editing text Liz had read the previous year. But whereas the text advocates reducing the number of "to be" verbs and prepositional phrases in one's prose, Liz seems to have interpreted the rules more absolutely, or had them so interpreted for her by overzealous professors and teaching assistants. Several other rules could also stem from the text (e.g., Writing is not good if it's not clear, vibrant prose; If you can singsong your writing it's not good stylistically). The balance of Liz's rules possibly come from other, earlier texts and teacher comments: writing has to be logical; word choices should not be too simple . . . too easy; school writing should not be too colloquial; and the puzzling "you can't start a sentence with 'says'" (a rule that is related to Liz's injunction against the colloquial; at one point she equated "says" with colloquiality).

While a rule like "you can't start a sentence with 'says'" is a strange one indeed and "if you can singsong your writing, it's not good stylistically" is questionable, most of Liz's other rules are legitimate and could be functional if they were not invoked at so early a point in the composing process. A further problem with some of these rules emerged when Liz was asked what they meant; she didn't really know. Finally, though one should not automatically equate the language with which a rule is expressed with the manner of that rule's enactment, Liz did express a number of her rules with an absolutism that could suggest a dysfunctional rigidity—an absence of context, purpose, and audience qualifiers that turns heuristic guidelines into narrow injunctions.

ENACTMENT OR REJECTION OF PREMATURE EDITING

Liz was .6 of a standard deviation above the Premature Editing mean. (Her "Occasionally" response to "My first paragraph has to be perfect before I'll go on" pulled her closer to the mean, and as was seen, Liz did not dwell on her first paragraph, but shifted to glossing the case study and framing further "blocks of information.") Liz's other responses to items in the Premature Editing subscale ("Often," "Sometimes," "Almost Always") suggest that she does have problems with early editing, and the stimulated-recall study confirmed this. Questionnaire items were constructed to tap general manifestations of a behavior, process, or attitude, but the items are not numerous or multifaceted enough to tap idiosyncratic variations such as the grabbag of rules that lead to Liz's early editing. Still, Liz very clearly edited prematurely, composing with the aid of a number of rules—some absolutely expressed, some not fully understood—which are appropriate to determine the final texture of prose but which are very inappropriate when one is working out ideas in rough draft or simply glossing an assignment sheet. The result, as was seen, is not only limited production but an actual stymieing and even forgetting of one's thoughts.

INTERPRETIVE AND WRITING STRATEGIES FOR COMPLEXITY

Though she could understand the Jaspers quotation and the case study and was achieving some success in structuring complex notions in possible topic sentences, Liz never did arrive at an overall focus and plan for her essay. She reported that she rarely outlines or writes some other form of structured plan before writing; rather, she often follows a mental plan and sometimes simply works out ideas as she writes. The last approach characterized her work on the essay under consideration. But that approach was not successful. Perhaps Liz needed more time to think through the issues; the 60-minute limit forced her to write before she was ready, and, thus, the reader gets a stream of preliminary and protean thought. Pertinent here is Liz's questionnaire response of "Almost Always" to "It is hard for me to write on topics that could be written about from a number of angles." (This was the only Strategies for

Complexity item she so answered. She was at the mean on this subscale.) This response suggests that though time might have been a factor here, Liz frequently has trouble formulating and structuring multifaceted topics. Given that difficulty, it is a little surprising that she continues to plan so incrementally, that she does not rely on lists, crude planning sketches, or even some form of outline. Her responses to queries about planning strategies are telling:

> RESEARCHER: You say it's difficult to organize and get all these associations straight, and yet it's interesting that you never work out any kind of outline.
>
> LIZ: I've tried that a couple of times. . . . It works on a specific kind of paper.
>
> RESEARCHER: What kind of paper?
>
> LIZ: It works on the kind of paper where you're supposed to . . . report on six or seven things, what somebody said, and that's easy.
>
> RESEARCHER: What kind of an outline did you use?
>
> LIZ: I just put [the points] in order.
>
> RESEARCHER: You mean number 1, number 2?
>
> LIZ: Yeah, 1, 2, 3, and then I tried to, well, I tried to do it like you're supposed to, with the 1 and the A.
>
> RESEARCHER: But for other sorts of papers, . . . you tend not to outline?
>
> LIZ: Sometimes if I've got a . . . real tough paragraph, I'll try and do it for that one paragraph.
>
> RESEARCHER: Does that help?
>
> LIZ: I don't know. . . . I think it's probably a pretty good tool. It's just that I don't know how to use it. . . . I wouldn't know how to outline something [in a way] that would benefit me.
>
> RESEARCHER: Didn't . . . grammar school teachers teach you an outline form?
>
> LIZ: Well . . . they didn't tell you why you put in I, A, B, C, . . . It's like a research paper where they . . . tell us "O.K. write a research paper of about 12 pages." And the way they told us to do it was just to get quotes and string them together. So this paragraph is from this book. This paragraph is from that book. This paragraph is from that book.

The above excerpt suggests that Liz does not rely on pen-and-paper structuring and focusing aids because she does not have them in her repertoire. The outline she knows (but claims not to fully understand) is the old standard. She does not possess other techniques (such as, for example, those discussed by Linda Flower) that are flexible and suited for generating and guiding complex discourse.[1] In a sense, then, she lacks the quintessential strategy for complexity: an aid to balancing intertwining or conflicting issues. Perhaps this lack explains why she plans in increments, in "blocks of information" not unlike the disconnected quotations in her research paper analogy.

But Liz has read a lot and written a lot; though not a distinguished English major, her work is competent. It is possible, then, that though she cannot articulate a variety of planning strategies, she might well possess them tacitly.[2] If this is so, is there any other reason to explain her affinity for non-pen-and-paper strategies? The protocol offers one possibility, a belief in unstructured discovery: "I do believe that most of the time there is an answer to a question. And if you . . . start out a paper without really being aware of that [fact] and just say 'Well, I'll just go through this structure . . .' [you think] you've answered the question [but] you haven't. You've just kind of skirted around it." Her logic might be odd, but Liz's belief is fairly clear: structure a paper in advance and you do not truly penetrate a question and might not arrive at the best answer. Earlier in the protocol, Liz had noted that when she is interested in a paper, she wants to "let it say itself." A similar advocacy of the spontaneous is implied above. Perhaps this belief contributes to Liz's use of incremental strategies. And perhaps her inadequacy as a pen-and-paper planner determines the belief. But whether Liz's planning style results from inadequacy or preference or some interaction of the two, the result is the same, pithily expressed by Liz at the end of the protocol:

> **RESEARCHER:** It sounds like sometimes you don't really know what [your paper] is going to look like and what it's going to be about until you're fairly long into it. Is that correct?
>
> **LIZ:** Yeah. Cross your fingers.

CONFLICTING RULES, PLANS, STRATEGIES, AND ASSUMPTIONS

As was noted, a number of Liz's rules conflicted with each other at specific instances of composing—e.g., a particular line is good because it is rhythmic but bad because it contains a prepositional phrase, the prepositional phrase, of course, adding to the rhythm of the sentence.

More global conflict existed between Liz's need for extended prewriting time—"boiling down," as she called it—and her premature editing. Premature editing also conflicted with her belief in spontaneity and discovery. How can one freely explore and uncover when one is assessing each word?

THE EVALUATION OF WRITING AND ATTITUDES TOWARD WRITING

Liz's negative evaluations of her writing were always aimed at specific phrases and clauses: "that sounds bad"; "that's really bad, bad writing." These evaluations were connected to one or more of her many rules—e.g., the latter evaluation was a reaction to prepositional phrases in the sentence: "Jaspers attributes the personal unhappiness of people like Cacci to the non-creative nature of their jobs." Note the overreaction. The sentence is not as lean as it could be, but it certainly is not "bad, bad writing."

Though Liz mentioned several times that certain English teachers made her conscious of aspects of her writing, she never voiced concern over the evaluation of others. If Liz's concern for others' evaluation is expressed at all here, it is manifested covertly through her embrace of her professors' and textbooks' rules.

Liz was asked if she enjoyed writing. She replied, "Sometimes, sometimes I do an awful lot." Asked why she concerned herself so much with editing on early drafts, Liz said she likes "monkeying around": "People always tell me . . . you should write your first draft . . . just do it . . . but I always enjoy the process of it." Liz also seems to like the play of ideas that accompanies composing: "Sometimes . . . I start thinking about something else that I find interesting, and I stop and think about that for awhile." Though writing does not come easy to her, Liz enjoys it, enjoys tinkering with language and exploring ideas. The videotape graphically displays this involvement: Liz bent over the page, her hand measuring out language; Liz sitting back, reflective with lit cigarette, only to snap her fingers, blurt "Ah ha!" or "That's it!" and quickly return to the page.

DISCUSSION

Some high-blockers would be identified by the questionnaire Blocking subscale but would fall outside the identifying criterion (1 [or .8] standard deviation from the mean) for other subscales. Such writers, if videotaped, might well reveal complex idiosyncratic composing behaviors, processes, and attitudes that would account for their blocking. Liz was chosen because she fell 1.88 and 1.4 standard deviations above the means respectively on the two behavioral subscales, Blocking and Lateness, but registered less than .8 of a standard deviation on Premature Editing (.6), Complexity (.05), and Attitude (.1). In fact, her protocol did reveal the suspected process idiosyncrasies. She, for example, fell only .6 of a standard deviation above the mean on Premature Editing because, to the degree one can generalize from the present study, she seems willing to abandon a first paragraph before it is "perfect." Otherwise, though, she does edit prematurely, and with an array of rules to which the questionnaire at its present level of generality, could never be sensitive.

So Liz reported herself a high-blocker and, in fact, during the study, produced a very short draft. But why did she block? It seems for the same reason so many people block, from undergraduate to student lawyer to professional novelist—a thorny problem is confronted and cannot be solved, in some cases cannot even be clearly conceived. In Liz's case, she faced a point of view (Jaspers') with which she, during most of the session, could not agree. Furthermore, she had to carry out an analysis with that point of view. Undergirding Liz's dilemma is what Linda Flower and John Hayes have labeled the rhetorical problem.[3] How does a writer convert an assignment's request into an appropriately "elaborate construction" that both honors the assignment and allows the writer to exercise his or her beliefs and abilities? Though she finally framed a topic sentence, the protocol revealed that the assignment's rhetorical problem was one Liz never solved.

But Liz's difficulties did not begin or end with the above dilemma. Though she might have purely and simply been stuck intellectually, a number of factors made it all the more difficult (even impossible) for her to become unstuck, for her to solve her particular rhetorical problem:

1. It seems likely that the 60-minute deadline forced Liz to write before she was ready. She might have needed more of the "boiling down" time she reported relying on at home. If Liz's composing at home is significantly different—temporally and qualitatively—from her composing in this study, then her troubles could be chalked up to the pressures of a 60-minute parameter alone and little more need be said. But, though unconfirmed self-report, Liz's composing in the present study was, in her words, "The way [she] do[es] it at home." She obviously gives herself more than 60 minutes (thus has more "boiling down" time), but then her assignments are considerably longer (I saw some of them), and she allows herself limited time to complete them. Why place such restrictions on herself? "Pressure helps" her push away the jumble of notes, the ruminations and diversions, and push toward the writing desk. "The way I do it at home" seems to refer to daydreaming, the generation of disjointed notes, pauses for cigarettes, coffee, and whatever else, battling deadlines and sometimes losing (remember, she was 1.4 standard deviations above the Lateness mean), and limited, sometimes stymied production.

This is not to say that the deadline was not responsible for Liz's writing before she had her thoughts clarified; it is only to suggest that her thoughts might often not be formulated before the clock forces her to begin writing the kinds of segmented notes produced in this study.

2. Another factor interfering with Liz's composing is her paucity of planning strategies. Certainly, pen-and-paper plans, as Janet Emig and others have shown, are not prerequisite to good writing,[4] but for Liz's incremental planning style to be effective she would need both a sense of academic discourse (with Liz's senior status in English, this can be assumed) and a fairly unconfounded, though even general, notion of what one wants to say (Liz lacked this). She set out, trying to frame "blocks of information" when either freewriting (which she preferred not to do) or outlining or sketching (which she claimed not to know how to do) might have freed up, possibly clarified, her thinking. She was left with few alternatives with which to solve the rhetorical problem she confronted—she could ruminate, generate her "blocks of information," or return to reading and marking assignment materials, but that was it. Her options were limited—no freewriting, no heuristics, no sketches or outlines.

3. Perhaps because of the 60-minute pressure but also perhaps because of habitual composing behaviors, Liz was fairly unmethodical in her approach to the assignment: she knew "boiling down" helped her, but she dove into writing "blocks of information" and attempts at topic sentences. The result? "I really didn't think it out well enough." She also knew glossing helped her "get her best ideas," but for reasons she could not pinpoint, she did not begin glossing the case history until the hour was half over and until she had attempted topic sentences.

4. Still, other students compose without the aid of plans and with jumbled ideas and in unmethodical ways and yet sometimes write themselves out of their conceptual jungles, even under the pressure of 60-minute essay exams. (See, for example, the upcoming case of Glenn.) But the final stymieing touch for Liz was her concentration on verbal surface—concentrating on the minutiae of surface

even before a fundamental confusion about topic was resolved, even while gloss-ing assignment materials in search of ideas.

The question that must be forming by now is "Why doesn't Liz know better?" She is a senior English major in good standing; she must have learned more about writing than the scramble of factors presented above would sug-gest. But before one begins questioning Liz's abilities, several facts need to be pointed out.

a. Liz holds a set of assumptions and preferences that could undergird her planning style, her unmethodical approach to composing, and, to some degree, her premature editing. She advocates a fairly spontaneous approach to compos-ing and distrusts carefully plotted attempts to compositionally solve problems. (Though she does believe in mulling over, "boiling down," issues involved in the assignment.) She also gets pleasure out of "monkeying around with words" and toying with ideas, apparently at the expense of production and, occasionally, at the expense of deadlines.

b. Liz's embracement of so many rules—often to the detriment of her fluency—seems odd unless one considers her situation. She had been told by sev-eral teachers to read an editing text; that would, the teachers putatively claimed, rid her of some nagging wordiness problems. Now, the textbook is wittily and forcefully written; it would take a fairly self-assured student to ignore it. What is more, the confusion Liz evinced vis-à-vis textbooks and teacher injunctions could reflect conflicts between the graders she encounters: "They said, 'Don't use "I."' But those have always been the papers I've gotten the best grades on. . . . When I use 'I,' they give me an 'A,' and when I don't, they don't." A pilot study by Gary Sloan and a more extensive piece of research by Rosemary Hake and Joseph Williams suggest that faculty can champion one standard and grade by another,[5] so Liz's statement, if accurate self-report, might not simply be unfounded complaining.

Liz never could resolve the conceptual and rhetorical problem presented by the assignment, for, as was seen, a number of process barriers and possi-bly a deadline stood in her way. It seems she should know better, and there might be reasons other than cognitive ones to explain why she does not, but, as her protocol comments suggest, she holds to certain assumptions and finds herself in certain situations that seem to interact with each other and with aspects of her composing process in ways that pretty convincingly impede her fluency.

A Low-Blocker: Glenn

Glenn is a sophomore Theater Arts major with a 600 VSAT and a 3.85 GPA. His writing experience placed him in category 6. He received a score of 23.75 on his essay. His questionnaire results follow: 1 standard deviation below the Blocking mean; .4 of a standard deviation below the Lateness mean; 1.1 stan-dard deviations below the Premature Editing mean; .9 of a standard deviation below the Strategies for Complexity mean; .9 of a standard deviation below the Attitude mean.

Glenn's Essay

Several elements of Jaspers' quote deal directly with Angelo Cacci's case. Cacci's loss of caring for his girlfriends, his view of his job as "O.K.," his history in general all seem to point to a lack of commitment. And without commitment there can be no continuity in reference to the man of modern times and his job. The job is performed and then forgotten. This relates directly to Cacci's view of his job as "O.K." He is noncommital about it. He probably has no feelings about it. It is only a way to get a few bucks and pay the bills. Angelo won't say "I hate it, but I need the money." This would require employment of an emotion. It seems Angelo has forgotten emotion. This is further exampled in the fact that he won't say he was in love with his girlfriend. He further discounts the relationship by comparing it to a past girlfriend. "I've been through this before," he says, relegating his feelings for the girl to something commonplace, unexciting.

As Jaspers claims that modern man lives a life of ephemeral activities—he builds a product and moves on to something new without a second thought—so Angelo lives his life without thought or emotion. He is a near robot. He has been at his job for ten years, has a good employment record, and, if he were to stop and look at his work, would probably realize that he is bored stiff. But as Jaspers says, Angelo—modern man—won't or can't look up from the machine long enough to see what's going on.

Angelo says that his relationship began O.K. with his girlfriend, "but after a while it fizzled. I just didn't feel that much for her anymore." He couldn't retain any emotion for her. He probably became afraid of what he was feeling, afraid to let any emotion into his life. Or perhaps he began to feel there was no point in expending the energy required for the relationship. Perhaps the answers to why he acts as he does are in his past—who knows? But his biggest problem, as Jaspers says about modern man, is that his life has no continuity. The only thing that is constant in Angelo's life is his lack of caring, his apathy toward his surroundings. He can't make any commitments.

Angelo's dream seems to illustrate his view of himself as noncommital. The dog that is injured in his dream is aided not by him, but by another man. "Love for things and human beings wanes and disappears," as Jaspers says. Maybe Angelo feels he should help the injured dog, but he doesn't. And through acts like these in his real life, ultimately his love and feeling for things dries up and vanishes.

A great deal of speculative answers to Angelo's problems can be drawn from his past—his mother's gradual growth into a spiritless t.v. freak, his father's leaving—and perhaps these facts are important in determining Angelo's present lifestyle. But Angelo must ultimately be made to realize that he possesses a brain and a heart and is not merely an "element of an apparatus," as Jaspers claims. Angelo must see that it is wrong to avoid emotion, to block out feeling, or one becomes divorced from oneself. He must seek, in Jaspers' words, "an expansion of the selfhood."

Glenn's Session

Overview. Given his attenuated composing time, Glenn was the most fluent writer of the 10 students. He did not begin writing until 11½ minutes into the hour and finished 12½ minutes before the 60-minute deadline. Though he paused 72 times during the 36 minutes of his composing, 24 of those pauses lasted five seconds or less. Only three pauses exceeded one minute. Glenn's longer pauses tended to come at the beginning of paragraphs as he thought through the direction of his discourse; once past those foundational sentences he wrote quickly, pausing briefly as he poured out two and three sentences at a time. He did not appear rushed, but rather at ease, assured, in control.

During the first 11½ minutes of the session, Glenn read and reread the materials; though he was "looking for things that the two sources have in common," he did not mark the Jaspers quotation or case history in any way. Glenn would eventually arrive at a solid understanding of Jaspers' vision and Angelo's situation, but that understanding did not come without some difficulty. Five minutes into the hour he was "just really confused": "I was trying to think of something to . . . connect it all together. At this point I don't know. It seemed really fragmented to me." Through the second five minutes of the hour, he unsuccessfully shifted his attention once again to the case history: "I was trying to get a general line of thought in the essay and I wasn't finding it, actually. This whole thing about his past, and then all these things about the girlfriends and his present life." And the quotation turned out to be more broadly philosophical than the kind of material he was used to working with:

> GLENN: Again I think I am just trying to tie in what I've just read, what I have gathered from the . . . case study . . . I am looking for this quote to be a concrete, matter-of-fact thing.
>
> RESEARCHER: And it's not working out that way?
>
> GLENN: No. He is saying things like, "His life has no continuity." "What he does has no purpose."
>
> RESEARCHER: That's pretty broad?
>
> GLENN: Yes. Just general ideas.

Glenn's expectations were thrown. He had more experience analyzing "really concrete" prose to which he could readily apply a standard five-paragraph pattern: "I remember this diagram that they drew for us a million times; there is the inverted triangle [on top] and then three rectangles and then the triangle at the bottom."

As he neared the 10-minute mark, Glenn did not have the thesis he could readily present (the inverted triangle) or the three points from which three paragraphs (the three rectangles) could be generated. He became conscious of the time. How to start:

> Some times I just think, "All right, what I'm going to do . . . is just start writing and it will come." [Other times I think,] "No, I am going to

search until I find a really good starting point that I am really confident of and go from that." And that is what I am doing right now is deciding which of those to use.

But after 10 minutes of reflection, an approach began to gel:

I think it is starting to come together, what I think the person who wrote the question wants. I am looking to the question. Specifically, "Does Jaspers' passage shed any light on Angelo's situation?" It is starting to come generally that Angelo is the modern man Jaspers is talking about.

At this point, the introductory phrase of Glenn's first paragraph ("Several elements of Jaspers' quote") "just popped into [his] brain," and he began writing, choosing to commence writing with a general direction but not with "a really good starting point."

Glenn then paused for 23 seconds ("Now I am thinking, 'Well, O.K., let's name the elements' ") and wrote his second sentence, looking back at the case history to make sure he was not forgetting any major points. As he was writing the second sentence ("Cacci's loss of caring for his girlfriends, his view of his job as 'O.K.,' his history in general all seem to point to a lack of commitment"), Glenn "just wanted to spew [the three topics] out, get them out and see where I could go from there," but was also aware that what was emerging would set him up for three paragraphs: "Right now, that is running through my brain, that classic essay pattern that I have."

The next three sentences came quickly. At this juncture, Glenn became concerned about "whether the things I was writing were really just the way I am feeling right now in my life . . . or whether they were really actual connections between the two [passages]." At first he worried about the evaluators' reaction, "but then I quickly got rid of that and wrote the way I wanted to." Still, at points throughout composing he expressed mild concern about his penchant for possibly subjective interpretation. ("I think it is the big problem with the whole paper.") Therefore, he often worked in a reference to or quotation from Jaspers or the case history, "trying to get it back to the factual."

The next seven sentences, hastily written, all short and rhythmically repetitious, developed by description rather than by analysis, support Glenn's contention that Angelo views his job with little emotion. Asked about the speed of the writing here, Glenn replied:

When I'm through, when the idea is finally washed out of my brain and onto the paper, and I feel safe that I am not going to lose it by putting in the punctuation, then I go back and put it in . . . I just really want to get the ideas out and just go, go, go with that, and something good will come out of it, and then [I'll] go back and worry about whether it's grammatically perfect or not.

Glenn's next statement revealed a self-assurance that undergirds his willingness to conceptually sprint through his essay and worry about grammar later: "I think I am confident enough about my abilities and grammar . . . that, you know, I feel safe enough that I can go ahead and just get all the ideas out and then worry about that."

But several sentences later, Glenn wrote, "He further discounts the relationship by comparing it to his"; he stopped, crossed out "his" and continued, "an older girlfriend." Glenn paused briefly, crossed out "older" and substituted "past." Questioned about what could be seen as a contradiction to his "go, go, go" injunction, Glenn explained: "I was thinking that the reader would interpret that as a girlfriend who was older than him . . . 'his' made it sound like it was his only girlfriend. He had two girlfriends." So while Glenn does not seem to be concerned about grammatical infelicities as he writes, he is very much concerned with even a single word's effect on his reader and does not leave the change, in this case anyway, for some after-the-fact editing period. Perhaps reader response (to a display of verbal prowess) is also behind the one other time Glenn stopped to ponder a single word. While composing the last sentence of paragraph one, he stopped after the clause "relegating his feelings for the girl": "I just really drew a blank. I started looking back at the word 'relegating.' I really like that word. . . . [But] I was looking back at it thinking 'it doesn't fit . . .' then I drifted off." After a 1½ minute pause, a phrase "just came and it sounded really good to [him]." The phrase ("to something commonplace, unexciting") allowed him to "use relegating in this sentence."

About to start paragraph two, Glenn again voiced concern "that I am not really connecting the two sources" and thus resorted to one of his favorite cohesive devices—a reference to Jaspers ("As Jaspers claims"). Throughout this paragraph, Glenn will oscillate between what he terms "the factual" and the expression of his "own feelings." He veers off, at times repetitively, into his own response to Angelo's situation, but continually pulls himself back to the texts with transitional phrases ("But as Jaspers says") or with direct quotations. Glenn discussed a similar but more conceptually elaborate technique while viewing the production of the sixth and seventh sentences of paragraph three. The sixth sentence grants a possibility, but the seventh expresses another point of view, one, by the way, that ties the discussion once again to Jaspers and cohesively back to the first paragraph's notion of absence of continuity: "That was another element of that perfect essay. In your first paragraph, you address the pros, you address the cons of the issue. You directly address what people might say against your topic, and you try to disprove them. Then you go on to what you feel . . . that is what this is, even though it comes at the middle of the paper when it would usually come at the very beginning."

Glenn's first attempt at a fourth paragraph resulted in an optimistic interpretation of Angelo's dream. Though Glenn deleted only three words in his first three paragraphs, he deleted this entire paragraph after finishing it and rereading the case history. (This was, by far, the largest deletion made by any of the 10 students.) "This paragraph's not too bad," he observed, "[but] it turns out to be totally wrong . . . when I read the dream the first time, I thought, 'an element of hope here,' . . . but I went back . . . and it doesn't show that at all." Glenn can express personal and, as one reader put it, "self-indulgent" views and then tie his discussion back to Jaspers and Angelo. But here he apparently transgressed some personal standard of objectivity and appropriateness. His second version of paragraph four—one that offers a bleaker interpretation of Angelo's dream—seemed more accurate to him: "The paragraph I wrote before . . . I must have known wasn't true, and that's what made me go back and read it." But Glenn's revision should not be seen as evidence of a deeply felt commitment to one point of view. He was pleased that though the original paragraph was "totally wrong," it was still "not too bad . . . which is one thing I like about my writing." Asked to elaborate, he explained: "I don't need a total commitment behind my writing . . . I could write on something that I did not really feel strongly about."

Beginning his last paragraph, Glenn was "trying to decide . . . whether there is anything new I can bring in . . . 'Is it time for a conclusion, or is there anything else I can bring up?' And, I am bored." Queried on how he was going to approach this conclusion, Glenn explained: "I am looking for one more really strong point, and I did not find it. So I wrote . . . a sort of tying-up of the ideas, addressing what maybe were the answers. That is another option to restating all of the old factors with no new ideas. That is what I did here—offer possible solutions to the problem." Asked if he learned his problem/solution approach when he learned his "classic essay pattern," Glenn said: "That is an option that I have adapted. I don't think they want us to do that in . . . this little ideal structure for an essay . . . It probably came out of that twelfth grade class [self-expressive writing] that I had . . . which [encouraged] getting your own ideas into the paper a little more." These deliberations resulted in Glenn's longest pause—three minutes and seven seconds. But after composing his first sentence, Glenn became concerned about violating his "little ideal structure": "I was thinking about the fact that I am not supposed to be bringing in any new ideas according to that ideal essay—God, I can't believe I still retain that thing—but I go ahead and do it anyway because I like the flow of what I'm writing." Having made his decision to follow the success of emerging production rather than an abstract ideal, Glenn produced two more sentences interrupted by five pauses. Then, while composing his fourth and final (and most rhetorically effective) sentence, he paused for 22 seconds:

> GLENN: I was really aware of ending with a quotation because that is another thing I have learned somewhere along the line. You never end with a quotation. You always end with your own words. Your interpretation of a quotation is all right, but you never end with a quotation.
>
> RESEARCHER: Then why did you end with a quotation?
>
> GLENN: Because it worked. It just worked there.

Glenn finished the sentence, smiled, and wrote "The End" at the bottom of the page. He did not proofread, though during each third of his composing time he did pause to reread several sentences or more of previous production: "I almost never proofread a paper . . . I feel this purging when I write—this 'get it all out, it's all done, I don't want to look at it anymore'—and I just hand it in."[6] Asked if he meant he was a one-draft writer he said "yes" and added: "They tried to get me into [rewriting] in high school . . . we would turn a paper in, get it back, do another draft, and turn it back in. I think I just did not see that many results or much change. I don't know how to rewrite is probably the problem. I don't know how to do it. I don't know how to go back over something and make it work better."

But though Glenn could probably present his much-considered audience with a more appealing essay if he proofread and revised accordingly, he is still a facile and effective—if somewhat unfocused and self-indulgent—student writer. At the end of the session I asked Glenn about writer's block; he answered with an assurance that characterized his composing: "I can't really remember a time when I sat down and it was like, 'My God! I don't know what the hell all this is.' Whereas my roommate does that all the time. So does the guy downstairs. It freaks me out. What's the problem. 'Here are all the sources. Let's go kids. Write!' "

The Invoking or Denial of Functional and Nonfunctional Composing-Process Rules and Assumptions

Glenn has a multioptional rule to direct him when facing the blank page—at times he "just starts writing and it will come," at other times he waits for "a really good starting point" before composing. The demands of the writing situation seem to determine which option he follows. In the present case, he used both: he thought through the assignment until his initial confusion was resolved ("Angelo is the modern man Jaspers is talking about") but waited no longer and began, working out a firmer direction through the first half of paragraph one.

In two instances, Glenn mentioned rules (Don't introduce new ideas in the last paragraph; Don't end the last paragraph with a quotation) but rejected them because they ran counter to the success of what he was producing. (In the case of the first rule, Glenn also had past instruction that encouraged him to question the rigid five-paragraph structure, though, it will be recalled, not without some conflict.) This rejection of rules in the face of success suggests, though this is conjecture, that Glenn composes with a high-level "meta-rule" which directs him to consider the context and effectiveness of his writing before acting on text or teacher rules. A statement of his suggests that such a rule might reflect something essential in his personality. "That is pretty much my attitude about everything. To hell with it if it does not work."

Three other rules, though not directly stated, can be inferred from repeated behaviors and protocol commentaries. One grants priority to getting ideas on paper rather than to grammatical correctness. Another gives the reader a central role in the composing process. The third is a complex, apparently flexible rule that directs a balance between personal observation and fidelity to assignment materials. The rule also presents options for maintaining fidelity: transitional references to authors, direct quotations, etc.

ENACTMENT OR REJECTION OF PREMATURE EDITING

Only one time in the protocol did Glenn concentrate on verbal surface to the sacrifice of his thought. The word "relegated" stumped him, and he drifted into reverie. Otherwise, both his behavior and his previously cited commentary gave precedence to ideas hitting paper. Felicities can be taken care of later. (And, in some cases, not at all, for while Glenn might have proofread sporadically, he did not do so methodically.)

Glenn's confidence in his grammatical skill could be an important variable here. Perhaps some such assurance frees writers up, allows them to concentrate on ideational substance, knowing all the while they can later clean up their flow of ideas. Certainly the reverse is true. Sondra Perl found that her basic writers were so concerned about their grammatical skills that they could not produce a single sentence without stopping a dysfunctional number of times to judge the correctness of their language.[7]

INTERPRETIVE AND WRITING STRATEGIES FOR COMPLEXITY

Glenn completed the essay with the aid of three effective strategies: an interpretive strategy that sought similarities between Jaspers and the case study, an organizational strategy that resembled the five-paragraph pattern he learned in high school, and a development/cohesion strategy, loosely adapted from argumentation, that resulted in a "granted this, but that" pattern within paragraphs. But Glenn did not gloss his materials in any way, and that absence of strategy (given his further reluctance to generate a written plan) might have negatively affected the organization and development, though obviously not the fluency, of his essay by making information somewhat inaccessible to him as he composed.

Pertinent to this study was Glenn's strategic flexibility. This flexibility was manifested in three ways.

1. Glenn "sometimes" makes outlines but, confused as he was during the session's first 10 minutes, decided not to: "I was looking at the information, and I was thinking that an outline wouldn't help me with this." Instead, he waited until he saw a connection between Jaspers and Angelo and then began to write, working out "a substitute for an outline" in the second sentence of his essay.

2. Though Glenn referred to his "classic essay pattern" three times in the protocol, he modified it as he brought it to bear on the assignment. He did not build inductively to a thesis—placed last—in his introductory paragraph; he did not refrain from bringing in new information in his conclusion. He modified or abandoned these characteristics of his "ideal essay pattern" as his barriers and discoveries demanded. (This does not mean to say that his adaptation was expertly effected. He failed to adequately explain all three of his subtopics within his first

paragraph, and he [I would guess inadvertently] did not develop those topics in the order presented in sentence two.)

3. In discussing his adaptation of a "pro-con" technique from his "ideal essay pattern" (and, in fact, he might be confusing two essay modes here — the expository and the argumentative), Glenn explained that the technique "would usually come at the very beginning" but that he needed it within the essay to bring him back to "the factual." Though Glenn might be working with a confused pattern, the important thing is that he can veer from it, modify it as need dictates. Again, this does not mean that his adaptation is without flaw. Though he competently executes his pro-con strategy at the sub-paragraph level, the entire essay seems to embody an argumentative thrust that is not really grounded in concrete opposition and never truly gels. It might well be that the argumentative approach allowed Glenn to best deal with the rhetorical problem presented by the essay. The way he solved the problem allowed him to bring an effective pro-con strategy to bear on his intra-paragraph fluctuations between personal indulgence and factual accuracy, but he was not able to expertly turn the entire discussion into solid argument.

Conflicting Rules, Plans, Strategies, and Assumptions

Glenn's protocol was free of any conflict. This was surprising, given the number of disparate rules and plans he mentioned. What is important, though, was that Glenn's rules and plans — as he expressed them — either embodied alternatives or were subject to situational exigencies.

One other potential conflict not mentioned above and only alluded to in the Overview was the possible clash between Glenn's concern for audience and his predilection to "get the ideas out and just go, go, go." A concern for audience could stymie some student writers, forcing a hyper-scrutinizing of every sentence generated. This was the case with one young woman in my pilot study, "Rigid Rules." But whereas she did not seem to have a clear notion of what her audience wanted or of how to integrate concern for audience into her composing process, Glenn seemed to have both a feel for his audience and an ability to use his audience awareness to aid his composing choices: "I had a really great idea in my brain, but I was feeling, 'Hum, this sentence isn't really getting my ideas out . . .' I guess I think a lot about the person who is going to be reading this paper. I try to think of the voice I am creating in the paper for the reader. . . . It gives me a really good focus which is really important when I'm writing." With the possible exception of Glenn's conflict over "relegating," his awareness of audience served to guide rather than block the flow of his prose. It did not force him to anxiously ponder the effect of every phrase.

The Evaluation of Writing and Attitudes Toward Writing

Glenn was very much aware of audience reaction to his work and several times expressed concern about reader response to his self-indulgence. (Though once he quickly countered his concern and "wrote the way [he] wanted to.") But, on the whole, he was pleased with his writing and assumed his reader would be as well.

As for Glenn's attitude toward writing, his questionnaire responses to "Even though it is difficult at times, I enjoy writing" and "I like having the opportunity to express my ideas in writing" were "Often" and "Almost Always," respectively. Yet, as was discussed earlier, Glenn can detach himself from his prose, almost, one feels, with a touch of cynicism. ("I could write on something that I did not really feel strongly about.") This does not mean to say that Glenn will write anything with equal abandon; as was seen, he felt better about a new, more accurate, fourth paragraph than about a falsely optimistic original. Asked about the motive for this revision, he replied, "I am interested in my own mind." Still, "I am just really lazy, most of the time, in my writing. I go a lot for what will sound good and sometimes it works. Usually it works." Asked why he thinks he seldom blocks, he replied, "I will settle for second best.[8] . . . Sometimes I feel like people can't really tell if it is the second-best idea . . . look at those papers I wrote in high school—all those A's." Glenn is a competent writer who has been reinforced for his efforts and who gets some pleasure out of exercising his skill. But his investment of personal energy stops there: "I don't feel my expository writing is going to be the way I ultimately want to express myself. It is not really that important to me."

DISCUSSION

Both readers had some positive things to say about Glenn's paper, and the average of their scores yielded the study's third highest evaluation. But the readers also pinpointed some obvious flaws: the treatment of Angelo and Jaspers, in one reader's words, "tends to be repetitive, to fail analytically." The essay never pulls its argumentative edges together. Development falters at several points. Infelicities and awkward constructions occasionally mar the prose. Perhaps the essay would have been tighter if Glenn had glossed his materials and attempted some sort of written plan. Perhaps the infelicities and awkward constructions would have been caught during careful proofreading. Whatever the case, Glenn did not make best use of his prewriting time nor did he proofread. His essay is intelligent but flawed. But it was produced quickly, displays fluency, and is relatively effective.

It would be difficult to deny that one explanation of Glenn's facility can be found in his lucky combination of competence and absence of self-imposed pressure. He is willing to settle for less than perfection because expository writing is "ultimately" not the way he wants to "express himself." (It turns out that songwriting is.) Taking what Glenn values into account, one still cannot deny the importance of the rules he has that spark production and offer context-dependent alternatives and the importance of his ability to abandon potentially rigid rules when he sees that they run counter to the flow or effect of his discourse. Also important are his planning and discourse strategies and his ability to extract, modify, and apply techniques from them. One could easily imagine a student who shared Glenn's attitude toward academic exposition but who lacked the linguistic skill and/or the cognitive flexibility that enabled Glenn to succeed as he did.

It seems as though Glenn's fluency and adaptability are rooted in two not unrelated high-level concerns: the importance of displaying his mental facility and his interest in the reaction of his reader. Though Glenn effects a certain distance between himself and his page ("I could write on something that I did not really feel strongly about"), it is important to him that what he writes is not "totally wrong" and that he balances his "subjectivity" with "objective" elements from an assignment's materials. He seems to take pride in his ability to produce academic writing. It seems, as well, that Glenn is very concerned with sounding intelligent, with weaving discourse that cleverly connects to a clever reader. This ultimately rhetorical concern significantly influences his composing: he won't edit prematurely because it might interrupt the flow of his thoughts. He won't hold to rigid rules like "don't end your last paragraph with a quotation" because they will subvert the felicitous effects he's creating. He'll adapt a strategy like the give and take of argument if it seems effective in its new guise. Glenn might well hold to fundamental assumptions about school writing that are not all that different from the rhetorician's assumption that discourse is a social act.

NOTES

[1] Linda Flower, *Problem Solving Strategies for Writing* (New York: Harcourt, 1981).

[2] Michael Polanyi, *Personal Knowledge* (Chicago: Univ. of Chicago Pr., 1962).

[3] Linda Flower and John R. Hayes, "The Cognition of Discovery: Defining a Rhetorical Problem," *College Composition and Communication* 31 (1980): 21–32.

[4] Janet Emig, *The Composing Processes of Twelfth Graders* (Urbana: National Council of Teachers of English, 1971).

[5] Gary Sloan, "Predilections for Plethoric Prose," *College English* 39 (1978): 860–65; Rosemary L. Hake and Joseph M. Williams, "Style and Its Consequences: Do as I Do, Not as I Say," *College English* 43 (1981): 433–51.

[6] Earlier Glenn said that after he pours an idea out onto paper he can "go back and worry about whether its grammatically perfect or not," yet here he says he "almost never proofread(s) a paper." (And, in fact, he did not methodically proofread the present essay.) These two statements might not be contradictory. Glenn could mean that after dashing out a particular sentence, he'll tend to quickly look back over it and clean it up (the tape displayed some behavior of this sort), but that after an essay is done, he rarely rereads the entire text for error.

[7] Sondra Perl, " 'Five Writers Writing': Case Studies of the Composing Processes of Unskilled College Writers" (Ph.D. diss., New York Univ., 1978).

[8] Before we label this statement immature or complacent, we should consider a further statement, one by William Stafford: "There are never mornings when I can't write. I think there are never mornings that anybody 'can't write.' I think that anybody could write if he would have standards as low as mine." *Writing the Australian Crawl* (Ann Arbor: Univ. of Michigan Pr., 1978), 104. There are times when settling for second-best might aid more than limit our composing.

AUTHOR'S NOTE: Details on the development of the questionnaire and of the statistical analyses accompanying it can be found in Rose, 1981 and 1984. Let me add here that since its development, the questionnaire has been used in other studies and has been translated into Spanish (Betancourt and Phinney, 1988) and Chinese (Lee and Krashen, 2003). To my knowledge, all further applications of it have confirmed its conceptual and statistical validity. The reader should feel free to copy and use it.

Appendix A: Writer's Block Questionnaire

Below are 24 statements about what people do or how they feel when they write. Under each is a five-point scale describing degrees of agreement or disagreement with the statement. We would like you to fill in the dot under the degree of agreement or disagreement that best describes your own writing behavior. For example, if the statement reads:

<blockquote>Like Hemingway, I write standing up.</blockquote>

and if you rarely or never write standing up, you should respond in the following way:

THIS DESCRIBES WHAT I DO OR HOW I FEEL:

ALMOST ALWAYS (90 to 100% of the time)	OFTEN (75% of the time)	SOMETIMES (50% of the time)	OCCASIONALLY (25% of the time)	ALMOST NEVER (0 to 10% of the time)
○	○	○	○	●

If another statement reads:

<blockquote>I write with #2 pencils.</blockquote>

and if you sometimes do (that is, not always and not rarely but about half the time), you should respond:

THIS DESCRIBES WHAT I DO OR HOW I FEEL:

ALMOST ALWAYS (90 to 100% of the time)	OFTEN (75% of the time)	SOMETIMES (50% of the time)	OCCASIONALLY (25% of the time)	ALMOST NEVER (0 to 10% of the time)
○	○	●	○	○

This questionnaire requires that you reflect on your writing behavior. Some items will be easy to answer, but others might be a little difficult because you'll have to analyze what you do by habit. It would probably be best to recall exactly what you did when you wrote a recent paper. This way you can *report what you actually do, not what you wish you could do*. Obviously, you will not be graded on this. Therefore, you can feel free to candidly report what you do and feel when you write. Again, don't report what you would like to do and feel but what you *actually* do and feel. For that fact, as you work through the questionnaire you might realize that an earlier response wasn't right. If that happens, it is OK to go back and change your answer to make it more accurate.

1) Even though it is difficult at times, I enjoy writing.
THIS DESCRIBES WHAT I DO OR HOW I FEEL:

ALMOST ALWAYS (90 to 100% of the time)	OFTEN (75% of the time)	SOMETIMES (50% of the time)	OCCASIONALLY (25% of the time)	ALMOST NEVER (0 to 10% of the time)
○	○	○	○	○

2) I've seen some really good writing, and my writing doesn't match up to it.

ALMOST ALWAYS	OFTEN	SOMETIMES	OCCASIONALLY	ALMOST NEVER
○	○	○	○	○

3) My first paragraph has to be perfect before I'll go on.

ALMOST ALWAYS	OFTEN	SOMETIMES	OCCASIONALLY	ALMOST NEVER
○	○	○	○	○

4) I have to hand in assignments late because I can't get the words on paper.

ALMOST ALWAYS	OFTEN	SOMETIMES	OCCASIONALLY	ALMOST NEVER
○	○	○	○	○

5) It is hard for me to write on topics that could be written about from a number of angles.

ALMOST ALWAYS	OFTEN	SOMETIMES	OCCASIONALLY	ALMOST NEVER
○	○	○	○	○

6) I like having the opportunity to express my ideas in writing.

ALMOST ALWAYS	OFTEN	SOMETIMES	OCCASIONALLY	ALMOST NEVER
○	○	○	○	○

7) There are times when I sit at my desk for hours, unable to write a thing.

ALMOST ALWAYS	OFTEN	SOMETIMES	OCCASIONALLY	ALMOST NEVER
○	○	○	○	○

8) I'll wait until I've found just the right phrase.

ALMOST ALWAYS	OFTEN	SOMETIMES	OCCASIONALLY	ALMOST NEVER
○	○	○	○	○

9) While writing a paper, I'll hit places that keep me stuck for an hour or more.

ALMOST ALWAYS	OFTEN	SOMETIMES	OCCASIONALLY	ALMOST NEVER
○	○	○	○	○

10) My teachers are familiar with so much good writing that my writing must look bad by comparison.

ALMOST ALWAYS	OFTEN	SOMETIMES	OCCASIONALLY	ALMOST NEVER
○	○	○	○	○

11) I have trouble figuring out how to write on issues that have many interpretations.

ALMOST ALWAYS	OFTEN	SOMETIMES	OCCASIONALLY	ALMOST NEVER
○	○	○	○	○

12) There are times when it takes me over two hours to write my first paragraph.

ALMOST ALWAYS   OFTEN   SOMETIMES OCCASIONALLY ALMOST NEVER
○   ○   ○   ○   ○

13) I think my writing is good.

ALMOST ALWAYS   OFTEN SOMETIMES OCCASIONALLY ALMOST NEVER
○   ○   ○   ○   ○

14) I run over deadlines because I get stuck while trying to write my paper.

ALMOST ALWAYS   OFTEN SOMETIMES OCCASIONALLY ALMOST NEVER
○   ○   ○   ○   ○

15) There are times when I'm not sure how to organize all the information I've gathered for a paper.

ALMOST ALWAYS   OFTEN SOMETIMES OCCASIONALLY ALMOST NEVER
○   ○   ○   ○   ○

16) I find myself writing a sentence then erasing it, trying another sentence, then scratching it out. I might do this for some time.

ALMOST ALWAYS   OFTEN SOMETIMES OCCASIONALLY ALMOST NEVER
○   ○   ○   ○   ○

17) It is awfully hard for me to get started on a paper.

ALMOST ALWAYS   OFTEN SOMETIMES OCCASIONALLY ALMOST NEVER
○   ○   ○   ○   ○

18) Each sentence I write has to be just right before I'll go on to the next sentence.

ALMOST ALWAYS   OFTEN SOMETIMES OCCASIONALLY ALMOST NEVER
○   ○   ○   ○   ○

19) I find it difficult to write essays on books and articles that are very complex.

ALMOST ALWAYS   OFTEN SOMETIMES OCCASIONALLY ALMOST NEVER
○   ○   ○   ○   ○

20) I think of my instructors reacting to my writing in a positive way.

ALMOST ALWAYS   OFTEN SOMETIMES OCCASIONALLY ALMOST NEVER
○   ○   ○   ○   ○

21) Writing is a very unpleasant experience for me.

ALMOST ALWAYS   OFTEN SOMETIMES OCCASIONALLY ALMOST NEVER
○   ○   ○   ○   ○

22) There are times when I find it hard to write what I mean.

ALMOST ALWAYS   OFTEN SOMETIMES OCCASIONALLY ALMOST NEVER
○   ○   ○   ○   ○

23) I have trouble with writing assignments that ask me to compare and contrast or analyze.

ALMOST ALWAYS   OFTEN SOMETIMES OCCASIONALLY ALMOST NEVER
○   ○   ○   ○   ○

24) Some people experience periods when, no matter how hard they try, they can produce little, if any, writing. When these periods last for a considerable amount of time, we say the person has a writing block. Estimate how often you experience writer's block.

ALMOST ALWAYS   OFTEN SOMETIMES OCCASIONALLY ALMOST NEVER
○   ○   ○   ○   ○

Appendix B: Assignment Materials for Stimulated-Recall Study

INSTRUCTIONS

1. Read the case history of Angelo Cacci (it's attached to this sheet) and the quotation from Karl Jaspers printed below.

2. Write an essay in which you discuss Angelo Cacci's situation in terms of the quotation from Jaspers. That is, does Jaspers' passage shed any light on Angelo's situation? If it does, explain how. If it doesn't, explain that as well. Supply evidence from the case history and the quotation to support your assertions.

It has been said that in modern times man has been shuffled together with other men like a grain of sand. He is an element of an apparatus in which he occupies now one location, now another, . . . He has occupation, indeed, but his life has no continuity. What he does is done to good purpose, but is then finished once and for all. The task may be repeated after the same fashion many times, but it cannot be repeated in such an intimate way as to become, one might say, part of the personality of the doer; it does not lead to an expansion of the selfhood . . . Love for things and human beings wanes and disappears. The machine-made products vanish from sight as soon as they are made and consumed; all that remains in view is the machinery by which new commodities are being made. The worker at the machine, concentrating upon immediate aims, has no time or inclination left for the contemplation of life as a whole.

THE CASE OF ANGELO CACCI

A young man visited a local counseling center because he was feeling "very down in the dumps." Angelo Cacci was 32 years old, lived alone, and was employed as a clerk in a large insurance company. The counselor noted that Angelo was fairly good looking, clean-shaven, and dressed nicely, though not expensively. He spoke articulately, though not with any particular flair; however, the lack of emphasis in his speech could have been related to his depression. He seemed to be willing to discuss his history and his feelings.

Angelo stated that he had had passing periods of the "blues" before, but that his present feelings of depression were more severe. Several months earlier, Angelo had broken up with his girl friend. "It just wasn't working out," he explained. "We used to go out—go to the park, a ball game, the movies—but after a while it fizzled. I just didn't feel that much for her any more." He added that a similar event had occurred with a different woman five years earlier.

Angelo talked a great deal about his past. He came from an Italian, working-class family. He has a brother and sister but doesn't see either one any longer. His brother was transferred to another large city because the automotive industry was booming there. His sister moved out west after she got married. When Angelo was younger, the Cacci family lived in a predominately Italian neighborhood. Both of the paternal grandparents died when Angelo was quite young. Still, some of Angelo's fondest memories were of his grandfather. The old man used to take him fishing outside the city. Angelo's father, on the other hand, didn't have much time for his children. Mr. Cacci supported the family as a dockworker, but he left when Angelo was 11. After the separation, Mrs. Cacci got a job in a clock factory, and she has worked there ever since.

Angelo explained that his childhood was a very unhappy period. His father was seldom home, and when he was present, he was constantly fighting with Mrs. Cacci. Mrs. Cacci usually became sullen and withdrawn after an argument, refused to speak to her husband, and became uncommunicative with her children. Angelo remembered that many times as a child he was puzzled because it seemed that his mother was angry with him too. Sometimes after an argument, Mrs. Cacci told her children that she ruined her life by marrying a "truckdriver." Angelo went on, explaining that his mother rarely smiled or laughed and did not converse very much with the children. When she came home from work she would usually put on her robe, cook dinner, and spend the evening watching television. This pattern continued well into Angelo's young adulthood.

After high school, Angelo went into the Army where he developed good typing, clerical, and basic accounting skills. He describes the Army as being uneventful. He put in his time and was honorably discharged.

Angelo characterized his job as being, "O.K." "It pays the bills and leaves me a decent amount for entertainment." His particular task is to certify damage claims by checking customer estimates against insurance investigator reports. This provides the company with the information it needs to challenge possibly exaggerated or even fraudulent claims. On an average day, Angelo said he examines and registers twenty to twenty-five estimates and reports. The counselor noted that Angelo's work record must be a good one. He has been with the company for ten years and regularly gets the raises afforded employees in good standing.

The reason for Angelo's visit to the counseling center, his depression, puzzled him. He recounted a dream he has had several times in the last month, wondering if it is connected to his depression. The counselor described the dream in Angelo's case history, but, though she might have offered an interpretation, she didn't write it down. In the dream Angelo and a man from another department in the insurance firm are walking in an open field. Horses are roaming the area as are several large dogs. One of the dogs seems to be injured and limps by Angelo and his friend. A third man appears and begins attending to the dog. Here either the dream fades or Angelo wakes up. Angelo then turned to other aspects of his life, but didn't see any immediate connection between them and his situation. "Sure I broke up with my girl," he speculated, "but I wasn't in love with her. Besides, I've been through this before." As for his job, "like I explained, it's all right. I've got a good record and the pay is satisfactory." As for his mother, "I go to see her now and then. She's still gloomy as always, but I realize there's little I can do about it. She's been that way for a long time."

3

Complexity, Rigor, Evolving Method, and the Puzzle of Writer's Block: Thoughts on Composing Process Research

1985

AUTHOR'S NOTE: Sometime in early 1982, I was asked by Linda Flower and John Hayes to edit a volume in a series on writing research they were coordinating for Guilford Press. They suggested a collection that would follow the lead of my writer's block study and address problems with composing. I would solicit original essays and would write an introduction and conclusion. I agreed, and the resulting book was titled *When a Writer Can't Write: Studies in Writer's Block and Other Composing-Process Problems.*

This was my first crack at editing something like this, and it proved to be a powerful experience, by turns frustrating and instructive. For starters, most of the contributors were more established than I was, some much more, so it felt awkward to be sending manuscripts back and asking for further revision and elaboration. In all, the project took much longer (several years) and required much more effort than I could have imagined. I would not recommend taking on such a task to young scholars, unless — as was the case here — it provides an opportunity to shape an area of inquiry. Editing *When a Writer Can't Write* gave me a lot of respect for people who put together collections of original work.

But the project did bring me into close contact with people whom I admired, people who thought quite differently about writing than I did — particularly in regard to the cognitive framework I was using at the time. This diversity of views was valuable beyond words for me and pushed my own thinking for this concluding chapter, especially about issues of research methodology.

I reprint the first four paragraphs of the preface to give a better sense of the collection, which included works by people who are well known to the composition community: David Bartholomae, Lynn Bloom, John Daly, Donald Graves, Muriel Harris, Donald Murray, and Cynthia Selfe. Bartholomae's essay "Inventing the University" would become one of the most cited articles in composition studies. Here is the opening of the book:

No one writes effortlessly. Our composing is marked by pauses, false starts, gnawing feelings of inadequacy, crumpled paper. Many of these dead ends are necessary; they occur when we've come up short on information or hit a knotty conceptual problem, when we can't quite arrive at the most effective way to organize material or we're trying to go beyond staid and stereotypic phrasing. Would that more writers understood such tangles for what they are: signs that they've hit a critical moment in composing. And would that more writers honored these moments—took the time to struggle with the conceptual or rhetorical challenge they present. Our reading would be made sweeter by their efforts.

But some writers with some tasks seem unduly vexed. Thoughts won't come, and when they do they evanesce as the writer tries to work them into written language. Pauses become longer and longer and transmogrify into avoidances. Inner conflicts manifest themselves in jumbled syntax and unclear diction. The demands of one's life and the ways one has been taught to deal with them interfere again and again with writing. The conventions of a genre or a discipline baffle and intimidate rather than guide. The very way one composes contains within it narrow or rigid assumptions and procedures that stymie production. And so goes the painful litany.

Distinguishing the necessary, productive dead end from the intractable composing-process problem is difficult and is ultimately a judgment that must be made after some consideration of an individual's writing history and current practice. There is no quick definition of writer's block, no facile description of the stymied writer. It is into this uncertain territory that the authors in this volume venture, and while no single author arrives at an easy formula, together they provide the reader with a good sense of what can go wrong as the writer writes.

This volume marks an attempt, the first of its kind really, to bring together a number of investigations focusing on composing-process problems. The essays address various cognitive and emotional dimensions of disrupted composing and describe some of the situational variables that can contribute to it. One of the strengths of the collection is the variety of methods the investigations include: naturalistic inquiry, survey procedures, tracing of cognitive process, clinical–experimental techniques, text analysis, and literary analysis. These investigations involve children, adolescents, college students, and academic and professional writers and are concerned with both theory and practice.

It took me a long time to think through and write my contribution to this collection, at least six or seven months as I remember it. There was the challenge of saying something original and, to be sure, some anxiety about wanting to do right by the contributors I had leaned on so hard. Linda Flower, as one of the general editors, proved to be a great help to me in my own struggles.

Looking back at the essay, I see several developments in it. Though it remains pretty much within a psychological paradigm, I was trying to expand its framework to include emotion and the writer's situational context. Unfortunately, as I note in the essay, I could only do some of this speculatively because of the limited information I had about the student who was the focus of the case study. From where I stand now — and where the field is — it's a pretty bounded articulation of context. The last fifteen or so years have seen the further development of other methodologies in composition that could be fruitful here. It would be revealing, for example, to consider the student, Stephanie, through a feminist perspective, one that puts gender in the center of focus. To do that perspective justice, we would need more information about Stephanie's history as a student, her interaction with her family around school and writing, and her composing process(es) with other kinds of writing. Also, some of the constraints of the present study would be altered to enable a different kind of interaction with me and to explore a wider range of topics and forms, spoken and written.

Still, for all its limits, I can see me moving, within disciplinary limitations, toward the contextual and social. Soon after completing the draft of this chapter, I would begin researching "The Language of Exclusion: Writing Instruction at the University," which would lead me to the use of a broader historical analysis in writing about writing.

The second development I see in "Complexity, Rigor" is the focus on research methodology. To be sure, my dissertation (especially working with a guy like Rich Shavelson) contains a lot of discussion of method, but in this essay method takes center stage. I realize that some readers of this book will not find the orientation of the essay particularly compelling, but what I hope maintains value is the endorsement of multiple methods and perspectives and the systematic and cautious way I try to develop the essay's argument. I would later bring some of the lessons learned here — particularly that close articulation of method — to bear on discussions of the thought processes of basic writers in the article "Narrowing the Mind and Page: Remedial Writers and Cognitive Reductionism." And, as I reread the endnotes — which provide detail on various research methods — I'm struck by the ways they prefigure the orientation of much later work, like " 'Our Hands Will Know' " (p. 335) and "The Working Life of a Waitress" (p. 362).

Considering the three pieces together — "Rigid Rules," the two case studies from *Writer's Block*, and "Complexity, Rigor" — I'm proud of the linkages among them. Work in the classroom and the tutoring center was the source of experience that led to the informal inquiry of the first essay, and that inquiry led, in turn, to the more rigorous writer's block study, and that study made possible broader speculation on research methodology itself. I doubt that no one part of this sequence would have been possible without the other.

I

When I first became interested in writer's block as a dissertation topic, several influential faculty at my school tried to dissuade me. They said the problem was too complicated, too messy, or, to be a little more precise, too uncontrollable to be explored with the tools of traditional educational research. I ignored them, went my way, and now six years later must admit that they were right. As the contributors to the present volume make very clear, a writer can be stymied for all sorts of reasons; and any one of those reasons, if isolable, would itself be difficult to explore. And then there's the thorny problem of definition. As Donald Murray warns, "Not writing can be writing." There are all sorts of necessary mulling and rehearsing periods in our composing processes; differentiating them from true blocks is difficult, perhaps in some cases impossible. And there's a related issue: Writing blocks are usually defined in negative terms. Should they be? Donald Graves suggests that some blocks are a necessary by-product of growth. Should we then even approach writer's block as a difficulty? Questions like these make clear that writer's block is one messy problem or, more likely, a web of problems. The temptation, of course, is to render it manageable, reduce it, define it in reductive ways (as, for example, the psychoanalyst Edmund Bergler did by labeling it a breakdown of unconscious defenses against oralmasochistic conflicts) or examine it in reductive ways (for example, by recording its behavioral manifestations — time spent pausing, number of words produced, etc.). Now, certainly, some delimiting, some selecting, some excluding of cases is necessary for any inquiry to proceed — whether the inquiry be ethnographic, cognitive-process tracing, or classically experimental. All research sets limits. But there comes a point past which the limiting of a problem changes the problem. The question, then, was how to explore this very real and thus very messy problem without unduly sacrificing its complexity. The rest of this chapter will be an attempt to provide — through example as well as speculation — some answers to this question.

Clearly, whatever formal research decisions I made in planning my study had to grow out of the preliminary, to a large extent "soft," information about writing blocks I already had: observations as a teacher, anecdotes, hunches, and simple pilot studies. This information was revealing a number of problems that seemed to be primarily cognitive rather than primarily emotional. The more I read in cognitive psychology — and the more I adapted and analogized it to the writing process — the more sense I was making of some of my students' behaviors (Rose, 1980). These early investigations were instructive, but a truly comprehensive exploration of the cognitive dimension of writer's block would require more scope and more rigor. Now, the issue of rigor raises the problem about reductive limiting I mentioned earlier. Rigor in traditional educational investigation is often equated with experimental designs; but, at this early stage of investigation, I didn't have enough information to enable

From *When a Writer Can't Write: Studies in Writer's Block and Other Composing Process Problems.* Ed. Mike Rose. New York: Guilford, 1985. 227–60.

me to effectively use such designs. Furthermore, even with richer information, traditional designs alone—though they offer more latitude than is often thought[1]—might have proved to be too constraining to illuminate the richness of a multifaceted composing problem. Was there another kind of rigor that wouldn't sacrifice complexity? The answer that my chairman, Richard Shavelson, and I arrived at was to use multiple methods that, since they would all be focused on the same problem, might reveal different dimensions of the problem or provide multiple readings of the same dimension, each reading confirming or qualifying the other. This strategy provided the kind of rigor one attains with multidiagnostic procedures in clinical medicine, with "triangulation" in sociology (Denzin, 1970; Webb, Campbell, Schwartz, & Sechrest, 1966), and with the more eclectic interpretive approaches in literary criticism. A rigor of multiple sightings rather than a rigor of singular constraints.

Let me now briefly summarize the study to illustrate the kinds and sequence of methods we used and suggest ways that the various methods enhanced each other. This summary will provide a starting point for my proposal of a comprehensive composing-process research framework.

We began by framing a questionnaire from information gained during my preliminary observations and pilot studies. One reason we needed a questionnaire was to enable us to identify large numbers of stymied or fluent writers, but we had other reasons for framing the questionnaire as well. First of all, we had to arrive at some identifying behavioral characteristics of writer's block. How else would we (or other teachers and researchers) know what to look for? Since I had conducted a number of conferences with students who reported themselves (or were referred) as being stymied or fluent writers, I had a sense of what general behaviors accompanied writer's block and also a sense of the variety of ways that students themselves used the term. For example, one student was bored with school; her assignments—in or outside of composition class—didn't spark much interest, and she didn't spend much, if any, time on them. Out of the blue she said, "I guess I've got a writing block." Responses like this gave me some sense of the term's popular usage but also made me realize that some delimiting boundaries had to be established. Otherwise "writer's block" would mean everything—and nothing. The pilot interviews revealed some broad behavioral indicators of writer's block (e.g., a number of stymied writers seemed to spend a good deal of time editing a sentence before going on to the next sentence). These indicators would allow us to identify students who fit our consensus of what "writer's block" meant and exclude cases, like that of the disenchanted student, that seemed more rooted in lack of motivation, boredom, uncertainty about one's career goals, and so on.

Another reason for framing a questionnaire was to gain further information about the cognitive dimension of writer's block. If we created subscales (subcategories of questionnaire items) that tapped behaviors and attitudes that provided further clues about cognition, then our questionnaire inquiry could be a bit more refined. That is, we could say more than "the student reports blocking behaviors like spending long periods of time without getting words on paper." We could also say, for example, "The student reports problems with organizing complex discourse or with evaluating his/her own writing." Via statistical analyses, we would then be able to explore the relationships among blocking behaviors and these other difficulties.

We administered the questionnaire over the year to six different groups of undergraduates at the University of California (Los Angeles), who ranged in English experience, class standing, and major. After each administration, we interviewed a small subsample of students and, as well, conducted statistical analyses. We used both sources of information to refine the instrument. (A much fuller discussion of the questionnaire as well as other artifacts and procedures of the study can be found in Rose, 1984.)

But questionnaires, no matter how refined, provide only one kind of report on behavior and attitude. We needed to find out what lay behind these responses. We chose 10 students from extreme ends of the 351 undergraduates who took the fifth version of the questionnaire. The 10, 6 high-blockers and 4 low-blockers, varied in English experience, class standing, major, and response to the different subscales. I closely explored the writing behaviors of these students via a technique adapted from decision-making research, "stimulated recall." The way I used it, stimulated recall worked as follows: Each student was presented with a university-level writing topic and was given some time to become familiar with it. Each was then given one hour to compose, and while composing each was alone. Two videotape cameras—one partially concealed across the room, another behind the student—respectively recorded the student from the waist up and the student's text emerging on the page. When the hour was over, I returned to the room and played the tapes to the student. What the student saw was a split screen: he or she on one side, the emerging text on the other. I stopped the tape at every pause, lining out, rescanning, and so on, and questioned these behaviors. The student, too, could stop the tape and comment. Our entire series of questions and answers was recorded on audiotape and later transcribed. The transcription, called a "protocol," could then be analyzed.

With the assistance of an independent rater, I analyzed the protocols, identifying and tallying, among other things, composing rules; plans used to interpret the assignment; assumptions about composing; instances of conflict among rules, plans, and assumptions; instances of editing at inappropriate times during composing; and, finally, positive and negative evaluations voiced by the student about the text he or she was creating.

We further decided that the fullest picture of blocking would emerge if we computed additional quantitative measures from the videotapes and from the students' written productions, measures that, taken alone, are pretty reductionistic, but that could provide one more perspective on blocking or fluency: We recorded time spent prewriting and planning and time spent in various kinds of pauses; we tallied words written and deleted on assignment materials, scratch paper, and drafts. Finally, we had the essays evaluated by two independent raters.

In the final, comprehensive analysis, then, we brought all our data to bear on the puzzle of writer's block. In summary, the data included questionnaire self-reports; tallies of prewriting, pausing, and planning time; tallies of words produced and deleted; reader evaluations of essays; the tracing and tabulation of a variety of cognitive-behavioral entities and processes, including rules, plans, assumptions, premature editing, conflict, and self-evaluations; and, finally, observations of mannerisms and other behaviors that would not be caught by the more circumscribed quantitative analyses. These data were presented in tabular as well as discursive formats and also were written up as case studies. The variety of methods and presentations checked and complemented each other. Tallies of pauses and of words produced and deleted helped make precise the qualitative observations, and observations fleshed out simple tallies as well as measures of cognitive processes. Empirical counts confirmed or checked questionnaire self-reports. Observations of the writers at work provided context for what the writers produced and for what the readers said about those productions. And so on. One single method would have been inadequate to reveal the complexities of writer's block or to verify, qualify, or reject our speculations about it. But multiple methods enabled us to gain a rich array of perspectives on a complicated composing problem and allowed us to formulate a theory about certain kinds of blocking.

The above narrative gives a sense of what we did, of how we used a varied methodology to reveal a dimension of a complex writing behavior. But the narrative, it seems to me, raises two concerns. First, it appears that we treated all methods as equals, picked them happily out of the researcher's bag of tricks as we needed them. Yet it is common knowledge that methods carry with them particular assumptions about reality and knowledge. Did we consider the philosophical roots of the methods we combined? This question is important and is central to one of the conclusions of this chapter, so I'll save it for the final section. The second concern, and I'll address it now, involves the limited focus of my study.

II

The study was successful in that it demonstrated a complex dimension of blocking that was primarily cognitive, mapped that dimension, modeled it, and derived from it practical implications for instruction. But, clearly, no complex composing behavior is purely cognitive; so, while this study was broad in scope, it was still constrained in that its primary purpose was to explore the heretofore neglected cognitive dimension of writer's block. Affective and sociocultural data were recorded and briefly discussed but were not fully explored. Further studies or networks of studies would have been required to investigate these dimensions. Now, this recognition implies more than the obvious fact that a single study can accomplish only so much; it also suggests that, where writer's block or any other complex writing behavior is concerned, a broad conceptual research framework (as well as an array of methods) is needed. This framework should have both structural value (it can assist in the organization of studies and of information gained from those studies) and heuristic value (it can serve as a reminder about kinds of information that must be sought out). I suggest that one such powerful framework would be the cognitive/affective/social-contextual trinity that organizes the present volume. This framework contains the traditional two domains of human mental reality and the social context that influences and is influenced by that reality. Let me quickly describe each of these dimensions, orienting each brief description in a direction consonant with the aims of this book. I will then qualify the framework's use and demonstrate its utility with a preliminary case study.

The Social-Contextual Dimension

Because writing can be such a private act, we tend to forget that it is also, paradoxically, a social act. Writing is learned; it isn't naturally acquired as is speech (though speech, too, needs a social context to develop). And as it's learned, learned as well are the myriad explanations, opinions, and biases of the immediate societies of teachers and family and the larger societies of institutions and communities that teach and receive writing. Even the solitary diarist manifests vestiges of the environment in which he or she learned to write: stylistic turns, images of past audiences, and so on.

The social sphere provides, in most cases, the prompt to write: school essays, business reports, editor's proposals, letters of request or complaint, personal letters. And any prompt carries with it specific constraints (e.g., deadline, mode) as well as general atmosphere (e.g., supportive, critical). Then the social sphere again has its say by responding to the writing that is produced. Response is critical. What Donald Graves tells us about the young writer's life remains true, in different guises, throughout a writer's growth: The responses of others can foster or limit the development of mechanical, grammatical, and rhetorical competence. And social influences do not begin or end with the immediate responses. There exist institutionally based criteria and expectations (tacit or articulated) like those discussed by David Bartholomae; and there exist, as well, broad cultural expectations that might well find expression within a particular setting—for example, the notions about women and the academy that seem to hamper the female graduate students that Lynn Bloom discusses.

In an attempt to arrive at an understanding of general mental processes, many traditional psychological/educational studies try to remove or control for social and environmental interferences. Yet, though situational variables can obscure or be mistaken for individual cognitive or emotional effects, they can also be powerful determiners and shapers of those effects. "Human behavior is complexly influenced by the context in which it occurs," notes Stephen Wilson (1977, p. 253); and Elliot Mishler boldly asks, " 'Meaning in context'—is there any other kind?" (Mishler, 1979). Even those who were major figures in the development of traditional social science experimental designs now question the attempt to exclude context from the derivation and interpretation of experimental data (Campbell, 1974, 1979; Cronbach, 1975). It seems, then, that composing-process researchers need to keep in mind the fact that the situation—both the immediate writing context as well as the larger school and social environment—plays into a study's results, needs to at least be acknowledged as part of the data.

Affect and Cognition

Because of the fundamental interplay of mind and social context, the elements of one's setting interact with, are filtered through, modify or are modified by, one's knowledge of and beliefs, assumptions, and theories about the world: one's skills and one's fears, one's predilections and one's interpretations. We now, of course, enter the realm of individual differences.

One longstanding Western convention for talking about mental reality has been to separate cognition from affect, intellect from feeling. Certainly, this convention has not gone without its philosophical and literary challenges. And a number of contemporary personality and clinical theorists have proposed a complex interweaving of cognition and affect (see, e.g., Ellis, 1959; Kelly, 1963; and Shapiro, 1965); several have even argued for the cognitive bases of emotional states (see Beck, 1976, on depression; and Lazarus & Averill, 1972, on anxiety) and for the emotional dimension of acts usually thought to be cognitive (Maslow, 1968, 1969). Such complex interweaving certainly manifests itself in composing. A fear of taking chances with one's writing, for example, might well stem from the way one assesses one's skills; and rigid planning strategies could be tied to feelings of inadequacy as a writer. Still, there is value, both theoretical and pedagogical, in speaking of some mental activities as being *primarily* cognitive (e.g., planning strategies) and others as *primarily* affective (e.g., fearing writing), as long as it is remembered that emotion cannot always be neatly stripped away from the way we deal with information.

The Affective Dimension

Writers don't simply process information in computer-like fashion. Professional writers often speak of the emotionally charged core of material that they then shape into the literature we read (see, e.g., the interviews in Cowley, 1977; Plimpton, 1977, 1981). And all of us have had the experience of being excited or dispirited as we've produced a piece of writing. The topic, setting, and constraints of a writing task each has the potential to arouse a variety of feelings. And there are times when these feelings can be overpowering. A writer's conflicts and fears can subvert the composing process. Some students get apprehensive when facing school-based writing assignments. Peitzman (1981) found that an emotionally loaded topic stymied one of her student writers. A very competent student writer whom I studied (Rose, 1981) got anxious during the study and reduced her normally complex planning and organizing strategies to an associational stream of ideas. Writers, then, can experience some level of discomfort—of anxiety, anger, or depression; and, if sufficiently pronounced, the discomfort can lead to a variety of observable responses: an agitated or flat style; an inability to get anything on paper; even, as Holland's (1980) work suggests, an avoidance of certain writing tasks altogether.

These reactions, to borrow an important distinction of Spielberger's (1972), can be "state-specific," that is, particular to a given environment, kind of writing task, or kind of topic, or can be more generalized, or a "trait" of the individual's personality—a wide variety of writing tasks trigger a negative response. This distinction is extremely important, for we have a tendency to make generalizations about people's emotional responses from limited observations. The case of a student of Sondra Perl's (1979) serves as a good reminder here. Though Louella did get apprehensive about school-based writing assignments, she wrote letters easily enough. Emotional reactions are more often than not specific to the situation and are not evidence of general affective traits. This recognition should be central to our theory-building as well as to our teaching.

The Cognitive Dimension

Writing involves the shaping, structuring, refining, and evaluating of thought. To affirm this complex and deliberate series of processes is not to deny the fact that some composing also involves flashes of insight, seemingly unconscious connections, and the feel of rightness or wrongness. It is simply to say that composing, particularly the shaping of thought to utterance (Britton, 1980) and whatever subsequent refining of that utterance that may occur, involves conscious linguistic-cognitive behaviors: planning and rehearsing, organizing and structuring according to various formal conventions, weighing the fit of formal or lexical options, reading with an attention to graphic-mechanical errors, and so on. Bereiter (1980), Graves (1982), and Scardamalia (1981) have shown how these complex abilities, and a higher level ("metacognitive") awareness of them, develop. Cooper and Matsuhashi (in press) have outlined some of the linguistic and cognitive decisions writers make during the production of sentential and extrasentential discourse. D'Angelo (1979) has suggested that the enactment of basic rhetorical strategies is related to the enactment of fundamental patterns of thinking. Flower and Hayes (1980, 1981) have mapped the planning processes of adult writers. Bridwell (1980) and Sommers (1980) have demonstrated the different ways that professional and student writers conceive of and enact revision.

When writing proceeds fluently, cognitive and linguistic processes interact in complex, productive ways. But there are times when a writer's cognitive and linguistic repertoire comes up short or when that writer's composing rules or planning strategies or assumptions about writing don't match the constraints of a particular task. In the study of mine summarized at the beginning of this chapter, students who reported a high degree of blocking, versus those who did not, displayed a number of rigid composing rules (e.g., "You're not supposed to have passive verbs"), and some of the rules conflicted with others. They also tended to plan rigidly or inadequately, and half of them expressed assumptions about writing that were inappropriate or inaccurate (e.g., that planning subverts spontaneity and thus "sacrifices truth and real feelings"). It is possible, then, that some of our rules, strategies, assumptions, decision sequences, and so on can impede writing as well as make it possible.

Some theorists attempt to generalize beyond specific cognitive processes and pose broad orientations to problem solving. These orientations are usually discussed in terms of extremes at either end of a continuum; for example, some people seem to depend on the field surrounding an object when perceiving that object, others tend to perceive the object independently of the field (Witkin, Moore, Goodenough, & Cox, 1977); some people tend to approach intellectual problems impulsively, others reflectively (Kagan, Moss, & Sigel, 1963); some serially, others holistically (Pask & Scott, 1972); and so on. There may be value in posing general cognitive orientations to composing, and my studies led me in fact to speculate about composing styles: Several writers seemed to compose cautiously, reflectively, while others wrote much more spontaneously; and each group expressed rules and assumptions that were consonant with their different approaches. Asked how typical these orientations were of their writing on other assignments, they said they were fairly typical (Rose, 1984). Now, if (and this is a very big "if") a number of other observations in varied settings with varied tasks over time were to confirm these preliminary observations and self-reports, then perhaps we could posit a notion like "composing styles," general orientations to writing that are based on fundamental assumptions and broad composing strategies. One would have to make such assessments cautiously, however, since writing behavior, like any complex behavior, is tremendously variable and can play itself out in different ways, given different settings, tasks, materials, constraints, and moods.

In one sense, the above research framework presents the obvious. It doesn't reveal anything other than what we've already learned from day-to-day living: People act and react intellectually and emotionally and do so in situations that trigger, shape, and quell those behaviors. But I would suggest that it is precisely this "obviousness," this commonsense validity that gives the framework its value as a *research* paradigm. We are forced to at least acknowledge in our research projects the complexity that we live by. The framework reminds us to be alert to the possibility of interactions of the cognitive, the affective, and the situational.

There is good reason, then, to believe that the cognitive/affective/ contextual framework could inform and enrich composing-process research; but, before going further, I must attach two qualifiers to its application, both of which stem from a fundamental characteristic of systematic inquiry. "All research," Egon Guba reminds us, "sets constraints" (Guba, 1978, p. 6). While the comprehensiveness of the cognitive/affective/contextual framework forces us to honor complexity, it would, if *fully* played out, make most research efforts impossible. There are two reasons why this would be so, one practical, the other conceptual.

1. Perhaps the ideal composing-process research project would be one that extended over years; involved large and diverse numbers of subjects; fully explored the cognitive, affective, and situational dimensions of their writing across a wide sample of public and private writing tasks; involved multiple researchers and studies to reduce experimenter bias and methodological limitations; and so on. But, of course, no investigation—from the artistic and literary to the scientific— has attained such comprehensiveness. The costs, the demands on personnel, the

sheer bulk of data would be prohibitive. So, for the most practical of reasons, we must "set constraints" — focus our research, make strategic decisions about what to include and what to exclude.

2. But there are also conceptual reasons for setting limits. A good deal of research, from the literary to the scientific, involves the analysis of constituent elements. Such analysis derives from the notion that a complex system — whether of language or organic compounds — may need to be explored, at least initially, by attempting to focus on the separate pieces of its puzzle. This strategy becomes especially compelling when one faces a problem whose components are so intertwined that one cannot get even a moderately clear sense of their nature or of how they interact. The strategy exposes us again, of course, to the danger of reductionism that I have been discussing. The interplay of elements within a system helps define these elements and, ultimately, the system itself. Thus one can misrepresent a system by envisioning it as a mere aggregate of constituent parts. But if componential analysis is carried out with the awareness that elements of most systems are not neatly isolable, then the examination of constituents can more likely be conducted and reported in a way that is appropriately qualified, that admits the possibility of modification via involvement in the system, and that suggests what, ultimately, to look for in less artificial settings (Cronbach, 1975). The analysis, to borrow and adapt a distinction made by the mathematician Ralph Strauch (1976), becomes a perspective on the phenomenon rather than a surrogate for it.

With these two qualifiers about necessary limits in mind, we can consider the utility of the cognitive/affective/contextual framework. It reminds us that any composing act could result from and be shaped by intellect, feeling, and setting. When our research projects necessitate a focus on one of these dimensions, the framework would make us mindful of possible influences and interactions of other dimensions: We could note such influences and interactions when they occur, even though we couldn't explore them fully; or we could speculate on how our present data might be interpreted if we were to consider them in the light of another of these perspectives. And, then, there would be circumstances where the framework could serve as more than a conceptual check and balance. It could inform an entire study, become a complex lens that brings cognitive, affective, and situational dimensions equally into focus. Let me illustrate the value of the latter — the use of the framework to fully inform investigation -- with a brief case study, that of Stephanie, taken from the research project of mine described earlier.

Stephanie's case was interesting from the beginning, for as her writing process unfolded via stimulated recall and as she sketched out her writing history, it became clear that, for her, a cognitive paradigm alone had limited explanatory power. Her writing problems were resulting from a complex interplay of cognitive, affective, and situational factors. I'll begin her brief case study with some general data and with the essay she wrote during the composing session. Then I'll offer a descriptive overview of what transpired during that session. I'll follow the description with an analysis of selected problems in her composing process.

III: THE CASE OF STEPHANIE

Stephanie was a freshman who had not decided on a major. Her verbal score on the Scholastic Aptitude Test was 400 and her grade point average was 2.18. Her scores on our university's written placement test had exempted her from the university's remedial English requirement. She had not yet taken the standard composition course. Her questionnaire results suggested that she did have trouble with writer's block and that she tended to turn in papers late. The results also suggested some, though not dramatic, tendencies to overedit her papers and a good deal of trouble structuring written responses to complex topics. (A fuller analysis is provided in Rose, 1981.)

For the stimulated-recall phase of the study, Stephanie had to work with the following assignment: She was given a three-page case history of a man named Angelo Cacci who visited a counseling center with complaints of depression. Her task was to interpret the man's situation in light of a passage from Karl Jaspers's *Man in the Modern Age*, a passage attributing the cause of contemporary malaise to alienating work. (The entire assignment can be found in the Appendix.) She was given time to adjust herself to the artificial writing setting and to read the materials; she was then asked to write for 60 minutes. The (unfinished) essay she produced is reprinted here. Nothing is corrected, though words Stephanie lined out are not included. Some of these deletions will be discussed in the upcoming overview of her writing session. The overview will contain a number of quotations. Most will be Stephanie's comments from the stimulated-recall protocol, though my questions, passages from the essay, and readers' comments will also be incorporated.

Stephanie's Essay

In the case history of Angelo Cacci it's rather obvious that he hasn't ever been and isn't now very fulfilled or satisfied with his life. His occupation is that of an average middle-class man, a job where you do the same thing over and over again, not very exciting. Carl Jaspers quotation seems to describe this sort of lifestyle but this is only one part of a life. It is true that people seem to be shuffled together but this is inevitable in the society in which we live, for survival is the first priority. It isn't because Angelo is put in this situation that he should suffer of the "blues" as he does. If the other parts of Angelos life were more fulfilling then perhaps his discription of his job would not be settling for something he doesn't want.

In everyones life there are things we must do that we don't really want to do; having a job of unimportance or having a job at all may be one of them. But what we do with the rest of our time is more important, having a relationship, keeping family ties . . . In Angelos case he doesn't have a fulfilling relationship with anyone and he never got or gave much love in his family. There is always time for those things after the work is done. The memories of his grandfather were the only thing that didn't have anything to do with working and surviving. After his grandfather died he didn't experience this kind of love, of doing things outside of the mechanical life of the city. His occupation seems to be the main stream of his life because there isn't much else, and since what Jasper says about being pushed together with others without much meaning in part of your life is true, then anyone would have the "blues" in his position. However, what Jasper says about not having any time left for thinking about life isn't true. If people don't have

Stephanie's Session

Stephanie began the session by slowly rereading the Jaspers quotation. She then shifted to the case history, mentally rephrasing its events "as if [she] were telling someone about this case history of Angelo Cacci, so [she] could explain it to [her]self better." But her retelling of Angelo's life was not comprehensive; she sidestepped the dream because "it didn't make much sense" to her, and, keeping Jaspers in mind, was "trying to pick out . . . more important points, trying to separate the points that related to the quotation from those that didn't." Stephanie intermittently spoke aloud while reading, and later while writing. Though she claimed she had a "lousy memory," she left the assignment materials virtually unmarked. (She underlined a string of five words in the case history: "grandfather. The old man used to"). Asked why, if she considered her memory so poor, she did not gloss or underline the Jaspers quotation and the case history she explained, "the ideas are put so clearly that I can just refer back" to the materials. After 8 minutes and 44 seconds of rereading, Stephanie began to write.

But Stephanie's first sentence did not come without some difficulty: "I'm trying to think of something to start with. I'm never satisfied with much. . . . I hate starting out papers, you know, in the usual." Though she "was trying to think of something better," she finally did rely on a stock opening because "it's easier for [her] to just put something down and start and then come back later." Halfway through her first sentence, however, she did pause 45 seconds to make a rhetorical change (she was going to write "that he hasn't had a fulfilling life" but instead wrote "that he hasn't ever been and isn't now very fulfilled or satisfied with his life"). "It was just another way of wording it," she explained; but it was clear that once started, she was trying to give her sentence the flair she earlier decided to forgo: "See, my . . . parents are both good writers and my brother's a good writer, and so I want that something, you know, that something a little extra that doesn't just make it a . . . clear sentence, but makes it a good, clear sentence."

Completing her first sentence, Stephanie paused for 58 seconds and rescanned what she had written, wondering if it was "irrelevant or not." Asked if she had a general idea of what was to come, she explained, "No. I don't really, because I'm writing, hoping that the more I write, the more it will come together . . . I never get the whole idea before I start writing."

Stephanie began her second sentence with "He is," paused, crossed it out, and wrote the existing version ("His occupation is . . ."). She wanted to "phrase it a different way." After writing, "His occupation is that of an average middle-class man," Stephanie paused and scanned the case history to verify her labeling of Angelo as middle-class: "I was checking back to see what his job was, and a lot of times I'm not sure if the word I'm using is right to describe something." At three other junctures in the protocol, Stephanie similarly checked the accuracy of her descriptions of Angelo's life.

Commenting on the production of her third sentence, Stephanie said she "wanted to bring the quotation into it somehow" in order to anchor her discussion in the assignment materials. She began her sentence ("Carl Jaspers quotation seems to") and paused, then came up with "describe." "I couldn't think of a word to put down," she explained; "my vocabulary is not that large." She continued the sentence—"describe this sort of lifestyle"—and paused for 60 seconds before completing the sentence with a clause that would qualify her agreement with Jaspers: "but this is only one part of a life." She then scanned the Jaspers quotation: "Some things, I think, in the quotation were right, and some I don't . . . I'm just trying to interpret it right because . . . that's where my biggest problem is, interpreting information." As she continued, a fundamental difficulty in dealing with complex information emerged: "I have a hard time knowing exactly what I'm thinking . . . I would rather write about something that only has one subject instead of having to give my opinion, because whenever it comes to giving my opinion, my opinion always goes two ways."

Through sentences four, five, and six, Stephanie continued to express disagreement with Jaspers—the crux of her argument being that mechanical work alone does not automatically result in alienation, for there are other factors (particularly that of family) in one's life that could allay or intensify that alienation. But Stephanie did not forge a solid direction for her disagreement, and at several points she said she was confused about "exactly what she wanted to say." Stephanie's drafting of the sixth and final sentence in the first paragraph revealed the semantic and conceptual difficulties she was having. She had originally written, "If the other parts of Angelos life were more fulfilling then perhaps this robot-like"; she paused, deleted "this robot-like," and continued, "perhaps his discription of his job would have more"; she paused again, deleted "have more," and continued, "not be so robot-like"; she paused once more, scanned the case history, deleted "so robot-like," and continued, "settling for something he doesn't want," a phrase that she enclosed in parentheses—her way of indicating that she believed her language was not quite right. Stephanie's trails with writing about "robot-like" behavior and her parenthesizing of "settling for something he doesn't want" suggest that she was having trouble clarifying her argument, mentally and scribally. She put it this way:

STEPHANIE: The job was bad, but that wasn't his reason for feeling blue. . . . It was that he was lacking something else that caused his life to be like that.

RESEARCHER: Why didn't you say it the way you just said it to me?

STEPHANIE: Well, 'cause what I just said wasn't even that clear . . . some things you can say, but they just don't sound right on paper.

Asked what would happen if she were at home and found herself in the just-witnessed difficulty, she said she "might ask my Mom to . . . rephrase the sentence for me."

Before beginning her second paragraph, Stephanie rescanned her first paragraph "just to keep the idea fresh in [her] mind." Except for its last few sentences, the construction of this second paragraph proceeded fairly un-eventfully, though three behaviors are worth noting: (a) The rhetorical play of the first sentence's second clause ("having a job of unimportance or having a job at all may be one of them") resulted in a positive self-evaluation: "I know when you read a paper, you look to see if it sounds good. If I come up with something like that . . . it's pleasing." (b) Questioned about omitted apostro-phes, Stephanie replied, "I always have that problem . . . so I just leave them out and then ask my mom." (c) After completing her sixth sentence of the second paragraph, Stephanie wrote, "His family worried about," paused, deleted the clause, and reread her entire essay: "Just to get the stream of it be-cause sometimes when I can't think of anything to write, I'll just . . . read it back and forth. . . . It'll trigger off something hopefully, eventually." Though Stephanie's rationale for rescanning is legitimate, the reason for the pause is telling: She was going to continue discussing Angelo's family, making the point that "all his family worried about was survival." But "if I had said that, it would've been putting too much of my opinion, making a judgment, too much of a judgment on the [case history] because I didn't really have enough information to say it." Her vigilance about including her opinion is interest-ing because, as she said a few minutes prior to the last comment (and echo-ing a much earlier explanation), she read the case history in a way that recast it in somewhat personal terms: "I read the case history, and I just sort of changed it into my own, you know, just as if I could see the person and so on. And that [way it's] not so hard to remember."

I don't have enough direct information on Stephanie's reading and mem-orizing strategies to say what follows with certainty, but it seems that her method of interpreting and of committing to memory did not lead smoothly to her composing. Angelo's history was, perhaps, a little too selectively read and personalized to make it accessible for an assignment that Stephanie per-ceived as demanding some sort of academic objectivity.[2] Maybe this conflict contributed to the fact that her second paragraph was part rehash, part loose development of previously stated ideas. In one reader's words:

> The student has shot [her] bolt rather early and has set up a structure of dreadful repetition. . . . Since the student is really offering an oppos-ing theme, [she] needs to be more precise about her area of attack or emphasis.

Stephanie might not have been aware of her repetitiousness, but she did be-lieve that her "main part . . . the idea [she] wanted to work on" was still not precisely stated; so, oddly enough, she generated two more repetitive sen-tences in an attempt to clarify. These last two sentences gave her more trou-ble than any other sentences in the essay and revealed the difficulty she was having structuring her disagreement with Jaspers. Of her second to last sentence, she said, "If I said everything I wanted to say, the sentence would just be too long; it wouldn't make sense . . . I put three ideas in one sentence [and] I didn't succeed . . . In my mind . . . everything [got] so confusing." She untangled herself by "writing one word . . . and [taking] it from there"; but, by her own admission, her rambling sentence "is sort of unclear." The confusion she noted in the production of her penultimate sentence was also present as she drafted her final sentence—she parenthesized "isn't true" and put a question mark in the margin: "I didn't want to say that it's not true, because it's his opinion." She was writing another sentence, a further elaboration on the previous two, when the clock ran out.

Discussion

I must begin this section by emphasizing the fact that, in the contextual realm particularly, I am speculating from very limited data. I did not observe Stephanie at home and did not study her production of a variety of kinds of writing. Furthermore, for practical reasons, I will focus this discussion on only two aspects of Stephanie's composing: her difficulty in structuring complex discourse and her feeling of discomfort in doing so. This investigation, then, is a preliminary rather than a definitive one and is intended as a sketch rather than a full illustration of the kind of analysis the cognitive/affective/contextual framework can help produce. The particular value of the framework here is that it enables us to see the way Stephanie's cognitive and linguistic difficulties (e.g., inadequate argumentative structure; reliance on relatively uncomplex syntactic structures) were intertwined with emotional issues (e.g., her reluctance to assert her opinion) and to further see how these problems may have been more or less pronounced, depending on the nature of the writing situations she found herself in. But the framework also allows us to ponder the successful play of Stephanie's skills. Despite her conflicts and limitations, she did not stare at a blank page but produced the beginnings of a decent enough essay and, as I'll suggest, did so because of a particularly empowering interplay of cognitive, affective, and contextual factors.

It would be difficult to understand Stephanie's compositional difficulties without considering her relationship *as a writer* with her family. She mentioned her family at nine different junctures in the protocol. At each point, she commented on the superior skills of her father, mother, or brother; or on how one of them could help her out of the particular grammatical, stylistic, or structural jam she was presently in; or on how she would like to match their prowess on a particular composing task before her. Two of her comments are particularly revealing:

> All the time I was growing up, I depended on my parents a lot, and my parents . . . are rather bright. . . . And my mother is an excellent writer, and she loves to help out. It's something I sort of got used to in elementary school and high school, and whenever I'm mixed up about something, I'll always ask my parents to explain it to me. And then maybe I'll

go from there because I'm sort of insecure with my own idea about something, even like how to interpret a quotation. . . . I know whatever my father interprets is going to be correct.

In high school a lot of times . . . at the last minute I would ask my mom to help me with something. It's hard to get out of that pattern because my mom puts it [in] her typewriter and . . . she types an essay for me in about 15 minutes.

But Stephanie was no longer at home. She was in the midst of her third quarter at UCLA and, as her mediocre grade point average (2.18) suggests, was moving through her classes without much distinction. She put off papers and missed deadlines. Now that Stephanie was on her own and her writing assignments (e.g., for classical art history) were more research-oriented and more ambitious than those she grew up with, she could not as easily rely on her family and, as her essay suggests, lacked the discourse strategies and perhaps the self-confidence needed to structure and take a position on complex information. I couldn't get much data on her schooling, but the home writing environment Stephanie grew up in didn't sufficiently guide her toward engaging in the kind of independent thinking and framing of complex discourse her new environment demanded. Given this conflict, the present writing task, based as it was in the academy, might well have sparked feelings of inadequacy and some of the kinds of blocking behaviors she had reported on the questionnaire.

But the interesting thing is that, though Stephanie may have felt inadequate and though while composing she displayed some of the behaviors that she had reported stymie her during other assignments, she did nonetheless write. I'd suggest three general reasons for her relative fluency. The first reason is cognitive: She had a variety of techniques to help spark the flow of prose. She would test a few words ("I'll start writing maybe one word"); place parentheses around inadequate language, in hope of returning to it ("I would work towards [that] later"); scan what she had already written ("It'll trigger off something, hopefully"); or follow alternatives ("I can't think of the right way to say it, so [I'll] move to something else"). These behaviors suggest the presence of a powerful and multifaceted heuristic rule that presents a number of options to the stymied writer. This rule seems associated with and potentiated by an assumption about discovery: "The more I write, the more it will come later."

The second reason, and this one is more guesswork on my part than are the other two, has to do with her feelings and beliefs about Karl Jaspers's passage. Though Stephanie felt uncomfortable disagreeing with Jaspers, she did disagree, taking issue with the focus on work and alienation in his analysis. She objected on the grounds that routine work alone cannot explain alienation; she found more explanation for Angelo's dilemma in his family situation. (I think it is interesting that the only words Stephanie underlined in Angelo's case history were "grandfather. The old man used to.") Stephanie often spoke of her family and of her closeness to it. It is possible, then, that Angelo's situation combined with Jaspers's theory sparked feelings strong enough to impel her to write.

The third reason concerns an artifact of the present writing context: the deadline. Stephanie reported that she normally procrastinated and thus produced rushed, inadequate essays. (Her high "lateness" score on the questionnaire and her low grade point average lend some credence to this report.) Though Stephanie produced a relatively flawed essay for the present study, she did not block. She attributed her fluency to the time limit; if she had been at home it would have taken her "hours and hours and hours," for she would not have been "satisfied" with her ideas. The pressure of the deadline, however, seemed to help her override her insecurities, dissatisfactions, and mechanical and structural limitations. She produced a two-paragraph essay of 300 words.

Stephanie's performance on this study's assignment, then, suggests that, if she did feel inadequate to frame complex arguments or to interpret information, there were—at least in this case—cognitive, affective, and situational variables that could help her overcome her reservations. The problem that remained, though, was primarily a cognitive-linguistic one. Stephanie constructed a first paragraph that inductively led to a thesis, but her second paragraph did little to develop it. Though she did use some argumentative conventions (e.g., granting Jaspers's thesis some legitimacy before taking issue with it), she seems to have had trouble with the overall structure of the argument. The thrust of the essay dissipates into repetitive, loosely connected sentences that don't hypotactically subordinate issues one to the other but paratactically string together issues of varied relevance with simple connectives. As protocol excerpts have illustrated, Stephanie was most confused and conflicted when writing the particular sentences that embodied her not-quite-honed, sometimes rambling disagreement with Jaspers. Though she could occasionally turn a phrase, she had trouble with larger rhetorical concerns.

William Perry (1970) has suggested that college students develop along a series of "positions," the first few being characterized by difficulty in dealing with ambiguity, with multiple acceptable answers to a problem, and with intellectual and moral complexity. Stephanie doesn't neatly fit into Perry's early positions, for she was able to accept Jaspers's viewpoint as one opinion and put hers forth as another. But she was not comfortable with this complexity and with asserting her position within it ("whenever it comes to giving my opinion, my opinion always goes two ways") or with the interpretive activity that was central to it ("that's where my biggest problem is, interpreting information"). These struggles were complicated by her apparent lack of skill in working complex information and opinion into appropriately complex syntactic structures and in framing an argument. Her uncertainties, her conceptual dilemmas with Jaspers, and her discourse limitations all interacted to vex her composing. Picture this web of difficulties against the backdrop of a home writing environment that, if her reports are accurate, had protected her from rather than aided her through the intellectual and linguistic difficulties that attend academic development. This protection, as we've seen, had both affective and cognitive consequences. Simon and Simon (1978) discuss the confidence that experienced problem-solvers acquire and the way that that confidence aids them in understanding a problem and executing a solution. Stephanie lacked such confidence. She was able to disagree with Jaspers but seemed trapped within his framework and tended to waffle and repeat herself, never bringing her argument to a clear focus. Hand in glove with the foregoing was her paucity of the syntactic and global discourse skills that would have enabled her to adequately structure the disagreements she was able to articulate.

It is possible, though this is speculation based on her commentary, that Stephanie's difficulties with writing could have been leading to a general distrust in or avoidance of writing. She preferred speaking to writing. For example, she said she "enjoys reading case histories" but would "rather talk about them than write about them"; she used to keep a journal, but it was "too time-consuming." "If I could put it on tape it would be a lot easier." And, most pervasively, she preferred speech because she could always qualify what she believed would be irreversible in print. It is valuable here to consider one reader's remarks.

> The writer is good at commenting at first, but [she] draws back. Probably she thinks [her] reader will disagree. She needs, I think, more courage to stick to [her] argument.

Place this evaluation alongside two comments of Stephanie's.

> A lot of times the reason I'd rather . . . sit and talk out loud about a topic is because then I can say something, and can say, "No. That's not right." But you can't do that on paper.

> I'm sort of insecure with my own idea about something. . . . I wait to see what the teacher's thing is or my parents' opinion is . . . so I'll know what's good of mine. 'Cause a lot of times I can't tell myself.

Stephanie might well have preferred speaking to writing because she could continually amend the ideas she had never been taught to trust. She preferred speaking to writing as well because she did not have to wrestle with internalized parental standards that she was never given the painful freedom to confront and possibly go beyond. And finally, in informal speech, Stephanie was freed from the complex syntactic and formal conventions that are so central to academic writing.

IV

I began this chapter with the suggestion that we can rigorously yet nonreductively investigate complex composing-process problems by using multiple and converging methods. I then suggested that we can further honor the full scope of writing behavior by espousing a broad research framework that interweaves the cognitive, affective, and situational dimensions of composing. Then came the case of Stephanie. One of the things that I hope her story illustrates is the complementarity of a multipronged methodology and a cognitive/affective/contextual framework, for in fact each implies the need for the other. The various dimensions of the framework cannot be adequately explored by any single method. And the presence of the framework reminds the researcher of cognitive, affective, and contextual variables that a single method would probably not reveal. There is one issue I have yet to deal with, one I raised earlier and temporarily set aside: the philosophical foundations of methodology.

People in composition studies are beginning to seriously examine the methods that are available to them and are particularly concerned with the historical and philosophical traditions that certain orientations and methods represent (see, e.g., Berthoff, 1981; Bizzell, 1979; Connors, 1983; Emig, 1982). The issue is this: Research methods develop out of particular historical and philosophical contexts and thus are defined by, or at least are associated with, particular sets of assumptions about human nature and human knowledge. This truism often leads people to embrace or reject methods because of the origins of those methods. Classical experimental designs smack of positivism and are held at arm's length by some humanists, just as some behavioral scientists question ethnographic investigations as being unrigorous, fuzzy phenomenology.

While admitting the legitimacy of an historical critique of the origins of method (one would be philosophically naive to reject such examination), I would like to suggest that certain methods, anyway, might not be as constrained by their origins as at first seems to be the case and that methods that are constraining or reductive with certain kinds of problems or at certain stages of research might be used to good effect with other problems, at other stages. Let me illustrate these assertions.

• Some methods are less constrained by their origins and their structures than are others. Pre-post experimental designs and procedures involving the tallying and classifying of observed behaviors both grew out of the empiricist-behaviorist tradition. Yet the first set of methods is much more constrained, historically and structurally, than the second. The process of recording and classifying behaviors has been readily adapted by ethnographers working in a phenomenological-anthropological, rather than a behaviorist, tradition.

• Some methods lend themselves to the earlier stages of particular research endeavors, others to later stages. Naturalistic observation, as has often been noted (see, e.g., Guba, 1978; Kantor, Kirby, & Goetz, 1981; Reichardt & Cook, 1979), can provide enough information to develop hypotheses that might then be explored by more controlled procedures. And, in turn, more controlled techniques might assist in identifying problems, the play of which can then be observed in more natural settings. Stephanie provides a good case in point. She was identified by a questionnaire (a pretty contrived research device), and then her writing process was studied in a relatively artificial setting. The results of these investigations, though, suggest a complex interaction of processes, feelings, and settings that could now be fruitfully explored by naturalistic observation techniques.

• It can be instructive to use several methods simultaneously or in close sequence, even (perhaps especially) methods traditionally seen as uncomplementary.

Methods used in this way can check and enhance each other. A nice example of the successful fusion of two fairly disparate methods can be found in David Bartholomae's study of the error patterns of basic writers (1980). He blends error analysis from applied linguistics with literary theory's hermeneutics in a way that allows each to empower the other. Error analysis lends precision to the examination of a student's text, but also underscores the places at which linguistic analysis falls short and must be supplemented by the methods of literary interpretation.

Methods from behavioral science, anthropology, and literary studies, then, need not be seen as incompatible, for it is possible that some of them in some settings can be combined in creative ways.[3] But even as I write that last sentence, I realize that to speak in primarily combinatorial terms of the selection and application of methods leaves out a further, very important dimension of the process. Methods are not only combined, even combined innovatively; they can also evolve. Methods stem from one period of history but, like any artifact of culture, become part of historical processes; thus the possibility is always there that they may be modified and changed by new concerns, new environments, new definitions of knowledge. Let me make this point more concrete with an example from the work of the Russian psychologist Lev Vygotsky.

Vygotsky reacted against the predominate behaviorist experimental method of his time by insisting on the importance of exploring the mental processes that people go through while solving problems versus simply quantifying some end product of that problem-solving. In reaction he created a number of new methods, one of which was really a modification of a standard experimental design: He kept the trappings of behaviorist method (set tasks, systematic controls on stimuli, manipulable conditions) but freed up the outcome constraints. For example, subjects had to perform certain tasks that tested memorial strategies and capacity but could solve these tasks in whatever way they wanted. Their attempts to solve the memory problems — their processes — became the data. This approach, termed "experimental-developmental" by Vygotsky, fused the situational control of the experimental design with the open-ended data collection of more naturalistic methods. He created methods to suit the questions he was asking, and some of those creations were in fact evolved from older, more rigid procedures.

I want to be very clear here. I am not denying the fact that research methods develop out of particular historical contexts nor that some of those contexts pose a model of human beings and definitions of knowledge that some of us in composing-process research find very troubling. I also don't want to deny that some methods are close to being procedural incarnations of these bothersome assumptions (or as Vygotsky put it, "Experimental procedures become surrogates for psychological processes"; 1981, p. 67). What I am arguing is that some methods from psychology and anthropology (and literary criticism, which, lest we forget, has had its own moments of philosophical and procedural narrowness) are not necessarily limited to the constraints of their origins and can be adopted and even revamped to serve other problems built on models of human beings and definitions of knowledge different from those that gave birth to such methods. To return to an earlier example, tallying and classifying observable behaviors becomes epistemologically reductionistic in the behaviorist paradigm because such quantification is defined as the only legitimate knowledge from which to build theory. In other paradigms — for instance, the phenomenological-ethnographic — this method, combined with others, serves a less restricted model of knowledge.

A discipline is defined by the problems it embraces and the questions it asks of those problems. And questions, in turn, result in investigative action when methods are incorporated into them. We in composing-process research, though we draw on the rich traditions of rhetoric and psychology, are really just beginning to identify the problems and formulate the questions by which we will define ourselves. But this development could be cut short or narrowed if we constrain our questions by a too early dismissal of methodological options. Such a limiting of disciplinary growth could easily happen; in some ways, I fear it has already begun. There is some division among us into literary and social science camps: The literary camp attributes to itself philosophical and interpretive sophistication, while the other congratulates itself on its empirical rigor. This separation — the exaggerated separation of polemics — falsely dichotomizes ways of thinking about writing. It threatens to rarify our theories and trivialize our observations.[4]

More than most other fields, ours — because of the complexity of the phenomena it studies and because of its many connections with both theoretical and applied concerns — demands the convergence of insight and method from multiple disciplines. This convergence can be simplistic, a mechanical overlay of one discipline's methods onto another's problems; or, as I've tried to suggest in this chapter, the convergence can be enlightening and generative, can lead to the creation of new investigative procedures. As researchers ask new and increasingly ambitious questions about the composing process, methods from philosophical, rhetorical, and literary study, psychology and cognitive science, anthropology and sociology will combine and fuse in special ways. And new methods, new research frameworks will emerge as they must when unique problems are investigated in ways that don't sacrifice their complexity.

[See Appendix B of "Two Case Studies" on pp. 54–55 for the assignment.]

ACKNOWLEDGMENTS

I would like to thank Michael Havens, Linda Flower, and Richard Shavelson for their generous comments on earlier versions of this chapter. Along the way, I also had helpful conversations with Peggy Atwell, Al Hutter, Karin Mack-Costello, Sondra Perl, and Sandy Thompson.

NOTES

[1]My experience is that many people in humanities and composition studies are not familiar with the range of research methods available to the educational and social science researcher. Though a footnote is hardly the place to attempt a survey of those methods, it might prove helpful to at least sketch out a few of the options.

Fundamental to certain kinds of social science investigation is the experimental design, and the most celebrated — and perhaps most notorious — experimental design is the "pretest-posttest control group design." An experimental design, like the "pre-post design," is defined by two characteristics: (a) It has one or more experimental groups (groups receiving some treatment) and one or more control groups (similar groups not receiving the treatment); and (b) people are randomly assigned to each of the groups. Some social scientists consider the experimental design the ultimate research design because it provides them with the most assurance in making causal interpretations from data. The reasoning is straightforward: Similarity of subjects is assured by randomly assigning people to experimental groups (for example, groups receiving training in sentence-combining) and to control groups (similar groups not receiving sentence-combining instruction); if the experimental group subjects display some statistically significant outcome effect that the control group subjects do not (e.g., increased syntactic maturity), then it seems probable that, all other things being equal, outcome effects resulted from the treatment.

The proper use of an experimental design depends on the researcher's ability to exercise a good deal of control over the people and the phenomenon he or she is studying. But such control isn't easily obtained, especially for researchers interested in complex educational phenomena. More latitude is provided by a further set of designs called "quasi-experimental designs." These designs, like the classic experimental designs, rely on one or more experimental and one or more control groups; but, unlike the classic designs, they do not involve random assignment of subjects. Two examples: In the "nonequivalent control group design," the researcher conducts a pre-post experimental and control group study using subjects who have *not* been assigned randomly but are naturally assembled — as in a classroom. In the "time-series design," the researcher uses the same group of subjects as, so to speak, both a control and an experimental group. A series of measurements is taken over time to provide a baseline (say, to stick with my earlier illustration, of syntactic maturity); then a treatment is given (say, instruction in sentence-combining), and the series of measurements continues. The researcher notes whether, after treatment began, any changes occurred in the phenomenon in question (e.g., the syntactic complexity of sentences) and tests their significance via statistical analysis. Though they must do so with caution, those using quasi-experimental designs can posit causal relationships between treatments and effects. (See Campbell & Stanley, 1963, for the classic treatment of experimental and quasi-experimental designs; and see Filstead, 1979, and Guba, 1978, for critical assessment of these designs.)

Experimental and quasi-experimental designs are appropriate for probing certain kinds of questions about phenomena that can be delimited and controlled. Survey research methods provide a very different set of procedures for probing different sorts of questions. The survey researcher uses questionnaires (either administered orally or in writing) to gain information on attitudes, habits, and behavioral patterns. Large samples are used, and questionnaires typically go through multiple stages of refinement. The researcher uses the data to describe specific attitudes, opinions, or habits of a particular population. It is not uncommon for the researcher to then correlate his or her findings with other measures of opinion, achievement, or behavior. (For an introduction to survey research, see Babbie, 1983.)

Single correlational studies, like those resulting from survey research, do not allow the researcher to make statements about causality, only about co-occurring phenomena. However, one can examine patterns of relationships in a number of correlational studies and, given an appropriate theory, derive possible causal relationships between variables. The procedure for doing this, "causal modeling" or "structural equation modeling," involves systems of correlations (or regression coefficients) in formal statistical models that allow one to test a particular causal interpretation against other, competing interpretations. (For a discussion of causal modeling, see Pedhazur, 1982.)

One criticism of experimental and quasi-experimental designs (and, by implication, of survey research and correlational studies) is that they provide some measure of a behavioral outcome, or attitude or opinion, or pattern of relationships, but they typically do not allow exploration of the mental processes that lead to them. Thus it is that an increasing number of cognitively oriented psychologists and educational researchers are relying on what has come to be called "process-tracing." The goal of process-tracing is to render the nature and sequence of the mental processes a subject goes through while solving a problem rather than simply to record, as one would in experimental and quasi-experimental designs, the end result of that problem-solving. One popular process-tracing technique is speaking-aloud protocol analysis: The researcher trains a person to speak aloud while solving problems, records that speech, and then analyzes the resulting transcript (called a "protocol") for traces of mental processes. The researcher follows guidelines for determining the validity of the person's reports and attempts to render an approximation of what happened cognitively as that person engaged in problem solving. (See Ericsson

& Simon, 1980, for a theoretical defense of this procedure, and Hayes & Flower, 1983, for an application of the procedure to composition studies.)

Other social science researchers, particularly those in anthropology, wish less intrusion into the lives of their subjects than results from either experimental or quasi-experimental designs or from process-tracing procedures; furthermore, such researchers wish to observe their subjects' behavior in natural rather than research settings. These researchers rely on various naturalistic inquiry procedures: They live with their subjects over time, develop and refine various methods to categorize the behaviors they observe, ask questions of the subjects to determine their perception of the events being observed, and so on. The results are often, though by no means always, written up as case studies. (See Guba, 1978, for an overview of these naturalistic observation methods; Stake, 1978, for a theoretical defense of the case study; and Kantor, Kirby, & Goetz 1981, for an application of naturalistic inquiry to composition studies.)

[2]Allow me to play out this speculation a bit further. As Stephanie commented throughout the protocol on her reading of the case history, three comprehension strategies emerged: (a) She read the case history with the Jaspers quotation in mind to develop links between the two; (b) she tried to imagine the history's events in terms of her own life; and (c) she imagined she was telling Angelo's story to others "to explain it to [her]self better." All three strategies represent effective ways to actively engage in the reading of a text, and the last two—which seem related—could certainly have enhanced comprehension and recall by incorporating the case history's events into Stephanie's own experience. The use of these last two strategies, combined with the fact that the case history's events are fairly vivid, could explain why—though she felt that she had a "lousy memory"—Stephanie didn't underline the text of the history. The events were clear, and she tried to make them her own. Anything that was hazy, she could double-check. (And in fact she did refer back to the case history four times during the session.)

But it's possible that the way she read the case history, while active and involving, was also problematic. Though schema theorists are right to insist that we best comprehend and remember that which we can relate to prior knowledge (Rumelhart, 1980; Spiro, 1977, 1980), the nature of that prior knowledge and the manner in which we relate new knowledge to old are important variables in determining the quality and appropriateness-to-task of our comprehension and recall. It is possible that Stephanie so incorporated the history's events into her own experience—saw them so much in terms of her own life—that she felt conflicted when she had to present those events "objectively." Thus she kept "wanting to bring a quotation" into her discussion. She knew she had to be faithful to the text of the history but also knew she had recast the history in personal terms. Perhaps in the heat of the timed assignment, her conflict intensified and fed into her more general uncertainty about her stance toward Karl Jaspers.

[3]I have spoken so far about the conceptual-investigative advantages of selecting from and combining a variety of methods. There is, of course, another advantage to such methodological flexibility, a political-rhetorical one. Whenever evaluation is a goal of a research project, the investigator has to consider the audience who will receive the data, for, as Ernest House reminds us, evaluation is an "act of persuasion" (House, 1977, p. 5). An evaluator of programs and curricula must use methods that are most sensitive to that which is being evaluated, but must also consider what kinds of methods will have the most persuasive impact on those who have requested the investigation. (Or the evaluator has to persuade the recipients to accept the methods he or she has chosen.) Where evaluation is a concern, then, methods cannot be adopted or rejected without considering the political-rhetorical context of a particular investigation.

[4]One current variation of this battle finds some humanists embracing the phenomenological-ethnographic paradigm and rejecting all other approaches as intrusive and artificial. Any research involving set tasks and/or procedural constraints is counterposed to naturalistic inquiry which is thought to preserve the integrity of the phenomena being studied and which is admired for being built on philosophical underpinnings compatible with humanistic study. While there is little doubt that naturalistic inquiry provides a much-needed balance to traditional quantitative approaches and thereby greatly enriches composition research, there are problems with the way this particular saga of methodological heroes and villains is playing itself out. First of all, there is potential danger in elevating any method. The fascination with naturalistic inquiry can lead, on the part of some, to a habit of uncritical acceptance (not unlike the unquestioning acceptance of experimentalism in the American academic psychology of a generation ago). In such uncritical embrace, naturalistic methods are trivialized and are used to legitimize work that, in one ethnographer's words, is "poorly conducted and ill-conceived" (Rist, 1980, p. 8). Second, not all methods using set tasks and procedural constraints are equally limiting (see footnote 1); and the distinction between "qualitative" and "quantitative" paradigms might not be as neat as it seems, for the approaches share more characteristics than the polemicists would have us believe (see Reichardt &

Cook, 1979, for further discussion). Third, when it comes to the study of cognitive processes, naturalistic methods alone will most likely come up short. It is important to keep in mind the fact that the two most influential researchers of cognitive development in our time, Vygotsky and Piaget, found it necessary to tamper with their subjects' natural settings in order to gain their rich data on the way children solve problems.

One last thought. This polarization of naturalistic and quantitative methods also results in a limiting of the ways we can write about writing. The naturalistic camp champions interpretation, rich detail, "thick description," while the more experimentally oriented camp insists on measurements, numerical analysis, the discussion grounded in statistics. The ideal text for the first group becomes the case study; for the second, it's the research article with its attendant tables and charts. But why must these be the two primary choices—two extremes pitted against each other? I would suggest that the most enlightening and comprehensive writing about writing would fuse these two approaches, would weave statistics into descriptions and provide interpretive human contexts for measurements. We in composing-process research need a way to write about our findings that blends the interpretive and metaphoric with the baldly referential and notational. How else will we render the richness of the writing act?

REFERENCES

Babbie, E. R. (1983). *The practice of social research*. Belmont, CA: Wadsworth.

Bartholomae, D. (1980). The study of error. *College Composition and Communication, 31,* 253–269.

Bartholomae, D. (1985). Inventing the university. In M. Rose (Ed.), *When a writer can't write: Studies in writer's block and other composing process problems* (pp. 134–165). New York: Guilford.

Beck, A. T. (1976). *Cognitive therapy and the emotional disorders*. New York: International Universities Press.

Bereiter, C. (1980). Development in writing. In L. W. Gregg & E. R. Steinberg (Eds.), *Cognitive processes in writing* (pp. 73–93). Hillsdale, NJ: Erlbaum.

Berthoff, A. E. (1981). *The making of meaning*. Montclair, NJ: Boynton/Cook.

Bizzell, P. (1979). Thomas Kuhn, scientism, and English studies. *College English, 40,* 764–771.

Bloom, L. (1985). Anxious writers in context: Graduate school and beyond. In M. Rose (Ed.), *When a writer can't write: Studies in writer's block and other composing process problems* (pp. 119–133). New York: Guilford.

Boice, R. (1985). Psychotherapies for writing blocks. In M. Rose (Ed.), *When a writer can't write: Studies in writer's block and other composing process problems* (pp. 182–218). New York: Guilford.

Bridwell, L. S. (1980). Revising strategies in twelfth grade students' transactional writing. *Research in the Teaching of English, 14,* 197–222.

Britton, J. (1980). Shaping at the point of utterance. In A. Freedman & I. Pringle (Eds.), *Reinventing the rhetorical tradition* (pp. 61–65). Conway, AR: Language and Style Books.

Campbell, D. T. (1974). *Qualitative knowing in action research*. Paper presented at the meeting of the American Psychological Association, New Orleans, LA.

Campbell, D. T. (1979). "Degrees of freedom" and the case study. In T. D. Cook & C. S. Reichardt (Eds.), *Qualitative and quantitative methods in evaluation research* (pp. 49–67). Beverly Hills, CA: Sage.

Campbell, D. T., & Stanley, J. C. (1963). *Experimental and quasi-experimental designs for research*. Chicago: Rand McNally.

Connors, R. J. (1983). Composition studies and science. *College English, 45,* 1–20.

Cooper, C., & Matsuhashi, A. (in press). A theory of the writing process. In E. Martlew (Ed.), *The psychology of writing*. New York: John Wiley & Sons.

Cowley, M. (Ed.). (1977). *Writers at work* (1st Series). New York: Penguin.

Cronbach, L. J. (1975). Beyond the two disciplines of scientific psychology. *American Psychologist, 30,* 116–127.

Daly, J. A. (1985). Writing apprehension. In M. Rose (Ed.), *When a writer can't write: Studies in writer's block and other composing process problems* (pp. 43–82). New York: Guilford.

D'Angelo, F. J. (1979). Paradigms as structural counterparts of topoi. In D. McQuade (Ed.), *Linguistics, stylistics, and the teaching of composition* (pp. 41–51). Akron, OH: University of Akron Press.

Denzin, N. K. (1970). *The research act*. Chicago: Aldine.

Ellis, A. (1959). Rationalism and its therapeutic applications. *Annals of Psychotherapy, 1,* (Monograph No. 2), 55–64.

Emig, J. (1982). Inquiry paradigms and writing. *College Composition and Communication, 33,* 64–75.

Ericsson, K. A., & Simon, H. A. (1980). Verbal reports as data. *Psychological Review, 87,* 215–251.

Filstead, W. J. (1979). Qualitative methods: A needed perspective in evaluation research. In T. D. Cook & C. S. Reichardt (Eds.), *Qualitative and quantitative methods in evaluation research* (pp. 33–48). Beverly Hills, CA: Sage.

Flower, L. S., & Hayes, J. R. (1980). The dynamics of composing: Making plans and juggling constraints. In L. W. Gregg & E. R. Steinberg (Eds.), *Cognitive processes in writing* (pp. 31–50). Hillsdale, NJ: Erlbaum.

Flower, L. S., & Hayes, J. R. (1981). Plans that guide the composing process. In C. H. Frederiksen & J. F. Dominic (Eds.), *Writing: The nature, development, and teaching of written communication* (Vol. 2, pp. 39–58). Hillsdale, NJ: Erlbaum.

Graves, D. (1982). *A case study observing the development of primary children's composing, spelling, and motor behaviors during the writing process.* Washington, DC: Educational Resources Information Center. (ERIC Document Reproduction Service No. ED 218 653)

Graves, D. H. (1985). Blocking and the young writer. In M. Rose (Ed.), *When a writer can't write: Studies in writer's block and other composing process problems* (pp. 11–18). New York: Guilford.

Guba, E. (1978). *Toward a methodology of naturalistic inquiry in educational evaluation* (Monograph Series in Evaluation, No. 8). Los Angeles: University of California, Center for the Study of Evaluation.

Hayes, J. R., & Flower, L. (1983). Uncovering cognitive processes in writing: An introduction to protocol analysis. In P. Mosenthal, L. Tamor, & S. Walmsley (Eds.), *Research in writing: Principles and methods* (pp. 207–220). New York: Longman.

Holland, Morris. (1980, July). *The state of the art: The psychology of writing.* Paper presented at the Inland Area Writing Project's summer writing conference, University of California, Riverside.

House, E. R. (1977). *The logic of evaluative argument* (Monograph Series in Evaluation, No. 7). Los Angeles: University of California, Center for the Study of Evaluation.

Kagan, J., Moss, H. A., & Sigel, I. E. (1963). Psychological significance of styles of conceptualization. In J. C. Wright & J. Kagan (Eds.), *Basic cognitive processes in children* (pp. 73–112). *Monographs of the Society for Research in Child Development, 28.*

Kantor, K. J., Kirby, D. R., & Goetz, J. P. (1981). Research in context: Ethnographic studies in English education. *Research in the Teaching of English, 15,* 293–309.

Kelly, G. A. (1963). *A theory of personality.* New York: Norton.

Lazarus, R. S., & Averill, J. R. (1972). Emotion and cognition with special reference to anxiety. In C. D. Spielberger (Ed.), *Anxiety: Current trends in theory and research* (Vol. 2, pp. 241–283). New York: Academic Press.

Maslow, A. H. (1968). *Toward a psychology of being* (2nd ed.). New York: Van Nostrand Reinhold.

Maslow, A. H. (1969). *The psychology of science.* Chicago: Henry Regnery.

Mishler, E. G. (1979). Meaning in context: Is there any other kind? *Harvard Educational Review, 49,* 1–19.

Murray, D. M. (1985). The essential delay: When writer's block isn't. In M. Rose (Ed.), *When a writer can't write: Studies in writer's block and other composing process problems* (pp. 219–226). New York: Guilford.

Pask, G., & Scott, B. C. E. (1972). Learning strategies and individual competence. *International Journal of Man-Machine Studies, 4,* 217–253.

Pedhazur, E. J. (1982). *Multiple regression in behavioral research* (2nd ed.). New York: Holt, Rinehart and Winston.

Peitzman, F. (1981). *The composing processes of three college freshmen: Focus on revision.* Unpublished doctoral dissertation, New York University.

Perl, S. (1979). Unskilled writers as composers. *New York University Education Quarterly, 10,* 17–22.

Perry, W. G., Jr. (1970). *Forms of intellectual and ethical development in the college years.* New York: Holt, Rinehart and Winston.

Plimpton, G. (Ed.). (1977). *Writers at work* (2nd, 3rd, 4th Series). New York: Penguin.

Plimpton, G. (Ed.). (1981). *Writers at work* (5th Series). New York: Penguin.

Reichardt, C. S., & Cook, T. D. (1979). Beyond qualitative versus quantitative methods. In T. D. Cook & C. S. Reichardt (Eds.), *Qualitative and and quantitative methods in evaluation research* (pp. 7–32). Beverly Hills, CA: Sage.

Rist, R. C. (1980). Blitzkrieg ethnography: On the transformation of a method into a movement. *Educational Researcher, 9,* 9–10.

Rose, M. (1980). Rigid rules, inflexible plans, and the stifling of language: A cognitivist analysis of writer's block. *College Composition and Communication, 31,* 389–401.

Rose, M. (1981). *The cognitive dimension of writer's block: An examination of university students.* Unpublished doctoral dissertation, University of California, Los Angeles.

Rose, M. (1984). *Writer's block: The cognitive dimension.* Carbondale: Southern Illinois University Press.

Rumelhart, D. E. (1980). Schemata: The building blocks of cognition. In R. J. Spiro, B. C. Bruce, & W. F. Brewer (Eds.), *Theoretical issues in reading comprehension* (pp. 33–58). Hillsdale, NJ: Erlbaum.

Scardamalia, M. (1981). How children cope with the cognitive demands of writing. In C. H. Frederiksen & J. F. Dominic (Eds.), *Writing: The nature, development, and teaching of written communication* (Vol. 2, pp. 81–103). Hillsdale, NJ: Erlbaum.

Shapiro, D. (1965). *Neurotic styles.* New York: Basic Books.

Shavelson, R. J., Webb, N. M., & Burstein, L. (in press). Measurement of teaching. In M. Wittrock (Ed.), *Handbook of research on teaching* (3rd ed.). New York: Macmillan.

Simon, D. P., & Simon, H. A. (1978). Individual difference in solving physics problems. In R. S. Siegler (Ed.), *Children's thinking: What develops?* (pp. 325–348). Hillsdale, NJ: Erlbaum.

Sommers, N. (1980). Revision strategies of student writers and experienced adult writers. *College Composition and Communication, 31,* 378–388.

Spielberger, C. D. (Ed.). (1972). *Anxiety: Current trends in theory and research* (Vols. 1 & 2). New York: Academic Press.

Spiro, R. J. (1977). Remembering information from text: The "state of schema" approach. In R. C. Anderson, R. J. Spiro, & W. E. Montague (Eds.), *Schooling and the acquisition of knowledge* (pp. 137–165). Hillsdale, NJ: Erlbaum.

Spiro, R. J. (1980). Constructive processes in prose comprehension and recall. In R. J. Spiro, B. C. Bruce, & W. F. Brewer (Eds.), *Theoretical issues in reading comprehension* (pp. 245–278). Hillsdale, NJ: Erlbaum.

Stake, R. E. (1978). The case study method in social injury. *Educational Researcher, 7,* 5–8.

Strauch, R. (1976). A critical look at quantitative methodology. *Policy Analysis, 2,* 121–144.

Vygotsky, L. S. (1981). *Mind in society* (M. Cole, V. John-Steiner, S. Scribner, & E. Souberman, Eds.). Cambridge, MA: Harvard University Press.

Webb, E. J., Campbell, D. T., Schwartz, R. D., & Sechrest, L. (1966). *Unobtrusive measures.* Chicago: Rand McNally.

Wilson, S. (1977). The use of ethnographic techniques in educational research. *Review of Educational Research, 47,* 245–265.

Witkin, H. A., Moore, C. A., Goodenough, D. R., & Cox, P. W. (1977). Field-dependent and field-independent cognitive styles and their educational implications. *Review of Educational Research, 47,* 1–64.

4

Sophisticated, Ineffective Books — The Dismantling of Process in Composition Texts

1981

AUTHOR'S NOTE: In closing this section, let me offer two articles on composition textbooks that emerged from the work I was doing with cognitive psychology. In the 1970s Richard Lanham and Richard Ohmann had published trenchant critiques of composition textbooks — Lanham from the perspective of a scholar of stylistics, Ohmann as part of a larger Marxist analysis of the profession of English in America.[1] These critiques set the stage for further scrutiny. It seemed to me that there were some basic questions to raise about learning and writing, questions the cognitive perspective would help me frame.

This was also the time I was developing first-year writing curricula for the Educational Opportunity Program and, later, UCLA Writing Programs, so that work figures in here, as well. In fact, the second half of "Sophisticated, Ineffective Books" ("Insular Approaches to School Writing") and some of the concerns raised in "Speculations on Process Knowledge and the Textbook's Static Page" (p. 95) would inform a curriculum that, years later, would be published as *Critical Strategies for Academic Thinking and Writing*. I'll discuss that textbook in the next section.

The writer's block study led me to look beyond the students I was interviewing to the contexts in which they learned to write academic prose. In the late 1980s and early 1990s, I would partner with Glynda Hull to look at context in a fuller way, but here my attention was on textbooks as one source, one window onto writing instruction. Muriel Harris had written a fascinating article on the contradictory rules about writing voiced by college freshmen and wondered if such rules originated in the writing classroom. I was curious about textbooks. Were there ways that writing was typically represented that might contribute to the development of rigid composing rules and inflexible or ineffective strategies, or to problematic beliefs and assumptions about how one should write? Composition textbooks are filled with declarations about thinking and writing, and I wanted to consider those statements through the cognitive lens.

NOTE

[1]Lanham (1974); Ohmann (1976).

84

Ⅰn a now-famous critique, Richard Ohmann took composition textbook authors to task for envisioning student writing ahistorically and for administering rather than liberating the composing process ("Freshman Composition and Administered Thought," in *English in America* [New York: Oxford Univ. Press, 1976], pp. 133–171). A few years earlier, Richard Lanham had gleefully ripped into the condescension and vague precepts in the writing texts that lined his shelf (*Style: An Anti-Textbook* [New Haven: Yale Univ. Press, 1974]).[1] Their criticism implied that better textbooks could be written. But I have come to believe that even if ahistoricity, coddling, and fingerwagging disappeared from composition texts, they would still be an ineffective way to teach writing. They are, by nature, static and insular approaches to a dynamic and highly context-oriented process, and thus are doomed to the realm of the Moderately Useful. Let me explain further by tracing the steps that led me to my conclusion.

STATIC APPROACHES TO PROCESS

Elsewhere I have suggested that the cause of some students' writer's block might not be fear of exposure and evaluation, but, rather, the use of narrow or otherwise inappropriate composing rules and plans ("Rigid Rules, Inflexible Plans, and the Stifling of Language," *College Composition and Communication, CCC,* 31 [December, 1980], 389–401). One student, for example, would struggle up to five hours with an introductory paragraph because she believed that "your first paragraph must grab your reader's attention. Until you can do that, there's no use going on." Another student believed that an outline had to be meticulously constructed and, once constructed, should not be modified. The students claimed they had learned these rules and strategies from textbooks or teachers. My hunch was that such dysfunctional approaches weren't read or taught directly, but resulted from misinterpretation. Still, misinterpretation can begin in the expression of the message. Muriel Harris had already shown that teachers can be the source of absolute, often contradictory, injunctions,[2] so I turned to composition textbooks, witchhunting for "rigid rules" and "inflexible plans." I made it hard on myself by sidestepping possibly unsophisticated secondary school texts, examining instead recently written or revised freshman composition texts sent as promotional enticements. Surely these would be the best the field has to offer; if I found questionable advice in this best of textual worlds, then Lord knows what might lie in older, less contemporary books. My students would have been vindicated. I randomly selected twenty texts and began.[3]

My initial discovery and biggest surprise was that these texts made good sense and with few exceptions were not condescending. In fact, most were conceptually sophisticated. Grammar and usage sections were informed by

From *College Composition and Communication* 32 (February 1981): 65–74.

linguistics and sociolinguistics, and discussions of writing were guided by current notions of prewriting and invention, writer-audience relations, writing as thinking, and writing as process. My reformer's zeal was dampened; these were obviously not the same kinds of texts that had triggered Lanham's adrenalin seven years ago.

But even here I found rigid rules, unqualified restrictive statements about the composing process or the written product. I offer ten:

> If you can't list at least six points (for any topic) then select another topic.
>
> Every word in your essay must lead the reader back to your thesis.
>
> The clearest and most emphatic place for your thesis sentence is at the end — not at the beginning — of the [introductory] paragraph.
>
> This is the basic principle for organizing the middle of your essay. Save the best for last. It's as simple as that.
>
> > (supported with a little chart presumably to add scientific clout)
>
> Nearly all good papers begin with what the writers think is least important (though perhaps catchy) and work up to what they consider most important.
>
> You will need to make at least two drafts before submitting any paper.
>
> In the first place, outlines freeze most writers.
>
> Begin (your essay) with a simple sentence.
>
> A thesis should not be written in figurative language.
>
> Do not inject a new idea into your concluding paragraph.

Certainly, these rules were sparked by difficulties the authors had seen again and again in student essays, but common errors do not justify dicta.

How many articles in this issue of *CCC* make at least six points about a topic? Where in such injunctions to tally are considerations of the *quality* of points, the weight of one piece of evidence over another?

Every word in an essay does not lead back to a thesis — that's semantically impossible. Halliday and Hasan's rigorous investigation of cohesion clearly shows that semantic relations of particular (not all) words across sentence boundaries result in tightly structured texts (*Cohesion in English* [London: Longmans, Green, 1976]). Again, quality blended with quantity, not just word counts alone.

The clearest and most emphatic place for a thesis sentence is not necessarily at the end of an introductory paragraph. Students writing essay exams had better demonstrate and direct their knowledge as soon as possible. How often have we scrawled "get to the point" alongside our students' linguistic traipsing?

And so on. In the midst of good sense I found the kinds of arbitrary prescriptions that some students could read as rigid rules. And the problem went beyond one- and two-line absolutes. Larger-scale discussions of the composing process, outlining, revision, and modes of discourse, though tempered with qualifiers and alternatives, were often presented in a way that implied a rigidity, a fixedness that is simply not borne out in the way writers, mediocre to talented, write. This new generation of texts was sensibly modified with the best of new ideas, but the modification was, for the most part, superficial. (Fifteen of the twenty texts used were, to my mind, not appreciable deviations from what Fogarty long ago tagged "the current-traditional rhetoric."[4]) Whether or not these discussions of composing, outlining, revision, and discourse also contribute to writer's block, I can't say. But what I do hope to show is that they profoundly constrict a student's notion of the writing process. That constriction could lead to blocking or to a number of the difficulties that mar student writing.

Some illustrations:

The Composing Process.   Though our own experience, interviews with creative writers, and a burgeoning composing process literature all attest to the highly complex, non-neatly sequential nature of the composing process, textbooks continue to begin with "Chapter 1: Generating Ideas" and move through a sequence of chapters that end with "Revising." Though most of these texts admit that writing doesn't always proceed in this orderly a fashion, their overall structure stands as a more potent statement than scattered caveats. Their structure expresses an ultra-rational spirit more appropriate to analytic logic than to composing. One text, for example, lists, then discusses, the following stages of the composing process:

1. Selecting the topic
2. Narrowing the topic
3. Thinking through the topic
4. Gathering and organizing material
5. Outlining
6. Writing the first draft
7. Revising the first draft
8. Preparing the final copy

Again, the intent here is legitimate—freshman writers often fly into assignments helter-skelter and need to learn more efficient approaches. But reductionistic schema like the above leave out one of the most obvious facts about composing—even moderately skilled freshman writers think through a topic while gathering, organizing, and rejecting information. For that fact, how is it cognitively possible to "narrow" and "think through" a topic without acquiring (or retrieving from memory) and weighing information? Furthermore, outlining and preliminary drafting often lead to further deletions and additions.

Not only are stage models inaccurate, they can mislead. Nancy Sommers, for example, has suggested that linear conceptualizations of composing have reduced revision to "an isolated, non-creative activity, as interesting, perhaps, as an autopsy."[5]

Outlining.   All but two of the textbooks devote two to ten pages to outlining. Six of the books sensibly warn of the abuses of the outline (e.g., "Your outline is only a guide for writing, not the final word") and four cite variations like the "scratch" outline. But most books, even those that offer cautions or alternatives, present in detail the formal outline and elaborate its conventions. One text even lists "12 Rules for Outlining" (e.g., "Center the title above the outline in capital letters," "Use no end punctuation in a topic outline," etc.). Pilot research of mine suggests that moderately to highly skilled students effectively use a variety of organizing strategies—mental schemes to simple written lists to formal outlines. The texts do not take individual differences like these into account. Worse yet, the texts, as I note above, treat the outline as a static genre rather than as an ordering strategy, a sketch, plan, logical map whose sole purpose is to aid composing. No wonder students groan at the mention of outlines; these form-for-form's sake antiques are not usually presented, and thus not seen, as flexible, alterable, discardable aids to process. No wonder, too, that some students don't take advantage of new ideas that pop up as they compose; if the idea is not listed under II-B-1, then there's no place for it in the essay.

Revision.   Revision is narrowly conceived in all but two of the texts, and as Nancy Sommers and Ronald Schleifer contend,[6] the result could well be that students misunderstand the possibilities of re-vision. By presenting composing in terms of stages, textbooks imply that once a topic is selected and limited, major discovery and re-thinking are completed. Second, texts often discuss revision as though it were synonymous with editing: "deleting, reordering, substituting," notes one text. Another equates revision with adding transitional words and other refinements to a first draft. These approaches lead the student to see an essay as a product to be cleaned up rather than as an investigative/communicative gesture that is always potentially reconceivable.

Discourse Modes.   So much criticism has been leveled against the traditional narration, description, exposition, argumentation division that it surprises me to find the quartet, complete with qualifiers naturally ("in actuality, most writing is a mixture of all four"), still appearing in the texts. Newer taxonomies are occasionally offered, for example: self-expressive, expository, persuasive, imaginative—again with hedging.

Discourse categories—and the authors are candid here—are not mutually exclusive. But what the authors don't seem to question is the categories' value. Certainly they are not useful in literary criticism and most certainly not in history, biology, psychology, etc. How, then, do these apples-and-oranges taxonomies aid student writing? They don't. My suspicion is that they confuse students, force them to classify the unclassifiable, and—major concern—narrow or muddle their vision of what they can do when an instructor tells them to "argue" or "explain" an issue. A Freshman Composition student who will have to write for, say, political science might come to think that persuasion doesn't explain or that exposition doesn't have a persuasive edge. Viewing discourse in this narrow way could detach process from audience and result in attenuated products—the student writing the argumentative essay puts all his energy into pleas and exhortations, neglecting the bit of description or the section of narration, or the weighing and explaining of facts, that foster connection with a reader.

The inclusion of prewriting, invention, discovery begins to resolve some of Ohmann's process, though not political, concerns, and only two of the texts contain the "be honest," "be sincere" platitudes that so riled Lanham. But, as I've tried to show, profound problems remain and, given textbooks as we know them, cannot be remedied. Texts reduce the complex, dynamic, non-linear process of composing to rules, stages, and operations that belie the richness of writing behavior, for writing is one process that cannot be dissected and directed in static print.

Few textbook writers from other disciplines try to teach process. Other than composition texts, only mathematics texts, lab manuals, and some sections of physics and chemistry texts aim at process. But the difference between composition texts and the others is significant. Take *Introduction to Calculus*, for example. The student is led through a series of steps in an operation that, if followed, will yield an answer. The operation, and sometimes the answer, can then be used in further operations. The operations do not vary; the rules that govern them are algorithmic—they always yield the same results. Here a process can be taught via static print because the outcomes are predictable and verifiable. Writing is obviously not that neat. There are no uni-directional operations, no algorithmic rules, no right and wrong answers. At best, composition texts offer heuristic rather than algorithmically rigid rules, options (e.g., "there are five ways to start an essay"), references to context (e.g., "passive voice is sometimes required in scientific writing"). At worst, they list pronouncements rooted in the authors' biases and offer static conceptions of composing. But in either case text authors are forced to reduce the multiplicity of composing options to a manageable number, and convert multi-directional possibilities to a set of rules or patterns or diagrams or lists. Caveats about the tenuousness of these rules and patterns might be present but, as with my students experiencing writing blocks, are sometimes misunderstood or go unnoticed. Certainly exercises help, but they aren't successful because they focus on a too discrete and disembodied aspect of the total essay ("Write 5 topic sentences," "Circle the words that unify this paragraph"), or are too broad and uninstructive (e.g., "you've just read a compare/contrast essay; now write one of your own").

A useful strategy would be to show students step by step how to construct particular kinds of essays. One of the texts does this admirably. Van Nostrand et al.'s *Functional Writing* devotes its 378 pages to guiding the student through the process of constructing the "argumentative" essay. Each chapter carefully builds on the previous one as explanations and qualifications are nicely mixed with extended and increasingly sophisticated exercises. But toward the end of the book a difficulty arises, one that is perhaps inevitable when process is taught in print: process and product begin to merge in potentially confusing ways:

> In order to develop your organizing idea, you must allow an expanding sequence to occur. This sequence permits new discoveries. It allows for a conclusion that is more significant than any assertion that leads up to it. This conclusion represents your new awareness of the importance of your subject. (p. 233)

> The broader base of the writer's pyramid represents the bonus of a conclusion that you did not anticipate when you began to write. (p. 343)

Some students might well read this to mean that their essays should contain all the pertinent *and* irrelevant steps they went through to reach their conclusion. Furthermore, it could lead them to save the best for last, a disastrous strategy with some kinds of assignments for some kinds of professors.

Lest I seem like a nitpicking crank, let me repeat again: these textbooks say some very sensible things about writing, don't degrade the student, include some of the valuable insights offered by linguistics and sociolinguistics, by newer rhetorical investigations, etc. My concern runs deeper — writing is simply too complex and unwieldy a process to be taught from a textbook. Good teachers know this. Thus they continually skip around in texts, qualify pronouncements, and supplement with sheet after sheet of handouts. Texts or the methods they espouse aren't responsible for systematic improvement in writing — they work or don't work with different students in the hands of different teachers in different classrooms on different days. (See the continually inconclusive or contradictory studies on textbook and method that help to fill *Dissertation Abstracts* and even some issues of *Research in the Teaching of English*.) What works, as I'll suggest at the end of this essay, is a learning relationship between teacher and student that accounts for individual differences, the process of composing, and the demands of audience. That late-60's promotional hook "teacherproof materials" epitomized a misguided technological cockiness.

INSULAR APPROACHES TO SCHOOL WRITING

The effectiveness of composition textbooks is also diminished because they present student writing and its audiences in insular, sometimes naive ways.

In a recent survey of composition readers, Laurence Behrens found an inordinate number of what he labeled "meditations" and "reminiscences" ("Meditations, Reminiscences, Polemics: Composition Readers and the Service Course," *College English*, 41 [January 1980], 561–570). Excerpts from such essays also served as models in most of the composition textbooks I examined. But, as Behrens argues, our students aren't really equipped to write such prose,[7] and even if they were they wouldn't be asked to meditate and reminisce in courses outside Freshman Composition.

Fifty percent of the texts, in an effort to provide models less removed from a student's skills, offered student essays, but again they were essentially belletristic and, quite often, all too simplistic. A sample:

AN UNFORGETTABLE EXPERIENCE

During the summer between my seventh and eighth grades in junior high, my parents sent me to a YWCA camp at Grass Lake. I was happy to go because I liked all the activities of boating, swimming, and crafts that would be provided. Although I did not know any other girls who were going to that particular camp, I felt confident that I would soon make friends. I imagined that the camp experience would be free and joyous; it was to be my first summer away from home and my expectations of youthful pleasures, happiness, and shared enthusiasms were great. When I arrived I was assigned to a cabin with five other girls. Nothing occurred during the early hours to make me less enthusiastic. Although none of my cabin mates were very friendly, I felt that any reserve would disappear in the camp experience. . . .

Sit in on classes. Listen to students comment on these essays: "It's clever." "It's interesting." "Something like that happened to me." "She could have started it differently." Two minutes of this and the teacher, hunting desperately for some substance, points out a clever trope and that's it. The same comments could have been made by these students in their freshman year in high school. Here Lanham's attack on condescension still holds.

A further problem: take belletristic essays, student or professional. Combine them with prescriptions like "Good writing is authentic"; "Rely on your own first-hand observation"; "You can never go wrong and certainly make readers grateful, if you try to create interest." The result is the plague of freshman writing: the substitution of vague reflection for mastery and orderly presentation of information. A first-rate student in my American Novel class wrote a pretty inept midterm on *A Farewell to Arms*. Her essay opened with a "War is Hell" sort of threadbare philosophic introduction and continued with a peppering of "I don't think Catherine Barkley was her own person" asides. When we talked about the exam it became clear that she thought good writing should both entertain me as well as reveal something about her. These are noble goals and, quite honestly, I respect the Macrorie/Elbow insistence on finding voice that underlies them. But I must also firmly say that there is nothing immoral in teaching young people how to assimilate, organize, and render information. We can show respect for students by honoring their intellects as well as their feelings.

Another indication of the insularity of the texts is found in their treatment of invention, finding a topic, prewriting. I asked faculty, teaching assistants, and graduate student tutors from seventeen disciplines (including English) to give me samples of paper topics and essay examination questions. Every one of the 445 topics and questions I received were specific. Invention, at this level, is unnecessary. It is only in Composition, and, for that matter, rarely there, that our students need to "find a topic." The invention or prewriting techniques that students really do need have much more to do with weighing and focusing large bodies of information already known. But this was not treated in any of the texts.[8]

Finally, and this brings me full-circle back to the beginning of this section, there is the narrow and, in fact, inaccurate discussion of audience. The audience of student writing is also assumed to be a literary audience who like the clever turn, the building on suspense, the scintillating image. One text urged originality, suggesting, for example, that a student quote Abigail van Buren rather than Patrick Henry. ("Even if your essay is not that good, by its very originality the teacher will be startled, revived, and refreshed.") Another much more sophisticated and admirable text followed a discussion of audience with Walter Ong's notion that though a writer must consider audience, the audience also becomes what the writer intends. But while this is true for literary text, it is not necessarily true for student-to-teacher text. In fact most of these textbook discussions of audience are unnecessary: every student knows exactly who his or her audience is—Mr. Jones, Ms. Smith, Professor Simpson. What the student needs to know is that Mr. Jones, Ms. Smith, and Professor Simpson might have very different tastes and standards. Yet only two texts offered a sentence worth of practical advice on how to determine an audience's stylistic and formal biases. Texts should offer sound advice on variation in academic audiences and further advice on how, purely and simply, to determine those audiences' demands.[9]

How, then, should Freshman Composition be taught? Through a program that acknowledges both the complexity of the composing process and the dilemma of the student as a stranger in a strange land of academic discourse and academic audiences.

The best teacher would:

conceive of writing as a thinking, learning, shaping process and would, therefore, involve students in an intensive series of thinking and rethinking, prewriting, and rewriting exercises;

understand, diagnose, and honor functional individual differences in composing process;

be aware of the ranges of audiences in an academic setting and use materials from a variety of disciplines for class discussions and writing assignments;

make students aware of stylistic and formal conventions across the disciplines and explain how to determine and respond to them.

What would replace the texts I've criticized?

Publishing houses (with NCTE possibly leading the way) could print books for teachers that condense our best research on the composing process and its individual variations. These texts-for-teachers would also offer information on academic writing situations and audience demands. And, of course, a variety of curricula to bring this all to life would be included. For students the houses would publish packets of process exercises and interdisciplinary materials. Teachers could then more sensibly teach prewriting, structuring, rethinking by selecting appropriate exercises for appropriate students. Writing assignments would be based on a range of materials: lists of facts, compilations of data, excerpts from essays and books, articles. Writing in composition would then approximate writing in other *English* and non-English courses. Students would learn to fuse thinking and writing in the ways they must with the kinds of materials they must use once their writing careers begin outside the doors of English Composition.

NOTES

[1]In a more recent article, Ohmann hits stylistic maxims like "use definite, specific, concrete language," speculating that they might lead students away from abstraction and analysis and toward the fragmented and concrete ("Use Definite, Specific, Concrete Language," *College English*, 41 [December 1979], 390–397). Other current critiques: Jeffrey Youdelman pillors remedial texts (and curricula) for limiting that which a student can write, and thus think, about ("Limiting Students: Remedial Writing and the Death of Open Admissions," *College English*, 39 [January 1978], 562–572). Donald C. Stewart suggests that texts have not been appreciably influenced by recent rhetorical theory ("Composition Textbooks and the Assault on Tradition," *College Composition and Communication*, 29 [May 1978], 171–176). Ellen Strenski observes that texts rely on model sentences that convey a world-view of cynicism and despair ("Grammar Sample Sentences and the Power of Suggestion," *College English*, 40 [January 1979], 512–516).

[2]Some examples: "Extend your vocabulary"/"Avoid big words"; "Keep sentences short"/"Sentences shouldn't be short, but long and interesting" (Muriel Harris, "Contradictory Perceptions of Rules for Writing," *College Composition and Communication*, 30 [May 1979], 218–220).

[3]I will list the texts but except in one instance will not cite specific titles in my discussion. Citation might be interpreted as individual attack and that is not my purpose. I should mention that of the 20 texts, two appeared in Ohmann's survey, one in Lanham's. In all three cases, however, I chose newer editions.

Adams, W. Royce. *TRRPWR*. 2nd ed. New York: Holt, Rinehart and Winston, 1979.

Baker, Sheridan. *The Complete Stylist and Handbook*. New York: Crowell, 1976.

Corder, Jim W. *Contemporary Writing: Process and Practice*. Glenview, Ill.: Scott, Foresman, 1979.

Cowan, Gregory, and McPherson, Elisabeth. *Plain English Rhetoric and Reader*. 2nd ed. New York: Random House, 1977.

Crews, Frederick. *The Random House Handbook*. 2nd ed. New York: Random House, 1977.

D'Angelo, Frank J. *Process and Thought in Composition*. Cambridge, Mass.: Winthrop, 1977.

Grasso, Mary Ellen, and Maney, Margaret. *You Can Write*. Cambridge, Mass.: Winthrop, 1975.

Guth, Hans P. *Words and Ideas — A Handbook for College Writing*. 4th ed. Belmont, Cal.: Wadsworth, 1975.

Hall, Donald. *Writing Well*. 3rd ed. Boston: Little, Brown, 1979.

Janis, J. Harold. *College Writing*. New York: Macmillan, 1977.

Langan, John. *English Skills*. New York: McGraw-Hill, 1977.

Macrorie, Ken. *Telling Writing*. 2nd rev. ed. Rochelle Park, N.J.: Hayden, 1976.

Optner, Ruth L. *Writing from the Inside Out*. New York: Harper and Row, 1977.

Roberts, Edgar V. *A Practical College Rhetoric*. Cambridge, Mass.: Winthrop, 1975.

Smith, William F., and Liedlich, Raymond D. *From Thought to Theme*. 5th ed. New York: Harcourt Brace Jovanovich, 1977.

Tibbetts, A. M., and Tibbetts, Charlene. *Strategies of Rhetoric*. 3rd ed. Glenview, Ill.: Scott, Foresman, 1979.

Van Nostrand, A. D., Knoblauch, C. H., McGuire, Peter J., and Pettigrew, Joan. *Functional Writing*. Boston: Houghton Mifflin, 1978.

Willis, Hulon. *Logic, Language, and Composition*. Cambridge, Mass.: Winthrop, 1975.

Winkler, Anthony C., and McCuen, Jo Ray. *Rhetoric Made Plain*. 2nd ed. New York: Harcourt Brace Jovanovich, 1978.

Winterowd, W. Ross. *The Contemporary Writer — A Practical Rhetoric*. New York: Harcourt Brace Jovanovich, 1975.

[4]Daniel J. Fogarty, S. J., *Roots for a New Rhetoric* (New York: Teacher's College, Columbia University, 1959).

[5]Nancy Sommers, "The Need for Theory in Composition Research," *College Composition and Communication*, 30 (February 1979), 48.

[6]Nancy Sommers and Ronald Schleifer, "Means and Ends: Some Assumptions of Student Writers," *Composition and Teaching* (in press).

[7]". . . the meditation, particularly in its more private or idiosyncratic forms, is an inappropriate mode to put as a model before college freshmen, who for the most part have neither lived long enough, nor experienced, nor read widely or deeply enough, nor developed sufficient maturity of insight to compose meditations of any significance or general interest (a fact they are generally well aware of, which is why they consider assignments to write meditations so futile and meaningless)" (Behrens, p. 565). There is an almost Wordsworthian assumption behind these reflective, meditative assignments; it is succinctly expressed by one of the textbook authors: "Really, we have enough memory packed away by the age of 18 to keep us writing until we are 70." This is misleading. Memory offers us the rawest of materials; it takes considerable skill to mould it into memorable prose.

[8]I suspect that the tagmemists' particle/wave/field heuristic could be useful here. Though presented in several texts, this heuristic was not applied to accumulated data or events.

[9]For a comprehensive theoretical justification, see Ruth Mitchell and Mary Taylor, "The Integrating Perspective: An Audience-Response Model for Writing," *College English,* 41 (November 1979), 247–271.

5

Speculations on Process Knowledge and the Textbook's Static Page

1983

AUTHOR'S NOTE: In this second article on composition textbooks, I extend the argument in "Sophisticated, Ineffective Books" (p. 84) and raise the fundamental question "Can we learn complex processes [like composing] from written materials?" What surprised me was that, at that point, no work had been done on this issue as it related to composing. Though there was some technical communication and human factors research on the effects of variation in textual format and illustration on the assembly of machinery, I couldn't find anything relevant to the more open-ended, and arguably more complex, tasks that students can encounter in freshman comp. Some of the questions raised in this article might be considered in a fresh way in the current composition studies environment, one rich in dynamic electronic media and interest in professional and technical writing, information systems, and visual rhetoric. All this raises again basic questions about reading and writing, learning and instruction.

A tremendous amount of energy goes into the contracting, developing, marketing, and revising of composition textbooks. And a significant amount of energy goes into criticizing them.[1] More than we critics would like to admit, editors — good editors anyway — try to respond to this criticism. Thus we are seeing a new generation of textbooks that incorporate current work in rhetoric, psycho- and sociolinguistics, the composing process, and writing across the curriculum. But the surprising thing is that such innovation goes on in the absence of fundamental research into what happens when students read current *or* traditional textbooks. True, some authors conduct field tests, but, for reasons that I hope will become clear in this essay, field testing provides limited answers to basic questions. We need more basic research than we now have into the interaction of reader and text when the text is one intended to teach a complex process. Without such research, we will never know whether or not our improvements — our attempts to revise and revitalize textbooks — are really contributing to growth in composing.

From *College Composition and Communication* 34.2 (May 1983): 208–13.

But is such research really necessary, or would it simply be a desirable but ultimately "academic" exercise? Won't textbooks continue to become more effective as our knowledge about composing increases? Not necessarily, for we have good reason to suspect that knowledge of any complex process—like knowledge about composing—cannot be adequately conveyed via static print. As soon as such knowledge hits the page of a text, its rich possibilities are narrowed and sometimes rigidified. While I certainly don't want to suggest that no student learns from composition textbooks, I do want to raise the possibility that students learn about the process of writing from a textbook less frequently and less effectively than many of us think. To argue the legitimacy of the foregoing assertion, I'll begin with general speculation on the value of textbook discussions of writing and move toward more specific consideration of problem-solving in the act of composing. Though I will state my thoughts with some assurance, I intend the essay to be read as an extended hypothesis set forth to be confirmed or rejected. I hope that the negative thrust of my speculation will underscore the seriousness of the issue and the reasons why we need closer investigation of the meeting of student and page. At the end of the essay, I'll briefly suggest some advances in instructional materials that could result from the sort of basic research I'm advocating.

One way textbook authors attempt to help students grow as writers is to discuss, often carefully and sometimes gracefully, various aspects or phases of the composing process: the value, even the excitement, of prewriting. The nature and methods of invention. Writing as discovering. The importance of revision. The audience-based nature of writing. And so on. Let me offer a brief excerpt from one such discussion; this deals with revision:

> Experienced authors will tell you, furthermore, that revision is often their best means of finding out what they wanted to say. This may seem like a strange remark after all the emphasis I've put on planning, but it's true nonetheless. Composition is a continual struggle against a wish to keep your familiar bearings, and originality is possible only when this struggle has been won. In order to challenge a reader you must first suffer a little disorientation yourself. Sometimes the habit of thinking in clichés prevails over every contrary effort until a slight change of wording allows a suppressed idea to burst through. . . . [2]

This is writing about writing. It discusses—even celebrates—rather than shows how. Perhaps such discussion sparks for our students a greater appreciation of composing. That would be wonderful, but we have, to my knowledge, no research on whether or not attitudes about writing change as a result of reading even the most eloquent reflection on composing. I suspect that such passages do more for us than for our freshmen—we already know how to, in this case, revise, and we appreciate reflection on the energy and the craft of re-seeing. But do our students learn from reading such reflections?

Such discussions are often followed by examples, so perhaps it's through illustration that the student is shown how to revise. Yet static examples are an uncertain means of teaching a highly complex and fluid process skill. Again, consider revising: one popular example presents initial and revised drafts of a student's paper. These pre-post samples illustrate that change in product has occurred, but they do not teach how to conceive of the need for change nor how to effect changes beyond sentence-level emendations.

Perhaps most of us would agree that general discussions, even with examples, have little specific pedagogic value. But more precise and richly detailed discussions might have a great deal of value. They teach students specific strategies and routines. But my earlier concern remains: can someone be taught highly complex strategies via textual discussions and explanations, even if they are detailed and illustrated? Our students might be able to parrot back or paraphrase or even carefully summarize what the textbook said about these strategies, but can they *practice* the gist of what they've read? All too often, they cannot, for, as Bloom, Gagné,[3] and others who research hierarchies of cognitive processes remind us, there's a wide gap between memorizing and recalling knowledge and putting that knowledge into play.

And there's a further issue here. Because anything complex is best explained in print by reducing complexity, what often happens is that a process is reduced to a list, a series of steps. That reduction might work with "closed" problems like, say, testing the pH of a solution in a chemistry lab, but it is less likely to work when the problem is complex and "open-ended" — that is, when there are multiple ways to achieve results (and multiple kinds of acceptable results) — as there are with virtually all discourse problems. One text I recently reviewed — one billed as an innovative process text that had been widely field-tested — attempted to teach the student how to prewrite. It did so by guiding students through *eight* "prewriting and planning" steps (e.g., "timed writing," then "free associating," then "listing") before suggesting that they begin writing their *first* drafts. How, essentially, is this different from, say, forcing students to write complete outlines before commencing writing? Both cases reduce process to prescriptive formulae, to static steps. I would suggest that similar reduction often lies at the heart of discussions of inventing, analyzing one's audience, organizing information, and so forth.

But let's say it were possible to discuss aspects of the composing process in a fuller, less reductive way as, in fact, some admirable new textbooks do. A fundamental — perhaps *the* most fundamental — difficulty would remain, and that has to do with both the problem-solver and the problem when the problem is highly complex and "open-ended." The effective "open-ended" problem-solver internalizes a method in idiosyncratic ways and then further adapts and modifies it when facing idiosyncratic tasks. For purposes of illustration, suppose that — contrary to my earlier reservations — a textbook author succeeded in conveying the intricacies of the tagmemists' particle/wave/field heuristic. Still, of necessity, different students would represent this heuristic to themselves — come to conceive of it and understand it — in slightly to significantly different ways. Human beings simply don't internalize a complex process identically. Now, by their very nature, texts can perhaps present a method, but they cannot represent all the possible ways each one of us makes that method work. One student, for example, might best comprehend the tagmemists' heuristic via physics or biology models. Another might rely on physical, sensual experiences or metaphors. Some students might best play out the heuristic in its suggested order—seeing a phenomenon as particle, then as wave, then as field. Others might use it most effectively when they reverse the order or start in the middle. But the text cannot respond to all these options. In most cases, it presents a single approach. One (or one's teacher) cannot look to the book for confirmation of the myriad individual ways a strategy is made one's own. Furthermore, complex "open-ended" tasks demand individual modification of any method. Let me illustrate by contrast. If a task is relatively simple and "closed"—for example, determining the pH balance in the chemistry lab—the student is guided toward mastery by the restricted, sequential nature of the activity and the verifiability of its successful completion. If the student doesn't apply her strategy one right way, she won't get results. But when the task is less constrained—as are all discourse tasks—there are multiple ways of achieving success. Varied writing tasks—ranging from a reflection on a personal experience to an analysis of the Cuban missile crisis to an explication of "Among School Children"—might well demand numerous variations, even fundamental changes, even distortions of (to stick with our earlier example) the tagmemic heuristic. The textbook, of course, cannot represent the variations the heuristic could effectively take. In summary, the textbook cannot respond to individual differences in the learner or in the task. Yet heuristics, by definition, must be flexible, yielding, multi-optioned, even alterable. How can the static page convey those properties?

Certainly now's the time for someone to say: "It's not the text's purpose to convey such complexity. That's what teachers do. Texts are simply source-books, compendia of advice and techniques which teachers gloss and energize and alter and supplement." And that's certainly true—for good teachers. But, in fact, how many teachers do use texts so creatively? How many, sad to say, simply assign chapters and then discuss rather than amplify those chapters' contents? "But," someone could further rejoin, "that's the teacher's fault, not the text's." Perhaps. But consider with me for a moment what the very existence of a textbook for composition can imply. Begin by considering what textbooks—any discipline's textbooks—represent in our culture. In general, textbooks are the repository of our knowledge on a given subject at a given time. That knowledge is usually knowledge of a certain kind: facts, data, information, theories.[4] Not so much knowledge of how to do but knowledge of what is known or is currently surmised. Now, as I've tried to suggest, composition texts hold knowledge of a kind different from that found in history or literature or biology or astronomy texts. It is process knowledge for solving complex, open-ended problems. This makes the composition text a rare kind of text, indeed. My fear is that it is not perceived by some teachers and many students as rare in that way. That is, they might see it as a text like the culture's other texts—full of knowledge to be memorized, hopefully understood on some level, and recalled.[5] And to the degree that teacher or student treats knowledge about composing this way, whatever limitations the composition textbook has cannot be overcome.

At the core of all the foregoing speculation has been a central, and I think fascinating, question: can we learn complex processes from written materials? One would think that some answers to this question could be found in experimental and educational psychology. But, in fact, the relevant work being done is with complex but relatively closed problems — e.g., How do people best learn to build moderately complex machinery from prose texts? Do diagrams help? Do pictures?[6] Composing is much more complex and open than the problems these psychologists explore; thus their findings, while to some degree pertinent, are not directly applicable to our present inquiry. What is interesting, and in a way shocking, is that, to my knowledge, there are no direct studies of how the advice in a text on composing is converted into practice. Let me repeat my call for such a line of research.

The composition textbook is a book with all sorts of historical/political intricacies in its tradition, but with no fundamental research into its function — into what happens when a student reads its pages, attempts to represent to him or herself what its pages say, and then attempts to put what is represented into practice. This sort of research would be different, more basic, from the one kind we do have: field testing. For the most part, field testing is a nonsystematic way of working out the kinks in already-developed materials. That is, field testing usually does not include experimental tests of the effectiveness of alternative text versions, nor does it include more cognitively-oriented studies of the ways students individually make the author's text their own. But how can we expect a rich development of composition pedagogy without this kind of more basic research? Wouldn't all of us — editors, researchers, teachers, students — be better served if the mad scramble for new textbooks and new authors was slowed down and true research and development took the place of the current marketing whirlwind? True, such research could confirm some of my bleak speculation and force us to look hard at a number of our assumptions about learning from textbooks. But textbook research could also disconfirm or qualify my hunches and in the process suggest ways to improve instructional materials. Some examples: We could test variations in the language, organization, formatting, and illustration of textbooks as we now know them. (I'm reminded here of Janet Emig's suggestion that we depict the multi-levelled, recursive nature of composing by using the sort of transparent overlays found in textbooks in the life sciences.) We could study and adapt procedures used in other fields that must also teach complex "open-ended" problem solving; medicine and the teaching of diagnosis via clinical-pathologic case studies come to mind. We could develop other kinds of printed materials, ones that encourage teachers to assess students' needs and determine the best ways to meet those needs. An example here would be packets that present alternate versions of the same lesson. The teacher could choose the version that best fit an individual student's learning style and needs. We could move beyond print technology and develop audio and video tapes and interactive computer software to actually show and guide students through, say, the process of revision. In addition to all this, we might be forced to admit—and force our publishers to see—the tremendous need for carefully done texts and tapes for teachers that condense the best, most applicable current theoretical and research knowledge.

We now approach the fundamental issue of textbook development traditionally—revise the text, make it more current, include new knowledge, hire the best people to do the writing. But all this goes on in absence of research on what happens cognitively when students face these texts. I don't think it's being overly dramatic to say that we can't afford (in all senses of that word) to proceed this way, for composition textbooks are potentially the culture's most important textbooks. They deal with our grandest means of exploring and rendering reality. Certainly the development of such books deserves the best research scrutiny we can provide.

ACKNOWLEDGMENTS

The author expresses gratitude to Peggy Atwell, Linda Bannister, Dave Cohen, Steve Duarte, Barbara Hayes-Roth, Ruth Mitchell, and Richard Shavelson for their helpful discussions of the issues presented in this paper. An earlier version of this paper was read at the 1982 CCCC, San Francisco, California.

NOTES

[1]See, for example, Richard Lanham, *Style: An Anti-Textbook* (New Haven: Yale University Press, 1974); Linda Bannister, "Anti-Writing: Phase One in the Composing Process," unpublished manuscript, University of Southern California, 1975; Richard Ohmann, *English in America* (New York: Oxford University Press, 1976) and "Use Definite, Specific, Concrete Language," *College English*, 41 (December, 1979), 390–397; Jeffrey Youdelman, "Limiting Students: Remedial Writing and the Death of Open Admissions," *College English*, 39 (January, 1978), 562–572; Donald C. Stewart, "Composition Textbooks and the Assault on Tradition," *College Composition and Communication*, 29 (May, 1978), 171–176; Ellen Strenski, "Grammar Sample Sentences and the Power of Suggestion," *College English*, 40 (January, 1979), 512–516; Mike Rose, "Sophisticated, Ineffective Books—The Dismantling of Process in Composition Texts," *College Composition and Communication*, 32 (February, 1981), 65–74.

[2]Frederick Crews, *The Random House Handbook* (New York: Random House, 1977), 45.

[3]Benjamin S. Bloom, Max D. Engelhart, Edward J. Furst, Walker H. Hill, and David R. Krathwohl, ed., *Taxonomy of Educational Objectives. Handbook I: Cognitive Domain* (New York: David McKay, 1956); Robert M. Gagné, *The Conditions of Learning*, Second Edition (New York: Holt, Rinehart, and Winston, 1970).

[4]Thomas Kuhn, *The Structure of Scientific Revolutions*, Second Edition (Chicago: University of Chicago Press, 1970); David R. Olson, "Writing: The Divorce of the Author from the Text," in Barry M. Kroll and Roberta Vann, ed., *Exploring Speaking-Writing Relationships* (Urbana, IL: National Council of Teachers of English, 1981), pp. 99–110.

[5]Some of the readers of earlier versions of this paper raised the following very legitimate point: current theories of reading comprehension stress that reading is a complex, active, generative interchange between reader and text, yet I seem to be suggesting that students reading composition textbooks are relatively passive in their comprehension. That is, they are not going beyond the static boundaries of the discussions in textbooks and generatively assimilating them into their own prior knowledge. Let me show how my speculations do not violate what we know about reading. First, I'm not saying that the reader cannot actively comprehend textbook discussions (or that texts with summaries, embedded questions, and certain kinds of exercises might not aid comprehension); I'm saying that, in line with Bloom and Gagné (see footnote #3), "comprehension" doesn't imply ability to creatively apply what is comprehended. Second, not all reading behavior is broadly active and generative. For all sorts of reasons, we might not read a text deeply, fully. Our own psychological states (e.g., anxiety or boredom) as well as the nature of the text (e.g., novel vs. repair manual) as well as situational cues (e.g., the culture's or profession's or individual

teacher's conception of textbooks) all contribute to our disposition to read in a particular way — whether deeply or superficially.

⁶Thomas L. Crandell and Marvin D. Glock, *Technical Communication — Taking the User into Account*, Report No. 5, Series B. Reading Research Group, Department of Education, College of Agriculture and Life Sciences, Cornell University, 1981; David E. Stone and Marvin D. Glock, "How Do Young Adults Read Directions With and Without Pictures?" *Journal of Educational Psychology*, 73 (June, 1981), 419–426.

PART TWO

Teaching Academic Writing, 1979–2001

Introduction to Part Two

My approach to teaching freshman composition was heavily influenced by my work in preparatory programs. The goal of the Veteran's Program was to get students with poor academic records ready for college, and the tutorial center at UCLA served students who were already admitted to the university but whose writing suggested trouble ahead. The goals were immediate and pragmatic, and the way I addressed them was to use the college curriculum itself as the context for instruction, to try to simulate in the writing classroom the discourse demands of the typical lower-division course of study—as I understood them at the time. Two particularly thorny problems students faced were working with nonfiction, informational texts and structuring typical academic responses to them: summarizing and synthesizing them, systematically comparing them, analyzing them. My personal experience and my experience in the classroom led me to believe strongly that students could engage in serious intellectual work and, given the right curriculum, could learn the conventions of academic writing. Furthermore, they could come to understand something about how these conventions function, the circumstances of their use, and their benefits and limitations.

The specifics of my approach to curriculum, as I noted, emerged from my reading in cognitive and educational psychology and from writing-across-the-curriculum. Then, a bit later, I encountered applied linguistics, particularly English for Special or Academic Purpose, which attempts to analyze the micro and macro discourse features of disciplinary prose, often with an eye toward instruction.

Though some of it is dated, the material in this section addresses issues that are very much alive in composition studies today. There seems to be a heightened interest in developing ways to help students gain competency in writing for the academy, and, for that matter, for other professional settings that share at least some of the academy's frames of mind and rhetorical strategies. There is also interest in helping students read and write from difficult texts.

There have long been tensions and objections within our field related to the teaching of academic writing. One concern is that such instruction directs the focus away from student experience and expression and toward a mimicking of academic convention. Another, not unrelated, concern is that an academic writing curriculum runs the risk of assimilating students to the disciplinary status quo rather than engendering in them a critical stance toward it. These are legitimate concerns and caution against an unthinking appropriation of conventions.

The unfortunate thing is that these concerns and the debates arising from them are sometimes framed as linguistic or political binaries, either/or pedagogical choices: assimilationist versus critical, accommodationist versus oppositional, instrumentalist versus reflective. As a number of people have pointed out recently,[1] the binaries keep us from imagining overlap and synthesis. A curriculum can be both instrumental — it includes what students need to know to succeed — and reflective in that it fosters analysis of the function and goals of the writing students are doing. The binaries also make it hard to account for the many examples of scholarly writing that rely on disciplinary conventions of argumentation, evidence, and citation, and that are highly critical of the social order. I'm looking up at rows of examples on my bookshelf right now, from James P. Anderson's *The Education of Blacks in the South — 1860–1935* to Cynthia Eagle Russett's *Sexual Science: The Victorian Construction of Womanhood*.

As well, the binaries play into the academy's dismissal of the applied and practical (I thank Irv Peckham for pointing this out to me) by marking the technical and instrumental dimensions of writing as intellectually and ideologically suspect. Finally, the binaries themselves erase the situated complexity of language use: the importance of context, of time, place, and motive. How is academic writing taught, to what end, to what population, and so on? A curriculum can't be judged in a vacuum.

My hope is that, collectively, the selections I include here can provide a set of heuristics for developing a writing curriculum that honors the tensions I mentioned and that assists students in developing the discursive competence they'll need to engage the academy.

Here are some of the questions the selections might help one frame:

- What is academic writing?

- Is it a single discourse? Many discourses? If many, are there shared characteristics?

- How might one find out? Through surveys, interviews, text analysis?

- What are the common difficulties that students have with such writing?

- How might one make instructional sense of the preceding questions? What knowledge and training is needed to provide this instruction? What curricular options and pedagogies might one create?

- Whose responsibility is it to teach academic writing? In what structure and venue? Through a single program? Distributed throughout the curriculum?

- Politically and institutionally, how will these questions be resolved? What local mechanisms are available to achieve consensus and commitment? How does writing and the teaching of writing get defined in the process?

NOTE

[1]See, for example, Beech (2004); Durst (1999); Horner (2000); and D. Seitz (2004).

6

From When Faculty Talk about Writing

1979

AUTHOR'S NOTE: In April, 1979, we in the Writing Research Project held a two-day, in-house conference at UCLA, bringing together faculty, staff, and teaching assistants to talk about student writing. I reprint here a few pages on the conference, drawn from the first article I published in composition studies. Much of the article concerns UCLA responses, too local and dated to merit full inclusion here. To be honest, I shake my head at my naiveté about possible institutional outcomes. And I cringe at some of the phrasing about students and writing. And at the occasional flourish. It would take awhile for me to sharpen my perspective and get my own academic journal style under control. But I'd like to give the reader a sense of the kinds of things we learned about the environments in which students wrote.

If I was developing a cognitive orientation to the teaching of writing, projects like the conference were also highlighting for me the importance of institutional context. What were the demands on students? What methods might help them effectively respond? And how can they develop a critical frame of mind in and through that response?

Gatherings like the 1979 conference can be a valuable source of information about writing outside of one's own department and can also serve a pedagogical and political function. Other faculty come to reflect on the uses of writing in their courses, and the writing program can form alliances that advance its own agenda. I should add that about four years later, our writing program held a further conference, but this time we focused on faculty writing as an entrée to thinking in fresh ways about student writing. So, for example, one thing we did was to invite faculty to bring the early drafts of an article they were currently writing and engage in a discussion across disciplines about their processes of discovery and composing—at least as manifest in this piece. Later in the day, we used that discussion as a bridge to talk about invention and how faculty might frame their assignments to better assist students in their own composing. I still like the idea of such a conference.

From *College English* 41.3 (November 1979): 272–74.

U CLA had a writing conference. No noted scholars were jetted in. No high-paid consultants offered workshops. Ninety-six faculty, staff, and teaching assistants from thirty-eight departments were simply brought together for a day-and-a-half in April. The reason should come as no surprise to any college instructor: an alarming number of students cannot write effectively; a small number are sadly inept. And if any comprehensive effort is going to be made to remedy this situation, it will have to come from within the institution, from a wide range of departments and student service units.

Current remedies at UCLA and most other campuses emanate primarily from English departments and learning centers. Secondary responses come, usually in ad hoc fashion, from individual departments in the form of tutorials, writing labs, additional TA assignments, etc. The results, of course, are fragmented programs, academic finger-pointing ("Why isn't the English department doing its job?" "Why doesn't Psychology assign more papers?"), a good deal of frustration, and a disheartening encapsulation of personal and programmatic knowledge ("Why, I had no idea Economics had instituted a writing lab"). Clearly, these people need to talk to one another. So UCLA's Writing Research Project (WRP)[1] held a local conference.

A brief survey identified faculty, teaching assistants, and student services personnel interested in student writing; WRP selected 139 of them and, with invitation, sent a questionnaire to gather information on workload, grading standards, and stylistic biases. Of the 139, ninety-six replied. They ranged from faculty in political science, fine arts, mathematics, and management to twenty-five teaching assistants representing eighteen departments to ten learning skills specialists and Educational Opportunity Program tutors. To my knowledge, so diverse a group had never been convened to discuss the student writing problems of a single campus.

During the conference, participants split their time between full-group activities and small-group discussions. The morning of the first day was spent discussing one topic: What kinds of writing problems were teachers encountering and what kinds of responses could they or their departments provide? The afternoon of the first day offered a varied agenda. Each group considered different topics (e.g., "The Evaluation of Writing," "Writing Research," "The Organization of Writing Instruction at UCLA"). The second day was entirely spent in large groups. Minutes of the previous afternoon's discussions were presented, and further exchange was encouraged. The conference ended with the formation of a communications network for writing problems, the first of its kind on our campus. I will be glad to provide procedural details to anyone who wishes to organize a similar conference.

As one would expect, the first stages of the conference were shot through with commiseration and superficial agreement. But as meetings wore on, significantly divergent opinions—particularly about style—emerged. These were argued, and some surprisingly balanced resolutions were voiced. At the risk of losing a good deal of the excitement of dialogue, I will distill this conflict and its resolution below. Later I will move beyond the dialogue to its implications.

Faculty Preference and Practice: The Evaluation of Student Prose.   A major section of our questionnaire asked participants to rate the importance of the features of a written product: spelling and simple punctuation errors, basic grammatical problems like those of agreement and reference, awkward construction and problems with coherence, appearance, quality of thought, organization, form, diction, usage, factual accuracy. The English department responses were similar to those from other departments: organization and quality of thought were rated highest (even over factual accuracy); length, appearance, form were lowest. The one significant variation came with diction and style; the English department, logically enough, weighted that category much more heavily than did other disciplines. Such agreement suggests that the UCLA community is of fairly similar mind on composition matters. This implication, however, did not hold.

First, though organization and quality of thought were ranked far above factual accuracy on the WRP questionnaire, TAs (the true graders of much student prose) from several disciplines stated that it was unwritten departmental policy to sift through poorly written, haphazardly organized prose, particularly on examinations, to find facts. If the facts were accurate, the student did well. Though this tolerance was licensed for the most pragmatic or well-intentioned of reasons ("Why penalize a good student for poor writing skills?"), the quality of student writing became very much a secondary, even moot, issue. For that matter, many non-English faculty admitted that as class enrollments grew and general literacy seemed to diminish, they had decreased the number and breadth of their writing assignments.

Second, although departments other than English ranked diction and style fairly low, style, broadly defined, did in fact emerge as a major concern. One professor of management, for example, was critical of the prose written by graduate students who had majored in the humanities as undergraduates:

> Students come to us writing over-academic, highly embroidered prose. We, in turn, have to retrain them to write simple, direct reports for companies, reports that someone will feel like reading.

Much undergraduate writing is fashioned out of the exigencies of a teacher-student relationship in which the student is trying to impress a professor with knowledge the professor, for the most part, already has. But in management, students must explain a personnel dilemma or a marketing strategy to a business audience that usually does not possess the writer's knowledge, and that wants, therefore, clear, straightforward information. Another, more specific, stylistic concern was voiced by faculty in psychology and sociology who must spend time shoving the passive voice back down the throats of students who have been conditioned in composition courses to gag over hidden subjects.

These are major differences indeed. Facts are seen by some as having an existence of their own; they can be extricated from tangled prose. Others cry "No," citing authorities from Aristotle to Richards and Frye on the importance of context and presentation. Certain formal and stylistic conventions are espoused by some, denounced, even ridiculed, by others. Even so circumscribed a community as a community of scholars could not agree. One distinguished professor of linguistics threw up his hands in exasperation:

> There is no such thing as "good" writing that can be taught in one course in the university and work equally well for physicists, linguists, and social workers.

It seems we are caught in an inevitable result of segmenting knowledge. Students are taught a "service course" housed in one department and then are expected to exercise their skills in others that may not share the assumptions and conventions of the first. And though professors from departments of psychology, biology, management, mathematics, and English talk to each other daily, their professional paths, particularly in journals, infrequently cross.

Bleak. How can the evaluation of writing occur except in the most idiosyncratic, insular of ways? But the truth is that evaluation goes on daily and students and faculty manage to communicate passably well. "I can't imagine," said one TA, "that the skills learned in freshman composition — developing a thesis, organizing material, providing evidence — are not transferable to other courses in other disciplines." She expressed concisely the conclusion of most of the groups in the conference. In fact, because of broad characteristics of school-based prose, most of us can follow and understand the work of our students (and our extra-departmental colleagues). Our disagreements come over form and style and felicities. But our true befuddlements arise from the vague thesis, the sloppy argument, the missing evidence — and most of us can agree on these. The next step, recommended at the conference but beyond its scope, would be to hammer out evaluative schema for thesis, evidence, organization. This would be done by an inter-disciplinary group at the university senate level. Perhaps, then, we would be able to judge our students' prose with some regularity. . . .

NOTE

[1]The Writing Research Project is an interdisciplinary group of UCLA faculty and staff from English, Psychology, the Educational Opportunity Program, and the Learning Skills Center. It is funded by the associate vice-chancellor for Undergraduate Affairs, and is charged with conducting both basic and applied research on the writing process.

7

Remedial Writing Courses: A Critique and a Proposal

1983

AUTHOR'S NOTE: The purpose of this article was to call attention to and analyze the assumptions driving the practices of traditional remedial writing programs—like the one that existed at UCLA before the changes of the early 1980s—and to offer an alternative vision of what a "remedial" curriculum could be. The five main points of the article (summarized in the first paragraph), unfortunately, seem as legitimate today as they did to me in 1983. Though there are currently a number of fine programs that provide, in some form, a rich and challenging curriculum, the situation I describe is all too common. (For one overview of the current basic writing landscape, see Linda Adler-Kassner and Susanmarie Harrington's *Basic Writing as a Political Act.*) I still get inquiries from people who read this article in an anthology or find it in a search of the literature. It continues to strike a nerve.

As with the early pieces in Part One, this essay relies on some research that I would no longer use if I were writing it today. But rereading it, I recall the excitement of the time. Many of the rhetoric and composition people of my generation and just before were producing original and important work: James Kinneavy's *A Theory of Discourse* and Cooper and Odell's book on evaluating writing, for example, or David Bartholomae and Joseph Williams on error, or all the composing process research.[1] And as I looked in other related areas—text linguistics, reading research, cognitive and educational psychology—I found material that was also relevant to my concerns. Ideas were in the air. I felt like things were falling into place as I tried to fashion a principled critique of practices that seemed so damaging—and present an alternative to them.

One of the things I regret about the article is that, in my frustration with the typical remedial writing assignments of the day, I glibly characterized assignments built on students' personal experience. I reprint a response by David Peck and Elizabeth Hoffman, for they call me on my blunder, provide a good counterweight, and enable me to clarify my position. I worry that the typical "personal" topics students get are poorly thought out—a default curriculum—and are built on assumptions about cognition and motivation that are in need of examination. Furthermore, the assignments do not often lead beyond themselves, are not part of a curriculum that, for example, integrates personal and academic writing or that leads to some broader social or political analysis. More than a few people over the years have thought my position to be an odd one, given my use of personal material in a book like *Lives on the Boundary*, but the personal accounts in that book become part of a broader argument about educational policy. I'll say more about *Lives on the Boundary* in Part Four.

There's one more issue to consider before moving on, and that has to do with the very existence of remedial or basic writing courses themselves. There have long been attempts at the college and university level to eradicate such courses or to move them to the community college. (I'll discuss this in "The Language of Exclusion.") Over the last decade or so, however, motivated by different concerns, there has *within* the composition community been debate about the function and consequences of remedial courses. The criticism is that the establishment of remedial courses stigmatizes those students placed in them (Ira Shor calls the practice "our apartheid") and creates barriers to students' advancement, for the courses lock in place another level of requirement, one that some students have a difficult time fulfilling. These are powerful criticisms, and I hope that the content of "Remedial Writing Courses" and other things I've written aligns with them. Over the past decade, some masterful alternatives to placement in remedial courses have been developed — from the City College of New York to Chico State in California — that do not separate students out, yet still provide the additional assistance they need.

Still, I would raise two cautions about the eradication of remedial courses and programs across the board. One I offer in an exchange with Peter Elbow. He had written a response to an article that comes later in the book ("Remediation as Social Construct," p. 252), but I'll print the exchange here, since it applies. Basically, I argue for the importance of institutional context in considering the dismantling of remedial courses — that such a move could work well in some places, yet in others could lead to the compromising or loss of any instructional space for students who need extra, focused assistance.

My second caveat is this: Institutional structures can be modified, but — as a lot of case studies of organizational change illustrate[2] — shifts in attitudes and beliefs don't necessarily follow. So in addition to changes in program structure, the kinds of assumptions discussed in "Remedial Writing Courses" would have to be raised to the level of analysis as well. This analysis would include assumptions about language, cognition, and motivation. And, given the institution in question, it could also include assumptions about particular populations of students, the groupings dependent on local conditions: assumptions about race and ethnicity, about immigrant status, about English language proficiency, about first-generation college goers, about transfer or nontraditional students, about social class or regional variation, and so on. Changing the structure of a place can be a necessary but not sufficient condition for change in its culture.

NOTES

[1]Kinneavy (1971); Cooper and Odell (1977); Bartholomae (1980); Williams (1981). Composing process research: see footnote 1 in the Introduction, p. 10.

[2]See, for example, the case of Douglas Aircraft Co. in Wilms (1996).

M

any of our attempts to help college remedial[1] writers, attempts that are often well-intentioned and seemingly commonsensical, may, in fact, be ineffective, even counterproductive, for these attempts reduce, fragment, and possibly misrepresent the composing process. I believe we may be limiting growth in writing in five not unrelated ways. 1) Our remedial courses are self-contained; that is, they have little conceptual or practical connection to the larger academic writing environment in which our students find themselves. 2) The writing topics assigned in these courses—while meant to be personally relevant and motivating and, in their simplicity, to assist in the removal of error—in fact might not motivate and might not contribute to the production of a correct academic prose. 3) The writing teacher's vigilance for error most likely conveys to students a very restricted model of the composing process. 4) Our notion of "basic skills" has become so narrow that we attempt to separate the intimately related processes of reading and thinking from writing. 5) In some of our attempts to reform staid curricula we have inadvertently undercut the expressive and exploratory possibilities of academic writing and have perceived fundamental discourse strategies and structures as restricting rather than enhancing the production and comprehension of prose.

At various places in my speculations I will offer potential solutions to the problems I pose. For the most part, these solutions come from programs I run at UCLA, though I should mention that some of these solutions were spawned during my days as a teacher of "developmental" writers in special programs for returning Vietnam veterans, parole aids, and newly released convicts. So, though this paper is primarily addressed to teachers of traditional college "remedial" writers vs. truly "basic" writers of the sort we saw and continue to see during periods of open admissions, many of the ideas I will present grew out of my work with students from both camps. I strongly believe, therefore, that what I am about to say has, with appropriate modification, broad applicability to that large, complex stratum of writers who have been labeled "substandard."

REMEDIAL COURSES ARE SELF-CONTAINED

Many remedial courses do not fit conceptually and practically into the larger writing environment in which students find themselves. Much of the writing we have our students do is distressingly like that Arthur Applebee found in his survey of secondary education—phrase to paragraph length fill-ins or brief responses, often in workbooks or on worksheets (*Writing in the Secondary School* [Urbana, Ill.: National Council of Teachers of English, 1981]). When fuller assignments are given, the topics are most often personal and simple. They are meant to be relevant and accessible but in fact

From *College English* 45.2 (February 1983): 109–28.

are usually old-hat and unacademic—a unique artifact of the composition classroom. Furthermore, though some courses and programs give the student more than a class period to work on a paper, a number of others (shades of Applebee's report again) limit writing to twenty to fifty-minute in-class sprints.[2] The end result, of course, is that our students' papers are flawed, not only by the writers' current compositional inadequacies but also by the writers' very composing situations. These papers are then returned to their source: composition teachers. But how can we teachers honestly provide an engaged response to spurts of writing on topics like "Describe a favorite place or event" or "Give your opinion of X"—X being some broad, complex social issue about which students are usually ill-informed? Clearly these topics and these situations are not preparing students for their university lives. In all too many cases we have created a writing course that does not lead outward toward the intellectual community that contains it. And that's a pity, for a remedial writing curriculum must fit into the overall context of a university education: students must, early on, begin wrestling with academically oriented topics that help them develop into more critical thinkers, that provide them with some of the tools of the examined life, and that, practically, will assist them in the courses they take. I am sure that many of my colleagues would agree, but establishing such a context is easier said than done.

Let me suggest one way to lay groundwork for a meaningful context, and this is, in fact, the procedure we used in developing UCLA's Freshman Preparatory Program. (I should add that we thought it important to explain our procedure to our students. Freshman writers should know the origins of their curriculum.) Here is what we did: we wanted to find out what our students were being asked to do when they wrote for university classes, so we collected 445 essay and take-home examination questions as well as paper topics from seventeen departments and performed some relatively simple analyses. (We hope eventually to collect more assignments—and the essays resulting from them—from more campuses and conduct a more sophisticated analysis.) Our (rather predictable) findings:

1. We determined what discourse mode the questions and topics seemed to require. Most called for exposition—transaction in James Britton's scheme, reference in James Kinneavy's (*Language and Learning* [Harmondsworth: Penguin, 1970]; *A Theory of Discourse* [New York: Norton, 1980]). The balance required argument (Britton's conative mode, Kinneavy's persuasive), but a special kind of argument I will label academic argument, that is, not a series of emotionally charged appeals and exhortations, as one often finds in oratorical persuasion, but a calculated marshalling of information, a sort of exposition aimed at persuading.[3]

2. It was also obvious that, in their writing, students had to work with large bodies of information garnered from lectures and readings and often had to write from texts. There were simply no assignments calling for the student to narrate or describe personal experiences, to observe relatively immediate objects or events like the architecture of campus buildings, to express a general opinion on something not studied closely, to reflect on self.

3. While in-class essay examinations clearly required a quick, nearly regurgitative — albeit structured — response, the students' other assignments assumed the ability to reflect on a broad range of complex material, to select and order information, and to see and re-see data and events in various contexts.

4. Our surveys also suggested that various academic audiences write and read with an elaborate and — unfortunately for our students — often subtle, even tacit set of philosophical and methodological assumptions that determine what they will consider acceptable or unacceptable reasoning, presenting of evidence, and inferring.[4] For example, an individual's reflections on personal events are considered legitimate evidence in many areas of sociology and anthropology, but are considered much less legitimate by behavioristic psychologists. Developing a sensitivity to the plurality of these assumptive foundations and the conventions that arise from them is crucial, for they shape the complex rhetorical relationship between writer and reader in the academy.

5. In another, related, survey (Mike Rose, "When Faculty Talk About Writing," *College English*, 41 [1979–80], 272–279), we found that some of the stylistic information we had been giving students in English composition simply did not reflect any sort of broad consensus among even as limited an audience as academics. Now, while it was no big surprise to find out that our concerns about, say, writing in the first person and avoiding passive constructions were not fervently shared by other disciplines, it was sobering to hear remarks like the following — this one from a professor of management:

> Students come to us writing over-academic, highly embroidered prose. We, in turn, have to retrain them to write simple, direct reports for companies, reports that someone will feel like reading. ("When Faculty Talk About Writing," p. 273)

Felicitous techniques like the Christensen cumulative sentence (which Christensen primarily derived from studying fiction) or the topic sentence seductively placed at the end rather than the beginning of a paragraph, for some readers in some contexts, hampered rather than enhanced or enlivened communication.

Considering the complex discourse demands our surveys revealed, our students and our courses fell pitifully short. We needed a remedial program that slowly but steadily and systematically introduced remedial writers to transactional/expositional academic discourse; that relied on texts and bits of texts, preferably from a variety of disciplines so that students would learn how to work with data presented in social science exposition as well as with detail from a short story; that created full, rich assignments which, again slowly and systematically, encouraged the student to develop his or her structural, rhetorical, stylistic facility; that alerted students to stylistic/ rhetorical variation within the university.

SIMPLE TOPICS, MOTIVATION, AND THE ELIMINATION OF ERROR

One of the aspects of traditional remedial curricula that I have questioned is the simple, personal topic. But clearly teachers do not assign topics like "Describe your favorite place" because they hold some deep affection for them. They have reasons. One very popular reason is best expressed thus: "I want to make the topic simple so if the student writes poorly, I'll know it had nothing to do with the strain of a complicated topic." Another popular reason concerns motivation: "If I can give them success experiences, they'll feel better about writing and want to write more." The reasoning behind assigning simple, personal topics, then, often lies in beliefs about cognitive interference and motivation. Let me deal with the issue of motivation first.

Certainly it is a sound motivation and learning principle to begin with the simple—let the student experience success—and then move toward the more complex. No argument. But we should not assume that the successful completion of an assignment the student might well perceive as being simple, even juvenile, is going to make him feel better about himself or his writing. Let me illustrate with a brief anecdote. My colleague at UCLA, George Gadda, is currently attempting to phase into our orientation program a more university-oriented set of diagnostic topics. He still gives a typical "Describe your favorite object" topic, but also gives a topic, with a brief academically oriented reading passage, that requires summarizing or analyzing skills. Though it is seemingly more difficult, a number of students reported via questionnaire that they preferred the academic topic because, as one student succinctly put it, "This is the real thing." Motivation to achieve in writing is much more complex than some composition theorists suppose. Personal topics are not necessarily more relevant than academic ones, and some of our students—particularly those from certain minority cultures—might not feel comfortable revealing highly personal experiences. Current work on achievement motivation has shown it to be a highly complex cognitive-affective phenomenon that includes such dimensions as perception of the difficulty of a task and perception of the role of luck or skill in completing the task.[5] Add to these perceptions psychodynamic variables such as the degree of comfort with the content of a task, and it is no longer clear that simple and personal topics are most motivating.

Now to the issue of cognitive overload and the concentration on error. It makes sense to assume that if we reduce the interfering strain of the challenging topic, or, put another way, if we give students a topic for which they already have information (e.g., "Describe an important person in your life"), they and we can more readily focus on grammatical problems. But this might be a case of common sense misleading us, for we have evidence to suggest that while a writer might eventually produce grammatically correct prose for one kind of assignment, that correctness might not hold when she faces other kinds of tasks. Brooke Nielson, for example, found that when her sample of traditional writers shifted registers from the informal (writing to peers) to the formal (writing to an academic audience), their proficiency fell apart ("Writing as a Second Language: Psycholinguistic Processes in Composing," Diss., University of California at San Diego, 1979). I suspect that similar difficulties arise when the student shifts from simpler discourse structures to more complex ones and from simpler to more complex topics. So we might guide a student to the point where she writes with few errors about her dorm room, but when she is asked, say, to compare and contrast two opinions on dormitory housing, not to mention two economic theories, the organizational demands of comparing and contrasting and the more syntactically complicated sentences often attending more complex exposition or argument[6] put such strain on her cognitive resources and linguistic repertoire that error might well reemerge. Error, in short, is not something that, once fixed in a simple and clean environment, will never emerge again. It is not a culture we can isolate and alter in a petri dish. What we must do, therefore, is carefully define and describe the kind of writing demanded of students in the academy (which — lest this suggestion seems mind-shackling — is also the kind of writing students would use to challenge the academy), and then focus on that kind of writing, scaling our assignments down and building slowly, but scaling and building within the same discourse domain. For we cannot assume a simple transfer of skills across broadly different discourse demands.

There is a related issue here. When we think that simple topics coupled with concentration on error will lead to the correction of error, we might be misleading ourselves. As any one who has read large numbers of remedial-level exams knows, there is a nagging doubt that one reason one sees, say, fewer comma splices or misspelled words in post-tests is that the students have simply stopped writing complex sentences or using tricky words. I don't know if the following study has ever been attempted, but I would wager that a careful examination of remedial students' pre- and post-tests would show that pre-tests evince more ambitious lexical to sentential attempts gone awry than would cleaner post-tests. We may be training students to be simple and safe rather than urging them toward the ambitious experimentation that will enhance their linguistic repertoire.

Creating simple topics to aid in the correction of error, then, might be a less successful strategy than we think — error cannot be isolated and removed; it can reemerge whenever a student moves onto a task that challenges him or her in new ways. Furthermore, we might be demoralizing our students by giving them the same kind of topic they have been writing on for so many years. I would suggest that we develop curriculums that offer academically oriented topics, the difficulty of each being systematically gradated so that the student is continually challenged in ways that don't overwhelm. (I will give examples of such assignments later.) Until students begin to develop some familiarity with such topics, we will not be able to help them in their attempts to write a relatively correct university prose.

ERROR VIGILANCE AND REDUCTIONISTIC MODELS OF COMPOSING

Our concern for error leads us to create overly simple topics, but I suspect it also results in something even more counterproductive. We might be unwittingly passing on an extremely constricted notion of what composing is. This occurs on three broad levels: the process, the conceptual, the rhetorical. Many of our students come to see the writing process itself as a matter of framing a thought in correct language. The results of such perception are disastrous. Sondra Perl, for example, noted that the basic writers she studied wrote in halting spurts and produced extremely truncated products. They were, she discovered, so vigilant for error, so concerned with placing every bit of language in its correct place, that their writing processes were stymied—they could not get the flow of their thoughts onto paper ("Five Writers Writing: Case Studies of the Composing Processes of Unskilled College Writers," Diss., New York University, 1978). The possibilities in writing—even "incorrect" writing—for discovering, connecting, playing were lost. Conceptually, our students come to believe that what counts is not the thought they give to a topic but how correctly that thought is conveyed. The results? Clean but empty papers. Barbara Tomlinson (personal communication, 1982) reports that even though the remedial writers' papers she studied for her doctoral dissertation were relatively error-free, her independent evaluators were "stunned" by the vapidity of the contents of the essays. The papers said nothing. On the rhetorical level students may not grow beyond their limited notions of connecting thought to reader, not because they are—to cite one current misapplication of the Piagetian developmental framework—egocentric, but rather because the local to global semantic and syntactic devices that establish that connection have not been opened up to them and, perhaps worse, the social base of making meaning and conveying it has not been established in their writing classroom. Just about the only rhetorical connection the correctness model establishes is the negative sociolinguistic one: don't err lest ye be judged. That is sound advice, but not when it becomes the only rhetorical advice students get.

In closing this section, let me cite a chilling—though admittedly preliminary—study conducted by Patrick Hartwell ("Writers as Readers," paper presented at the Conference on College Composition and Communication, March, 1981). He asked elementary, secondary, and college students labeled by their teachers as weaker readers/writers and better readers/writers to respond to the question, "What do people do when they write?" Notice the model of writing implied in the typical responses of weaker elementary readers/writers (I corrected the few misspellings in their responses): "They hold the pencil tightly." "Move their fingers. And write neat." Of weaker secondary readers/writers: "They put the point of the pencil to the paper and start making words and letters." Of weaker college readers/writers: "People write through English grammar, punctuation, etc." "First you pick your topic, then you make sure that you have enough information. Then you rewrite and check the spelling and copy it down." The responses of better readers/writers were qualitatively different. A few examples. The primary level: "They think of what they are going to write. They ask a person if it sounds good." The secondary level: "They get stuff across to other people." The college level: "People explain their ideas, theories, stories and imagination to each other." Because these data are preliminary and because Hartwell has not yet shown whether these self-reports are linked to actual writing behaviors, I do not want to make too much of this. Though I must admit that because my own investigations of stymied writers revealed the power of rigid rules and inaccurate assumptions ("The Cognitive Dimension of Writer's Block: An Examination of University Students," Diss., UCLA, 1981), I find it hard to take these self-reports lightly. It seems safe to say that the impressions of these selected weaker student writers implies a very limited notion of what composing is, a notion based on simple behaviors, narrow linear steps, and shriveled rhetorical possibilities. This notion might reflect their limited skills (i.e., writers fixate on error because they keep erring), but it also stands as a barrier to their improving. If they continue to conceive of writing as holding a pencil tightly and using correct grammar, how will they grow beyond those constraints?

But let me be quick to point out that I am not trying to lay blame on the remedial writing teacher alone, if at all. For there are powerful reasons to explain why some teachers reduce the process, conceptual, and rhetorical possibilities of composing. The public, spurred by an often misconceived "back to basics" movement and the misinformed, but profitable, arrogance of "pop grammarians" like John Simon and Edwin Newman, make a teacher feel negligent and vulnerable if he or she does not attempt to clear up error. Furthermore, as Patricia Laurence points out in "Error's Endless Train: Why Students Don't Perceive Errors" (*Journal of Basic Writing* [Spring, 1975], 23–42), our scholars have not provided us with a comprehensive theory of error—a rich perceptual/cognitive/linguistic framework that will enable us to study error, see patterns in our students' errors, and provide guidelines on how to assist most effectively the student in understanding and remedying them. (And, I suspect, such a theory would also tell us when to ignore error.) Thus there is little for the conscientious teacher to do but keep marking. To do less in the absence of any other guidelines seems like shirking responsibility.

And there is a third reason for excusing us teachers. It seems to me that, in general, we have been offered pretty limited definitions of "writing skills." The reasons for the emergence of these narrow definitions are historically and sociologically complex. But one powerful reason lies in the energetic movement of the 1920s and 30s to insure mass education by reducing all learning to discrete steps, stages, bits of information and then holding teachers accountable for imparting fixed numbers of these steps, stages, bits during a given period of time. This "cult of efficiency," as Raymond Callahan called it (*Education and the Cult of Efficiency* [Chicago: University of Chicago Press, 1962]), found its theoretical constructs and evaluative devices in the storehouse of a burgeoning educational psychology that was rapidly devising methods and models for quantifying and structuring knowledge. In this milieu writing was reduced to text production and text to its most salient constituent parts. And though we currently hold to more advanced notions about composing and don't expect, for example, teachers to teach x number of grammar rules per week, we still are partially entrapped by reductionistic models and measures. Look, for example, at current evaluation procedures— for evaluation schemes reveal powerful assumptions about the object of evaluation.

Many of our evaluation schemes focus on product alone, do not incorporate issues of writer's intention and the actual playing out of that intention in the process of composing the essay, nor do they take account of a writer's relation to audience in any full way.[7] Furthermore, in all too many cases, crucial dimensions of any meaningful communication — like the accuracy of information and the legitimacy of the writer's reasoning with it — are put aside so that the felicity of the writing itself can be evaluated.[8] (Such separation, of course, only communicates to the student that cleanliness and charm matter. Accuracy and sense do not.) These procedures, for the most part, suggest that what counts most is a fixed and final and fairly limited product, a product containing or lacking certain countable features or broad structural relationships or specific connections to the writing task. Now this sounds like a limited and fragmented notion of writing skills to me — perhaps *conceptually* not far removed from earlier rigid product notions, the kinds of seriously limited and perhaps limiting notions that emerged in Hartwell's pilot study.

Clearly we need to rethink our definitions of writing skills and make special efforts to change the models of composing our students have internalized. It is possible, for example, that our remedial classes — at least some significant portion of them — should be very process-oriented. This does not simply mean that we would have our students freewrite daily, though there is certainly value in that. It also means that we would help our students experience the rich possibilities of the writing process. We could lead them to see the value of writing as an ordering and storing aid by making them amateur ethnographers and turning them loose on a campus event with pad and pencil in hand. We could break them of conceiving of their written texts as static by introducing exercises like our Preparatory Program's "Revision Scramble." In this exercise students are given a five- to ten-minute lecture on an academic topic, must take notes, and then must write either a summary or a critical reaction. In the next class they are given a further brief lecture on the same topic but with new information included. They must revise their summary or reaction in ways that account for the new. Thus they come to see that texts can — even must — evolve. We get them to experience writing as making meaning for self and others by engineering group projects that necessitate collaborative research, composing, and editing, thus moving them through process to product. A nice illustration of this is provided by my Preparatory Program colleague Bill Creasy. He gives his entire class the task of preparing a brief guidebook for incoming Preparatory Program students. Teams of two to three students are each assigned aspects of campus life: dormitories, athletics, ethnic study centers. Throughout the quarter the class collects and selects information (by interviewing officials, reading pamphlets and brochures, distributing questionnaires to seniors), writes it up, puts it on a word processor, and edits it. Professor Creasy provides assistance as it is needed at each point along the way.

Sure, these assignments must be carefully structured, scaled down, and built upon, and, yes, for a while our students will struggle, and some will produce very flawed papers. But we will have to train ourselves to wait, to live with uncertainty and comma splices. Some students may leave our classes writing papers that aren't as clean as some of us would like them to be, but at least these students will hold conceptions of composing that will foster rather than limit growth in writing.[9]

THE SEPARATION OF WRITING FROM READING AND THINKING

In our attempts to isolate and thereby more effectively treat "basic skills" we have not only reduced discourse complexity, we have separated writing from reading and thinking.

When I bring up "thinking skills" I sometimes get responses like the following: "Yes, we used to teach the syllogism, but it didn't carry over to the students' writing." Presenting students with intellectually worthwhile problems, assisting them as they work through them, offering them strategies with which to explore them, showing them how to represent and, when necessary, reduce them, seems to have been equated with formal Aristotelian logic and relegated to the philosophy department. What a disservice. We should help remedial writers become familiar with heuristic routines, too often saved for standard composition, that will enhance their interpretive powers. (Stripped of its theoretical baggage, the tagmemist's particle/wave/field heuristic comes to mind as a particularly useful technique.) And if certain of us question heuristics as being too gimmicky, there is good old-fashioned patient and careful guidance with assignments requiring classifying, comparing, analyzing. In any case—and this is why formal logic always failed in the composition classroom—"thinking skills" must not be taught as a set of abstract exercises (which, of course, they will be if they are not conceived of as being part of writing), but must be intimately connected to composition instruction. Otherwise students hear one more lecture on isolated mental arabesques.

When I bring up the need to incorporate reading into our basic courses, and particularly when I suggest we have our students work from a simple passage in writing their diagnostics (thereby making their diagnostics more equivalent to the academic writing tasks they will face), here is what I hear: "If you do that, you'll confound reading skills and writing skills. You'll never know why they make the mistakes they do. Is it because they can't read or they can't write?"[10] Yes, reading and writing are different processes, but it is simply not true that they are unconnected. Anthony Petrosky explains how current theories present reading as a kind of "composing process"; people construct meaning from text rather than passively internalize it. Teun Van Dijk points out that while we need to know the conventions, structures, and intentions of particular discourses to produce them, we likewise need such knowledge to comprehend them. And Stephen Krashen suggests that one's repertoire of discourse skills is built slowly and comprehensively through reading.[11] Reading and writing are intimately connected in ways we are only beginning to understand. Furthermore, even if they weren't, a major skill in academic writing is the complex ability to write from other texts—to summarize, to disambiguate key notions and useful facts and incorporate them in one's own writing, to react critically to prose. Few academic assignments (outside of composition) require a student to produce material ex nihilo; she is almost always writing about, from, or through others' materials.

It seems to me that we have no choice but to begin—and to urge the scholars who have sequestered themselves in segmented disciplines to begin—conceiving of composition as a highly complex thinking/learning/reading/writing skill that demands holistic, not neatly segmented and encapsulated, pedagogies.[12]

The Narrowing of Exploratory Discourse and the Misperception of Discourse Structures

But not all causes of a narrowed model of and curriculum for composing stem from an overzealous vigilance for error or from limited conceptualizations of writing skill. Ironically, one cause might inadvertently have come from some of the most serious critics of standard composition fare, for in their eagerness to torpedo staid and wrong-headed notions about composing, they sometimes polarize issues that in fact lie along a continuum. I suspect that when Ken Macrorie inveighs against "Engfish" and William Coles against "theme-writing," when politically conscious critics like John Rouse complain that teaching standard patterns of discourse socializes and thus regiments minds, when Stephen Judy says "the best student writing is motivated by personal feelings and experience," when Janet Emig distinguishes between extensive and reflexive writing[13]—when all these critics express their observations, they establish in the minds of some of their readers an essentially false set of dichotomies: to write in a voice other than one's most natural is to write inauthentically, to master and use strategies like comparing and contrasting is to sacrifice freedom, to write on academic topics that don't have deep personal associations is to be doomed to mechanical, lifeless composing, and to write expositional, extensive academic prose is to sabotage the possibility of reflexive exploration. Again, let me restate that Coles, Judy, et al. do not necessarily make distinctions this rigidly. Many folks who cite them do.

What does this polarization do to the remedial writer's curriculum? At least two things: The reflexive, exploratory possibilities of engaging in academic (vs. personal) topics are not exploited, and instruction in more complex patterns of discourse is delayed or soft-pedaled.

Reflexive, exploratory discourse has been too exclusively linked to "personal" writing, writing that deals with making sense of one's own feelings and experiences. In fact, making meaning for the self, ordering experience, establishing one's own relation to it is what informs any serious writing. A student writing a paper on Rousseau or on operant conditioning could, and should be encouraged to, engage in a good deal of self-referenced writing to make sense of difficult notions and, possibly, to weigh these notions against other readings, personal experience, and values. If we don't see all the possibilities for exploration inherent in academic writing, we won't encourage our writers to talk to each other and to us, to plumb their own thoughts, to freely explore the conceptual intricacies of a topic. Again, it is not Emig who would disagree. But in my experience many teachers who read—or misread—her would.

When we delay or insufficiently emphasize the writing of complex discourse, we deprive writers of a chance to learn what coherent, extended texts should look like, what shape or structure they will take. And until they possess a sense of the form of such texts, they cannot write them. Textlinguists like Van Dijk and Robert de Beaugrande have begun to demonstrate the reality of global discourse structures. Margaret Atwell has shown the central role discourse structures can play in the production of coherent text. Frank D'Angelo has recently suggested that these structures, or "paradigms" as he calls them, could well be related to Aristotelian topoi, the classical orator's repository of generating and structuring aids.[14]

The sad truth is that many of our students, particularly remedial students, do not get that much opportunity to read or write extended academic discourse before reaching us[15] and thus are not afforded the chance to develop a wide repertoire of discourse structures or schemata, as they are called by cognitive psychologists. (Lately there has been a proliferation of labels for these discourse representations: superstructures, paradigms, frames, plans, schemata. For consistency's sake, I will stick to schemata, but because I am interested both in the investigative, interpretive capability of schemata as cognitive strategies as well as the role of schemata in the production of written discourse, in certain contexts I will interchange "strategies" with "structures" or "patterns.") The lack of appropriate schemata, of course, will have disastrous results as remedial writers are asked to produce structurally complex prose by readers who, according to Sarah Freedman in "Why Do Teachers Give the Grades They Do?" (*CCC*, 30 [1979], 161–164), evaluate student writing with a good deal of emphasis on organization, a product feature resulting from appropriate discourse schemata.[16] We have little choice, then, but to teach these schemata. And I should stress here that we have no reason to believe that a student has to have every pronoun and antecedent correctly in place before he can learn discourse structures. Sentence level mechanics and discourse structures are not developmentally lockstepped.

Now some would agree that students must master these complex schemata and add that a sensible remedial approach would be to begin with "simpler" patterns like narration and then eventually shift to higher order discourse. But, as I suggested earlier, we have reason to doubt that work on narration or on description will build in students a repertoire of more abstract and complex schemata, schemata, that is, that are not based on chronological sequences or spatial arrangements.[17] Academic expositional discourse seems to be more cognitively demanding than simple narration or description;[18] it seems to embody global syntactic and semantic structures that are different from those found in narration and description;[19] and it requires kinds of sentences that, on the average, tend to be syntactically different from those found in narration and description.[20] The studies that support the aforementioned propositions only represent beginnings in the exploration of the cognitive demands and structural features of different kinds of discourse, but though beginnings they should make us wary of assuming that mastering, say, narrative structure will enable students to construct analytic essays.

I suggest, therefore, that we determine the organizational patterns required of our students in academic discourse, and slowly and systematically teach these patterns. They should not be conceived of or taught as "modes" of discourse or as rigid frameworks but, simultaneously, as strategies by which one explores information and structures by which one organizes it. It would not restrict students' freedom to learn these strategies/structures; in fact, such learning would enhance their freedom, afford them more discourse options. Without these options much academic discourse (the very kind of discourse written by critics like Rouse) will be beyond these writers. For that fact they are essential to the making and conveying of meaning in our culture. The question is, how should they be taught? The two most natural ways to assimilate or learn these patterns are by reading a good deal of discourse containing them (see Krashen's essay cited in footnote 11, and Mellon's cited in footnote 15), and experiencing the need for them as one encounters barriers while writing. The trouble is, of course, that our remedial writers don't have much time. They are enrolled in other classes, some of which demand structurally complex written responses to complex assignments. And while we can suspend concern about, say, comma splices, we can't wait for students to assimilate these global structures—they are essential to reader comprehension. Students need them now. Yet we don't want to put our students through one more lifeless and disembodied drill on the "compare/contrast mode." What to do? I propose a four-tiered plan:

A. *Make sure that the patterns/strategies are real.* That is, that they are derived not from the theorist's speculations on how discourse ought to be taxonomized, but from writing situations the students face daily. In the aforementioned surveys of university assignments, I found calls or cues for a number of global discourse strategies or patterns. These were either explicitly requested or seemed to be the best approaches to apply to purposely ambiguous or to simply poorly written questions. I will list the most salient of them now and illustrate the teaching of several of them momentarily: definition, seriation, classification, summary, compare/contrast, analysis, academic argument. With the exception of analysis and academic argument—which I define in special ways—these patterns are too familiar for comfort. We see some combination of them in our rhetorics and readers, and they have, in all too many hands, come to represent much that stifles our pedagogy. But—and here I'll look for support to D'Angelo's speculation about the connection of schemata to topoi—the problem is not that these patterns are inherently rigid or unuseful, but that they have not been taught as thinking strategies as well as discourse structures. (I am tempted, therefore, to write out definition, classification, etc., with participial endings to stress their actively strategic nature.) I would speculate—and at this stage, it *is* speculation—that the reason these strategies/structures appeared so frequently in our surveys of academic writing situations (and, my colleague Ruth Mitchell tells me, in her surveys of business and professional writing as well) is that they are so central to the way we explore, order, and present information when we are engaged in transactional/referential discourse.[21]

B. *Create a meaningful context for their use.* Here I would like to raise again the issues of the context of writing and the motivation to write. It is usually assumed that for writing to be meaningful, it must generate from issues and experiences that centrally involve the student. This assumption, as I suggested earlier, can result in some pretty superficial curricula, but can also lead to challenging pedagogies like Coles', that leads students to examine their own writing as ways of knowing and becoming (see footnote 13), or like David Bartholomae's, that weaves academic writing into students' reflections on, for example, their coming of age and requires them to turn an analytic eye onto their own and others' autobiographies ("Teaching Basic Writing: An Alternative to Basic Skills," *Journal of Basic Writing* [Spring/Summer 1979], pp. 85–109). I believe, though, that another meaningful context for student writing is the very academic environment in which students find themselves; it is a strange, complicated place, at times feared in its newness, at others, appreciated, a place of promise and a place of limitation, sometimes cynically apprehended, sometimes enjoyed. If the discourse schemata I have listed are, on one hand, pragmatically offered as being central to success in the university and, on the other, offered as investigative tools necessary for examining reality, for examining the academic environment itself, then it seems to me we have established a motivating and meaningful context for their use.

C. *Teach the schemata as strategies as well as structures.* Classifying or comparing/contrasting can be taught in cookbook formulaic fashion, and with writers who hold few complex schemata in their repertoire, this patterned instruction might be necessary. At first. We would then want to show students other uses, other shapes, to wean them from learning an inflexible discourse pattern. But we also want to teach comparing and contrasting as a cognitive strategy, as a way to explore things, events, phenomena as well as a way to organize what we discover about them. Note the difference from usual textbook treatment—no static modes, but, borrowing Linda Flower's words, "ways to think systematically about complex topics" (*Problem-Solving Strategies for Writers* [New York: Harcourt Brace Jovanovich, 1981], p. 74).

D. *Sequence the schemata appropriately.* In teaching these structures/strategies, we need to keep the importance of proper sequencing in mind. Educational theorists like Benjamin Bloom and Robert Gagné[22] repeatedly show the benefits of arranging tasks in ways that allow subsequent tasks to build on previously learned ones, and in our own field Britton and his colleagues have noted:

> Our experience suggests that there is likely to be a hierarchy of kinds of writing which is shaped by the thinking problems with which the writer is confronted. (James Britton, Tony Burgess, Nancy Martin, Alex McLeod, Harold Rosen, *The Development of Writing Abilities (11–18)* [London: Macmillan, 1975], p. 52)

Considering the schemata I presented, this discussion of sequencing suggests that we offer students tasks that require, for example, the presenting of steps in a series before confronting them with tasks requiring summarizing before assigning tasks involving argument. And, as frequently as possible, a previously learned structure/strategy should be incorporated into the preliminary stages of a new assignment (e.g., have the student summarize a theory that she will need for an assignment requiring analysis) or should become part of the assignment itself. It is possible to sequence assignments and the schemata they embody so that they lead to highly complex discourse like analyzing and arguing.

Teaching these schemata allows students to begin writing academic discourse early on. They are able, even crudely, to construct a complicated essay into which they can weave their reading. They are participating in an academic context.[23]

Let me illustrate the above discussion by providing three kinds of assignments from our Freshman Preparatory Program.

Seriation. For one seriation assignment the teacher reads a brief account of a burn patient's daily routine of hydrotherapy, medication, meals, etc. Late in the day the patient experiences chills, nausea, and dizziness. The students take notes and then, in groups, write a brief paper retelling the day's events. In a somewhat related assignment students take notes while the teacher reads a description of the reduplication process of an intestinal virus. Then they are given a list of the steps in the reduplication process, but the steps are scrambled. In groups, students have to order the steps correctly and write a brief paper detailing the accurate sequence of process steps. Another seriation assignment has the teacher and a colleague extemporaneously act out five minutes of a psychotherapy session. Students become clinical observers and take notes on the interaction. Again, in groups, the students write an essay presenting the stages of the interaction. For all assignments students must underline and orally or in footnotes explain the function of each connective and transition they use. In this way they become sensitive to the differences among simple concatenation vs. correlation vs. causality. For example, can they say the medication "caused" the patient's reaction, or must they be cautious and say the reaction "followed" the medication, physical therapy, and meals?

Classification. One classification assignment calls for students to view twenty slides of the human form—Raphael to Rivera. They are shown the slides two or three times and are told to observe as keenly as possible, jotting down notes on whatever characteristics of each painting strike them. They are not told anything about era, school, or painter. Then they are told to decide, with the aid of their notes, whether or not any two or more paintings could be grouped under the same characteristic. (For teachers so inclined, this can be done in small groups.) At first, students tend to offer very general observations: "Paintings #1, 3, 10, 19 are all very bright." "2, 8, 20 don't look like human beings." The teacher does not criticize and puts all characteristics on the board. What she does begin doing is asking questions to point out similarity or generality in the categories. Students are led to refine, collapse, subdivide categories. What the students finally arrive at is their own classificational system. They are then asked to write a brief essay that proposes the system and illustrates it with specific paintings. In subsequent exercises they work with items from a personality inventory, a list of definitions of genius, and a collection of first paragraphs from novels, textbooks, and articles. In this way students actually experience the process of classification as well as learn how to present its results.

Analysis. Textbook authors usually define analysis as a careful exploration that breaks an artifact, event, or phenomenon down to its constituent parts. What they don't mention is that no analyzer operates without some belief or value system, without some exploratory framework.[24] Toward the end of our program we introduce students to this complex nature of analysis. We give them a list of raw data, or a description of an event, or a scene or story, or we show them a film. To enhance pedagogical effect, the data, descriptions, or episodes are in some way puzzling or incomplete. We encourage discussion about them. Then we provide a theoretical framework of some sort and ask them to assume it and analyze and explain the data, event, film, etc. Thus their analysis is informed by another's perspective. Finally, we ask them to criticize the perspective, to consider ways it might be lacking in accuracy, explanatory power, or comprehensibility. In these ways we introduce students to the fact that analyses are always founded on assumptions and orientations—from personal analyses of moral issues to statistical analyses of biological data—and that any given analysis is open to investigation once its informing framework is made specific. Some examples: Students are given a newspaper account of a suicide. They discuss it, providing their own interpretations. They are then offered an explanation of depression and "learned helplessness." They investigate the suicide with the aid of the latter clinical theory, noting how it illuminates and how it comes up short. Students are given a list of U.S. immigration statistics from 1820 to 1977. This is followed by a quotation from *Das Kapital* on exploitation of labor. They are shown *An Andalusian Dog*, and it is followed by a definition of surrealism. They are given the Barthelme short story "Game" (a story of two deranged soldiers locked indefinitely in a missile bunker) and then given a series of quotations on the environmental etiology of insanity. And so on. Thus it is that students are shown the power and limitation of an explanatory framework, the crucial role some such framework plays in analysis (and that no analysis takes place atheoretically), how to assume—and question—an analytic framework, and how to present the result of that analysis in writing. In writing up their analysis they usually have to rely on previously learned strategies: serializing, summarizing, comparing, etc.

Our institutions create deplorable conditions for our remedial writing programs and our students—labeled intellectually substandard, placed in the conceptual basements of English departments, if placed in the department at all, ghettoized. No need to polemicize further; we all know the complaints. But what we teachers must remember is that the very nature of many remedial writing courses contributes to institutional insularity, to second-class citizenship and fragmented education, to a limiting of our students' abilities to grow toward intellectual autonomy. Oddly enough, the nature of our programs is nearly synchronized with the narrow reality created for them by our institutions.

Clearly we must work to change our institutions, but we must also question our assumptions about our students' abilities and the pedagogies we have built on these assumptions. All too often these days we hear that remedial writers are "cognitively deficient," locked, for example, at the Piagetian level of concrete (vs. formal) operations. These judgments are unwarranted extrapolations from a misuse (or overuse) of the developmental psychologist's diagnostic instruments, for as Jean Piaget himself reminded us in one of his final articles, if we are not seeing evidence of formal operations in young adults, then we should either better acquaint them with our diagnostics or find more appropriate ones ("Intellectual Evolution from Adolescence to Adulthood," *Human Development*, 15 [1972], 1–12). The problem might well lie with our tools rather than with our students' minds. We must assume, Piaget warns, that in their daily lives our students can generalize and analyze, can operate formally.[25] What they can't do—applying this to the writing teacher's domain—is successfully operate within the unfamiliar web of reasoning/reading/writing conventions that are fundamental to academic inquiry. Our students are not cognitvely "deficient" in the clinical sense of the term; if they were, they wouldn't be able to make the progress they do. Our students are not deficient; they are raw. Our job, then, is to create carefully thought-out, appropriate, undemeaning pedagogies that introduce them to the conventions of academic inquiry. Bartholomae presents one such pedagogy. The foundations for another can be found in Shaughnessy's seventh chapter of *Errors and Expectations* (see footnote 21). At various points in the present essay, I have suggested a third approach;[26] let me summarize it here.

In my opinion, a remedial writing curriculum must fit into the intellectual context of the university. Topics should have academic substance and, when possible, should require the student to work from text. The expressive, exploratory dimension of writing ought to be exploited here—academic topics as much as personal ones demand a working through, a talking to and making meaning for the self. The richness of the composing process must be revealed. Too many of our students come to us with narrow, ossified conceptions of writing. Our job is to create opportunities so they can alter those conceptions for themselves. We have to allow our writers to be ambitious and to err. Error vigilance creates safe, not meaningful, prose. We need to integrate thinking and reading and writing, and we must pressure our training institutions to give us fuller, richer definitions of writing competence. Finally, we should seriously consider the central role discourse schemata play in discovering, organizing, and presenting information. It is these structures/strategies, rather than sentence-level error, which should be the fundament of our courses.

How flat some of our remedial courses feel. And how distant the eyes of too many of our students. We sometimes take this flatness, this distance as signs of intellectual dullness. They are more likely the signs of boredom, humiliation, even anger. But in my experience anyway the flatness dispells and the distant gazes revitalize when students are challenged, engaged, brought fully into the milieu they bargained for. Yes, we teachers will work slowly, scale carefully, provide as much assistance as we can. But we will still be creating an edge to our "remedial" classroom. Our students will grumble about the strain — grumbling is part of the student's drama — but they will know they are participating in the university. And that is a strain that can make one feel worthwhile.

ACKNOWLEDGMENTS

Gratitude is due Ruth Mitchell and Barbara Tomlinson for their insightful comments on that earlier version. Professor Rose also wishes to thank the teachers who worked with him in the Freshman Preparatory Program: Bill Creasy, Carol Edwards, Mike Gustin, Mal Kiniry, Faye Peitzman, Ellen Strenski, David Ward. Acknowledgment is also due Charles Cooper and his graduate students for several long discussions of the Freshman Preparatory Program curriculum. Special thanks must go to Mal Kiniry, who has significantly revised the sourcebook of interdisciplinary materials used in the program.

NOTES

[1] I will use the adjective "remedial" and occasionally the adjective "basic" throughout this essay. I should note, though, that I use them with some reservation, for they are often more pejorative than accurately descriptive.

[2] Many think this fifty-minute limit prepares students for essay exams. But not so. In those situations students already have a wealth of information to spew forth. In the remedial course they are expected to retrieve, give meaning to, and organize information that, in some cases, they simply do not have.

[3] For some additional and informative discussion of argument in the academy, see Charles Kneupper, "Teaching Argument: An Introduction to the Toulmin Model," *College Composition and Communication*, 29 (1978), 237–241; Patricia Bizzell, "The Ethos of Academic Discourse," *CCC*, 29 (1978), 351–355; and Paul Bator, "Aristotelian and Rogerian Rhetoric," *CCC*, 31 (1980), 427–432.

[4] A good general introduction to this complex assumptive plurality is Philip Phenix's *Realms of Meaning* (New York: McGraw-Hill, 1964).

[5] Bernard Weiner, "Achievement Motivation, Attribution Theory, and the Educational Process," *Review of Educational Research*, 42 (1972), 203–215; Bernard Weiner, ed., *Achievement Motivation and Attribution Theory* (Morristown, NJ: General Learning Press, 1974).

[6] Marion Crowhurst, "Syntactic Complexity and Teachers' Quality Ratings of Narrations and Arguments," *Research in the Teaching of English*, 14 (1980), 223–231.

[7] Lee Odell and Charles R. Cooper, "Procedures for Evaluating Writing: Assumptions and Needed Research," *College English*, 42 (1980), 35–43; Anne Ruggles Gere, "Written Composition: Toward a Theory of Evaluation," *CE*, 42 (1980), 44–58. See also Ruth Mitchell and Mary Taylor, "The Integrating Perspective: An Audience-Response Model for Writing," *CE*, 41 (1979), 247–271.

[8] Barbara Gross Davis, Michael Scriven, and Susan Thomas, *The Evaluation of Composition* (Inverness, CA: Edgepress, 1981).

[9] I am not suggesting that teachers should completely turn their backs on error. There is little doubt that many academic readers and, as Maxine Hairston reminds us, readers outside the university react strongly to grammatical/mechanical errors ("Not All Errors Are Created Equal: Non-Academic Readers in the Professions Respond to Lapses in Usage," *CE*, 43 (1981), 794–806). We wouldn't want our students to blithely write their ways into the dens of the error-vigilant. What I am suggesting is that we might better serve our students if we free them from dulling and limiting notions of composing and then focus and refocus on correctness as an editing, not generating and producing, concern. If we run out of time — if some of our students still have not mastered points of mechanics and usage when they leave us — they will at least be open to writing as a discovering/ordering/communicating process. And if we taught the editing process well, they will know how to use dictionaries, handbooks, and a friend with a copy-editor's eye to help them clean up their final drafts.

[10] Anthony Petrosky, "From Story to Essay: Reading and Writing," *CCC*, 33 (1982), 19–36. Petrosky reports similar artificial encapsulation of reading and writing skills. In his case evaluators were telling him that to have students write about their reading would muddy the assessment of their "reading" ability.

[11]Petrosky, "From Story to Essay"; Van Dijk, *Macrostructures* (Hillsdale, NJ: Erlbaum, 1980); Krashen, "The Role of Input (Reading) and Instruction in Developing Writing Ability," unpublished manuscript, Department of Linguistics, University of Southern California, 1981.

[12]Several other writers have recently called for variations of such integrated pedagogies; Charles Bazerman, "A Relationship between Reading and Writing: The Conversational Model," *CE*, 41 (1980), 656-661; Marilyn S. Sternglass, "Assessing Reading, Writing, and Reasoning," *CE*, 43 (1981), 269-275.

[13]Macrorie, *Uptaught* (New York: Hayden, 1970); Coles, *Composing* (Rochell Park, NJ: Hayden, 1974); Rouse, "Knowledge, Power and the Teaching of English," *CE*, 40 (1979), 473-491; Judy, "The Experiential Approach: Inner Worlds to Outer Worlds," in *Eight Approaches to Teaching Composition*, ed. Timothy R. Donovan and Ben W. McClelland (Urbana, IL: National Council of Teachers of English, 1980), pp. 37-51; Emig, *The Composing Processes of Twelfth Graders* (Urbana, IL: NCTE, 1971).

[14]Van Dijk, *Macrostructures*; de Beaugrande, *Text, Discourse, and Process* (Norwood, NJ: Ablex, 1980); Atwell, "The Evolution of Text: The Inter-relationship of Reading and Writing in the Composing Process," Diss., Indiana University, 1981; D'Angelo, "Paradigms as Structural Counterparts of Topoi," in *Linguistics, Stylistics and the Teaching of Composition*, ed. Donald McQuade (Akron, OH: University of Akron, 1979), pp. 41-51; D'Angelo, "Topoi, Paradigms, and Psychological Schemata," in *Proceedings of the Inaugural Conference of the University of Maryland Junior Writing Program*. University of Maryland, 1981, pp. 9-23.

[15]Arthur Applebee, *Writing in the Secondary School*, NCTE Research Report Report 21 (Urbana: NCTE, 1981). John Mellon, "Language Competence," in *The Nature and Measurement of Competency in English*, ed. Charles Cooper (Urbana, IL: NCTE, 1981), pp. 21-64.

[16]Relying on an analysis of variance. Freedman found that her evaluators were most affected by the content of an essay, then its organization. Mechanics ranked third. Interestingly, mechanics were most influential when organization was strong. To my mind, these findings lend further credence to a point I made earlier: clean but empty (or directionless) papers count for little. Correctness begins strongly to affect a reader once he or she has substantial and sensible prose to read. Let me close this note with a quote from Freedman's article:

> if society values content and organization as much as the teachers in this project did, then according to the definition of content and organization I used in this study, a pedagogy for teaching writing should aim first to help students develop their ideas logically . . . . Then it should focus on teaching students to organize the developed ideas so that they would be easily understood and favorably evaluated. . . . It seems today that many college-level curricula begin with a focus on helping students correct mechanical and syntactic problems rather than with the more fundamental aspects of the discourse. (pp. 163-164)

[17]Writers often resort to narrative frameworks when they are unable to execute more complex or abstract discourse schema. Narration becomes a substitute rather than a building block: see Suzanne E. Jacobs and Adela B. Karliner, "Helping Writers to Think," *CE*, 38 (1976-77), 484-505; Linda Flower, "Writer-based Prose: A Cognitive Basis for Problems in Writing," *CE*, 41 (1979-80), 19-37.

[18]Jim Williams and Micky Riggs, "Subvocalization During Writing," unpublished manuscript, Department of English, University of Southern California, 1981; Ann Matsuhashi, "Producing Written Discourse: A Theory-based Description of the Temporal Characteristics of Three Discourse Types from Four Competent Grade 12 Writers," Diss., State University of New York at Buffalo, 1979.

[19]Van Dijk, *Macrostructures*; C. Cooper and A. Matsuhashi, "A Theory of the Writing Process," in Elizabeth Martlew, ed., *The Psychology of Writing* (New York: Wiley, in press).

[20]Crowhurst, "Syntactic Complexity"; Joseph Williams, "Defining Complexity," *CE*, 40 (1978-79), 595-609; Sandra Thompson, "Grammar and Discourse: The English Detached Participial Clause," in Flora Klein, ed., *Discourse Approaches to Syntax* (Norwood, NJ: Ablex, in press).

[21]For compatible viewpoints presenting somewhat different lists of strategies, see Chapter Seven of Mina Shaughnessy, *Errors and Expectations* (New York: Oxford University Press, 1977) and Anne Ruggles Gere and Eugene Smith, *Writing and Learning* (New York: Macmillan, in press).

[22]Bloom, ed., *Taxonomy of Educational Objectives, Handbook I: Cognitive Domain* (New York: David McKay, 1956); Gagné, *The Conditions of Learning*, 2nd ed. (New York: Holt, Rinehart, and Winston, 1970).

[23]I realize I am asking that we teach discourse structures often assumed to be beyond the grasp of remedial writers. One way to teach such complicated structures has been suggested throughout this fifth section. The approach simply entails a scaling down of potentially complex tasks and a gradual building of skill through carefully sequenced, increasingly complex assignments. But it would also prove helpful to have some idea of the written discourse sophistication students possess

when they enter our classes. The following procedure could provide such information: During the first few days of class, the teacher gives an assignment that requires students to bring into play a discourse structure that will be dealt with at some later point in the course. In reading the students' responses, the teacher would suspend concern with sentence-level error and attempt to estimate the discourse sophistication of each student's essay. If, for example, the task called for comparing and contrasting, did a student attempt to organize the essay in a way that indicates comparison? How adequate was the attempt? Did the student rely on simpler—inadequate—structures like narration? Certainly this procedure will not provide clear entry to the complexities of a student's discourse repertoire, but—especially if repeated with one further assignment—it can offer some suggestions as to the level of particular students' discourse sophistication. Thus the teacher will have an indication of where and how he or she needs to begin instruction on discourse frameworks.

[24]This point is convincingly made by Karl Popper in *Conjectures and Refutations: The Growth of Scientific Knowledge* (New York: Harper and Row, 1968). After working up my analysis exercises, I discovered Marc Belth's *The Process of Thinking* (New York: David McKay, 1977). Belth equates *all* thinking with the bringing to bear of models, metaphors, analogies onto internal and external events.

[25]I will quote from Piaget's article:

> In our investigation of formal structures we used rather specific types of experimental situations which were of a physical and logical-mathematical nature because these seemed to be understood by the school children we sampled. However, it is possible to question whether these situations are, fundamentally, very general and therefore applicable to any school or professional environment. . . . It is highly likely that [young adults] will know how to reason in a hypothetical manner in their speciality, that is to say, dissociating the variables involved, relating terms in a combinatorial manner and reasoning with propositions involving negations and reciprocities. They would, therefore, be capable of thinking formally in their particular field, whereas faced with our experimental situations, their lack of knowledge or the fact they have forgotten certain ideas that are particularly familiar to children still in school or college, would hinder them from reasoning in a formal way, and they would give the appearance of being at the concrete level. (p. 10)

For further evidence that many of our young adults are not "deficient"—that is, that once appropriately exposed to Piagetian diagnostic procedures they can evince "formal" operations—see Fred W. Danner and Mary Carol Day, "Eliciting Formal Operations," *Child Development*, 48 (1977), 1600–1606; and Deanna Kuhn, Victoria Ho, and Catherine Adams, "Formal Reasoning Among Pre- and Late-Adolescents," *Child Development*, 50 (1979), 1128–1135. (My thanks to Professor Deborah Stipek, a former post-doctoral fellow at Piaget's Geneva Institute, for her helpful conversations on these issues.)

Since Piagetian tests of formal operations are based on mathematics, formal logic, and physics, I wonder how many of us—being as far removed as we are from our college physics labs—would fumble about with them and be labeled "concrete" thinkers.

[26]This third approach is essentially that embodied in the regular year Freshman Preparatory Program composition courses offered at UCLA. During the summer, however, we employ a variation of this approach in our Freshman Summer Program, an adjunct program in which composition courses are linked to introductory breadth courses. I will be glad to mail a description of the Freshman Summer Program to interested readers. Send requests to Mike Rose, Department of English, 2225 Rolfe Hall, UCLA, 405 Hilgard Avenue, Los Angeles, California 90024.

Comment on "Remedial Writing Courses"

DAVID PECK AND ELIZABETH HOFFMAN

Many of the ideas in Mike Rose's "Remedial Writing Courses: A Critique and a Proposal" (*CE*, February 1983) are good and necessary, but we do find fault

From *College English* 46.3 (March 1984): 302–8.

in some of his methods. Certainly more and more remedial teachers and programs are stressing, as Rose advocates, process over product, the importance of reading, a deemphasis on surface errors, and a concern for critical thinking. All necessary. The problem is that Rose makes these points through an exclusive focus on "correct academic prose," and a consequent dismissal of all "personal" writing.

While Rose acknowledges that "it is a sound motivation and learning principle to begin with the simple — let the student experience success — and then move toward the more complex," he concludes this key paragraph by asserting that "it is no longer clear that simple and personal topics are most motivating" (p. 113). The mistake Rose makes here is in equating "personal" with "simple." Narrative and descriptive writing assignments (as research shows) can teach writing structures and strategies as effectively as any other rhetorical forms. A paper on "A Neighborhood Problem" or "Ways My Life Will Differ from My Parents" may be as complex and analytical as any "academic" topic. "In fact," as Rose later admits, "making meaning for the self, ordering experience, establishing one's own relation to it is what informs any serious writing" (p. 120).

The advantage of such "personal" writing is not only that it is "relevant and motivating" (which Rose denies) but that it allows remedial students to draw from the well of their own lives — their own experiences and culture.[1] By doing such "personal" writing early in a remedial course, through journals and freewriting, students can gain confidence in their writing as they examine their experiences and analyze their ideas. By generating and exploring their own topics, they discover resources within themselves which they can later tap for more formal papers. Much "academic" writing is of course awful: vague, boring, and artificial. How much better to be teaching our students clear, interesting, and committed writing through narratives and descriptions of their own experience.

What Rose ignores in his article is where his students come from and what their background is. Many of the students we shepherd into college remedial classes have "done time" in overcrowded high-school English classes where they avoided writing. They have little confidence in their own writing skills because they have not written much, and what they have written has been faulted for surface errors and/or lack of ideas. Such students are going to flounder in a class that immediately demands "a correct academic prose." What they really need from a remedial class is the encouragement to write and the time to do it. Yes, remedial students need to be prodded toward analytical topics (and many of Rose's writing activities would help students to this end), but not until they have built a base of confidence and writing in themselves.

Actually, the title of Rose's article should have been, "What Will We Do in English 100?" If we teach everything that Rose suggests in our remedial classes, what will be left to do in regular freshman composition? Certainly one of the advantages we have as teachers of remedial writing is that we know most of our students will go from our classes into another freshman composition class. That knowledge allows us to omit certain elements from our syllabus (rhetorical modes, fine discussions of diction and style) and to concentrate instead on giving our students the foundation in writing skills and confidence they lack, the very foundation that should help them be successful in the next, regular writing class where they will be asked to write more formal, academic papers.

The University of California system, within which Rose administers his program, enrolls only 15% of the full-time students in California public institutions. (30% are in the California State University and College system, while 55% attend the vast network of community colleges.) This 15% figure represents the top 12% academically of all California high school graduates. Rose's UCLA students are better prepared and face richer occupational futures than the hundreds of thousands of students in state universities and junior colleges in California (to say nothing of similar public institutions across the country). What works for this elite minority at UCLA may not always work for the remaining 88%. Rose should recognize that those of us who teach this majority face larger tasks that may take longer.

One final note. We used an earlier version of Rose's article (in the proceedings from a 1982 conference) in a faculty workshop for our remedial writing staff at California State University at Long Beach. Both versions of this article contain good ideas and classroom activities that we can use. Rose only needs to recognize that he does not have to dismiss experiential writing—and the reasons we use it—in order for us to agree on the same goals. As he explains, "We needed a remedial program that slowly but steadily and systematically introduced remedial writers to transactional/expositional academic discourse" (p. 112). Perhaps our argument comes down to the word "slowly." We feel that by forcing our remedial students too quickly and exclusively into "academic discourse," we may just be guaranteeing their eventual failure in a form that has already assigned them to this remedial writing class.

NOTE

[1]For a recent experiment with this Freirian concept, see Kyle Fiore and Nan Elsasser, "'Strangers No More': A Liberatory Literacy Curriculum," *College English*, 44 (1982), 115–128.

MIKE ROSE RESPONDS

Let me begin by thanking Professors Peck and Hoffman for the kind things they say about my article. Let me also say that, in general, I read their response as a necessary counterstatement to several issues I raise in my critique of remedial writing courses. There are, however, two or three points they make that I feel I should qualify, for I was either misunderstood or didn't state my case with sufficient clarity.

Though I use the phrase "correct academic prose" in the first paragraph of my article, the context of its use does not imply that I would "immediately demand" such writing. For that fact, much of the essay advises that we suspend concerns about correctness and move students gradually toward an appropriate academic prose.

Perhaps I was overzealous while questioning the transfer of skills from narrative and descriptive writing to typically academic writing. And Peck and Hoffman are absolutely right to call me on my glib coupling of "simple" and "personal." Clearly a personal topic can call forth very complex cognitive and emotional responses.

What I would challenge, though, is Peck and Hoffman's assertion that research shows that "narrative and descriptive writing assignments . . . can teach writing structures and strategies as effectively as any other rhetorical forms." Yes, narrative and descriptive assignments can certainly lead to the development of narrating and describing skills, but we simply don't have much evidence that such assignments will effectively result in the development of other, fairly different rhetorical structures. (Studies to support this assertion are listed in footnotes 17–20 of "Remedial Writing Courses.") The mastery of one cognitive skill—as the long history in educational psychology of studies of "transfer of training" has made depressingly clear—does not necessarily lead to the development of other, even moderately distinct cognitive skills. Let me be clear here. I'm not saying that such transfer never happens; I'm suggesting that "we have reason to doubt" the ease and frequency of its occurance, and thus should be wary of any curriculum based on the assumption that the personal narrative or the descriptive rendering leads in some necessary developmental-cognitive way to the more impersonal expositional discourse required in the academy.

The above does not mean that, for example, narrative skills cannot be incorporated into the framing of, say, an academic argument. (In laying out the art slides classification assignment in my article, I relied on a narrative technique.) And it also does not mean that certain kinds of curricula might not be able to structure assignments in ways that guide students from personal narratives to other kinds of writing. The program by Bartholomae that I cite—or that of Fiore and Elsasser cited by Peck and Hoffman—are good examples of such curricula. They take students from personal narratives and descriptions toward critical analyses of the narrative/descriptive material. But what we're talking about here is the gradual movement away from one skill and the shaping and manipulating toward another—not a transfer. This distinction is not a picky or trivial one, for it would profoundly influence the nature and sequencing of assignments and the way earlier tasks are incorporated into later ones.

Finally, I want to be clear on the issue of motivation. I did not unilaterally dismiss the motivational potential of the personal/experiential topic. What I wanted to challenge is the assumption that the closer the topic is to one's own life experience, the more interest it will necessarily hold for the student. Human motivation is more complex than that assumption suggests, and I was trying to balance the pedagogical scales in the direction of topics that might not directly involve the personal. I hope the qualifications in my language support my attempt to undercut any unidimensional theory of motivation: "personal topics are not *necessarily* more relevant than academic ones," "*some* of our students . . . *might* not feel comfortable revealing highly personal experiences."

As Peck and Hoffman point out, we agree on the same goals. If we were carrying on this conversation over beer rather than in the pages of *College English*, our disagreements would be quickly superseded by our agreements, and, while I pulled the old trick of going through my pockets, Peck would spring for another pitcher.

Yes, experiential topics can contribute to our mutually held goals: increased control of critical discourse, participation in rather than exclusion from institutions of power, and so on. But I would like to raise the possibility that personal topics can limit as well as liberate. I mentioned in "Remedial Writing Courses" that, before coming to UCLA, I worked in several developmental literacy programs. During that time I saw a number of curricula built on personal/expressive writing. As far as I could tell, they didn't lead toward any carefully thought-out end and certainly not toward the kind of critical awareness that Professors Peck and Hoffman, and I, in our own ways, argue for. The topics were built on assumptions about cognition and motivation that to my mind kept students locked in a prisonhouse of their own experience. It was in those settings that I first became suspicious of the assumptions underlying some remedial curricula and started tinkering with the curriculum presented in my article.

O.K. I've had my say. Let me, then, again affirm Peck and Hoffman's response as a necessary counterstatement. They remind us that personal topics can have an important part in a curriculum that aims toward the development of critical sophistication; they check my too-ready equating of the personal with the simple; and they underscore the importance of a slow and gradual movement toward critical analysis, a movement that won't overwhelm and alienate but, rather, enhance and empower.

Peter Elbow Responds to "Remediation as Social Construct"[1]

I commend and admire your article. You give us a helpful and detailed picture of how a teacher comes to perceive a student as having a serious cognitive deficit, when the student's problem seems really to be that she has a way of engaging in conversational turn-taking that the teacher found inappropriate and in fact annoying. Part of her problem seemed to be that she

From *College Composition and Communication* 44.4 (December 1993): 587–89.

behaved too much like a peer and wasn't sufficiently deferential. This recalls the research by Sarah Freedman on how teachers respond negatively to student writing that is not deferential ("The Registers of Student and Professional Expository Writing," *New Directions in Composition Research*, ed. Richard Beach and Lillian Bridwell, Guilford, 1984).

By the way, I also appreciate *your* deference toward teachers: you don't paint the teacher as bigoted ogre—in fact you imply that all of us would probably be embarrassed at what would come to light in such a searching analysis of our teaching (I'm sure I would). I take that to be your point: circumstances tempt all of us into misguided behavior; your essay helps us with our task of greater vigilance.

But you never got around to the question your article most aroused in me: why and how was Maria ever *placed* in a remedial class when she'd written a novel, been on the debate team, and loved writing? For it was her placement in a *remedial* class which tempted the teacher into seeing a cognitive deficit where there was just an odd or even annoying way of talking. If the setting had been a regular course, the teacher would have just seen the behavior as "behavior." And imagine if Maria had been in an honors section: "Lord, aren't all these smart kids *pushy!* Sometimes I just get *tired* of them interrupting all the time and trying to steer the conversation their way."

So my question is what moral or conclusion do you draw from this patently "bad placement" of Maria? It seems as though the *minimal* implication of your study is that we've got to be more careful when we place students in remedial tracks or classes. But I would be sad if this is your moral. For you know that almost no colleges or universities would be willing to spend the time and money needed for a genuinely responsible process of placement. This would mean looking at two or more texts by each student, written in two or more genres produced on two or more occasions (with of course two or more readers). Most colleges aren't even willing to pay for a responsible assessment process even for exit or graduation testing, much less placement testing.

And even if colleges had an *ideal* placement process, what would that give us? We'd be blessed with remedial classes where all the students really *are* extremely poor writers; none who just *seem* poor when we first look at some of their writing. What kind of promised land is this? The teachers of these "ideal" remedial classes would be even *more* tempted to see cognitive deficits where perhaps there is just lack of training or skill. At least under the present half-assed conditions, most teachers of remedial classes are on the look out for bad placements.

You open your essay by saying you want to "examine remediation as a social construct" (299) and you go on to say you want to make us question "our assumptions about remediation and remedial writing" (316). I hear you, then, suggesting a more far-reaching moral to your story—but I wish you would say it outright: that we in higher education must be willing to take a few steps down the path blazed by so many elementary, middle, and high-school teachers—that is, in learning to teach mixed-ability classes. Surely there is a much *wider* range of abilities in many middle and secondary schools than there is in most colleges and universities. Think of all the students who don't go on to college.

What justification do you see, really, for remedial classes at the college level, or at least for remedial classes for students who are capable of vigorous language use — students who can say what they mean, who can look at data and reach conclusions, and who can get meaningful words down on paper — *even* if they write extremely poorly? Why should very poor writers be taught in some different place and manner from very strong ones? And even if we conclude that very poor writers need special or different treatment, why should we assume that the special treatment should take the form of segregating them to themselves — instead of giving them *supplementary* help while they are in classes with writers of all abilities?

Note these passages from the recent resolution passed by NCTE: "RESOLVED, that NCTE support curricula, programs, and practices that avoid tracking, a system which limits students' intellectual, linguistic, and/or social development; that NCTE urge educators and other policy makers to reexamine curricula, programs, and practices which require or encourage tracking of students in English language arts; that NCTE support teachers in their efforts to retain students in or return students to heterogeneous English language arts placement . . ." (*College English*, Jan. 1992, 40). As long as five years ago, sixty representatives of the seven main professional organizations in English at the English Coalition Conference discussed tracking at length and voted unanimously to urge colleagues to move against it. *But*, as an indication that we seem to have more trouble imagining heterogeneous classrooms in colleges than in schools, the Conference resolution is titled "Tracking at the Elementary and Secondary Level," and there was an unpublished paragraph in the full report that exempted college teachers from having to teach heterogeneous classes. (See *The English Coalition Conference*, ed. Richard Lloyd-Jones and Andrea Lunsford, NCTE and MLA, 1989, 40; and Peter Elbow, *What Is English*, MLA and NCTE, 1991, 32–38 and note 3, 42.)

I know that it would seem a large and radical step to move away from remedial writing classes in colleges. To draw the minimal implication from your story would seem to me at once too timid — yet impossible: in effect, "Let's segregate poor writers to themselves in remedial classes, but let's make sure their teachers never treat them as cognitively deficient." Lots of luck! Especially when teachers of remedial classes are often the least well paid and the least respected.

I hear your admirable research suggesting a goal that would in fact be *easier* to attain, yet far more exciting: heterogeneous writing classes. Of course this would involve some deep rethinking of how we teach, and some restructuring of various curricular and bureaucratic arrangements. Certainly poor writers should get supplementary help; certainly they should have to meet the same standards; probably many of them would have to stay longer in the course or meet more days a week. But isn't rethinking what your article is all about?

Besides, think of how much money and time colleges and universities spend on placement testing—all for a dubious process. That money could be used to help us begin to learn from many of our colleagues in elementary, middle, and secondary schools how to teach heterogeneous writing classes.

I would appreciate some of your thinking on these matters.

REPLY BY GLYNDA HULL, MIKE ROSE, KAY M. LOSEY, AND MARISA CASTELLANO

We thank Peter Elbow for his kind words about our article and for the thoughtful way he raises a very critical issue. The short form of our response is this: while we think Professor Elbow paints remedial programs with too broad a brush—some programs are better than others and some are sites of valuable work—we agree in principle with a lot of what he says. We hope his letter stimulates further comment. One possible next step would be to collect descriptions of college programs where there has been an attempt to disband remedial courses and create heterogeneous courses in their place. Then we could talk from cases.

We do have one concern, however, and we raise it not to diminish Professor Elbow's suggestion, but to place it in a broader institutional context. As problematic and counter-productive as some remedial programs and courses can be—and several of us have been very critical of them—they, in general, assure a place in the curriculum for instruction geared toward a wider range of student need than is typically addressed in the lower-division course of study. It is here where the analogy with tracking in the schools, though certainly apt, begins to strain a bit. As schools detrack, they are still held *legally* responsible—thanks to a range of hard-won state and federal legislation—for providing assistance to various groups of students with special needs. There is no such legal imperative compelling post-secondary institutions. In fact, there are strong forces in many colleges and universities to limit access to students who are underprepared, or at least to restrict or diminish their services. If remedial programs were disbanded, other permanent structural—not ad hoc or experimental—guarantees would have to be put in place. Tutorial centers, as Professor Elbow suggests, could play a major role here. They certainly have the expertise to do so. But many centers are not in a position—and even with additional staff would not be in a position—to provide a coordinated, consistent, and ongoing adjunct to a major instructional program. The passing on to a tutorial center of responsibilities that should be met in the curriculum complicates instruction. Students can get lost in the process, and the program itself—because it involves multiple departments and units—is vulnerable to turf wars, shifts in budget priorities, and institutional inertia.

A related concern. Remedial programs provide at least the possibility of a space within the faculty (marginal though it may be) where people interested in working with underprepared students can come together. Though some of the practices and theories that one finds in remedial programs are problematic, even harmful, there is no other departmental niche that provides the opportunity to discuss and advocate for these issues.

If we could think about Professor Elbow's proposal while keeping these institutional dynamics in mind, then we could begin to reconceive remediation, and, as he suggests, that would be exciting. But such reconceptualization, to our way of thinking, would have to include basic structural — if not legal — guarantees that the thrust toward access and achievement for students from a wide range of backgrounds will not be compromised.

NOTE

[1]"Remediation as a Social Construct," *College Composition and Communication* 42 (Oct. 1991): 299–329. Reprinted on pp. 253–82 of this volume.

8

"A Sociology Assignment: The Phases of Culture Shock" from Critical Strategies for Academic Thinking and Writing

WITH MALCOLM KINIRY

1998

AUTHOR'S NOTE: The assignments offered at the end of "Remedial Writing Courses" came early in my and my colleagues' thinking about curriculum. I would like, therefore, to present an assignment that comes farther down the line of development and is more fully formed but draws on the same principles articulated in the 1983 article. This is taken from a textbook Malcolm Kiniry and I authored. It comes from the section on *classifying*. In some assignments in this section, students are asked to develop classification schemes and then critique them. (One assignment, for example, is similar to the images of the human form exercise described on p. 126.) In other assignments, students are given a classification scheme of some kind and asked to apply it—and then to reflect on their application. The present assignment is of the second variety. The reader will recognize in it a number of the issues raised in "Remedial Writing Courses."

In our textbook, *classifying* is treated as both a technology and a rhetorical strategy—that is, as a way of organizing objects, events, experiences, or verbal or visual artifacts (e.g., the scheme that the authors of the opening passage use to define and understand the experience of "culture shock") and as a way to write about that understanding (the structure of the passage). Once familiar with this strategy, students can turn it back on itself, ask questions about the legitimacy of its use, consider what it does to human experience, and analyze what happens to one's thinking as one applies it. To use a current term, one operates "metacognitively," examining one's own thinking and the way the technology of classifying affects it. Finally, we have here the option that students test a theory against their own experience, blending personal or family experience and academic material in a way that, we hope, leads to both a reflection on experience as well as a critical perspective on intellectual work, on the way knowledge gets generated.

From *Critical Strategies for Academic Thinking and Writing, Third Edition.* Ed. Mike Rose and Malcolm Kiniry. Boston, MA: Bedford/St. Martin's, 1998. 331–47.

I would like to say a little more about teaching an assignment like this, and then reflect on the process of creating the book that contained it, given the issues I raise in the two articles on textbooks in Part One. Any reader who finds the assignment of interest is welcome to use it.

Critical Strategies is aimed at freshman composition, but I have taught assignments from it—or similar to those in it—in settings where students are less prepared. Also, other teachers working with students in community college remedial courses or with high school students have used the book or have created new assignments based on the book's principles. (The Education Trust has used these principles to create curricula for high schools in Pennsylvania and California.) I am not trying to peddle the book here or its general approach, but I do feel strongly about the capacity of a wide range of students to handle difficult material.

When I've used assignments like this one on culture shock with less-prepared students, I'll spend more time setting it up. Through information provided by me or generated through discussion (as a class or in groups), students are given background material to understand the opening passage. This can include anything from vocabulary ("quaint," "indigenous," "ethnocentrism"), to the notion of "culture shock" itself, to the use of stage or phase theories in social science. We then turn to each of the portraits of immigrants, discussing students' sense of them, what the portraits convey factually (there's a focus on details here) and what feelings they evoke. The discussion typically involves a good deal of personal opinion and example flowing though analysis and interpretation. Also, there is the interplay of oral and written work in all this—for example, having students take five minutes to write for themselves a definition of "culture shock" or to verbally offer a brief summary of the Brink and Saunders passage. This preparation sets up the class for the assignment itself, which can involve the same mix of personal and academic material and of talking and writing. Clearly, for an assignment involving this much effort to be useful, it would need to fit logically into a broader curriculum, be preceded by assignments that, in some way, lead to it, and followed by assignments that build on what is learned from it. Kiniry and I offer such sequences in *Critical Strategies*.

There is some discussion these days—and several new books—about the creation of alternative (or hybrid or mixed) academic discourses, the intention being to afford more options for expression and intellectual work.[1] The present assignment provides students with the possibility of creating such discourse, and if Kiniry and I were writing *Critical Strategies* today, we would undoubtedly provide more, and more varied, options.

But let me admit that my inclination, for better or worse, has been to focus on traditional academic writing, for it, in its various manifestations, typically presents such significant problems both for students and teachers, particularly for students from less-than-privileged backgrounds. The majority of assignments that students will encounter in their first year or two of college will be pretty conventional in style and form, and draw from textbooks and texts that, generally, fall within a particular discipline's borders. This is what I and my coworkers found in our surveys of the lower-division curriculum, and it is supported by a recent study of a range of faculty by Christopher Thaiss and Terry Myers Zawacki. The challenge, in my opinion, is to develop curricula that prepare students for such work in ways that foster rhetorical flexibility, a reflective cast of mind, and a sense of linguistic agency.

Let me close with a few thoughts about writing a textbook. To take the task seriously, especially if you're trying to do something a bit different, involves every ounce of pedagogical skill that you possess. You have this idea — and it can seem so fresh, even bold — and then you begin the process of playing it out, materializing it in assignments, and selections, and surrounding text. You face not only your own limits of imagination but also the constraints of the genre and the market. It's in a publisher's best interest to issue something new, but it can't be too new or atypical, or the sales force will have a hard time describing it, categorizing it — is it country and western or rock'n'roll? And then there's the market. There are obviously many instructors who experiment with their pedagogy and seek out new materials, but more often than we in rhetoric and composition would like to think, there is a tendency toward the familiar. There are many reasons for this tendency, from working conditions that make it hard to abandon one's routines to convictions about student ability. All this creates further constraints on the textbook author, constraints one tries to work within while pushing on them. And, then, if you accept the line of argument in "Speculations on Process Knowledge," there are limits on trying to render and get people to engage complex cognitive-rhetorical processes through print.

The rhetorical strategies Mal Kiniry and I selected to structure the book were conceived and presented as thinking and writing strategies rather than as modes of discourse, and we tried to frame the assignments in ways that called for reflection on one's thinking and writing. It might be close to impossible to render complex composing processes in print, we reasoned, but perhaps we could provide a collection of materials that simulate some of the writing demands of the lower division and spark reflection on them. With the help of exceptional editors (in turn, Ellen Darion, Jane Betz, Beth Castrodale), we put the book through three substantial revisions, trying to get closer to what we had in mind. As much as I like the third edition especially, I'm not sure we ever got the book right. After going through the process, I have no doubt of the legitimacy of the claim made by Ernest Boyer in *Scholarship Reconsidered* and espoused for some time by the Conference on College Composition and Communication: Writing a textbook can be "a significant intellectual endeavor" (Boyer, 1990, p. 35). It is certainly an endeavor that puts theories about writing and teaching to a kind of test, and thus can be a hugely instructive as well as humbling experience. For Kiniry and me, it was a way to continue the development of the materials we and others at UCLA had been struggling with and to provide for a wider audience a concrete illustration, an "existence proof" of our beliefs about what students could do.

NOTE

[1]See, for example, Schroeder, Fox, and Bizzell (2002).

A SOCIOLOGY ASSIGNMENT

Culture shock is a general term for describing the problems that people experience in making the transition from a familiar to an unfamiliar setting. The first reading is an excerpt from a book written for nurses by nursing professors Pamela J. Brink and Judith Saunders. The authors define four distinct phases of culture shock. Each of the phases of culture shock becomes a kind of category of experience, a way to classify patterns of feelings and behaviors—and Brink and Saunders theorize that these phases come in a particular order.

Brink and Saunders's piece is followed by readings portraying the experiences of five people adjusting to life in the United States: Wood Chuen Kwong came to San Francisco from Canton, China, as an adult in 1979; Amitar Ray, who received a medical degree in his native India, immigrated to the United States, where there was a shortage of physicians, in 1972; Negi, a young girl whose story is told in Esmeralda Santiago's memoir, *When I Was Puerto Rican*, moved with her mother, sister, and brother to her grandmother's home in Brooklyn, where she had to adjust to a new school and a new way of life; Alex Bushinsky, a Russian Jew, immigrated to New York for work in 1976 and faced many economic and cultural challenges; finally, Haroutioun Yeretzian, an Armenian from Lebanon, also arrived in America in 1976 and eventually opened an Armenian bookstore in Hollywood.

As you read each passage, ask yourself two things: Do the feelings and behaviors of the central character or characters fit those feelings and behaviors described in any of the phases described by Brink and Saunders? If they do, do they come in the order suggested by the theory? Then write an essay using specific details from the readings to discuss the legitimacy of Brink and Saunders's portrayal of culture shock.

In a separate, brief paper—one that can be rough and experimental—reflect on the act of trying to apply a classification scheme and a theoretical model to particular cases: the ways this process helped you understand people's experience and the ways it narrowed or misrepresented their experience.

For those of you who immigrated to the United States or have spent a significant amount of time in another culture, we offer a further option: Write an essay discussing your own experience of crossing cultures using Brink and Saunders's model, specifically considering the ways the model fits and illuminates your experience and the ways it doesn't.

The Phases of Culture Shock

PAMELA J. BRINK AND JUDITH SAUNDERS

[The researcher] Oberg's original paper isolated and described four phases of culture shock and named the first phase the "Honeymoon Phase." . . . The other three phases were described but not named. The following discussion is an attempt to name and extend Oberg's discussion.

Phase One.   "The Honeymoon Phase" is marked by excitement. The desire to learn about the people and their customs is great; sightseeing is anticipated with pleasure; and getting to work and accomplishing all the goals envisioned at home provide the basis for this phase. Travelers, visiting dignitaries, and other temporary functionaries may never experience any other phase but this one.

Phase Two.   "The Disenchantment Phase" generally does not begin until the individual has established residence, i.e., when he begins to become aware of the setting as his area of residence. This sense of awareness often is associated with the realization that one is "stuck here" and cannot get out of the situation. What was "quaint" may become aggravating. Simple tasks of living are time consuming because they must be done in a different way. This beginning awareness often results in frustration—either frustration because the indigenous population is too stubborn to see things your way or frustration because you can't see things their way and are constantly making social errors. Embarrassment coupled with feelings of ineptness attack self-image or self-concept.

Particular, individual styles of behavior are developed over the years through the principles of inertia and economy. Usually the individual is unaware of the operation of these principles and their effect on him. They form part of ethnocentrism: "The way I do things is the right way (and perhaps for some the only way) to do things." The disenchantment phase directly threatens ethnocentrism because the host country believes exactly the same way about its customs and sees no reason to change its ways. Phase two includes a reexamination of one's self from the vantage point of another set of values. In this phase failure often outweighs success.

To this, add loneliness. No one knows you well enough to reaffirm your sense of self-worth. The distance from home is magnified. Home itself assumes the aura of Mecca—distant, unattainable, beautiful. This form of nostalgia for the past and the familiar seems to have two effects. Mail and visitors from home assume immense importance as a contact with people who believe in you and think you are important. To protect yourself from these feelings of loneliness and lack of self-esteem, you attack the presumed cause of these feelings—the host country. Feelings of anxiety and inadequacy are often expressed through depression, withdrawal, or eruptions of anger at frustration; or by seeking out fellow countrymen to the exclusion of the indigenous population. This period in the culture shock syndrome is the most difficult to live through and this is the period where people "give up and go home."

Phase Three. "The Beginning Resolution Phase." Oberg described this phase . . . as the individual seeking to learn new patterns of behavior appropriate to the setting, attempting to make friends in the indigenous population, and becoming as much of a participant-observer as possible in the ceremonies, festivals, and daily activities of the new setting.

This phase seems to be characterized by the reestablishment of a sense of humor. Social errors no longer are devastating to the ego. The host culture no longer is considered all bad and home all wonderful. This phase seems to be facilitated greatly by the arrival of fellow countrymen who are "worse off" and need help. You can show off what you have learned, you are important because you are sought for advice, you feel needed by the newcomer.

At this point also, the individual becomes aware that things seem easier; friendships are being developed; home is still distant, but less relevant. Letters from home somehow seem peripheral to current interests and concerns. Letters to home become more superficial; explanation of what is becoming familiar would take up too much time. Current friendships have the same frame of reference for conversation, a frame of reference that is unknown at home.

Without really becoming aware of the process one slowly adapts to the new situation. Each small discovery, each small victory in learning the new rules is satisfying, and helps to restore one's sore and damaged ego.

Phase Four. "The Effective Function Phase." This means being just as comfortable in the new setting as in the old. Having achieved this phase, the individual will probably experience reverse culture shock when he returns home. Or, the individual may decide only to go home for visits, but make the new culture his own.

From New Immigrants: Portraits in Passage

THOMAS BENTZ

Wood Chuen Kwong

"I wouldn't leave Chinatown, even if I were offered a job somewhere else," said Wood Chuen Kwong from his apartment in the heart of the world's largest Chinese community outside of Asia. This city is wonderfully textured with the Chinese sensibility. Graceful calligraphy blinks brilliantly from neon signs on banks, fish markets, and boutiques. The Chinese language is spoken at every turn and other aspects of Chinese culture are seen everywhere. Chinatown is like a haven between hemispheres, an oasis of the Orient firmly planted on our western shore.

"I wanted to stay in San Francisco for a year or two, to get acquainted, to get to know the people here. It is such a beautiful city and the weather is wonderful. But it is very difficult to find a job." For now, Wood and his son, Ching Yu, work as dishwashers and busboys, but they hope this is only temporary. Wood is a mechanical engineer and has an extensive background in electronics.

"In Canton, I was a radio repairman for thirty-two years in my spare time. The locally made radios and parts were easy to come by in China, and we always saved any extra parts. In America I see people who are so wasteful. They will throw out a radio if a single part breaks down. All these electric gadgets you have here are luxuries you don't need. We had to cook in China on a messy coal stove. It would be very helpful to have what you have here, the Japanese-made electric frying pans, rice cookers, and toasters. But there the people couldn't afford them even if they were available. Here you have useless electric razors and toothbrushes too.

"In Canton our whole family was allowed only 10 kilowatts of electricity each month. One 40-watt lightbulb and one 60-watt fan were all we could afford. All our work and reading had to be done by that one bulb. We also had one 3-watt fluorescent lamp we could put in the socket for dim and minimal lighting. There was, of course, no air-conditioning in our apartment, or anywhere else in Canton, even though the heat hit 90 degrees in the autumn and 100 degrees in the summer.

"Living in China, you have to learn how to fix almost anything and everything in your household. For others to fix what you have would take too long and cost too much. So I learned carpentry and began to make tables and chairs. If a leg on something broke, or our bed broke down, I had to fix it. Soon I had repaired a whole house. So did all the other workers that I knew who got about $40 a month for their normal labors.

"All the people were willing to help. If you needed to move something or paint a wall, you could just call on your friends and they would all come and give you a hand to do anything or go anywhere. And they didn't need to be paid." It is just this sort of cooperation between people that Wood finds to be lacking in the United States. Even though he and his wife, Foong Ying Dang, and their son, Ching Yu, and daughter, Ming Yu, feel relatively secure within the cultural haven of Chinatown, they know that they are now living in more threatening surroundings. Rival Chinese street gangs have been trying to assert their dominance, and their presence breeds fear in the new and old residents alike.

"I would not come home late at night, or go out of Chinatown," admitted Wood. "I have never had any trouble, but I don't feel safe. In China I knew everybody who lived on our block, but here, even people in the same building don't say hello. There may not be enough freedom in China but there is too much here. They have far less crime, very little theft or murder, because the offender in China is handled much more thoroughly and properly. Picking someone's pocket there would get you twenty days to three months in jail. Burglary draws at least two years, armed robbery is ten to twenty years. Murder is for life, with no probation. When the rule and punishment are straight and strong, then you can have restraint. There is no gambling in China because the people don't have the greed that makes them want to take what doesn't belong to them instead of earning it themselves."

Wood takes pride in being able to earn what his family needs though he has known disappointment along these lines and understands that fairness and justice are not always available to everyone. "For about eight years in the 1950s I took part in a Chinese government-promoted plan to provide housing, employment, and services. We put our money in the bank, and with the interest the government built homes and left the principal in the bank for future investment. No one person in China could build or afford to buy a house. So the money made some housing available. And each new year we drew lots and several people won the houses. The Cultural Revolution wiped this out before I could win my house. But you know, if the savings and loans in San Francisco would follow that scheme, there would be lots of investors and we could both build houses and provide employment for people in the process."

Wood can see that there is good and bad in both countries. He knows that China could certainly use some American technology and suspects that the U.S. would do well to have more of the will and spirit that the Chinese worker has. "Opening trade has been and will continue to be beneficial to both the U.S. and China. If China doesn't look to the U.S. for technical progress it will never catch up to the new and better ways that the world can work. And if the U.S. doesn't meet the real spirit of the Chinese people, it will never get out of its old red-devil fear. We are different, but each of us has good points and weaknesses. If we come together we can learn to complement each other."

"I just finished a manpower training program in the Chinatown Resources Development Center and I have already had several interviews for jobs. I've just applied and taken a written examination in English for a government position that I have high hopes for. It is a civil service mechanical technician at $800 a month."

In Canton he made much less money, $113 a month, but his expenses were much less too. His food cost about $10 a month and his rent, for a three-bedroom apartment, was $13.49 a month. He was not dissatisfied with his life there and though he applied for a visa to come here for six years, he only wanted to visit and to see his parents. However the Chinese government refused his requests. Finally his father's influence made the difference.

"My father had studied at Ohio State University before spending his life teaching, first in Canton and then from 1946 to 1968 in Hong Kong. In 1952 one of my sisters and her husband came to the United States. In 1968, my parents followed after my sister's petition for reunification was accepted. None of the rest of us seven children could come out of China with them then.

"In 1979 my father petitioned for me to come out because of the special case of his illness. He was also a commissioner on the housing authority in San Francisco, so through his connections, my case was expedited. I was able to come and be with him before he died. It had been so difficult to get out of China just for a visit that I decided that once I came here I would want to stay. I am now a permanent resident alien. I think I'll decide after five years whether I want to become a U.S. citizen."

Meanwhile one of his sisters has no such choice. She is now a permanent resident alien in a country she doesn't want to be in. She came out of China to Hong Kong at the same time that Wood flew to San Francisco to be with his father. "Father also petitioned for Kin. But when she came out of China in June of 1979, a lot of other people were going to Hong Kong to be processed for America. So the U.S. consulate just listed people in the order of the requests for immigration. She was put way back on the list. When our father died, so did his petition for Kin. The case was closed. Now she cannot come to America nor can she go back to China.

"Kin was a doctor in China, but she can't get recognized in Hong Kong, so she works as an aide in a school for the blind. Her husband was an X-ray specialist in China, but he can't find a job in Hong Kong. They have a very difficult life now. I don't know who is to blame. I often write to her and send money to help. I don't know what else to do."

Amitar Ray
From Immigrant America: A Portrait

ALEJANDRO PORTES AND RUBÉN G. RUMBAUT

After finishing medical school, Amitar Ray confronted the prospect of working *ad honorem* in one of the few well-equipped hospitals in Bombay or moving to a job in the countryside and to quick obsolescence in his career. He opted instead for preparing and taking the Educational Council for Foreign Medical Graduates (ECFMG) examination, administered at the local branch of the Indo-American Cultural Institute. He passed it on his second attempt. In 1972, there was a shortage of doctors in the United States, and U.S. consulates were directed to facilitate the emigration of qualified physicians from abroad.

Amitar and his wife, also a doctor, had little difficulty obtaining permanent residents' visas under the third preference of the U.S. immigration law, reserved for professionals of exceptional ability. He went on to specialize in anesthesiology and completed his residence at a public hospital in Brooklyn. After four years, nostalgia and the hope that things had improved at home moved the Rays to go back to India with their young daughter, Rita. The trip strengthened their professional and family ties, but it also dispelled any doubts as to where their future was. Medical vacancies were rare and paid a fraction of what he earned as a resident in Brooklyn. More important, there were few opportunities to grow professionally because he would have had to combine several part-time jobs to earn a livelihood, leaving little time for study.

At fifty-one, Amitar is now associate professor of anesthesiology at a midwestern medical school; his wife has a local practice as an internist. Their combined income is in the six figures, affording them a very comfortable lifestyle. Their daughter is a senior at Bryn Mawr, and she plans to pursue a graduate degree in international relations. There are few Indian immigrants in the mid-sized city where the Rays live; thus, they have had to learn local ways in order to gain entry into American social circles. Their color is sometimes a barrier to close contact with white middle-class families, but they have cultivated many friendships among the local faculty and medical community.

Ties to India persist and are strengthened through periodic trips and the professional help the Rays are able to provide to colleagues back home. They have already sponsored the immigration of two bright young physicians from their native city. More important, they make sure that information on new medical developments is relayed to a few selected specialists back home. However, there is little chance that they will return, even after retirement. Work and new local ties play a role in this, but the decisive factor is a thoroughly Americanized daughter whose present life and future have very little to do with India. Rita does not plan to marry soon; she is interested in Latin American politics, and her current goal is a career in the foreign service.

Negi
From When I Was Puerto Rican

ESMERALDA SANTIAGO

Uniformed women with lacquered hair, high heels, and fitted skirts looked down on us, signalled that we should fasten our safety belts, place parcels under the seat in front of us, and sit up.

"Stewardesses," Mami said, admiring their sleek uniforms, pressed white blouses, stiff navy ribbons tied into perfect bows in their hair. None of them spoke Spanish. Their tight smiles were not convincing, did not welcome us. In our best clothes, with hair combed, faces scrubbed, the dirt under our nails gouged out by Mami's stiff brush, I still felt unclean next to the highly groomed, perfumed, unwrinkled women who waited on us.

"Someday," Mami mused, "you might like to be a stewardess. Then you can travel all over the world for free." . . .

The sky darkened, but we floated in a milky whiteness that seemed to hold the plane suspended above Puerto Rico. I couldn't believe we were moving; I imagined that the plane sat still in the clouds while the earth flew below us. The drone of the propellers was hypnotic and lulled us to sleep in the stiff seats with their square white doilies on the back. . . .

I dozed, startled awake, panicked when I didn't know where I was, remembered where we were going, then dozed off again, to repeat the whole cycle, in and out of sleep, between earth and sky, somewhere between Puerto Rico and New York.

It was raining in Brooklyn. Mist hung over the airport so that all I saw as we landed were fuzzy white and blue lights on the runway and at the terminal. We thudded to earth as if the pilot had miscalculated just how close we were to the ground. A startled silence was followed by frightened cries and *aleluyas** and the rustle of everyone rushing to get up from their seats and out of the plane as soon as possible.

Mami's voice mixed and became confused with the voices of other mothers telling their children to pick up their things, stay together, to walk quickly toward the door and not to hold up the line. Edna, Raymond, and I each had bundles to carry, as did Mami, who was loaded with two huge bags filled with produce and spices *del país.*** "You can't find these in New York," she'd explained.

We filed down a long, drafty tunnel, at the end of which many people waited, smiling, their hands waving and reaching, their voices mingling into a roar of *hello*'s and *how are you*'s and *oh, my god, it's been so long*'s.

"Over there," Mami said, shoving us. On the fringes of the crowd a tall woman with short cropped hair, a black lace dress, and black open-toed shoes leaned against a beam that had been painted yellow. I didn't recognize her, but she looked at me as if she knew who I was and then loped toward us, arms outstretched. It was my mother's mother, Tata. Raymond let go of Mami's hand and ran into Tata's arms. Mami hugged and kissed her. Edna and I hung back, waiting.

"This is Edna," Mami said, pushing her forward for a hug and kiss.

"And this must be Negi," Tata said, pulling me into her embrace. I pressed against her and felt the sharp prongs of the rhinestone brooch on her left shoulder against my face. She held me longer than I expected, wrapped me in the scratchy softness of her black lace dress, the warmth of her powdered skin, the sting of her bittersweet breath, pungent of beer and cigarettes.

---

aleluyas: Hallelujahs (Spanish) [Eds.].
**del país:* Literally, "from the country" (Spanish) [Eds.].

Behind her loomed a man shorter than she, but as imposing. He was squarely built, with narrow eyes under heavy eyebrows, a broad nose, and full lips fuzzed with a pencil mustache. No one would have ever called him handsome, but there was about him a gentleness, a sweetness that made me wish he were a relative. He was, in a manner of speaking. Mami introduced him as "Don Julio, Tata's friend." We shook hands, his broad, fleshy palm seeming to swallow mine.

"Let's get our things," Mami said, pulling us into a knot near her. "You kids, don't let go of each others' hands. It's crazy here tonight."

We joined the stream of people claiming their baggage. Boxes filled with fruit and vegetables had torn, and their contents had spilled and broken into slippery messes on the floor. Overstuffed suitcases tied with ropes or hastily taped together had given way, and people's underwear, baby diapers, and ratty shoes pushed through the stressed seams where everyone could see them. People pointed, laughed, and looked to see who would claim these sorry belongings, who could have thought the faded, torn clothes and stained shoes were still good enough for their new life in Brooklyn.

"That's why I left everything behind," Mami sniffed. "Who wants to carry that kind of junk around?"

We had a couple of new suitcases and three or four boxes carefully packed, taped at the seams, tied with rope, and labelled with our name and an address in New York that was all numbers. We had brought only our "good" things: Mami's work clothes and shoes, a few changes of playclothes for me, Edna, and Raymond, some of them made by Mami herself, others bought just before we left. She brought her towels, sheets, and pillowcases, not new, but still "decent looking."

"I'll see if I can find a taxi," Don Julio said. "You wait here."

We huddled in front of the terminal while Don Julio negotiated with drivers. The first one looked at us, counted the number of packages we carried, asked Don Julio where we were going, then shook his head and drove along the curb toward a man in a business suit with a briefcase who stood there calmly, his right hand in the air as if he were saluting, his fingers wiggling every so often. The second driver gave us a hateful look and said some words that I didn't understand, but I knew what he meant just the same. Before he drove off, Mami mumbled through her teeth *"Charamanbiche."* Don Julio said it was illegal for a driver to refuse a fare, but that didn't stop them from doing it.

Finally, a swarthy man with thick black hair and a flat cap on his head stopped, got out of his taxi, and helped us load our stuff. He didn't speak Spanish, none of us spoke English, and, it appeared, neither did he. But he gave us a toothy, happy smile, lifted Raymond into Mami's lap, made sure our fingers and toes were inside the taxi before he closed the doors, then got in with a great deal of huffing and puffing, as his belly didn't fit between the seat and the steering wheel. Tata and Don Julio sat in the front seat with the driver, who kept asking questions no one understood.

"He wants to know where we're from," Mami figured out, and we told him.

"Ah, Porto Reeco, yes, ees hot," he said. "San Juan?"

"Yes," Mami said, the first time I'd ever heard her speak English.

The driver launched into a long speech peppered with familiar words like America and President Kennedy. Mami, Tata, and Don Julio nodded every once in a while, uhhuhed, and laughed whenever the taxi driver did. I wasn't sure whether he had no idea that we didn't understand him, or whether he didn't care.

Rain had slicked the streets into shiny, reflective tunnels lined with skyscrapers whose tops disappeared into the mist. Lampposts shed uneven silver circles of light whose edges faded to gray. An empty trash can chained to a parking meter banged and rolled from side to side, and its lid, also chained, flipped and flapped in the wind like a kite on a short string. The taxi stopped at a red light under an overpass. A train roared by above us, its tiny square windows full of shapes.

"Look at her," Tata laughed from the front seat, "Negi's eyes are popping out of her head."

"That's because the streets are not paved with gold, like she thought," Mami teased.

The taxi driver grinned. I pressed my face to the window, which was fogged all around except on the spot I'd rubbed so that I could look out.

It was late. Few windows on the tall buildings flanking us were lit. The stores were shuttered, blocked with crisscrossed grates knotted with chains and enormous padlocks. Empty buses glowed from within with eerie gray light, chugging slowly from one stop to the next, their drivers sleepy and bored.

Mami was wrong. I didn't expect the streets of New York to be paved with gold, but I did expect them to be bright and cheerful, clean, lively. Instead, they were dark and forbidding, empty, hard. . . .

[We pick up after Negi, her mother, brother, and sister have arrived at Tata's house.]

There were angels on the ceiling. Four fat naked cherubs danced in a circle, their hands holding ivy garlands, their round buttocks half covered by a cloth swirling around their legs. Next to me, Mami snored softly. At the foot of the bed, Edna and Raymond slept curled away from each other, their backs against my legs. The bedroom had very high ceilings with braided molding all the way around, ending in a circle surrounded by more braid above the huge window across from the bed. The shade was down, but bright sunlight streaked in at the edges. The cherubs looked down on us, smiling mysteriously, and I wondered how many people they had seen come in and out of this room. Slowly I crawled over Mami, out of bed.

"Where are you going?" she mumbled, half asleep.

"To the bathroom," I whispered.

The bed was pressed into the corner against the wall across from the window, next to a wide doorway that led into the next room. A long dresser stretched from the doorway to the window wall, leaving an aisle just wide enough to open the drawers halfway out.

It was six in the morning of my first day in Brooklyn. Our apartment, on the second floor, was the fanciest place I'd ever lived in. The stairs coming up from Tata's room on the first floor were marble, with a landing in between, and a colored glass window with bunches of grapes and twirling vines. The door to our apartment was carved with more bunches of grapes and leaves. From the two windows in the main room we could look out on the courtyard we had come through the night before. A tree with broad brown leaves grew from the middle of what looked like a well, circled with the same stones that lined the ground. Scraggly grass poked out between the cracks and in the brown dirt around the tree. The building across from ours was three stories high, crisscrossed by iron stairs with narrow landings on which people grew tomatoes and geraniums in clay pots. Our building was only two stories high, although it was almost as tall as the one across the courtyard. We, too, had an iron balcony with a straight ladder suspended halfway to the ground. It made me a little dizzy to look down. . . .

The first day of school Mami walked me to a stone building that loomed over Graham Avenue, its concrete yard enclosed by an iron fence with spikes at the top. The front steps were wide but shallow and led up to a set of heavy double doors that slammed shut behind us as we walked down the shiny corridor. I clutched my eighth-grade report card filled with A's and B's, and Mami had my birth certificate. At the front office we were met by Mr. Grant, a droopy gentleman with thick glasses and a kind smile who spoke no Spanish. He gave Mami a form to fill out. I knew most of the words in the squares we were to fill in: NAME, ADDRESS (CITY, STATE), and OCCUPATION. We gave it to Mr. Grant, who reviewed it, looked at my birth certificate, studied my report card, then wrote on the top of the form "7–18."

Don Julio had told me that if students didn't speak English, the schools in Brooklyn would keep them back one grade until they learned it.

"Seven gray?" I asked Mr. Grant, pointing at his big numbers, and he nodded.

"I no guan seven gray. I eight gray. I teeneyer."

"You don't speak English," he said. "You have to go to seventh grade while you're learning."

"I have A's in school Puerto Rico. I lern good. I no seven gray girl."

Mami stared at me, not understanding but knowing I was being rude to an adult.

"What's going on?" she asked me in Spanish. I told her they wanted to send me back one grade and I would not have it. This was probably the first rebellious act she had seen from me outside my usual mouthiness within the family.

"Negi, leave it alone. Those are the rules," she said, a warning in her voice.

"I don't care what their rules say," I answered. "I'm not going back to seventh grade. I can do the work. I'm not stupid."

Mami looked at Mr. Grant, who stared at her as if expecting her to do something about me. She smiled and shrugged her shoulders.

"Meester Grant," I said, seizing the moment, "I go eight gray six mons. Eef I no lern inglish, I go seven gray. Okay?"

"That's not the way we do things here," he said, hesitating.

"I good studen. I lern queek. You see notes." I pointed to the A's in my report card. "I pass seven gray."

So we made a deal.

"You have until Christmas," he said. "I'll be checking on your progress." He scratched out "7–18" and wrote in "8–23." He wrote something on a piece of paper, sealed it inside an envelope, and gave it to me. "Your teacher is Miss Brown. Take this note upstairs to her. Your mother can go," he said and disappeared into his office.

"Wow!" Mami said, "you can speak English!"

I was so proud of myself, I almost burst. In Puerto Rico if I'd been that pushy, I would have been called *mal educada** by the Mr. Grant equivalent and sent home with a note to my mother. But here it was my teacher who was getting the note, I got what I wanted, and my mother was sent home.

"I can find my way after school," I said to Mami. "You don't have to come get me."

"Are you sure?"

"Don't worry," I said. "I'll be all right."

I walked down the black-tiled hallway, past many doors that were half glass, each one labelled with a room number in neat black lettering. Other students stared at me, tried to get my attention, or pointedly ignored me. I kept walking as if I knew where I was going, heading for the sign that said STAIRS with an arrow pointing up. When I reached the end of the hall and looked back, Mami was still standing at the front door watching me, a worried expression on her face. I waved, and she waved back. I started up the stairs, my stomach churning into tight knots. All of a sudden, I was afraid that I was about to make a fool of myself and end up in seventh grade in the middle of the school year. Having to fall back would be worse than just accepting my fate now and hopping forward if I proved to be as good a student as I had convinced Mr. Grant I was. "What have I done?" I kicked myself with the back of my right shoe, much to the surprise of the fellow walking behind me, who laughed uproariously, as if I had meant it as a joke.

Miss Brown's was the learning disabled class, where the administration sent kids with all sorts of problems, none of which, from what I could see, had anything to do with their ability to learn but more with their willingness

---

mal educada: Rude or bad-mannered (Spanish); usually written as one word [Eds.].

to do so. They were an unruly group. Those who came to class, anyway. Half of them never showed up, or, when they did, they slept through the lesson or nodded off in the middle of Miss Brown's carefully parsed sentences.

We were outcasts in a school where the smartest eighth graders were in the 8-1 homeroom, each subsequent drop in number indicating one notch less smarts. If your class was in the low double digits (8–10 for instance), you were smart, but not a pinhead. Once you got into the teens, your intelligence was in question, especially as the numbers rose to the high teens. And then there were the twenties. I was in 8–23, where the dumbest, most undesirable people were placed. My class was, in some ways, the equivalent of seventh grade, perhaps even sixth or fifth.

Miss Brown, the homeroom teacher, who also taught English composition, was a young black woman who wore sweat pads under her arms. The strings holding them in place sometimes slipped outside the short sleeves of her well-pressed white shirts, and she had to turn her back to us in order to adjust them. She was very pretty, with almond eyes and a hairdo that was flat and straight at the top of her head then dipped into tight curls at the ends. Her fingers were well manicured, the nails painted pale pink with white tips. She taught English composition as if everyone cared about it, which I found appealing.

After the first week she moved me from the back of the room to the front seat by her desk, and after that, it felt as if she were teaching me alone. We never spoke, except when I went up to the blackboard.

"Esmeralda," she called in a musical voice, "would you please come up and mark the prepositional phrase?"

In her class, I learned to recognize the structure of the English language, and to draft the parts of a sentence by the position of words relative to pronouns and prepositions without knowing exactly what the whole thing meant.

The school was huge and noisy. There was a social order that, at first, I didn't understand but kept bumping into. Girls and boys who wore matching cardigans walked down the halls hand in hand, sometimes stopping behind lockers to kiss and fondle each other. They were *Americanos* and belonged in the homerooms in the low numbers.

Another group of girls wore heavy makeup, hitched their skirts above their knees, opened one extra button on their blouses, and teased their hair into enormous bouffants held solid with spray. In the morning, they took over the girls' bathroom, where they dragged on cigarettes as they did their hair until the air was unbreathable, thick with smoke and hair spray. The one time I entered the bathroom before classes they chased me out with insults and rough shoves.

Those bold girls with hair and makeup and short skirts, I soon found out, were Italian. The Italians all sat together on one side of the cafeteria, the blacks on another. The two groups hated each other more than they hated Puerto Ricans. At least once a week there was a fight between an Italian and a *moreno*,* either in the bathroom, in the school yard, or in an abandoned lot near the school, a no-man's-land that divided their neighborhoods and kept them apart on weekends.

The black girls had their own style. Not for them the big, pouffy hair of the Italians. Their hair was straightened, curled at the tips like Miss Brown's, or pulled up into a twist at the back with wispy curls and straw straight bangs over Cleopatra eyes. Their skirts were also short, except it didn't look like they hitched them up when their mothers weren't looking. They came that way. They had strong, shapely legs and wore knee socks with heavy lace-up shoes that became lethal weapons in fights.

It was rumored that the Italians carried knives, even the girls, and that the *morenos* had brass knuckles in their pockets and steel toes in their heavy shoes. I stayed away from both groups, afraid that if I befriended an Italian, I'd get beat up by a *morena*, or vice versa.

There were two kinds of Puerto Ricans in school: the newly arrived, like myself, and the ones born in Brooklyn of Puerto Rican parents. The two types didn't mix. The Brooklyn Puerto Ricans spoke English, and often no Spanish at all. To them, Puerto Rico was the place where their grandparents lived, a place they visited on school and summer vacations, a place which they complained was backward and mosquito-ridden. Those of us for whom Puerto Rico was still a recent memory were also split into two groups: the ones who longed for the island and the ones who wanted to forget it as soon as possible.

I felt disloyal for wanting to learn English, for liking pizza, for studying the girls with big hair and trying out their styles at home, locked in the bathroom where no one could watch. I practiced walking with the peculiar little hop of the *morenas*, but felt as if I were limping.

I didn't feel comfortable with the newly arrived Puerto Ricans who stuck together in suspicious little groups, criticizing everyone, afraid of everything. And I was not accepted by the Brooklyn Puerto Ricans, who held the secret of coolness. They walked the halls between the Italians and the *morenos*, neither one nor the other, but looking and acting like a combination of both, depending on the texture of their hair, the shade of their skin, their makeup, and the way they walked down the hall.

Alex Bushinsky
From Today's Immigrants, Their Stories

THOMAS KESSNER AND BETTY BOYD CAROLI

"I always thought of going to the States. The American Jews I met (mainly at the Moscow Synagogue) impressed me. They were so smart, so businesslike,

---

*moreno: Literally, a brown person. Often used to refer to black people (Spanish) [Eds.].

so warm, educated, polite. I loved them. But in the end I went to Israel. Officially that is the only place to which you can emigrate but it is possible to come to America. Still, I felt if you claim you are Jewish you go to your country, join your own people, speak your own language. I was a moderate Zionist. And America was more distant. It was scary to think of getting a job without perfect English. My parents told me that competition was so high that I would not succeed. We thought of America as a prosperous country, but where a Russian would be a second-class citizen.

"Israel has to be a disappointment. You expect so much. All the happiness you did not have. I got a terrific job in computer programming. But when things began to change in the organization and it seemed that I might lose this job, I started to lose my good feeling for the country. I realized that my good feeling toward Israel was because I was happy in general. I had a good job, good status, a nice environment, and friends. When this was threatened my attitude changed. Later, in the United States, I was once on a plane with a woman from San Diego. I asked her if she liked San Diego. She said she hated it. Why? She started to tell me, 'Well you know I got divorced and. . . .' and I realized that she hated it because that's where she became unhappy.

"I learned about Judaism in Israel. I met a fine, very good man. He was Russian and he managed even in Russia to be religious. He was so righteous. He devoted so much time to teach me from the beginning. Of course this was not for money. Now I had a religion.

"Then I was invited by an American company to the States to try a job with the company. In Russia I was sometimes a technical translator and I came into contact with Americans. I kept up the friendships and now they got me an invitation to try out for a job and the company would pay my expenses for two months. I did not really expect to stay. I did not close the idea that I might stay, but I didn't think I would be so attracted to the States.

"I was delayed for half a year in Israel because of the incredible bureau-cracy there. So I arrived here late. The same day I arrived they told me, 'Listen we waited too long so we cannot give you the job now. It is not available anymore.' They didn't feel sorry. They made $30,000 or $40,000 — when I wrote to them that I made $500 a month, they wrote back you probably mean $500 a week. They felt I had money, that I could get a job just like that.

"I had only $300 with me. I was scared. I spoke to the lawyer for the company. I told him I don't have money. He told me, 'If you want money why don't you just go to work?' I had no choice, I had to go to work. I bought a *New York Times*. I saw an ad with all my skills listed. I went there. It was an agency. The secretary asked for my résumé and in a few minutes an agent came out and said, 'Hi, my name is so and so, I have arranged several inter-views for you already, and I am expecting some more calls.' He gave me a list of nine companies — Irving Trust Company, Chemical Bank, Automated Con-cept, Sperry Univac, Salomon Bros., Royal Globe Insurance, and some others. I got a job. Three days after coming to America I had a job. I was fascinated by working for an American company.

"My first exposure to New York impressed me. It turned out to be clean somehow. Later I learned it's not clean, but when I came it was clean. I expected huge piles of garbage but it wasn't that bad. I liked the tall buildings. They were gleaming from the sun. In the first two days I hated the city. I lost a job. I had no money. Definitely I hated it. I felt insecure, terrible. But in five days when I saw I could get a job just like that, I started to work and half a month later I realized my prospects were much better here than in Israel. Within a month I got a second job teaching a class in data processing at a university.

"This was a new world for me. There were so many things I did not have: language, American education; I was an American immigrant, a Russian, and still I got a job. I decided to remain here (I usually like to stay until things get worse), because of the tremendous opportunities and the freedom.

"I was lucky. The Russians had copied all of the computer software from the States and I knew the necessary languages. Today I have a position as systems analyst. It is very satisfying. I have confidence in my career and I am satisfied with my salary. I have every right that you have except the right to vote and at the moment that does not concern me too much. I feel so comfortable, completely at home. I could not go anywhere after the States.

"I knew I wouldn't get a break in Russia because I was a Jew. It would be hard to get a good job, an apartment. Here, I got a job in a few days. It needed furniture. I got it in a week. Later, I wanted a vacation, so I went for twenty-four days. I took my paycheck and a little money out of the bank and I went across the United States, and saw the nice things. Terrific. It didn't take a year's salary. I appreciate it. I really do. In Russia you make peanuts, usually your parents help support you even after you are married. I was lucky. My father used to be a director of a factory and when I wanted to take a vacation he gave me money. Here I took fourteen different trips by plane. I changed reservations daily. Still I failed to confuse the American airlines. I even got a letter saying because of round-trip fares I am entitled to a $12 refund. In Russia I would not change anything (or I would lose my trip). I would never, never get money back. It could happen that you wait ten years to have a telephone installed in Russia, really, ten years.

"I don't mind all the different types of people and the mixed cultures. The greatest thing in New York is that it is the capital of immigrants. An immigrant feels at home. In the first place he sees a lot of immigrants around. In the second place he realizes Americans have a good stereotype of foreigners, that they are professionals, and that they work hard and that they are smart. They don't care about your English. You are equal. You feel it. A foreigner and still equal.

"This is New York's asset. You can find any society. In my office you have Japanese, Chinese, Greek, Spanish, and Italian. More immigrants than Americans. Tens of different accents. They are all managers and you speak better English than they do. Of course you feel at home.

"There are a few Russian communities in New York, especially in Brighton Beach, Brooklyn. I did not live in that area of mostly Odessa Jews.

I am not married and have no relatives here so I do not have a very strong connection with the Russian community. It's not really a community. People from Moscow, Leningrad, and Odessa do not mix in the States. It's not just a city. It's a type. In Israel there are circles by the year you come. The 1972 circle. The 1973 circle. Psychologically it is easy to understand. In the beginning it is difficult to adjust, to form your credo, your point of view. It is painful to have to go over this stage again with somebody just arriving. It is new for him and he needs to discuss his problems. You have been through it already. It is hard to go through the beginning again. . . .

"People ask if it is difficult to come from a Marxist Communist State and adapt to American capitalism. I would say Russians are more materialist than Americans. Could you believe that? For example, I still cannot understand that people voluntarily go to demonstrate or vote. In Russia we do not do anything voluntarily, we don't believe we can affect the destiny of the country. When you see thousands of people waving flags at Brezhnev at an airport welcoming him, they were transported there by State buses, from work. They were even given the flags. Here and in Washington I marched in some demonstrations for Soviet Jewry and the fact that people keep coming voluntarily amazes me. In Russia you do not do anything voluntarily or they think you are crazy. In this capitalist country you have volunteer work and charity.

"I was amazed that Americans do not work hard except where they are building a career. The office empties at five o'clock. We are paid overtime, a lot of money, and still almost no one works. It looks like they do not need the money. When there was a big snow I was the only one to come to work. Many lived nearby — they could take the subway, the underground subway — like I did. Yet they lived in Manhattan and they did not come. In Russia you come. The weather could be even worse, you still come. Even if you are sick you come in and say you are sick and they send you home.

"There are problems in New York: crime, the race problem, and the weather, but my basic needs are satisfied. When I went to California I found nice clean communities and the climate is just perfect. Life looks much easier. It looks like this. I'm not sure it's exactly like this. I know someone who left New York and went to live there and came back in three months. She said people were too easy going there, not serious enough, and they are very materialistic. After three days in San Francisco I could not stand the idea of New York's dirt, climate, and crowds. But I came back.

"The biggest problem in New York I think is fear of crime. People pay for a 'good' neighborhood. They live in ugly homes, in less attractive areas, and make many other compromises but the area is 'exclusive.' People are afraid and nervous. Perhaps many people do not even experience it, but they cannot escape an awareness of it from television, radio, the newspapers and this keeps them from doing things. There may be more crime here than in Russia (there is plenty of crime and street violence there too) but this shows me a level of freedom and civilization somehow. Really. But yes, it does make me tense. I have to be careful. That is the way New York is.

"It is overcrowded, dirty, and the climate—I hate the climate. It is also very competitive, very tense. The city has a high standard of living. It creates new desires for things you never thought you needed before. It offers museums, theaters, everything.

"I am here now. I feel very far away from Russia. I have a very good job, a good salary. I am Jewish, I know *Yiddishkeit*. I am not afraid that this will keep me back. I am in America, in New York, and it is good, it is good for the important things.

Haroutioun Yeretzian
From The New Americans: Immigrant Life in Southern California

ULLI STELTZER

The main immigration of Armenians into this country took place over 100 years ago, at the time of the massacres.* Most of these immigrants were poor people. They came here to help their families back in Armenia. Their children were unable to fight the American culture, they became assimilated. All they kept was the Armenian church and Armenian food. We call them the shish kebab generation. The election of (George) Deukmejian as governor of California was instrumental in bringing the older Armenians back to their roots. But it is the influx of Armenians from the Middle East during the last ten years that has brought the culture back on a big scale. Now we are publishing in Los Angeles maybe more than twelve newspapers—dailies, weeklies, monthlies—in the Armenian language.

I started out with a monthly magazine when I first came here in 1976. Then I started a small printing shop to print that magazine. During that period of time people kept coming by asking about books. That gave me the idea that there is an interest. This is the first Armenian commercial bookstore in Hollywood. Of course it is more a community service than a business. People don't buy books every day, but they know where to go. They know I am here.

Many Armenian kids can't afford the Armenian private schools. In Hollywood, Pasadena, and Glendale, where most of the Armenian community is living, the public schools have special Armenian instructors teaching the language, history, and culture to the Armenian students. I know that, because all these schools come to buy books from me.

---

*For years, Armenians struggled under Turkish (and Russian) domination, sometimes culminating in violence, as in the 1894–1896 massacre of Armenians under Sultan Abdul. The worst single massacre of Armenians, however, came during deportation by the Turks between 1915 and 1918 [Eds.].

My son goes to an Armenian school. When he comes home from school he immediately turns on the TV. We fight with him every day; learn your Armenian lessons! He studies his English, his math, his social science, everything, but not the Armenian language, because it is very difficult. There is a difference between learning what you want to know, as grown-ups do, and being forced to learn something you did not choose for yourself. How the kids feel, having to make that extra effort, we don't know. But we know how important it is to keep our language, our culture, alive so that one day the Armenian people will be able to go back to their homeland.

9   A Call for the Teaching of Writing in Graduate Education

WITH KAREN McCLAFFERTY

2001

AUTHOR'S NOTE: This final and more recent article was written for an audience concerned with the training of graduate students in education. I include it here for two reasons.

First, it extends the discussion of academic writing to a new institutional domain and thus provides a different context for some of the ideas expressed earlier in this section: The importance of grounding a curriculum and pedagogy in a particular setting. The interpersonal and political work of legitimizing it within a school or department. The mix, the interconnectedness, of the elements of writing sometimes separated out—from grammar and genre to audience, voice, and academic identity. (A question about sentence structure can quickly lead to a discussion of the assumptions behind a student's research design.) And there is the persistence of concerns about "remediation," the ongoing institutional anxiety over the teaching of nonfiction writing, that it violates the academic mission of the college or university. I'll address this theme in "The Language of Exclusion," but one thing I want to note here is the value gained by the way we in the UCLA Graduate School of Education and Information Studies locate and define our writing courses.

There are five divisions within Education (e.g., Psychological Studies, Urban Schooling, etc.), and I am in Social Research Methodology. Our division focuses on social science methodology itself, so we offer both the introductory and advanced courses in statistics, qualitative methods, educational measurement, and program evaluation. When I entered the division in 1995 and gradually began developing our writing course, I was able to position it as a methods course, arguing that writing was as much a social science methodology as was linear regression. I think this really helped to define the course in a certain way, define writing as something more than a "skill" (see "The Language of Exclusion"), and address the concern about remediation. Again, as I've been noting throughout this section, the context of course and curriculum development is as important as any characteristic of the curriculum itself.

Second, the essay may be of use to some writing program administrators if they try to make a case for courses at the graduate level. I remember a period of time in the mid- to late 1980s when UCLA Writing Programs was conducting a few courses for graduate students in the sciences. The courses were well received, but the dean of graduate study objected to them, claiming that (1) such courses were remedial, and (2) the graduate faculty in each department were already responding to the writing needs of their students. I think that "A Call for the Teaching of Writing" addresses both objections.

A coda: Not that long ago, about ten years back, I was applying for a fellowship, and the foundation required a "career history" as part of the application. I wasn't sure what that meant, but I attempted to summarize the professional things I had done up to that point. Before submitting it, I sent it to a friend who was much more senior than I, and who had won one of these awards in the past. He faxed it back covered in ink, noting the clumsy places and slamming the tone. "This should not read like a press release," he grumbled in bold script. I was an accomplished writer, and yet this unfamiliar task taxed my competence. Some of the sentences were ungraceful, and the tone was all wrong.

James Seitz in his *Motives for Metaphor* wonders why we don't appreciate that even apparently elementary literacy practices "are endlessly negotiated and discovered anew" (p. 17). There seems to be a reductive developmental model of writing at work in the academy, at least where students are concerned, a linear model in which basics, once mastered, are assumed to be set in place and built upon, not needing revisiting. The model doesn't account for variation in context, genre, purpose, or audience or for the cognitive demands that new tasks can place on already-learned conventions—as when the unfamiliar demands of the "career history" tangled with my sentence-level syntactic fluency. I see evidence that disconfirms this model every time I teach the course described in the upcoming article or, for that fact, whenever a colleague asks me to read a paper—or when I sit down with some new writing of my own.

INTRODUCTION

Let us begin with a vignette from a class in professional writing that one of us has been teaching for about four years now. It is a graduate-level workshop with 12 students from diverse disciplines. The class has been discussing three pages of a student's literature review, and zeroes in on those times when she offers strings of citations. Another student wonders if she needs all those citations. The instructor suggests the possibility of offering selected important or summative studies, with the use of "for example." The writer then says:

> STUDENT ONE: I have a question. When do you use "e.g." and when do you use "i.e."?

> STUDENT TWO: I think you use "e.g." when you're offering examples and "i.e." when you're re-phrasing something you've just said.

> INSTRUCTOR: That's right. In either case, it's followed by a comma.

> STUDENT FOUR: Ah. Thank you.

From *Educational Researcher* (March 2001): 27–33.

Student Four adds a comma to her paper. Several others take a note.

STUDENT THREE: I noticed that you used the phrase "many researchers" to give credibility to your argument. (To instructor) When do you have to give examples of who those researchers are?

A brief conversation ensues, where five students in the class share their own experiences with and opinions about the question. Finally, the instructor suggests, in this case, to use "e.g." and include several examples. He adds:

INSTRUCTOR: It's my belief that you can have too many citations. Too often, we see an overreliance on citation to establish authority in academic writing, a shopping bag of sources rather than building an argument. It's true that citation is the coin of the realm, but ask yourself what you're trying to achieve with your citations, what's your purpose?

The conversation continues with Student Two referring to her academic advisor, whom we will call Harry:

STUDENT TWO: This is a Harry comment, but you have to ask yourself, if someone is reading this paper, why should they take your word for it? How do they know you've read what you're supposed to read? You have to show that you've read the important background material.

STUDENT ONE: O.K., but I still need help summarizing exactly what's important.

The class then turns back to a paragraph in her paper.

During these not atypical few minutes in the workshop, a student and her colleagues struggle with an issue of summary and citation—which includes a discussion of usage and punctuation. Fairly quickly the discussion turns to broader issues of academic standards and of rhetorical purpose. Then the conversation comes to involve a moment of professional attribution and the consideration of the identity, style, and thinking of a mentor. The conversation moves from microlevel graphical conventions to issues of authority and identity; all are interrelated, and all represent key aspects of the scholarly writing process. What we think is especially important here is that issues like these are being addressed in the students' training in an explicit and sustained way.

Writing is an activity in which all academics engage. It is an activity that consumes a great deal of our time, both in the production of scholarship and in the teaching and mentoring of students. There is a small but growing research literature on writing at the graduate level, most of it dealing with the appropriation of disciplinary discourse conventions by graduate students during their course of study (e.g., Berkenkotter, Huckin, & Ackerman, 1988; Blakeslee, 1997; Prior, 1995). But there is little professional discussion of what we can do to help our students write more effectively.[1] And though some graduate faculty spend a good deal of time working with their students on their writing, there are few proposals to address writing specifically in the graduate curriculum. (One reason for the reluctance might be concerns that such an effort smacks of remediation, an issue we will address shortly.) The irony here is that the quality of scholarly writing is widely bemoaned, both outside and inside the academy (e.g., Limerick, 1993; Rankin, 1998), yet we seem to do little to address the quality of writing in a systematic way at the very point where scholarly style and identity is being shaped. So, in 1996, Mike Rose instituted a course in professional writing housed in the Social Research Methodology Division of our Graduate School of Education & Information Studies.[2] In this article we would like both to describe what gets done in the course—and could be transferable to other institutions—and to reflect on what an explicit focus on writing instruction might provide to a graduate program in education.[3]

Several faculty have taught the course since its creation, and each does it a bit differently, but the essential structure is that of a writing workshop. The primary texts for the course are student writing, and, while there may be one or two initial common assignments, most of the course is spent focusing on the writing students are doing for a range of courses and a range of purposes. The students come from any of the five divisions in our school (Social Sciences & Comparative Education, Social Research Methodology, Psychological Studies in Education, Urban Schooling, and Higher Education & Organizational Change), and, depending on the particular academic quarter, can range from first-year students to those writing their dissertations. Demand for the course has consistently exceeded its capacity. Often, at the discretion of the instructor, extra sections are created to accommodate as many students as possible.

The pedagogical specifics will vary by instructor, but basically during any given class session a certain number of students bring in three to five pages of their writing. The students distribute this work either within small groups or to the workshop at large, read it aloud and give their assessment of it, and then engage in discussion with peers and the instructor about it. Such a structure requires that the instructor create an atmosphere of reading and response that is both rigorous and considerate, calling on all students to respond to their peers' work in thoughtful and useful ways.

Let us note several things about the foregoing description. As is suggested in the opening vignette, the topic of discussion can range widely from issues of mechanics, grammar, and organization, to style and audience, to evidence and argument, to research design, to broad issues of conceptualization, to the very place of one's work and one's scholarly identity in a field. As well, students are working in a variety of genres—from the class paper, to an essay for practitioners, to the dissertation—adding to the richness of the conversation. Additionally, the course provides one of the few places in the curriculum where students from a range of backgrounds get to hear about and respond to each other's work, and provides a wider audience than is usually available within the confines of a course within a division.

Mike Rose has taught the writing seminar eight times. Karen McClafferty is a former student in the course and is now a postdoctoral fellow at UCLA. We thought there would be value in combining our two perspectives and articulating what we believe to be the issues surrounding graduate-level writing instruction, and the benefits of it. To aid in this articulation, Rose reviewed several years' worth of student work, and McClafferty sat in on a new offering of the course, taking notes on both content and interaction. Both of us reviewed tape recordings of class discussions from a previous year. And we benefited from participants' written evaluations and from student comments on an earlier draft of this article. The issues we identified through these activities cluster around six thematic strands: the interrelation of formal and rhetorical elements of writing; writing as craftwork; writing as a method of inquiry; audience; becoming a critic; and writing and identity. We have organized and labeled these themes into distinct categories, but the reader will note significant overlap among them. This complexity is inevitable, and it is reflective of the nature of the course, where students move swiftly among topics of discussion. We will discuss each of these themes in turn, and then discuss problems and questions emerging from the course.

THE INTERRELATION OF GRAMMAR, STYLE, LOGIC, VOICE

As evidenced by the opening vignette, students rely on this course to gain competency in a wide range of topics. The topics play off each other, interconnect. From an attempt to revise an awkward sentence comes a question that reveals confusion over a paper's key concept. A discussion about comma and semicolon usage reveals buggy rules about punctuation and sparks a further discussion about the rhetorical value of varying sentence length. A thorny research design leads to questions about the value of a project, and an attempt to structure a literature review raises questions about how one locates oneself in a field. And a student's desire for more "voice" in her writing takes the class back to sentence length and semicolons, and to the use of vignette, metaphor, and analogy. This wide range of shuttling occurs quite naturally, as students begin to form their identities as scholarly writers. They are not only receptive to the natural connectedness of all of these areas—they seem eager for forums in which to integrate them.

This raises interesting questions about remediation. When we talk about writing instruction, especially at the graduate level, there is often an assumption that we are talking about remedial intervention, that is, a course that is addressing topics that students should have mastered in previous schooling. To be sure, some students enter the course with such problems: Though highly literate by most any common measure, these students have not had the kinds of education that require extended writing about scholarly texts coupled with systematic feedback. Let's consider the kinds of problems we typically see.

Some students are new to their fields and, consequently, to the material they are attempting to synthesize and write about. Similarly, they are often not that familiar with the traditions and conventions of social science writing and/or with organizing and discussing quantitative or qualitative data—and the result can be some pretty awkward prose. Some report that writing has always been hard for them, they've never taken to it, and they face it now with anxiety—and with a variety of linguistic and rhetorical misconceptions. A lot of students are unsure about various mechanical and grammatical rules, and have been told conflicting things over the span of their education. And some students are not native speakers of English and, though literate in two or more languages, display in their writing a range of common ESL errors.

The debate among university faculty about what of the foregoing should or should not be considered remedial has gone on for most of this century. Different faculties at different institutions in different eras have arrived at various positions about it (Rose, 1985). A graduate faculty considering the creation of writing courses would need to have this discussion among themselves. Our faculty did in 1996 as our writing course was being developed, and many faculty members from across departmental divisions participated in the conversation. The topic touched nerves and needs, as faculty expressed exasperation about the quality of student writing ("I'm absolutely burned out") and widely acknowledged the importance and necessity of some sort of systematic writing instruction. The outcome was support for the course—and the overall endeavor of addressing writing directly and comprehensively—because, as one professor put it, "it's part of [students'] ongoing development." "Students [in our division] are required to take three statistics courses," added another, "and writing is no less important for their professional success." "It's an issue of methods training," said a third.

Still, there is the fact that some of what goes on in a writing course like ours is pretty basic stuff—perhaps too basic to have a place in a graduate program. And though we do agree with the opinion expressed by one of the participants in that 1996 meeting—"the students are here, so it's our responsibility"—we think there's a more compelling argument against the label of simple remediation. Basics of grammar or sentence structure or paragraph organization do arise and are treated in the course. Students often begin their own self-critiques with questions about punctuation, grammar, or word choice. But these conversations almost always lead to or occur within the context of a broader issue that is not remedial. To use again the example of semicolon rules, the rules are presented, but are frequently interconnected to rhetorical and stylistic concerns, which quickly can lead to issues of purpose and argument. Seen this way—which reflects the actual dynamics of the workshop—distinctions between what is basic and what is not become harder to make. And students become more aware of the complex interrelation of the elements of written language.

LISTENING TO WRITING, CRAFTING WRITING

It is common to hear poetry read out loud, or fiction, but fairly uncommon to hear scholarly prose. Yet reading one's prose out loud animates what too often is a dry, unengaged production and use of text. You *hear* your writing. And others hear, as well as read, it too. One immediate effect is that reading aloud enables one to catch a number of grammatical errors and instances of stylistic awkwardness or conceptual confusion. It is common for a student to pause while reading and say: "Oh, that doesn't work well at all, does it?" Such moments give rise to talk—from the writer, from others in the class—about how to revise, and this helps everyone become more attuned to and articulate about particulars of grammar and style. One student gave cogent expression to this process:

> I learned quite a bit from . . . talking about problems in the writing of other students. A major problem in someone's work was sometimes a problem of a lesser degree in mine (e.g., needing to add more flesh to numbers in text or writing better topic sentences). Even when a flaw in another's writing was [not one of mine] there were times that thinking about a solution made me more aware of an important stylistic device or writing strategy.

Over time, students begin to see writing as craftwork, rather than as an innate gift or an inaccessible science of grammatical and analytic rules that must be mastered before writing can begin. The participants in these seminars range in skill, experience, and comfort with writing, but what is interesting to us is the number of students who hold counterproductive beliefs about it—beliefs that complicate or mystify the writing process or that attribute skill to unattainable sources. And these beliefs interact with everyone's struggle to appropriate scholarly genres and languages.

This is not the place to discuss attribution theory or to debate the sources of skill in writing, but what we can say is that as students continue to listen to and read writing out loud and talk in specific ways about how to make it better, their sense of agency toward it seems to change. They come to understand that writing is something you can *work on*. In very specific ways, you can move the parts of a sentence around; you can try addressing the reader more directly; you can talk about and try out some of the stylistic things a peer does that appeal to you. We think here of a student who could write the prose of experimental psychology well—could summarize research literature and present results pretty competently—but who felt her writing "was lifeless." During one class meeting, another student's paper intrigued her, and she zeroed in on the way that student used a metaphor in discussing results. The instructor asked her, then, to see if she could create one or two metaphors in the text she was preparing for the next meeting. A specific, manipulable technique—and she could judge what effect it had on her writing. We do not want to claim that 10 weeks in a seminar and a few tricks will make someone a confident and graceful writer. The experience, however, does provide knowledge and tools and a sense that one can do things to one's writing to make it more effective.

Writing as Method

In addition to experiencing writing as a craft, students also have multiple opportunities to understand the ways writing is central to their inquiry. Researchers working within an ethnographic tradition, of course, view writing as methodology, as do historians, who would most likely include in their training a course in historical writing and historiography. But for many other students, writing is thought of as simply a vehicle or a conduit for delivering one's findings (cf. Lanham, 1983, Ch. 5 and Reddy, 1979).

To counter the vehicle analogue, the course instructor talks about the ways writing can help one think through a problem—and provides examples from his or her own and others' writing lives. But, as well, the continued, shared, specific discussion of students' writing processes combined with the course's emphasis on rewriting contributes to a sense that writing is not simply an inert means of representation, but is a vital element of inquiry. There is the intimate connection of writing and conceptualizing. There is the use of writing to test an idea—an instructor might tell a student who is tentatively suggesting an idea "to go down that road, to write it out, and see where it takes you." There is the way writing makes thought visible—and thus open to examination for coherence, for flaws in logic, for worth and value. ("Writing fixes thought on paper," observes phenomenologist Max van Manen, 1990, p. 125.) There is the rich potential interplay of different semiotic systems (words, numbers, graphics), and course participants come to see that numbers need to tell a story, that even a list reveals a rhetoric, that a series of sentences can have a tight propositional logic to them. Writing becomes a means to articulate thought and test it. All this, of course, can go on in any class and in any encounter between a faculty member and a student over a piece of writing. But it is sustained and made explicit in a course that focuses on writing.

AUDIENCE AWARENESS

As students immerse themselves in scholarly literature, trying both to understand and use it and to acquire its conventions in their own work, complex issues of audience arise. To whom are they writing? To a professor or a committee, of course, but only to them? Students are socialized to believe they're writing for a scholarly community, but that's usually a heterogeneous group and, to boot, a pretty inchoate notion—and a hard audience to write for when one is working overtime to acquire the linguistic and rhetorical conventions of that community. "It paralyzes me," observed one of the students. (There is the further problem that the quality of scholarly writing itself varies widely.) And what if one also wants to be able to write about one's work for broader audiences, for teachers or policymakers or the public at large?

By presenting their work to each other on a regular basis, students are faced with an audience that sits across the table, ready to respond, question, and advise immediately. Students will occasionally pause as they read their writing aloud, noting that, as they revised the document, they had a particular classmate in mind. A student might say, "I knew Dave was going to ask me what my big point was here, so I tried to say it right up front." In the end, the physical presence of an audience plays out in two ways. First, students read their writing directly to their audience and receive immediate feedback.

Second, students may recall or imagine interactions with their peers as they compose—whether for this course or for other purposes—a practice that seems to encourage them to explain, define, and be more precise.

Adding to the strength of the audience presence is the fact that the group is not only composed of students at a variety of levels, but it is also interdisciplinary. By bringing together students from diverse disciplines, the course allows for more dynamic discussions about students' work. Students do not necessarily arrive with the same background knowledge or accompanying assumptions. As a result, conversations often revolve around clarification of concepts that may seem basic or straightforward to the writer but are new and complicated to the readers. The result is that the writer is compelled to communicate his or her ideas more clearly and with less jargon, and this can lead to some very specific and useful rhetorical tricks of the trade: learning to present a technical term followed by a precise definition or quick example, elaborating on tables and charts in the body of the text, creating apt illustrative metaphors or analogies, and so on. Finally, a student learns how to make scholarly writing accessible to a wider audience, while honoring the conventions of his or her discipline. Thinking back over the offerings of the course and our investigation of it, we suspect that the course's most significant benefit is the fostering of a rhetorical sense, that writing acts on a reader and that—recalling craft work—the writer can influence that response. As one student put it: "The course got me to think of my writing as strategic. Who am I writing to? Where do I want to take them with my argument? How can I get them there?"

BECOMING A BETTER READER OF OTHER PEOPLE'S WRITING

If the dynamics work right, the writing workshop becomes a small community maintained by students' face-to-face responses to each other's writing. This encourages both a seriousness as well as a certain consideration of one's peers. In a sense, a writing workshop might strive toward becoming a microcosm of the ideal scholarly community, where colleagues thoughtfully respond to each other's work, and there is a press toward greater articulation and understanding. We saw elements of this intellectual camaraderie throughout the course.

Just as students gain confidence in their ability to talk about writing, they also become more certain of their skills in reading and commenting on each other's work. They become co-instructors—guiding, prodding, pushing, and encouraging each other to write more effectively and more authoritatively. And they progressively are able to integrate grammatical nuts-and-bolts conversations (which are necessary and important in their own right) with broader issues of voice, method, and conceptualization. Considering that many will go on to teach—at the college and university level or elsewhere—this effect of the writing course has further benefit. If these students carry their sensibilities and editing skills over into their own instruction, it will enhance their effectiveness as teachers. Similarly, once these students graduate, they will be called upon to read colleagues' writing, whether as friends, as reviewers, or as members of editorial boards. Improved skills as readers enable them to carry out these tasks with greater efficiency and effectiveness.

There are, of course, many ways to go about creating a scholarly atmosphere that is conducive to good, thoughtful work on writing, and every instructor will have his or her own inclination as to how to achieve this goal. Though there will be variation, we can suggest several qualities—based on Karen McClafferty's observations and queries to students—that course participants see as important in fostering this atmosphere. The instructor, of course, must be knowledgeable about scholarly conventions and writing and model precise and humane response, but also be willing to have authority distributed across the workshop, be able to move to the periphery of discussion, attending to it while encouraging student exchange. (If the workshop is composed of students from across divisions, this move to the periphery will occur naturally, for some of the participants will know more about a given topic than will the instructor.) Students need the discursive space to jointly make sense of a piece of writing and assist in improving it. The instructor should also have an interest in, be curious about, the way scholarly conventions and writing skill are acquired, be able to assess the effectiveness of a piece of student writing but be able as well to shift to a developmental perspective, viewing that piece of writing in terms of a student's (as yet partial) socialization into a discipline. (We'll say more about this issue when we discuss grades under "Problems and Questions.") Put another way, the instructor needs to consider the cognitive and interpersonal dynamics necessary to create a scholarly atmosphere that is specific, systematic, and rigorous while being attentive to the intellectual intentions of the student author—and considerate of how difficult the task of writing is and how much of one's sense of self can be invested in it. Isn't this, in fact, the web of concern that should be at the heart of any attempt to create a scholarly community?

THE WRITING PROCESS AS A PROCESS OF SCHOLARLY IDENTITY FORMATION

All of the strands discussed so far tie to this final one: the creation of a scholarly identity. Writing is one of the primary sites where scholarly identity is formed and displayed. Whether through papers written for coursework, for conferences or journals, or simply correspondence, scholars often form their impressions of their colleagues based on the written word. This may be even more the case as greater proportions of interactions take place across e-mail. Graduate students are part of all this as they begin to form their own scholarly identities through their choices about what they research, whose work they cite, and how they communicate their own ideas. The opportunity to reflect on their writing is additionally (and importantly) an opportunity to reflect on themselves.

The course plays an important role in this process, assisting students as they establish and refine their own relationships to their work. Some students come to the course seeking a greater connection with their research and writing. Many have been taught (or have simply assumed) that scholarly writing requires a distance, even disassociation, that absents the author. For other students, academic work is so intimately connected with issues of personal history and identity that a greater amount of distance is necessary if the work is to have broader implications. For each of these kinds of students, the course can provide the opportunity to find an integration of authorial presence and scholarly convention.

We are taken by this coupling of writing and identity—by how many of the issues raised in the course, exchanges, and engagements with revision of text could be understood in terms of identity development. We find moments when, implied or explicit, questions like these emerge: What kind of work do I want to do; what issues and problems compel me? What methods seem most effective and appropriate, and which methods suit my own beliefs and dispositions? How do I locate myself in this field I've chosen—where, to pick specific examples, is my presence felt in a literature review or in a detailing of method? How can I sound even a little distinctive? How can I get some style into my writing, a "voice"?

How do these questions emerge in the context of a writing workshop? Often, they follow directly from conversations about what styles, formats, and methods of writing are acceptable in the academic world, and what approaches must be transformed, or abandoned altogether. Through these conversations, students come to realize the ways in which their writing ties the personal beliefs they hold about the work they do and the people or phenomena they study to the public ways in which they present these beliefs to others. As they increasingly see the written word as their primary method of communication—and as a medium over which they can have mastery and control—they become more expert at questioning and understanding just what it is they want to communicate. In short, they more consciously shape their own scholarly identities, construct meaningful relations to their disciplines.

PROBLEMS AND QUESTIONS

There are problems with our course—limitations and design flaws. Let us now discuss six of them and offer our partial solutions.

First, though there is clear value in writing for a diverse audience—and such an audience, as we suggest, can provide helpful feedback—scholarly writing is grounded in domain knowledge. Thus there will be times in the discussion of a student's work when an expert's knowledge is required. (An example would be the methods section of a quantitative paper, where the technical detail of an advanced statistical procedure is explained.) Though a non-expert audience can be helpful in providing a test for clarity of expression, that audience would be of limited help in the specifics of how expression could be clarified and still maintain technical accuracy. The heterogeneous composition of the course often yields two or more students from the same division, and thus with at least generally related training. So the instructor orchestrates response and/or forms sub-groups in ways that utilize this shared training.

Second, there is, as one would expect, a diversity of audiences and expectations within the faculty of our Department of Education, and that variation plays out in the writing course. The instructor needs to be mindful of this diversity. It is not uncommon, then, for the instructor to contact a student's advisor—with the student's permission—to clarify the advisor's expectations and/or to check the advice the student is getting in class. (This can have a valuable secondary effect in that issues of writing are explicitly discussed among the faculty.) It is also valuable to turn this diversity of expectation itself into a topic of class discussion with invited faculty and/or among the class participants. This foregrounds the issue of audience and lays it open for analysis.

Third, the focus on three to five pages of writing works against a consideration of the overall structure of a paper, and problems at that level are commonplace in graduate education. This limitation is somewhat circumvented when a student works on the same project—a proposal, a thesis chapter—throughout the course. Thus we encourage extended work on one or two projects, though, typically, about a quarter of the class participants are not working on such projects when they take the course.

Fourth, an academic quarter goes by quickly—a semester is somewhat better—and improving one's writing is not a quick-fix enterprise. Students' writing skill, understanding of the process, and rhetorical savvy does change over the quarter, along the lines discussed above, but in some respects the course is just a beginning. The course can be taken more than once, and a few students do—for example, in their first or second year and then again when writing a proposal or a thesis. And the instructor encourages students to form writing groups once the course is over—and some do.

This point leads to a further, important issue: the possibility that the regular offering of a course in professional writing can generate a heightened attention to writing beyond the boundaries of the course itself. Whether or not this happens, of course, would depend on a number of contextual factors. It seems that at UCLA the course over time has had a catalyzing effect. We've instituted a further course, a special topics course in writing and rhetoric, and through it have offered seminars in advanced ethnographic writing, new rhetorical theory, and the writing of the OpEd piece. We are also experimenting with writing tutorials for non-native speakers of English. Some students are taking the initiative and forming writing groups themselves. Students have always formed informal study groups around exams and support groups for dissertations, but we are seeing an emphasis within those groups on writing, and the formation of groups with an explicit focus on writing. And, finally, some faculty seem to be talking frequently and forcefully about writing and are expressing interest in addressing it more effectively. Several divisions are increasing the attention paid to writing in their newly revised core courses or research practica. Faculty are requesting workshops on responding to student writing, and we are beginning to organize gatherings where we discuss both student and faculty writing together.[4]

One of the reviewers of this article raised the fifth question: Who would teach the course? "There are too many demands already on faculty, and there are actually very few faculty who would be good at teaching such a course." While discussing the creation of a scholarly community, we offered some thoughts on the qualities that might make someone a good fit to teach the course. Let us now think through the politics of getting people to teach it. One reason to convene the aforementioned schoolwide meeting of the faculty is to collectively discuss the issues of teaching load and resource allocation— thus the chair or dean should be present. The course does come with a price tag, and at UCLA we initially had to piece together resources to pull it off, and then subject it to further faculty review. So some on-the-ground work, public discussion, and course development and review might be needed. This combination generated at UCLA advocacy from a number of quarters— necessary to give the effort some roots and staying power.

Finding appropriate instructors is a concern, but it is possible that there will be some faculty who have a professional interest in developing and teaching a graduate-level writing course. Writing instruction is too often thought of as a simply technical enterprise and as a service, but, as we hope we've shown, it can be intellectually engaging—rich rhetorically, theoretically, methodologically—and it could easily intersect with research interests in a number of ed school domains: from language and literacy, to the sociology of knowledge, to professional development. Finding such connection will also contribute to the stability of the course, grounding it in the school's intellectual culture.

Sixth: grading. Another reviewer raises "the thorny issue of grading developing writing." "What are the students' perspectives on being graded," the reviewer asks, "while simultaneously being asked to take risks with their writing?" Grading *is* a thorny issue. We would be disingenuous to not acknowledge the tensions among institutional requirements, professional standards, and developing writing. One solution, of course, would be to offer the course *pass/no pass*. If letter grades are given, the instructor has several options that could honor the nature of the course. Grading could be phased in, with qualitative assessments recorded for earlier assignments and letter grades for later pieces, as proficiency improves. Another approach would be to develop evaluation criteria that reward the multiple elements that comprise effective writing and editing: the quality of response to others' writing, the incorporation of feedback, the attempts at experimentation, the linguistic sophistication of one's prose—with attention to patterns of development, and so on. One could grade by portfolio, whereby students select the pieces they think display various competencies and write further commentary on them—thus aligning assessment with the development of rhetorical self-awareness. (It strikes us that this issue of grading performance in a graduate writing workshop could be a terrific topic of discussion for a school's language and literacy, evaluation, and measurement faculties.) One thing that was clear in students' responses to grading was that they appreciated a multidimensional approach to assessment—that each piece of writing wasn't treated as a final product for summative assessment, and that risk and possible blunder would be appreciated and accounted for . . . which takes us back, again, to the issues raised in the discussion of the creation of a scholarly community.

In closing, let us offer a thought that is not directly related to writing but, we think, emerges from a sustained consideration of it. A focus on writing provides a place in the curriculum where students can slow down a bit, reflect on what they're doing and why, and think about the language they're using to represent it. For example, students will sometimes bring to class a piece of writing that was presented to a research group or seminar, and use the class as a vehicle to unpack and think through the group's reaction. In the midst of all the pressures to become part of and publish within a discipline, students are able to stop and think, to try new things, even to be playful in their thinking and writing. The writing workshop is a formal course, and students receive a grade at its end, so we wouldn't want to claim that participants see it as a free zone. But because it's outside of their discipline, because in most cases their advisor isn't present, and because everyone in a sense feels they're in the same boat—struggling to make their writing better— because of all these factors, the workshop does seem to have an unusual place in the course of study. The academic profession, like so many other kinds of work and ways of living, has speeded up and intensified (Cassuto, 1998; Hampel, 1995). This pace can yield heightened productivity, but it brings with it a rush to closure that can work against reflection and experimentation. Writing, really thinking about writing and practicing its craft, demands a slowing down, a deliberation, and students need—we all need—a place in our professional lives for that.[5]

NOTES

[1]There are exceptions. A notable one is the effort of Howard Becker, leading to his 1986 book *Writing for Social Scientists*.

[2]There were precedents. Professor Sol Cohen taught a seminar in scholarly writing and Professors James Catterall and Amy Stuart Wells taught several non-credit workshops to prepare students in their division for qualifying examinations. These folks provided helpful guidance as the new writing course was being developed.

[3]Some would argue that the ability to write scholarly prose is best acquired and refined through immersion in scholarly practice, in apprenticeship situations, via extended experience in research projects with a mentor. Explicit focus on scholarly writing in a separate course might undercut such processes and, as well, constrain a student's own discovery and creative impulses (cf. Hunt, 1989). We would surely not dispute the value of the apprenticeship and the acquisition processes operating therein, but there is both research evidence (e.g., Blakeslee, 1997; Casanave, 1995) as well as the testaments of our students that explicit—at times even quite direct— instruction in writing, particularly with unfamiliar genres, is helpful.

[4]We believe that discussing writing produced by students and by faculty within the same workshop can help faculty consider student writing from a different perspective—find parallels and correspondences—and, as well, can generate a broader understanding of their own composing.

[5]We want to acknowledge course participants Dan Battey, Shiva Golshani, Jolena James, Terri Patchen, David Silver, and Ash Vasudeva for their very helpful feedback on an earlier version of this paper, and want to acknowledge, as well, Professor Diane Durkin, who has taught the course, and Professors William Sandoval and Michael Seltzer for helping us think through the interplay of writing and method. We also want to thank the three anonymous *Educational Researcher* referees; their thoughtful reviews began the exchange we would like the article to foster.

REFERENCES

Becker, H. S. (1986). *Writing for social scientists: How to start and finish your thesis, book, or article.* Chicago: University of Chicago Press.

Berkenkotter, C., Huckin, T. N., & Ackerman, J. (1988). Conventions, conversations, and the writer: Case study of a student in a rhetoric Ph.D. program. *Research in the Teaching of English, 22*(1), 9–44.

Blakeslee, A. M. (1997). Activity, context, interaction, and authority: Learning to write scientific papers in situ. *Journal of Business and Technical Communication, 11*(2), 125–169.

Casanave, C. P. (1995). Local interactions: Constructing contexts for composing in a graduate sociology program. In D. Belcher & G. Braine (Eds.), *Academic writing in a second language: Essays on research and pedagogy* (pp. 83–110). Norwood, NJ: Ablex.

Cassuto, L. (1998, November 27). Pressures to publish fuel the professionalization of today's graduate students. *The Chronicle of Higher Education*, p. B4.

Hampel, R. L. (1995). Overextended. *Educational Researcher, 24*(3), 29–30, 38.

Hunt, R. A. (1989). A horse named Hans, a boy named Shawn: The Herr von Osten theory of response to writing. In C. M. Anson (Ed.), *Writing and response: Theory, practice, and research* (pp. 80–100). Urbana, IL: NCTE.

Lanham, R. A. (1983). *Literacy and the survival of humanism.* New Haven: Yale University Press.

Limerick, P. N. (1993, October 31). Dancing with professors: The trouble with academic prose. *The New York Times Book Review*, pp. 3, 23–24.

Prior, P. (1995). Tracing authoritative and internally persuasive discourses: A case study of response, revision, and disciplinary enculturation. *Research in the Teaching of English, 29*(3), 288–325.

Rankin, E. (1998, April 3). Changing the hollow conventions of academic writing. *The Chronicle of Higher Education*, p. A64.

Reddy, M. (1979). The conduit metaphor—A case of frame conflict in our language about language. In A. Ortony (Ed.), *Metaphor and thought* (pp. 284–324). Cambridge: Cambridge University Press.

Rose, M. (1985). The language of exclusion: Writing instruction at the university. *College English, 47*(4), 341–359.

van Manen, M. (1990). *Researching lived experience: Human science for an action sensitive pedagogy.* Albany: SUNY Press.

PART THREE

Integrating the Cognitive and the Social: Critical Perspectives on Writing Instruction, 1985–1991

Introduction to Part Three

This was a rich period for me, filled with wide reading and engaging writing projects. I wrote *Lives on the Boundary*, a book on the underprepared student that led me to experiment with style and form. I taught for a semester at Carnegie Mellon, and I spent a good deal of time at the University of Pittsburgh, which was close by, benefiting immensely from both schools' faculty and graduate students. I also hooked up with Glynda Hull, who had completed her dissertation at Pitt and, by the end of the eighties, was teaching at Berkeley. Looking back on it all, I can't believe how much I learned, thanks to the places I found myself in and the people I met—a reminder of how profoundly environment and resources affect achievement.

I include two articles from the collaboration with Glynda, and I will say more about each and about the collaboration when we get to them. And in the next section, I'll address *Lives on the Boundary*. But here I'd like to discuss one of the courses I taught at Carnegie Mellon, for it ended up being such a significant experience.

There was no specialization in writing, rhetoric, or literacy at UCLA— neither in English nor in the ed school—and the positions I held there were administrative. What teaching I was able to do came through the tutorial center or as an adjunct lecturer in the English Department. So I taught freshman composition, introductions to literature and to the American novel, and creative writing. I really enjoyed the teaching—it frankly kept me going through the sometimes disheartening administrative work—but none of it directly incorporated the topics and material I was covering in my scholarly writing. The visit to CMU—which had by then developed an important program in writing and rhetoric—required me to think about all this research material as a teacher. How could I pull it together as a course? What were the organizing themes in it? Could I present it in a way that engages people? As often happens when we have to teach a new course, the needs of instruction led to purposeful thinking about a wide sweep of reading.

The result was a course I called "Literacy, Cognition, and the Teaching of Writing." Here's the opening paragraph of the syllabus:

> Our research and our teaching are built on assumptions about literacy and cognition, and the purpose of this seminar is to consider,

from multiple perspectives, some of the assumptions that currently seem most prevalent in our professional literature.

I broke the course into five overlapping sections: overview and current issues, historical perspectives, cognition and literacy, sociopolitics and literacy, and developmental perspectives (i.e., children's literacy). The students and I read a lot together: from Harvey Graff's "Reflections on the History of Literacy" and M. T. Clanchy's *From Memory to Written Record: England 1066–1307*; to Scribner and Cole and Shirley Brice Health; to Robert Connors, Flower and Hayes, and Paolo Friere.[1] One of the features I liked about the course was the use of a pair of readings to open each of the five sections:

> My hope is that the coupling will make a few sparks fly, not set a rigid agenda for the section following the pair, but generate stimulating issues that have direct bearing on the teaching and researching of writing in our time.

So, for example, we began the course by pairing the 1975 *Newsweek* article "Why Johnny Can't Write" (influential in the 1970s and 1980s national discourse about a literacy crisis) with John Szwed's "The Ethnography of Literacy." Szwed's essay provides one of the earlier (1981) discussions of literacy as a social practice and calls for close observation of the ways people actually use literacy in everyday settings. Another pairing matched E. D. Hirsch's "Cultural Literacy" with David K. Cohen's "Loss as a Theme in Social Policy." Cohen's essay argues for the role that an evocation of a sense of loss, often coupled with a golden age mythology, plays in the crafting of social policy, and I thought it might be illuminating to consider Hirsch's proposal through the lense Cohen provides.

These are not point-counterpoint pairings; the pieces have no direct relation to each other. But one could provide a perspective or a frame onto the other that, I hoped, would be generative, would help us think about a pedagogical or policy issue in a new way.

Looking at the syllabus after all these years, it's clear how important it was becoming to me to try to create the conditions for people to see things differently, to create the conditions for reflection. You could say it was my interest in cognition manifesting itself in another form. Thinking back on it, there were traces of this interest in my teaching with the veterans and then in the tutorial center. One early writing assignment—that would eventually make its way into *Critical Strategies*—had the students in the Veterans Program comparing an aboriginal creation myth with a passage on the "big bang" from an astronomy textbook. What happens when you place them side by side? What might you come to understand about science, about myth, and about the human desire to make meaning? These kinds of pedagogical concerns would play out in the CMU course and, later, in the various editions of *Critical Strategies*. And they would lie behind the experimentation with form in *Lives on the Boundary*.

Teaching all this material on literacy and cognition—crafting a curriculum from it—would also lead to a collaboration with Eugene Kintgen and

Barry Kroll (Gene was at the same time teaching a course on literacy at Indiana) to produce an anthology *Perspectives on Literacy* (SIU Press, 1988). (Ten years later, Ellen Cushman joined us to begin a new volume, *Literacy: A Critical Sourcebook.*) The collaboration helped me to further broaden my knowledge of the research on literacy and to get a better sense of the major questions in the field and of the scope and sweep of the disciplines involved. This knowledge would be immensely helpful as I worked, during the last year of the writing, on certain key sections of *Lives on the Boundary*, those where I try to frame the book's personal and classroom vignettes within a larger argument about language, literacy, and underpreparation.

Reading again the articles in this section, I see overarching themes, present in the earlier work, but more developed or extended here:

- A concern with research methodology
- An attempt to fuse the cognitive and the social perspectives
- An interest in institutional and professional language and the way it shapes practice
- Exploration of the ways that belief and practice—at the individual, classroom, or institutional level—open up or close down the opportunity to learn

NOTE

[1]Graff (1981); Clanchy (1979); Scribner and Cole (1981); Heath (1983); Connors (1986); Flower and Hayes (1984); Friere (1970).

10   *The Language of Exclusion: Writing Instruction at the University*

1985

AUTHOR'S NOTE: I still like this article a lot, for it marked a turn to historical study and, through history, to a more pointed analysis of the institutional language that informs the teaching of writing. To repeat a point I made in the Introduction, administering a program—even the mundane aspects of it— can give rise to opportunities to write about broader rhetorical, cultural, or political issues. The resistance we met from faculty and the things they would say about student writing had a pattern to it, common themes, and I wanted to explore them in print.

Over the few years that preceded "The Language of Exclusion," I had been working with Richard Lanham, a scholar of Renaissance stylistics and rhetorical theory who directed UCLA Writing Programs, and he tended to take a long view of disciplines and institutions. And I had recently edited David Bartholomae's "Inventing the University," so I can't help but wonder if that essay's focus on discourse influenced me as well. When I was a graduate student in English, I had done both historical research and close analysis of texts, but now I began to appreciate how such methods could apply to the study of institutions.

I threw myself into the history of the American college and university, of the postsecondary curriculum, and of English as a school subject. I kept a little, cloth-covered notebook during this time, and, rereading it, I see myself trying to make sense of this history, trying to bring it into a coherent argument with the day-to-day events of running a writing program.

The notebook presents a mix of entries: notes on meetings of the academic senate, where, for example, faculty argue for the removal of half-credit from a remedial course or express displeasure and some shock at a proposal for a second quarter of freshman composition. There are also clippings from the *Los Angeles Times* or *The Chronicle of Higher Education*. "Law Ends Remedial Courses at 8 Florida Universities," one reads. "If students need those kinds of courses," said a Florida legislator, "they shouldn't have to get them at the University level." There are also notes of informal talk on campus. At a retirement party for the fellow who had supervised UCLA's remedial writing course for years, the host, a senior professor of English, toasted him as a stalwart soldier "who has read more bad prose than anybody." All of this is interspersed among passages from books like Frederick Rudolph's *Curriculum: A History of the American Undergraduate Course of Study Since 1636*, or Arthur Applebee's

Writing in the Secondary School, or Laurence Veysey's *The Emergence of the American University*. Such reading was invaluable—I can't recommend it highly enough—in helping me to understand, to frame in a bigger picture, the ordinary, often irritating, talk and practice that surrounds a writing program.

I think that something I wrote in the prefaratory note to "Remedial Writing Courses" applies here as well. Though "The Language of Exclusion" is dated in its particulars, the issues that it raises, sad to say, are very much with us today.

One last thing: a word on the upcoming discussion of "skill," of the defining of writing as a skill (versus, say, a discipline) and the problems that definition creates for it in a university context. I think my point still holds, though I would probably address the issue a bit differently today, given the further research I've done on "skill" for *The Mind at Work*. One of the things I try to do in the book is explore the Western cultural assumptions that lead us to define a skill in opposition to a conceptual pursuit, to oppose hand to brain. As I worked on the book, my appreciation for the richness and complexity of "skill" increased. I'll say more about *The Mind at Work* in Part Five.

"How many '*minor* errors' are acceptable?"

"We must try to isolate and define those *further* skills in composition . . ."

". . . we should provide a short remedial course to patch up any deficiencies."

"Perhaps the most striking feature of this campus' siege against illiteracy . . ."

"One might hope that, after a number of years, standards might be set in the high schools which would allow us to abandon our own defensive program."

These snippets come from University of California and California state legislative memos, reports, and position papers and from documents produced during a recent debate in UCLA's Academic Senate over whether a course in our freshman writing sequence was remedial. Though these quotations—and a half dozen others I will use in this essay—are local, they represent a kind of institutional language about writing instruction in American higher education. There are five ideas about writing implicit in these comments: Writing ability is judged in terms of the presence of error and can thus be quantified. Writing is a skill or a tool rather than a discipline. A number of our students lack this skill and must be remediated. In fact, some percentage of our students are, for all intents and purposes, illiterate. Our remedial efforts, while currently necessary, can be phased out once the literacy crisis is solved in other segments of the educational system.

From *College English* 47.4 (April 1985): 341–59.

This kind of thinking and talking is so common that we often fail to notice that it reveals a reductive, fundamentally behaviorist model of the development and use of written language, a problematic definition of writing, and an inaccurate assessment of student ability and need. This way of talking about writing abilities and instruction is woven throughout discussions of program and curriculum development, course credit, instructional evaluation, and resource allocation. And, in various ways, it keeps writing instruction at the periphery of the curriculum.

It is certainly true that many faculty and administrators would take issue with one or more of the above notions. And those of us in writing would bring current thinking in rhetoric and composition studies into the conversation. (Though we often—perhaps uncomfortably—rely on terms like "skill" and "remediation.") Sometimes we successfully challenge this language or set up sensible programs in spite of it. But all too often we can do neither. The language represented in the headnotes of this essay reveals deeply held beliefs. It has a tradition and a style, and it plays off the fundamental tension between the general education and the research missions of the American university. The more I think about this language and recall the contexts in which I've heard it used, the more I realize how caught up we all are in a political-semantic web that restricts the way we think about the place of writing in the academy. The opinions I have been describing are certainly not the only ones to be heard. But they are strong. Influential. Rhetorically effective. And profoundly exclusionary. Until we seriously rethink it, we will misrepresent the nature of writing, misjudge our students' problems, and miss any chance to effect a true curricular change that will situate writing firmly in the undergraduate curriculum.

Let us consider the college writing course for a moment. Freshman composition originated in 1874 as a Harvard response to the poor writing of *up*-*per*classmen, spread rapidly, and became and remained the most consistently required course in the American curriculum. Upper division writing courses have a briefer and much less expansive history, but they are currently receiving a good deal of institutional energy and support. It would be hard to think of an ability more desired than the ability to write. Yet, though writing courses are highly valued, even enjoying a boom, they are also viewed with curious eyes. Administrators fund them—often generously—but academic senates worry that the boundaries between high school and college are eroding, and worry as well that the considerable investment of resources in such courses will drain money from the research enterprise. They deny some of the courses curricular status by tagging them remedial, and their members secretly or not-so-secretly wish the courses could be moved to community colleges. Scientists and social scientists underscore the importance of effective writing, yet find it difficult—if not impossible—to restructure their own courses of study to encourage and support writing. More than a few humanists express such difficulty as well. English departments hold onto writing courses but consider the work intellectually second-class. The people who teach writing are more often than not temporary hires; their courses are robbed of curricular continuity and of the status that comes with tenured faculty involvement. And the instructors? Well, they're just robbed.

The writing course holds a very strange position in the American curriculum. It is within this setting that composition specialists must debate and defend and interminably evaluate what they do. And how untenable such activity becomes if the very terms of the defense undercut both the nature of writing and the teaching of writing, and exclude it in various metaphorical ways from the curriculum. We end up arguing with words that sabotage our argument. The first step in resolving such a mess is to consider the language institutions use when they discuss writing. What I want to do in this essay is to look at each of the five notions presented earlier, examine briefly the conditions that shaped their use, and speculate on how it is that they misrepresent and exclude. I will conclude by entertaining a less reductive and exclusionary way to think — and talk — about writing in the academy.

BEHAVIORISM, QUANTIFICATION, AND WRITING

A great deal of current work in fields as diverse as rhetoric, composition studies, psycholinguistics, and cognitive development has underscored the importance of engaging young writers in rich, natural language use. And the movements of the last four decades that have most influenced the teaching of writing — life adjustment, liberal studies, and writing as process — have each, in their very different ways, placed writing pedagogy in the context of broad concerns: personal development and adjustment, a rhetorical-literary tradition, the psychology of composing. It is somewhat curious, then, that a behaviorist approach to writing, one that took its fullest shape in the 1930s and has been variously and severely challenged by the movements that followed it, remains with us as vigorously as it does. It is atomistic, focusing on isolated bits of discourse, error centered, and linguistically reductive. It has a style and a series of techniques that influence pedagogy, assessment, and evaluation. We currently see its influence in workbooks, programmed instruction, and many formulations of behavioral objectives, and it gets most of its airplay in remedial courses. It has staying power. Perhaps we can better understand its resilience if we briefly survey the history that gives it its current shape.

When turn-of-the-century educational psychologists like E. L. Thorndike began to study the teaching of writing, they found a Latin and Greek-influenced school grammar that was primarily a set of prescriptions for conducting socially acceptable discourse, a list of the arcane do's and don'ts of usage for the ever-increasing numbers of children — many from lower classes and immigrant groups — entering the educational system. Thorndike and his colleagues also found reports like those issuing from the Harvard faculty in the 1890s which called attention to the presence of errors in handwriting, spelling, and grammar in the writing of the university's entering freshmen. The twentieth-century writing curriculum, then, was focused on the particulars of usage, grammar, and mechanics. Correctness became, in James Berlin's words, the era's "most significant measure of accomplished prose" (*Writing Instruction in Nineteenth-Century American Colleges* [Carbondale: Southern Illinois University Press, 1984], p. 73).

Such particulars suited educational psychology's model of language quite well: a mechanistic paradigm that studied language by reducing it to discrete behaviors and that defined language growth as the accretion of these particulars. The stress, of course, was on quantification and measurement. ("Whatever exists at all exists in some amount," proclaimed Thorndike.)[1] The focus on error—which is eminently measurable—found justification in a model of mind that was ascending in American academic psychology. Educators embraced the late Victorian faith in science.

Thorndike and company would champion individualized instruction and insist on language practice rather than the rote memorization of rules of grammar that characterized nineteenth-century pedagogy. But they conducted their work within a model of language that was tremendously limited, and this model was further supported and advanced by what Raymond Callahan has called "the cult of efficiency," a strong push to apply to education the principles of industrial scientific management (*Education and the Cult of Efficiency* [Chicago: University of Chicago Press, 1962]). Educational gains were defined as products, and the output of products could be measured. Pedagogical effectiveness—which meant cost-effectiveness—could be determined with "scientific" accuracy. This was the era of the educational efficiency expert. (NCTE even had a Committee on Economy of Time in English.) The combination of positivism, efficiency, and skittishness about correct grammar would have a profound influence on pedagogy and research.

This was the time when workbooks and "practice pads" first became big business. Their success could at least partly be attributed to the fact that they were supported by scientific reasoning. Educational psychologists had demonstrated that simply memorizing rules of grammar and usage had no discernible effect on the quality of student writing. What was needed was application of those rules through practice provided by drills and exercises. The theoretical underpinning was expressed in terms of "habit formation" and "habit strength," the behaviorist equivalent of learning—the resilience of an "acquired response" being dependent on the power and number of reinforcements. The logic was neat: specify a desired linguistic behavior as precisely as possible (e.g., the proper use of the pronouns "he" and "him") and construct opportunities to practice it. The more practice, the more the linguistic habit will take hold. Textbooks as well as workbooks shared this penchant for precision. One textbook for teachers presented a unit on the colon.[2] A text for students devoted seven pages to the use of a capital letter to indicate a proper noun.[3] This was also the time when objective tests—which had been around since 1890—enjoyed a sudden rebirth as "new type" tests. And they, of course, were precision incarnate. The tests generated great enthusiasm among educators who saw in them a scientific means accurately and fairly to assess student achievement in language arts as well as in social studies and mathematics. Ellwood Cubberley, the dean of the School of Education at Stanford, called the development of these "new type" tests "one of the most significant movements in all our educational history."[4] Cubberley and his colleagues felt they were on the threshold of a new era.

Research too focused on the particulars of language, especially on listing and tabulating error. One rarely finds consideration of the social context of error, or of its cognitive-developmental meaning — that is, no interpretation of its significance in the growth of the writer. Instead one finds W. S. Guiler tallying the percentages of 350 students who, in misspelling "mortgage," erred by omitting the "t" vs. those who dropped the initial "g."[5] And one reads Grace Ransom's study of students' "vocabularies of errors" — a popular notion that any given student has a more or less stable set of errors he or she commits. Ransom showed that with drill and practice, students ceased making many of the errors that appeared on pretests (though, unfortunately for the theory, a large number of new errors appeared in their post-tests).[6] One also reads Luella Cole Pressey's assertion that "everything needed for about 90 per cent of the writing students do . . . appears to involve only some 44 different rules of English composition." And therefore, if mastery of the rules is divided up and allocated to grades 2 through 12, "there is an average of 4.4 rules to be mastered per year."[7]

Such research and pedagogy was enacted to good purpose, a purpose stated well by H. J. Arnold, Director of Special Schools at Wittenberg College:

> [Students'] disabilities are specific. The more exactly they can be located, the more promptly they can be removed. . . . It seems reasonably safe to predict that the elimination of the above mentioned disabilities through adequate remedial drill will do much to remove students' handicaps in certain college courses. ("Diagnostic and Remedial Techniques for College Freshmen." *Association of American Colleges Bulletin*, 16 [1930], pp. 271–272)

The trouble, of course, is that such work is built on a set of highly questionable assumptions: that a writer has a relatively fixed repository of linguistic blunders that can be pinpointed and then corrected through drill, that repetitive drill on specific linguistic features represented in isolated sentences will result in mastery of linguistic (or stylistic or rhetorical) principles, that bits of discourse bereft of rhetorical or conceptual context can form the basis of curriculum and assessment, that good writing is correct writing, and that correctness has to do with pronoun choice, verb forms, and the like.

Despite the fact that such assumptions began to be challenged by the late 30s,[8] the paraphernalia and the approach of the scientific era were destined to remain with us. I think this trend has the staying power it does for a number of reasons, the ones we saw illustrated in our brief historical overview. It gives a method — a putatively objective one — to the strong desire of our society to maintain correct language use. It is very American in its seeming efficiency. And it offers a simple, understandable view of complex linguistic problems. The trend seems to reemerge with most potency in times of crisis: when budgets crunch and accountability looms or, particularly, when "non-traditional" students flood our institutions.[9] A reduction of complexity has great appeal in institutional decision making, especially in difficult times: a scientific-atomistic approach to language, with its attendant tallies and charts, nicely fits an economic/political decision-making model. When in doubt or when scared or when pressed, count.

And something else happens. When student writing is viewed in this particularistic, pseudo-scientific way, it gets defined in very limited terms as a narrow band of inadequate behavior separate from the vastly complex composing that faculty members engage in for a living and delve into for work and for play. And such perception yields what it intends: a behavior that is stripped of its rich cognitive and rhetorical complexity. A behavior that, in fact, looks and feels basic, fundamental, atomistic. A behavior that certainly does not belong in the university.

ENGLISH AS A SKILL

As English, a relatively new course of study, moved into the second and third decades of this century, it was challenged by efficiency-obsessed administrators and legislators. Since the teaching of writing required tremendous resources, English teachers had to defend their work in utilitarian terms. One very successful defense was their characterization of English as a "skill" or "tool subject" that all students had to master in order to achieve in almost any subject and to function as productive citizens. The defense worked, and the utility of English in schooling and in adult life was confirmed for the era.

The way this defense played itself out, however, had interesting ramifications. Though a utilitarian defense of English included for many the rhetorical/conceptual as well as the mechanical/grammatical dimensions of language, the overwhelming focus of discussion in the committee reports and the journals of the 1920s and 1930s was on grammatical and mechanical error. The narrow focus was made even more narrow by a fetish for "scientific" tabulation. One could measure the degree to which students mastered their writing skill by tallying their mistakes.

We no longer use the phrase "tool subject," and we have gone a long way in the last three decades from error tabulation toward revitalizing the rhetorical dimension of writing. But the notion of writing as a skill is still central to our discussions and our defenses: we have writing skills hierarchies, writing skills assessments, and writing skills centers. And necessary as such a notion may seem to be. I think it carries with it a tremendous liability. Perhaps the problem is nowhere more clearly illustrated than in this excerpt from the UCLA academic senate's definition of a university course:

> A university course should set forth an integrated body of knowledge with primary emphasis on presenting principles and theories rather than on developing skills and techniques.

If "skills and techniques" are included, they must be taught "primarily as a means to learning, analyzing, and criticizing theories and principles." There is a lot to question in this definition, but for now let us limit ourselves to the distinction it establishes between a skill and a body of knowledge. The distinction highlights a fundamental tension in the American university: between what Laurence Veysey labels the practical-utilitarian dimension (applied, vocational, educationalist) and both the liberal culture and the research dimensions — the latter two, each in different ways, elevating appreciation and pure inquiry over application (*The Emergence of the American University* [Chicago: University of Chicago Press, 1965]). To discuss writing as a skill, then, is to place it in the realm of the technical, and in the current, research-ascendant American university, that is a kiss of death.

Now it is true that we commonly use the word *skill* in ways that suggest a complex interweaving of sophisticated activity and rich knowledge. We praise the interpretive skills of the literary critic, the diagnostic skills of the physician, the interpersonal skills of the clinical psychologist. Applied, yes, but implying a kind of competence that is more in line with obsolete definitions that equate skill with reason and understanding than with this more common definition (that of the *American Heritage Dictionary*): "An art, trade, or technique, particularly one requiring use of the hands or body." A skill, particularly in the university setting, is, well, a tool, something one develops and refines and completes in order to take on the higher-order demands of purer thought. Everyone may acknowledge the value of the skill (our senate praised our course to the skies as it removed its credit), but it is valuable as the ability to multiply or titrate a solution or use an index or draw a map is valuable. It is absolutely necessary but remains second-class. It is not "an integrated body of knowledge" but a technique, something acquired differently from the way one acquires knowledge — from drill, from practice, from procedures that conjure up the hand and the eye but not the mind. Skills are discussed as separable, distinct, circumscribable activities; thus we talk of subskills, levels of skills, sets of skills. Again writing is defined by abilities one can quantify and connect as opposed to the dynamism and organic vitality one associates with thought.

Because skills are fundamental tools, basic procedures, there is the strong expectation that they be mastered at various preparatory junctures in one's educational career and in the places where such tools are properly crafted. In the case of writing, the skills should be mastered before one enters college and takes on higher-order endeavors. And the place for such instruction — before or after entering college — is the English class. Yes, the skill can be refined, but its fundamental development is over, completed via a series of elementary and secondary school courses and perhaps one or two college courses, often designated remedial. Thus it is that so many faculty consider upper-division and especially graduate-level writing courses as de jure remedial. To view writing as a skill in the university context reduces the possibility of perceiving it as a complex ability that is continually developing as one engages in new tasks with new materials for new audiences.

If the foregoing seems a bit extreme, consider this passage from our Academic Senate's review of UCLA Writing Programs:

> ... it seems difficult to see how *composition* — whose distinctive aspect seems to be the transformation of language from thought or speech to hard copy — represents a distinct further step in shaping cogitation. There don't seem to be persuasive grounds for abandoning the view that composition is still a *skill* attendant to the attainment of overall linguistic competence.

The author of the report, a chemist, was reacting to some of our faculty's assertions about the interweaving of thinking and writing; writing for him is more or less a transcription skill.

So to reduce writing to second-class intellectual status is to influence the way faculty, students, and society view the teaching of writing. This is a bitter pill, but we in writing may have little choice but to swallow it. For, after all, is not writing simply different from "integrated bodies of knowledge" like sociology or biology? Is it? Well, yes and no. There are aspects of writing that would fit a skills model (the graphemic aspects especially). But much current theory and research are moving us to see that writing is not simply a transcribing skill mastered in early development. Writing seems central to the shaping and directing of certain modes of cognition, is integrally involved in learning, is a means of defining the self and defining reality, is a means of representing and contextualizing information (which has enormous political as well as conceptual and archival importance), and is an activity that develops over one's lifetime. Indeed it is worth pondering whether many of the "integrated bodies of knowledge" we study, the disciplines we practice, would have ever developed in the way they did and reveal the knowledge they do if writing did not exist. Would history or philosophy or economics exist as we know them? It is not simply that the work of such disciplines is recorded in writing, but that writing is intimately involved in the nature of their inquiry. Writing is not just a skill with which one can present or analyze knowledge. It is essential to the very existence of certain kinds of knowledge.

REMEDIATION

Since the middle of the last century, American colleges have been establishing various kinds of preparatory programs and classes within their halls to maintain enrollments while bringing their entering students up to curricular par.[10] One fairly modern incarnation of this activity is the "remedial class," a designation that appears frequently in the education and language arts journals of the 1920s.[11] Since that time remedial courses have remained very much with us: we have remedial programs, remedial sections, remedial textbooks, and, of course, remedial students. Other terms with different twists (like "developmental" and "compensatory") come and go, but "remedial" has staying power. Exactly what the adjective "remedial" means, however, has never quite been clear. To remediate seems to mean to correct errors or fill in gaps in a person's knowledge. The implication is that the material being studied should have been learned during prior education but was not. Now the reasons why it was not could vary tremendously: they could rest with the student (physical impairment, motivational problems, intelligence), the family (socio-economic status, stability, the support of reading-writing activities), the school (location, sophistication of the curriculum, adequacy of elementary or secondary instruction), the culture or subculture (priority of schooling, competing expectations and demands), or some combination of such factors. What "remedial" means in terms of curriculum and pedagogy is not clear either. What is remedial for a school like UCLA might well be standard for other state or community colleges, and what is considered standard during one era might well be tagged remedial in the next.

It is hard to define such a term. The best definition of remedial I can arrive at is a highly dynamic, contextual one: The function of labelling certain material remedial in higher education is to keep in place the hard fought for, if historically and conceptually problematic and highly fluid, distinction between college and secondary work. "Remedial" gains its meaning, then, in a political more than a pedagogical universe.

And the political dimension is powerful—to be remedial is to be substandard, inadequate, and, because of the origins of the term, the inadequacy is metaphorically connected to disease and mental defect. It has been difficult to trace the educational etymology of the word "remedial," but what I have uncovered suggests this: Its origins are in law and medicine, and by the late nineteenth century the term fell pretty much in the medical domain and was soon applied to education. "Remedial" quickly generalized beyond the description of students who might have had neurological problems to those with broader, though special, educational problems and then to those normal learners who are not up to a particular set of standards in a particular era at particular institutions. Here is some history.

Most of the enlightened work in the nineteenth century with the training of special populations (the deaf, the blind, the mentally retarded) was conducted by medical people, often in medical settings. And when young people who could hear and see and were of normal intelligence but had unusual—though perhaps not devastating—difficulties began to seek help, they too were examined within a medical framework. Their difficulties had to do with reading and writing—though mostly reading—and would today be classified as learning disabilities. One of the first such difficulties to be studied was dyslexia, then labelled "congenital word blindness."

In 1896 a physician named Morgan reported in the pages of *The British Medical Journal* the case of a "bright and intelligent boy" who was having great difficulty learning to read. Though he knew the alphabet, he would spell some words in pretty unusual ways. He would reverse letters or drop them or write odd combinations of consonants and vowels. Dr. Morgan examined the boy and had him read and write. The only diagnosis that made sense was one he had to borrow and analogize from the cases of stroke victims, "word blindness," but since the child had no history of cerebral trauma, Morgan labelled his condition "*congenital* word blindness" (W. Pringle Morgan, "A Case of Congenital Word Blindness," *The British Medical Journal*, 6, Part 2 [1896], 1378). Within the next two decades a number of such cases surfaced; in fact another English physician, James Hinshelwood, published several books on congenital word blindness.[12] The explanations were for the most part strictly medical, and, it should be noted, were analogized from detectable cerebral pathology in adults to conditions with no detectable pathology in children.

In the 1920s other medical men began to advance explanations a bit different from Morgan's and Hinshelwood's. Dr. Samuel Orton, an American physician, posed what he called a "cerebral physiological" theory that directed thinking away from trauma analogues and toward functional explanations. Certain areas of the brain were not defective but underdeveloped and could be corrected through "remedial effort." But though he posed a basically educational model for dyslexia, Dr. Orton's language should not be overlooked. He spoke of "brain habit" and the "handicap" of his "physiological deviates."[13] Though his theory was different from that of his forerunners, his language, significantly, was still medical.

As increasing access to education brought more and more children into the schools, they were met by progressive teachers and testing experts interested in assessing and responding to individual differences. Other sorts of reading and writing problems, not just dyslexia, were surfacing, and increasing numbers of teachers, not just medical people, were working with the special students. But the medical vocabulary—with its implied medical model—remained dominant. People tried to *diagnose* various *disabilities, defects, deficits, deficiencies*, and *handicaps*, and then tried to *remedy* them.[14] So one starts to see all sorts of reading/writing problems clustered together and addressed with this language. For example, William S. Gray's important monograph, *Remedial Cases in Reading: Their Diagnosis and Treatment* (Chicago: University of Chicago Press, 1922), listed as "specific causes of failure in reading" inferior learning capacity, congenital word blindness, poor auditory memory, defective vision, a narrow span of recognition, ineffective eye movements, inadequate training in phonetics, inadequate attention to the content, an inadequate speaking vocabulary, a small meaning vocabulary, speech defects, lack of interest, and timidity. The remedial paradigm was beginning to include those who had troubles as varied as bad eyes, second language interference, and shyness.[15]

It is likely that the appeal of medical-remedial language had much to do with its associations with scientific objectivity and accuracy—powerful currency in the efficiency-minded 1920s and 30s. A nice illustration of this interaction of influences appeared in Albert Lang's 1930 textbook, *Modern Methods in Written Examinations* (Boston: Houghton Mifflin, 1930). The medical model is quite explicit:

teaching bears a resemblance to the practice of medicine. Like a successful physician, the good teacher must be something of a diagnostician. The physician by means of a general examination singles out the individuals whose physical defects require a more thorough testing. He critically scrutinizes the special cases until he recognizes the specific troubles. After a careful diagnosis he is able to prescribe intelligently the best remedial or corrective measures. (p. 38)

By the 1930s the language of remediation could be found throughout the pages of publications like *English Journal*, applied now to writing (as well as reading and mathematics) and to high school and college students who had in fact learned to write but were doing so with a degree of error thought unacceptable. These were students—large numbers of them—who were not unlike the students who currently populate our "remedial" courses: students from backgrounds that did not provide optimal environmental and educational opportunities, students who erred as they tried to write the prose they thought the academy required, second-language students. The semantic net of "remedial" was expanding and expanding.

There was much to applaud in this focus on writing. It came from a progressive era desire to help *all* students progress through the educational system. But the theoretical and pedagogical model that was available for "corrective teaching" led educators to view writing problems within a medical-remedial paradigm. Thus they set out to diagnose as precisely as possible the errors (defects) in a student's paper—which they saw as symptomatic of equally isolable defects in the student's linguistic capacity—and devise drills and exercises to remedy them. (One of the 1930s nicknames for remedial sections was "sick sections." During the next decade they would be tagged "hospital sections.") Such corrective teaching was, in the words of H. J. Arnold, "the most logical as well as the most scientific method" ("Diagnostic and Remedial Techniques for College Freshmen," p. 276).

These then are the origins of the term, remediation. And though we have, over the last fifty years, moved very far away from the conditions of its origins and have developed a richer understanding of reading and writing difficulties, the term is still with us. A recent letter from the senate of a local liberal arts college is sitting on my desk. It discusses a "program in remedial writing for . . . [those] entering freshmen suffering from severe writing handicaps." We seem entrapped by this language, this view of students and learning. Dr. Morgan has long since left his office, but we still talk of writers as suffering from specifiable, locatable defects, deficits, and handicaps that can be localized, circumscribed, and remedied. Such talk reveals an atomistic, mechanistic-medical model of language that few contemporary students of the use of language, from educators to literary theorists, would support. Furthermore, the notion of remediation, carrying with it as it does the etymological wisps and traces of disease, serves to exclude from the academic community those who are so labelled. They sit in scholastic quarantine until their disease can be diagnosed and remedied.

ILLITERACY

In a recent meeting on graduation requirements, a UCLA dean referred to students in remedial English as "the truly illiterate among us." Another administrator, in a memorandum on the potential benefits of increasing the number of composition offerings, concluded sadly that the increase "would not provide any assurance of universal literacy at UCLA." This sort of talk about illiteracy is common. We hear it from college presidents, educational foundations, pop grammarians, and scores of college professors like the one who cried to me after a recent senate meeting, "All I want is a student who can write a simple declarative sentence!" We in the academy like to talk this way.[16] It is dramatic and urgent, and, given the current concerns about illiteracy in the United States, it is topical. The trouble is, it is wrong. Perhaps we can better understand the problems with such labelling if we leave our colleagues momentarily and consider what it is that literacy means.

To be literate means to be acquainted with letters or writings. But exactly how such acquaintance translates into behavior varies a good deal over time and place. During the last century this country's Census Bureau defined as literate anyone who could write his or her name. These days the government requires that one be able to read and write at a sixth-grade level to be *functionally* literate: that is, to be able to meet—to a minimal degree—society's reading and writing demands. Things get a bit more complex if we consider the other meanings "literacy" has acquired. There are some specialized uses of the term, all fairly new: computer literacy, mathematical literacy, visual literacy, and so on. Literacy here refers to an acquaintance with the "letters" or elements of a particular field or domain. And there are also some very general uses of the term. Cultural literacy, another new construction, is hard to define because it is so broad and so variously used, but it most often refers to an acquaintance with the humanistic, scientific, and social scientific achievements of one's dominant culture. Another general use of the term, a more traditional one, refers to the attainment of a liberal education, particularly in belles-lettres. Such literacy, of course, is quite advanced and involves not only an acquaintance with a literary tradition but interpretive sophistication as well.

Going back over these definitions, we can begin by dismissing the newer, specialized uses of "literacy." Computer literacy and other such literacies are usually not the focus of the general outcries we have been considering. How about the fundamental definition as it is currently established? This does not seem applicable either, for though many of the students entering American universities write prose that is grammatically and organizationally flawed, with very few exceptions they can read and write at a sixth-grade level. A sixth-grade proficiency is, of course, absurdly inadequate to do the work of higher education, but the definition still stands. By the most common measure the vast majority of students in college are literate. When academics talk about illiteracy they are saying that our students are "without letters" and cannot "write a simple declarative sentence." And such talk, for most students in most segments of higher education, is inaccurate and misleading.

One could argue that though our students are literate by common definition, a significant percentage of them might not be if we shift to the cultural and belletristic definitions of literacy or to a truly functional-contextual definition: that is, given the sophisticated, specialized reading and writing demands of the university—and the general knowledge they require—then it might be appropriate to talk of a kind of cultural illiteracy among some percentage of the student body. These students lack knowledge of the achievements of a tradition and are not at home with the ways we academics write about them. Perhaps this use of illiteracy is more warranted than the earlier talk about simple declarative sentences, but I would still advise caution. It is my experience that American college students tend to have learned more about western culture through their twelve years of schooling than their papers or pressured classroom responses demonstrate. (And, of course, our immigrant students bring with them a different cultural knowledge that we might not tap at all.) The problem is that the knowledge these students possess is often incomplete and fragmented and is not organized in ways that they can readily use in academic writing situations. But to say this is not to say that their minds are cultural blank slates.

There is another reason to be concerned about inappropriate claims of illiteracy. The term illiteracy comes to us with a good deal of semantic baggage, so that while an appropriately modified use of the term may accurately denote, it can still misrepresent by what it suggests, by the traces it carries from earlier eras. The social historian and anthropologist Shirley Brice Heath points out that from the mid-nineteenth century on, American school-based literacy was identified with "character, intellect, morality, and good taste . . . literacy skills co-occurred with moral patriotic character."[17] To be literate is to be honorable and intelligent. Tag some group illiterate, and you've gone beyond letters; you've judged their morals and their minds.

Please understand, it is not my purpose here to whitewash the very real limitations a disheartening number of our students bring with them. I dearly wish that more of them were more at home with composing and could write critically better than they do. I wish they enjoyed struggling for graceful written language more than many seem to. I wish they possessed more knowledge about humanities and the sciences so they could write with more authority than they usually do. And I wish to God that more of them read novels and poems for pleasure. But it is simply wrong to leap from these unrequited desires to claims of illiteracy. Reading and writing, as any ethnographic study would show, are woven throughout our students' lives. They write letters; some keep diaries. They read about what interests them, and those interests range from rock and roll to computer graphics to black holes. Reading, for many, is part of religious observation. They carry out a number of reading and writing acts in their jobs and in their interactions with various segments of society. Their college preparatory curriculum in high school, admittedly to widely varying degrees, is built on reading, and even the most beleaguered schools require some kind of writing. And many of these students read and even write in languages other than English. No, these

students are not illiterate, by common definition, and if the more sophisticated definitions apply, they sacrifice their accuracy by all they imply.

Illiteracy is a problematic term. I suppose that academics use it because it
is rhetorically effective (evoking the specter of illiteracy to an audience of
peers, legislators, or taxpayers can be awfully persuasive) or because it is
emotionally satisfying. It gives expression to the frustration and disappointment in teaching students who do not share one's passions. As well, it af-
firms the faculty's membership in the society of the literate. One reader of
this essay suggested to me that academics realize the hyperbole in their illiteracy talk, do not really mean it to be taken, well, literally. Were this invari-
ably true, I would still voice concern over such exaggeration, for, as with any
emotionally propelled utterance, it might well be revealing deeply held attitudes and beliefs, perhaps not unlike those discussed by Heath. And, deeply
felt or not, such talk in certain political and decision-making settings can dramatically influence the outcomes of deliberation.

The fact remains that cries of illiteracy substitute a fast quip for careful
analysis. Definitional accuracy here is important, for if our students are in
fact adult illiterates, then a particular, very special curriculum is needed. If
they are literate but do not read much for pleasure, or lack general knowledge that is central to academic inquiry, or need to write more than they do
and pay more attention to it than they are inclined to, well, then these are
very different problems. They bring with them quite different institutional
commitments and pedagogies, and they locate the student in a very different
place in the social-political makeup of the academy. Determining that place is
crucial, for where but in the academy would being "without letters" be so
stigmatizing?

THE MYTH OF TRANSIENCE

I have before me a report from the California Postsecondary Education
Commission called *Promises to Keep*. It is a comprehensive and fair-minded assessment of remedial instruction in the three segments of California's public
college and university system. As all such reports do, *Promises to Keep* presents
data on instruction and expenses, discusses the implications of the data, and
calls for reform. What makes the report unusual is its inclusion of an historical
overview of preparatory instruction in the United States. It acknowledges the
fact that such instruction in some guise has always been with us. In spite of its
acknowledgement, the report ends on a note of optimism characteristic of
similar documents with less historical wisdom. It calls for all three segments
of the higher education system to "implement . . . plans to reduce remediation" within five years and voices the hope that if secondary education can be
improved, "within a very few years, the state and its institutions should be
rewarded by . . . lower costs for remediation as the need for remediation declines." This optimism in the face of a disconfirming historical survey attests
to the power of what I will call the myth of transience. Despite the accretion of
crisis reports, the belief persists in the American university that if we can just

do x or y, the problem will be solved—in five years, ten years, or a generation—and higher education will be able to return to its real work. But entertain with me the possibility that such peaceful reform is a chimera.

Each generation of academicians facing the characteristic American shifts in demographics and accessibility sees the problem anew, laments it in the terms of the era, and optimistically notes its impermanence. No one seems to say that this scenario has gone on for so long that it might not be temporary. That, in fact, there will probably *always* be a significant percentage of students who do not meet some standard. (It was in 1841, not 1985 that the president of Brown complained, "Students frequently enter college almost wholly unacquainted with English grammar . . ." [Frederick Rudolph, *Curriculum: A History of the American Undergraduate Course of Study* (San Francisco: Jossey-Bass, 1978), p. 88].) The American higher educational system is constantly under pressure to expand, to redefine its boundaries, admitting, in turn, the sons of the middle class, and later the daughters, and then the American poor, the immigrant poor, veterans, the racially segregated, the disenfranchised. Because of the social and educational conditions these groups experienced, their preparation for college will, of course, be varied. Add to this the fact that disciplines change and society's needs change, and the ways society determines what it means to be educated change.

All this works itself rather slowly into the pre-collegiate curriculum. Thus there will always be a percentage of students who will be tagged substandard. And though many insist that this continued opening of doors will sacrifice excellence in the name of democracy, there are too many economic, political, and ethical drives in American culture to restrict higher education to a select minority. (And, make no mistake, the history of the American college and university from the early nineteenth century on could also be read as a history of changes in admissions, curriculum, and public image in order to keep enrollments high and institutions solvent.[18] The research institution as we know it is made possible by robust undergraduate enrollments.) Like it or not, the story of American education has been and will in all likelihood continue to be a story of increasing access. University of Nashville President Philip Lindsley's 1825 call echoes back and forth across our history: "The farmer, the mechanic, the manufacturer, the merchant, the sailor, the soldier . . . must be educated" (Frederick Rudolph, *The American College and University: A History* [New York: Vintage, 1962], p. 117).

Why begrudge academics their transience myth? After all, each generation's problems are new to those who face them, and people faced with a problem need some sense that they can solve it. Fair enough. But it seems to me that this myth brings with it a powerful liability. It blinds faculty members to historical reality and to the dynamic and fluid nature of the educational system that employs them. Like any golden age or utopian myth, the myth of transience assures its believers that the past was better or that the future will be.[19] The turmoil they are currently in will pass. The source of the problem is elsewhere; thus it can be ignored or temporarily dealt with until the tutors or academies or grammar schools or high schools or families make the changes they must make. The myth, then, serves to keep certain fundamental recognitions and thus certain fundamental changes at bay. It is ultimately a conservative gesture, a way of preserving administrative and curricular status quo.

And the myth plays itself out against complex social-political dynamics. One force in these dynamics is the ongoing struggle to establish admissions requirements that would protect the college curriculum, that would, in fact, define its difference from the high school course of study. Another is the related struggle to influence, even determine, the nature of the high school curriculum, "academize" it, shape it to the needs of the college (and the converse struggle of the high school to declare its multiplicity of purposes, college preparation being only one of its mandates). Yet another is the tension between the undergraduate, general education function of the university vs. its graduate, research function. To challenge the myth is to vibrate these complex dynamics; thus it is that it is so hard to dispel. But I would suggest that it must be challenged, for though some temporary "remedial" measures are excellent and generously funded, the presence of the myth does not allow them to be thought through in terms of the whole curriculum and does not allow the information they reveal to reciprocally influence the curriculum. Basic modifications in educational philosophy, institutional purpose, and professional training are rarely considered. They do not need to be if the problem is temporary. The myth allows the final exclusionary gesture: The problem is not ours in any fundamental way; we can embrace it if we must, but with surgical gloves on our hands.

There may be little anyone can do to change the fundamental tension in the American university between the general educational mission and the research mission, or to remove the stigma attached to application. But there is something those of us involved in writing can do about the language that has formed the field on which institutional discussions of writing and its teaching take place.

We can begin by affirming a rich model of written language development and production. The model we advance must honor the cognitive and emotional and situational dimensions of language, be psycholinguistic as well as literary and rhetorical in its focus, and aid us in understanding what we can observe as well as what we can only infer. When discussions and debates reveal a more reductive model of language, we must call time out and reestablish the terms of the argument. But we must also rigorously examine our own teaching and see what model of language lies beneath it. What linguistic assumptions are cued when we face freshman writers? Are they compatible with the assumptions that are cued when we think about our own writing or the writing of those we read for pleasure? Do we too operate with the bifurcated mind that for too long characterized the teaching of "remedial" students and that is still reflected in the language of our institutions?

Remediation. It is time to abandon this troublesome metaphor. To do so will not blind us to the fact that many entering students are not adequately prepared to take on the demands of university work. In fact, it will help us perceive these young people and the work they do in ways that foster appropriate notions about language development and use, that establish a framework for more rigorous and comprehensive analysis of their difficulties, and that do not perpetuate the raree show of allowing them entrance to the academy while, in various symbolic ways, denying them full participation.

Mina Shaughnessy got us to see that even the most error-ridden prose arises from the confrontation of inexperienced student writers with the complex linguistic and rhetorical expectations of the academy. She reminded us that to properly teach writing to such students is to understand "the intelligence of their mistakes."[20] She told us to interpret errors rather than circle them, and to guide these students, gradually and with wisdom, to be more capable participants within the world of these conventions. If we fully appreciate her message, we see how inadequate and limiting the remedial model is. Instead we need to define our work as transitional or as initiatory, orienting, or socializing to what David Bartholomae and Patricia Bizzell call the academic discourse community.[21] This redefinition is not just semantic sleight-of-hand. If truly adopted, it would require us to reject a medical-deficit model of language, to acknowledge the rightful place of all freshmen in the academy, and once and for all to replace loose talk about illiteracy with more precise and pedagogically fruitful analysis. We would move from a mechanistic focus on error toward a demanding curriculum that encourages the full play of language activity and that opens out onto the academic community rather than sequestering students from it.

A much harder issue to address is the common designation of writing as a skill. We might begin by considering more fitting terms. Jerome Bruner's "enabling discipline" comes to mind. It does not separate skill from discipline and implies something more than a "tool subject" in that to enable means to make possible. But such changes in diction might be little more than cosmetic.

If the skills designation proves to be resistant to change, then we must insist that writing is a very unique skill, not really a tool but an ability fundamental to academic inquiry, an ability whose development is not fixed but ongoing. If it is possible to go beyond the skills model, we could see a contesting of the fundamental academic distinction between integrated bodies of knowledge and skills and techniques. While that distinction makes sense in many cases, it may blur where writing is concerned. Do students really *know* history when they learn a "body" of facts, even theories, or when they act like historians, thinking in certain ways with those facts and theories? Most historians would say the latter. And the academic historian (vs. the chronicler or the balladeer) conducts inquiry through writing; it is not just an implement but is part of the very way of doing history.

It is in this context that we should ponder the myth of transience. The myth's liability is that it limits the faculty's ability to consider the writing problems of their students in dynamic and historical terms. Each academic generation considers standards and assesses the preparation of its students but seems to do this in ways that do not call the nature of the curriculum of the time into question. The problem ultimately lies outside the academy. But might not these difficulties with writing suggest the need for possible far-ranging changes within the curriculum as well, changes that *are* the proper concern of the university? One of the things I think the myth of transience currently does is to keep faculty from seeing the multiple possibilities that exist for incorporating writing throughout their courses of study. Profound reform could occur in the much-criticized lower-division curriculum if writing were not seen as only a technique and the teaching of it as by and large a remedial enterprise.

The transmission of a discipline, especially on the lower-division level, has become very much a matter of comprehending information, committing it to memory, recalling it, and displaying it in various kinds of "objective" or short-answer tests. When essay exams are required, the prose all too often becomes nothing more than a net in which the catch of individual bits of knowledge lie. Graders pick through the essay and tally up the presence of key phrases. Such activity trivializes a discipline; it reduces its methodology, grounds it in a limited theory of knowledge, and encourages students to operate with a restricted range of their cognitive abilities. Writing, on the other hand, assumes a richer epistemology and demands fuller participation. It requires a complete, active, struggling engagement with the facts and principles of a discipline, an encounter with the discipline's texts and the incorporation of them into one's own work, the framing of one's knowledge within the myriad conventions that help define a discipline, the persuading of other investigators that one's knowledge is legitimate. So to consider the relationship between writing and disciplinary inquiry may help us decide what is central to a discipline and how best to teach it. The university's research and educational missions would intersect.

Such reform will be difficult. True, there is growing interest in writing adjuncts and discipline-specific writing courses, and those involved in writing-across-the-curriculum are continually encouraging faculty members to evaluate the place of writing in their individual curricula. But wide-ranging change will occur only if the academy redefines writing for itself, changes the terms of the argument, sees instruction in writing as one of its central concerns.

Academic senates often defend the labelling of a writing course as remedial by saying that they are defending the integrity of the baccalaureate, and they are sending a message to the high schools. The schools, of course, are so beleaguered that they can barely hear those few units ping into the bucket. Consider, though, the message that would be sent to the schools and to the society at large if the university embraced — not just financially but conceptually — the teaching of writing: if we gave it full status, championed its rich relationship with inquiry, insisted on the importance of craft and grace, incorporated it into the heart of our curriculum. What an extraordinary message that would be. It would affect the teaching of writing as no other message could.

ACKNOWLEDGMENT

Author's note: I wish to thank Arthur Applebee, Robert Connors, Carol Hartzog, and William Schaefer for reading and generously commenting on an earlier version of this essay. Connors and Hartzog also helped me revise that version. Bill Richey provided research assistance of remarkably high caliber, and Tom Bean, Kenyon Chan, Patricia Donahue, Jack Kolb, and Bob Schwegler offered advice and encouragement. Finally, a word of thanks to Richard Lanham for urging me to think of our current problem in broader contexts.

NOTES

[1]Quoted in Lawrence A. Cremin, *The Transformation of the School: Progressivism in American Education* (New York: Alfred A. Knopf, 1961), p. 185.

[2]Arthur N. Applebee, *Tradition and Reform in the Teaching of English: A History* (Urbana, IL: National Council of Teachers of English, 1974), pp. 93–94.

[3]P. G. Perrin, "The Remedial Racket," *English Journal*, 22 (1933), 383.

[4]From Cubberley's introduction to Albert R. Lang, *Modern Methods in Written Examinations* (Boston: Houghton Mifflin, 1930), p. vii.

[5]W. S. Guiler, "Background Deficiencies," *Journal of Higher Education*, 3 (1932), 371.

[6]Grace Ransom, "Remedial Methods in English Composition," *English Journal*, 22 (1933), 749–754.

[7]Luella Cole Pressey, "Freshmen Needs in Written English," *English Journal*, 19 (1930), 706.

[8]I would mislead if I did not point out that there were cautionary voices being raised all along, though until the late 1930s they were very much in the minority. For two early appraisals, see R. L. Lyman. *Summary of Investigations Relating to Grammar, Language, and Composition* (Chicago: University of Chicago Press, 1924), and especially P. G. Perrin, "The Remedial Racket," *English Journal*, 22 (1933), 382–388.

[9]Two quotations. The first offers the sort of humanist battle cry that often accompanies reductive drill, and the second documents the results of such an approach. Both are from NCTE publications.

"I think . . . that the chief objective of freshman English (at least for the first semester and low or middle—but not high—sections) should be ceaseless, brutal drill on mechanics, with exercises and themes. Never mind imagination, the soul, literature, for at least one semester, but pray for literacy and fight for it" (A University of Nebraska professor quoted with approval in Oscar James Campbell, *The Teaching of College English* [New York: Appleton-Century, 1934], pp. 36–37).

"Members of the Task Force saw in many classes extensive work in traditional schoolroom grammar and traditional formal English usage. They commonly found students with poor reading skills being taught the difference between *shall* and *will* or pupils with serious difficulties in speech diagraming sentences. Interestingly, observations by the Task Force reveal far more extensive teaching of traditional grammar in this study of language programs for the disadvantaged than observers saw in the National Study of High School English Programs, a survey of comprehensive high schools known to be achieving important results in English with college-bound students able to comprehend the abstractions of such grammar" (Richard Corbin and Muriel Crosby, *Language Programs for the Disadvantaged* [Urbana, IL: NCTE, 1965], pp. 121–122).

[10]In 1894, for example, over 40% of entering freshmen came from the preparatory divisions of the institutions that enrolled them. And as late as 1915—a time when the quantity and quality of secondary schools had risen sufficiently to make preparatory divisions less necessary—350 American colleges still maintained their programs. See John S. Brubacher and Willis Rudy, *Higher Education in Transition: A History of American Colleges and Universities, 1636–1976*, 3rd ed. (New York: Harper and Row, 1976), pp. 241 ff., and Arthur Levine, *Handbook on Undergraduate Curriculum* (San Francisco: Jossey-Bass, 1981), pp. 54 ff.

[11]Several writers point to a study habits course initiated at Wellesley in 1894 as the first modern remedial course in higher education (K. Patricia Cross, *Accent on Learning* [San Francisco: Jossey-Bass, 1979], and Arthur Levine, *Handbook on Undergraduate Curriculum*). In fact, the word "remedial" did not appear in the course's title and the course was different in kind from the courses actually designated "remedial" that would emerge in the 1920s and 30s. (See Cross, pp. 24–25, for a brief discussion of early study skills courses.) The first use of the term "remedial" in the context I am discussing was most likely in a 1916 article on the use of reading tests to plan "remedial work" (Nila Banton Smith, *American Reading Instruction* [Newark, Delaware: International Reading Association, 1965], p. 191). The first elementary and secondary level remedial courses in reading were offered in the early 1920s; remedial courses in college would not appear until the late 20s.

[12]James Hinshelwood, *Letter-, Word-, and Mind-Blindness* (London: Lewis, 1902); *Congenital Word-Blindness* (London: Lewis, 1917).

[13]Samuel Orton, "The 'Sight Reading' Method of Teaching Reading, as a Source of Reading Disability," *Journal of Educational Psychology*, 20 (1929), 135–143.

[14]There were, of course, some theorists and practitioners who questioned medical-physiological models, Arthur Gates of Columbia Teacher's College foremost among them. But even those who questioned such models — with the exception of Gates — tended to retain medical language.

[15]There is another layer to this terminological and conceptual confusion. At the same time that remediation language was being used ever more broadly by some educators, it maintained its strictly medical usage in other educational fields. For example, Annie Dolman Inskeep has only one discussion of "remedial work" in her book *Teaching Dull and Retarded Children* (New York: Macmillan, 1926), and that discussion has to do with treatment for children needing health care: "Children who have poor teeth, who do not hear well, or who hold a book when reading nearer than eight inches to the eyes or further away than sixteen. . . . Nervous children, those showing continuous fatigue symptoms, those under weight, and those who are making no apparent bodily growth" (p. 271).

[16]For a sometimes humorous but more often distressing catalogue of such outcries, see Harvey A. Daniels, *Famous Last Words* (Carbondale: Southern Illinois University Press, 1983), especially pp. 31–58.

[17]Shirley Brice Heath, "Toward an Ethnohistory of Writing in American Education," in Marcia Farr Whiteman, ed., *Writing: The Nature, Development, and Teaching of Written Communication*, Vol. 1 (Hillsdale, NJ: Erlbaum, 1981), 35–36.

[18]Of turn-of-the-century institutions, Laurence Veysey writes: "Everywhere the size of enrollments was closely tied to admission standards. In order to assure themselves of enough students to make a notable "splash," new institutions often opened with a welcome to nearly all comers, no matter how ill prepared; this occurred at Cornell, Stanford, and (to a lesser degree) at Chicago" (*The Emergence of the American University*, p. 357).

[19]An appropriate observation here comes from Daniel P. and Lauren B. Resnick's critical survey of reading instruction and standards of literacy: "there is little to go back to in terms of pedagogical method, curriculum, or school organization. The old tried and true approaches, which nostalgia prompts us to believe might solve current problems, were designed neither to achieve the literacy standard sought today nor to assure successful literacy for everyone . . . there is no simple past to which we can return" ("The Nature of Literacy: An Historical Exploration," *Harvard Educational Review*, 47 [1977], 385).

[20]Mina Shaughnessy, *Errors and Expectations* (New York: Oxford University Press, 1977), p. 11.

[21]David Bartholomae, "Inventing the University," in Mike Rose, ed., *When a Writer Can't Write: Studies in Writer's Block and Other Composing Process Problems* (New York: Guilford, 1985); Patricia Bizzell, "College Composition: Initiation into the Academic Discourse Community," *Curriculum Inquiry*, 12 (1982), 191–207.

11

Narrowing the Mind and Page: Remedial Writers and Cognitive Reductionism

1988

AUTHOR'S NOTE: As with "Complexity, Rigor" (p. 56) — though in quite a different way and for a different purpose — this article puts questions of research methodology at the center of analysis. In "Complexity, Rigor" I was trying to sketch out an approach that could broaden the scope of composing process research; here I'm using what I had learned about social science methodology as a vehicle of critique. Because issues related to cognition, to how people think, are often enmeshed in issues of race, class, or gender, the cognitive perspective can aid in examining the way people are defined and represented.

One important influence as I was beginning to frame this article was Stephen Jay Gould's *The Mismeasure of Man,* a biting critique of the abuses of mental measurement that combines historical study with methodological and conceptual analysis. Writing the article took me into some new disciplinary territory, and so I also benefited from a number of consultations with experts in linguistics, psychiatry and neurology, developmental psychology, and classical studies. Few of us can master multiple disciplines, and, as I hope the article shows, there can be a danger in selectively applying research outside of one's area of competence to student writing. But there can also be real benefit in a focused consultation across disciplines, where an expert can draw the conceptual landscape, guide your reading, answer questions about methods, warn of pitfalls. I would rely on such consultation increasingly, certainly for a book like *The Mind at Work,* which draws not only on multiple disciplines but also on the working knowledge held by different tradespersons and service providers.

Skimming the notebook I kept while I was researching "Narrowing the Mind and Page," I see a technique developing that I would use in the article and in later writing: a testing of big theoretical claims against the everyday. (Mal Kiniry and I would incorporate this technique into *Critical Strategies;* see p. 140.) Here the basic move involves asking the question "How would this claim manifest itself in a student's thinking and writing?" So if the notion of cognitive style is relevant to composing, how would it play out? How would any set of freshmen essays reveal it? How would we know it when we see it?

To be sure, there can be a parochialism to this move, a stubborn reductive empiricism, and one needs to guard against it. So there should be some counterquestions to ask: What does the claim open up to us? What do we see if we examine a paper with the claim in mind? What I think is valuable about this line of questioning and counterquestioning is that it reminds us that, finally, we're talking about real people, actual language use, everyday behavior. What we claim about people's minds and words has significant consequences.

This is an article with a number of concepts and references to its argument, lots of trees, so let me pull back to forest-altitude and suggest some broader issues that inform it:

- To use Harvey Graff's phrase, "the tyranny of conceptual dichotomies"

- The importance of purpose, function, context

- The danger of overgeneralizing

- The need to test theory against human particulars, to seek disconfirming cases, to be skeptical of the grand claim

- The rich variability of human behavior

In closing, let me say that I would like to see someone write this kind of article today, for the general tendencies I describe are enduring ones. And with the heightened interest in social theory over the past decade, there is danger of the conceptual leaps I worry about in this article. We in rhetoric and composition have moved away from some of the models of mind discussed here — you won't hear much about brain hemisphericity or Piagetian developmental theory. But you do hear talk about learning styles (a popular notion in educational circles). And, as some newer scholarship is pointing out, analysis of race, language, and identity; or class and cultural practices; or gender, sexual orientation, and epistemology, though progressive in intention, can veer toward overgeneralized and dichotomous ways of explaining complex and variable human behavior.[1] As our field, as the humanities and social sciences generally, has taken a critical turn, are there aspects of our current cultural, linguistic, or political theories that unwittingly lead us into the kinds of conceptual problems I examine here? The tendencies I describe are hard to see sometimes; they are part of the cultural surround and can morph into new guise.

NOTE

[1]See, for example, Gilyard and Nunley (2004); Holmes (2004); and Malinowitz (1995).

There has been a strong tendency in American education—one that took modern shape with the I.Q. movement—to seek singular, unitary cognitive explanations for broad ranges of poor school performance. And though this trend—I'll call it cognitive reductionism—has been challenged on many fronts (social and political as well as psychological and psychometric), it is surprisingly resilient. It re-emerges. We see it in our field in those discussions of basic and remedial writers that suggest that unsuccessful writers think in fundamentally different ways from successful writers. Writing that is limited to the concrete, that doesn't evidence abstraction or analysis, that seems illogical is seen, in this framework, as revealing basic differences in perception, reasoning, or language.[1] This speculation has been generated, shaped, and supported by one or more theories from psychology, neurology, and literary studies.

Studies of cognitive style suggest that people who can be characterized as "field-dependent" (vs. those who are "field-independent") might have trouble with analytical tasks. *Popular articles on brain research* claim a neurophysiological base for some humans to be verbal, logical, analytical thinkers and for others to be spatial, holistic, non-verbal thinkers. *Jean Piaget's work on the development of logical thought* seems pertinent as well: some students might not have completed their developmental ascent from concrete to abstract reasoning. And *orality-literacy theorists* make connections between literacy and logic and suggest that the thinking of some minority groups might be affected by the degree to which their culture has moved from oral to literate modes of behavior.

The applications of these theories to poor writers appear in composition journals and papers at English, composition, and remedial education conferences. This is by no means the only way people interested in college-age remedial writers talk about thinking-writing connections, but the posing of generalized differences in cognition and the invoking of Piaget, field dependence and the rest has developed into a way of talking about remediation. And though this approach has occasionally been challenged in journals, it maintains a popular currency and encourages a series of bold assertions: poor writers can't form abstractions; they are incapable of analysis; they perceive the world as an undifferentiated whole; the speech patterns they've acquired in their communities seriously limit their critical capacity.

I think we need to look closely at these claims and at the theories used to support them, for both the theories and the claims lead to social distinctions that have important consequences, political as well as educational. This is not to deny that the theories themselves have contributed in significant ways to

From *College Composition and Communication* 39.3 (October 1988): 267–302.

our understanding of mental processes (and Piaget, of course, shaped an entire field of research), but their richness should not keep us from careful consideration of their limits, internal contradictions, and attendant critical discussions and counterstatements. Consideration of the theories leads us naturally to consideration of their applicability to areas beyond their original domain. Such application often overgeneralizes the theory: Ong's brilliant work on orality and literacy, for example, moves beyond its history-of-consciousness domain and becomes a diagnostic framework. A further problem — sometimes inherent in the theories themselves, sometimes a result of reductive application — is the tendency to diminish cognitive complexity and rely on simplified cognitive oppositions: independent vs. dependent, literate vs. oral, verbal vs. spatial, concrete vs. logical. These oppositions are textbook-neat, but, as much recent cognitive research demonstrates, they are narrow and misleading. Yet another problem is this: these distinctions are usually used in a way meant to be value-free (that is, they highlight differences rather than deficits in thinking), but, given our culture, they are anything but neutral. Social and political hierarchies end up encoded in sweeping cognitive dichotomies.

In this article I would like to reflect on the problems with and limitations of this particular discourse about remediation. To do this, I'll need to provide a summary of the critical discussion surrounding each of the theories in its own field, for that complexity is too often lost in discussions of thought and writing. As we move through the essay, I'll point out the problems in applying these theories to the thought processes of poor writers. And, finally, I'll conclude with some thoughts on studying cognition and writing in less reductive ways.

COGNITIVE STYLE: FIELD DEPENDENCE-INDEPENDENCE

Cognitive style, broadly defined, is an "individual's characteristic and consistent manner of processing and organizing what he [or she] sees and thinks about" (Harré and Lamb 98). In theory, cognitive style is separate from verbal, quantitative, or visual intelligence; it is not a measure of how much people know or how well they mentally perform a task, but the manner in which they perform, their way of going about solving a problem, their style. Cognitive style research emerges out of the study of individual differences, and there have been a number of theories of cognitive style proposed in American and British psychology since the late 40's. Varied though they are, all the theories discuss style in terms of a continuum existing between two polar opposites: for example, reflectivity vs. impulsivity, analytic vs. global, complexity vs. simplicity, levelling vs. sharpening, risk-taking vs. cautiousness, field-dependence vs. field-independence. Field dependence-independence, first described by Herman A. Witkin in 1949, is, by far, the most researched of the cognitive styles, and it is the style that seems to be most discussed in composition circles.

The origins of the construct are, as Witkin, Moore, Goodenough, and Cox note, central to its understanding. Witkin's first curiosity concerned the degree to which people use their surrounding visual environment to make judgments about the vertical position of objects in a field. Witkin devised several devices to study this issue, the best known being the Rod and Frame Test. A square frame on a dark background provides the surrounding visual field, and a rod that rotates within it is the (potentially) vertical object. Both the frame and the rod can separately be rotated clockwise or counter-clockwise, and "[t]he subject's task is to adjust the rod to a position where he perceives it as upright, while the frame around it remains in its initial position of tilt" ("Field-Dependent" 3). Witkin, et al.'s early findings revealed some interesting individual differences:

> For some, in order for the rod to be apprehended as properly upright, it must be fully aligned with the surrounding frame, whatever the position of the frame. If the frame is tilted 30 [degrees] to the right, for example, they will tilt the rod 30 [degrees] to the right, and say the rod is perfectly straight in that position. At the opposite extreme of the continuous performance range are people who adjust the rod more or less close to the upright in making it straight, regardless of the position of the surrounding frame. They evidently apprehend the rod as an entity discrete from the prevailing visual frame of reference and determine the uprightness of the rod according to the felt position of the body rather than according to the visual frame immediately surrounding it. ("Field-Dependent" 3–4)

A subject's score is simply the number of degrees of actual tilt of the rod when the subject claims it is straight.

Witkin and his associates later developed another measure—one that was much less cumbersome and could be given to many people at once—The Embedded Figures Test.[2] Witkin, et al. considered the Embedded Figures Test to be similar to the Rod and Frame Test in its "essential perceptual structure." The subject must locate a simple geometric design in a complex figure, and "once more what is at issue is the extent to which the surrounding visual framework dominates perception of the item within it" (6). A subject's score on the test is the number of such items he or she can disembed in a set time.

The "common denominator" between the two tests is "the extent to which the person perceives part of the field as discrete from the surrounding field as a whole, rather than embedded in the field; or the extent to which the organization of the prevailing field determines perception of its components" (7). Put simply, how strong is our cognitive predisposition to let surrounding context influence what we see? Witkin soon began to talk of the differences between field dependence vs. independence as differences between articulated (or analytic) vs. global perception:

> At one extreme there is a consistent tendency for experience to be global and diffuse; the organization of the field as a whole dictates the manner in which its parts are experienced. At the other extreme there is

a tendency for experience to be delineated and structured; parts of a field are experienced as discrete and the field as a whole organized. To these opposite poles of the cognitive styles we may apply the labels "global and articulated." ("Psychological Differentiation" 319)

Witkin's tests were tapping interesting individual differences in perception and cognition, but the really tantalizing findings emerged as Witkin and his colleagues began pursuing a wide-ranging research agenda that, essentially, sought correlations between performance on field dependence-independence tests and performance on a variety of other cognitive, behavioral, and personality tests, measures, and activities. Hundreds of these studies followed, ranging from the insightful (correlating cognitive style with the way teachers structure social science concepts) to the curious (correlating cognitive style with the shortness of women's skirts). Some of the studies yielded low correlations, and some were inconclusive or were contradictory — but, in general, the results, as summarized by educational psychologist Merlin Wittrock, resulted in the following two profiles:

- To the degree that people score high on field independence they tend to be: "relatively impersonal, individualistic, insensitive to others and their reinforcements, interested in abstract subject matter, and intrinsically motivated. They have internalized frames of reference, and experience themselves as separate or differentiated from others and the environment. They tend to use previously learned principles and rules to guide their behavior" (93).

- To the degree that people score low on field independence they are, by default, field-dependent, and they tend to be: "more socially oriented, more aware of social cues, better able to discern feelings of others from their facial expressions, more responsive to a myriad of information, more dependent on others for reinforcement and for defining their own beliefs and sentiments, and more in need of extrinsic motivation and externally defined objectives" (93).

The tendency of the field-independent person to perceive particular shapes and orientations despite context, and the tendency of the field-dependent person to let "the organization of the field as a whole dictate the manner in which its parts are experienced" seemed to be manifesting themselves in motivation, cognition, and personality. A few relatively simple tests were revealing wide-ranging differences in the way people think and interact.

The psychometric neatness of this work seems a little too good to be true, and, in fact, problems have been emerging for some time. My discussion of them will be oriented toward writing.

You'll recall that it is central to the theory that cognitive style is not a measure of ability, of how well people perform a task, but a measure of their manner of performance, their style. If we applied this notion to writing, then, we would theoretically expect to find interesting differences in the way discourse is produced, in the way a rhetorical act is conceived and executed: maybe the discourse of field independents would be more analytical and impersonal while field-dependent discourse would be richer in social detail. But these differences should not, theoretically, lead to gross differences in quality. By some general measure, papers written by field-dependent and field-independent students should have equal possibility of being acceptable discourse. They would just be different. However, the most detailed and comprehensive cognitive style study of college-level writers I've yet seen yields this: papers written by field-dependent students are simply poor papers, and along most dimensions—spelling, grammar, development (Williams). This doesn't fit. Conclusions emerge, but they don't jibe with what the theory predicts.

Such conceptual and testing perplexities are rooted, I believe, in the field dependence-independence work itself. My review of the psychological literature revealed seven problems with the construct, and they range from the technical to the conceptual level.

For cognitive style to be a legitimate construct, it has to be distinct from general intelligence or verbal ability or visual acuity, because cognitive style is not intended to be a measure of how "smart" someone is, but of the manner in which she or he engages in an intellectual task. Unfortunately, there are a number of studies which suggest that field dependence-independence significantly overlaps with measures of intelligence, which are, themselves, complex and controversial. As early as 1960, Lee J. Cronbach wrote in his authoritative *Essentials of Psychological Testing:* "General reasoning or spatial ability accounts for much of Embedded Figures performance as does difficulty in handling perceptual interference" (549). In 1972, Philip Vernon, also a prominent researcher of individual differences, reviewed studies that investigated relations between scores on field dependence-independence and various measures of "visual intelligence." He concluded that "the strong positive correlation with such a wide range of spatial tests is almost embarrassing" (368). And after conducting his own study, Vernon declaimed that Embedded Figures Tests "do not define a factor distinct from general intelligence . . . and spatial ability or visualization" (386). Things become more complicated. Vernon, and other researchers (see, for example, Linn and Kyllonen), present factor-analytic data that suggest that determining the position of the rod within the frame and disembedding the hidden figures tap *different* mental constructs, not the unitary construct Witkin had initially postulated.[3] It is possible, of course, that different aspects of field dependence-independence are being tapped by the different tests and that two of them should be administered together—as Witkin, in fact, recommended. But even if researchers used multiple measures (as few have—most use only the Embedded Figures Test because of its utility), the problem of overlap with measures of intelligence would remain. In short, it's not certain just what the field dependence-independence tests are measuring, and it's very possible that they are primarily tapping general or spatial intelligence.

There is a further testing problem. In theory, each pole of a cognitive style continuum "has adaptive value in certain circumstances . . . neither end of [a] cognitive style dimension is uniformly more adaptive . . . adaptiveness depends upon the nature of the situation and upon the cognitive requirements of the task at hand" (Messick 9). Now, there have been studies which show that field-dependent people seem to attend more readily than field-independent people to social cues (though the effects of these studies tend to be small or inconsistent—see McKenna), but it is important to note that Witkin and his colleagues have never been able to develop a test that *positively* demonstrates field dependence. The Rod and Frame Test, the Embedded Figures Test—and all the other tests of field dependence-independence—assess how well a person displays field *in*dependence. Field dependence is essentially determined by default—the more a person fails at determining the true position of the rod or the slower he is at disembedding the figure, the more field dependent he is. This assessment-by-default would not be a problem if one were testing some level of skill or intellectual ability, say, mechanical aptitude. But where a bipolar and "value-free" continuum is being assessed—where one is not "deficient" or "maladaptive" regardless of score, but only different, where both field-independent and field-dependent people allegedly manifest cognitive strengths as well as limitations—then it becomes a problem if you can't devise a test on which field-dependent subjects would score well. Witkin, et al. admit that the development of such a test is "an urgent task" (16). It has not yet been developed.

But even if a successful test of field dependence could be created, problems with assessment would not be over. All existing tests of field dependence-independence are, as Paul L. Wachtel points out:

> in certain respects poorly suited for exploration of the very problem [they were] designed to deal with—that of style. It is difficult to organize ideas about different directions of development upon a framework which includes only one dimension, and only the possibility of "more" or "less." (186)

Consider the notion of style. It would seem that style is best assessed by the observation and recording of a range of behaviors over time. Yet the Rod and Frame and Embedded Figures Tests don't allow for the revelation of the cognitive processes in play as the person tries to figure them out. That is, there is no provision made for the subject to speak aloud her mental processes or offer a retrospective account of them or explain—as in Piagetian method—why she's doing what she's doing. We have here what Michael Cole and Barbara Means refer to as the problem of drawing process inferences from differences in task performance (65). It would be unfair to lay this criticism on Witkin's doorstep alone, for it is a general limitation with psychometric approaches to cognition. (See, for example, Hunt.) But Witkin's work, since it purports to measure style, is especially vulnerable to it.

Let us now rethink those composite profiles of field-independent vs. field-dependent people. You'll recall that the correlations of all sorts of measures suggest that field-dependent people are more socially oriented, more responsive to a myriad of information, etc., while field-independent people tend to be individualistic, interested in abstract subject matter, and so on. These profiles can be pretty daunting; they're built on hundreds of studies, and they complement our folk wisdom about certain kinds of personalities. But we must keep in mind that the correlations between tests of field independence and personality or cognitive measures are commonly .25 to .3 or .4; occasionally, correlations as high as .5 or .6 are recorded, but they are unusual. That means that, typically, 84% to 94% of the variance between one measure and the other remains to be accounted for by factors other than those posited by the cognitive style theorist. Such studies accrue, and eventually the theorist lays them all side by side, notes the seeming commonalities, and profiles emerge. You could consider these profiles telling and veridical, but you could also consider them webs of thin connection.

We in the West are drawn to the idea of consistency in personality (from Renaissance humors to Jungian types), and that attraction, I think, compels us to seek out similar, interrelated consistencies in cognition. Certainly there are regularities in the way human beings approach problems; we don't go at our cognitive tasks willy-nilly. But when cognitive researchers try to chart those consistencies by studying individual people solving multiple problems they uncover a good deal of variation, variation that is potentially efficient and adaptive. William F. Battig, for example, found in his studies of adult verbal learning that most subjects employed different strategies at different times, even when working on a single problem. At least in the cognitive dimension, then, it has proven difficult to demonstrate that people approach different problems, in different settings, over time in consistent ways. This difficulty, it seems to me, presents a challenge to the profiles provided by cognitive style theorists.

There are, finally, troubling conceptual-linguistic problems with field dependence-independence theory, and they emerge most dramatically for me when I try to rephrase some of Witkin's discussions of the two styles. Here is one example:

> Persons with a global style are more likely to go along with the field "as is," without using such mediational processes as analyzing and structuring. In many situations field-independent people tend to behave as if governed by general principles which they have actively abstracted from their experiences ... In contrast, for field-dependent people information processing systems seem to make less use of such mediators. (Witkin, et al. 21)

Statements like this are common in Witkin, and they flow along and make sense in the discussion he offers us—but you stop cold if you consider for a minute what it might mean for people to have a tendency to operate in the world "without using such mediational processes as analyzing and structuring" or, by implication, to not "behave as if governed by general principles which they have actively abstracted from their experiences." These seem like pretty extreme claims, given the nature and limitations of tests of cognitive style. All current theories of cognition that I'm familiar with posit that human beings bring coherence to behavior by abstracting general principles from experiences, by interpreting and structuring what they see and do. When people can't do this sort of thing, or can only do it minimally, we assume that something is seriously wrong with them.

Witkin and his colleagues faced the dilemma that all theory builders face: how to find a language with which to express complex, abstract ideas. (For a Wittgensteinian analysis of Witkin's language, see Kurtz.) And given the nature of language, such expression is always slippery. I think, though, that Witkin and company get themselves into more than their fair share of trouble. The language they finally choose is often broad and general: it is hard to operationalize, and, at times, it seems applicable post hoc to explain almost any result (see Wachtel 184–185). It is metaphoric in troubling ways. And it implies things about cognition that, upon scrutiny, seem problematic. I would suggest that if we're going to apply Witkin's notions to the assessment of writing and cognition we'll need more focussed, less problematic definitions. Now, Witkin does, in fact, occasionally provide such definitions, but they raise problems of a different order. And here again we see the complications involved in connecting Witkin's theory to composing.

In an admirably precise statement, Witkin, et al. note:

> The individual who, in perception, cannot keep an item separate from the surrounding field—in other words, who is relatively field-dependent—is likely to have difficulty with that class of problems, and, we must emphasize, *only* with that class of problems, where the solution depends on taking some critical element out of the context in which it is presented and restructuring the problem material so that the item is now used in a different context. (9)

Consider rhetoric and the production of written language. For Witkin's formulation to apply, we would have to define rhetorical activity and written language production as *essentially* involving the disembedding of elements from contexts and concomitant restructuring of those contexts. It seems to me that such application doesn't hold. Even if there were a rhetorical-linguistic test of cognitive style—and there isn't; the tests are visual, perceptual-orientational—I think most of us would say that while we could think of linguistic-rhetorical problems that might fit Witkin's description, it would be hard to claim that it characterizes rhetorical activity and linguistic production in any broad and inclusive way.

Second of all, it's important to remember that Witkin is talking about a *general* disembedding skill, a skill that would be effective in a wide range of contexts: engineering, literature, social relations. A number of contemporary students of cognition, however, question the existence of such general cognitive skills and argue for more domain-specific strategies, skills, and abilities (see, for example, Carey; Fodor; Gardner, *Frames*; Glaser; Perkins). Given our experience in particular domains, we may be more or less proficient at disembedding and restructuring problem areas in literature but not in engineering. Our ability to disembed the hidden geometric figures in Witkin's test may be more related to our experience with such visual puzzles than to some broad cognitive skill at disembedding. If a student can't structure an essay or take a story apart in the way we've been trained to do, current trends in cognitive research would suggest that her difficulties have more to do with limited opportunity to build up a rich network of discourse knowledge and strategy than with some general difference or deficit in her ability to structure or analyze experience.

HEMISPHERICITY

The French physician Paul Broca announced in 1865 that "we speak with the left hemisphere"; neurologists have had clinical evidence for some time that damage to certain areas of the left side of the brain could result in disruptions in production or comprehension of speech—aphasia—and that damage to certain areas of the right could result in space and body orientation problems; laboratory experiments with healthy people over the last 25 or so years have demonstrated that particular linguistic or spatial capacities seem to require the function of regions in the left or right brain respectively (though it is also becoming clear that there is some degree of right hemisphere involvement in language production and comprehension and left hemispheric involvement in spatial tasks); and radical neurosurgery on a dozen or so patients with intractable epilepsy—a severing of the complex band of neural fibers (the commissures) that connect the left and right cerebral hemispheres—has provided dramatic, if highly unusual, illustration of the anatomical specialization of the hemispheres. It is pretty much beyond question, then, that different areas of the brain contribute to different aspects of human cognition. As with any biological structure there is variation, but in 98% of right handers and 70% of "non-right" handers, certain areas of the left hemisphere are critical for the processing of phonology and syntax and for the execution of fine motor control, and certain areas of the right hemisphere are involved in various kinds of visual and spatial cognition.

These conclusions evolve from either clinical observation or experimental studies. Most studies fit the following paradigm: a set of tasks is presented to a subject, and the tasks are either isomorphic with the process under investigation (e.g., distinguishing nonsense syllables like "pa," "ta," "ka," "ba" as a test of phonetic discrimination) or can be assumed, in a common sense way, to tap the activity under investigation (e.g., mentally adding a list of numbers as a test of serial processing). The subject's speed or accuracy is recorded and, in some studies, other measures are taken that are hypothesized to be related to the mental processes being studied (e.g., recording the brain wave patterns or blood flow or glucose metabolism of the cerebral hemispheres while the subject performs the experimental task).

Studies of this type have enabled researchers to gain some remarkable insight into the fine neuropsychological processes involved in understanding language and, to a lesser degree, in making spatial-orientational discriminations. But it is also true that, ingenious as the work has been, the field is still at a relatively primitive state: many studies are difficult to duplicate (a disturbing number of them yield conflicting results), and the literature is filled with methodological quarrels, competing theories, and conceptual tangles. (For a recent, and very sympathetic, overview see Benson and Zaidel.)

In spite of the conflicts, there are various points of convergence in the data, and, in the yearning for parsimony that characterizes science, the areas of agreement have led some neuroscientists to seek simple and wide-ranging characterizations of brain function. They suggest that beneath all the particular findings about syntax and phonetics and spatial discrimination lie *fundamental* functional differences in the left and right cerebral hemispheres: each is best suited to process certain kinds of stimuli and/or each processes stimuli in distinct ways. A smaller number of neuroscientists—and many popularizers—go a step further and suggest that people tend toward reliance on one hemisphere or the other when they process information. This theory is commonly referred to as "hemisphericity" (Bogen, DeZure, TenHouton, and Marsh). And a few sociologically oriented theorists take another, truly giant, step and suggest that entire dominant and subdominant groups of people can be characterized by a reliance on left or right hemispheric processing (Ten-Houten). We have, then, the emergence of a number of cognitive dichotomies: the left hemisphere is characterized as being analytic while the right is holistic (or global or synthetic); the left is verbal, the right non-verbal (or spatial); the left a serial processor, the right a parallel processor—and the list continues: focal vs. diffuse, logical vs. intuitive, propositional vs. appositional, and so on.

The positing of hemispheric dichotomies is understandable. Human beings are theory-makers, and parsimony is a fundamental criterion by which we judge the value of a theory: can it account for diverse data with a simple explanation? But, given the current state of brain research, such generalizations, to borrow Howard Gardner's phrase, leapfrog from the facts ("What We Know" 114). Gardner is by no means alone in his criticism. My reading of the neuroscientific literature reveals that the notion of dichotomous hemispheric function is very controversial, and the further notion of hemisphericity is downright dismissed by a broad range of neuroscientists, psychologists, psycholinguists, and research psychiatrists:

> [T]he concepts [analytic/synthetic, temporal/spatial, etc.] are currently so slippery that it sometimes proves impossible to maintain consistency throughout one paper. (John C. Marshall in Bradshaw and Nettleton 72)

> [M]uch of perception (certainly of visual perception) is very difficult to split up this way. The alleged dichotomy [between temporal-analytic and spatial-holistic] is, if it exists at all, more a feature of laboratory experiments than of the real world. (M. J. Morgan in Bradshaw and Nettleton 74)

> [T]he idea of hemisphericity lacks adequate foundation and . . . because of the assumptions implicit in the idea of hemisphericity, it will never be possible to provide such a foundation. The idea is a misleading one which should be abandoned. (Beaumont, Young, and McManus 191)

The above objections rise from concerns about method, subjects, and conceptualization. Let me survey each of these concerns.

A significant amount of the data used to support hemisphericity—and certainly the most dramatic—is obtained from people in whom accident or pathology has highlighted what particular sections of the brain can or can't do. The most unusual group among these (and they are much-studied) is the handful of people who have had severe and life-threatening epilepsy alleviated through a radical severing of the neural fibers that connect the right and left hemispheres. Such populations, however, present a range of problems: tumors and wounds can cause disruptions in other areas of the brain; stroke victims could have had previous "silent strokes" and could, as well, be arteriosclerotic; long disease histories (certainly a characteristic of the severe epileptics who underwent split-brain surgery) can lead to compensatory change in brain function (Bogen, "The Dual Brain"; Whitaker and Ojemann). Furthermore, extra-pathological factors, such as education and motivation, can, as Bradshaw and Nettleton put it, also "mask or accentuate the apparent consequences of brain injury" (51). And, as a final caution, there is this: the whole enterprise of localizing linguistic function through pathological performance is not without its critics (see Caplan).

Studies with healthy subjects—and there are increasing numbers of these—remove one major difficulty with hemisphericity research, though here methodological problems of a different sort arise. Concern not with subjects but with instruments and measures now comes into focus. Space as well as my own technological shortcomings prohibit a full review of tools and methods, but it might prove valuable to briefly survey the problems with a representative research approach: electroencephalographic methods. (Readers interested in critical reviews of procedures other than the one I cover can consult the following: Regional Cerebral Blood Flow: Beaumont; Lateral Eye Movements: Ehrlichman and Weinberger; Tachistoscopic Methods: Young; Dichotic-Listening Tests: Efron.)

If you hypothesize that certain kinds of tasks (like discriminating between syllables or adding a list of numbers) are primarily left-brain tasks and that others (like mentally rotating blocks or recognizing faces) are primarily right-brain tasks, then neuroelectric activity in the target hemisphere should vary in predictable ways when the subject performs the respective tasks. And, in fact, such variation in brain wave activity has been empirically demonstrated for some time. Originally, such studies relied on the electroencephalogram (EEG)—the ongoing record of brain wave activity—but now it is possible to gain a more sophisticated record of what are called event-related potentials (ERP). ERP methods use the electroencephalographic machinery, but rely on computer averaging and formalization to more precisely relate brain wave activity to repeated presentations of specific stimuli (thus the waves are "event-related"). The advantage of EEG and ERP methods is that they offer a direct electrophysiological measurement of brain activity and, especially in the case of ERP, "can track rapid fluctuation in brain electrical fields related to cognitive processing . . ." (Brown, Marsh, and Ponsford

166). Such tracking is important to hemisphericity theorists, for it can lend precision to their claims.

There are problems, however. EEG/ERP methods are among the most technically demanding procedures in psychology, and that technical complexity gives rise to a number of difficulties involving variation in cortical anatomy, electrode placement, and data analysis (Beaumont; Gevins, Zeitlin, Doyle, Schaffer, and Callaway). And, when it comes to the study of language processing—certainly an area of concern to writing researchers— ERP procedures give rise to problems other than the technical. Most ERP studies must, for purposes of computer averaging, present each stimulus as many as 50 times, and such repetition creates highly artificial linguistic processing conditions. Even relatively natural language processing studies have trouble determining which perceptual, linguistic, or cognitive factors are responsible for results (see, e.g., Hillyard and Woods). So, though hemispheric differences in brain wave patterns can be demonstrated, the exceptional technical and procedural difficulties inherent in the EEG/ERP studies of language processing make it hard to interpret data with much precision. Cognitive psychophysiologists Emanuel Donchin, Gregory McCarthy, and Marta Kutas summarize this state of affairs:

> [A]lthough a substantial amount of clinical data support the theory of left hemisphere superiority in language reception and production, the ERP data regarding this functional asymmetry are far from consistent. The methodological and statistical shortcomings which exist in some of the studies cited [in their review article] along with inconsistencies in the others render any decision about the efficacy of ERP's as indices of linguistic processing inconclusive. (239. For similar, more recent, assessments, see Rugg; Beaumont, Young, and McManus.)

In considering the claims of the hemisphericity theorists, we have reviewed problems with subjects, techniques, and procedures. There is yet a further challenge to the notion of hemisphericity. Some hemisphericity theorists believe that since people can be characterized by a tendency to rely on one hemisphere or the other, then such reliance should manifest itself in the way people lead their lives: in the way they solve problems, in the jobs they choose, and so on. Yet the few studies that have investigated this dimension of the theory yielded negative results. Hemisphericity advocates Robert Ornstein and David Galin failed to find overall systematic EEG differences between lawyers (assumed to be left hemispheric) and sculptors and ceramicists (assumed to be right hemispheric). In a similar study, Dumas and Morgan failed to find EEG differences between engineers and artists, leading the researchers to conclude that "the conjecture that there are 'left hemispheric' people and 'right hemispheric' people seems to be an oversimplification" (227). In a more ambitious study, Arndt and Berger gave graduate students in law, psychology, and sculpture batteries of tests to assess verbal analytic ability (for example, a vocabulary test) and spatial ability (for example, a figure recognition test), and, as well, tests to assess hemisphericity (letter and facial recognition tachistoscopic tasks). While they found — as one would expect — a significant correlation between verbal or spatial ability and occupation (e.g., sculptors scored better than lawyers on the spatial tests), they *did not* find significant correlations between the verbal or spatial tests and the hemisphericity task; nor did they find significant correlation between the hemisphericity task and occupation.

A postscript on the above. Failures to find hemispheric differences between individuals of various occupational groups — along with the methodological difficulties mentioned earlier — throw into serious doubt the neurosociological claim that entire *groups* of people can be characterized as being left or right hemispheric. The neurosociological literature makes some remarkable speculative leaps from the existence of left-right dualities in cultural myth and symbol to asymmetries in left-right brain function, and relies, for empirical support, on the results of individual verbal and spatial tests (like the sub-tests in I.Q. assessments) — precisely the kinds of tests that a number of psychologists and neurologists have shown to be limited in assessing left or right hemispheric performance (see, e.g., DeRenzi).

Let me try to draw a few conclusions for rhetoric and composition studies.

It is important to keep in mind that the experimental studies that do support hemispheric specialization suggest small differences in performance capacities, and the differences tend to be of degree more than kind: in the range of 6–12%. Researchers have to expose subjects to many trials to achieve these differences. (One hundred and fifty to two hundred is common; one facial recognition study ran subjects through 700 trials.) And the experiments deal with extremely specific — even atomistic — functions. (Researchers consider the distinguishing of homonyms in a sentence — "bear" vs. "bare" — to be a "complex verbal task.") It is difficult to generalize from results of this type and magnitude to broad statements about one hemisphere being the seat of logic and the other of metaphor. What happens, it seems, is that theorists bring to very particular (though, admittedly, very important) findings about phonology or syntax or pattern recognition a whole array of cultural beliefs about analytic vs. synthetic thinking and logic vs. creativity and apply them in blanket fashion. There is a related problem here, and it concerns the hemisphericity theorists' assumption that, say, distinguishing phonemes is an analytical or serial or propositional task while, say, facial recognition is synthetic or holistic or appositional. These assumptions are sensible, but they are not proven. In fact, *one could argue the other way around*: e.g., that recognizing faces, for example, is not a holistic but a features analysis task. Unfortunately, neuroscientists don't know enough to resolve this very important issue. They work with indirect measures of information processing: differences in reaction time or variations in electrophysiological measures. They would need more direct access than they now have to the way information is being represented and problems are being solved.

Because the accounts of cerebral asymmetry can be so dramatic — particularly those from split-brain studies — it is easy to dwell on differences.

But, in fact, there is wide-ranging similarity, overlap, and cooperation in the function of the right and left hemispheres:

> Complex psychological processes are not 'localized' in any one hemisphere but are the result of integration between hemispheres. (Alexander Luria cited in LeDoux 210)

If Luria's dictum applied anywhere, it would certainly be to the "complex psychological processes" involved in reading and writing. Under highly controlled laboratory conditions researchers can show that phoneme discrimination or word recognition can be relatively localizable to one hemisphere or the other. But attempts to comprehend or generate writing—what is perceived or produced as logical or metaphoric or coherent or textured—involve a stunning range of competencies: from letter recognition to syntactic fluency to an understanding of discourse structure and genre (see, e.g., Gardner and Winner 376–380). And such a range, according to everything we know, involves the whole brain in ways that defy the broad claims of the hemisphericity theorists. When students have trouble structuring an argument or providing imagistic detail, there is little neurophysiological evidence to support contentions that their difficulties originate in organic predisposition or social conditioning to rely on one hemisphere or the other.

Jean Piaget and Stages of Cognitive Development

Piaget's theory of cognitive development is generally held to be, even by its revisors and detractors, the modern West's most wide-ranging and significant account of the way children think. The theory, which Piaget began to articulate over 50 years ago, covers infancy to adolescence and addresses the development of scientific and mathematical reasoning, language, drawing, morality, and social perception; it has shaped the direction of inquiry into childhood cognition; and it has led to an incredible number of studies, a good many of which have been cross-cultural. In holding to the focus of this article, then, there's a lot I'll have to ignore—I'll be limiting myself to those aspects of Piaget's theory that have been most widely discussed in reference to college-age writers.

Though Piaget and his colleagues adjusted their theory to account for the wealth of data being generated by researchers around the world, there are several critical features that remain central to the theory. Piaget's theory is a stage theory. He posits four general stages (some with substages), and all children pass through them in the same order. A child's reasoning at each stage is *qualitatively* different from that at earlier or later stages, though the knowledge and strategies of earlier stages are incorporated into later ones. During any given stage, the child reasons in *similar* ways regardless of the kinds of problems she or he faces, and Piaget tended to rule out the possibility that, during a given stage, a child could be trained to reason in much more sophisticated ways. Passage, evolution really, from one stage to the next occurs over time, an interaction of genetic processes and engagement with the world. The child continually assimilates new information which both reshapes and is reshaped by the knowledge structures the child currently has — and, as the child continues to interact with the world, she or he experiences discontinuities between the known and the new, and these discontinuities lead to further development of knowledge of how things work. Thinking, then, gradually evolves to ever more complex levels, represented by each of the stages.

It is important to keep in mind that Piaget's perspective on cognition is fundamentally logical and mathematical. Late in his life he observed that he did not wish "to appear only as a child psychologist":

> My efforts, directed toward the psychogenesis of thought, were for me only a link between two dominant preoccupations: the search for the mechanisms of biological adaptation and the analysis of that higher form of adaptation which is scientific thought, the epistemological interpretation of which has always been my central aim. (in Gruber and Vonèche xi)

With this perspective in mind, let us very briefly consider the stages of Piaget's theory that are appropriated to discussions of college-age remedial writers.

• *Concrete Operational* (6–7 to 11–12 years). The cognitive milestone here is that children are freed from immediate perception and enter the realm of logical — if concrete — operations. They can use logic to solve everyday problems, can take other points of view, can simultaneously take into account more than one perspective. In many ways, though, the child's reasoning is still linked to the environment, to tasks that are concrete and well-specified: "Tasks that demand very abstract reasoning, long chains of deduction, or the recognition that the available evidence is insufficient to reach any conclusion are thought to be beyond the reach" of children at the concrete operational stage (Siegler 89). Children have trouble separating out and recombining variables, performing sophisticated conservation tasks, and solving proportionality problems. They also have trouble planning systematic experiments and understanding "purely hypothetical questions that are completely divorced from anything in their experience" (Siegler 90).

• *Formal Operational* (11–15 years). During this stage, children develop into sophisticated logical thinkers — Piaget compared them to scientists — and can solve problems that throw concrete-operational children: like the pendulum task described below. Flavell summarizes the ability of the formal-operational child this way: "His thinking is *hypothetico-deductive* rather than *empirico-inductive*, because he creates hypotheses and then deduces the empirical states of affairs that should occur if his hypotheses are correct ... The older individual's thinking can ... be totally abstract, totally formal-logical in nature." (145. For a critical discussion of the notion of stages, see Brainerd.)

Piaget and his colleagues developed a number of tasks to distinguish concrete from formal operational thinking. The pendulum task is representative:

> Children observed strings with metal balls at their ends swinging from a metal frame. The strings varied in length and the metal balls varied

in how much they weighed; the task was to identify the factor or combination of factors that determined the pendulum's period. Plausible hypotheses included the weight of the metal balls, the length of the strings, the height from which the strings were dropped, and the force with which they were pushed. Although the length of the string is in fact the only relevant factor . . . 10- and 11-year-olds almost always concluded that the metal ball's weight played a key role, either as the sole determining factor or in combination with the string's length. Thus the children failed to disentangle the influence of the different variables to determine which one caused the effect. (Siegler 89–90)

In the 1970's a number of studies appeared reporting that up to 50% of American college freshmen could not solve formal-operational problems like the pendulum task. The conclusion was that an alarming number of our 18-year-olds were locked at the level of concrete operations, a stage Piaget contends they should have begun evolving beyond by early and certainly by mid-adolescence. These data quickly found their way to a more general readership, and some people in composition understandably saw relevance in them and began to use them to explain the problems with the writing of remedial students. With support of the data, they wrote that up to 50% of college freshmen were locked into the level of the concrete, couldn't think abstractly, couldn't produce logical propositions, couldn't conceptualize — and, borrowing further from Piagetian terminology, they speculated that these students couldn't decenter, couldn't take another's point of view, were cognitively egocentric. The last two stages of the Piagetian framework became in application a kind of cognitive dichotomy unto themselves. If students couldn't produce coherent abstractions in writing, if they wrote about what was in front of them and couldn't express themselves on the conceptual level, if they described something in writing as though their reader shared their knowledge of it — then those limits in written expression suggested something broad and general about the state of their thinking: they might be unable to form abstractions . . . any abstractions; they couldn't decenter . . . at all. There are problems with this line of reasoning, however, and they have to do with the application of the framework as well as with the framework itself.

As any developmental psychologist will point out, there are major conceptual problems involved in applying a *developmental* model to adults. Piaget's theory was derived from the close observation of infants, children, and early- to mid-adolescents; it was intended as a description of the way thinking evolves in the growing human being. Applying it to college-age students and, particularly, to adult learners is to generalize it to a population other than the one that yielded it. There are more specific problems to consider as well, and they have to do with testing.

It is important to underscore the fact that Piaget implies broad limitations in cognition from specific inadequacies on a circumscribed set of tasks. This is not an unreasonable induction — all sorts of general theories are built on the performance of specific tasks — but it must be pointed out that we are dealing with an inference of major consequence. As developmental psychologist

Rochelle Gelman put it: "The child is said to lack cognitive principles of broad significance simply because he fails a particular task involving those principles" (326). It is, then, an inferential leap of some magnitude to say that because college students fail to separate out variables and formally test hypotheses in a few tasks typical of the physics lab, they cannot conceptualize or abstract or tease out variables in any other sphere of their lives. Piaget himself said as much in one of his late articles:

> In our investigation of formal structures we used rather specific types of experimental situations which were of a physical and logical-mathematical nature because these seemed to be understood by the school children we sampled. However, it is possible to question whether these situations are, fundamentally, very general and therefore applicable to any school or professional environment . . . It is highly likely that [people like apprentice carpenters, locksmiths, or mechanics] will know how to reason in a hypothetical manner in their speciality, that is to say, dissociating the variables involved, relating terms in a combinatorial manner and reasoning with propositions involving negations and reciprocities. (10)

Piaget's tests are clever and complex. To assist in replication, Piaget and his colleagues provided explicit instructions on how to set up the tests, what to say, and how to assess performance. This clarity contributed to the welter of Piagetian studies conducted over the years, many of which supported the theory. A significant body of recent research, however, has raised serious questions about the social conditions created when these tests are given. Most of this research has been done with younger children, and probably the best summary of it is Donaldson's. The thrust of this work is contained in one of Donaldson's chapter titles; when a child performs poorly on a Piagetian task, is it because of a "failure to reason or a failure to understand"? The tasks might be unfamiliar; the child might misunderstand the instructions; because psychological experiments are new to her, she might confuse the experimenter's intentions and "not see the experiment as the experimenter hopes [she] will" (Gelman 324). (See also philosopher Jonathan Adler's Grician critique of Piagetian testing.) What psychologists like Donaldson have done is keep the formal requirements of Piagetian tasks but change the particular elements to make them more familiar (e.g., substituting a toy policeman and a wall for a doll and a mountain), provide a chance for children to get familiar with the tasks, and rephrase instructions to make sure children understand what is being asked. Children in these conditions end up performing remarkably better on the tasks; significantly higher percentages of them can, for example, adopt other points of view, conserve quantity and number, and so on. What limited some children on Piaget's tasks, then, seems to be more related to experimental conditions rather than some absolute restriction in their ability to reason.

A somewhat related set of findings has do with training — one of the more controversial issues in Piagetian theory. This is not the place to recap the controversy; suffice it to say that a large number of studies has demonstrated that brief training sessions can have dramatic results on performance. One such study has direct bearing on our discussion. Kuhn, Ho, and Adams provided training to college freshmen who failed at formal-operational tasks. After training, the students were once again presented with the tests, and "most of the college subjects showed immediate and substantial formal reasoning." The authors go on to speculate that the absence of formal-operational performance "may to a large extent reflect cognitive processing difficulties in dealing with the problem formats, rather than absence of underlying reasoning competencies" (1128).

I will conclude this brief critique by considering, once again, the mathematico-logical base of Piaget's theory. There is a tradition in the 20th century West—shaped by Russell, Whitehead, Carnap, and others—to study human reasoning within the framework of formal, mathematical logic, to see logic not only as a powerful tool, but as a representation of how people actually reason—at least when they're reasoning effectively. This tradition had a strong influence on Piaget's theory. In Toulmin's words, Piaget's "overall intellectual goal" was to:

> discover how growing children "come to *recognize the necessity* of" conforming to the intellectual structures of logic, Euclidean geometry, and the other basic Kantian forms. (256)

And as Inhelder and Piaget themselves said: "[R]easoning is nothing more than the propositional calculus itself" (305).

Mathematical logic is so privileged that we tend to forget that this assumption about logic being isomorphic with reasoning is highly controversial; it lies at the center of a number of current debates in cognitive psychology, artificial intelligence, and philosophy. Here is one of many counterstatements:

> Considerations of pure logic . . . may be useful for certain kinds of information under certain circumstances by certain individuals. But logic cannot serve as a valid model of how most individuals solve most problems most of the time. (Gardner, *Mind's New Science* 370)

Formal logic essentially strips away all specific connections to human affairs and things of the world; it allows us to represent relations and interactions within a wholly abstract system. Our elevation of this procedure blinds us to the overwhelming degree to which powerful and effective reasoning can be practical, non-formal, and concrete. As psychologist Barbara Rogoff puts it, "thinking is intricately interwoven with the context of the problem to be solved" (2). She continues:

> Evidence suggests that our ability to control and orchestrate cognitive skills is not an abstract context-free competence which may be easily transferred across widely diverse problem domains but consists rather of cognitive activity tied specifically to context. (3)

Much problem-solving and, I suspect, the reasoning involved in the production of most kinds of writing rely not only on abstract logical operations, but, as well, on the rich interplay of visual, auditory, and kinesthetic associations, feeling, metaphor, social perception, the matching of mental representations of past experience with new experience, and so on. And writing, as the whole span of rhetorical theory makes clear, is deeply embedded in the particulars of the human situation. It is a context-dependent activity that calls on many abilities. We may well need to engage in formal-logical reasoning when writing certain kinds of scientific or philosophical papers or when analyzing certain kinds of hypotheses and arguments, but we cannot assume that the ability or inability to demonstrate formal-operational thought on one or two Piagetian tasks has a necessary connection to our students' ability or inability to produce coherent, effective discourse.

ORALITY-LITERACY

Orality-literacy theory draws on the studies of epic poetry by Milman Parry and Albert Lord, the classical-philological investigations of Eric Havelock, the wide-ranging theoretical work of Walter Ong, and, to a lesser degree, on the compelling, though dated, cross-cultural investigations of thought in primitive, non-literate cultures. The work is broad, rich, and diverse—ranging from studies of the structure of the epic line to the classification schemes of unlettered rural farmers—but as it comes to those of us in composition, its focus is on the interrelation of language and cognition. Various scholars say it in various ways, but the essential notion is that the introduction of literacy into a society affects the way the members of the society think. There seem to be strong and weak versions of this theory.

The strong version states that the acquisition of literacy brings with it not only changes in linguistic possibilities—e.g., subordinative and discursive rather than additive and repetitive styles, less reliance on epithets and maxims and other easily remembered expressions—but *necessarily* results in a wide variety of changes in thinking: only after the advent of literacy do humans possess the ability to engage in abstraction, generalization, systematic thinking, defining, logos rather than mythos, puzzlement over words as words, speculation on the features of language. And these abilities, depending on who you read, lead to even wider changes in culture, summarized, not without exasperation, by social historian Harvey Graff:

> These characteristics include, in typical formulations or listings, attitudes ranging *from* empathy, innovativeness, achievement orientation, "cosmopoliteness," information and media awareness, national identification, technological acceptance, rationality, and commitment to democracy, *to* opportunism, linearity of thought and behavior, or urban residence. ("Reflections" 307)

The operative verb here is "transformed." Writing *transforms* human cognition.

The weak version of the oral-literate construct acknowledges the role literacy plays in developing modes of inquiry, building knowledge, etc., but tends to rely on verbs like "facilitate," "favor," "enable," "extend"—the potential of human cognition is extended more than transformed. Here's Jack

Goody, an anthropologist who is often lumped in with those holding to the "strong version," but who, at least in his late work, takes issue with the oral-literate dichotomy. In discussing various differences between literate and oral expression, for example, he warns that such differences "do not relate primarily to differences of 'thought' or 'mind' (though there are consequences for these) but to differences in the nature of communicative acts" (26). So though Goody grants that writing "made it possible to scrutinize discourse in a different kind of way" and "increased the potentiality for cumulative knowledge" and freed participants from "the problem of memory storage" dominating "intellectual life," (37) he also insists that:

> Even in non-literate societies there is no evidence that individuals were prisoners of pre-ordained schemes, of primitive classifications, of the structures of myth. Constrained, yes; imprisoned, no. Certain, at least, among them could and did use language in a generative way, elaborating metaphor, inventing songs and "myths," creating gods, looking for new solutions to recurring puzzles and problems, changing the conceptual universe. (33)

The theory is a sensible one: literacy must bring with it tremendous repercussions for the intellect. The problem is that when the theory, particularly the strong version, is applied to composition studies, it yields some troubling consequences. Late twentieth-century American inner-city adolescents and adults are thought to bear cognitive resemblance to (ethnocentric notions of) primitive tribesmen in remote third-world cultures (or these adolescents and adults think like children, and children think like primitives): they don't practice analytic thinking; they are embedded in the context of their lives and cannot analyze it; they see things only as wholes; they think that printed words are concrete things; they cannot think abstractly.

A little reflection on this application of orality-literacy theory—given its origins—reveals a serious problem of method. The theory emerges from anthropological work with primitive populations, from historical-philological study of Homeric texts, from folkloric investigations of non-literate taletellers, and from brilliant, though speculative, literary-theoretical reflection on what might have happened to the human mind as it appropriated the alphabet. It is, then, a tremendous conceptual leap to apply this theory to urban-industrial Americans entering school in the penultimate decade of the twentieth century. We have here a problem of generalizability.

Now one could admit these problems yet still see some analogic value in applying the oral-literate construct with a hedge—for it at least, as opposed to the other theories we've been exploring, is directly concerned with written language. Fair enough. Yet my reading has led me to doubt the strength and utility of the theory on its own terms. (My concern rests primarily with the strong version. The weak version makes less dramatic claims about cognition, though some of what I found would qualify weak versions as well.) There are problems with what the theory implies about the way written language emerges in society and the role it plays in determining how people lead their linguistic lives and conduct their cognitive affairs. This is not to deny the profound effects literacy can have on society; it is to question the strength of the orality-literacy construct in characterizing those effects. Let me briefly survey some of the difficulties.

Literacy and Society.   The historical record suggests that the technology and conventions of literacy work their way slowly through a society and have gradual—and not necessarily linearly progressive—influence on commerce, politics, bureaucracy, law, religion, education, the arts. (See, e.g., Marrou; Clanchy; Cressy.) Furthermore, it is hard to maintain, as the strong version does, that literacy is the primum mobile in social-cultural change. What emerges, instead, is a complex interaction of economic, political, and religious forces of which literacy is a part—and not necessarily the strongest element. Though there is no doubt that literacy shapes the way commerce, government, and religion are conducted, it, as John Oxenham puts it: "would have followed, not preceded, the formation of certain kinds of society" (59). And Harvey Graff, pointing out all the "discontinuities" and "contradictions" in linear, evolutionary assumptions about the spread of literacy, emphasizes that "[n]either writing [n]or printing alone is an 'agent of change'; their impacts are determined by the manner in which human agency exploits them in a specific setting" ("Reflections" 307).[4]

Another way to view the problems with the transformational claims about literacy is to consider the fact that a number of societies have appropriated literacy to traditional, conservative purposes. In such societies literacy did not trigger various cultural-cognitive changes—changes in mores, attitudes, etc.—but reinforced patterns already in place. Again, John Oxenham:

> We have always to bear in mind that there have been literate social groups, who so far from being inventive and trusting, have been content merely to copy their ancient scriptures and pass them on virtually unaltered. It may be, then, that literate people can respond more readily to leadership for change in culture, technology, social mores, but that literacy by itself does not induce appetites for change, improvement or exploration. (52)

There are a number of illustrations of this; one specific case-study is provided by Kenneth Lockridge, whose inquiry into the social context of literacy in Colonial New England leads him to conclude:

> [T]here is no evidence that literacy ever entailed new attitudes among men, even in the decades when male literacy was spreading rapidly toward universality, and there is positive evidence that the world view of literate New Englanders remained as traditional as that of their illiterate neighbors. (4)

It is even difficult to demonstrate causal links between reading and writing and changes in the economic sphere—an area that "modernization theorists" generally thought to be particularly sensitive to gains in literacy.

Harvey Graff's study of social mobility in three mid-19th century towns revealed that "systematic patterns of inequality and stratification . . . were deep and pervasive and relatively unaltered by the influence of literacy." He continues:

> Class, ethnicity, and sex were the major barriers of social inequality. The majority of Irish Catholic adults, for example, were literate . . . but they stood lowest in wealth and occupation, as did laborers and servants. Women and blacks fared little better, regardless of literacy . . . social realities contradicted the promoted promises of literacy. (*The Literacy Myth* 320–321)

Similar assertions are made closer to home by Carman St. John Hunter and David Harmon, whose overview of the research on contemporary adult illiteracy leads to this conclusion:

> For most persons who lack literacy skills, illiteracy is simply one factor interacting with many others—class, race and sex discrimination, welfare dependency, unemployment, poor housing, and a general sense of powerlessness. The acquisition of reading and writing skills would eliminate conventional illiteracy among many but would have no appreciable effect on the other factors that perpetuate the poverty of their lives. (9–12. See also Ogbu.)

The oral-literate distinction can help us see differences in the communicative technologies available to the members of a society, to get a sense of formats, means, and forums through which communication occurs (Enos and Ackerman). But it appears to be historically, culturally, and economically reductive—and politically naive—to view literacy as embodying an automatic transformational power. What is called for is a contextual view of literacy: the ability to read or to write is a technology or a method or a behavior, a set of conventions that interact in complex ways with a variety of social forces to shape society and culture. It is, to use Harvey Graff's phrasing, a "myth" to assume that literacy necessarily sparks social change.

Literacy and Cognition.   Let us move now from the social-cultural realm to some of the claims made about cognition. These come from two highly diverse sources: classical philological studies of epic poetry and anthropological studies of thought and language. There are problems with both.

The key work in the classicist vein is Eric Havelock's investigation of Greek culture before and after the advent of the alphabet. In books ranging from *Preface to Plato* (published in 1963) to *The Muse Learns to Write* (1986) Havelock has made the strong claim that pre-alphabetic Greeks, ingenious as they were, were barred from philosophical thought because oral discourse could not generate abstract, propositional language or self-conscious reflection on language as language. To be sure, there are times when Havelock's claims are less extreme, but even in *The Muse Learns to Write*, a tempered book, one finds questions and statements like these: "May not all logical thinking as commonly understood be a product of Greek alphabetic literacy?" (39) and "it is only as language is written down that it becomes possible to think about it" (112). And such theorizing quickly leads to a troublesome alphabetic determinism.

Havelock's work is compelling, but we must remember that when it comes to cognition, he is operating very much in the realm of speculation. That is, he infers things about cognitive processes and the limits of reasoning ability from the study of ancient texts, some of which represent genres that one would not expect to give rise to philosophic inquiry. Furthermore, even if we accepted his method, we could find powerful counterstatements to his thesis — and some of these are contained in a festschrift issued by the Monist Press. Examining the same texts from which Havelock built his case, University of Chicago classicist Arthur W. H. Adkins provides evidence of abstraction, verbal self-consciousness, and the linguistic resources to engage in systematic thinking. He concludes that:

> Havelock has not as yet demonstrated any *necessary* link between literacy and abstract thought ... he has not as yet demonstrated that *in fact* the stimulus to abstract thought in early Greece was the invention of writing; [and] some features denied by Havelock to be available in oral speech are found in the Homeric poems. (220. See also Margolis.)

The other line of argument about literacy and cognition comes from twentieth-century anthropological studies of the reasoning of rural farmers and primitive tribesmen. These studies tend not to be of literacy-orality per se, but are appropriated by some orality-literacy theorists. A good deal of this cross-cultural research has involved classification tasks: a set of objects (or a set of pictures of the objects) is given to a tribesman, and the investigator asks the tribesman to group the objects/pictures. The key issue is the scheme by which the tribesman completes the grouping: does he, for example, place a hoe with a potato and offer the *concrete* reason that they go together because you need one to get the other, or does he place the hoe with a knife because he reasons *abstractly* that they are both tools? The Western anthropologist considers concrete reasoning to be less advanced than abstract reasoning, and orality-literacy theorists like to pose literacy as the crucial variable fostering abstract reasoning. It is because the tribesman lacks letters that he is locked into the concrete. This is an appealing conjecture, but, as I hope the previous discussion suggests, literacy is too intertwined with schooling and urbanization, with economics, politics, and religion to be able to isolate it and make such a claim. There are other problems too, not just with the causal linking of literacy and abstraction, but with traditional comparative research itself. Cole and Means put it this way:

> [D]epartures from the typical performance patterns of American adults are not necessarily deficits, but may indeed be excellent adaptions to the life circumstances of the people involved ... Which type of classification is preferable will depend upon the context, that is, the number of different types of objects to be grouped and the way in which the materials are going to be used ... preference for one type of grouping over another is really no more than that — just a matter of preference. (161–162)

In line with the above, it must be kept in mind that because "primitive" subjects tend to classify objects in ways we label concrete does not necessarily mean that they can think in no other way. Consider, as we close this section, a wonderful anecdote from anthropologist Joseph Glick, as retold by Jacqueline Goodenow:

> The investigators had gathered a set of 20 objects, 5 each from 4 categories: food, clothing, tools, and cooking utensils . . . [W]hen asked to put together the objects that belonged together, [many of the tribesmen produced] not 4 groups of 5 but 10 groups of 2. Moreover, the type of grouping and the type of reason given were frequently of the type we regard as extremely concrete, e.g., "the knife goes with the orange because it cuts it." Glick . . . notes, however, that subjects at times volunteered "'that a wise man would do things in the way this was done.' When an exasperated experimenter asked finally, 'How would a fool do it?' he was given back groupings of the type . . . initially expected—four neat piles with foods in one, tools in another." (170–171. For fuller cross-cultural discussions of concrete vs. abstract reasoning see Ginsburg; Lave; and Tulkin and Konner.)

Literacy and Language.   It is problematic, then, to claim that literacy necessarily causes a transformation of culture, society, or mind or that societies without high levels of literacy are barred from the mental activities that some theorists have come to associate with literacy: verbal self-consciousness, abstraction, etc. Perhaps, though, the orality-literacy construct does have value if one strips away the cultural-cognitive baggage; its real benefit might be its ability to help us understand the nature of the language experiences students received in their homes and communities and further help to distinguish between the oral and literate features in their writing. But even here there are problems, for the reality of speaking-writing relationships seems to be more complex than the oral-literate distinction suggests.

Certainly, there are bioanatomical and perceptual differences between speech and writing—differences in the way each is acquired, produced, and comprehended. And if you examine very different types of language (e.g., dinner-table conversation vs. academic prose), you will find significant grammatical and stylistic differences as well. (See, for example, Chafe.) But the oral-literate construct leads us to focus attention too narrowly on the channel, the mode of communication, in a way that can (a) imply a distinctive uniformity to oral modes vs. written modes and (b) downplay the complex interaction among human motive, language production, and social setting. Linguists currently working with oral narratives and written texts suggest that the notion of an oral narrative itself is problematic, for oral traditions can differ in major ways (Scollon and Scollon); that the narrative variations we see may have less to do with literateness than with cultural predispositions (Tannen, "A Comparative Analysis"); that features often defined as literate are frequently found in oral discourse and vice versa (Polanyi; Tannen, "Relative Focus"); that characteristics identified by some as a mark of preliterate discourse—e.g., formulaic expressions—are woven throughout the language of literate people (Fillmore); that while spoken sentences can be shown to differ from written sentences, they are not necessarily less complex grammatically (Halliday); and so on. Finally, it seems that many of the differences we can find between stretches of speech and writing might, as Karen Beamon suggests, depend on factors such as genre, context, register, topic, level of formality, and purpose as much as whether the passage is spoken or written.

These closer examinations of a wide variety of texts and utterances should make us wary of neat, bipolar characterizations—whether dichotomies or simple continua—of oral vs. written language. And it seems to me that this caution about the linguistic reality of the oral-literate distinction could lead to reservations about its contemporary social reality—that is, can we accurately and sensitively define, in late twentieth-century America, entire communities and subcultures as being oral and others as being literate? By what criteria, finally, will we be able to make such a distinction? In asking these questions, I am not trying to downplay the obvious: children enter school with widely different degrees of exposure to literacy activities and with significantly different experiences as to how those activities are woven into their lives. And these differences clearly have consequences for schooling.

What I do want to raise, though, is the possibility that the oral-literate continuum does not adequately characterize these differences. The continuum, because it moves primarily along the single dimension of speech-print, slights history and politics—remember, it weights literacy as *the* primary force in cognitive development and social change—and it encourages, because of its bipolarity, a dichotomizing of modes where complex interweaving seems to exist. Finally, the orality-literacy construct tends to reduce the very social-linguistic richness it is meant to describe. Here is Shirley Brice Heath on the language behaviors of two working-class communities in the Carolinas:

> The residents of each community are able to read printed and written materials in their daily lives and, on occasion, they produce written messages as part of the total pattern of communication in the community. In both communities, the residents turn from spoken to written uses of language and vice versa as the occasion demands, and the two modes of expression serve to supplement and reinforce each other. Yet, in terms of the usual distinctions made between oral and literate traditions, neither community may be simply classified as either "oral" or "literate." (*Ways with Words* 203)

Work like Heath's challenges the sociological and linguistic utility of the orality-literacy construct; in fact, elsewhere Heath directly criticizes "current tendencies to classify communities as being at one or another point along a hypothetical [oral-literate] continuum which has no societal reality" ("Protean Shapes" 116).

What is most troubling on this score is the way the orality-literacy construct is sometimes used to represent language use in the urban ghetto. What emerges is a stereotypic characterization of linguistic homogeneity—all the residents learn from the sermon but not the newspaper; they run the dozens but are ignorant of print. The literacy backgrounds of people who end up in remedial, developmental, or adult education classes are more complex than that: they represent varying degrees of distance from or involvement with printed material, various attitudes toward it and skill with it, various degrees of embracement of or complicated rejection of traditions connected with their speech. Important here is what Mina Shaughnessy and Glynda Hull so carefully demonstrate: some of the most vexing problems writing teachers face are rooted in the past attempts of educationally marginalized people *to make sense of the uses of print*. Print is splattered across the inner city, and, in effective and ineffective ways, people incorporate it into their lives.

There is a related problem. Some theorists link Piagetian notions of cognitive egocentrism with generalizations about orality and conclude that without the language of high literacy, people will be limited in their ability to "decenter," to recognize the need to "decontextualize" what they are communicating, to perceive and respond to the social and informational needs of the other. Certainly, people with poor educations will have a great deal of trouble doing such things in writing, but one must be very cautious about leaping from stunted and limited texts to inferences about deficits in social cognition or linguistic flexibility. Developmentally and sociologically oriented linguists have demonstrated for some time that human beings are not locked into one way of speaking, one register, and develop, at quite a young age, the recognition that different settings call for different kinds of speech (Hudson). Poor writers are not as a population cognitively egocentric; they are aware of the other, of "audience" — some disenfranchised people acutely so. What they lack are the opportunities to develop both oral and written communicative facility in a range of settings. Or they may resist developing that facility out of anger or fear or as an act of identity. They may prefer one way of speaking, most of us do, and thus haven't developed a fluency of voices. But rather than being cognitively locked out of other registers, other linguistic roles, other points of view, they are more likely emotionally and politically barred from them.

It is obvious that literacy enables us to do a great deal. It provides a powerful solution to what Walter Ong calls "the problem of retaining and retrieving carefully articulated thought" (34). It enables us to record discourse, scan and scrutinize it, store it — and this has an effect on the way we educate, do business, and run the courts. And as we further pursue intellectual work, reading and writing become integral parts of inquiry, enable us to push certain kinds of analysis to very sophisticated levels. In fact, as investigations of academic and research settings like Latour and Woolgar's *Laboratory Life* suggest, it becomes virtually impossible to tease writing and reading out of the conduct and progress of Western humanistic *or* scientific inquiry. One of the values of the orality-literacy construct is that it makes us aware of how central literacy is to such inquiry. But, finally, the bipolarity of the construct (as with the others we've examined) urges a way of thinking about language, social change, and cognition that easily becomes dichotomous and reductive.

"The tyranny of conceptual dichotomies," Graff calls it ("Reflections" 313). If writing is thought to possess a given characteristic — say, decontextualization or abstraction — then the dichotomy requires you to place the opposite characteristic — contextualization, concreteness — in the non-writing category (cf. Elbow). We end up splitting cognition along linguistic separations that exist more in theory than in social practice.

CONCLUSION

Witkin uncovered interesting perceptual differences and led us toward a deeper consideration of the interrelations of personality, problem solving, and social cognition. Hemisphericity theorists call our attention to the neurological substrate of information processing and language production. Piaget developed an insightful, non-behaviorist method to study cognitive growth and, more comprehensively than anyone in our time, attempted to articulate the changes in reasoning we see as children develop. And the orality-literacy theorists give us compelling reflection on spoken and written language and encourage us to consider the potential relations between modes of communication and modes of thought. My intention in this essay is not to dismiss these thinkers and theories but to present the difficulties in applying to remedial writers these models of mind. For there is a tendency to accept as fact condensed deductions from them — statements stripped away from the questions, contradictions, and complexities that are central to them. Let me summarize the problems I see with the theories we've been considering.

First, the theories end up levelling rather than elaborating individual differences in cognition. At best, people are placed along slots on a single continuum; at worst they are split into mutually exclusive camps — with one camp clearly having cognitive and social privilege over the other. The complexity of cognition — its astounding glides and its blunderous missteps as well — is narrowed, and the rich variability that exists in any social setting is ignored or reduced. This reductive labelling is going on in composition studies at a time when cognitive researchers in developmental and educational psychology, artificial intelligence, and philosophy are posing more elaborate and domain-specific models of cognition.

Second, and in line with the above, the four theories encourage a drift away from careful, rigorous focus on student writing and on the cognitive processes that seem directly related to it, that reveal themselves as students compose. That is, field dependence-independence, hemisphericity, etc., lead us from a close investigation of the production of written discourse and toward general, wide-ranging processes whose link to writing has, for the most part, been *assumed rather than demonstrated*. Even orality-literacy theory, which certainly concerns language, urges an antagonism between speech and writing that carries with it sweeping judgments about cognition.

The theories also avert or narrow our gaze from the immediate social and linguistic conditions in which the student composes: the rich interplay of purpose, genre, register, textual convention, and institutional expectation

(Bartholomae; Bizzell; McCormick). When this textual-institutional context is addressed, it is usually in simplified terms: the faculty—and their discourse—are literate, left-hemispheric, field-independent, etc., and under-prepared students are oral, right-hemispheric, and field-dependent. I hope my critical surveys have demonstrated the conceptual limits of such labelling.

Third, the theories inadvertently reflect cultural stereotypes that should, themselves, be the subject of our investigation. At least since Plato, we in the West have separated heart from head, and in one powerful manifestation of that split we contrast rational thought with emotional sensibility, intellectual acuity with social awareness—and we often link the analytical vs. holistic opposition to these polarities. (I tried to reveal the confusion inherent in such talk when discussing cognitive style and hemisphericity.) These notions are further influenced by and play into other societal notions about independence and individuality vs. communal and tribal orientations and they domino quickly toward stereotypes about race, class, and gender.

Let me say now that I am not claiming that the research in cognitive style or hemisphericity or any of the other work we surveyed is of necessity racist, sexist, or elitist. The conclusions that can be drawn from the work, however, mesh with—and could have been subtly influenced by—cultural biases that are troubling. This is an important and, I realize, sensitive point. Some assert that student writers coming from particular communities can't reason logically or analytically, that the perceptual processes of these students are more dependent on context than the processes of white, middle-class students, that particular racial or social groups are right-hemispheric, that the student writers we teach from these groups are cognitively egocentric.

A number of recent books have amply demonstrated the way 19th and early 20th century scientific, social scientific, and humanistic assessments of mental capacity and orientation were shaped by that era's racial, gender, and class biases (see, for example, Gilman; Gould; Kamin; and Valenstein). We now find these assessments repellent, but it's important to remember that while some were made by reactionary social propagandists, a number were made as well by thinkers operating with what they saw as rigorous method—and some of those thinkers espoused a liberal social philosophy. This is a powerful illustration of the hidden influences of culture on allegedly objective investigations of mind. We all try to make sense of problematic performance—that's part of a teacher's or a researcher's job—but we must ask ourselves if speculation about cognitive egocentrism and concrete thinking and holistic perception embodies unexamined cultural biases about difference—biases that would be revealed to us if we could adopt other historical and social perspectives.

These summary statements have a number of implications for research.

The leap to theory is a privileged move—it is revered in the academy and allows parsimonious interpretations of the baffling variability of behavior. But a theory, any theory, is no more than a best guess at a given time, simultaneously evocative and flawed. Especially when it comes to judging cognition, we need to be particularly aware of these flaws and limitations, for in our culture judgments about mind carry great weight. A good deal of careful, basic descriptive and definitional work must be done before we embrace a theory, regardless of how compelling it is.

A series of fundamental questions should precede the application of theory: Is the theory formulated in a way that allows application to writing; that is, can it be defined in terms of discourse? Given what we know about writing, how would the theory be expected to manifest itself — i.e., what would it mean textually and dynamically for someone to be a field-dependent writer? What will the theory allow us to explain about writing that we haven't explained before? What will it allow us to do pedagogically that we weren't able to do as well before? Will the theory strip and narrow experience and cognition, or does it promise to open up the histories of students' involvement with writing, their rules, strategies, and assumptions, the invitations and denials that characterized their encounters with print?

Beyond such general questions are more specific guidelines for those of us doing psychological research. Once we undertake an investigation of cognition we must be careful to discuss our findings in terms of the kinds of writing we investigate. Generalizing to other tasks, and particularly to broad cognitive processes, is not warranted without evidence from those other domains. If theories like the four we discussed, but others too (e.g., theories of moral development, social cognition, metacognition, etc.), are appropriated that are built on particular tests, then researchers must thoroughly familiarize themselves with the tests beneath the theories and consult with psychologists who use them. People who are going to administer such tests should take the tests themselves — see what they're like from the inside. My mentor Richard Shavelson also urges researchers to administer the tests to individual students and have them talk about what they're doing, get some sense of how students might interpret or misinterpet the instructions, the various ways they represent the task to themselves, what cognitive processes seem to come into play as the students work with the tests. Furthermore, it must be remembered that the results of testing will be influenced by the degree of familiarity the students have with the tests and by the social situation created in the administration of them. How will these conditions be adjusted for and acknowledged? Finally, the resulting data must be discussed as being specific to the students tested. Generalizing to others must be done with caution.

A special word needs to be said here about comparative studies. If we employ hi-lo designs, expert-novice studies, and the like — which can be powerfully revealing designs — we need to consider our design and our results from historical and sociopolitical perspectives as well as cognitive ones. That is, if class, gender, or race differences emerge — and they certainly could — they should not automatically be assumed to reflect "pure" cognitive differences, but rather effects that might well be conditioned by and interpreted in light of historical, socio-political realities. There is currently a lot of talk about the prospect of forging a social-cognitive orientation to composition research (see, for example, Freedman, Dyson, Flower, and Chafe; Bizzell and Herzberg). One of the exciting results of such an endeavor could be an increased sensitivity to the social forces that shape cognitive activity. I've argued elsewhere for a research framework that intersects the cognitive, affective, and situational dimensions of composing and that involves the systematic combination of multiple methods, particularly ones traditionally thought to be antagonistic. My assumption is that the careful integration of, say, cognitive process-tracing and naturalistic observation methods can both contribute to fresh and generative insight and provide a guard against reductive interpretation (Rose, "Complexity").

Much of this essay has concerned researchers and theoreticians, but at the heart of the discussion is a basic question for any of us working with poor writers: How do we go about judging the thought processes involved with reading and writing when performance is problematic, ineffective, or stunted? If I could compress this essay's investigation down to a single conceptual touchstone, it would be this: Human cognition—even at its most stymied, bungled moments—is rich and varied. It is against this assumption that we should test our theories and research methods and classroom assessments. Do our practices work against classification that encourages single, monolithic explanations of cognitive activity? Do they honor the complexity of interpretive efforts even when those efforts fall short of some desired goal? Do they foster investigation of interaction and protean manifestation rather than investigation of absence: abstraction is absent, consciousness of print is absent, logic is absent? Do they urge reflection on the cultural biases that might be shaping them? We must be vigilant that the systems of intellect we develop or adapt do not ground our students' difficulties in sweeping, essentially one-dimensional perceptual, neurophysiological, psychological, or linguistic processes, systems that drive broad cognitive wedges between those who do well in our schools and those who don't.[5]

NOTES

[1]For presentation, qualification, or rebuttal of this orientation see, for example: Ann E. Berthoff, "Is Teaching Still Possible?" *College English* 46 (1984): 743–755; Thomas J. Farrell, "I.Q. and Standard English," *CCC* 34 (1983): 470–485 and the replies to Farrell by Greenberg, Hartwell, Himley, and Stratton in *CCC* 35 (1984): 455–478; George H. Jensen, "The Reification of the Basic Writer," *Journal of Basic Writing* 5 (1986): 52–64; Andrea Lunsford, "Cognitive Development and the Basic Writer," *College English* 41 (1979): 38–46 and Lunsford, "Cognitive Studies and Teaching Writing," *Perspectives on Research and Scholarship in Composition*, Ed. Ben W. McClelland and Timothy R. Donovan, New York: MLA, (1986): 145–161; Walter J. Ong, "Literacy and Orality in Our Times," *Profession 79*, Ed. Jasper P. Neel, New York: MLA, 1979: 1–7; Lynn Quitman Troyka, "Perspectives on Legacies and Literacy in the 1980s," *CCC* 33 (1982): 252–262 and Troyka, "Defining Basic Writers in Context," *A Sourcebook for Basic Writing Teachers*, Ed. Theresa Enos, New York: Random House, 1987: 2–15; James D. Williams, "Coherence and Cognitive Style," *Written Communication* 2 (1985): 473–491. For illustration of the transfer of this issue to the broader media, see Ellen K. Coughlin, "Literacy: 'Excitement' of New Field Attracts Scholars of Literature," *The Chronicle of Higher Education* 29 (9 Jan. 1985): 1, 10.

[2]For a description of the other tests—the Body Adjustment Test and the rarely used auditory and tactile embedded figures tests—see Witkin, et al.

[3]Witkin later revised his theory, suggesting that the rod and frame test and the embedded figures test were tapping different dimensions of the field dependence-independence construct. This revision, however, gives rise to further problems—see Linn and Kyllonen.

[4]Educators and evaluators often seem locked into a nineteenth-century linear progress conception of the way both societies and individuals appropriate literacy. Graff presents a provocative

historical challenge to such notions; here's Vygotsky on individual development: "together with processes of development, forward motion, and appearance of new forms, we can discern processes of curtailment, disappearance, and reverse development of old forms at each step . . . only a naive view of development as a purely evolutionary process . . . can conceal from us the true nature of these processes" (106).

[5]Particular sections of this paper were discussed with or reviewed by specialists who provided a great deal of expert help: Susan Curtiss (neurolinguistics), Richard Leo Enos (classical studies), Sari Gilman (research psychiatry), John R. Hayes, Richard Shavelson, and Catherine Stasz (cognitive and educational psychology), Thomas Huckin (linguistics), Robert Siegler (developmental psychology). David Bartholomae, Linda Flower, Glynda Hull, David Kaufer, and Stephen Witte commented generously on the entire manuscript. The project benefited as well from rich conversation with Mariolina Salvatori and Kathryn Flannery. Versions of the paper were read at Carnegie Mellon, Pitt, Indiana University of Pennsylvania, UCLA, Berkeley, CCCC (Atlanta), Penn State, and UCSD. My thanks for all the ideas generated at those conferences and colloquia. Finally, appreciation is due to Sally Magargee for her research assistance and the Carnegie Mellon Department of English and the Spencer Foundation for their support.

REFERENCES

Adkins, Arthur W. H. "Orality and Philosophy." Robb 207–227.

Adler, Jonathan. "Abstraction is Uncooperative." *Journal for the Theory of Social Behavior* 14 (1984): 165–181.

Arndt, Stephen, and Dale E. Berger. "Cognitive Mode and Asymmetry in Cerebral Functioning." *Cortex* 14 (1978): 78–86.

Bartholomae, David. "Inventing the University." Rose, *When a Writer Can't Write* 134–165.

Battig, William F. "Within-Individual Differences in 'Cognitive' Processes." *Information Processing and Cognition.* Ed. Robert L. Solso. Hillsdale, NJ: Erlbaum, 1975. 195–228.

Beamon, Karen. "Coordination and Subordination Revisited: Syntactic Complexity in Spoken and Written Narrative Discourse." Tannen, *Coherence in Spoken and Written Discourse* 45–80.

Beaumont, J. Graham. "Methods for Studying Cerebral Hemispheric Function." *Functions of the Right Cerebral Hemisphere.* Ed. A. W. Young. London: Academic Press, 1983. 113–146.

Beaumont, J. Graham, A. W. Young, and I. C. McManus. "Hemisphericity: A Critical Review." *Cognitive Neuropsychology* 2 (1984): 191–212.

Benson, D. Frank, and Eran Zaidel, eds. *The Dual Brain: Hemispheric Specialization in Humans.* New York: Guilford, 1985.

Berthoff, Ann E. "Is Teaching Still Possible?" *College English* 46 (1984): 743–755.

Bizzell, Patricia. "Cognition, Convention, and Certainty: What We Need to Know about Writing." *Pre/Text* 3 (1982): 213–244.

Bizzell, Patricia, and Bruce Herzberg. *The Bedford Bibliography for Teachers of Writing.* Boston: Bedford Books, 1987.

Bogen, Joseph. "The Dual Brain: Some Historical and Methodological Aspects." Benson and Zaidel 27–43.

Bogen, Joseph, et al. "The Other Side of the Brain: The A/P Ratio." *Bulletin of Los Angeles Neurological Society* 37 (1972): 49–61.

Bradshaw, J. L., and N. C. Nettleton. "The Nature of Hemispheric Specialization in Man." *Behavioral and Brain Sciences* 4 (1981): 51–91.

Brainerd, Charles J. "The Stage Question in Cognitive-Development Theory." *The Behavioral and Brain Sciences* 2 (1978): 173–181.

Brown, Warren S., James T. Marsh, and Ronald E. Ponsford. "Hemispheric Differences in Event-Related Brain Potentials." Benson and Zaidel 163–179.

Caplan, David. "On the Cerebral Localization of Linguistic Functions: Logical and Empirical Issues Surrounding Deficit Analysis and Functional Localization." *Brain and Language* 14 (1981): 120–137.

Carey, Susan. *Conceptual Change in Childhood.* Cambridge: MIT P, 1985.

Chafe, Wallace L. "Linguistic Differences Produced by Differences in Speaking and Writing." Olson, Torrance, and Hildyard 105–123.

Clanchy, M. T. *From Memory to Written Record: England 1066–1307.* Cambridge: Harvard UP, 1979.

Cole, Michael, and Barbara Means. *Comparative Studies of How People Think.* Cambridge: Harvard UP, 1981.

Cressy, David. "The Environment for Literacy: Accomplishment and Context in Seventeenth-Century England and New England." *Literacy in Historical Perspective.* Ed. Daniel P. Resnick. Washington: Library of Congress, 1983. 23–42.

Cronbach, Lee J. *Essentials of Psychological Testing.* New York: Harper and Row, 1960.

DeRenzi, Ennio. *Disorders of Space Exploration and Cognition.* London: Wiley, 1982.

Donaldson, Margaret. *Children's Minds.* New York: Norton, 1979.

Donchin, Emanuel, Gregory McCarthy, and Marta Kutas. "Electroencephalographic Investigations of Hemispheric Specialization." *Language and Hemispheric Specialization in Man: Cerebral Event-Related Potentials.* Ed. John E. Desmedt. Basel, NY: Karger, 1977. 212–242.

Dumas, Roland, and Arlene Morgan. "EEG Asymmetry as a Function of Occupation, Task and Task Difficulty." *Neuropsychologia* 13 (1975): 214–228.

Efron, Robert. "The Central Auditory System and Issues Related to Hemispheric Specialization." *Assessment of Central Auditory Dysfunction: Foundations and Clinical Correlates.* Ed. Marilyn L. Pinheiro and Frank E. Musiek. Baltimore: Williams and Wilkins, 1985. 143–154.

Ehrlichman, Howard, and Arthur Weinberger. "Lateral Eye Movements and Hemispheric Asymmetry: A Critical Review." *Psychological Bulletin* 85 (1978): 1080–1101.

Elbow, Peter. "The Shifting Relationships Between Speech and Writing." *CCC* 34 (1985): 283–303.

Enos, Richard Leo, and John Ackerman. "*Letteraturizzazione* and Hellenic Rhetoric: An Analysis for Research with Extensions." *Proceedings of 1984 Rhetoric Society of America Conference.* Ed. Charles Kneupper, forthcoming.

Fillmore, Charles J. "On Fluency." *Individual Differences in Language Ability and Language Behavior.* Ed. Charles J. Fillmore, Daniel Kempler, and William S.Y. Wang. New York: Academic Press, 1979. 85–101.

Flavell, John H. *Cognitive Development.* Englewood Cliffs: Prentice-Hall, 1977.

Fodor, Jerry A. *The Modularity of Mind.* Cambridge: MIT P, 1983.

Freedman, Sarah, et al. *Research in Writing: Past, Present, and Future.* Berkeley: Center for the Study of Writing, 1987.

Gardner, Howard. *Frames of Mind.* New York: Basic Books, 1983.

_____. *The Mind's New Science.* New York: Basic Books, 1985.

_____. "What We Know (and Don't Know) About the Two Halves of the Brain." *Journal of Aesthetic Education* 12 (1978): 113–119.

Gardner, Howard, and Ellen Winner. "Artistry and Aphasia." *Acquired Aphasia.* Ed. Martha Taylor Sarno. New York: Academic Press, 1981. 361–384.

Gelman, Rochelle. "Cognitive Development." *Ann. Rev. Psychol* (1978): 297–332.

Gevins, A. S., et al. "EEG Patterns During 'Cognitive' Tasks." *Electroencephalography and Clinical Neurophysiology* 47 (1979): 704–710.

Gilman, Sandor. *Difference and Pathology.* Ithaca, NY: Cornell UP, 1985.

Ginsburg, Herbert. "Poor Children, African Mathematics, and the Problem of Schooling." *Educational Research Quarterly* 2 (1978): 26–44.

Glaser, Robert. "Education and Thinking: The Role of Knowledge." *American Psychologist* 39 (1984): 93–104.

Goodenow, Jacqueline. "The Nature of Intelligent Behavior: Questions Raised by Cross-Cultural Studies." *The Nature of Intelligence.* Ed. Lauren B. Resnick. Hillsdale, NJ: Erlbaum, 1976. 168–188.

Goody, Jack. *The Domestication of the Savage Mind.* London: Cambridge UP, 1977.

Gould, Stephen Jay. *The Mismeasure of Man.* New York: Norton, 1981.

Graff, Harvey. *The Literacy Myth.* New York: Academic Press, 1979.

_____. "Reflections on the History of Literacy: Overview, Critique, and Proposals." *Humanities and Society* 4 (1981): 303–333.

Gruber, Howard E., and J. Jacques Vonèche, eds. *The Essential Piaget.* New York: Basic Books, 1977.

Halliday, M. A. K. "Differences Between Spoken and Written Language." *Communication through Reading.* Vol. 2. Ed. Glenda Page, John Elkins, and Barrie O'Connor. Adelaide, SA: Australian Reading Association, 1979. 37–52.

Havelock, Eric. *The Muse Learns to Write.* Cambridge: Harvard UP, 1986.

_____. *Preface to Plato.* Cambridge: Harvard UP, 1963.

Harré, Rom, and Roger Lamb. *The Encyclopedic Dictionary of Psychology.* Cambridge: MIT P, 1983.

Heath, Shirley Brice. "Protean Shapes in Literacy Events: Ever-Shifting Oral and Literate Traditions." *Spoken and Written Language.* Ed. Deborah Tannen. Norwood, NJ: Ablex, 1982. 91–117.

_____. *Ways With Words.* London: Cambridge UP, 1983.

Hillyard, Steve A., and David L. Woods. "Electrophysiological Analysis of Human Brain Function." *Handbook of Behavioral Neurobiology.* Vol. 2. Ed. Michael S. Gazzaniga. New York: Plenum, 1979. 343–378.

Hudson, R. A. *Sociolinguistics*. Cambridge: Cambridge UP, 1986.

Hull, Glynda. "The Editing Process in Writing: A Performance Study of Experts and Novices." Diss. U of Pittsburgh, 1983.

Hunt, Earl. "On the Nature of Intelligence." *Science* 219 (1983): 141–146.

Hunter, Carman St. John, and David Harmon. *Adult Illiteracy in the United States*. New York: McGraw-Hill, 1985.

Inhelder, Barbel, and Jean Piaget. *The Growth of Logical Thinking from Childhood to Adolescence*. Trans. Anne Parsons and Stanley Milgram. New York: Basic Books, 1958.

Jensen, George H. "The Reification of the Basic Writer." *Journal of Basic Writing* 5 (1986): 52–64.

Kamin, Leon J. *The Science and Politics of I.Q*. Hillsdale, NJ: Erlbaum, 1974.

Kuhn, Deanna, Victoria Ho, and Catherine Adams. "Formal Reasoning Among Pre- and Late Adolescents." *Child Development* 50 (1979): 1128–1135.

Kurtz, Richard M. "A Conceptual Investigation of Witkin's Notion of Perceptual Style." *Mind* 78 (1969): 522–533.

Latour, Bruno, and Steve Woolgar. *Laboratory Life*. Beverly Hills, CA: Sage, 1979.

Lave, Jean. "Cognitive Consequences of Traditional Apprenticeship Training in West Africa." *Anthropology and Education Quarterly* 8 (1977): 177–180.

LeDoux, Joseph E. "Cerebral Asymmetry and the Integrated Function of the Brain." *Functions of the Right Cerebral Hemisphere*. Ed. Andrew W. Young. London: Academic Press, 1983. 203–216.

Linn, Marcia C., and Patrick Kyllonen. "The Field Dependence-Independence Construct: Some, One, or None." *Journal of Educational Psychology* 73 (1981): 261–273.

Lockridge, Kenneth. *Literacy in Colonial New England*. New York: Norton, 1974.

Margolis, Joseph. "The Emergence of Philosophy." Robb 229–243.

Marrou, H. I. *A History of Education in Antiquity*. Madison, WI: U of Wisconsin P, 1982.

McCormick, Kathleen. *The Cultural Imperatives Underlying Cognitive Acts*. Berkeley: Center for The Study of Writing, 1986.

McKenna, Frank P. "Field Dependence and Personality: A Re-examination." *Social Behavior and Personality* 11 (1983): 51–55.

Messick, Samuel. "Personality Consistencies in Cognition and Creativity." *Individuality in Learning*. Ed. Samuel Messick and Associates. San Francisco: Jossey-Bass, 1976. 4–22.

Ogbu, John U. *Minority Education and Caste*. New York: Academic Press, 1978.

Olson, David R., Nancy Torrance, and Angela Hildyard, eds. *Literacy, Language, and Learning*. New York: Cambridge UP, 1981.

Ong, Walter J. *Orality and Literacy: The Technologizing of the Word*. New York: Methuen, 1982.

Ornstein, Robert E., and David Galin. "Psychological Studies of Consciousness." *Symposium on Consciousness*. Ed. Philip R. Lee et al. New York: Viking, 1976. 53–66.

Oxenham, John. *Literacy: Writing, Reading, and Social Organisation*. London: Routledge and Kegan Paul, 1980.

Perkins, D. N. "General Cognitive Skills: Why Not?" *Thinking and Learning Skills*. Ed. Susan F. Chipman, Judith W. Segal, and Robert Glaser. Hillsdale, NJ: Erlbaum, 1985. 339–363.

Piaget, Jean. "Intellectual Evolution from Adolescence to Adulthood." *Human Development* 15 (1972): 1–12.

Polanyi, Livia. *Telling the American Story: A Structural and Cultural Analysis of Conversational Storytelling*. Norwood, NJ: Ablex, 1985.

Robb, Kevin, ed. *Language and Thought in Early Greek Philosophy*. LaSalle, IL: Monist Library of Philosophy, 1983.

Rogoff, Barbara. *Everyday Cognition*. Cambridge: Harvard UP, 1984.

Rose, Mike. "Complexity, Rigor, Evolving Method, and the Puzzle of Writer's Block: Thoughts on Composing Process Research." Rose, *When a Writer Can't Write* 227–260.

———, ed. *When a Writer Can't Write: Studies in Writer's Block and Other Composing Process Problems*. New York: Guilford, 1985.

Rugg, Michael D. "Electrophysiological Studies." *Divided Visual Field Studies of Cerebral Organisation*. Ed. J. Graham Beaumont. New York: Academic Press, 1982. 129–146.

Scollon, Ron, and Suzanne B. K. Scollon. "Cooking It Up and Boiling It Down: Abstracts in Athabascan Children's Story Retellings." Tannen, *Coherence in Spoken and Written Discourse* 173–197.

Shaughnessy, Mina. *Errors and Expectations*. New York: Oxford UP, 1977.

Siegler, Robert S. "Children's Thinking: The Search For Limits." *The Function of Language and Cognition*. Ed. G. J. Whitehurst and Barry J. Zimmerman. New York: Academic Press, 1979. 83–113.

Sperry, Roger W. "Consciousness, Personal Identity, and the Divided Brain." Benson and Zaidel 11–26.

Tannen, Deborah, ed. *Coherence in Spoken and Written Discourse.* Norwood, NJ: Ablex, 1984.

_____. "A Comparative Analysis of Oral Narrative Strategies: Athenian Greek and American English." *The Pear Stories.* Ed. Wallace Chafe. Norwood, NJ: Ablex, 1980. 51–87.

_____. "Relative Focus on Involvement in Oral and Written Discourse." Olson, Torrance, and Hildyard 124–147.

TenHouten, Warren D. "Social Dominance and Cerebral Hemisphericity: Discriminating Race, Socioeconomic Status, and Sex Groups by Performance on Two Lateralized Tests." *Intern J. Neuroscience* 10 (1980): 223–232.

Toulmin, Stephen. "Epistemology and Developmental Psychology." *Developmental Plasticity.* Ed. Eugene S. Gollin. New York: Academic Press, 1981. 253–267.

Tulkin, S. R., and M. J. Konner. "Alternative Conceptions of Intellectual Functioning." *Human Development* 16 (1973): 33–52.

Valenstein, Elliot S. *Great and Desperate Cures.* New York: Basic Books, 1986.

Vernon, Philip. "The Distinctiveness of Field Independence." *Journal of Personality* 40 (1972): 366–391.

Vygotsky, L.S. *Mind in Society.* Cambridge: Harvard UP, 1978.

Wachtel, Paul L. "Field Dependence and Psychological Differentiation: Reexamination." *Perceptual and Motor Skills* 35 (1972): 174–189.

Whitaker, Harry A., and George A. Ojemann. "Lateralization of Higher Cortical Functions: A Critique." *Evolution and Lateralization of the Brain.* Ed. Stuart Dimond and David Blizard. New York: New York Academy of Science, 1977. 459–473.

Williams, James Dale. "Coherence and Cognitive Style." Diss. U of Southern California, 1983.

Witkin, Herman A., "Psychological Differentiation and Forms of Pathology." *Journal of Abnormal Psychology* 70 (1965): 317–336.

Witkin, Herman A., et al. "Field-Dependent and Field-Independent Cognitive Styles and Their Educational Implications." *Review of Educational Research* 47 (1977): 1–64.

Wittrock, Merlin. "Education and the Cognitive Processes of the Brain." *Education and the Brain.* Ed. Jeanne S. Chall and Allen S. Mirsky. Chicago: U of Chicago P, 1978. 61–102.

Young, Andrew W. "Methodological and Theoretical Bases of Visual Hemifield Studies." *Divided Visual Field Studies of Cerebral Organisation.* Ed. J. Graham Beaumont. New York: Academic Press, 1982. 11–27.

12   *"This Wooden Shack Place": The Logic of an Unconventional Reading*

WITH GLYNDA HULL

1990

AUTHOR'S NOTE: The intention here (and in the upcoming "Remediation as Social Construct") is to get in close to a moment of pedagogical interaction, to dwell on it in hopes of understanding its complexity and drawing something instructive from it.

The thing I value about this article is the way Glynda and I try to present and consider the logic of the student Robert's interpretation of a poem, at least as it emerges in dialogue with me, his teacher. There are some similarities between this paper and my earlier writer's block studies, in that both attempt to understand the thinking that informs student work and to involve students themselves in that process. But in both this piece and the "Social Construct" article, there is an explicit blending of the cognitive and the social-cultural — and that blending became a major goal of the work Glynda and I did together.

We thought it was important to examine the interaction between Robert and me, for it is precisely in the everyday exchanges between teachers and students where judgments about cognition are made. One interesting thing here, we think, is that both teacher and student share a working-class background, and yet it is partly around class that the teacher's misperception arises. His disciplinary training trumps other perspectives he might have taken on the poem's landscape and imagery. Without that disciplinary lens, the student reads the poem in a different way.

Let me say a little about method. There can be great value in the kind of close analysis of instructional discourse evident here and in the "Social Construct" article. It enables the researcher to be precise and, if successful, to give a sense of the interactional dynamics that attend teaching, learning, and assessment. Because of the level of detail, however, one must select passages from longer events, so selection becomes critical and raises its own set of questions: Is the passage typical, representative? (In this case, Robert did tend to respond in the manner captured here.) If the passage is unusual, why does the researcher think it is important to examine, and is that rationale convincing?

The writing of such analyses can also be tricky. The danger is that the researcher can get lost in the detail, lose sight of the big idea, the larger claim that the details are intended to support.

The reader can judge the next two essays on these criteria. I appreciate the fact that pieces like these (especially the longer one) can get tedious.

There is another methodological issue that I want to raise here, and it has to do with the relation of research question to method. I'm fond of a quip from physicist Percy Bridgman, who offered that method "is doing one's damnedest with one's mind, no holds barred." We tend to think of research methods, quantitative, qualitative, or critical interpretive, as a set of techniques or conceptual moves that we master and then apply. And they are. Each tradition brings with it established procedures, ways of doing things, and with them all sorts of constraints and cautions. These procedures define method, make inquiry systematic and principled.

But I also want to consider the inventive side of method, the "doing one's damnedest with one's mind" that is often necessary to explore multifaceted problems. The kinds of things we in writing and rhetoric try to get at—like the process of literary interpretation—may call for combining methods, or altering them, or coming up with a novel technique. (Patricia Sullivan and James Porter make a nice argument for this approach when studying literacy in the workplace.) One small example in the present article is my playing back the tape of my and Robert's interaction and trying to cue my own recall of what was going on as I spoke with Robert. Since the interplay between teacher expectation and student response is such an important part of classroom life, I wanted to get as good a sense as I could of my own expectations during the exchange.

It's not easy to be aware of what we bring to our teaching and tutoring encounters, and it's even more difficult to apprehend the train of thought, the logic behind another person's statements, in mathematics or in poetry. Yet, the logic that emerges may be revelatory, may yield something fresh, or it may be in need of reflection and revision. But until it's evident, not much real dialogue and education can go on.

This is a paper about student interpretations of literature that strike the teacher as unusual, a little off, not on the mark. When we teachers enter classrooms with particular poems or stories in hand, we also enter with expectations about the kind of student responses that would be most fruitful, and these expectations have been shaped, for the most part, in literature departments in American universities. We value some readings more than others — even, in our experience, those teachers who advocate a reader's free play. One inevitable result of this situation is that there will be moments of mismatch between what a teacher expects and what students do. What interests us about this mismatch is the possibility that our particular orientations and readings might blind us to the logic of a student's interpretation and the ways that interpretation might be sensibly influenced by the student's history.

From *College Composition and Communication* 41.3 (October 1990): 287–98.

The two of us have been involved for several years in a study of remedial writing instruction in American higher education, attempting to integrate social-cultural and cognitive approaches to better understand the institutional and classroom practices that contribute to students being designated remedial (Hull and Rose). One of the interesting things that has emerged as we've been conducting this research is the place of reading in the remedial writing classroom, particularly at a time when composition professionals are calling for the integration of reading and writing while affirming, as well, the place of literature in remedial instruction (Bartholomae and Petrosky; Salvatori, "Reading and Writing"). As this integration of reading, and particularly the reading of literature, into the remedial writing classroom continues, composition teachers will increasingly be called on to explore questions of interpretation, expectation, and background knowledge—particularly given the rich mix of class and culture found in most remedial programs. We would like to consider these issues by examining a discussion of a poem that was part of a writing assignment. Specifically, we will analyze a brief stretch of discourse, one in which a student's personal history and cultural background shape a somewhat unconventional reading of a section of a poem. We will note the way the mismatch plays itself out in conversation, the logic of the student's reading and the coherent things it reveals about his history, and the pedagogical implications of conducting a conversation that encourages that logic to unfold.

The stretch of discourse we're going to analyze comes from a conference that immediately followed a classroom discussion of a poem by the contemporary Japanese-American writer Garrett Kaoru Hongo. The class is designated as the most remedial composition class at the University of California; it is part of a special program on the Los Angeles campus (the Freshman Preparatory Program) for students determined by test scores to be significantly at-risk. (The SAT verbal scores of this particular section, for example, ranged from 220 to 400.) Mike Rose taught the class at the time he was collecting data on remedial writing instruction at the university level, and though his class was not the focus of his research, he did keep a teaching log, photocopy all work produced by the class, and collect sociohistorical and process-tracing data on several students and tape record selected conferences and tutorial sessions with them. For reasons that will shortly be apparent, a student named Robert was one of those Rose followed: he will be the focus of this paper. Let us begin this analysis with the poem Robert and the others in the class read; the discussion took place during the third week of the fall quarter:

And Your Soul Shall Dance
for Wakako Yamauchi

Walking to school beside fields
of tomatoes and summer squash,
alone and humming a Japanese love song,
you've concealed a copy of *Photoplay*
between your algebra and English texts.

Your knee socks, saddle shoes, plaid dress,
and blouse, long-sleeved and white
with ruffles down the front,
come from a Sears catalogue
and neatly complement your new Toni curls.
All of this sets you apart from the landscape:
flat valley grooved with irrigation ditches,
a tractor grinding through alkaline earth,
the short stands of windbreak eucalyptus
shuttering the desert wind
from a small cluster of wooden shacks
where your mother hangs the wash.
You want to go somewhere.
Somewhere far away from all the dust
and sorting machines and acres of lettuce.
Someplace where you might be kissed
by someone with smooth, artistic hands.
When you turn into the schoolyard,
the flagpole gleams like a knife blade in the sun,
and classmates scatter like chickens,
shooed by the storm brooding on your horizon.
                              —GARRETT KAORU HONGO

The class did pretty well with "And Your Soul Shall Dance." They followed the narrative line, pictured the girl, and understood the tension between her desires (and her dress) and the setting she's in. The ending, with its compressed set of similes and metaphors, understandably gave them some trouble—many at first took it literally, pictured it cinematically. But, collaboratively, the class came to the understanding that the storm meant something powerful and disquieting was brewing, and that the girl—the way she looks, her yearning for a different life—was somehow central to the meaning of the storm. The class was not able, however, to fit all the pieces together into one or more unified readings. And during the discussion—as members of the class focused on particular lines—some students offered observations or answers to questions or responses to classmates that seemed to be a little off the mark, unusual, as though the students weren't reading the lines carefully. Rose wondered if these "misreadings" were keeping the students from a fuller understanding of the way the storm could be integrated into the preceding events of the poem. One of these students was Robert.

A brief introduction. Robert is engaging, polite, style-conscious, intellectually curious. His father is from Trinidad, his mother from Jamaica, though he was born in Los Angeles and bears no easily discernible signs of island culture. His parents are divorced, and while he spends time with both, he currently lives with his mother in a well-kept, apartment-dense area on the western edge of central Los Angeles. Robert's family, and many of their neighbors, fall in the lower-middle-class SES bracket. He was bused to middle and high school in the more affluent San Fernando Valley. His high-school GPA was 3.35; his quantitative SAT was 410, and his verbal score was 270. In class he is outgoing and well-spoken—if with a tinge of shyness—and though his demeanor suggests he is a bit unsure of himself, he volunteers answers and responds thoughtfully to his classmates.

During the last half hour of the class on the Hongo poem, the students began rough drafts of an interpretive essay, and in his paper Robert noted that his "interpretation of this poem is that this girl seems to want to be different from society." (And later, he would tell his teacher that Hongo's poem "talked about change.") Robert clearly had a sense of the poem, was formulating an interpretation, but he, like the others, couldn't unify the poem's elements, and Rose assumed Robert's inability was caused by his misreading of sections of the poem. Here is Rose's entry in his teacher's log:

> Robert was ok on the 1st third of the poem, but seemed to miss the point of the central section. Talk with the tutor—does he need help with close reading?

Rose decided to get a better look, so he moved his regularly-scheduled conference with Robert up a week and tape-recorded it. In the three-minute excerpt from that conference that follows, Robert is discussing the storm at the poem's conclusion—the foreboding he senses—but is having some trouble figuring out exactly what the source of this impending disruption is. Rose asks Robert if—given the contrast between the farming community and the girl's dreams and appearance—he could imagine a possible disruption in her not-too-distant future. We pick up the conversation at this point. To help clarify his own expectations, Rose replayed the stretch of tape as soon as Robert left, trying to recall what he intended in asking each of his questions.

1a. ROSE: What do you think . . . what, you know, on the one hand what might the reaction of her parents be, if she comes in one day and says, "I, I don't like it here, I want to leave here, I want to be different from this, I want to go to the city and . . ." [*Expectation:* Robert will say the parents will be resistant, angry—something rooted in the conservative values associated with poor, traditional families.]

1b. ROBERT: Um, that would basically depend on the wealth of her family. You'd wanna know if her parents are poor . . . (mumbling) . . . they might not have enough money, whereas they can't go out and improve, you know . . . [Responds with a *qualification* that complicates the question by suggesting we need to know more. This further knowledge concerns the family's economic status, something Rose had assumed was evident.]

2a. ROSE: OK. OK. [*Acknowledges with hesitation*] From what we see about the background here and the times and the look, what can . . . can we surmise, can we imagine, do you think her parents are wealthy or poor?

[*Focuses* on the poem, asking for a conjecture. *Expectation*: Robert's attention will be drawn to the shacks, the hand laundering, the indications of farm labor.]

2b. ROBERT: I wouldn't say that they're wealthy but, again, I wouldn't say that they are poor either. [Responds with a *qualification*]

3a. ROSE: OK. [*Acknowledges with hesitation*] And why not? [Requests *elaboration. Expectation:* Robert will provide something from the poem, some line that explains the ambiguity in his answer.]

3b. ROBERT: Because typical farm life is, you know, that's the way that you see yourself, you know, wear jeans, just some old jeans, you know, some old saddle shoes, boots or something, some old kinda shirt, you know, with some weird design on the shoulder pad . . . [Responds by creating a *scenario*]

3c. ROSE: Uh huh . . . [*Unsure about direction,* but *acknowledges*]

3d. ROBERT: . . . for the guys. And then girls, probably wear some kind of plain cloth skirt, you know, with some weird designs on it and a weird shirt. I couldn't really . . . you really wouldn't know if they're . . . whether they were rich or not. Cause mainly everyone would dress the same way . . . [Continues *scenario* leading to an observation]

4a. ROSE: Yeah. [Sees the purpose of the scenario] That's right, so you wouldn't be able to tell what the background is, right? [*Confirms* Robert's observation and *reflects back*] Let's see if there's anything in the poem that helps us out. (pause) "All of this sets you apart . . ." this is about line twelve in the poem, "All of this sets you apart from the landscape: / flat valley grooved with irrigation ditches, / a tractor grinding through alkaline earth, / the short stands of windbreak eucalyptus / shuttering the desert wind / from a small cluster of wooden shacks / where your mother hangs the wash." [*Focuses* on poem] Now if she lives with her mother in a wooden shack, a shack . . . [*Begins line of reasoning*]

4b. ROBERT: OK. OK. Oh! [*interrupts*] Right here — is it saying that she lives with her mother, or that she just goes to this wooden shack place to *hang* her clothes? [*Challenges* teacher's line of reasoning]

4c. ROSE: Oh, I see. So you think that it's possible then that her mother . . . [*Reflects back*]

4d. ROBERT: [*picks up thought*] washes her clothes probably at home somewhere and then walks down to this place where the wind . . . the wind . . . so the eucalyptus trees block this wind, you know, from . . . [*Elaborates*]

4e. ROSE: [*picks up thought*] so that the clothes can dry.

4f. ROBERT: Right. [*Confirms*]

5a. ROSE: Well, that's certainly possible. That's certainly possible. [*Confirms*] Um, the only thing I would say if I wanted to argue with you on that would be that that's possible, but it's also the only time that this writer lets us know anything about where she might live, etc. . . . [*Begins to explain his interpretation* — an interpretation, we'd argue, that is fairly conventional: that the family is poor, and that poverty is signaled by the shacks, the place, most likely, where the family lives]

Certainly not all of Robert's exchanges—in classroom or conference—are so packed with qualification and interruption and are so much at cross purposes with teacher expectation. Still, this stretch of discourse is representative of the characteristics that make Robert's talk about texts interesting to us. Let us begin by taking a closer look at the reasoning Robert exhibits as he discusses "And Your Soul Shall Dance." To conduct this analysis, we'll be intersecting socioeconomic, cognitive, and textual information, bringing these disparate sources of information together to help us understand Robert's interpretation of sections of "And Your Soul Shall Dance," explicating not the poem, but a particular reading of it in a particular social-textual setting.

Here are a few brief comments on method:

Our data comes from the stretch of discourse we just examined, from other sections of the same conference, from a stimulated-recall session (on an essay Robert was writing for class) conducted one week prior to the conference,[1] and from a follow-up interview conducted four months after the conference to collect further sociohistorical information.

To confirm our sense of what a "conventional" reading of this section of the poem would be, we asked six people to interpret the lines in question. Though our readers represented a mix of ages and cultural backgrounds, all had been socialized in American literature departments: two senior English majors—one of whom is Japanese-American—two graduate students—one of whom is African-American—and two English professors—one of whom is Mexican-American. Regardless of age or cultural background, all quickly offered the same interpretation we will be suggesting is conventional.[2]

Analysis

1a–1b

1a. ROSE: What do you think . . . what, you know, on the one hand what might the reaction of her parents be, if she comes in one day and says, "I, I don't like it here, I want to leave here, I want to be different from this, I want to go to the city and . . ."

1b. ROBERT: Um, that would basically depend on the wealth of her family. You'd wanna know if her parents are poor . . . (mumbling) . . . they might not have enough money, whereas they can't go out and improve, you know . . .

Robert claims that the reaction of the girl's parents to "I want to leave here . . . [and] go to the city . . ." would "depend on the wealth of her family." This qualification is legitimate, though the reasoning behind it is not quickly discernible. In the follow-up interview Robert elaborates: "[If she goes to the city] she's gonna need support . . . and if they're on a low budget they won't have that much money to be giving to her all the time to support her." The social context of Robert's reasoning becomes clearer here. He comes from a large family (11 siblings and half-siblings), some members of which have moved (and continue to move) across cultures and, to a degree, across class lines. It is the parents' obligation to help children as they make such moves, and Robert is aware of the strains on finances such movement brings—he is in the middle of such tension himself.

2a-4f This segment includes Robert's qualified response to "do you think her parents are wealthy or poor?," his farm fashion scenario, and his perception of the "small cluster of wooden shacks." As we've seen, we need to understand Robert's perception of the shacks in order to understand his uncertainty about the parents' economic status, so we'll reverse the order of events on the transcript and deal first with the shacks.

> 4a. ROSE: Yeah. That's right, so you wouldn't be able to tell what the background is, right? Let's see if there's anything in the poem that helps us out. (pause) "All of this sets you apart . . ." this is about line twelve in the poem, "All of this set you apart from the landscape: / flat valley grooved with irrigation ditches, / a tractor grinding through alkaline earth, / the short stands of windbreak eucalyptus / shuttering the desert wind / from a small cluster of wooden shacks / where your mother hangs the wash." Now if she lives with her mother in a wooden shack, a shack . . .

> 4b. ROBERT: OK. OK. Oh! Right here—is it saying that she lives with her mother, or that she just goes to this wooden shack place to *hang* her clothes?

Those of us educated in a traditional literature curriculum, and especially those of us trained in an English graduate program, are schooled to comprehend the significance of the shacks. We understand, even if we can't readily articulate them, the principles of compression and imagistic resonance that underlie Hongo's presentation of a single image to convey information about economic and historical background. Robert, however, isn't socialized to such conventions, or is only partly socialized, and so he relies on a model of interpretation Rose had seen him rely on in class and in the stimulated-recall session: an almost legalistic model, a careful, qualifying reasoning that defers quick judgment, that demands multiple sources of verification. The kind of reasoning we see here, then, is not inadequate. In fact, it's pretty sophisticated—though it is perhaps inappropriately invoked in a poetic world, as Rose begins to suggest to Robert in 5a. We'll come back to this momentarily, but first we want to address one more issue related to Robert's uncertainty about the income level of the girl's parents.

We would like to raise the possibility that Robert's background makes it unlikely that he is going to respond to "a small cluster of wooden shacks" in quite the same way—with quite the same emotional reaction—as would a conventional (and most likely middle-class) reader for whom the shacks might function as a quickly discernible, emblematic literary device. Some of Robert's relatives in Trinidad still live in houses like those described in the poem, and his early housing in Los Angeles—further into central Los Angeles than where he now lives—was quite modest. We would suggest that Robert's "social distance" from the economic reality of poor landscapes isn't as marked as that of the conventional/middle-class reader, and this might make certain images less foreign to him, and, therefore, less emotionally striking. This is certainly *not* to say that Robert is naive about his current position in American society, but simply to say that the wooden shacks might not spark the same dramatic response in him as in a conventional/middle-class reader. The same holds true for another of Hongo's indicators of economic status—the hanging of the wash—for Robert's mother still "likes to wash her clothes by hand." Paradoxically, familiarity might work against certain kinds of dramatic response to aspects of working-class life.

In line with the above assertion, we would like to consider one last indicator of the girl's economic status—the mention of the Sears catalogue. The Sears catalogue, we believe, cuts two ways in the poem: it suggests lower-income-level shopping ("thrifty," as one of our readers put it) and, as well, the importing of another culture's garments. But the catalogue also carries with it an ironic twist: it's not likely that conventional readers would consider a Sears catalogue to be a source of fashion, so there's a touch of irony—perhaps pity mixed with humor—in this girl fulfilling her romantic dreams via Sears and Roebuck. We suggest that Robert's position in the society makes it difficult for him to see things this way, to comply with this conventional reading. He knows merchandise from Sears is "economical" and "affordable," and, to him, there's nothing ironic, pitiable, or humorous about that. When asked if he sees anything sad or ironic about the girl buying there he responds, "Oh, no, no," pointing out that "some of the items they sell in Sears, they sell in other stores." He then goes on to uncover an interesting problem in the poem. He uses the Sears catalogue to support his assertion that the family isn't all that poor (and thus doesn't necessarily live in those shacks): "She couldn't be really poor because she has clothes from the Sears catalogue." Robert knows what real poverty is, and he knows that if you have enough money to buy at Sears, you're doing OK. He goes on to speculate—again with his careful, qualifying logic—that if she is as poor as the shacks suggest, then maybe the Sears clothes could be second-hand and sent to her by relatives, in the way his family sends clothes and shoes to his relatives in Trinidad. Hongo's use of the Sears catalogue is, in some ways, undercut by other elements in his poem.

> 3b. ROBERT: Because typical farm life is, you know, that's the way that you see yourself, you know, wear jeans, just some old jeans, you know, some old saddle shoes, boots or something, some old kinda shirt, you know, with some weird design on the shoulder pad . . .
>
> 3c. ROSE: Uh huh . . .
>
> 3d. ROBERT: . . . for the guys. And then girls, probably wear some kind of plain cloth skirt, you know, with some weird designs on it and a weird shirt. I couldn't really . . . you really wouldn't know if they're . . . whether they were rich or not. Cause mainly everyone would dress the same way . . .

Now we can turn to the farm fashion scenario. Given that the "small cluster of wooden shacks" doesn't seem to function for Robert as it might for the conventional reader, he is left more to his own devices when asked: "do you think her parents are wealthy or poor?" What begins as a seeming non sequitur—and a concrete one at that—does reveal its purpose as Robert plays it out. Though Robert has a frame of reference to understand the economics of the scene in "And Your Soul Shall Dance" and the longing of its main character, he is, after all, a city boy, born and raised in central Los Angeles. What he does, then, when asked a question about how one determines the economic background of people moving across a farm landscape is to access what knowledge he does have about farm life—things he's read or heard, images he's gleaned from movies and television shows (e.g., *The Little House on the Prairie*)—and create a scenario, focusing on one indicator of socioeconomic status: fashion. (And fashion is a sensible criterion to use here, given the poem's emblematic use of clothing.) Classroom-observational and stimulated-recall data suggest that Robert makes particularly good use of visual imagery in his thinking—e.g., he draws pictures and charts to help him comprehend difficult readings; he rehearses sentences by visualizing them before he writes them out—and here we see him reasoning through the use of scenario, concluding that in certain kinds of communities, distinctions by readily discernible indicators like dress might not be all that easy to make.

> 4d. **ROBERT:** washes her clothes probably at home somewhere and then walks down to this place where the wind . . . the wind . . . so the eucalyptus trees block this wind, you know, from . . .
>
> 4e. **ROSE:** so that the clothes can dry.
>
> 4f. **ROBERT:** Right.

This section also involves the wooden shacks, though the concern here is Robert's assertion that the mother doesn't have to live in the shacks to hang the wash there. Robert's reasoning, again, seems inappropriately legalistic. Yes, the mother could walk down to this place to hang her clothes; the poem doesn't specify "that [the girl] lives with her mother, or that [the mother] just goes to this wooden shack place to *hang* her clothes." But to Rose during the conference this seemed like a jurisprudential rather than a poetic reading. In the follow-up interview, however, Robert elaborated in a way that made Rose realize that Robert might have had a better imagistic case than his teacher first thought—for Rose missed the full visual particulars of the scene, did not see the importance of the "tractors grinding through alkaline earth." Robert elaborates on "this place where . . . the eucalyptus trees block this wind." He describes this "little shack area where the clothes can dry without being bothered by the wind and dust . . . with all this . . . the tractor grinding through the earth. That brings up dust." Robert had pictured the surrounding landscape—machines stirring up grit and dust—and saw the necessity of trees to break the dust-laden wind so that wash could dry clean in the sun. The conventional reader could point out that such a windbreak would be necessary as well to protect residents, but given Robert's other interpretations, it makes sense, is coherent, to see the shacks—sheds of some kind perhaps or abandoned housing—as part of this eucalyptus-protected place where women hang the wash. What's important to note here is that Robert was able to visualize the scene—animate it, actually—in a way that Rose was not, for Rose was focusing on the dramatic significance of the shacks. Robert's reading may be unconventional and inappropriately jurisprudential, but it is coherent, and it allows us—in these lines—to animate the full landscape in a way that enhances our reading of the poem.

CONCLUSION

We hope we have demonstrated the logic and coherence of one student's unconventional reading. What we haven't addressed—and it could certainly now be raised—is the pedagogical wisdom of encouraging in a writing classroom the playing out of such unconventional readings. Reviewing the brief stretch of Rose's and Robert's discourse, we see how often teacher talk is qualified, challenged, and interrupted (though not harshly), and how rarely teacher expectations are fulfilled. If the teacher's goals are to run an efficient classroom, cover a set body of material, and convey certain conventional reading and writing strategies to students who are on the margin of the academic community, then all these conversational disjunctions are troubling.

What we would like to suggest, though, is that the laudable goal of facilitating underprepared students' entry into the academic community is actually compromised by a conversational pattern that channels students like Robert into a more "efficient" discourse. The desire for efficiency and coverage can cut short numerous possibilities for students to explore issues, articulate concerns, formulate and revise problems—all necessary for good writing to emerge—and can lead to conversational patterns that socialize students into a mode of interaction that will limit rather than enhance their participation in intellectual work.[3] We would further suggest that streamlined conversational patterns (like the Initiation-Comment-Response pattern described by Mehan) are often reinforced by a set of deficit-oriented assumptions about the linguistic and cognitive abilities of remedial students, assumptions that are much in need of examination (Hull et al.; Rose, *Lives*).

We would pose instead a pedagogical model that places knowledge-making at its center. The conversational techniques attending such a model are not necessarily that demanding—Robert benefits from simple expressions of encouragement, focusing, and reflecting back—but the difference in assumptions is profound: that the real stuff of belonging to an academic community is dynamic involvement in generating and questioning knowledge, that students desperately need immersion and encouragement to involve themselves in such activity, and that underprepared students are capable— given the right conditions—of engaging in such activity. We would also underscore the fact that Robert's reading (a) does bring to light the problem with the Sears catalogue and (b) animates the landscape as his teacher's reading did not do. Finally, we would suggest that engaging in a kind of "social-textual" reading of Robert's reading moves us toward deeper understanding of the social base of literary interpretation (cf. Salvatori, "Pedagogy").

In calling for a richer, more transactive model of classroom discourse, we want to acknowledge that such a model removes some of the control of teacher-centered instruction and can create moments of hesitance and uncertainty (as was the case with Rose through the first half of the transcript). But hesitancy and uncertainty—as we all know from our own intellectual struggles—are central to knowledge-making. Furthermore, we are not asking teachers to abandon structure, goals, and accountability. A good deal of engineering still goes on in the transactive classroom: the teacher focusing discussion, helping students better articulate their ideas, involving others, pointing out connections, keeping an eye on the clock. Even in conference, Rose's interaction with Robert is clearly goal-driven, thus Rose's reliance on focusing and reflecting back. Rose operates with a conventional reading in mind and begins moving toward it in 5a—and does so out loud to reveal to Robert the line of such reasoning. Robert's interpretation, though, will cause his teacher to modify his reading, and the teacher's presentation of his interpretation will help Robert acquire an additional approach to the poem. (In fact, the very tension between academic convention and student experience could then become the focus of discussion.) This, we think, is the way talk and thought should go when a student seems to falter, when readings seem a little off the mark.[4]

NOTES

[1]In stimulated recall, a student's writing is videotaped and, upon completion, replayed to cue recall of mental processes occurring during composing. For further discussion of the procedure and its advantages and limitations, see Rose, *Writer's Block*.

[2]Frankly, we had trouble arriving at a way to designate the readings we're calling conventional and unconventional. And we're not satisfied yet. Certain of Robert's responses seem to be influenced by class (e.g., his reaction to the wooden shacks and Sears), and we note that, but with reluctance. We don't want to imply that class is the primary determiner of Robert's reading (vs., say, socialization into an English department—which, we realize, would correlate with class). We also don't want to imply that middle-class readers would, by virtue of class, automatically see things in a certain way, would have no trouble understanding particular images and allusions. One of the people who read this paper for us, Dennis Lynch, suggested that we use Wayne Booth's notion of "intended audience"—that Robert is simply not a member of the audience for whom the poem was written, thus he offers a reading that differs from the reading we're calling conventional. The notion of intended audience makes sense here, and fits with our discussion of socialization. Hongo, like most younger American poets, honed his craft in an English department and an MFA program, places where one's work is influenced by particular audiences—fellow poets, faculty, journal editors, etc. But, finally, we decided not to use the notion of intended audience, for it carries with it a theoretical framework we're not sure does Robert or Hongo full justice here. We use words like "conventional" and "middle-class," then, with reserve and invite our readers to help us think through this problem.

[3]For two different but compatible perspectives on this claim see Shor; Tharp and Gallimore.

[4]We would like to thank Linda Flower, Kay Fraser, Marisa Garrett, Jonathan Lovell, Dennis Lynch, Sandra Mano, Cheryl Pfoff, Mariolina Salvatori, Melanie Sperling, and Susan Thompson-Lowry for their comments on this paper. We benefited from a discussion at a meeting of the directors of the California Writing Project, and we would also like to acknowledge three anonymous CCC reviewers who gently guided us toward an understanding of the gaps and blunders in the essay. This work has been supported by grants from the McDonnell Foundation Program in Cognitive Studies for Educational Practice and the Research Foundation of the National Council of Teachers of English.

REFERENCES

Bartholomae, David, and Anthony Petrosky, eds. *Facts, Counterfacts and Artifacts: Theory and Method for a Reading and Writing Course.* Upper Montclair: Boynton, 1986.

Hongo, Garrett Kaoru. "And Your Soul Shall Dance." *Yellow Light.* Middletown: Wesleyan UP, 1982. 69.

Hull, Glynda, and Mike Rose. "Rethinking Remediation: Toward a Social-Cognitive Understanding of Problematic Reading and Writing." *Written Communication* 6 (Apr. 1989): 139–154.

Hull, Glynda, Mike Rose, Kay Losey Fraser, and Marisa Garrett. "The Social Construction of Remediation." The Tenth Annual Ethnography in Education Forum. University of Pennsylvania, Feb. 1989.

Mehan, Hugh. *Learning Lessons.* Cambridge: Harvard UP, 1979.

Rose, Mike. *Lives on the Boundary: The Struggles and Achievements of America's Underprepared.* New York: Free Press, 1989.

_____. *Writer's Block: The Cognitive Dimension.* Carbondale: Southern Illinois UP, 1984.

Salvatori, Mariolina. "Pedagogy: From the Periphery to the Center." *Reclaiming Pedagogy: The Rhetoric of the Classroom.* Ed. Patricia Donahue and Ellen Quandahl. Carbondale: Southern Illinois UP, 1989. 17–34.

_____. "Reading and Writing a Text: Correlations between Reading and Writing Patterns." *College English* 45 (Nov. 1983): 657–666.

Shor, Ira. *Empowerment: Education for Self and Social Change.* (forthcoming).

Tharp, Roland G., and Ronald Gallimore. *Rousing Minds to Life.* New York: Oxford UP, 1989.

13

Remediation as Social Construct: Perspectives from an Analysis of Classroom Discourse

WITH GLYNDA HULL, KAY LOSEY FRASER,
AND MARISA CASTELLANO

1991

AUTHOR'S NOTE: Much of what I wrote in the prefatory note to " 'This Wooden Shack Place' " applies here. This, too, is an essay about teacher assumptions and expectations and the effect those can have on the evaluation of a student's efforts. What we try to demonstrate — with the assistance of two of Glynda Hull's graduate students — is the way that a teacher's assumptions, played out over time, can contribute to the defining, the social construction, of a student as someone who is cognitively deficient and in need of substantial remediation.

There are several important methodological issues in this paper. I think it was one of the first in composition studies to use conversational analysis, at least in this way. (Marisa Castellano was the expert here.) The challenge, then, was both to introduce this complicated method to a new audience and to use it as the central analytic technique. The value of conversational analysis is that it provides a close examination of classroom talk as it proceeds, rendering some of its dynamic qualities: intonation, pausing, overlapping speech, and so on. We thought that it was in these dynamics that some aspects of the social construction of the student, Maria, was occurring.

The second methodological issue worth mentioning is our continuing attempt to blend the individual and the social, "micro" and "macro" levels of analysis. In this case, what broader institutional and cultural conditions might help explain the assumptions the teacher holds and the evaluations she makes from them? Put another way, if the language and beliefs I try to document in "The Language of Exclusion" and "Narrowing the Mind and Page" are real and have consequence, then they should affect practice. We should be able to show their effects on particular teachers and students. Trying to make such connections across planes of activity or levels of analysis is a delicate business, so we move cautiously. If the reader finds the attempt to make such connections of interest, I recommend Frederick Erickson's *Talk and Social Theory*.

I am sometimes asked about the teacher and student in this article, particularly if they read it and if we did anything to intervene. Such questions have special meaning now, since there is a heightened awareness among writing and rhetoric folk about the ethics of doing research in classrooms. Glynda was the primary researcher on this project; she was observing the class and working with Maria. The first thing to say is that she and Kay Losey Fraser went to some lengths to disguise the setting, the assignments, and the identifying features of the participants. Though we did not show the final paper to the teacher or student, Glynda worked with Maria, providing regular tutoring. And she shared the videotapes, transcripts, and her observations with the teacher — in fact, at several places in the transcripts printed in the article, Glynda is voicing a qualification to the teacher's interpretation. Back then, we believed, perhaps wrongly, that this was the best way to intervene.

It is an audacious thing to observe a classroom and to analyze what you see. You are in the room at the courtesy of the teacher. Yet, you may see things that trouble you and that might not be in the best interest of the students involved. What do you do? We struggled over this issue, and if we were doing this research today, we might do some things differently, given the development of thinking about such matters in our field. At the time, it seemed important to demonstrate and analyze the beliefs about cognition, writing, and speaking that apparently informed the teacher's actions and assessments. Our work, individually and as a team, was increasingly suggesting the salience of such beliefs, that such belief systems were in the institutional air we breathe and needed to be articulated and examined.

In closing, I would like to call attention to the final section of the article. In it, Glynda and I try to think through our field's various approaches — complicated and contradictory — to the issue of cultural differences. On rereading it, I think it has resonance with some recent discussions in feminist theory, rhetoric and ethnicity, and gay and lesbian studies.

I n this paper, we examine remediation as a social construct, as the product of perceptions and beliefs about literacy and learning, and we illustrate some ways in which inaccurate and limiting notions of learners as being somehow cognitively defective and in need of "remedy" can be created and played out in the classroom. We will look closely at one student in one lesson and detail the interactional processes that contribute to her being defined as remedial — this specific case, however, is also representative of common kinds of classroom practices and widespread cultural assumptions, ones we've seen at work in our other studies (Hull and Rose, "Rethinking"). In order to better understand these cultural assumptions and the ways they can affect classroom practices, we will attempt to combine an empirical, fine-grained analysis of classroom discourse with broader historical and cultural analyses. We want to place a teacher's instructional and evaluative language in the contexts that we believe influence it, that contribute to the practice of defining students as remedial.

From *College Composition and Communication* 42.3 (October 1991): 299–329.

We write this paper believing that, however great the distance our profession has come in understanding the students and the writing we call "remedial," we have not yet come far enough in critically examining our assumptions about our students' abilities — assumptions which both shape the organization of remedial programs and orient daily life in remedial classrooms. Engaging in such an examination is not so easy, perhaps because as teachers of remedial writing, we have good intentions: we look forward to our students' growth and development as writers; we want to teach our students to be literate in ways sanctioned by the academy and the community beyond. And, knowing our intentions, we can forget to examine our assumptions about remediation — assumptions that are deeply held and so ingrained as to be tacit, that can, without much conscious choice on our part, drive the way we structure a course and circumscribe the learning that students will do in it. Our hope, then, is that this paper will be an occasion to reflect on the ways we, as teachers, can inadvertently participate in the social construction of attitudes and beliefs about remediation which may limit the learning that takes place in our classrooms, and to consider some ways in which we can begin to examine these basic assumptions, building from a different ground our notions about our students' abilities and the nature of literacy learning.

ANALYZING CLASSROOM DISCOURSE

The centerpiece of our discussion — a fifty-minute classroom lesson on writing conducted in a remedial classroom at an urban college[1] — was one of several that we videotaped across a semester. As regular observers in the class, we also collected field notes and records of reading and writing assignments and homework and essays. We conducted interviews with students and teachers as well, sometimes asking them to comment on the videotapes we had recently made of classroom lessons. Outside of class, we served as tutors and thereby were able to audiotape our conferences with students and to elicit additional writing and reading performances.

In our studies, we have worked only with teachers rated highly by their departments and students. The teacher in this study was June, a recent and respected graduate of a long-standing composition program and a candidate for an advanced degree in literature. Our work with June confirmed her commitment to teaching. She spent a great deal of time responding to papers at home and meeting with students in conferences, and she was interested in discussing composition research and finding ways to apply it in her classroom. In fact, she volunteered to participate in our study because she saw it as an occasion to be reflective about her own teaching and to improve instruction for students in remedial classes.

The composition program in which June had studied was also a part of the college and included reading on and discussion of new composition theory and practice. The size of the class she taught was reasonable (approximately 15 students), though June taught three sections requiring two different preparations while completing graduate school. A remedial writing course and a complementary reading course were required for entering students depending on their scores on entrance tests. In the writing course, students kept a journal, made summaries of short reading passages, and wrote essays on assignments common to the program. Most of these assignments asked students to read short passages as background material and to use them as the basis for writing an essay on a specified topic related to the reading. One of these assignments gave rise to the classroom talk that we will analyze.

In this lesson, which took place the fourth week of the semester, June held a discussion to prepare students to write an essay on music videos and their appropriateness for viewers. The essay assignment consisted of a set of brief readings: a magazine article describing recently released and acclaimed rock videos; an editorial from a local newspaper on censorship; a review of the music video, *Thriller;* a list of recent music videos with brief descriptions. The assignment then asked students to take part in current debates about the regulation of music videos, developing a position on the issue perhaps by arguing that videos ought to be banned from television, or that there should be no censorship, or that some kind of rating system should be developed. The assignment emphasized that students should justify their arguments and make clear their reasoning.

In the class, June introduced the topic of music videos and, in preparation for the writing assignment, led a class discussion on accessibility and censorship issues. The discussion was, then, a kind of "pre-writing" activity, an attempt, June told us, to help students access their own knowledge and experiences and to draw upon them when writing an academic essay. "Many of these students don't have a lot to bring with them in terms of academic experience," she explained, "but they do have some life experiences to bring with them." What we want to do in our analysis of this lesson is to look closely at the conversation June had with her class, characterizing it in terms of its interactional patterns and the kinds of classroom discourse such patterns allow, and to consider the relationship between one student's pattern of talk and the teacher's perception of her cognitive abilities.

Let us explain why we have chosen to examine talk as a way to study this writing class. In *The Social Construction of Literacy,* Jenny Cook-Gumperz reminds us that literacy learning consists of more than the acquisition of cognitive skills; it also involves the "social process of demonstrating knowledgeability" (3). In other words, competence in classrooms means interactional competence as well as competence with written language: knowing when and how and with whom to speak and act in order to create and display knowledge. In the same way, then, that there are cultural "rules" for how to have conversations in particular contexts — the kinds of replies that are appropriate, the points at which it is acceptable to interrupt, the ways one might indicate attentiveness and interest — so there are rules for the talk that goes on in classrooms, rules students will need to know, at least tacitly.[2] From a significant amount of research on Western schooling, it is clear that a great deal of classroom talk is led by the teacher, and that a particular kind of participant structure — or way of arranging verbal interaction (Philips) — dominates classroom conversations.

This structure consists of a tripartite series of turns in which a teacher *initiates*, a student *replies*, and the teacher *evaluates* the student's response — the IRE sequence (Cazden; Mehan, *Learning;* Sinclair and Coulthard).[3] In the initiation, or opening turn, the teacher can inform, direct, or ask students for information. The student's reply to this initiation can be non-verbal, such as raising a hand or carrying out an action, or it can be a verbal response. In the evaluation turn, the teacher comments on the student's reply.

Here is an example of an IRE sequence in which June asks about music videos that students have seen lately. We first provide a plain transcript of this brief stretch of talk between teacher and students, and then we follow it with a second transcript (Figure 1) in which we attempt to capture some of the elements of speech that are lost when talk is written down — pauses, stress, and tempo, for instance — elements which suggest a speaker's communicative intentions. Such features, known as contextualization cues (Gumperz, "Contextualization," *Discourse*), signal how an utterance is to be understood, including how it relates to what precedes or follows. According to this system, speakers' turns are segmented into idea or information units[4] on the basis of both semantics and intonation (rising or falling contours). Other features are also represented: lexical prosody, such as vowel elongation or fluctuation, and overlapping speech, where more than one person talks at a time. We think this method enhances the understanding of classroom interaction, and we will incorporate it into our discussion accordingly.[5]

TRANSCRIPT #1

Initiation	*Reply*	*Evaluation*
1. Teacher: How 'bout *I Want Your Sex*, Matt? What would [you rate] that?		
	2. Matt: R.	
		3. Teacher: R. All right. The title of it might indicate right off the bat that it should be an R rated video. Okay.
4. Teacher: How 'bout some of the rest of you?		
	5. Maria: I, I, just seen *Like a Prayer.*	
		6. Teacher: Okay, *Like a Prayer.* All right, good.
7. Teacher: What, do you know what the rating would be on that one?		

Here is the same segment of classroom talk, this time with contextualization cues marked. The most prominent symbols in this segment are slash marks (/ and //), which signal a drop in voice tone and the end of a speaker's turn; double equal signs (= =), which indicate overlap (that more than one person is speaking at once—e.g., lines g, h, and i in Figure 1) or latching (that they are speaking in rapid succession—e.g., lines a and b in Figure 1); asterisks (*), which label words that speakers are stressing; and indications of volume, pitch, and tempo in brackets—e.g., [p] means quieter speech, [f] means louder speech, [hi] means high-pitched speech.

FIGURE 1   Transcript with Contextualization Cues Marked

a Teacher: how about i want your sex matt what would you rate that?
b Matt: = = r/
c Teacher: r// alright//
d   the *title of it might-
e Maria: = = [laughs] = =
f Teacher: = = indicate right
             off the bat that it should be . . an r rated video, okay/
g   how 'bout some of the rest = = of you?
h Unidentified Speaker: = = (all last = = summer)
i Maria: = = {[f] uh
             uh} . . i i just seen like a pray {[laugh]er}/
j Teacher: = = okay like *a prayer alright, {[hi] *good}/
k   what-, do you know what the rating would be {[p] on that one}?

Selected Contextualization Cues

Symbol	Significance
//	turn—final falling intonation
/	slight falling intonation suggesting more to come
. .	pauses of less than .5 seconds
<2>	pauses timed precisely (=2 second pause)
= =	overlapping or latching speech
~	fluctuating intonation
*	accent, normal prominence
CAPS	accent, extra prominence
( )	unintelligible speech
(xxx)	unclear word, each "×" = one syllable
[ ]	non-lexical phenomena which interrupts the lexical stretch
{[ ]}	non-lexical phenomena which overlays the lexical stretch, such as:
	[p] quieter speech
	[f] louder speech
	[hi] high pitch
	[lo] low pitch
	[ac] accelerated speech

In this exchange, we see a series of initiations in the form of teacher questions, student replies, and teacher evaluations of those replies—these evaluations often signalled by the word "okay." Throughout the semester, we noticed that "okay" was June's most frequent evaluation token—whether or not a student's response was acceptable—but early on we learned to differentiate her positive "okays" from negative ones by means of intonation patterns. Here the first "okay" was pronounced with a slight falling intonation—a signal that the student's response had been appropriate. (Contrast this positive or at least neutral intonation pattern with the negative one for "okay" found below in line e of Figure 2.) Also apparent from Figure 1, but not from Transcript 1, is that there is a fair amount of simultaneous talk going on. Note that Maria overlaps her teacher's talk with a laugh in line e and then again in line i, but more loudly the second time, as she attempts to gain the floor. Paying attention to these kinds of contextualization cues helped us more confidently understand and interpret the dynamics of talk and interaction that characterized this particular lesson.

The majority of the conversational turns which occurred in this lesson—some 52 percent—followed the IRE pattern. There were portions of the class time, however, which did not strictly fit this pattern—such as teacher lectures, student initiations, and teacher responses to student initiations. One particularly salient participant structure we call the "mini-lecture." Teacher evaluations often led into these pieces of extended discourse, which served either to elaborate on information already provided or discussed, or to introduce new material. A noticeable feature of mini-lectures was that during them June did not acknowledge interruptions or entertain questions. Students who attempted to interrupt were not given the floor. Of the six attempts to interrupt her lectures during this particular class, June gave only one of these any attention, and that one just enough to work the topic into the mini-lecture.

The predominance of IRE sequences and mini-lectures suggests a discourse that is very much teacher-led. And, in fact, of all the exchanges that occurred during this lesson, 83 percent were directed by June. Two of the twelve students in the class, Andrea and Maria, made the majority of student initiations and responses—19 percent and 16 percent, respectively—and also the majority of student responses to teacher initiations—24 percent and 20.5 percent. For the most part, the rest of the class sat quietly—at times they whispered or laughed to each other—but they answered few of June's questions, and they asked fewer questions still. In other words, they adhered to the participant structures that normally characterized interaction in this classroom.

Except, that is, for Maria. We now want to look closely at the talk of one student whose discourse patterns stood out, who did not always abide by the tacit rules that governed talk in this classroom. In fact, she often and obviously pressed at the boundaries of what was permissible conversationally. Of Spanish and Italian descent, Maria was born in El Salvador and moved to the United States with her parents when she was almost two years old. Although all her schooling had taken place in the United States, her first language was Spanish, and through a bilingual program in elementary school she had learned to read and write Spanish before she learned English. Maria told us that her parents don't speak English very well today, although they have been in the United States since 1971, and Spanish continues to be the language of their home, except between Maria and her thirteen-year-old sister.

What Maria told us about her experiences in school prior to college suggests that there she had been a successful student, particularly in English and foreign language classes. She claimed to enjoy writing and said that she had written a romance novel in high school. Her worst subject in high school, she reported, was math, in which she improved from a C to a B (suggesting that she was at least a B student in her other subjects). Maria told us that she had traveled with her high-school speech team and had won a $1000 scholarship to college. As a college freshman, she still enjoyed writing, especially short stories, and she also kept a journal regularly, writing in it about once a week.

Maria sat in the front row of her remedial writing class. She attended every class and turned in all of her homework on time. She also chose to get tutoring when it was offered. In many respects, then — her scholastic history, her engagement in the course, her goals for the future — she seemed very much the dutiful student, dedicated to schooling and willing to work hard. But as we will illustrate with examples of talk from this lesson, her rules for classroom discourse did not map well onto the norm for this class, particularly her strategies for gaining the floor. And this mismatch, this small but noticeable discontinuity, was to work to her disadvantage.

The difficulty was with turn-taking. In ordinary conversation, the potential exists for the speaker to change after every speaker's turn. That is, once a person has concluded her turn, unless she designates the next speaker, then anyone can take a turn (Sacks, Schegloff, and Jefferson). There are differences, of course, in conversational style: "high involvement" speakers tend to take more turns, talk more, and overlap their speech more than other speakers (Tannen). Generally, though, in an ordinary conversation, a speaker has the opportunity to talk after the current speaker finishes. But this state of affairs does not, as we illustrated above, exist in certain kinds of classroom conversations. When a teacher initiates, he takes the floor, his students reply, and then the teacher takes the floor back as he evaluates the reply. This IRE structure, this set of interactions, constitutes an integral unit. The appropriate time for students to gain access to the floor is after an IRE sequence. It's not appropriate in an IRE classroom for students to speak after any speaker's turn except the teacher's initiation, and certainly not during a turn. But this is what Maria does.

Maria not only speaks before an IRE sequence has been completed, interjecting between an initiation and a directed response, she also, on occasion, interrupts during a mini-lecture — an extended piece of teacher discourse which is supposedly non-interruptable — with an "Ohhh!" or "Huh Hmmm!" loud enough to be picked up by the audio recorder. Here is an example of such an interruption. Following a lively discussion of a potential rating system for music videos, June begins an explanation of the writing assignment:

TRANSCRIPT #2

1. TEACHER: Yeah, all right. Very frightening, traumatic, (kind of) blood and gore. [Laughter from the class.] Okay, yeah. All right, yeah. And they, yeah, there's a problem with the accessibility of music videos on television right now, and that's really what we're going to be dealing with in this essay, is the issue of music videos that is being considered right now, and you're going to have a chance to . . .

2. MARIA: Oh.

3. TEACHER: . . . try to convince your audience of your position. Okay?

When we analyzed this excerpt—in the manner of Figure 1—it was clear that June/the teacher intends this explanation of a new writing assignment to be non-interruptable: she completes the sentence she had begun as if Maria had not spoken. While Maria's "Oh" is not a lengthy interruption, it is a loud one, and we can also note that she is the only student to interrupt mini-lectures during this lesson.

In addition to interrupting the IRE sequence and mini-lectures inappropriately, Maria sometimes pursued topics for a longer time than June seemed to prefer, continuing to initiate statements about a topic after June was ready to move on. In fact, in the example above, when Maria interrupts the beginning of the mini-lecture with her "Oh," she seems to do so because she is still pursuing a topic that she had initiated moments earlier. Here is the larger context for that interruption, several turns both preceding and following it:

TRANSCRIPT #3

1. TEACHER: Any other music videos that you feel should have been rated in some way or another? [6 second pause]

2. MARIA: How about those scary ones like, um, *Thriller?*

3. TEACHER: Okay. All right. How could-, well, how could you rate those?

4. MARIA: Uh, R. But they're, the, the, they're very, very—I don't like them 'cause they're very scary.

5. TEACHER: Okay.

6. ANDREA: That's why we should create another rating between R and X, 'cause it would-

7. MARIA: No, because it's not only about, um, sex, about that, but it's those, those, those, those traumatic-

8. TEACHER: Okay.

9. MARIA: You hear about blood and-[Laugh]

10. TEACHER: Yeah, all right. Very frightening, traumatic, (kind of) blood and gore.
[Laughter from the class.]
Okay, yeah. All right, yeah.
And they, yeah, there's a problem with the accessibility of music videos on television right now, and that's really what we're going to be dealing with in this essay, is the issue of music videos that is being considered right now, and you're going to have a chance to . . .

11. MARIA: Oh.

12. TEACHER: . . . try to convince your audience of your position. Okay?

13. MARIA: When I saw the first part of *Thriller* and that, that part when the first part about that corpse?

14. TEACHER: Mmhmm.

15. MARIA: And, and, he jumped up with blood and that was, I, I haven't seen a scene like that in a video before. (It was) scary. Very scary!

[Laughter]

16. TEACHER: Yeah, I can tell just from the publicity which videos I'm gonna avoid just because of those kinds of scenes. So, okay. Wh-, tell me a little about whether you think music videos that you have seen should be allowed on TV. What kinds of things . . . um . . . should determine whether they can be on TV?

17. ANDREA: Language.

18. TEACHER: Okay, language . . .

The contextualization cues at the opening of the transcript suggest that something may be amiss conversationally right from the start. Note the overlap between June's and Maria's speech in lines b, c, and d, and the fluctuating intonation of June's "okay" and "all right" in line e, the intonation indicating that, in this teacher's repertoire, these are not affirmative responses.

We can see from the extended portion of classroom talk in Transcript 3 that Maria interrupts the mini-lecture apparently to continue talking about a topic that she had brought up just moments earlier — the frightening violence

FIGURE 2   Section of Transcript with Contextualization Cues Marked

a Teacher: {[f] any other music videos that you felt should . . . be rated, that should have been rated in some way or another?} <6> b Maria: = = how about = = those scary ones- c Teacher: = = (×××) = = d Maria: = = like um, thriller? e Teacher: ok~ay, all r~ight/ {[hi] how could, well how could you rate those?}

in the video *Thriller*—but that June had discouraged. In fact, Maria pursues this topic quite persistently: she ignores June's question in turn 3 about how such movies are rated to comment further on their frightfulness in turn 4; she heads off Andrea's comment about a new rating proposal in turn 6 to argue for the salience of trauma over sex in turn 7; and she interrupts June's mini-lecture (which starts in line 10) to describe a particularly scary incident from *Thriller* in turn 13. We can see June responding to Maria's initiations with brief or disapproving responses (see turn 3/line e; see also turn 16) and finally taking hold of the discourse once again.

We think June's response in this instance is understandable: Maria appears to be reintroducing a topic that had been completed; June had shifted from discussion of specific videos to the essay question of whether or not music videos should be regulated. It is interesting to note, though, that the question June asks to bring the discourse round again to the essay topic— what kinds of things should determine whether a video could be aired on television?—was answered implicitly by Maria in her discussion of the violence in *Thriller*, but her contribution wasn't explicitly acknowledged.

In fact, June didn't appear to value what seemed to us appropriate responses from Maria, even when those responses did fit the pattern of classroom talk. Toward the end of Transcript 3 (turn 16), June asked what might determine how a movie video would be rated. In response to her question, students suggested "language," "sex," and "violence," and there were brief discussions of each in turn. June then asked the question again, for the fourth time, and when there was no response for several seconds, she explained that nudity might be another factor and explained how it's not to be confused with sexual scenes. Then, again, she asks the "what else" question; there's a long pause, and Maria replies:

TRANSCRIPT #4

1. TEACHER: Okay, can you think of anything else that might, they might consider when they're trying to decide how to rate a music video? (pause)

2. MARIA: Um, is it like . .(. .). . something to do with somebody that criticizes somebody else, like political issues, something like that?

3. TEACHER: Um, I don't know, um, that-

4. MARIA: Seems like, um, yeah-

5. TEACHER: That's not a widely recognized one but it might be one that is sort of subtle that's-

6. MARIA: Yeah. Like talking about like if you ( ) somebody, like race or something like that, ( ) video ( ) something like that.

7. TEACHER: Um, I don't know. Um, who would that kind of a video appeal to?

8. MARIA: Um, I don't know, um.

9. TEACHER: Would that appeal to children?

10. MATT: What music video is this?

11. TEACHER: If, a music video about some kind of a political issue.

12. MARIA: Yeah.

13. MATT: Oh, you mean like *Graceland* or something by U2?

14. TEACHER: Yeah, something like that. Now is that the kind of video that would really appeal to children?

15. ANDREA: No.

16. TEACHER: Or who would that appeal to?

In the following analysis of turns 1–7, notice that after line a, there is a long pause—one that perhaps gives Maria and the rest of the class enough time to provide thoughtful responses. It's also noteworthy that in line b we see some indications—from her pauses, soft voice, and tentative questions—that Maria is struggling to articulate a partly-formed idea. Notice, though, that in line f Maria takes on steam as she thinks of race as a possible example and speeds up her talk.

In this exchange, it seems to us that Maria brings up a new way to think about what influences ratings: a video with political overtones certainly could arouse concern or anger. Maria's comment, then, could have been an occasion for a discussion of censorship. For such a discussion to happen, however, June would need to provide some assistance, some verbal scaffolding, for Maria is struggling to express a partly formed idea about the importance of political contexts for music videos. But June does not assist this potential contribution; in fact, she disallows Maria's answer by undercutting it. (Notice June's use of "I don't know" in the evaluation slot in contrast to

FIGURE 3   Section of Transcript with Contextualization Cues Marked

a Teacher: ... okay, {[hi] can you think of anything else that might}-, they might consider when they're trying to decide how to rate a music video?<5>

b Maria: Uhhm, is it like <4> {[p] ( ) uh <3> something to do with . . . somebody that criticizes somebody else}, like . . . political issues? something like that?

c Teacher: uh [sigh] <2.5> i don't know/ um = = that-

d Maria: = = seems like um, yeah-

e Teacher: = = {[f] that's not a widely recog}nized one but . . . it might be one that is sort of subtle that's-

f Maria: y~eah like {[ac] [p] talking about like if you ( ) somebody, like race or something like that ( ) video ( ) something like that}

g Teacher: {[p] mm hmm/} uhhm, {[hi] i don't know}/

h   um, WHO would that kind of video appeal to?

her usual, more ostensibly neutral, "Okay.") June shifts the discussion away from political censorship and toward the issue of age by asking an unexpected question: "Who would that kind of a video appeal to?" (In line h this shift is signaled by June's intonation, a specific use of a contextualization cue that we observed at other places in the lesson.) This question departs from the pattern she had earlier established—the repeated question of "what else" might determine how a video gets rated—and it has a silencing effect on Maria. The conversation gets short-circuited, and Maria's moment for contributing a piece of knowledge is lost, and so is an opportunity for the class to consider an important issue.

Soon after the lesson, June viewed the videotape we had made of it, and she commented on Maria's classroom talk:

> Maria is becoming to me the Queen of the Non Sequiturs. You know, she really is just not quite. . . . That's, that's why I'm sort of amazed at times at, at her writing level, which is not really too bad. . . . Because her thinking level seems to be so scattered that I would expect that her writing would be a lot more disorganized and disjointed.

June was amazed at the level of Maria's writing, which was "not really too bad," given the scattered cognition she surmised from Maria's oral performance in class. In fact, June actually awarded Maria's written logic and organization with steadily improving grades and positive comments on her essays: "I like the way you made distinctions between facts and opinions." "You are very thorough and your thinking about the advice is very clear and logical." But, in spite of such evidence, June seemed to be greatly influenced in her assessment of Maria's abilities by her talk in the classroom, using "talking" as a barometer for "thinking," labeling Maria the "Queen of the Non Sequiturs." At the end of the semester, when summing up her evaluations of students, June confided that Maria "was a sweet girl, but she drove me crazy." She accounted for the improvement Maria had made in her writing by surmising that she had probably gotten help from her parents. (This was unlikely, however, since Maria's parents spoke little English.) June then made a final comment about her thinking: "Maria has thinking continuity problems." She predicted Maria wouldn't pass the next writing class the first time through "because it requires coherent thinking."

We think we can outline the process by which June constructed her view of Maria. When we looked over our field notes and our videotapes, there was abundant evidence that Maria did violate some of this classroom's rules for talk. Over the course of the semester, Maria made twenty-eight statements that were recorded in our fieldnotes. Ten of these were responses that fit the IRE question/answer structure; the remaining eighteen were initiations in the form of questions, and of these questions, six were procedural—how long does our essay have to be? must we type or can we write by hand? what page did you say the exercises are on?—a type of question that may be bothersome, particularly if its timing is a little off and it occurs after the conversation has turned to other matters. And, in fact, June did notice Maria's questioning patterns, and commented at the end of the semester that Maria asked a lot of questions in class but didn't answer many that June had posed to her.

Maria did, then, seem to initiate more than she responded—asking questions, taking the floor, diverting the course of classroom talk—and hers was not exactly the expected posture for a student in an IRE classroom. There were times when her interjections did suggest that she was not paying attention or was involved in something else related to the class, like reading over the assignment sheet while June was talking. This, we would argue, led to June's construction of Maria as the "Queen of the Non Sequiturs," the student who could be trusted to make a comment that was inappropriate or off-target. Given the way Maria's conversational habits stood out, it seems likely that June's view of Maria as an inappropriate talker would eventually become salient enough to affect her perception of Maria even when she interjects in a way that is appropriate. Join this perception of a particular student with this teacher's strong predilection for an IRE participant structure, and you won't be surprised that Maria's chances to be heard would be undercut. The cycle continues as Maria's interactional patterns in class become not just an annoying conversational style, but the barometer by which to measure her cognitive abilities. Her bothersome conversational habits become evidence of a thinking problem—evidence that is so salient that it goes unqualified even in the face of counter-evidence that Maria, in fact, wrote rather well.

But though we can explain at least some of the steps in the construction of Maria as a scattered thinker, we are left with a troubling question: how is it that annoying conversational style can become a measure of intellectual ability? What we have seen here is a relatively minor disjunction between teacher expectation and student behavior, an irritating mismatch of styles that, perhaps, chafes at a teacher's sense of authority. But given that irritations with students can lead to a range of outcomes, what made June's judgment of cognitive deficiency possible? To answer this question, we believe we need to consider the broader educational and cultural context in which this teacher lives—the received language and frames of mind she works within. Put another way, we need to consider the ways our schools have historically judged mental ability from performance that is somehow problematic and the sanctioned paths of inference from behavior to cognition that emerge from such judgments. We will begin by describing what we think of as this larger context for remedial writing instruction with a brief history of "low achievers" in American education.

THE CULTURAL CONTEXT OF SCHOOL FAILURE

There is a long, troubling history in American education of perceiving and treating low-achieving children as if they were lesser in character and fundamental ability. Larry Cuban and David Tyack, citing work by Stanley Zehm, trace this history by examining the labels that have been attached to students who are low-achievers, for "contained in a name, either explicitly or implicitly, is both an explanation and a prescription" (4). In the first half of the nineteenth century the poor performer was a "dunce," "shirker," "loafer," "reprobate," or "wrong-doer" who was "stupid," "vicious," "depraved," "wayward," or "incorrigible." Some of these labels imply that students lacked intelligence, but the majority suggest a flawed character. Such assessments, note Cuban and Tyack, reveal "a set of religious and moral convictions that placed responsibility for behavior and achievement in the sovereign individual" (4). During the last half of the nineteenth century, the labels shifted somewhat toward intelligence rather than character, though with a developmental or organic cast: students were "born late," "sleepy-minded," "overgrown," "immature," "slow," or "dull." "The condemnatory, religious language used earlier was diminishing," note Cuban and Tyack, "but the notion that academic failure came from defects of character or disposition continued" (4). As we moved into the twentieth century, notions of developmental and intellectual normalcy — evident in the abnormalcy of labels like "born late" and "sleepy-minded" — continued to evolve and were applied, in a negative way, to poor performers. And with the advent of the IQ movement, the assessment of intelligence, as Stephen Jay Gould has observed, was pseudoscientifically reified into a unitary measure of cognitive — and human — worth. Class and race prejudice, xenophobia, and the social engineering of Social Darwinists and Eugenicists absorbed the new technology of mental measurement, and the deficiency of those who performed poorly in school could, it was said, be precisely and scientifically assessed.

Though the ways of thinking about thinking generated by the IQ movement are still very much with us, we have changed perspectives somewhat since the heyday of the Eugenicists. The social reform movements of the 50s and 60s shifted the discussion of school failure from the character and ability of the individual toward the society that produces "alienated" and "socially maladjusted" youth and, as well, toward the economic conditions that have a negative impact on a lower-class child's readiness for school. Yet such social theories often reflected the influence of the theories that preceded them. Cuban and Tyack point out that along with the sociologically oriented analyses of the 50s — with their discussion of "social maladjustment" and "dropping out" — came designations of students as "immature learners," "unwilling learners," and "dullards." And many of the economic analyses of the 60s discussed minority and working-class culture in terms of deficit and pathology. A number of linguistic, psychological, and social psychological studies — focused, to a great extent, on African Americans — were designed and interpreted in such a way as to demonstrate impoverishment of language, maladaptive mother-child interaction, inadequate environmental stimuli for the development of cognition, and so on. (See Mitchell for a good overview.) Education tried to move beyond the moralistic, characterologic, deficit orientation of a previous era only to enshrine such orientations in a seemingly reform-minded social science research — and to continue to fault children for educational failure.

Through the 70s and 80s, two other perspectives on school failure have emerged: the effect cultural differences can have on communication and learning in the classroom (see, e.g., Au; Heath; Philips), and the effect class- and race-based resistance to socialization into the mainstream can have on school performance (see, e.g., Chase; Everhart; Giroux; Ogbu and Matute-Bianchi; Willis). We see these perspectives as powerful advances and — like many researchers of our generation — have been deeply influenced by them. But what concerns us is the ease with which older deficit-oriented explanations for failure can exist side by side with these newer theories, and, for that fact, can narrow the way such theories are represented and applied, turning differences into deficits, reducing the rich variability of human thought, language, and motive (Rose, "Language"; "Narrowing").

We think here of another teacher at another school in our study — a very good teacher, respected by colleagues and warmly regarded by students — a teacher who, upon receiving an assignment to teach his institution's most "remedial" course, dutifully sought out the program's expert in applied linguistics and schooling. The expert told the teacher, among other things, about research on differences in socialization for schooling. Our teacher later told a colleague that he was "in despair," fearful that he "may not be able to help these kids." Given their early socialization patterns "they barely have a chance. They're doomed by the time they enter school." There may be a harsh truth in the teacher's despair — poor kids do fail in disproportionate numbers — but note how variability disappears as rich differences in background and style become reduced to a success-failure binary and the "problem" — as has been the tendency in our history — shifts from the complex intersection of cognition and culture and continues to be interpreted as a deficiency located within families and students. In this perspective, school performance, as Ronald Edmonds once put it, "derives from family background instead of school response to family background" (23).

It is difficult to demonstrate causal relationships across the level of individual functioning and the levels of social, cultural, and historical contexts, what Erickson calls "system levels" or "levels of organization" (166–167). It is difficult to demonstrate, in our case, that pervasive, shared assumptions about ability and remediation influenced a teacher's interaction with and assessment of a student. One way to gain some reasonable evidence of influence, however, is to look closely at the language the teacher uses, and we have done that. Another way is to find institutional mechanisms that might serve to instantiate influential cultural assumptions. One such mechanism seemed to be the college's training program in which this teacher participated. In such programs, readings on topics like the composing process, the social context of schooling, and error analysis are sometimes combined, we have observed, with skills-and-drills materials and deficit-oriented theories and assessments. From what we could tell from the teacher's discussion of the program with us, this mix seemed to obtain. In addressing it, we can treat more fully a point we made earlier: the lasting power of deficit notions in our society and the way they can blend with and subvert more forward-looking notions about language and cognition. This blend is evident in two excerpts from June's commentary on the videotapes of the previous lesson and a present one.

In the first, June and the interviewer have been talking about the difficulty her students have with academic writing, particularly papers requiring categorization and comparison:

> TEACHER: They don't have those skills. Many of them don't. And many don't have an attention to detail that's necessary for some kinds of things; for instance, for classification, uh, exercises there's a need to look at, at specifics and at detail at times in order to be thorough, you know, to deal with that. They just don't have the practice in doing that. Uh, I think what I'm trying to do is, um, make sure that I tie as much as I possibly can into their own experience. Um, because many of these students don't have a lot to bring with them in terms of academic experience, but they do have some life experience to bring with them so. . . .

> INTERVIEWER: Okay.

> TEACHER: So, for instance, what I did in class about, um, having them write about what they think the educational system should do. Uh, ideally I would have liked them to do that before they ever read the article on, uh, Wednesday, just to get them thinking about what they're, what they already know about it, what, you know, what experience has already shown them about the things or what they've heard somewhere. . . . A lot of these kids have problems with connections between things. They, they don't see the connection between what goes on in their lives and what happens in the classroom, what happens, uh, at home. . . .

June notes, accurately we think, that many of her students haven't had sufficient practice in writing academic papers in which they must classify phenomena and attend closely to detail. She then observes that while her students may not have had a certain kind of privileged education, they certainly do have life experience and a history of schooling—both of which can be tapped and reflected upon, activating background knowledge that can help them with college assignments. But then look at the interesting thing that happens—a move that we witnessed in a number of our studies—the leap is made from an accurate description of particular difficulties (students have trouble writing certain kinds of papers) to a judgment about a general cognitive capacity: "A lot of these kids have problems with connections between things." Note, as well, the acknowledgment of a problem with the educational system—the segmentation of home and school knowledge—but the locating of it within the individual's cognition ("They don't see the connection") rather than within the system.

Now to the second excerpt:

> INTERVIEWER: Maria said something real interesting today. I asked them . . . to tell me what they think good writing or good reading is, and . . . she just immediately said "Good writing is creative writing."

> TEACHER: She's written a novel—incredible!

> INTERVIEWER: Yes, she told me that (both laugh).

> TEACHER: She's written about it in her journal and I, I, you know I thought that was neat. . . .

INTERVIEWER: You know I asked her . . . if she tried to apply creativity in her writing, and she said, "Oh, Yes!"

TEACHER: Well, she doesn't. . . . (laughs) She doesn't understand the difference between creative writing and expository prose.

INTERVIEWER: I'm not sure.

TEACHER: Yet.

INTERVIEWER: I'm not sure.

TEACHER: Well, that's not really something they get until, um, English 20A anyway. We don't really start talking about those distinctions until then. . . .

June wants to "tie as much as [she] possibly can into [her students'] own experience"; she also thinks it's a good thing that Maria wrote about her novel in her journal. But almost in the same breath she devalues Maria's extra-institutional literary activity and negates the possibility that she could learn things about literacy from it. The closing remark about English 20A is telling, we think, for with it June suggests that it is only through a lockstepped, carefully segmented curriculum that students like Maria can eventually develop the ability to understand the characteristics of different literacies and make distinctions between them. Perhaps because this teacher views fundamental cognitive abilities as deficient—thinking continuity problems, problems seeing connections—she suggests that it is only through the remedial therapy of a series of self-contained, carefully sequenced treatments that literacy knowledge can be developed. In a different guise, this is a skills-and-drills philosophy in which instructional scaffolding is replaced by curricular prostheses.

The point we want to make is that June is not alone in her judgments. For almost two centuries the dominant way to think about underachieving students has been to focus on defects in intellect or character or differences in culture or situation that lead to failure, and to locate the causes within the mind and language of the individual.[6] We are primed by this history, by our backgrounds and our educations, to speak of students as deficient,[7] even as we attempt to devise curricula we call forward-looking,[8] and this is true despite the great awakening that has occurred since the publication of Shaughnessy's *Errors and Expectations* in 1977. To be sure, we have found ways to understand our students' writing and promote its development, even when that writing differs markedly from the academic standard; we have come to see our courses as entry points to the academy, safe ground where students who have not had sufficient experience with academic reading and writing can make up for lost time, and do so without censure. Often, however, these new understandings come mixed with deeply held, unarticulated assumptions about remediation and remedial students, deficit assumptions that have been part of educational thought for a long time. Our unexamined cultural biases about difference, our national habits of mind for sorting and labeling individuals who perform poorly, our legacy of racism and class bias—these are the frames of mind which make it possible, even unremarkable, to assume that talk that is occasionally non-synchronous with the talk in a classroom indicates some fundamental problem in thought, to assume "thinking continuity problems" from a difference in conversational style. In examining June's ways of assessing cognition, then, we hope to set the foundation for ongoing self-examination, for we are all enmeshed in culture, and, even as we resist them, we are shaped by its forces.

EXAMINING ASSUMPTIONS

How can we as teachers and researchers examine our assumptions about remediation and remedial writing and remedial students? How can we be alert to deficit explanations for the difficulties that students experience in our classrooms? We have four suggestions: remembering teacher development, attending to classroom discourse, making macro-micro connections, and rethinking the language of cultural difference.

Remembering Teacher Development

When basic writing was just emerging as a course worth a teacher's serious attention and commitment, Mina Shaughnessy pointed out that most work was focusing on what was wrong with students rather than with teacher development. The effect of this tendency was the erroneous notion "that students, not teachers, are the people in education who must do the changing" ("Diving In" 234). Shaughnessy reminded us that students aren't the only people in a classroom who develop and grow, and she proposed a kind of impressionistic developmental scale for teachers of basic writing, each stage of which she named with a common metaphor: "Guarding the Tower," "Converting the Natives," "Sounding the Depths," and "Diving In." The significant thing to us about these metaphors is that they focus on teachers' attitudes about students' abilities. Teachers who guard the tower are so stunned by fractured writing that they believe the students who produced it have no place in the academy, for they will never be able to live up to the ideal of academic prose. Once this shock abates, and teachers begin to believe that students are educable, they proceed with conversion by offering them a steady flow of "truth" without thinking too much about the skills and habits students bring with them, often unconsciously, to their interactions with texts. The third stage involves the recognition that the writing behavior these students display has a logic that merits careful observation. At this point, then, a teacher is moving away from deficit notions and towards an appreciation of students' abilities. The last stage takes place when a teacher is willing to "remediate himself, to become a student of new disciplines and of his students themselves in order to perceive both their difficulties and their incipient excellence" (239). It is not at all easy, cautioned Shaughnessy, for a college teacher to assume that the students in a class, already labeled "remedial," possess this incipient excellence.

We want to argue that the situation Shaughnessy described is still with us. Granted, we have made much progress in learning about the writing process, in conducting interdisciplinary research, in imagining liberatory pedagogies, even in establishing composition programs which include some kind of training for teachers.[9] But what we have been much less successful in doing is promoting teacher development of the sort Shaughnessy described. We have assumed, as a best-case scenario, that if new teachers are introduced to writing theory and research as a part of their graduate training, and if they have the chance to prepare and develop curricular materials for their classes (conditions that are all too rare), then they will necessarily acquire whatever it is they need to know about remedial students. Maybe we have also assumed that teachers automatically move from "guarding the tower" to "diving in" just as a function of experience. Our studies make us question these assumptions. Because deficit notions of abilities are so deeply ingrained in most of us, it seems very unlikely that most teachers, pressed as they are by constraints of time and curricula, will discover serendipitously more productive ways to view students' abilities.

And how we view students' abilities, we have tried to illustrate in this paper, can have profound effects. A great deal of research has shown that students whose teachers expect them to do well, tend to do well, while students whose teachers expect them to do poorly, do poorly. These findings hold firm, even in cases of mistaken placement or misinformation. That is, "bright" students who are mistakenly expected to perform poorly in the classroom will often do poorly, while students labeled "average" will often excel if their teacher believes that this is what they are supposed to do (Brophy). We have illustrated that Maria's discourse style did not fit well with the IRE participant structure of her remedial writing class. It also occurred to us that Maria's conversational patterns more closely resembled the talk that is allowed in classrooms geared to the honors student. Perhaps Maria, who placed in non-remedial classes in high school and was on the speech team, was accustomed to speaking up with her own opinion, which she expected to be acknowledged by her teachers and to be of some import to the lesson. She displays an eagerness to be involved, to interact with her teacher.[10] By the end of the semester, the mismatch between Maria's discourse style and that of the classroom seemed to be taking a toll. Maria told us in her last tutoring session that she now "had some problems with . . . English," that her writing had gotten "longer" but not necessarily better, and that she was "not a very good speaker." Perhaps it is also noteworthy that she expressed interest at the end of the semester in teaching students who were poor performers in the classroom. In any case, her negative self-assessments are very different from the successful Maria we saw at the beginning of the semester — the student who loved writing and who'd been a member of the speech team — and suggest that she had perhaps begun to internalize her teacher's opinions of her abilities.

Research on expectancy theory thus supports Shaughnessy's claims about teacher development: the beliefs we construct of our students' abilities can influence their lives in our classrooms and beyond in profound ways. We want to suggest that it would be unwise just to rely on process pedagogy and experience in the classroom to foster the development of non-deficit attitudes among teachers and teacher-trainees. We need to spend some time thinking about teacher development—not just what knowledge to impart about writing, but how to develop the ability to question received assumptions about abilities and performance, how to examine the thinking behind the curricula we develop and the assessments we make.[11]

We might, for a start, look closely at writing instruction to identify moments when teachers transcend deficit attitudes, when teaching serves to invite rather than to deny. Roger Simon has written about "the contradictory character of the work of teaching" (246), illustrating that "what teachers choose to signify at any particular moment in time may present meanings which are ideologically inconsistent with meanings present at other times" (248). He locates the origin of these contradictions not in the individual but in the larger social and institutional context, and he sees contradictory moments as potentially liberatory, for they make possible the inclusion of oppositional knowledge in educational practice. In a related way, we might think of teaching as an ongoing flow of moments of invitation and moments of denial. The better, the more effective the teaching, the richer and more frequent the moments of invitation, encouragement, and assistance (though no extended period of teaching will be free of constraint, limit, even rejection). What has interested us in this paper is the way in which culturally sanctioned, deficit-oriented assumptions about learning and cognition can tip the scale. But what we need to do as well is identify, understand, and learn to foster those moments in which teachers encourage rather than restrict their students' potential.

Attending to Classroom Discourse

One of the things we have learned in doing this paper is the value of looking closely at the talk that transpires in classrooms. We have been interested particularly in conversational patterns—rules for turn-taking and the special participant structure that characterizes so much of talk in school, the IRE sequence. But this work on turn-taking, interesting and revealing though it can be, was a means to another end. In the classroom, it is through talk that learning gets done, that knowledge gets made. Using conversational turns as a unit of analysis gave us a window on knowledge-making.

In the analysis reported in this paper, we focused on a moment when Maria didn't get to make knowledge, when her chance to contribute a special piece of information, one that would have deepened the discourse at hand, was denied. We have argued that the reason her contribution was denied had to do with her teacher's construction of her as a particular kind of remedial student, a scattered thinker, and that such a construction likely had its origin in longstanding, widespread beliefs about low-achieving students, beliefs that such students are deficient and that the locus of any academic difficulty they have lies within them. In this instance, then, we saw faulty notions about cognition being played out and reinforced within a certain participant structure, the IRE sequence.

This finding raised for us the possibility that the IRE sequence could be the vehicle for a discourse of remediation, a discourse where most questions have "known" answers, where the teacher maintains tight control over conversation, where students are not allowed to participate in free-ranging talk. In the literature on classroom talk, many objections have been raised about the IRE participant structure in terms of the role that more free-ranging talk can play in knowledge construction (see, e.g., Applebee; Barnes; Cazden; Dillon; Edwards and Furlong; Moffett; Tharp and Gallimore). We too see a place for free-ranging, student-led discussion (Hull and Rose, " 'This Wooden' ").[12] But we would also suggest that the IRE participant structure does not itself circumvent knowledge-making and engagement; the kinds of questions that teachers ask and the kinds of evaluations that they give to students' responses will more often affect what knowledge gets made and who makes it. Questions that are genuine questions, that don't have pre-specified answers, and evaluations that validate students' contributions are going to create a different kind of classroom discourse and a different level of engagement.[13]

Let us look at some bits of conversation from our classroom lesson which do just that.

> TEACHER: Well, tell me a little bit about what would go into determining how the music videos that you have seen might be rated. What kinds of things, um, would be used to determine how, what, how a movie gets rated?
>
> STUDENT: Language.
>
> TEACHER: Okay, language (writes it on the board). Like what, tell me, give examples. I mean . . . You don't have to swear but. . . .

In this IRE sequence, June asks a follow-up question, incorporating the student's answer into her next question in order to elicit an elaboration on the student's answer. She considers the student's answer important enough to spend time on it, to work it into the exchange, to allow it to modify the subsequent discussion. And in so doing, she bestows value on it.

> TEACHER: Or who would that appeal to?
>
> MATT: I don't think that—
>
> SUSAN: (   ) over 18.
>
> MATT: Children of what age level?
>
> TEACHER: Okay, that's a good question: children of what age?

Here June accepts a student's initiation and sanctions it as the topic of the next series of questions. This move shows, again, a willingness to accept students' ideas and to value them.

> TEACHER: What, what are some of the music videos you've seen recently?
>
> ANDREA: *Thriller.*

TEACHER: *Thriller.*

MATT: *Graceland.*

TEACHER: Okay, *Thriller* . . . and *Graceland.* I'll, I'll come back to that one, but *Thriller,* what's the rating on *Thriller?*

Here June acknowledges that a student's comment, although it cannot immediately be responded to, is nevertheless important and will eventually be discussed.

And those moments when June was able to shift out of the IRE pattern—mixing conversation styles, encouraging other modes of participation—gave rise to yet other opportunities for fruitful talk. For example, when one student proposes that music videos could be rated by a quantitative tally of objectionable language, June responds:

TEACHER: Okay. Now that's something I had not heard before, but that kind of makes sense.

Here, then, is an admission from June that a student knows something that she doesn't—an admission that might lessen the power differential in the classroom and make authentic discourse more possible. Another such moment occurred when a student points out that the same kind of violence that would result in a restrictive rating for a music video regularly occurs as part of on-the-scene reporting in newscasts—an assertion, by the way, that challenged the position June had adopted. The student then goes on to give an example of a murder shown recently on a local television news program:

MATT: I saw the shooting.

ANDREA: Yeah, I've seen the shooting.

JASON: Yeah, (   ) They shot 'im like from, from where I'm at to where you're at. . . .

Following the above excerpt, the conversation takes off and continues for another two pages in our transcript. June does evaluate a few times during this conversation, but she sees that it is clearly a topic of concern for the students—a number of different students initiate during this discussion—and she lets it go longer than any other student conversation in the lesson. She also becomes an "equal" participant at times, no longer evaluating but asking questions for which she doesn't have a particular answer in mind. These are not remarkable exchanges, but they were rare in the lessons we analyzed, and they do illustrate a capacity to engage in kinds of classroom conversation other than those we saw with Maria.

We want to recommend that attention be paid to the talk that goes on in our writing classrooms—analyses of the participant structures, whether they be IRE sequences or other patterns of interaction—with an eye for determining the kind of talk those structures allow. We have seen that discourse structures direct talk in particular ways and that certain moves within those structures can instantiate assumptions about cognition and undercut creative thinking and engagement. If we look closely at the talk we allow, we may also get a new sense of our own assumptions about our students' capabilities.

Making Macro-Micro Connections

What has frequently happened in the study of reading and writing is that researchers have conducted either fine-grained analyses of texts or of the cognitive processes involved in text comprehension and production *or* have produced studies of wider focus of the social and political contexts of reading, writing, and schooling. Such a separation isn't peculiar to literacy research, but characterizes as well divisions among disciplines. As anthropologist Frederick Erickson has pointed out, "Individual cognitive functioning has been largely the purview of cognitive psychologists who have often attempted to study thinking apart from the naturally occurring social and cultural circumstances of its use," while "the anthropology of education often has studied *anything but* deliberately taught cognitive learning" (173). Erickson goes on to suggest that "some rapprochement is needed, from the direction of the (more cognitively sophisticated) psychology of learning to the (more contextually sophisticated) anthropology of learning" (173).

Such calls to systematically integrate social and cognitive perspectives are increasing (Freedman, Dyson, Flower, and Chafe; Michaels; Rose, "Complexity"). Sociologist Aaron Cirourel argues that "the study of discourse and the larger context of social interaction requires explicit references to a broader organizational setting and aspects of cultural beliefs often ignored by students of discourse and conversational analysis" (qtd. in Corsaro 22). At the same time, educational anthropologist Henry Trueba reminds us, "the strength of ethnographic research [on school achievement] and its contribution to theory building . . . will depend on the strength of each of the microanalytical links of the inferential chains that form our macrotheoretical statements" (283). To adequately study language in society, then, one has to take into account "interrelationships among linguistic, cognitive, and sociocultural elements" (Cirourel quoted in Corsaro 23).

Moving between micro-level, close examination of oral or written discourse and macro-level investigations of society and culture—seeking connections between language, cognition, and context—is, we feel, particularly important in the case of students designated remedial and for our efforts to examine our assumptions about these students' abilities (Hull and Rose, "Rethinking"). Without the microperspective, one runs the risk of losing sight of the particulars of behavior; without the macroperspective, one runs the risk of missing the social and cultural logic of that behavior. In the case of Maria, micro-level analyses enabled us to examine closely the conversational processes by which a student was defined as a scattered thinker and the ways her opportunities to participate in and contribute to knowledge production were narrowed. Macro-level analyses can encourage a consideration of Maria's discourse processes in contexts other than the individual cognitive one provided by her teacher and, as well, encourage reflection on the very language June uses in making her assessment. So, let us now play out some macro-level considerations of Maria's conversational style.

Reproduction-resistance theorists and cultural-difference theorists, both mentioned earlier, would raise questions about the broader political and cultural contexts of Maria's behavior. The former group would wonder if Maria's conversational style was an attempt to resist an educational system that does not serve her well, while the latter group would wonder if Maria's conversational style reflected communication patterns shaped by her cultural inheritance and/or her family background. The focus of the "problem" of Maria's conversational style wouldn't automatically be on the isolated processes of her own cognition, but on the possible role played by other political or cultural influences. A somewhat related perspective would focus on Maria's history in classrooms — wondering what prior socializing experiences in school might have influenced her interactional style. A further perspective would tighten the contextual focus to the immediate psychosocial context of Maria's current instruction. Was there something about the way Maria expressed her need to be involved in the class and her teacher's conscious or unconscious reaction to it that affected Maria's conversational style?

In posing these perspectives, we do not want to suggest that each has equal explanatory power for Maria's case. For example, our data don't seem to support reproduction-resistance theory. Maria was an eager participant in the classroom community, taking part dutifully in virtually every aspect of her course. Her interruptions of classroom talk did not appear to us to be interruptions for the sake of disruption; rather she seemed to want to take part in class, to make a contribution, or to keep track of assignment information she may have missed. (The value of this perspective in Maria's case may be more general, however, in that it can lead one to examine the political context of schooling and the inequities of class in American educational history.) The applicability of the cultural-differences perspective is a more complicated issue. There may well be home/school differences at work in Maria's conversational style; unfortunately we were not able to visit Maria's home or collect information from other sources that could shed light on this hypothesis directly. One could argue, though, against the applicability of the cultural-differences hypothesis here in any strong way. While Maria may have operated with different cultural assumptions about communication when she first began elementary school in the United States, it seems unlikely that she would not have become aware of the dominant discourse of schooling, the IRE participant structure, by the time she entered college. Still, there is real value, it seems to us, in speculating on the possible conversational dynamics within Maria's family that might influence what she does in the classroom, especially under the pressure to articulate an idea. We have very limited data on the third perspective offered above — Maria's history of interaction with teachers — though this seems a good possibility to pursue, especially given her participation on a speech team, where somewhat more interactive conversational patterns could have existed. We think the fourth perspective — the psychosocial context of Maria and her teacher — is also promising, especially when we consider the less excitable Maria observed in our tutorial sessions.

Our best, and cautious, guess about the context of Maria's conversational style in this classroom, then, would be that three possible influences are at work: (a) Maria's previous experience in classrooms or other school contexts that were less teacher-centered, (b) characteristics of her non-classroom conversational style, possibly shaped by family dynamics, and (c) Maria's eagerness — perhaps tinged with anxiety — to do well and be part of things and the growing number of disapproving cues she picks up from her teacher, which could lead to further uncertainty and anxiety, and with that, further communicative missteps.

Attempting to link micro-level with macro-level analysis — shuttling in a systematic way between close linguistic and cognitive study and studies of broader contexts — can, we think, provide a richer understanding of the history and logic of particular behaviors. It might provide, as well, checks and balances on the assessments we make about ability, and perhaps it can lead us to raise to conscious examination our assumptions about the nature and cause of performance that strikes us as inadequate or unusual. But even as we use this micro-macro metaphor, we are unhappy with it, for we recognize that it still separates cognitive behaviors and social contexts into different domains. In fact, one reason for much recent interest in Vygotsky and the extension of his work called "activity theory" (Wertsch, Minick) is that his sociocultural theory of mind provides an alternative to the division of cognition from context, mind from culture, knowing from acting. We see a need to work toward holistic conceptions of the study of schooling and students' performance which take as a given that linguistic and cognitive behaviors occur within, and can best be understood within, their particular institutional, cultural, and historical milieus.

Rethinking the Language of Cultural Difference

Our last suggestion for examining our assumptions about remediation and remedial students is to work toward a conceptualization of discourse that undercuts easy thinking about difference. This call is difficult, for it requires an engagement of the very language currently available to us to discuss school failure in a progressive way.

Research on cultural and class differences in communication and learning styles has revealed the coherence, purposiveness, and richness of behavior that has puzzled mainstream educators and resulted in harmful explanations and assessments of poor performance. Such research has moved us significantly toward a more democratic vision of learning and schooling and, in some cases, has helped us successfully tailor instruction to fit students' needs (e.g., Au; Heath). But our time spent in remedial programs — reviewing curricula, talking to teachers and administrators, catching our own disturbing reactions to the literacy performances we saw — has made us uncomfortable with much of the research that focuses on differences, whether such difference grows out of the recognition that communication styles at school aren't like those at home or that people come to intellectual tasks in different ways. The problem is that all American educational research—ours and everyone else's—emerges from a culture in the grips of deficit thinking, and any analysis that delineates differences will run the risk of being converted to a deficit theory (Rose, "Narrowing"). We believe that a focus on differences, while potentially democratic and certainly instructive, can lead us to forget two things: (1) in fundamental ways, we all possess the means to use language to make meaning; we all participate in fundamental linguistic and cognitive processes by virtue of our common humanity and (2) human beings, given the right social conditions, are astoundingly adaptive, and to determine what works against this adaptability, we need to look at the social and instructional conditions in the classroom rather than assume the problem is to be found in the cultural characteristics students bring with them. Two research-based observations are pertinent here. The first is from Asa Hilliard, and the second comes from Luis Moll and Stephen Diaz:

> I do believe that greater sensitivity to [learning] style issues will make meaningful contributions to pedagogy in the future. Yet I remain unconvinced that the explanation for the low performance of culturally different "minority" group students will be found by pursuing questions of behavioral style. Since students are adaptable, the stylistic difference explanation does not answer the question of why "minority" groups perform at a low level. . . . [C]hildren . . . are failing primarily because of systematic inequalities in the delivery of whatever pedagogical approach the teachers claim to master—not because students cannot learn from teachers whose styles do not match their own. (Hilliard 68)

> Although student characteristics certainly matter, when the same children are shown to succeed under modified instructional arrangements it becomes clear that the problems . . . working-class children face in school must be viewed primarily as a consequence of institutional arrangements that constrain children *and* teachers by not capitalizing fully on their talents, resources, and skills. (Moll and Diaz 302)

It is useful here to recall Ray McDermott's discussion of the way our society "keep[s] arranging for school failure to be so visible." "We might do better," he continues,

> to ask how it is a part of the situation of every minority group that it has had to be explained, or about the degradation every minority group has had to suffer from our explanations. . . . By making believe that failure is something that kids do, as different from how it is something that is done to them, and then by explaining their failure in terms of other things they do, we likely contribute to the maintenance of school failure. (McDermott 362–363)

McDermott takes us all to task for our manufacture of failure, our entrapment in a way of thinking and of organizing society that virtually assures failure. We struggle within a discourse that yearns for difference, and difference, in our culture, slides readily toward judgment of better-or-worse, dominance, otherness.

Yet the moment we express our concerns about a focus on difference, we must stop short. Without such a focus one can easily forget that "intellectual development is socially and culturally based, and that what happens in the home, school, and local community . . . is crucial to understanding the learning processes and academic achievement of all children, including minority children" (Trueba 279). Such a perspective can lead to a greater appreciation of the richness of background, language, and gesture that comprise America. In fact, a focus on cognitive and linguistic *similarity* can shift readily to a leveling vision that not only reduces the variability that should be a cause for celebration, but, in its way, can also blind us to the political and economic consequences of difference. As Linda Brodkey puts it, a focus on similarity can distract us "from noticing the consequences of difference, namely, inequity" (599). Given a history of diminishment, of a devaluation and ridicule of difference, it is not surprising that some members of historically subjugated groups want to move beyond an embrace of cognitive and linguistic similarity to an elevation of difference. Within French feminism and African-American cultural studies, for example, some writers are arguing for the existence of distinctive female and Afrocentric epistemologies. Their move is to turn otherness on its head, to celebrate ways of knowing that have been reduced and marginalized.

Given the culturally received ways we have to think about school failure in America, it seems that we have to keep these two perspectives in dynamic tension, see them as elements in a complex dialectic, a dialectic that can lead us to be alert to the ease with which we can make limiting, harmful judgments about linguistic and cognitive ability, the ease with which rich differences can be ignored or converted to deficits, but the ease, as well, with which differences can be represented in essentialistic and deterministic ways that reduce human variability and adaptability. For that fact, we need to be vigilant that the very dialectic we want to honor does not degenerate into the kind of bipolar, better-worse scheme that has been so characteristic of our thinking about language use. To focus on the possible cultural or class differences of a student like Maria can both reveal the logic of her behavior and — given the ways we carry with us to react to difference — blind us to the shared cognitive and linguistic processes she displays. But to focus on the shared nature of Maria's cognitive and linguistic processes can blind us to the specifics of her background, and, further, can lead us to downplay variability and the way difference has been historically embedded in inequity. To talk about difference in America, given our legacy of racism and class prejudice, requires us to talk, as well, about the many reductive, harmful ways difference has historically been represented. What we need to develop are conceptual frameworks that *simultaneously* assert shared cognitive and linguistic competence while celebrating in a non-hierarchical way the play of human difference.[14]

NOTES

[1]The work reported here is part of a larger study, "Literacy, Underpreparation, and the Cognition of Composing." We gratefully acknowledge the support of the James S. McDonnell Foundation's Program in Cognitive Studies for Educational Practice, the Spencer Foundation, the National Center for the Study of Writing, and the National Council of Teachers of English Research Foundation.

[2]For other discussions of interactional classroom competence and reviews of previous work in this area, see Mehan ("Competent") and Corno.

[3]We should point out, however, that most of the research identifying the IRE sequence has been done with classrooms in the elementary grades. For an exception to this, and an example of how the IRE participant structure can be used to analyze writing conferences, see Freedman and Katz.

[4]The transcription conventions were developed by John Gumperz, with help from Wallace Chafe and Noreen Barantz. Gumperz has stressed that the system is more interpretive than descriptive, and that the key to its proper usage is consistency.

[5]In the interest of saving space, we haven't provided transcripts with contextualization cues for every stretch of classroom talk. Readers interested in seeing such transcripts can request a copy of Technical Report #44 from the National Center for the Study of Writing at the University of California, Berkeley.

[6]For another account of this history, see Robert Sinclair and Ward Ghory's *Reaching Marginal Students.*

[7]British researchers Michael Golby and John R. Gulliver make a related point in their critical review of remedial education in England and Wales: "In order to understand what exists, we must see remedial education firstly in its historical context, and secondly as a manifestation of ideologies obtaining not only within education but also having co-relative applications within wider social policy" (11). See also Michael Cole and Peg Griffin.

[8]For a related argument, see Sandra Schecter and Tamara Lucas's position paper on "Literacy Education and Diversity."

[9]A special issue of the *Journal of Basic Writing* (1981) was devoted to discussions of the kinds of programs that would best prepare basic writing teachers.

[10]This explanation of Maria's interactional patterns is developed more fully by Kay Losey Fraser in a paper delivered at the 1989 Conference on College Composition and Communication.

[11]To this end, with our colleague Cynthia Greenleaf, we are creating a set of cases and an interpretation of remedial education in America that we hope can be used to engage teachers in the kind of inquiry that leads one to trace the connections between the mind of the student and the classroom and the community beyond.

[12]We aren't, however, offering student-led discussion, collaborative groups, or peer conferencing as a panacea. Thomas Fox has illustrated that conversation between peers can be dramatically and negatively affected by gender and race relations. See also Trimbur.

[13]Martin Nystrand and Adam Gamoran at the University of Wisconsin–Madison are currently engaged in studies of classroom lessons aimed at characterizing high-quality instructional discourse.

[14]We would like to thank Carmen Colon Montes de Oca for helpful conversation and Cynthia Greenleaf, Kris Gutierrez, Rebekah Kaplan, Jacqueline Jones Royster, and Gloria Zarabozo for reading and commenting on the manuscript. We also benefitted from the comments of three anonymous reviewers for *CCC*. We appreciate Susan Thompson's assistance throughout the research project.

REFERENCES

Applebee, Arthur N. *Writing in the Secondary School: English and the Content Areas.* NCTE Research Report 21. Urbana: NCTE, 1981.

Au, K. "Participation Structures in a Reading Lesson with Hawaiian Children." *Anthropology and Education Quarterly* 11 (June 1980): 91–115.

Barnes, D. *From Communication to Curriculum.* London: Penguin, 1976.

Brodkey, Linda. "Transvaluing Difference." *College English* 51 (Oct. 1989): 597–601.

Brophy, Jere E. "Research on the Self-Fulfilling Prophecy." *Journal of Educational Psychology* 75 (Oct. 1983): 631–661.

Cazden, Courtney B. *Classroom Discourse: The Language of Teaching and Learning.* Portsmouth, NH: Heinemann, 1988.

Chase, Geoffrey. "Accommodation, Resistance and the Politics of Student Writing." *College Composition and Communication* 39 (Feb. 1988): 13–22.

Cole, Michael, and Peg Griffin. "A Sociohistorical Approach to Remediation." *Literacy, Society, and Schooling: A Reader*. Ed. S. de Castell, A. Luke, and K. Egan. Cambridge: Cambridge UP, 1986. 110–131.

Cook-Gumperz, Jenny. "Introduction: The Social Construction of Literacy." *The Social Construction of Literacy*. Ed. Jenny Cook-Gumperz. Cambridge: Cambridge UP, 1986. 1–15.

Corno, Lyn. "What It Means to be Literate about Classrooms." *Classrooms and Literacy*. Ed. David Bloome. Norwood, NJ: Ablex, 1989. 29–52.

Corsaro, William A. "Communicative Processes in Studies of Social Organization: Sociological Approaches to Discourse Analysis." *Text* 1 (1981): 5–63.

Cuban, Larry, and David Tyack. " 'Dunces,' 'Shirkers,' and 'Forgotten Children': Historical Descriptions and Cures for Low Achievers." Conference for Accelerating the Education of At-Risk Students. Stanford U, 1988.

Dillon, J. T. ed. *Questioning and Discussion: A Multidisciplinary Study*. Norwood, NJ: Ablex, 1988.

Edmonds, Ronald. "Effective Schools for the Urban Poor." *Educational Leadership* 37 (Oct. 1979): 15–24.

Edwards, A. D., and V. J. Furlong. *The Language of Teaching: Meaning in Classroom Interaction*. London: Heinemann, 1978.

Erickson, Frederick. "Taught Cognitive Learning in Its Immediate Environments: A Neglected Topic in the Anthropology of Education." *Anthropology and Education Quarterly* 13 (1982): 149–180.

Everhart, R. B. *Reading, Writing, and Resistance: Adolescence and Labor in a Junior High School*. Boston: Routledge, 1983.

Fox, Thomas. "Collaborative Learning, Literacy, and Conversational Analysis." Unpublished paper. Chico State U, 1989.

Fraser, Kay Losey. "Classroom Discourse and Perceptions of Cognitive Ability: An Analysis of Interaction in a Basic Writing Class." Conference on College Composition and Communication Convention. Seattle, 1989.

Freedman, Sarah Warshauer, Anne Haas Dyson, Linda Flower, and Wallace Chafe. *Research in Writing: Past, Present, and Future*. Technical Report 1. Center for the Study of Writing, U of California, Berkeley, and Carnegie Mellon U, Pittsburgh, 1987.

Freedman, Sarah Warshauer, and Anne Marie Katz. "Pedagogical Interaction During the Composing Process: The Writing Conference." *Writing in Real Time: Modeling Production Processes*. Ed. Ann Matsuhashi. Norwood: Ablex, 1987. 58–107.

Giroux, Henry. *Theory and Resistance in Education*. South Hadley: Bergin, 1983.

Golby, Michael, and John R. Gulliver. "Whose Remedies, Whose Ills? A Critical Review of Remedial Education." *New Directions in Remedial Education*. Ed. Colin J. Smith. London: Falmer Press, 1985. 7–19.

Gould, Stephen Jay. *The Mismeasure of Man*. New York: Norton, 1981.

Gumperz, John. "Contextualization and Understanding." *Rethinking Context*. Ed. A. Duranti. Cambridge: Cambridge UP, in press.

_____. *Discourse Strategies*. Cambridge: Cambridge UP, 1982.

Heath, Shirley Brice. *Ways with Words: Language, Life, and Work in Communities and Classrooms*. Cambridge: Cambridge UP, 1983.

Hilliard, Asa G. "Teachers and Cultural Styles in a Pluralistic Society." *NEA Today* 7 (Jan. 1989): 65–69.

Hull, Glynda, and Mike Rose. "Rethinking Remediation: Toward a Social-Cognitive Understanding of Problematic Reading and Writing." *Written Communication* 8 (April 1989): 139–154.

_____. " 'This Wooden Shack Place': The Logic of an Unconventional Reading." *College Composition and Communication* 41 (Oct. 1990): 287–298.

McDermott, R. P. "The Explanation of Minority School Failure, Again." *Anthropology and Education Quarterly* 18 (Dec. 1987): 361–364.

Mehan, Hugh. "The Competent Student." *Anthropology and Education Quarterly* 11 (June 1980): 131–152.

_____. *Learning Lessons: Social Organization in the Classroom*. Cambridge: Harvard UP, 1979.

Michaels, Sarah. *The Literacies Institute: Technical Proposal*. Newton, MA: Education Development Center, 1989.

Minick. Norris. *L. S. Vygotsky and Soviet Activity Theory: Perspectives on the Relationship between Mind and Society*. Technical Reports Special Monograph 1. Newton, MA: The Literacies Institute, 1989.

Mitchell, Jacquelyn. "Reflections of a Black Social Scientist: Some Struggles, Some Doubts, Some Hopes." *Harvard Educational Review* 52 (Feb. 1982): 27–44.

Moffett, James. *Teaching the Universe of Discourse*. Boston: Houghton, 1968.

Moll, Luis C., and Stephen Diaz. "Change as the Goal of Educational Research." *Anthropology and Education Quarterly* 18 (Dec. 1987): 300–311.

Nystrand, Martin, and Adam Gamoran. *Instructional Discourse and Student Engagement*. Madison: National Center on Effective Secondary Schools and the Wisconsin Center for Education Research, 1989.

_____. *A Study of Instruction as Discourse*. Madison: National Center on Effective Secondary Schools and the Wisconsin Center for Education Research, 1988.

Ogbu, John U., and Maria Eugenia Matute-Bianchi. "Understanding Sociocultural Factors: Knowledge, Identity, and School Adjustment." *Beyond Language: Social and Cultural Factors in Schooling Language Minority Students*. Los Angeles: Evaluation, Dissemination and Assessment Center of California State U, 1986. 73–142.

Philips, Susan U. *The Invisible Culture: Communication in Classroom and Community on the Warm Springs Indian Reservation*. New York: Longman, 1983.

Rose, Mike. "Complexity, Rigor, Evolving Method, and the Puzzle of Writer's Block: Thoughts on Composing Process Research." *When a Writer Can't Write: Studies in Writer's Block and Other Composing Process Problems*. Ed. Mike Rose. New York: Guilford, 1985. 227–260.

_____. "The Language of Exclusion: Writing Instruction at the University." *College English* 47 (April 1985): 341–359.

_____. "Narrowing the Mind and Page: Remedial Writers and Cognitive Reductionism." *College Composition and Communication* 39 (Oct. 1988): 267–302.

Sacks, H., E. A. Schegloff, and G. Jefferson. "A Simplest Systematics for the Organization of Turn-taking in Conversation." *Language* 50 (Dec. 1974): 696–735.

Schecter, Sandra R., and Tamara Lucas. "Literacy Education and Diversity. A Position Paper." Unpublished manuscript, U of California, Berkeley, 1989.

Shaughnessy, Mina. "Diving In: An Introduction to Basic Writing." *College Composition and Communication* 27 (Oct. 1976): 234–239.

_____. *Errors and Expectations*. New York: Oxford UP, 1977.

Simon, Roger I. "But Who Will Let You Do It? Counter-Hegemonic Possibilities for Work Education." *Journal of Education* 165 (Summer 1983): 235–256.

Sinclair, J. M., and R. M. Coulthard. *Toward an Analysis of Discourse*. New York: Oxford UP, 1977.

Sinclair, Robert L., and Ward J. Ghory. *Reaching Marginal Students: A Primary Concern for School Renewal*. Berkeley: McCutchan, 1987.

Tannen, Deborah. *Conversational Style: Analyzing Talk among Friends*. Norwood: Ablex, 1984.

Tharp, Roland G., and Ronald Gallimore. *Rousing Minds to Life: Teaching, Learning, and Schooling in Social Context*. Cambridge: Cambridge UP, 1989.

Training Teachers of Basic Writing. Special Issue of the *Journal of Basic Writing* 3.2 (Spring/Summer 1981).

Trimbur, John. "Consensus and Difference in Collaborative Learning." *College English* 51 (Oct. 1989): 602–615.

Trueba, Henry T. "Culturally Based Explanations of Minority Students' Academic Achievement." *Anthropology and Education Quarterly* 19 (Dec. 1988): 270–287.

Wertsch, James V. *Vygotsky and the Social Formation of Mind*. Cambridge: Harvard UP, 1985.

Willis, Paul. *Learning to Labor: How Working Class Kids Get Working Class Jobs*. New York: Columbia UP, 1977.

Zehm, Stanley J. "Educational Misfits: A Study of Poor Performers in the English Class 1825–1925." Diss., Stanford U, 1973.

PART FOUR

School and Society, 1989–1995

Introduction to Part Four

With *Lives on the Boundary* and continuing with *Possible Lives*, I began writing for audiences beyond the academy, trying to find a language and form that would reach a broader readership. Could I demonstrate as well as argue for the issues that mattered in composition studies, embody ideas, animate them? I'll say more about public writing in Part Six, but here I want to note that these books, though not typically academic in genre and diction, drew on all the academic work I had done before in graduate school and subsequent research projects. The books would not have been possible without that work.

The cognitive research, for example, provided an orientation to think about thinking, to want to explore the logic of a piece of tangled writing or to inquire about the decisions a teacher was making as she guided a class through a physics experiment. And the continual attempts to develop a social-cognitive perspective enabled the narrative depiction of the mind's work as lived, rich, culturally embedded. What I learned about the close analysis of instructional discourse helped as well — an understanding of how learning, academic identity, and intellectual competence is affected by the dynamics of classroom talk. Certainly, the historical and sociological literature on institutions — combined with all the on-the-ground administration and curriculum development — was essential in framing the larger arguments in both *Lives on the Boundary* and *Possible Lives*. Those larger arguments were enhanced as well by my earlier literary study that provided both an intellectual landscape and a sensitivity to language, invaluable when reading educational history or considering the word choice in institutional memoranda or policy reports.

The danger in the retrospection afforded by a book like *An Open Language* is that the writer is tempted to provide order, sequence, development where it may not have existed in the messy, scattered flow of life. I don't want to suggest a conscious and strategic bringing together of these disparate disciplinary orientations and modes of inquiry. As you'll see in the upcoming discussions, the two books took their shape in less determined ways. But it does seem clear to me now that all the foregoing work came to bear on *Lives on the Boundary* and *Possible Lives*. Directly or indirectly, we draw on what we know. How could it be otherwise?

I was lucky enough to find projects that invited this drawing together, this consolidation, projects that mattered and that forced a stretch and a synthesis. It's not uncommon that I meet graduate students or younger faculty who have switched fields of study or careers: the critical race theorist who was in statistics, the lawyer turned cognitive educational psychologist, the biology major who likes rhetoric. They often have regrets about the earlier pursuit, feeling it was time wasted en route to their true passion. Don't think that way, I tell them; you don't know how that earlier work might come into play. Look for resonance, connection. Does the earlier work by chance offer a fresh perspective on current projects? And are your current projects rich enough to benefit from it?

14

From *"The Politics of Remediation"* in Lives on the Boundary: The Struggles and Achievements of America's Underprepared

1989

AUTHOR'S NOTE: I get asked how I came to write *Lives on the Boundary*, so let me begin by saying a little about its origins.

For some time before I began my doctoral studies in education, I had been writing poetry. Much of it, especially the early stuff, wasn't all that good, but it brought me such pleasure, hiding away a few afternoons each week, unplugging the phone, and getting lost in the writing. I'd flip through favorite poets (Denise Levertov, Stephen Dunn) to prime the pump, dig into the dictionary or thesaurus to find the right word, move back and forth from legal pad to an old Olympia typewriter to see what a line looked like in print. It was a slow and peaceful pursuit. And, over time, the poems did get better, maturing from a young man's overwrought set pieces and beery romances to portraits of my family and the other Italian immigrants from their era:

Vertigo

Cabot's *Differential Diagnosis,*
Browne on Diseases of the Throat,
lace curtains, handwritten hours,
an alembic, porcelain bottles,
a soft voice explaining the inner ear.
Dr. DeSantis still sees patients.
A dumbwaiter locked into place
holds a cutaway of the vestibular canals.
His voice carries an old woman
through the curves and the delicate bones.
Vertigo.
The dizziness of old age.
The fear of an open street.
She stands on one foot.
DeSantis catches her.
Again. His arm snaps up.
The curtains rustle.
The doctor explains the winds
beginning on the street.

> How the bones are like sails.
> How she can leave her fear
> in his arms.
> How the wind heals
> with its own risky balance.

When in the late 1970s I started writing academic essays and research articles, I continued the poetry, eventually collecting it into a volume that I unsuccessfully sent around. These different kinds of writing overlapped — but did not intersect — for six or more years. Both were important to me, but each remained separate, separate in purpose, style, and audience.

Over time, however, this separation began to feel artificial, splitting life apart. I became curious about the possibility of combining the writing I was doing. Scholarship and research gave me a set of powerful analytic tools, and I worked hard to get better at using them, felt good about what they enabled me to do. And the poetry provided a medium to convert all the little pieces of daily life — from dreams to objects on a shelf — into written language, and with that conversion came the development of descriptive skill: the image, compression, rhythm, the dramatic turn.[1] Although composition studies afforded an increasingly important audience for me, the poetry offered a different sort of connection, one based more on an emotional and aesthetic response. I didn't want to lose any of this. Could analytic, even formal academic prose, be blended with poetry, with story?

One thing I did was to photocopy a few paragraphs on the structure of long-term memory from a cognitive psychology textbook and tape them on a large sheet of paper. Underneath them, I placed some lines of poetry I had written about events from my childhood: a discussion of memorial processes right next to a depiction of memories. Why not? It was this sort of fooling around with text and genre that would lead to the form of *Lives on the Boundary*. Over the next few months, I would shift from poetry to narrative vignette — about my own education and that of others as well — and in place of the textbook passages, there would be analysis of the kind I was writing for scholarly journals but without some of the academic conventions.

From the beginning of this experimentation, then, there was a desire to combine different kinds of writing, but for the first year or two of composing what I had were individual vignettes strung together on a chronological thread. Within each vignette, there would be descriptions of my neighborhood, of early literacy experiences, and of going to school — and these passages would be interspersed with psychological, sociological, or historical material drawn from my graduate study or subsequent research. So there was this mixing within sections of text, and it felt worthwhile. It was a different way to come at the issues of language and cognition that I was dealing with elsewhere, an attempt to illustrate research and theory through vignette. But there was no conceptual through-line, no overarching theme or argument.

Several things happened that began to move this writing toward a book. One of the people I met while shopping around my collection of poems — a

West Coast editor for Doubleday—followed up his failed submission of the poetry by asking if I had anything else. I showed him the early chapters, which he tried to pitch, again with no success. I can see why; at that point all I had was a (somewhat unusual) memoir of school days and early teaching. But the experience gave me hope and spurred me to imagine the material as a book.

What followed was a year or more of continued writing and submitting, only to get the manuscript rejected again and again, twelve times in all, I believe. But during that time, the increased national discussion of the alleged literacy crisis and the publication of books like Allan Bloom's *The Closing of the American Mind* and E. D. Hirsch's *Cultural Literacy* got me to thinking about my vignettes within a larger frame. This was crucial, for though there was an incipient argument within the vignettes, it was not fully developed and threaded through the pages. Put simply, what was the purpose of these blended stories, and what larger discussions in the culture were they tied to? Put even more simply, why should a reader who doesn't know me give a damn?

The section I reprint here comes toward the end of *Lives on the Boundary*, in a chapter entitled "The Politics of Remediation." It deals with issues related to college writing and tutorial centers, issues I had previously written about for a rhetoric and composition audience: the social and cognitive dimensions of underpreparation; the politics of remediation and the reductive beliefs and measures integral to those politics; the short shrift given to student learning and development in disciplinary specialization; and the intellectual stratification in the academy and the marginalizing of certain kinds of knowledge and practice. The reader can get a sense of how I tried to frame these issues for a larger audience.

NOTE

[1]In "The Craft, Practice, and Possibility of Poetry in Educational Research," Melissa Cahnmann (2003) argues for the use of poetic techniques in the writing of educational research.

During the time I was working with Denise and Lucia and the others, all hell was breaking loose in American education. The literacy crisis that has become part of our current cultural vocabulary was taking shape with a vengeance. It was in December 1975 that *Newsweek* informed America that Johnny couldn't write, and in the fall of 1976 the *Los Angeles Times* declared a "Drop in Student Skills Unequalled in History." California, the *Times* article went on to reveal, had "one of the most pronounced drops in achievement of all." Reports on the enrollment and retention of students are a long-standing tradition in the way education conducts its business, but it seemed that every month now a new document was appearing on my desk: reports from a vice-chancellor or the university president's office or from some analyst in the

From *Lives on the Boundary*. New York: Free Press, 1989. 185–202.

state legislature. What percentage of people from families below a certain income level were entering college? What were their SAT scores? What were the SAT scores of blacks? Chicanos? Asians? More locally, how many UCLA students were being held for remedial English? Remedial math? Were there differences by race or income?

This was a new way for me to look at education. My focus had been on particular students and their communities, and it tended to be a teacher's focus, rich in anecdote and observation. Increasingly, my work in the Tutorial Center required that I take a different perspective: I had to think like a policymaker, considering the balance sheet of economics and accountability. Chip would sit with me in the late afternoon, going over the charts and tables, showing me how to use them to argue for our programs, for in an academic bureaucracy admissions statistics and test scores and retention rates are valued terms of debate. All teaching is embedded in a political context, of course, but the kind of work I had done before coming to the Tutorial Center tended to isolate me from the immediate presence of institutions: working with a group of kids in the corner of a cafeteria, teaching veterans in a dingy satellite building. I was learning from Chip and from a shrewd vicechancellor named Chuck Ries how to work within the policy-maker's arena. And though it was, at times, uncomfortable for me and though I would soon come to question the legitimacy of the vision it fostered, it provided an important set of lessons. Probably the central value of being at the Tutorial Center was that it forced me to examine the broad institutional context of writing instruction and underpreparation.

The work in the center led to other projects, and during my four years in Campbell Hall, I would be invited to participate in them. One was the Writing Research Project, initiated by Vice-Chancellor Ries, and its purpose was to study the uses of writing and the way it was taught at UCLA. Another was the Freshman Summer Program, six intensive weeks before the freshman year during which students took a writing course linked to an introductory course in political science or psychology or history. There is a lot to tell about these ventures — the politics of evaluating a curriculum at a university, the strains of initiating a curriculum that requires people to cross departmental lines — but the most important thing about both projects was that they led me to do something rarely achieved at a research university. I had to stand on the borders of a number of disciplines and study the way knowledge is structured in the academy and, as well, detail what it means to be unprepared to participate in that disciplinary structure.

Students were coming to college with limited exposure to certain kinds of writing and reading and with conceptions and beliefs that were dissonant with those in the lower-division curriculum they encountered. And that curriculum wasn't doing a lot to address their weaknesses or nurture their strengths. They needed practice writing academic essays; they needed opportunities to talk about their writing — and their reading; they needed people who could quickly determine what necessary background knowledge they lacked and supply it in comprehensible ways. What began troubling me about the policy documents and the crisis reports was that they focused too narrowly on test scores and tallies of error and other such measures. They lacked careful analysis of the students' histories and lacked, as well, analysis of the cognitive and social demands of the academic culture the students now faced. The work I was doing in the Tutorial Center, in the Writing Research Project, and in the Summer Program was guiding me toward a richer understanding of what it meant to be underprepared in the American research university. It seemed to me there were five overlapping problem areas — both cognitive and social — that could be used to explain the difficulties experienced by students like Marita and James and Lucia. These by no means applied equally to all the students whom I came to know, but taken together they represent, better than pie charts and histograms, what it means to be underprepared at a place like UCLA. Many young people come to the university able to summarize the events in a news story or write a personal response to a play or a movie or give back what a teacher said in a straightforward lecture. But they have considerable trouble with what has come to be called critical literacy: framing an argument or taking someone else's argument apart, systematically inspecting a document, an issue, or an event, synthesizing different points of view, applying a theory to disparate phenomena, and so on. The authors of the crisis reports got tremendously distressed about students' difficulty with such tasks, but it's important to remember that, traditionally, such abilities have only been developed in an elite: in priests, scholars, or a leisure class. Ours is the first society in history to expect so many of its people to be able to perform these very sophisticated literacy activities. And we fail to keep in mind how extraordinary it is to ask *all* our schools to conduct this kind of education — not just those schools with lots of money and exceptional teachers and small classes — but massive, sprawling schools, beleaguered schools, inner-city schools, overcrowded schools. It is a charge most of them simply are not equipped to fulfill, for our educational ideals far outstrip our economic and political priorities.

We forget, then, that by most historical — and current — standards, the vast majority of a research university's underprepared students would be considered competently literate. Though they fail to meet the demands made of them in their classes, they fail from a literate base. They are literate people straining at the boundaries of their ability, trying to move into the unfamiliar, to approximate a kind of writing they can't yet command. And as they try, they'll make all the blunders in word choice and sentence structure and discourse strategy that regularly get held up for ridicule, that I made when I was trying to write for my teachers at Loyola. There's a related phenomenon, and we have research evidence of this: As writers move further away from familiar ways of expressing themselves, the strains on their cognitive and linguistic resources increase, and the number of mechanical and grammatical errors they make shoots up. Before we shake our heads at these errors, we should also consider the possibility that many such linguistic bungles are signs of growth, a stretching beyond what college freshmen can comfortably do with written language. In fact, we should *welcome* certain kinds of errors, make allowance for them in the curricula we develop, analyze rather than simply criticize them. Error marks the place where education begins.

Asked to produce something that is beyond them, writers might also fall back on strategies they already know. Asked to take a passage critically apart, they'll summarize it. We saw this with James, the young man distressed with his C–, but as with so much else in this book, the principle applies to more than just those labeled underprepared. I was personally reminded of it when I was writing my dissertation. My chairman was an educational research methodologist and statistician; my background straddled humanities and social science, but what I knew about writing tended to be shaped by literary models. When it came time to report on the procedures I was using in my study—the methods section of the dissertation—I wrote a detailed chronology of what I did and how I did it. I wanted to relay all the twists and turns of my investigation. About a week later I got it back covered with criticism. My chairman didn't want the vagaries of my investigative life; he wanted a compressed and systematic account. "What do you think this is," he wrote alongside one long, dancing stretch of narrative, "*Travels with Charley?*"

Associated with these difficulties with critical literacy are students' diverse orientations toward inquiry. It is a source of exasperation to many freshmen that the university is so predisposed to question past solutions, to seek counterexplanations—to continually turn something nice and clean and clear into a problem. English professor David Bartholomae recalls a teacher of his suggesting that, when stuck, student writers should try the following "machine": "While most readers of _____ have said _____, a close and careful reading shows that _____." The teacher's machine perfectly expresses the ethos of the university, a fundamental orientation toward inquiry. University professors have for so long been socialized into this critical stance, that they don't realize how unsettling it can be to students who don't share their unusual background.

There is Scott sitting in an Astronomy tutorial, his jaw set, responding to another student's question about a finite versus an infinite universe: "This is the kind of question," he says, "that you'll argue and argue about. It's stupid. No one wins. So why do it?" And there is Rene who can't get beyond the first few sentences of her essay for Speech. She has to write a critical response to an address of Ronald Reagan's. "You can't criticize the president," she explains. "You've gotta support your president even if you don't agree with him." When students come from other cultures, this discordance can be even more pronounced. Our tutors continually encouraged their students to read actively, to ask why authors say what they say, what their claims are, what assumptions they make, where you, the reader, agree or disagree. Hun's tutor is explaining this to him, then has him try it, has him read aloud so she can guide him. He reads a few lines and stops short. After two more abortive trials, she pulls out of Hun the explanation that what gets written in books is set in tradition, and he is not learned enough to question the authority of the book.

Remember Andrea? She was the distressed young woman who was failing chemistry. Andrea could memorize facts and formulas but not use them to solve problems—and her inability was representative of a whole class of difficulties experienced by freshmen. What young people come to define as intellectual competence—what it means to know things and use them—is shaped by their schooling. And what many students experience year after year is the exchange of one body of facts for another—an inert transmission, the delivery and redelivery of segmented and self-contained dates and formulas—and thus it is no surprise that they develop a restricted sense of how intellectual work is conducted. They are given Ancient History one year and American History the next, and once they've displayed knowledge of the Fertile Crescent and cuneiform and Assyrian military campaigns, there is little need for them to remember the material, little further opportunity to incorporate it, little reason to use these textbook facts to engage historical problems. Next year it will be American History: a new textbook, new dates and documents and campaigns, new tests—but the same rewards, and the same reasons to forget. John Dewey saw the difficulty long ago: "Only in education, never in the life of the farmer, sailor, merchant, physician, or laboratory experimenter, does knowledge mean primarily a store of information aloof from doing."

Students like Andrea are caught in a terrible bind. They come to the university with limited experience in applying knowledge, puzzling over solutions, solving problems. Many of the lower-division courses they encounter—their "general education" or "breadth" requirements—will involve little writing or speaking or application, will rely on so-called objective tests that, with limited exception, stress the recall of material rather than the reasoned elaboration of it. But the gatekeeper courses—the courses that determine entrance to a major—they up the intellectual ante. Courses like Andrea's bête noire, Chemistry 11-A, are placed like land mines in the uneven terrain of the freshman year. The special nature of their demands is not made the focus of attention that it should be; that is, the courses are not taught explicitly and self-consciously as courses on how to think as a chemist or a psychologist or a literary critic. And there are few opportunities for students to develop such ability before they enroll in those courses. The faculty, for the most part, do not provide freshmen with instruction on how to use knowledge creatively—and then penalize them when they cannot do so.

It is not unusual for students to come to the university with conceptualizations of disciplines that are out of sync with academic reality. Like the note taker in the lecture hall who opened this chapter, a lot of entering freshmen assume that sociology is something akin to social work, an applied study of social problems rather than an attempt to abstract a theory about social interaction and organization. Likewise, some think psychology will be a discussion of human motivation and counseling, what it is that makes people do what they do—and some coverage of ways to change what they do. It comes as a surprise that their textbook has only one chapter on personality and psychotherapy—and a half dozen pages on Freud. The rest is animal studies, computer models of thought, lots of neurophysiology. If they like to read novels, and they elect a literature course, they'll expect to talk about characters and motive and plot, but instead they're asked to situate the novel amid the historical forces that shaped it, to examine rhetorical and stylistic devices and search the prose for things that mean more than they seem to mean. Political science should be politics and government and current events—nuclear treaties, trade sanctions, the Iran-Contra scandal—but instead it's Marx and Weber and political economy and organizational and decision-making models. And so goes the litany of misdirection. This dissonance between the academy's and the students' definitions of disciplines makes it hard for students to get their bearings with material: to know what's important, to see how the pieces fit together, to follow an argument, to have a sense of what can be passed over lightly. Thus I would see notebooks that were filled—in frantic script—with everything the professor said or that were scant and fragmented, records of information without coherence.

The discourse of academics is marked by terms and expressions that represent an elaborate set of shared concepts and orientations: alienation, authoritarian personality, the social construction of the self, determinism, hegemony, equilibrium, intentionality, recursion, reinforcement, and so on. This language weaves through so many lectures and textbooks, is integral to so many learned discussions, that it's easy to forget what a foreign language it can be. Freshmen are often puzzled by the talk they hear in their classrooms, but what's important to note here is that their problem is not simply one of limited vocabulary. If we see the problem as knowing or not knowing a list of words, as some quick-fix remedies suggest, then we'll force glossaries on students and miss the complexity of the issue. Take, for example, *authoritarian personality*. The average university freshman will know what *personality* means and can figure out *authoritarian*; the difficulty will come from a lack of familiarity with the conceptual resonances that *authoritarian personality* has acquired in the discussions of sociologists and psychologists and political scientists. Discussion . . . you could almost define a university education as an initiation into a variety of powerful ongoing discussions, an initiation that can occur only through the repeated use of a new language in the company of others. More than anything, this was the opportunity people like Father Albertson, my Shakespeare teacher at Loyola, provided to me. The more comfortable and skillful students become with this kind of influential talk, the more they will be included in further conversations and given access to further conceptual tools and resources—the acquisition of which virtually defines them as members of an intellectual community.

All students require such an opportunity. But those coming to the university with less-than-privileged educations, especially those from the lower classes, are particularly in need. They are less likely to have participated, in any extended way, in such discussions in the past. They won't have the confidence or the moves to enter it, and can begin to feel excluded, out of place, put off by a language they can't command. Their social marginality, then, is reinforced by discourse and, as happened to me during my first year at Loyola, they might well withdraw, retreat to silence.

This sense of linguistic exclusion can be complicated by various cultural differences. When I was growing up, I absorbed an entire belief system—with its own characteristic terms and expressions—from the worried conversations of my parents, from the things I heard and saw on South Vermont, from the priest's fiery tales. I thought that what happened to people was preordained, that ability was a fixed thing, that there was one true religion. I had rigid notions about social roles, about the structure of society, about gender, about politics. There used to be a rickety vending machine at Manchester and Vermont that held a Socialist Workers newspaper. I'd walk by it and feel something alive and injurious: The paper was malevolent and should be destroyed. Imagine, then, the difficulty I had when, at the beginning of my senior year at Mercy High, Jack MacFarland tried to explain Marxism to us. How could I absorb the language of atheistic materialism and class struggle when it seemed so strange and pernicious? It wasn't just that Marxist terms-of-art were unfamiliar; they felt assaultive. What I did was revert to definitions of the social order more familiar to me, and Mr. MacFarland had to draw them out of me and have me talk about them and consider them alongside Marx's vision and terminology, examining points of conflict and points of possible convergence. It was only then that I could appropriate Marx's strange idiom.

Once you start to think about underprepared students in terms of these overlapping problem areas, all sorts of solutions present themselves. Students need more opportunities to write about what they're learning and guidance in the techniques and conventions of that writing—what I got from my mentors at Loyola. They need more opportunities to develop the writing strategies that are an intimate part of academic inquiry and what has come to be called critical literacy—comparing, synthesizing, analyzing—the sort of thing I gave the veterans. They need opportunities to talk about what they're learning: to test their ideas, reveal their assumptions, talk through the places where new knowledge clashes with ingrained belief. They need a chance, too, to talk about the ways they may have felt excluded from all this in the past and may feel threatened by it in the present. They need the occasion to rise above the fragmented learning the lower-division curriculum encourages, a place within a course or outside it to hear about and reflect on the way a particular discipline conducts its inquiry: Why, for example, *do* so many psychologists who study thinking rely on computer modeling? Why is mathematics so much a part of economics? And they need to be let in on the secret talk, on the shared concepts and catchphrases of Western liberal learning.

There is nothing magical about this list of solutions. In fact, in many ways, it reflects the kind of education a privileged small number of American students have received for some time. The basic question our society must ask, then, is: How many or how few do we want to have this education? If students didn't get it before coming to college—and most have not—then what are we willing to do to give it to them now? Chip and I used to talk about our special programs as attempts to create an Honors College for the underprepared. People would smile as we spoke, but, as our students would have said, we were serious as a heart attack. The remedial programs we knew about did a disservice to their students by thinking of them as *remedial*. We wanted to try out another perspective and see what kind of program it would yield. What would happen if we thought of our students' needs and goals in light of the comprehensive and ambitious program structures more often reserved for the elite?

∽

It was during one of our afternoon meetings that Chip confirmed the rumor. We had heard that some faculty members were questioning the money being spent on our programs. They were lobbying to have it shifted, Chip explained, to what they saw as "the legitimate research mission of the university." I had known for a while, for Chip had sensitized me to it, that our position in the university was a complicated one. Certain powerful administrators and some faculty were our strong supporters—for political, for pedagogical, for ethical reasons—but others were suspicious of us, even questioned our place at a prestigious university like UCLA. The kind of work we did was suspect. What exactly *did* we do? Were we qualified to do it? Did our students belong here—were we, in fact, keeping unqualified kids in school? We didn't have a faculty advisory board or any other institutional link with academic departments, so we had no systematic way to influence or gain support from the professoriat. Chip began loaning me to English free of charge to teach a few classes, seeking even the most superficial of connections.

As it turned out, Vice-Chancellor Ries applied his cunning and successfully countered this particular offensive against our budget, but the experience remained with me. When I took Chip Anderson up on his offer to come to UCLA, I had assumed that the rigorous intellectual methods of the academy would be focused on problems of student learning. But the truth was that, by and large, the research university focuses its collective intelligence on other matters. And the places designated to deal with such problems—tutorial centers and preparatory programs—are conceived of as marginal to the intellectual community. These conditions had direct effects on the young men and women who we came to know at the center.

One day, a professor of English turned to me in the food line and began telling me about an office meeting he had with one of our students. He thought that the fellow's paper on a Wordsworth poem was such a muddle that he simply wrote "see me" on the bottom of the last page. The student showed up and, in the professor's words, the meeting was a disaster. "It was as though I were talking to someone from another planet!" he exclaimed. "I showed him line by line how the poem should be explicated. I figured he just didn't know, so I'd show him. But when he said back to me what I had said to him, I could see that we were talking completely past each other." He stopped and shrugged his shoulders: "I never felt so hopeless."

Some faculty, I knew from my tutors, were especially good with our students, made attempts to understand the difficulties they were having, and seemed to enjoy working with them. But what was more striking, and I became increasingly aware of it as time went on, was the gulf that existed between so many professors and the students who frequented the Tutorial Center. A number of faculty were like the man from English: They wanted to help but didn't know how, and they found their inability very frustrating. Others were distant and aloof, didn't particularly care to help, and shunted freshmen off to teaching assistants. Of these, a small percentage had real problems with differences of class or race.

Reflecting on my own first awkward year at Loyola, I tended to explain this gulf between faculty and students in strictly social terms. Most faculty didn't share the backgrounds of our program's students, and, unless they made efforts to the contrary, they had increasingly spent time, as we all do, with people of similar persuasion. But as I became more familiar with the university, I began to see that while there certainly could be an ethnic or cultural dimension to these troubling encounters, there was something else going on as well, and it had to do with the very way people are socialized into academic life.

As young scholars progress through graduate study, they acquire more than knowledge and method: Strong allegiances are formed. It's a time of gradual yet powerful shaping of identity as a scholar, the increasing investment of self-worth in research and publication. Graduate study forces you to give a tremendous amount of thought to the development of your discipline, to its methods, exemplary studies, and central texts. People emerge from graduate study, then, as political scientists or astronomers or botanists—but not necessarily as educators. That is, though professors may like to teach, like to talk about the knowledge they've worked so hard to acquire, it is pretty unlikely that they have been encouraged to think about, say, the cognitive difficulties young people have as they learn how to conduct inquiry in physics or anthropology or linguistics, the way biological or historical knowledge is acquired, the reading or writing difficulties that attend the development of philosophical reasoning. These issues, if addressed at all in the academy, are addressed in schools of education, and most faculty hold schools of education in low regard.

I never heard in those years a professor—an anthropologist, for example—say of a poor exam, "There's a curious failed anthropology here," or "Look at the interesting missteps this person makes in trying to articulate the concept of liminality." Rather, the work is judged as legitimate, accurate, close to the current conversations in the discipline, the received wisdom, the canonical texts, or it is inaccurate, not close, a failure. The thrust of graduate training and the professorial commitment that follows from it are toward the preservation of a discipline, not the intellectual development of young people. That English professor had neither the training nor the inclination to see in his student's vexing Wordsworth paper the wealth of clues about the way literary inquiry develops and goes awry. And he didn't seem able to set things up so the student could reveal the twists and turns in that development. Rather, he saw the student's paper as a failed attempt, alien, as if from another planet. And he saw his job as monitoring the rightness or wrongness of incursions into his discipline.

Every so often at UCLA and other similar institutions, the delicious proposal is made to move lower-division instruction—the entire first two years, all the introductory courses—to the state and community colleges. This would allow the disciplinary focus of the university to emerge full-blown: Faculty would only teach students who have already declared their apprenticeships to mathematics or French or musicology. Fortunately, the proposal never gets very far. What's troubling is that among the counterarguments—which are mostly political and economic—you rarely hear concerns about the astounding inbreeding and narrowness that would result: a faculty already conceptually isolated along disciplinary lines talking in more self-referenced ways to less and less diverse audiences. Babel talk. The final isolation of inquiry.

The homiletic nod toward the interconnection of general education and research is commonplace. Yet a variety of investigations—from Laurence Veysey's standard history, *The Emergence of the American University*, to Gerald Graff's critique of English Studies, *Professing Literature*—all suggest that the American university has yet to figure out, conceptually or institutionally, how to integrate its general education mission with its research mission. An unresolved problem: How to interweave the social dimension of knowledge with the preservation of a discipline, how to make the advancement of a discipline go on in concert with the development of young minds.

This is not to deny that research universities have some passionate teachers. They want to excite young people about their discipline. They volunteer to teach introductory courses. But here they meet a powerful institutional reality. Regardless of what the university publicists say, faculty are promoted and given tenure and further promoted for the research they publish, not for the extent of their involvement in undergraduate, especially introductory-level, teaching. Yes, there are unusual cases. If someone's research record is right on the line, then student evaluations of the person's teaching are consulted: If they're exceptionally high or exceptionally low, then they might sway a decision. If the person made an extraordinary contribution to curriculum development, that might count—a little. Such cases are set forth as proof that undergraduate education counts, but by their paucity, they become the exception that proves the rule. Publish or perish. Like most universities, UCLA gives Distinguished Teaching Awards to its outstanding teachers. One very talented professor I knew had superlative student evaluations and was coming up for tenure; she pleaded with her department *not* to advance her for the Distinguished Teaching Award, for winning it, she thought, might bias her tenure committee, making them conclude that too much of her research time had gone into her teaching.

Consider, in the midst of all this, the Tutorial Center and the students who frequent it. Tutorial centers don't produce research—the coin of the realm—but, rather, provide a service. Most of those working in them are not in the professorial ranks and thus are not perceived as having developed the intellectual rigor that comes from such membership. The work the center does is not considered a contribution to a discipline, in fact, much of what tutors do is considered "remedial," work that isn't even part of disciplinary pursuit but preliminary to it. What emerges in the culture's institution that most touts humane, liberal learning is a rigid intellectual class system. Certain kinds of cognitive work are considered peripheral and tainted; those who perform the work become an intellectual underclass. These class divisions of the mind are so powerful that they can override and even contradict one's stated beliefs about the social order. Several faculty whose work embodied a radical critique of culture were dismissive of the work we did. And I heard remarkable stories of distinguished Marxist academics at other schools who flat out refused to teach undergraduate courses. In their scholarly articles, they pursued a critique of meritocratic capitalism, yet in their dealings with students, they replicated the very elitism they assailed in print. One of the simple indicators of our place in the university was the fact that, at least during my stay, not one professor visited the center. We would get occasional phone calls, some friendly, some quizzical, but no one came by to see how we tutored, to inquire about what we were uncovering as we worked with students, to talk about education. The deep divisions of intellectual work in the university kept all of us moving along different strata.

By not considering the kind of work tutorial centers or other preparatory programs do as being worthy of intellectual attention, the university encouraged a kind of loose, unrigorous talk about underpreparation and a reductive means of assessing it. Rather than questioning the local and national crisis reports that surrounded us—subjecting their claims to close investigation, probing their assumptions—the university marched to their apocalyptic drum. It even piped in. Yet the crisis reports were both reflecting and contributing to a set of misleading perceptions of underpreparation. The reports varied widely but tended to build their case on three sources of evidence: declines in scores on various national and local tests, rising enrollments in remedial classes, and observations from professors. These evidential strands combined in rhetorically powerful ways to spark alarm and anger—in legislators, in academics, in the public.

The reports listed scores from both broad national tests and more local, specific assessments, and inferred all sorts of dire things from them. The most famous national test is the Scholastic Aptitude Test—the bane of the college-bound high schooler, the SAT—and the decline in its scores was cited regularly and with assurance, as though the test were a geiger counter of the mind. But tests like the SAT are much more problematic than the public is led to believe. The fairness of the test, its legitimacy as a measure of literacy and academic potential, its use as a prerequisite for admission to college and as an indicator of the performance of the public schools have all been seriously challenged, at times by Educational Testing Service researchers themselves. And, as a further complicating irony, more recent studies of SAT and other national test scores suggest that, as one research team put it, "evidence for a massive, consistent skill decline . . . is much more mixed than the school critics have claimed."

Local assessments—studies of math or writing skills conducted by specific campuses or systems—were more specific and, in some ways, more legitimate. By their very proliferation, however, and by the academic community's reliance on them, they generated problems of a different order. The data in all the reports—and the charts and graphs that displayed them—became the vocabulary, the elements of a discourse for conducting the business of underpreparation. A vast and wealthy industry of educational institutes and consultants grew up around them. Things that seemed sensible, and in other contexts would never be challenged, now became questions to be solved by quantitative evaluation. The Tutorial Center was asked to demonstrate, with numbers, that getting individual guidance with material you don't understand is helpful, that having a chance to talk about what you're learning is beneficial. The drive to quantify became very strong, a reality unto itself, and what you couldn't represent with a ratio or a chart—what was messy and social and complex—was simply harder to talk about and much harder to get acknowledged. Patricia Cline Cohen, the historian of numeracy, notes that in America there is the belief that "to measure is to initiate a cure." But a focus on quantification—on errors we can count, on test scores we can rank-order—can divert us from rather than guide us toward solutions. Numbers seduce us into thinking we know more than we do; they give the false assurance of rigor but reveal little about the complex cognitive and emotional processes behind the tally of errors and wrong answers. What goes on behind the mistakes simply escapes the measurer's rule.

The second source of evidence for decline found in the crisis reports was statistics on remedial enrollments. The reports claimed that remedial courses were a new and alarming phenomenon, the flooding of the ivy halls with the intellectually unwashed. If anything sparked fear in the general public, these numbers did. But, in fact, courses and programs that we could call remedial are older than fight songs and cheerleaders. Since the mid-1800s, American colleges have been establishing various kinds of preparatory classes within their halls—it was, and is, their way of maintaining enrollments while bringing their entering students up to curricular par. (In 1894, for example, over 40 percent of entering freshmen came from the "preparatory divisions" of the institutions that enrolled them.) If the 1970s saw an increase in remedial courses and programs, the increase was measured in terms of very recent history and reflected the fact that universities had grown rapidly in the fifties and sixties and now had to scramble to fill their classrooms. So recruitment began for populations that had not traditionally come to college—working-class whites, blacks, and Hispanics, single parents, older folks—students who had, for the most part, received dreary educations down the line. And, yes, they would need special courses, "low-level" courses, remedial courses, but this was not the first taint of curricular sin on an otherwise pristine American university.

And then there were the faculty testimonials about decline. "These are the truly illiterate among us," said the dean. And in memos and public documents and interviews you'd read the judgments, somber and dramatic: "Simple reading is beyond them." "They have ceased to care about ideas." "What we have here is cultural illiteracy." "They have abandoned the word." This was the human side of the crisis reports, the weary battle cries from the front lines—grave and disconsolate. These pronouncements are still with us; they pepper our newspapers and magazines. No matter that the commentators are rarely on the front lines at all, listening closely as students work through an essay, probing for the logic of a sentence gone awry. Ask yourself if it is accurate to say that Lucia, the older student with the baby, can't read. That she is without culture? I'm not asking for softheartedness here—the accusation so often hurled when these questions are raised. I'm simply trying to force precision. Is it accurate to say that Marita, the girl accused of plagiarism, didn't care about ideas? The teacher who thought she was cheating missed completely the intellectual underpinnings of her action and—in a telling leap—leveled a moral judgment instead. The sad thing is that the somber one-liners are accepted, even encouraged, in the very place in the society that refuses to condone easy judgment. No academic would allow such superficial assessments in his or her own discipline.

The crisis reports conveyed a sense of tough-mindedness, but, in fact, they really weren't that intellectually rigorous at all. They lacked both historical perspective and sophistication about cognition and culture, and their alarmist tone distracted people from careful study of the students they assailed. Blaming the victim allowed institutional contributions to the crisis of underpreparation to be ignored. Stressing the "deficits," "deficiencies," and "handicaps" of the students, quantitatively displayed, diverted attention from the segmented dispensary that lower-division education has become. In the candid opinion of one university administrator:

> Almost uniformly throughout the lower division in the social sciences, I am convinced that the quality of education cannot at present be described as university-level.... Typically, 17- and 18-year-old freshmen, many if not most underprepared for the university, are herded together into large, anonymous lecture classes.... [They] take, at most, two machine-scored objective tests, with no homework assignments, no opportunity or necessity to communicate orally, no written work, and no direct contact of any kind with anyone in a teaching role, and all too frequently no human contact of any kind....

Because of the complex mix of cognitive and cultural factors we've seen, the EOP students felt most strongly the effects of this impersonal, fragmented education; they, truly, were the least prepared for it, though not necessarily for the reasons the crisis reports would have us believe. But their difficulties served to illuminate, to throw into relief, the problems a great number of students—not just ours—were having. The struggles of the underprepared were revealing the needs of the many.

15

From Introduction to Possible Lives: The Promise of Public Education in America

1995

AUTHOR'S NOTE: There were times during the writing of *Lives on the Boundary* — the last year or so especially — when I just couldn't figure out how to pull it off. Was I really making debates internal to composition studies accessible and interesting to a more general readership? How could I bring all the events and themes together in a workable conclusion? Some nights I would wake up in the grip of inadequacy, wondering what I was going to do, fretting, not seeing a solution. But for all that, the book provided some of the most engaging rhetorical challenges I'd yet experienced, and once it was done and in print, I found myself casting about for another project that also would involve a mix of kinds of writing and would be geared toward a larger audience. Working on *Lives on the Boundary* took me into issues of public policy, required further inquiry into social and educational issues on a national level. Context, so to speak, in the broadest terms. I suppose that set the stage for a book like *Possible Lives*, which deals with public education and the way we understand it and talk about it, with its role in a democracy and the kind of scrutiny that best advances it. Ultimately, the book becomes a defense of public, collective institutions at a time when they are being assaulted and the private sphere and free market idealized.

This framing of *Possible Lives* didn't come immediately. The first six or eight months of work involved some visits to classrooms, both within and beyond Los Angeles. I was captivated by them and the task of trying to render them — classrooms that I had nothing to do with, didn't know from the inside, as was the case in *Lives on the Boundary*. This was the closest I had come to ethnographic writing, a less ornate, more authorially distant prose than in *Lives on the Boundary*. I involved the teachers in the rendering, asking questions about their practice, checking details, showing them drafts, seeing if I got it right. And, from the beginning, the work became the occasion to learn volumes about teaching K–12, about school life and politics, and about the remarkably varied social and physical geography of the United States.

But the large argument that frames the book came as the visits to classrooms accrued. What I was seeing in these classrooms was complicating on many levels the intense national discourse about the failure of public education. Thus, the impulse that set me off on the project began to take shape as an argument, a counternarrative.

302

As with *Lives on the Boundary*, I had to develop a broad structuring device that would be adequate both to the individual cases and to the overarching themes. This is where a favorite book of mine provided a solution: William Least Heat-Moon's masterful *Blue Highways: A Journey into America*. The book is an account of Heat-Moon's journey across the country, traveling its smaller roads (printed in blue on old highway maps), visiting, talking, taking pictures, reflecting on the nature of the republic. I adapted the device of the journey for my developing book, a device that provided the organizing structure of the travelogue as well as a metaphor for investigating public education and for learning about America through its classrooms.

I have one more thing to say about the kind of critique I tried to fashion. Academic training is agonistic; graduate study instills in us the penchant for critique, and the disciplinary tools to do it. More generally, Western intellectual life is energized by attack and counterattack — just read the letters section of a magazine like *The Nation*. It is less common — and perhaps more difficult — to find shared concerns or seek collaborative resolution. (A classic essay of Peter Elbow's, "The Doubting Game and the Believing Game," offers a thoughtful take on all this.) It seemed to me that the negative discourse about public schools needed more than a counterargument, more than a dismantling of claims. The dismantling is valuable, of course — and David Berliner and Bruce Biddle do it well in *The Manufactured Crisis* — but, in itself, doesn't necessarily show us where to go from here. Another way to put it is this: In the midst of the loss of public confidence wrought by the negative critique, we need images of the possible.

The conundrum for me, however, was that there *is* so much wrong with public education — as a multitude of analyses (including *Lives on the Boundary*) has shown. How to counter the negative discourse about schools without swinging to a blanket defense? How to fashion an argument — and a broader narrative containing it — that was simultaneously critical and hopeful? The final paragraph of a reflection I wrote for *The Nation* (the whole text is in Part Six) sums up the challenge:

> An important project for the left — and though I focus on schools, this applies to a range of social issues — will be to craft a language that is critical without being reductive, that frames this critique in nuance and possibility, that honors the work good teachers do daily and draws from it broader lessons about ability, learning, and opportunity, that scrutinizes public institutions while affirming them.

I hope that these goals are evident in the upcoming selections from *Possible Lives*.

During a time when so many are condemning public schools — and public institutions in general — I have been traveling across the country, visiting classrooms in which the promise of public education is being powerfully realized. These are classrooms judged to be good and decent places by those closest to them—parents, principals, teachers, students—classrooms in big cities and small towns, preschool through twelfth grade, places that embody the hope for a free and educated society that has, at its best, driven this extraordinary American experiment from the beginning.

We seem to be rapidly losing that hope. Our national discussion about public schools is despairing and dismissive, and it is shutting down our civic imagination. I visited schools for three and a half years, and what struck me early on—and began to define my journey—was how rarely the kind of intellectual and social richness I was finding was reflected in the public sphere.

We have instead a strange mix of apocalyptic vignettes—violent classrooms, incompetent teachers, students who think Latin is spoken in Latin America—and devastating statistics: declines in SAT scores and embarrassing cross-national comparisons. We hear—daily, it seems—that our students don't measure up, either to their predecessors in the United States or to their peers in other countries, and that, as a result, our position in the global economy is in danger. We are told, by politicians, by pundits, that our cultural values, indeed our very way of life is threatened. We are offered, by both entertainment and news media, depictions of schools as mediocre places, where students are vacuous and teachers are not so bright; or as violent and chaotic places, places where order has fled and civility has been lost. It's hard to imagine anything good in all this.

Though researchers have for some time challenged the simplicity of these representations—reports from the Rand Corporation and the Sandia National Laboratories, for example, dispute the much-broadcasted declines in student achievement—their challenges rarely enter our public discourse in any significant way. We seem beguiled by a rhetoric of decline, this ready store of commonplaces about how awful our schools have become. "America's schools are the least successful in the Western world," declare the authors of a book on the global economy. "Face it, the public schools have failed," a bureau chief for a national news magazine tells me, offhandedly. "The kids in the Los Angeles Unified School District are garbage," a talk-radio host exclaims.

There are many dangers in the use of such language. It blinds us to the complex lives lived out in the classroom. It pre-empts careful analysis of one of the nation's most significant democratic projects. And it engenders a mood of cynicism and retrenchment, preparing the public mind for extreme responses: increased layers of testing and control, denial of new resources— even the assertion that money doesn't affect a school's performance—and the curative effects of free market forces via vouchers and privatization. What has been seen historically as a grand republican venture is beginning to be characterized as a failed social experiment, noble in intention but moribund now, perhaps headed toward extinction. So, increasing numbers of people

From *Possible Lives: The Promise of Public Education in America*. Boston: Houghton Mifflin, 1995. 1-10, 97-122.

who can afford to don't even consider public schools as an option for their children, and increasingly we speak, all of us, about the schools as being in decline. This is what is happening to our public discussion of education, to our collective vision of the schools.

But if you would travel with me to those classrooms in Baltimore or Kentucky or Chicago or LA, sit and watch those teachers work, listen in as students reason through a problem, walk around the neighborhoods to see what the schools provide—then the importance of public education and the limits of our portraits of it would become clear. To be sure, the visitor traveling through our nation's schools would find burned-out teachers, lost students, boredom, violence, inertia. But if our understanding of schooling and the conception we have of what's possible emerge primarily from these findings, then what we can imagine for public education will be terribly narrow and impoverished.

If, for example, we try to organize schools and create curriculum based on an assumption of failure and decay, then we make school life a punitive experience. If we think about education largely in relation to our economic competitiveness, then we lose sight of the fact that school has to be about more than economy. If we determine success primarily in terms of test scores, then we ignore the social, moral, and aesthetic dimensions of teaching and learning—and, as well, we'll miss those considerable intellectual achievements which aren't easily quantifiable. If we judge one school according to the success of another, we could well diminish the particular ways the first school serves its community. In fact, a despairing vision will keep us from fully understanding the *tragedies* in our schools, will reduce their complexity, their human intricacy. We will miss the courage that sometimes accompanies failure, the new directions that can emerge from burn-out, the desire that pulses in even the most depressed schools and communities.

Why are we thinking about our schools in such limited and limiting ways? To begin with, the way we perceive problems in schools is profoundly affected by our concerns about broad social conditions that exist well beyond the schoolhouse door. Since the mid-nineteenth century, that period when we began the standardization of the "common" elementary school and the development of the high school, most major periods of national concern about education—and the reform movements that have emerged from them—have coincided with periods of social and economic disruption, and in some ways have been responses to them. As historians David Tyack and Larry Cuban put it, "Americans have translated their cultural anxieties and hopes into dramatic demands for educational reform." The last fifteen years have seen conflict and uncertainty about economic competitiveness, changing demographics and national identity, and our position in the world order. These anxieties shape our perception of the schools—our schools have placed "our very future as a Nation and a people" at risk, states the most prominent of 1980s' reform documents—and manifest themselves in the sweeping but one-dimensional remedies we pose as a corrective, the remedies of siege and devastation.

There are other reasons for our limited perception; some are long-standing, others more immediate, all are interrelated. Though the teacher has been a respected figure in some communities, as a nation we have had little regard for teaching. It has been low-pay, low-status work, devalued as "women's work," judged to have limited intellectual content. In addition, we have little appreciation for the richness and mystery of "everyday cognition," for the small, commonplace intellectual challenges and achievements of the school day. It is also true that through most of this century our society has been in the grip of narrow conceptions of intellectual development and academic achievement; we operate with inadequate, even damaging notions of what it means to be "excellent." For all the hope we place in what school will do for our children—and we have always placed great hope in the benefits of education—we have a tendency to diminish the day-to-day practice of schooling. This has been especially true for our intellectual elite. Few discussions of schooling in policy papers, in legislation, in the endless flow of books by nonteachers telling us how to make it right, few of these discussions take us in close to teaching and learning. They tend to work at a high level of generality and opinion, thereby relying more easily on one-dimensional portrayals of the classroom. Class and race bias play into all this, keeping us from seeing the good in poor schools and orienting us toward stereotype and sweeping condemnation—and this distortion will get worse as public schools increasingly become the domain of the working classes, immigrants, and minorities. Contributing as well to our disillusion with the schools is a general loss of faith in public institutions and an idealization of the private sphere and the free market. Finally, these tendencies have been skillfully manipulated during the last decade by legislators, policy analysts, and entrepreneurs who want to restrict funding to public education, subject it to market forces, and, ultimately, privatize it.

I have written this book to help us think in a different way.

In doing so, I am not trying to ignore the obvious misery in our schools nor the limitations of too many of those who teach in and manage them. Nor have I disregarded the complaints of those whose schools are failing them; they have a strong voice in this book. This is not a call to abandon the critical perspective a citizenry should have when it surveys its institutions. What I am suggesting is that we lack a public critical language adequate to the task. We need a different kind of critique, one that does not minimize the inadequacies of curriculum and instruction, the rigidity of school structure, or the "savage inequalities" of funding, but that simultaneously open discursive space for inspired teaching, for courage, for achievement against odds, for successful struggle, for the insight and connection that occur continually in public school classrooms around the country. Without a multiplicity of such moments, criticism becomes one-dimensional, misses too much, is harsh, brittle, the humanity drained from it.

Public education demands a capacious critique, one that encourages both dissent and invention, fury and hope. Public education is bountiful, crowded, messy, contradictory, exuberant, tragic, frustrating, and remarkable. We need an expanded vocabulary, adequate to both the daily joy and daily sorrow of our public schools. And we are in desperate need of rich, detailed images of possibility. In the stories that follow, I try to provide some of those images. What begins to shape itself in our minds as we witness good work being done in the South Side of Chicago; in an auditorium just off the freeway in Monterey Park, on the east side of the LA Basin; in a computer lab in Floyd County, Kentucky; in a border town; in a one-room schoolhouse; on the second floor of a market on North Avenue in Baltimore? *Possible Lives* is part inquiry, part meditation, a tour and a discovery, an opportunity to reimagine ourselves through the particulars of people's lives, an attempt to envision the possible from the best of the present. . . .

~

Our journey begins in Los Angeles and the surrounding LA Basin. The movement of the chapter forecasts the movement of the book, traveling through region and community, finding good work in a range of places, arising out of specific histories and cultural conditions, abundant and varied. The LA chapter presents a number of classrooms in relatively quick succession, for I want at the outset to render the complexity of public education in urban America, the overwhelming needs of these schools condemned and abandoned by so many, yet the many kinds of teaching and learning achieved within them. Subsequent chapters proceed at a different pace, but the scheme is the same: a series of portraits of classrooms, each good on its own terms, yet part of a larger social fabric.

I also want to introduce during our time in Los Angeles some of the themes that will re-emerge as we continue the journey: the relation of classroom to community and learning to identity; the nature of a teacher's knowledge and the social and moral dimensions of that knowledge; the role of the teacher as culture broker, boundary mediator; the intricate mix of courage, hope, and thoughtfulness among our nation's youth and the threats to and misrepresentations of those riches; the grounding of the public school in local economy, politics, and social structure; the joy of intellectual work and the role of public institutions in fostering it. We will encounter as well the educational issues that were much in the news as I traveled through the LA Basin and across the country—school restructuring, standards and testing, multiculturalism, and the like—for they have become part of the sociopolitical terrain of schooling. Many treatments of them, unfortunately, tend toward the polemical or the sensational. They will emerge here in the more nuanced contexts of classrooms and the teacher-student encounter.

From Los Angeles I travel south to Calexico, California, a small city on the Mexican border that reveals some of the educational possibilities of bicultural life in the United States and presents, as well, an occasion to reflect on teacher education and development. The third stop in the journey, a long arc cross country from the base of California to the Chesapeake Bay, takes us along North Avenue in inner-city Baltimore, where science, reading, writing, and the African-American experience intersect in a first-grade classroom. Then a six-hundred-mile angle west and a little north to Chicago, the industrial Midwest. We'll make our way through a number of schools, observing, as we will throughout the journey, a range of teaching styles and classroom events, from an advanced placement class analyzing *As I Lay Dying* to a group of sixth-graders putting their day in order. All this takes place in the midst of chaotic school politics and a movement to reform the way schools are structured and governed. It is this reform impulse that takes me back across the Northeast to New York City, to interview nine first-year principals trying to create a new kind of public high school in the largest school system in the nation. There is much said about school reform these days, but we hear infrequently from the people struggling to make it work. We will get close to the day-to-day human reality of social change.

From New York, I fly south and west into one of the early frontiers of the Republic, the Commonwealth of Kentucky. We'll hear from young teachers about to begin their careers, the dreams and uncertainties that consume them, and then travel into the Eastern Coal Field to watch two veteran teachers work through their own uncertainty as they forge an American studies curriculum around independent research projects and computer technology. Farther south to Mississippi, via commuter plane and Greyhound bus to Tupelo, Hattiesburg, Jackson, and a series of small towns in the Delta, where physics, algebra, and the humanities provide the opportunity to consider race, gender, sexual orientation, and school prayer. From Mississippi in sharp angle over the Great Plains, into Western Montana, to a one-room schoolhouse near the ghost town of Polaris in Beaverhead County. The country school, the foundation of public education in rural America. From Polaris we travel to an experimental preschool in Missoula that integrates children with and without disabilities, providing them, at a young age, the opportunity to live across the boundaries of ability. Straight south, then, over the Rockies, to Tucson for a summer enrichment program at the University of Arizona, one example of the many ways colleges and universities—and other public and private institutions—can contribute to the public schools. Here students from the Navajo and Hopi reservations study Greek tragedy, Native American literature, and contemporary novels, writing, in the process, their own defining stories and poetry and plays.

Together, the chapters form an anthology of educational possibility, a series of occasions to think about the future of our public schools. So, though the chapters offer a number of portraits of good teachers, there is no single profile of the Good Teacher; though they offer a number of accounts of skilled practice, I recommend no final list of good practices, no curricular framework or set of instructional guidelines. Such profiles and lists have value: they can suggest direction and generate discussion. But they also have a tendency to be stripped of context, to become rigid prescriptions, at times reduced to slogan or commodity. As we move from classroom to classroom, along the packed hallways of the big city school, along the highway beyond the city, I hope not so much for prescription as for an opening up of the way we think and talk about public schools. What we come to know, we know by settling in, staying a while, watching and listening. There may be no uniform road signs on this journey, but there are rest stops, places to take stock, to reflect on the slowly developing landscape of decency and achievement, to try to leave behind the reductive charts and the stultifying, dismissive language, and ponder the intricate mix of mind and heart that defines the classroom.

The journey comes to a temporary stop in Chapter Ten; there I will try to pull some thoughts together. For all their variety, what do the classrooms share? How did they develop? What threatens them? How can we begin to talk about public schools so that we simultaneously capture their failures and articulate their potential? The kind of talk that comes from thoughtful work and leads to thoughtful action. As the chapter ends, the journey begins again, both across and inward, for public education is ongoing, unfinished, as the democratic state is ongoing, continually trying to realize its promise. "I refer," wrote Walt Whitman, "to a Democracy that is yet unborn"; these classrooms offer a collective public space in which America is being created.

16

From "Baltimore, Maryland" in Possible Lives: The Promise of Public Education in America

1995

AUTHOR'S NOTE: This selection comes from a chapter on a first-grade classroom in Baltimore. I include it for a number of reasons.

It offers a portrait of excellent teaching in science and language arts in the primary grades, the beginning of the educational pipeline. I thought that readers who study writing at the secondary and postsecondary level would find of particular interest the development of children's literacy, which is highlighted later in the selection.

At a time when multiculturalism and race-conscious curricula have become such hot-button issues — and the culture-war polemics around them generate more heat than light — this teacher's work represents the rich and layered possibilities of such an approach. Race is at the center of Stephanie Terry's pedagogy, in the books she selects, in the environment she creates, in her interactions with students and parents. But the centrality of race does not lead to an exclusionary course of study. Ms. Terry incorporates much from a range of sources — Dr. Seuss to Venn diagrams — into her curriculum.

I also include the chapter because it illustrates several core themes of *An Open Language*, again at the other end of the education pipeline: the richness of human language and cognition and the power of opportunity. But it also illustrates a key dilemma, both a political and rhetorical one: how to represent the opportunity opened up by good teaching (or any social intervention) while simultaneously representing the terrible threat to opportunity posed by a history of discrimination and poverty, how to insist on the possible while being clear-eyed about the devastation of inequality. As a nation, we find it difficult to hold both of these perspectives in sight simultaneously, to look on social issues with a binocular vision. Adopting this binocular vision is not unrelated to the task I advocated a moment ago of fashioning an institutional critique that contains both dissent and affirmation. People who study language and rhetoric should be especially equipped for such work.

From *Possible Lives: The Promise of Public Education in America*. Boston: Houghton Mifflin, 1995. 97–109, 112–22.

I

I imagined the tree frog wondering about these kneeling bipeds. Hunched down, hunkered down, faces right up against the glass of his classroom home. "I want some crickets," he might have thought, giving them a dull and sullen look. "Just give me the damned crickets." He didn't move—contemptuous, stolid, the color of the surrounding rocks and dead leaves, looking back at Mrs. Terry's curious first-graders with eyes half closed.

Stephanie Terry's students, thirty of them, were all African American, as was Mrs. Terry, and all lived close by Duke Ellington Primary School in Baltimore's inner city. Stephanie, in her early forties, wore her hair in elaborate braids, had a round, gentle face and a serious lingering gaze. She and her students, half of them boys and half girls, were in the middle of a science lesson on the tree frog, its eating habits and its ability to change skin color in response to the environment. They were about to feed it. But first Mrs. Terry wanted them to look very closely at the frog and its surroundings. "What do you see?" she asked. "Oh, oh, Miss Terry," Frank ventured, twisting around on his knees, "He's real gray now." "Yes, he is, isn't he?" Mrs. Terry said slowly, as if deep in thought. "How could that be?" "Because," Shereese said, looking up from the opposite side of the case, her beaded braids dangling, "he's in with the leaves and the rocks and they're all gray, too." "Hmmm, interesting. Yes. What do we call that ability to change colors?" Frank again, dimples, high forehead, eyes wide: "Ka-ka-meal-e-yon!" "All right. Very good, Frank." Mrs. Terry replied, pausing to let the word settle in the air. Then, "Boys and girls, what else do you see?" "Miss Terry," said Leon, brow furrowed, "the crickets, they're all gone." "No, no," piped up Shereese. "There's one under the cup. Look." And she pointed, tapping, while Leon and the rest of the group scooted around on knees and elbows to get a better look. Mrs. Terry leaned forward in her tiny chair. And there it was. A dead cricket, on its side, under a tilted dish of water. "Why won't he eat it, Miss Terry?" Leon asked, a trace of concern still in his voice. "Ain't he hungry no more?"

"That's a very good question, Leon. I wonder if anyone has any ideas. Let's assume the frog is hungry. After all, it's time to feed him, right?" A chorus of "uh-huh" and "right" and "yeah" and lots of nodding heads. "Well, then . . ." Rachel, who was not in the group of five immediately surrounding the case, asked tentatively from the wider circle where she, I, and the others sat, "Is it . . . maybe he only eats alive crickets?" Mrs. Terry nodded. "What do you think of that, class?" Some murmurings, and Dondi, a picture of Malcolm X and the word *study* on his T-shirt, asked how the frog could tell whether the cricket was dead or "just ain't moving cause he's scared." Mrs. Terry thought that was another good question and began to explain how the frog's eye and brain are set up such that he'll strike only at something moving. "In fact," she continued, "a frog could starve to death if we fed him only dead insects!" Almost all the eyes in the room were on Mrs. Terry now. Amazed. Disbelieving. Everyone's eyes but Leon's, who was still down on hands and knees looking at the frog, waiting for a clue. The frog looked back, impassive, waiting for crickets.

~

The crickets for that day's feeding were in a jar on the science table against the wall by the sink. The wall was covered with information, in big print, on the aquatic snail, the frog, the newt, the hermit crab, the praying mantis, the blackworm, and the tadpole—all the creatures Mrs. Terry kept in her class to pique curiosity and sharpen the eye. On the floor was a case with hermit crabs, the space for Mr. Frog's home (temporarily relocated to the center of the room), a fish tank with newts, a spotted frog, and a tiny African frog. Right by the science table was a box of books, a few scattered out on the rug: *Backyard Hunter: The Praying Mantis, Snails and Slugs, Pond Life, A House for Hermit Crab, The Tadpole and the Frog.*

The table itself was small and cluttered with the remnants of experiments past, the messiness of good science. There was a cluster of acorns and orange and yellow gourds, the head of a big sunflower, a bird's nest, some stray twigs, the corpse of a newt—carefully laid out on cardboard and labeled—five or six small magnifying glasses, several Audubon Pocket Guides, and a pile of crisp maple leaves.

Mrs. Terry walked over and picked up the pickle jar that held three lively crickets. She selected three students who hadn't yet had a chance to observe the frog closely. There was big excitement, but contained somehow, giddy seriousness. Shaquente went first, extending her thumb and forefinger into the jar like pincers, her face set somewhere between a smile and a grimace. She missed, oops, then missed again, the students around her watching, twitching their arms and shoulders with each of her failed attempts. Mrs. Terry suggested that she tilt the jar a little more, and when she did one cricket hopped up the side. She nabbed it, pressing its wings to its body. Mrs. Terry opened the lid of the case, and Shaquente gingerly dropped the cricket in and got down close to watch. The frog stirred, finally, dislodging itself from the leaves and rock. The cricket crawled around, over an old potato, over a twig, a rock, and the frog came off its hind legs in a flash and engulfed it in one swallow. The class squealed. A minute or so more, and the second cricket met its fate. The third somehow escaped the frog's field of vision and got a momentary reprieve. The frog went back to its niche and settled in. The students were against the case again. The frog closed its eyes.

~

Over the next few days, Stephanie's students performed experiments. Rachel wanted to see what would happen if Mrs. Terry put a bright color next to Mr. Frog. Would his skin change again? So Stephanie cut a three-inch-square piece of yellow art paper and placed it inside the case, close to the frog's corner. When the class looked again later in the day, nothing had happened.

"Why do you think the frog didn't turn yellow?" Mrs. Terry asked.

"Maybe the frog has to see the paper," Rachel said, raising a delicate hand.

"Do you think if we put the paper where he could see it, it would make a difference?"

"Let's try it, Miss Terry," suggested Frank in a half-bounce.

Stephanie reached carefully into the case, picked up the paper, and slid it along the glass, into the frog's field of vision.

The next morning, no change. The paper had become moist and dried with a warp. That's all.

"Miss Terry," Dondi offered, "maybe . . . maybe, he has to be *on* it."

"Hmm, that's interesting, Dondi. Let's see. Stephanie tried to slide the paper in as close to the frog as possible, a little under the stones and leaves. The frog stirred, but didn't hop away.

When the class looked again, just before lunch, there was no change.

"Why isn't anything happening?" Shaquente asked, disappointed.

"Well," said Mrs. Terry, "sometimes you have to wait. An important part of science is learning how to wait." Then she asked them to take out their journals and write about the experiment with the yellow paper.

For Stephanie Terry, doing science meant waiting and watching — and writing about what you saw. In fact, writing about Mr. Frog — or the newt or the hermit crab — fostered, she believed, a reflective cast of mind. And having Mr. Frog and the newts and the other creatures to write about fired up the kids to put pencil to paper, to practice print's difficult technology. Science and writing. C. P. Snow's two cultures merging in a primary school in inner-city Baltimore.

≈

Three or four days after the unsuccessful experiment with the frog and the yellow paper, Stephanie read to the students a book called *A House for Hermit Crab*. Hermit crabs inhabit empty mollusk shells, and as they grow, they leave old shells to find bigger ones. In this story, we accompany a cheery hermit crab in its search for a more spacious home. Over the year, Mrs. Terry's students had seen this behavior. The case containing the five crabs held thirteen shells of various sizes, and more than once students noticed that a shell had been abandoned and a new one suddenly animated. But as Stephanie read *A House for Hermit Crab*, she raised broader questions about where the creatures lived, and this led to an eager query from Kenneth about where you'd find hermit crabs. "Well," said Mrs. Terry, "let's see if we can figure that out."

She brought the case with the hermit crabs to the center of the room, took them out, and placed them on the rug. One scuttled away from the group, antennae waving; another moved in a brief half-circle; three stayed put. While this was going on, Mrs. Terry took two plastic tubes from the cupboard above the sink and filled one with cold water from the tap. "Watch the hermit crabs closely," she said, "while I go to the kitchen. Be ready to tell me what you saw." She went down the hall to get warm water from the women who prepared the children's lunches. Then she put both tubs side by side and asked five students, one by one, to put each of the crabs in the cold water. *Plop, plop, plop.* "What happened?" asked Mrs. Terry. "They don't move," said Kenneth. "They stay inside," added Miko.

Mrs. Terry gave the crabs a bit longer, then asked five other students to transfer the crabs to the second tub. They did, and within seconds the crabs started to stir. "Ooooo" from the class. Before long, the crabs were really moving, antennae dipping, legs scratching every which way at the plastic, two of the crabs even crawling over each other. "OK," said Mrs. Terry. "What happens in this water?" An excited chorus: "They're moving." "They're walking all over." "They like it." "They're happy like the crab in the book." "Well," said Mrs. Terry, standing up, placing her hands on the small of her back, and having a little stretch. "What does this suggest about where they like to live?"

That night the students wrote about the experiment, and the next day they took turns standing before the class and reading their reports.

Miko, whose skin was dark and lustrous, and whom Stephanie called "our scientist," went first: "I saw the hermit crab walking when it was in the warm water, but when it was in the cold water it was not walking. It likes to live in warm water."

Then Romarise took the floor, holding his paper way out in his right hand, his left hand in the pocket of his overalls: "(1) I observed two legs in the back of the shell. (2) I observed that some of the crabs changes its shell. (3) When the hermit crabs went into the cold water, they walked slow. (4) When the hermit crabs went into the warm water, they walked faster." One by one, the rest of the students read their observations, halting at times over their invented spellings, sometimes losing track and repeating themselves, but, in soft voice or loud, with a quiet sense of assurance or an unsteady eagerness, reporting on the behavior of the hermit crabs that lived against the east wall of their classroom.

~

The frog and the hermit crab and all of the other creatures in Mrs. Terry's class live in multiple domains: they live in their aquatic or blue gravel or leafy habitats; they live in books; they live in the children's discussion of them—"science talk," Stephanie called it—and, subsequently, they live in the writing that emerges from talk and observation. They live in ear and eye, in narrative, in fantasy. Think of Stephanie Terry's curriculum, then, as the overlay of domains usually separated.

One day Kenneth told a story about fishing with his grandfather. Catfish was the catch, and Kenneth dwelled on the details of their whiskers and their gutted innards—to the delight of the boys and the repulsion of the girls. *Oooo. Ugggh.* "That was a real good story," said Leon. That afternoon, Stephanie dug out one of the district's basal readers and read "New Friends for Catfish." In the story, a catfish is ridiculed by a seal and a turtle because he looks funny—a fish with whiskers!—and, in an escalation of nastiness, Seal and Turtle bully their way onto the sunken ship that is Catfish's home. But when Seal gets stuck in a porthole, Catfish swims back to save him, causing a change of heart in the malicious duo, and the last panel of the story shows Seal, Turtle, and Catfish, in pirate hats and striped bandannas, frolicking together on the deck of Catfish's home.

After getting the class's reaction to "New Friends for Catfish," Mrs. Terry recalled Kenneth's story from the morning. What did the class think of these two catfish stories together? As the boys and girls began making their comparisons, Stephanie reached over for an easel that held a large sketch pad. "Kenneth's Story" she wrote on one side of the page. "New Friends for Catfish," she wrote on the other, and drew a line down the middle. "OK," she said. "Let's start thinking about the differences between these two stories. What should I put here?"

"Miss Terry, Miss Terry," Frank volunteered. "Kenneth ate his catfishes, but nobody ate Catfish." "Good," said Stephanie, and she listed the difference. "Kenneth examined the catfish," Rachel then noted, recalling Kenneth's talk about those innards, "but nobody did that to Catfish." And over the next ten minutes, the students observed that Kenneth's story involved thirteen catfish, while "New Friends for Catfish" was about one, and that Kenneth and his grandfather cut off the catfish's whiskers, but Seal and Turtle did not cut off Catfish's whiskers. And so the list grew.

A few days later, Mrs. Terry read a story called "The Magic Fish." A poor fisherman catches but tosses back a magic fish, which, in turn, grants him a wish. The fisherman's wife, though, is greedy and makes the fisherman return to the sea over and over, asking for greater and greater wealth, finally breaking the magic fish's patience with a request to be "queen of the sun and the moon and the stars." When she finished the story, Mrs. Terry dragged her easel over and, on a fresh sheet of paper, drew a big Venn diagram. The Venn diagram is a simple logician's tool, two partly overlapping circles that illustrate shared properties—those listed within the area of overlap—and properties not held in common, those within each circle's unshared space. Over the circle on the left, Stephanie wrote "New Friends for Catfish," and over the circle on the right, "The Magic Fish."

The children, already familiar with the use of the diagram, started in. They noted shared properties: there was one fish in each story; the magic fish lived in water and so did Catfish; each story had a not-so-nice character. They noted differences: the fisherman had to go back to the sea, while Catfish had to go back to his boat; the fisherman's wife wanted to be in charge of the sun and the moon and the stars, while Seal and Turtle wanted to be in charge of Catfish's home. The children continued—Catfish is a catfish and the magic fish looks like a goldfish—and Mrs. Terry's neat script crammed against the borders of the circles. Kenneth's adventure with catfish had led to a comparison with a story in a basal reader, which led to a logical analysis with a further story: critical thinking emerging from personal experience, logic from fiction—all boundaries crossed in the service of the development of free-ranging thought.

∿

"She just walked into the kitchen and asked me if I had anything to make a circle, so I gave her the coffee can," Rachel's mother told me as she opened the large sheet of paper with the two overlapping circles. Over one side of the homemade Venn diagram was "Harriet Tubman," over the other was "Sojourner Truth," the subjects of two books Rachel had checked out of the school's small library. "Both were slaves," she had printed with a little waver to the letters. "Both earned their freedom." For distinctive properties, she noted that Tubman was born in the South, while Sojourner Truth was born in New York; she noted that Tubman died at ninety-three, but that Sojourner Truth didn't know exactly when she was born. What Stephanie Terry had set in motion, Rachel continued, crossing the line, using in her home what she had learned in school, incorporating an academic tool into a personal exploration of African-American history.

II

Every morning Rachel Ortiz's mother walked her to school. They walked past old brick row houses, some of them boarded up, condemned, or burned out. They avoided the corner where lost men stood around the porch of a dilapidated crack house. They walked with purpose and in the presence of Jehovah, talking about home, about church, about school. Duke Ellington Primary School, P.S. 117, occupied the second story of a long brick building on the west 800 block of North Avenue, near the Pennsylvania Avenue intersection of the Old West Side. The Old West Side was once the locus of vibrant small businesses, professional offices, an art scene, and jazz clubs, but deindustrialization, fractious and discriminatory city politics, and middle-class flight—the forces devastating so many of our cities—have left the area poor and dangerous.

Duke Ellington housed prekindergarten, kindergarten, and first grade. The first floor was a market—hand-lettered signs advertising neck bones and chitterlings and money orders were spread across the wall facing the street— and Rachel and her classmates reached the school by ascending concrete stairs at the rear of the building. At the base of the stairs was a sign reading DRUG FREE SCHOOL ZONE. On the landing another sign warned ATTACK DOGS LOOSE IN THIS AREA FROM DARK TO DAWN, a German shepherd, teeth bared, lunging from the rusted script. To the west and just behind the school was an asphalt area belonging to an adjacent apartment complex; it served as a playground for Duke Ellington. There was a hopscotch grid, worn from missteps, a diagram for a volleyball court—but no poles, no net—and a basketball backboard with the hoop torn away. When the teachers used the area, they avoided those places where broken glass from the night before lay scattered in the snow.

But once Rachel and the other children walked through the pitted metal doors of P.S. 117 and into the lobby, a different world opened up—and you were struck by it right away, felt it almost before your eyes could register the particulars: a feeling of warmth and invitation. The wall to one side of the lobby was an abstract mosaic of Duke Ellington's band, a geometric splash of African color: radiant diamonds, zigzagging swirls of triangles, bright saxophones and drums. The wall to the other side had a row of photographs of Ellington and company, black-and-white, neatly spaced, precise. Straight ahead were some small ferns and bromeliads, an American flag, a glass case displaying the children's art, and a long sign in bold computer script announcing DUKE Ellington is a school that reads. The place was immaculate, and you were usually greeted at the door by Mrs. Thompson, who worked with parent volunteers, or by one of those volunteers, like Mrs. Ortiz.

"The school encourages parent involvement," Mrs. Ortiz told me. "At first, some parents may feel intimidated, but we really try to bring them in." Moving through this school, turning right or left from the lobby to one row of classrooms or another—separated by partitions rather than walls—you'd see mothers helping teachers prepare art materials, putting children's work on display, or reading a story to a small group of kids. It was all this you were sensing when you stepped into the lobby. On the way to Duke Ellington, you occasionally saw a window in those row houses that had a lamp lit behind lace curtains or some flowers on a table. The school gave you the same feeling. It was a good place to be.

~

Her students would start appearing in Mrs. Terry's room fifteen or twenty minutes before class officially began. The parents often lingered, talking to Mrs. Terry about their kids while the children put their coats and boots in the crowded wooden cabinets along the south wall. Then they would find a book, or take out their journals and write, or check out the creatures in tanks and cases amid the science paraphernalia. "I want our classroom to be an interesting place," Stephanie told me when I first arrived. "I want it to be a place where children *want* to come . . . and where *I* want to come, too." She spent a lot of her time and money to make it a place that children enjoyed.

There was a table full of math games, the whole array of science materials and displays — and, of course, the African frog, tree frog, hermit crab, and all their associates. Alongside them were three reading carrels stacked with books: from *Green Eggs and Ham* and *Curious George* to fairy tales recast with Black characters — *Jamiko and the Beanstalk*, for example — to books on Native Americans, *Buffalo Woman* and *The People Shall Continue*. At the front of the room, Stephanie's blackboard looked like a paper mosaic: word lists, which the children consulted when writing in their journals; alphabet strings; work from the previous day, taped up for the children to examine; and checklists of the books the children were borrowing overnight. Past the next corner was the half wall of shelves separating Mrs. Terry's room from the first-grade classroom. The shelves were packed with district-issue basal readers, writing paper, art paper, scratch paper, scissors, glue, pencils, and crayons. Along the top shelf, Mrs. Terry had opened up for display a row of alphabet books: Lucille Clifton's *The Black ABC's*; *The Yucky Reptile Alphabet Book* (B is for *boa*, G is for *gila monster*); *The Calypso Alphabet* (C is for *Carib*, Y is for *yam*); Dr. Seuss's *ABC's*; and Margaret Musgrove's Caldecott winner, *Ashanti to Zulu*.

From the point where the full wall began again, all the way around to the edge of the wooden coat cabinets, Mrs. Terry had fashioned a big comfortable corner. There was a piano, scratched and dinged from years of service, several large pillows and corduroy backrests, a piñata shaped and colored like a rainbow, a box of books, mostly on prominent African Americans, a tape recorder with a box of tapes — airy instrumentals, gospel, and peace songs by Pete Seeger and Holly Near — and a wall display, decorated with colorful kente cloth that featured snapshots and sketches of African peoples: Egypt, Mali, Zaire, Mozambique. "We Are Beautiful People" it read across the top. Mrs. Terry and the children spent a lot of time in this corner: she read stories here, the children read their stories here (a little chair was labeled "Author's Chair"), they listened to music here, they shared experiences — like Kenneth's catfish expedition — here. And if a student wanted to be alone, spreading out a math game or leaning against a pillow to thumb through a book, this was a choice spot. There were no open windows in Duke Ellington — temperature was centrally regulated—but right behind the piano were two translucent, partly covered windows, and warm light suffused the pillows and rug.

Every morning Mrs. Terry would begin class by sitting on the rug by the piano and gathering the children around her in a full circle. With thirty students, the circle—the Morning Unity Circle, she called it—extended out past the coat cabinets and close to the math games and science displays. Mrs. Terry and her students would close their eyes and take a few deep breaths. Though there was the sound of the children in the class next door or a little late movement in the hall, the room would get very quiet. A calming, pleasant silence. Then Mrs. Terry, in a hushed voice, would begin reciting some variation of the following, and the children, softly, would recite along with her:

> I am a special person.
> My teacher knows I'm special.
> I can do great things.
> I shall do great things.
> I will learn all that I can to become all that I can.

Another pause, the children sitting cross-legged, eyes closed, one or two taking a peek or squirming into a more comfortable position, but meditative, serious. Then Mrs. Terry would say something like, "Let's think about all the good work we're going to do today," and lead the children in a further recitation:

> I will become a better writer.
> I will become a better thinker.
> I will really be ready for school today.

The children would turn to those next to them and say, "Good morning, I'm glad you're here today," and shake hands—lots of smiles and giggles, a few exaggerated pumps of the arm—and either go to their desks or gather in closer around Mrs. Terry to do science or share experiences or hear a story.

∿

One of the books Stephanie read during my visit was *Amazing Grace*. The title character was an African-American girl who loved good stories and enthusiastically acted them out: she became Joan of Arc, Hiawatha, the West African trickster, Anansi the Spider. So when Grace's school announced a production of *Peter Pan*, who else but Grace was expected to try out for the lead? But her desire was crushed. "Peter Pan's a boy," announced one child; "Peter Pan isn't Black," proclaimed another. Fortunately for Grace, the two strong women in her life came to the rescue. Her mother said a girl *can* be Peter Pan. Her grandmother, incensed, said Grace could be anything she wanted to be, and took her to see the Black ballerina Rosalie Wilkins in *Romeo and Juliet*. That did it. All weekend Grace, enraptured, leaped and twirled around the house, and when the auditions came, everyone agreed that only Grace had the moves to be Peter Pan.

The children loved *Amazing Grace*. Romarise was up on his haunches beside Mrs. Terry as she read, peering over her arm at the illustrations. Both

Kenneth, of catfish fame, and Rachel thought it was unfair of the other children to tell Grace she couldn't be Peter Pan. And Miko, the class scientist, pointed out that Grace practiced very hard, and that was why she got the part. In Miko's line of sight, on the wall just to the side of Mrs. Terry, were photographs of two Black NASA astronauts, Dr. Mae Jemison and Dr. Guion Bluford, Jr. Underneath the photographs was the crammed box of books that held the stories of Sojourner Truth, Frederick Douglass, Ida Wells, Paul Robeson, Thurgood Marshall, Dr. King, Malcolm X, and Rosa Parks. And on display or tucked away on the shelves and in the carrels and piled on the floor were folktales and alphabet guides and serious books about science and lyrical books about words—books written by Black Americans. Books and books. Evidence of achievement was all around the room. Not contested; no polemic; present in the deed. Present in what the children accomplished each day, present in the history of accomplishment that was part of the surround.

Right at the entrance to Stephanie's room was a sign:

> Each child is sent into this world with
> a unique message to share . . . a new song to
> sing . . . a personal act of love to bestow.
>
> Welcome to Grade I.
> I'm glad you're here.

There was no other way to think about yourself:

> I can do great things
> I will do great things

Stephanie Terry taught, by paradoxical logic, at the intersection of hope and despair. There were a host of probabilities that could lead one to believe that the academic future of her students would not be bright: the danger and seduction of the streets, the limited resources her students' families have for education, the overt restrictions and hidden injuries of class bias and racism. Yet Stephanie knew how profound was the desire in some of those row houses for achievement—knew from the inside the African-American legacy of self-help and self-improvement. She knew in her bones the brilliance of her people and believed, in the deepest way, in the promise of their children.

Stephanie assumed, therefore, that her students could "do better than many people expect them to," that "if you put good stuff in front of them, wonderful things will happen." She was always on the lookout for materials and techniques to interest and challenge them. Sometimes she drew on their immediate experience, sometimes on the legacies of their culture. But sometimes she called on more distant resources. Take, for instance, those Venn diagrams. About four years ago, Stephanie visited a "very exclusive private school" and watched a first-grade teacher skillfully use the diagram to enhance the way her students thought about the books they were reading. "I'd like to try some of that," she thought. "My kids might not be able to read as well, but they're just as verbal." Stephanie's science curriculum provided another illustration. Two years ago she joined a National Science Foundation project aimed at integrating science into the elementary school curriculum. Most of the participants came from schools different from Duke Ellington; several even expressed skepticism as to whether students from such schools could benefit from the project. Stephanie had no doubt, and by the following year her science curriculum was captivating Romarise, Miko, and the others. It was not uncommon, then, for Stephanie to move across educational boundaries, seeing what was done in more privileged settings, and asking herself how she could bring it to the children who came, full of energy, into her room each day.

~

Stephanie Terry grew up in a family that celebrated children. "Our house was always full of neighborhood kids. Every night, it seemed, there was an extra face at the dinner table, and my parents just made it known how lovely it was to have us . . . to have all of us around them." She and I were sitting in small chairs in the corner by the piano, right alongside the Author's Chair and a big box of books. "Kids came first, and as I grew older, I guess I never forgot that. It just felt very natural to be around a lot of young people . . . to enjoy them and support them." Stephanie was wearing a full purple dress, a swatch of kente cloth around her long, braided hair, and earrings from which crescent moons dangled. It was late afternoon, but there was still a soft light on things. A few pencils and some crumpled papers were scattered around us. The debris of thought. "Maybe," she said, "maybe that's why I always wanted to be a teacher. I've wanted to be a teacher for as long as I can remember."

She attended public schools in the city of her birth, York, Pennsylvania, then went to nearby Lock Haven State College (now a university) to major in teacher education. Since graduating, twenty-one years ago, she has taught in York, then in Trenton, New Jersey, then in Baltimore, where she has lived since 1977. About six years into her career, while still in Trenton, she was selected to participate in the planning of an experimental school, one that involved teachers in the development of curriculum and the structuring of the school day. The project gave her, at a young age, a sense of intellectual daring—she came to see teaching as an ongoing experiment, as inquiry. Once in Baltimore, she had the opportunity to participate in further educational experiments, one of which combined "regular" students with the "gifted and talented"—with the result that half of the regular students tested as gifted and talented, and reshaped their academic careers. This convinced her that "if your expectations were high and you put the right things in place in the classroom, a lot was possible." For some time, then, Stephanie Terry has pushed on limits, has taken risks—"stepping outside the district curriculum," she called it—has been instrumental in challenging assumptions about what poor, usually poor and Black, children can do. She shrugged her shoulders and brought her hands together as a cup. "I guess some see me as a bit of a renegade. But what else can I do?"

If Stephanie ventured beyond protocol, though, she did so with a quiet step. She spoke softly, deliberately, and as she talked about her students, she looked at you often, holding connection. She was intent on making herself understood: pulling out a piece of student writing to illustrate a point, telling a story, stopping momentarily to reflect on what she had just said, a slight lilt to her voice as she questioned herself, then starting off on a different tack. She was both focused and even-tempered, seeming to speak from some deep self-knowledge and a bedrock sense of peace. As Mrs. Ortiz put it, "Stephanie just seems to have a special quality."

"How does such a strong advocate," I asked her, "stay so calm?" She laughed, disavowing any hedge on serenity. But as we talked further through the afternoon, those translucent windows turning dark blue, the conversation taking casual and unexpected turns, Stephanie revealed three sources of her strength. There was, of course, her family. "My parents gave us a powerful sense that we were valuable, that we could accomplish whatever we set our mind to." Then, during the 1960s, she, like so many Black Americans of her generation, began to read the history of Africa and African Americans, and that reading sparked a life-long cultural and spiritual quest. That night, in fact, she was going to a rehearsal of an *a cappella* group she and three other women had formed called Rafiki Na Dada, Swahili for Friends and Sisters. The members included, beside Stephanie, a physician, an epidemiologist, and a lawyer, and they sang what Stephanie called songs of the African Diaspora: from South African freedom songs, to gospel, to rhythm and blues à la Marvin Gaye and the Pointer Sisters. "I think that when some folks hear about such an African-centered focus," Stephanie mused, "they think of White-hating, because that's what makes it into the papers. But I don't see it that way [she paused on each word] not   at   all.   I see it as positive. I'm interested in positive things . . . you know, like contributions to culture, family and spiritual values, respect for each other and for the earth."

And there was a third source of strength for Stephanie Terry. Meditation. For six or seven years, she had been a member of a study group organized to "read and talk about the intellectual dimension of Christianity and other religions." Though Stephanie's own religious affiliation was with the Heritage, United Church of Christ, she found something compelling in the meditation techniques of Eastern religions. And, in line with her experimental bent, she had wondered whether a kind of secularized meditation could assist her teaching. "A way, maybe, to begin the day with some sense of unifying, some focus . . . a sense that we've all come together for the same purpose." Thus was born the Morning Unity Circle.

Stephanie Terry lived and taught, then, out of the flux of the stable and the exploratory. "It's important for me to have my base as an African-American woman—and it's solid and steady—but I also have to be able to move out to find things for me and my classroom. I can't separate things into all sorts of compartments." To place her culture and personal history at the center was not to wall off movement. "With a solid base, you can travel far and wide. That's what I want to impart to my kids." In Stephanie's eyes, the center made movement possible. In life and work. Center. Movement. One enabling the other. . . .

III

. . .The Author's Chair might have come from an inexpensive set of kitchen furniture, if it weren't so small—housekeeping drilled and pressed in miniature. Steel tubing, blue-green speckled plastic seat and back rest. A sign, curled at the edges, was taped across the top: AUTHOR'S CHAIR. At least once a week, each student in Stephanie's class had the opportunity to sit in it and read something he or she had written, the rest of the class listening and responding. The students looked forward to the readings, letting out a moan when, for some reason, a scheduled session had to be canceled, or an athletic "yesssss"—hitting that s with brio—when Mrs. Terry announced that it was time for the authors to come forward.

Jamika's trip to the Author's Chair was typical. Jamika's parents were devout Jehovah's Witnesses, so it was not uncommon for Jamika to write on religious themes. She was small and serious and had the full cheeks that relatives yearn to pinch. Just before Jamika started to read, she inched forward on the chair so that her feet were steady on the ground:

> Saturday and Sunday I went to a Assembly. I ate breakfast in the Assembly's cafeteria. They gave me a chicken sandwich. I took my food home. When I was in the Assembly in the Auditorium I took off my shoes because my mother said I could. Lots of Brothers gave lots of talks. People got on the stage.

When she finished, she looked over the top of her paper, anticipating questions. "That was a good story," said Shaquente. "Thank you," replied Jamika, glancing at Mrs. Terry and smiling. "You gave a lot of details," said Leon from the back, standing up to be heard. "Thank you," Jamika said again. "Why did you take your sandwich home?" asked Frank, alert to the advent of lunch. "Because I wasn't hungry," explained Jamika. "Well, uh, maybe you could say that, too," he offered. "If you decide to say something more about your sandwich"—Mrs. Terry tapped her lip with her index finger, as if in thought—"where would you put it?" "I could put it where I say 'I took my food home,'" answered Jamika. "I could say, 'I took my food home because I wasn't hungry.'" "OK," replied her teacher. "Think about it."

Kenneth was next, shooting his hand up in the air, waving it, pressing his cheek against his arm. "Wa . . . what did the people do on the stage?" Stephanie waited a moment, then added that she was curious about that, too. Jamika set the paper on her lap. "They talked about the ministry, and they told stories from the scripture and . . ."—a pause here, looking at Mrs. Terry again—"and that's what I remember." "Well, Jamika," said Mrs. Terry, "I think your readers would like to know that," and leaned over to provide a quick assist to Jamika, who was fishing a pencil out of the pocket of her dress.

When Stephanie first introduced me to the children some days earlier, she told them I was a teacher and an author. "We're going to have an author staying with us for a while." "Ooooo, Miss Terry," Dondi offered, waving his hand, "we're authors too!" You couldn't be in Stephanie Terry's classroom for long before the children walked up to you, their dog-eared journals folded back, asking whether you'd like to hear a story. They saw themselves as writers. And, thanks to Mrs. Terry's feedback and the experience of the Author's Chair, a number of them were becoming reflective about their prose. Ciera came up to me—hair in cornrows, pretty, a little coy—and read me a description of her rings: "I have four rings. One has a whitish stone. One has a red stone. One is gold, one silver." She finished and looked up. I complimented her, and she said "Thank you," but then she paused, pursing her lips, and said, "I think I need more ideas, huh?" "Like what else?" I asked. Again a pause. "Maybe how I *got* the rings?" "Now that's a good idea," I said. She turned on her heel and ran off, still holding her paper in both hands. Six or seven minutes later and she came back, a big smile on her face. "OK," she said, "this is better." She read her original description and then her new sentences: "My mother got me the rings. She got two at Kmart and two at Sears."

Not too long ago, it was assumed that children couldn't learn to write until they had learned to read. It was—and in many classrooms still is—assumed that a critical awareness of one's writing and the impulse to revise should not be expected or encouraged until the later elementary grades. And in many settings it is assumed that the most effective language arts curriculum for poor kids, inner city or rural or immigrant, is one that starts with the alphabet, phonics, and lists of simple words, presented in sequence, learned through drills and packaged games, and builds slowly toward the reading of primer prose. Stephanie Terry's classroom challenged those assumptions.

Writing and reading were taught as related processes and were developed apace. Children did receive instruction in letter recognition and principles of phonics, both from Stephanie and from the school's reading teacher, Carol Hicks. Carol was, by her own description, "a traditionalist," who worked with Stephanie in her classroom and, together with Stephanie, planned supplemental instruction for those children "who may fall through the cracks." But while the students were learning about letter-sound correspondences, they were also learning to brainstorm, consider an audience, reflect on their writing, add detail, and revise. The development of these complex processes was not put on hold until more discrete language skills were perfected. So Ciera spelled "stone" as *stone* and "Sears" as *Sers*, and Jamika, who was the most proficient speller in the class, wrote *Sauterday* and *cafetereia* and *chiken*. Errors like these would gradually disappear as Ciera and Jamika read more and wrote more, as Stephanie and Carol gave them feedback on their work, as they received more direct instruction—from Stephanie, from Carol, from an aide—in phonics and spelling. Meanwhile, they were using language in full, rich ways to tell the stories they wanted to tell.

～

"It's all part of it," Stephanie had said to me. "Everything contributes to the writing. The animals, the books, the music, the things on the wall, the African themes and images—it all feeds into their journals. And the activities. They need lots of opportunities to talk, to hear good books, to ask questions, to share experiences with classmates, to help each other, to read the things they've written." So any given reading at the Author's Chair may grow from a number of sources, all part of the classroom environment.

There were, of course, the books. Each day, Stephanie read at least one book to the class: fairy tale or folktale, a story about children, biography, history, an account of other cultures, an explanation of the biology or ecology of the creatures living along the wall of the classroom. In any given month, then, the children might hear a tale set in the African rain forest, a linguistic romp by Dr. Seuss, an explanation of the Navajo cosmology, information on the newt or hermit crab, the life of Harriet Tubman or Rosa Parks, a story about a magic fish or a spirited girl or a trickster spider. A wide range of genres.

The children could check out any of the books overnight. In the front of the room, taped to the blackboard, was a long sign-out sheet, and at the end of each day, those children who wanted a book would line up and write in the title and their initials. This usually went surprisingly fast; the kids were used to the procedure. When they came in the next morning, they would, along with hanging their coats and other routines, put a check by their name and indicate, in one of three columns, whether the book was "easy," "just right," or "a challenge." Stephanie could thereby tell a lot at a glance. And the children had the chance to be with books. Reading them for a first or second or third time, or just looking at the illustrations — words and pictures feeding their imagination.

There was music. Some was instrumental — drums, harps, guitars, and birdsong to accompany that rain forest tale, for example. But most involved language play and storytelling: Taj Mahal's "Shake Sugaree," Sweet Honey in the Rock's "All for Freedom," "Yoruba Children's Tales," and a collection called "Peace Is the World Smiling." Picking up on the lyrics of the peace songs, Kenneth started one of his entries with "My Earth give us Love and Peace. You got to love the Earth just like you love your friends."

There were the creatures and all the print surrounding them. Words referring to their anatomies — *claw, antenna, gill* — to their habitats and birth cycles — which the children had observed — words about how to care for them ("In our room, we feed praying mantis nymphs apple bits"), and words on the ecological functions they served: "aquatic snails keep our aquarium clean." The language, for the most part, came from the children themselves — with a spelling assist from Mrs. Terry. (It was not uncommon to see children leave their desks to copy from the walls the correct spelling of a difficult word.) And there was all that talk, "science talk," the language of close observation that led to the creation of the children's own explanatory texts.

Another kind of generative talk was the daily recounting of the children's experience: fishing expeditions, trips to the zoo, church services, birthday parties, visits to relatives, neighborhood journeys with "best, very best" friends. These accounts were taken seriously as contributions to the linguistic environment. Children's oral stories were celebrated, analyzed, incorporated into discussions of written stories, and considered for further elaboration. And occasionally one student's story would find its way into another student's composing.

If the books and animals and the rest provided a multilayered content for the children's writing, the journals themselves offered the occasion to learn about the process. Each month, Stephanie passed out homemade stapled booklets filled with lined paper. The children wrote every day, sometimes on an assigned topic, more often on a topic of their choosing—but not infrequently with some kind of guiding principle that arose from other classroom work. If, for example, Stephanie had read a book that was especially rich in description, she might ask the children to try to "add lots of detail" to their own writing. And as Stephanie or an aide circulated around the room, they would give on-the-spot instruction in spelling or encourage a student to be a little more descriptive or point out an unhelpful repetition. All of this, of course, set the stage for revision.

Such work was done on the fly, but once or twice a week Stephanie drew from everything she saw to present a more formal demonstration of the composing process. Resting on an easel in the front of the room, right by the blackboard, was a three-foot-high version of a journal. On the front was Stephanie's self-portrait in crayon, braids twisting into the air. *Mrs. Terry's Journal*, it said across the top. With felt pen in hand, she would model how to get started and how to revise, and would provide opportunity for children to apply their editing skills. "Last week I went to the Baltimore Aquarium," she might say in mock consternation, "but, uh, but I don't know what to say about it." And the children would jump in: "Did you go alone?" "What fish did you see first?" "Did you have fun?" "These were the kinds of questions they heard when they were in the Author's Chair. Then Stephanie would start writing, making many simple errors—"on sunday i wnt to the aquarium"—and a chorus of her students would happily edit her writing: "Miss Terry, you need to start with a capital." "Miss Terry, there's a *e* between the *w* and the *n*." "Miss Terry, oooh, you didn't put a period at the end." As she proceeded, she repeated herself or put sentences out of logical sequence, and that would lead to discussion of broader revisions—as would a question like: "What else would you as a reader like to know about my trip?" With time, these questions and operations, and an awareness of the linguistic contexts that give rise to them, would gradually work their way into the children's composing process.

The journals encouraged another kind of work. At the table close to the door, Romarise leaned over and asked Kevin how to spell *night*. Kevin thought for a moment, then wrote *n-i-g-h-t* across the top of his page. A few minutes later, Kevin turned to Shereese. "Hey, Shereese, do you know how to spell *Friday?*" Shereese ticked off the letters, and Kevin wrote it out and thanked her. At another table Rachel had gotten up with her journal in her hand and was guiding Shaquente toward the comfortable section of rug and pillows by the piano. They settled in, and Rachel read to Shaquente her thoughts on the biography of Sojourner Truth that had been capturing her interest for the past week or so. Stephanie encouraged her students to work with one another: to write about each other's experiences, to help with spelling and punctuation, to share stories and elicit peer reactions. Individual writing, in her eyes, was enhanced by a community of writers.

It was all this that made possible Ciera's and Jamika's and Romarise's performances at the Author's Chair.

~

Another way to consider how Stephanie Terry's students grew as writers would be to look at their work over time, getting a sense of how growth happens in a curriculum of such sweep and embrace. I'll present two students: Kevin, whose writing would place him somewhere in the upper half, maybe third of this classroom's achievements, and Rachel, who, despite some trouble with spelling and mechanics, was one of the most accomplished writers in the class.

Kevin was one of four or five boys who, in another setting, might have been labeled a "behavior problem." He had large, soulful eyes and was usually pretty low-key, but he could easily slip from a task and turn his pencil into an imaginary airplane zipping noisily over his desk or surreptitiously pester the child sitting next to him. About once a day I would see Stephanie sitting with him, head to head, reminding him of the importance of his work, of the importance of his very presence here among the children. And he would usually calm down and get to it, writing a story, or helping other kids spell — for he was a decent speller — or finding a book to take home with him later that day.

The first few entries in Kevin's journal, those for early September, were simply his attempts to copy words he saw on the science displays:

> newtafricanfrog
> tadgole bloodwormS   *Sept. 9*

He had good control of his letters, though he ran words together and hadn't yet mastered capitalization. He also occasionally miscopied — as you can see with *tadgole* for *tadpole*.

About a month later, in early October, Kevin was still copying words but was getting them from all around the room and rearranging them. He was also making his first attempts to guess at the spelling of words he couldn't find on the walls:

> Beautiful   simWnPeat
> The Right crab mhTsnu
> Thing hermit crabs Rainbow   *Oct. 7*

Beautiful came from the "We Are Beautiful People" display, *hermit crabs* from the science area across the room, *Rainbow* from above the reading carrels, and *The Right* and *Thing* from the title of Spike Lee's movie, which Stephanie had spelled out in red and blue art paper letters over the sink by the science materials. He may or may not have been trying to tell a story with them. But by late October he was attempting to write stories like all the ones he was hearing and was relying solely on his own attempted spellings. The first line of one read:

> thet's Info. psw. wIgto psw   *Oct. 28*

What's interesting about these entries — which look a little like a printout from a haywire computer — is that they could be seen as a step backward, since there are no recognizable words here at all. Yet Kevin was experimenting with phonetic strings to try to communicate, experimentation that would, within a month, begin to yield simple written stories:

> Ie wint too The zooo.
> wif mi fe mly.
> wif mi murr.   *Nov. 22*

"I went to the zoo, with my family, with my mother." Kevin was getting the idea about word boundaries and punctuation, and his phonetic guesses were much improved. Here he used his developing skill to take a shot at creating a story common in the primary grades: the visit to an exciting place.

Over the next few months, Kevin's writing took a big leap forward. Here's another zoo story:

> I can go to the zoo with you
> but you can,t go to day with
> me Can i go now not yet
> you can go at the zoo at day
> With me you can to the zoo
> with me now.   *Jan. 16*

His printing was quite good by now, word boundaries were under control, and he was developing a repertoire of simple words. What caught my attention, though, was the experimentation with story structure. There were several voices at work here, possibly a result of all the dialogue Kevin was hearing in the books Stephanie read to the class. Kevin seemed to be using the basic frame of his zoo story to try out some new linguistic maneuvers.

By the time of my visit in March, six months after his first entry, Kevin had gained greater control over sentence boundaries and punctuation and was taking more adventurous chances with his vocabulary. And along with these skills, he was developing a sense of narrative:

> On friday we went on a trip. And it was
> fun at the trip. And we saw a man with
> firer. And he got a beloon and he bust
> the beloon.   *March 9*

Stephanie's next move with Kevin would be to encourage more of the nice detail in those last two sentences—fire and bursting balloons—and to help him develop other kinds of experiences, from inside or outside the classroom, into material for his journal.

~

Rachel looked delicate—thin arms and legs—but, during gym, had a quick, pumping sprint, and, though usually reserved, could match anyone's squeal when the tree frog zapped an unlucky cricket. She was not the most technically proficient writer in the class—Jamika would spell words like *sorrow* and *dwelling* for her—but she was the most inventive. She read all the time and wrote in a variety of settings and for a variety of purposes. She wrote copious entries in her journal, which she frequently took home with her; she copied out long stretches of books she liked; she took notes on church services in a little pad her mother had given her; and there was that Venn diagram on Harriet Tubman and Sojourner Truth. Rachel used writing to render experience and tell stories, to record and relish other people's prose, to keep track of speech, to conduct logical analyses.

The first entries in Rachel's journal showed some basic proficiency and an occasional touch, but it would have been hard to predict her future work from them. Take, for example, this passage:

> The FRogsdo not go
> rib rib rib and we ~~jump~~
> Did not see thoe jump   *Sept. 20*

Rachel had a sense of word boundaries and could spell some simple words. But it was interesting to see the way she used her writing to record an observation with a critical thrust: frogs do not make a *rib-it, rib-it* sound as kids are led to believe.

About three weeks later, Rachel began constructing basic narratives on her experiences:

> Me an my fin India are walling
> at the prak and I get sug
> by a bee an we ran hm   *Oct. 8*

Though Rachel had some trouble with spelling, increasingly she took chances in order to get her experience on paper: *fin* for *friend, walling* for *walking, prak* for *park*, and *sug* for *stung*. Stephanie would sometimes respond right on the journal page; here she wrote, "Oh no! What did you do then?" The question would urge Rachel to tell more, to extend the narrative she had written.

Rachel's reading and writing were developing together, and about a week after the bee-sting story there was an entry in her journal, pages and pages long, that recorded her favorite Dr. Seuss book:

> I am gon to tellw you
> The story By Dr. Seuss
> it is Green Eggs and
> Ham. that-Sam-I am
> that-Sam-I am I do not
> like that-Sam-I am do you
> like Green Eggs
> and Ham . . .   *Oct. 14*

The entry continued, Rachel seeming to enjoy writing the rhythmic words, making them her own. About a month later, there was another long entry. This time, though, Rachel tried to recount rather than copy stories, and, in an intriguing move, blended two in unlikely unison. The first was from Margaret Musgrove's alphabet book *Ashanti to Zulu*, which Stephanie had read to the class.

A. is for the ashot
people . . . the hoozl
people was running
after The ashot
people when The
ashot people got
to a river . . .

The retelling went on for a while; then, on the same line, Rachel picked up *Green Eggs and Ham* once again:

people could not
get them . . . Green
Eggs and ham By
Dr. Seuss . . . that Sam-
I-am that Sam-
I am   *Nov. 18–19*

The shift to Dr. Seuss continued to the end of the entry. I didn't get a chance to talk to Rachel about this, but she seemed to be playing with two stories she liked, connecting them in her own retelling.

Over the next two months, Rachel would gain better control of mechanics, sentence boundaries, punctuation, capitalization — and her spelling would improve.

I love my brother and my sister.
I love my mother and my father
they are apart of my family and
I love them all the same. If they
make me mad I will stil love them
beacus I know they did not meen
it. When somebody dose something
to you it doesn't mean do it
back.   *Jan. 17*

Through January and February, Rachel's entries were fairly straightforward, less experimental as she gained control over conventions. She tended to use her writing now to address a range of topics and to reflect on her own interests and on her developing competence:

I love all kinds of book.
I love Green eggs and ham.
I love Cinderella and Rapunzel.
Piggies. It don't matter what
book it is. It is so fun to read all
kinds of books.
I can read. I am somebody.
I am me.   *Feb. 24*

Roughly two weeks later, Rachel began a longer piece in the computer lab about the funeral of a family friend. Stephanie encouraged her to revise it, and she did so. Her phonetic guesses were improving, and she was beginning to catch and correct her own mistakes. The paper proved to be her most ambitious piece of writing to date:

> On saterday I went to the
> froonrol of Manerva Homes. It was
> sad to look at her. She had
> six girls and one boy. My
> family crid. When the froonrol
> was omost over we got to see
> her and I kissed her. She was
> like a grandmother to me and
> my brother and sister. I loved
> her so much. She helped my
> mother knit and everyday we
> went to see her. She was in the
> housbidol taking some pilse and
> deid in her sleep. We had
> he froonarol at the kingdom
> hall. We sanged song 15 and
> that says can you see with
> your minds eye people are
> dwelling togather. Sorrow has
> pass no need to weep or fear.
> sing out with joy of heart
> you too can have a part.
> Man and beast living in peace
> cause no harm to each other.
> Food will be there all will
> share in what our God pervids.   *March 11*

Rachel was doing some fascinating things here. She told the story of the funeral and of her feelings about the passing of Mrs. Homes, and, relying on the notes she took, she incorporated the psalm into her written text. Her earlier practice of copying favorite passages was being put to a rhetorical purpose, and she was using the notes she had taken in one setting to embellish a piece of writing being done in another.

Kevin and Rachel and the rest of the students kept their current journals at their desks; journals from earlier months were filed in a large box by the piano. So you could sit on the rug before class or after the children had gone home and flip back through the dog-eared pages, thin in places from vigorous erasure, and watch the print becoming more stable, the stories getting longer. Soon you would find places where something wonderful was going on: an experiment in narration, a new understanding of form, an unexpected increase in the kinds of words attempted. And you might, as I did, lay the journals down month by month and stretch out to get a longer view, no longer seeing the particular letters and erasures, but a flow of language, words and effort over time, the development of possible lives.

The Mind at Work: Researching the Everyday, 1999–2004

Introduction to Part Five

The travel and research that I did for *Possible Lives* enabled me to see so much of the country, meet so many people, get a sense firsthand of this complex and contradictory nation. The journey became—and I know this phrase is a cliché—a life-changing experience. I came to understand things about the country—not to mention about schooling—that I didn't understand before.

But *Possible Lives* was also an exhausting endeavor: the traveling, the sweep and scope, trying to make sense of it all. About a year after the book's publication, I started to think about the project that would become *The Mind at Work: Valuing the Intelligence of the American Worker*. The idea, which defined the project from the beginning, was to demonstrate the thought involved in physical work, the kind of work I grew up witnessing. But my early take on it, the feeling that was central to it, was to go small, to move from the wide-angle lens of *Possible Lives* to a tight focus. To consider the use of the hammer, let's say, or the saw, and the tactile and visual perception needed to handle such a tool, and the tricks of the trade that enable its effective use. Small, go small was the feeling. There was the desire to return to the kind of investigation that I did in the writer's block study, but within the richer cultural framework that had been developing over the intervening years.

Going small, of course, turned out to be impossible for reasons that I hope are evident in the pieces reprinted in this part: A tool or a technique or a routine of service has a history, and a sociology, and, well, there's nothing small about it. But that initial feeling, though it misled in some ways, would find expression in the kind of analysis I would employ: a close, detailed examination of the particulars of work. The argument for *The Mind at Work* had to be made through detail.

Looking back, what is interesting to me is that this concern about cognition and the working class emerged early in my graduate studies. I mentioned in the Introduction to this book a paper I wrote criticizing Basil Bernstein's theory of elaborated and restricted codes. In essence, the theory posits that the (British) working class tend to speak in ways more syntactically and semantically restricted than do middle-class folk, and these differences have cognitive and social consequences for their children. Bernstein's work is complex and has been interpreted at times unfairly, and I may have done the same. But I was troubled by the tendency I was seeing in social science (one that I would revisit in "Narrowing the Mind and Page") to characterize less-powerful social groups in reductive, dichotomous, deficit-oriented ways. So this new project continues in that vein: a critical look at the cognitive divides we make between kinds of work and between people based on the work they do.

The Mind at Work provides another way to consider social class, to come at class through the attributions we make about occupation and intelligence. My hope is that this perspective is unusual enough to spark fresh thought about the everyday labors of the kinds of people who populate the book: waitresses and welders, factory workers and hairstylists, carpenters, electricians, and plumbers.

The project might be of interest to some in rhetoric and composition in that it deals with the social context of cognition; with epistemology, embodied knowledge, and the privileging of certain kinds of knowledge over others; with expertise and identity; and with the use of print, numbers, and other symbol systems outside of school.

17

"Our Hands Will Know": The Development of Tactile Diagnostic Skill — Teaching, Learning, and Situated Cognition in a Physical Therapy Program

1999

AUTHOR'S NOTE: Fairly early in the project, it occurred to me to look at work that shared some characteristics with blue-collar labor — that is, the coordinated use of hand and body, a knowledge base of the physical as well as symbolic — but that held a different occupational status. For reasons that I explain in the upcoming article, physical therapy presented itself. (Six months later, I would spend a summer studying general surgeons.) This comparative focus, I hoped, would help me make the argument more broadly about the limitations of our long-standing Western categories: mental versus manual, abstract versus concrete, conceptual versus technical, academic versus vocational.

I chose to study physical therapy by observing students in their first clinical course — that is, a course where they must put into practice knowledge acquired mostly through text and lecture. It's in a clinical course where easy distinctions between mental and manual, abstract and concrete, begin to blur.

There is a big advantage to doing research in a clinical setting like this. Because students are required to perform techniques they're learning and explain what they're doing and why (to assess their clinical reasoning), because learning and assessment are interlinked and ongoing — because of all this, the particulars of thinking and learning are more available to observation than would typically be the case in other training settings and job sites.

The class, Orthopedic Management, had at its core an issue similar to the one I raised in the two early articles on textbooks, particularly in "Speculations on Process Knowledge and the Textbook's Static Page," p. 95. How do you convert or transform information in print (in this case on the structure and biomechanics of the human body) into practice? The students were top-notch; they knew how to "do school," how to memorize and apply material on a written test or even in a laboratory setting, which is a fairly regulated environment. But could they transform that knowledge into skilled physical performance? Not all could, including some who did very well on the school-based tasks.

What fascinated me about the course was the widely eclectic pedagogy that the instructors used to assist in this development: They lectured, demonstrated, modeled, had students test their own bodies and work on others, used props and graphics, visualization and metaphor. They directly intervened to correct faulty performance. They had students shift between modes of representation, had them verbally describe or draw a picture of what they felt when examining a classmate. They integrated assessment with learning and had students reflect on their own developing thinking. It is a pedagogy of multiple methods and symbol systems, and the use of language in all this is rich and complex and worthy of rhetorical study itself.

We in composition are very interested in pedagogy — we even have a journal of that name — so there could be merit in occasionally studying a range of classrooms and other settings where learning occurs, for it could broaden our discussion of learning and instruction. The Writing Across the Curriculum movement has encouraged this kind of exploration, and I think we've gained a lot from it. But the exploration tends to be through the compositional lens, both to understand what is going on with writing and to offer possible enhancement. It would be interesting, though, to consider other things as well: the organization and use of space and talk, the pedagogical methods and routines, the assumptions about language and cognition that drive it all.

Some in composition studies are adopting newer theoretical work in neo-Vygotskian activity theory, cultural psychology, practice theory, embodied knowledge, and situated cognition. Such readers will find "Our Hands Will Know" pertinent. It draws on those frameworks while, I hope, contributing to them. Of particular interest would be the way the instructors create within school an environment that simulates physical therapy practice, that reflects many characteristics of that practice, yet is, finally, not the real thing — it couldn't be, for reasons of safety and patient protection. This simple, self-evident observation I think raises theoretically interesting questions related to concepts like apprenticeship, legitimate peripheral participation, and community of practice. The setting is at one and the same time not a site of real practice, is filled with instructional artifice, yet involves authentic tasks and problems and has potentially profound effects on both students' knowledge and identity.

Jody and Martina were naturals for a program like this. Excellent students, they also had rich experience with physical performance and biomedicine. Martina was a volleyball player in college, majored in athletic training, and volunteered for over five years in a hospital acute care unit, assisting in physical therapy, helping patients become ambulatory, and the like. Jody majored in biology, was athletic, and volunteered for three years in a physical therapy clinic where she performed a number of tasks, administering ultrasound, doing "a little soft-tissue work," and so on. Their backgrounds were fairly typical of the 40 students enrolled in the graduate physical therapy program at Mount Saint Mary's College on the west side of Los Angeles, a rigorous 28-month mix of course work and clinical experience leading to a master's degree in physical therapy.[1] Jody and Martina were in their second semester of a curriculum that spans seven terms and includes courses in anatomy and physiology (gross anatomy, orthopedics, neurology, cardiopulmonary function, etc.), classes in the procedures and practice of physical therapy (these range from introductions to the field and its modes of treatment, to interpersonal and professional communication, to research methods, to ethics and the law), clinical courses in which students put biomedical knowledge into practice (e.g., orthopedic management, assessment of neurologic dysfunction, etc.), and a number of directed research practice and supervised clinical internships. Generally, these courses are sequenced by level of difficulty, and there is a cumulative thrust to them. So, for example, biomechanical concepts learned early on are revisited and elaborated in later courses, with the expectation that students will be able to reason about etiology and treatment in ever more complex ways. And this ability to reason clinically is a central, informing goal of the program.

The workload — seven or more courses of varied unit weight per semester — is, everyone agreed, daunting. But most agreed, as well, that the concerns students had about achievement were not equally distributed across this curriculum. Jody, Martina, and their peers had long histories of academic success; they knew how to "do school." So even the anatomy and physiology courses, which are about as information-heavy as those one would find in medical school, though certainly taxing, were familiar in their cognitive demands. Of particular interest to me are the courses that were less familiar, the clinical courses. It is primarily from time spent as an observer in one of these courses, Orthopedic Management II, that I write the present article, developing it from field notes, interviews, and course and program textual materials. It is courses like Ortho II, for reasons that will become clear as I proceed, that present some of the program's most challenging demands. But first I will provide some background on this project.

From *Anthropology & Education Quarterly* 30.2 (1999): 133–60.

For about a year and a half now, I have tried to gain a better understanding of the cognitive processes involved in skilled work, the array of conceptualizing, problem-solving, troubleshooting activities involved in carpentry, auto mechanics, electrical wiring, plumbing. To help me frame this research, I have observed high school students as they learned the fundamentals of this work, and I have interviewed their teachers and other experts in these trades. To provide bases for comparison, I have also spent some time observing and interviewing people involved in learning a "low-tech" skill, such as flower arranging, and people involved in several service industries, like waitressing and bartending, work that is not considered among the skilled trades but is known for the memory demands and other abilities it requires—planning on the fly, interpersonal adroitness—at least when it is done well. And, finally, these considerations have led me to examine work in several professions that, like all the above, require skills people tend to label "physical" or "tactile" as well as "conceptual" (I hope this article complicates the ease of that distinction), where problem formulation and problem solving occur in complex ways both "within" the individual and "out there" in the world—or, as one current school of thought would have it, in systems of activity (see, e.g., Wertsch 1995). Surgery is one such kind of pursuit, and physical therapy is another. This article will be developed, primarily, from my physical therapy data, though insights gained from my other research, and an occasional reference to it, will appear as well.

These pilot studies, and the fuller research that is emerging from them, touch on a number of issues currently in the burgeoning literature that is helping us reconsider cognition, learning, and teaching from a social and cultural perspective: situated cognition (e.g., Greeno 1998), apprenticeship (e.g., Brown et al. 1988), legitimate peripheral participation (e.g., Lave and Wenger 1991), and various articulations of cultural psychology (e.g., Cole 1996) and activity theory (e.g., Engeström 1993; Wertsch 1995). This literature informs my studies, and I hope that the present article contributes to it. The article analyzes an activity that, unlike those at the center of many recent studies, is, for all its sophistication, fairly low-tech in its practice. (I worry that the direction in a good deal of newer research toward managerial-industrial, military, and technology-intensive settings—though certainly legitimate settings to study—will skew our understanding of thought and action.) Also, by its nature and the way it is taught, physical therapy makes learning particularly open to observation, with some interesting implications for the way we articulate our social-cultural theories of learning and the pedagogies that issue from them.

As is the case with so many research projects, this one has a personal dimension to it. During the time I was commencing the pilot studies on skilled work, some old back trouble was stirring up, so I began seeing a physical therapist at an orthopedic rehabilitation unit attached to the University of California at Los Angeles Medical Center. His approach to therapy involved a good deal of musculoskeletal manipulation, observation of me performing various tasks, a fair amount of discussion of what I was feeling at any given point in movement, and an ongoing exercise routine. I started feeling better quickly, and I was struck by how much the guy knew about the body — anatomy but, more so, biomechanics — and how skillful he seemed to be at picking things up through touch, observation, and talk. I cannot recall exactly when, though it was not too long into treatment, it hit me that physical therapy provided interesting parallels with the knowledge and practice of the skilled work I was beginning to study. I started asking the therapist about his work and, through him, began meeting and informally observing several other therapists in the clinic. The clinic includes a small gym, and once my treatment was completed, I joined it and over the year continued my casual observation, striking up friendships with several of the therapists, having long talks about their work. My therapist assists in the master's program at the institution where he studied, nearby Mount Saint Mary's College, and, as my interests developed beyond curiosity, he arranged for me to observe a class.

Orthopedic Management II is a 14-week course — with an additional two-week field placement — that meets two days per week, three hours per meeting. It comprises lectures, demonstrations, and a good deal of hands-on practice by the students, who sit in pairs at padded tables, from which they take notes, observe demonstrations, and practice the techniques under discussion, usually on each other. It is taught by Nicole Christensen, a faculty member and orthopedic curriculum coordinator at the college who received her graduate education in a distinguished Australian program, and two physical therapists who assist Nicole: my therapist, Tim Gilleran, and Sydney Risser, who, along with Tim, works at the UCLA Rehab Center. Occasionally, a fourth physical therapist will visit to assist in giving students feedback on their practice. Nicole is responsible for the curriculum and the overall organization of the class and carries the primary weight of instruction. Tim and Sydney deliver lessons on particular topics and, along with Nicole, provide a great deal of individual assistance to the students, as all three move about the class during those considerable stretches of time — at least one-half of each class period — when students practice techniques.

The course covers a number of topics and considers them in reference to each of the major human musculoskeletal structures. So, for example, the topic of the "range of motion" of a structure, the play of its movement, is considered for the spinal vertebrae, the pelvic girdle, the knee, and so on. This topic and its application call up a significant amount of lecture and reading material from other course work in anatomy, biomechanics, and orthopedic pathology which must now be put into practice via techniques of manipulation — for example, palpating the spinal vertebrae, moving a patient's leg — and this practice must be proficient enough to avoid hurting the patient and to yield information to the therapist about a patient's condition, what might be causing it, and what might be done to treat it. Throughout this information gathering and after, the therapist must be able to engage in "clinical reasoning" — that is, diagnose the cause of a patient's problem and formulate a treatment plan in a systematic manner. In this article, I select one of the many key topics that emerged during my observation, the concept of resistance, and its application to the spine, hip, and knee. I begin my discussion by defining *resistance* and explaining its importance in manual physical therapy—though for present purposes I will simplify course content a bit and not rely on technical terminology. Then I will discuss the use of the novice physical therapist's body—the development of proper technique—in order to gain information about range of motion and resistance. From there I will cover, in two subsections, one of the key abilities—the ability to make fine tactile discriminations—that the novice must develop in order to gauge resistance accurately. Then I will discuss the overarching practice of clinical reasoning, which gives meaning to the work just listed. These topics are interrelated, and I break them out for convenience of discussion. Woven throughout will be descriptions of the various pedagogical techniques the instructors use to help students develop these skills and abilities. I will conclude with some thoughts on the theoretical significance of the above and on its implications for the way scholars talk about teaching and practice within the current reconsideration of cognition and learning.

I will make one more point before proceeding. Though physical therapy generally is built on the study of human movement and is directed at assessing, treating, and preventing movement dysfunction, it is a broad and complex field, composed of many areas of specialization and foci of treatment—orthopedics, neurology, cardiopulmonary, pediatrics, and so on—each of which contains further approaches and schools of thought, with attendant variation in belief about the specific causes of dysfunction and in favored techniques and routines. The class I observed reflects the manual or manipulative therapy approach to orthopedics, particularly as it has been developed in Australia. Australian manual therapy places strong emphasis on the systematic manipulation of musculoskeletal structures through an array of hands-on techniques that are used strategically as the therapist, through careful observation, questioning, and listening, develops a hypothesis about the source(s) of a patient's problems; tests, rejects, or refines the hypothesis; and formulates a treatment plan. Undergirding and guiding this approach are particular conceptualizations of the body and assumptions about our ability to be subjectively aware of it and to articulate that awareness in language—what one of manual therapy's key figures calls "the body's capacity to inform" (Maitland 1997:27). As well, there are beliefs, based on a history of clinical experience and empirical study, about the efficacy and interconnection of the techniques, routines, diagnostic frameworks, and modes of rationality that constitute manual physical therapy. All this forms the assumptive base and ideology of this approach and is thus central to its tradition of practice. In this article, therefore, these assumptions will be accepted as integral to this tradition, though other approaches to physical therapy, not to mention other critical disciplines outside of biomedicine, might take issue with one or more basic tenets.

RESISTANCE

Put simply, *resistance* refers to the stiffness of a musculoskeletal structure—the degree of flexibility or fluidity of movement of a knee or vertebrae—and a physical therapist tests resistance by manipulating the structure by hand (i.e., the patient does not perform the movement) through its potential range of motion. As a vertebra is being palpated or a leg lifted, the therapist tries to determine two particular points of resistance: r_1 is that point at which the therapist first feels any stiffness in motion—and this, for novices especially, can be subtle—and r_2, which is an end point, is the place where the structure can move no further without some other compensating movement. For example, in one of the tests for hip problems, the patient lies on her or his back, and the therapist, holding the leg straight, raises it—the therapist would exceed r_2 if the patient began to lift her or his pelvis or turn her or his torso. And, of course, resistance can be related to pain, which brings with it further medical, social-psychological, and ethical issues.

Resistance is a concept of key diagnostic importance, for it provides a way to conceptualize how severely a patient's mobility is restricted and provides information that contributes to diagnosis of cause and possible treatment. The concept is threaded throughout Orthopedic Management II as students continually try to refine their ability to assess r_1 and r_2. The instructors talk of "respecting a patient's resistance," underscoring the centrality of the concept in the professional relationship established with clients.

In the classes I observed, the instructors used a number of methods to help students comprehend, tactilely as well as conceptually, the notion of resistance. They assigned reading on resistance and defined and discussed the concept in lecture format before the whole class, and, during lecture, they referred to material the students learned in other classes, locating that more technical material in this context of practice. They related stories from their own clinical experience and, not infrequently, commented on each other's stories. They performed clinical demonstrations of techniques and talked out loud as they assessed r_1 and r_2. They alerted students to visual clues that indicate r_2 has been reached—for example, the aforementioned rotation of the pelvis during a leg raise. "Use your eyes," Sydney, the assistant instructor, said one day. "Use your eyes until your hands get more sensitive."

They also used graphic representations, drawn on the chalkboard, to formally depict resistance. A common one was some variation of the following, called a "movement diagram":

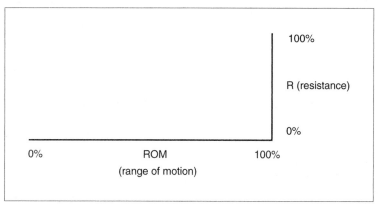

The horizontal axis represents the range of motion of the musculoskeletal structure, from no motion whatsoever (0%) to full motion (100%). The vertical axis represents the intensity of resistance as the therapist moves the structure through its range of motion. The instructors, after initially explaining the diagram, frequently asked students to graphically depict a manipulation they had conducted or a case the instructors had presented verbally. For example, a graph for a person whose leg moves easily through its range of motion, encountering a first point of resistance (r_1) fairly well along and an end point (r_2) when the leg is extended, would look like this:

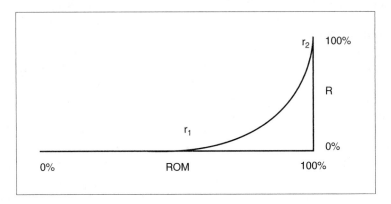

Whereas the graph for a patient with significantly limited mobility, whose r_2 comes pretty quickly, would look like this:

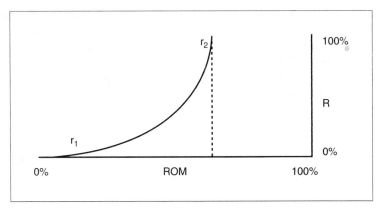

The instructors shifted back and forth from the tactile, to the verbal, to the graphic. So Nicole might draw a diagram and ask, "What would this feel like? Describe it in words." Or, once students had executed a technique, an instructor might ask what that execution would look like graphically. "I want you to think about what you just felt," Nicole would say, "and how you would draw a picture of it to show or explain it to someone."

There is more to say about resistance, but it would be helpful, first, to cover several other topics: the novice physical therapists' development of their bodies as diagnostic instruments and the refined tactile discriminations they learn to make. Before moving on, though, it is worth noting again how many conceptual, visual, and tactile pedagogical modes and techniques the instructors used in combination to help students come to understand the notion of resistance. As Nicole put it one day in lecture, "Sometimes it helps to see something three different ways."

THE BODY AS INSTRUMENT

The body becomes the physical therapist's instrument in several metaphoric senses of the word.[2] It is, first of all, the means by which physical therapists perform a technique, whether for diagnostic or for treatment purposes: it is with their palms and fingers that they palpate spinal vertebrae, and it is by stabilizing and lifting the leg that they check for problems with the hip or related structures. Therefore, to take the example of vertebral palpation, novice therapists have to learn how to position their bodies in order to perform the technique most effectively—that is, their shoulders up and over the patient's spinal column, so that the "lines of force" of palpation are precisely on target, producing optimal, controlled movement of the target vertebra. There is another reason for this care in the positioning of the body: to protect oneself from fatigue or injury. So there was a fair amount of talk in Ortho II about being in this "for the long haul" and the "efficiency" of one's motions—knowledge of biomechanics here applied to the protective use of one's own body. And bodies, of course, vary. So one concern that emerged throughout Ortho II was how an individual student learns to use *her* or *his* body, given height and weight, injuries or musculoskeletal limitations, and so on. During the period when the class was learning to use the fleshy part of their palms (with the other hand interlocked over the top) and their thumbs to palpate the spinal vertebrae, Sydney gave a brief impromptu lecture about variation in the flexibility of the thumb. She stood in the middle of the room, held her right hand high, and, with her left, bent her right thumb quite far back toward her wrist. Her thumbs, she said, were "wobbly." She called on Nicole, who was standing close by, to do the same with her thumb, which had much less bend to it. They talked informally and laughed for a minute or so about the difference, and, around the room, students did the same, bending their thumbs, talking, comparing. Sydney then offered several ways to compensate for a "wobbly" thumb. She placed the thumb of her one hand over the other, stabilizing the first thumb—and students did this too. Then she slipped what looked like a piece of jewelry off her middle finger—a thin, gold spiral—and put it on her thumb as a "thumb splint," a device to reinforce the body. The effective and efficient (two words I heard frequently in Ortho II) use of one's body, then, was a central goal in this class, and it involved a degree of bodily self-awareness that, for many, even for this quite physical group, was unusual. As Martina explained to me, "I'm more aware of myself in space, where my hands are, or is my elbow in the line of force, am I hurting myself?"

There is a second sense in which the body is the physical therapists' instrument: it is the primary means by which they get "good information" about a patient's condition — through feeling and seeing and listening to a patient's response to what happens when they perform a particular technique. Performing a technique effectively and efficiently, then, is important not only to protect the patient and oneself from injury (and eventually to provide good manual therapy) but also to gain tactile data — the therapist's body becomes both tool and gauge.

These various uses of the body are, of course, intimately related. Sydney was demonstrating the hip exam on one of the students, holding the prone student's leg lightly, bending it at the knee, moving the leg gently back and forth toward the torso. Sydney spoke throughout the demonstration, noting the way she positioned the student's body close to the edge of the examining table for ease of access and calling the class's attention to the movement of her own body, the way she rocked her body back and forth to move the leg, not using her arms a lot, thus not tiring herself: "stay in a stride stance," "keep your spine in neutral," "keep a nice, clean plane." And during this discussion of her own stance and movement, she talked about the information her efficient motion enabled her to gain. For example, "Move gentle, move slow, but get in close. The patient will let you get more information if you can get in close and move the leg."

As has been pointed out, the instructors used a range of pedagogical methods in Ortho II, and, accordingly, they helped students learn to use their bodies effectively and efficiently in a number of ways that include methods I have discussed: lecture and demonstration, the relating of personal anecdotes, and so on. In addition, during lecture and demonstration, they used visual metaphors. In describing and demonstrating to students the way to position themselves over a patient to perform the palpation of the spinal vertebrae, Nicole said, "You want to make a triangle from your shoulders to your hands." Another, related method is to connect a particular position and movement to the familiar. Sydney, working with a group of students, said, "Get your sternum over the spine. Think CPR."

There are further pedagogical strategies. Following a lecture demonstration and the attendant practice of a technique by the students, it was common for the instructors to check in with the entire class. After the students practiced the palpation of the vertebrae, Nicole asked, "Okay, how many of you feel you're using your wrist extensors a lot?" She waited for a response, then said, "You should not be activating your wrist extensors." Then, after more practice, she again checked in: "If your hands are sore, you're pushing too hard." During demonstrations, the instructors would sometimes use one of several plastic skeletons to pinpoint a particular structure, calling up work done in anatomy and biomechanics and connecting that knowledge to the particular manipulation techniques being learned at the moment. To help students get a better sense of where to place their thumbs when palpating the facets of the spinal vertebrae (those flat pieces of bone lying to either side of the raised central ridge of the vertebrae), Nicole had a student lie face down on a table and placed over his back a partial skeleton of the spine and rib cage. "Okay," she said to the class, "now you have X-ray vision," and she positioned herself over the spinal column, showing the students how to move their thumbs off of the (easily locatable) elevated ridges of the vertebrae and onto the less accessible facets.

As the instructors moved about the class to provide individual and small group assistance, they often intervened quite directly in the way students were using their bodies, placing their hands on shoulders, hips, forearms, and hands to adjust the students' positions. Nicole was having a student demonstrate on another student one element of the exam of the sacroiliac joint of the pelvis, a difficult exam. After he performed the technique, she placed her hand over his, which was on the other student's left pelvic bone, and turned his palm outward about ten degrees. As she did this, she explained to him and the class how this made "the lines of force more vertical." She and the student then talked for a few moments—he knew he was "coming in at an [ineffective] angle"—and he tried the technique again but still not exactly right. Nicole adjusted his hand again, explaining, at one point taking over and modeling the position, having him try again, staying with him until he got it. "Once you do it right," she said to the class, "you'll have a feeling for what it feels like done correctly. Then you need to do it on a lot of people."

And students practiced on each other, on some days for nearly an entire class. The following example comes from an introduction to the neurological examination, which, though not dealing with resistance directly, is necessary to establish a baseline of performance and to rule out neuropathology. Kim and Elizabeth were learning to test the reflex of the Achilles tendon with a reflex hammer (that little hammer with a triangular rubber head). Kim was the patient and was lying on her stomach, feet just over the edge of the table; Elizabeth was holding Kim's right foot, and, as Tim had demonstrated to the class earlier, had flexed Kim's foot and had the ball set lightly against her thigh. Elizabeth tapped Kim's tendon but got no response. She did it again— no response. Sydney came by, observed, and, asking for the hammer, demonstrated, tapping the tendon a little higher—and got the reflex response. Elizabeth tried it, and it worked. Sydney moved on to the next table. Elizabeth then began explaining to Kim where one has to hit the tendon, did it again, and, again, got a good response. "Whoa. Feel that?" she said. Then she talked to Kim about swinging the hammer with a light touch and the need to "try to stay consistent" in that movement. They switched places; Elizabeth was now the patient, Kim the therapist. Kim had a little trouble initially assuming the right position—"I can't quite get it," she said—so Elizabeth, propping up on one elbow, guided her. Then Kim tapped Elizabeth's tendon. "Does that feel like I'm hitting in the middle?" she asked. "No," Elizabeth told her, "you can go a little higher up." Then after several more attempts, Elizabeth observed, "You're a little bit better on the medial than on the lateral side," referring to the direction from which Kim was approaching the tendon. This kind of exchange in its precision and collaborative helpfulness was quite common and was, perhaps, the essential activity in helping students refine their technique. As Tim observed to the class, "You've got to try these [techniques] on each other. It doesn't make sense unless you try to feel it." One further element of this collaborative practice involved having one of the instructors perform the technique in question on one's own body—as we saw Sydney do with Kim in the above episode—so that, as Nicole put it, "You'll know what it feels like. Then you can give better feedback to your partner."

Reading the above vignette, Tim noted how hard it was to create the conditions for this kind of collaboration to occur. Students have to struggle publicly to express sensations and movements that are hard to express—an issue I return to later—and they must come to trust each other, admit uncertainty, venture being wrong—not an easy thing for such academically competitive folk. Establishing training space for these kinds of risks takes explicit curricular and pedagogical effort, both across the program and within Ortho II.

TACTILE INFORMATION

As is evident above, novice physical therapists work hard at mastering technique in order to get "good data" from their patients. As Tim explained one day, "No matter how smart you are, if you have bad information, you'll make a bad decision." It may sound a little odd initially—I know it struck me when I first heard it—to think of the tactile as data, but it is central to the manual physical therapist's profession to work with the information about the musculoskeletal structure that is yielded by the performance of effective and efficient technique. "Go slow," Nicole advised when students were first learning how to palpate the spinal vertebrae; "you get better information with your hands when you go slow." And one day, later in the month, Tim said to the class, "You need to get to where your technique is good and consistent, and then you go through your routine and get good information." Getting tactile information is central to the routines, protocols, and general habits of mind that the program refers to as clinical reasoning (which I will discuss shortly); "no matter how smart [one is]," no matter how much textbook anatomy one knows or how quickly one can list off the steps in the neurological exam, without good information, one will hypothesize and diagnose poorly and generate inadequate treatment plans: "You'll make a bad decision."

What is required, therefore, to return to the notion of the physical therapists' bodies as their instruments, is to, over time, continue to improve one's skill at executing manual techniques, refining one's sense of touch and motion in order to acquire increasing sensitivity to the feel of musculoskeletal processes and tissues. Efficient, just-right movement on the therapist's part is critical. Tim explained, "If there's too much of the therapist's movement in the system [i.e., the physical system of the therapist's and patient's interrelated bodies], then you're not going to get the clean movement" of the particular musculoskeletal structure being tested. The language is almost cybernetic here: the body cannot be an efficient instrument if one's movement is not fluid, is too pronounced, irregular, or exaggerated, because noise enters the system. Observing a student execute one of the techniques for the hip exam, whereby the therapist stabilizes the patient's leg and raises it, Tim offered a corrective metaphor as he assisted her: "You've got too many links in the chain. Picture yourself as one circular piece of steel, rocking. Otherwise, there's too much movement to confuse you."

Over time, one begins to discern a developmental trajectory in the use of the body as an information-collecting device. As Sydney explained to me, "When an experienced therapist works, you're thinking results, clinical pathways. When you begin, you're thinking techniques—did I do the test right? These students are having to think [about properly executing techniques] so much." (A student independently told me the same thing: "When you start, you're concentrating on getting your technique right.") This concerns the automatization of processes that comes with expertise (Bracewell and Witte 1997; Hutchins 1986). There are two interrelated issues here: The more one's attention can shift from executing a technique properly to what one is feeling, the more focused one can be on the information the technique is yielding. And the more efficient one is at executing technique, the less interfering "noise" there is in the information one acquires.

REFINING DISCRIMINATION

For a good while during my time in Ortho II, students would, in their words, "blow right past r_1" (the first indication of musculoskeletal resistance). Sydney observed one day, "Some of you guys go right to the end range" (that is, r_2). As Jody put it, "I'm not used to feeling for little changes." A different, though related, problem, one touched on at the end of the last section was succinctly expressed by one of the students: "I focus too much on r_2 and miss other things." If students miss the "little changes," they may also concentrate so intently on a particular technique or diagnostic moment (like r_2) that they miss the broader band of information a more experienced therapist might register. At heart, I am talking here about the development of an increasingly refined perceptual ability: the ability to make discrete distinctions in the feel of musculoskeletal structures. It is "finesse," Nicole told the class one day: "You'll start to feel more finely." A bit later in the class a student laughed and said, "Feeling is believing."

One of the things that makes the development of this refined tactile discrimination difficult, of course, is that the physical therapist works with a number of quite different musculoskeletal structures, each with its own range of motion—from the limited movement of spinal vertebrae to the wide swing of the shoulder—and each has its own tactile indicators of r_1 and r_2. But what seems to make the development of this refined tactile skill even more difficult is the fact that, as Sydney put it one day, "Every single person is going to have their own r_1 and r_2, though there's a normal range." Within a normal range, there is significant variation—and for each of the musculoskeletal structures. When the class was in its first few days of learning the technique for palpating the spinal vertebrae, one student said in frustration, "I can't get it. I do it on different people, and they're all different. I can't get it." He hit on one of the key challenges in the development of this keen discriminating ability: the need to establish a sense of a normal range, a kind of broad-banded "average" of mobility. As Sydney explained later in that same class meeting, "You need to try other people to get a feel for all the feels. Then you'll form an idea. You need to get an idea of the normal spine and get a sense of r_1 and r_2. You need to get a sense in your hand. You need to train your hand to feel." This knowledge in the hand, then, is not reducible to the finding of a correspondence for or the mapping of a particular feel onto a specific process or condition but, rather, seems to involve the development of a sense of a bounded range of sensations, a tactile concept, a kinesthetic "idea" of the feel of the normal spine, or hip, or knee. It is a complex business and yields in this setting a language of the tactile and abstract intertwined: Sydney's idea that develops through the hand.

How did the instructors create the conditions for their students to master these subtle discriminations? Much of what we have already seen was involved: from calling up textually derived knowledge of anatomy and biomechanics, to instructor modeling and explanation, to hands-on practice with peers. The development of keen discrimination emerges primarily from a manual pedagogy, but it is worth dwelling for a moment on the ways it also involves the visual, the graphic, and, especially, the verbal.

In the discussion of resistance, I quote Sydney calling a student's attention to the compensating movement of the hip after that student had raised a patient's leg past the end point of resistance, r_2. "Use your eyes," she said, "until your hands get more sensitive." At another time, one of the students showed me something an instructor had just shown him: how, when one has gone past r_2 on the third lumbar vertebra, the vertebrae above it descend slightly into the back—a visual tip that one has missed r_2. Jody speculated that because people tend to be more visual than tactile, it helps to use visual clues until, as Sydney said, they get better at feeling things. The visual becomes a kind of perceptual scaffold assisting the refinement of the tactile. And, it seems, though further study would be needed to explore this, that some students rely on mental visualization as they develop their tactile skill. Jody explained, "At this point, I just have to visualize [the r_1 and r_2 of vertebrae] before I can do it and believe eventually we'll move past having to visualize and just be able to go in there and know—our hands will know."

The graphic representations play in here as well. Tim told the class several times, and mentioned it to me more than once, that when he was a student, he and his peers drew movement diagrams a lot as a way to help them understand the different patterns of resistance and communicate what they were feeling to each other. As the instructors introduced the charts and other graphic conventions to the class, students began to use them. During the session when students were learning to palpate the spinal vertebrae, Nicole drew arrows on the board to illustrate an effective rhythm of palpation (its "oscillation"): pressing down on the vertebrae with the palm of the hand, then coming up, then "in a little deeper," then up again, "but don't come all the way out," then in until the end point, r_2, is hit. She drew the following:

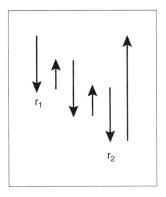

Toward the end of that class—after everyone had practiced the palpation and had an instructor model it, assist them, or, in some cases, do it on them—one of the students asked Tim about the differences she felt when he performed the technique on her versus what she believed was the way she performed it on her partner. It was a hard thing to express—a reminder of how difficult it is to find a tactilely apt language—and Tim did not quite get what she was asking. So she took him up to the chalkboard and explained, as she drew arrows, that she seemed to need to come farther back up in her oscillation than Tim did—the length of Tim's arrows was shorter, hers longer—in order to gauge r_1 and r_2. Her oscillation seemed gross and slow to her, and she used these graphics to try to convey to Tim a fairly discrete difference in oscillation. She had quickly appropriated this representational device to aid her attempt at articulation. Perhaps the graphics function as another scaffolding device in the refinement of technical skill and discrimination. What we see here is, I think, a particularly nice example of a phenomenon discussed by cultural-historical psychologists (e.g., Cole 1996): the acquisition of a culturally transmitted mediating device (variations of these graphic representations of movement are part of the conceptual and communicative tradition of Australian manual therapy) by a new member of the community, in a new context, to solve an emerging problem.

And there may be a developmental pattern to the use of the movement diagrams. Tim explained to me that though he no longer had need (or was required clinically) to draw movement diagrams, except in teaching, the process "now goes on in my head." And one day Nicole said to the class, "Will you be drawing these diagrams when you're out working on people? No. But you'll go through the process in your head." Exactly how the diagrams and the processes they embody get internalized and represented is hard to say—and some social scientists now suggest that graphics (or "inscriptions") can better be understood as a social rather than a cognitive/mental phenomenon (Roth and McGinn 1998)—but Tim and Nicole's comments suggest that, for some therapists, the diagrams function as an aid to the development of discriminating competence and the way they are used goes through some sort of transformation over time.

During the class when Nicole was introducing the movement diagrams, she drew a diagram with a line that had a slowly ascending trajectory. "What would this feel like?" she asked, "Describe it in words." There was a good deal of talk attached to the use of the graphics, and, in general, instructors were continually encouraging students to describe what they felt as they performed techniques and to give precise feedback on what a partner's technique felt like when it was performed on them. Following Nicole around the classroom as she observed students working on each other, I heard her asking continually, "Feel what that feels like. Can you feel the difference [between r_1 and r_2]? Try to put it in words." And she had students direct their answers to each other. These were attempts to articulate the kinesthetic, and language, then, became another mediating device in the attempt to refine the ability to make fine tactile discriminations. Cindy Moore, the chair of the program, had an interesting take on the use of language here. She suggested that this vocalizing of the sensual, difficult though it may be, acts to not only assist discrimination but to confirm it: "It's a way of validating that they're feeling what they're feeling. What they feel feels intuitive; it doesn't feel 'real.' To talk about it is a way of assuring that what you feel is not made up."

Finally, and not unrelated to the above, the instructors encouraged students to reflect on their own thinking and sensation — metacognition. Sometimes the encouragement was indirect as instructors modeled what might go on in their heads as they work on a patient. Talking about r_2 to the class, Nicole paused and, as though pondering, asked, "What's a normal 'end-feel'? So I'm thinking in my head, What's normal?" More often, the encouragement toward metacognition was direct. During the time when students were just learning how to palpate the spinal vertebrae and had just finished executing the technique on padded tables, Nicole asked everyone to take a moment and "think about what you just felt." And it was not uncommon for students to be encouraged to think out loud, making cognition public. "Take me through your thought process," Tim told a student, "so I can make sure I'm following you." As students articulated differences in sensation and their thoughts about them, the interior became open to the assessment of and feedback from peers and the instructors, whose responses could further socialize students into a clinical tradition, assisting them in making a particular kind of sense out of what they feel, one more mechanism by which their hands come to know.

CLINICAL REASONING

The orientation to manual physical therapy found in Orthopedic Management II is often referred to as the Australian approach, and a key figure in formulating that approach is Australian physiotherapist Geoffrey Maitland. Reading his core textbook, *Vertebral Manipulation* (1997, originally published in 1964), one encounters, within the first few pages, the following caveat about the manipulative techniques the students in Ortho II spent so much time trying to master: "When people talk about manipulative treatment, it seems impossible to avoid the problem of their putting inordinate emphasis on the techniques. . . . This is most unfortunate to say the least, because it prevents their seeing the *whole* picture" (1997:4, emphasis in original). The "whole picture" of manual therapy for Maitland is framed by what he calls "analytical assessment" and what Nicole referred to as "clinical reasoning," which she explains thus in a handout that students in Ortho II receive early on:

> Clinical reasoning can be defined as the cognitive processes, or thinking, used in the evaluation and management of patients (Jones, 1992). . . . The goal of clinical reasoning is "wise action" — i.e., making the best judgment in a specific context (Dutton, 1995). Clinical reasoning requires situational thinking, done "in the moment" as well as retrospectively.

The students were not yet at the place in their training where, even with supervision, they could do a comprehensive evaluation on a patient, though they already had been taught the rationale for and stages of assessment, as proposed in the Australian approach. The full protocol is somewhat elaborate, but, in essence, the therapist attempts to gather a patient's history; a precise understanding of the presenting problem from the patient's perspective; and, through the strategic use of procedures and techniques — like those we have seen — information on the physical factors that may be related to the problem. From all this, the therapist formulates a hypothesis about causality and a related treatment plan, but what is particularly important in the Australian approach is that each subsequent treatment becomes the occasion for further assessment. The initial hypothesis must be open to revision or refutation, "for even treatment is viewed as a form of hypothesis testing. Results of treatment serve to modify or reform hypotheses, contributing further to the therapist's evolving concept of the patient's problem" (Jones et al. 1994:94). Maitland's concerns about an overemphasis on his manipulative techniques becomes clear: technique has to be executed effectively and efficiently to yield good data, but data will be useless unless the therapist operates with a critical, reflective mind.

It is no surprise, then, that throughout Orthopedic Management II, students heard from Nicole and from Sydney and Tim about the importance of thinking things through, of using whatever academic and clinical knowledge one has combined with all a patient reveals to analyze and reanalyze possible causes of malady. When Nicole was introducing the pelvic girdle exam, she discussed a tendency a decade or so ago to rush to judgment and overdiagnose sacroiliac problems. Then, stressing the importance of a careful and thoughtful examination, she said, "We want you to be able to figure out when sacroiliac treatment is appropriate and when it isn't." A bit later, discussing the many variations and anomalies in the pelvic bones, she cautioned, "It is an error in your reasoning if you find a bony anomaly or odd alignment and assume it's related to mobility problems." Even a finding that seems clear-cut needs to be carefully considered and analyzed, for so many orthopedic problems are complex and nuanced. Sydney explained one day how X rays and more sophisticated computer-assisted imaging techniques (e.g., the MRI) that show a deformity or pathology—for example, a slightly herniated disc—may not reveal the cause producing a patient's symptoms, and, during that same class, she explained how local pain may have its source in other regions of the body. "Never assume," she said cryptically, "that a knee is a knee." So, though a central goal of Orthopedic Management II is the mastery of techniques and procedures that, given their precision and continued practice, could be seen as being "mechanical," the manner and purpose of their deployment is anything but mechanical. There is an ethos in Ortho II, a culture, if you will, of reflective thought, problem solving, troubleshooting—talk about clinical reasoning surrounds technique.

Central to this analytic habit of mind is the precise use of language and the fostering of effective communication between therapist and patient. Maitland's *Vertebral Manipulation* has an entire chapter on communication, and throughout the book he stresses "detail," "specificity," and "precision" in language and underscores the importance of careful listening and questioning, "believing that the body can inform the patient about aspects of her disorder that cannot be found by examination" (1997:9). The course of study at Mount Saint Mary's College is unusual, including four half-unit courses on "personal and professional communication," and throughout Ortho II the instructors, as we have seen, create the conditions for students to articulate what they are doing, their reasons for doing it, and what they are experiencing as someone works on them. It was telling that when I asked Jody what it was that characterized the expertise of the therapist who supervised her first clinical field placement, she quickly said that the therapist "really fosters good communication with her patients. She listens to them, explains things to them, includes them in the treatment." So every time an instructor asks a student to explain what he or she is thinking or experiencing and every time students tell each other what they are doing or feeling, this difficult push toward articulation of the tactile anticipates the give and take of language in professional practice.

There are powerful assumptions in the foregoing about subjectivity, cognition, language, communication, and hypothetico-deductive reasoning that, as I noted at the beginning of this article, could themselves be open to analysis—just the relation of language to thought has occupied a major place in 20th-century philosophy—but one can see the coherence of the assumptions and their relation to practice. And, for my purposes, it is important to understand that comprehending resistance, mastering techniques, developing the use of one's body, and refining one's tactile discrimination are all integrated and given meaning within an orientation to human movement, cognition, and language which defines and directs the tradition of practice that informs the work students do in Orthopedic Management II.

DISCUSSION

This article is an attempt to examine a classroom setting in which beginning physical therapy students develop the ability to use their bodies to make increasingly fine tactile discriminations about the resistance of musculoskeletal structures, an ability that is made sense of and deployed in the context of reasoning clinically about the possible causes of and treatments for a patient's problems with movement. The study is built from field notes, textual materials from the class and about the program, interviews (both during practice and post hoc) with instructors and selected students, interviews with the chair of the program, histories of manual physical therapy and books and articles from the field's professional literature, and informal observations and interviews with physical therapists not connected with the instruction of Ortho II.

As a number of researchers working within the frameworks of sociocultural psychology, activity theory, practice theory, and situated cognition have been recommending over the past decade (see, for example, Cobb and Yackel 1996; Cole 1996; Engeström 1993; Lave and Wenger 1991; Rogoff 1995), I have tried to consider these data along several interrelated analytic layers/domains (Hull and Rose 1989; Hull et al. 1991) or "planes of focus" (Rogoff 1995). The concepts, techniques, uses of language and other signs, and habits of mind we have seen have complex histories of development, and these technical, discursive, and cognitive practices can be understood as the "tools of the trade," transmitted by professional culture, that constitute the practice of the Australian approach to manual physical therapy. Each cohort of students that passes through Ortho II acquires these tools through guided and sustained practice; the students' learning is "situated," then, both in a tradition and, more immediately, in the conditions created by the instructors which enable them to develop competence. At times, the analysis has been at the level of the student, or a pair of students, or a student and instructor, focusing on the acquisition of particular techniques, procedures, or linguistic or cognitive skills and abilities. This analysis could have a fairly tight temporal focus—for example, Kim and Elizabeth learning the reflex exam for the Achilles tendon—or could be more developmental, considering a process over time. At other points in the article, analysis shifts to the classroom as a complex unit of activity: for example, when considering the ways the instructors created the conditions—through language, graphics, actions, and objects—for this cohort of students to participate in and acquire some of the practices of manual physical therapy. And the analysis, at times, considers the tradition of Australian manual physical therapy—a tradition comprising techniques, routines, guiding assumptions—and the way that tradition affects particular practices in Ortho II—for example, the role of communication and hypothetico-deductive reasoning in the development of technique and the refinement of tactile discrimination. Though provisionally isolable for purposes of analysis, all these domains or planes converge in the day-to-day activity of Orthopedic Management II. I will now consider in more detail several topics from within this activity.

A PEDAGOGY OF MULTIPLE METHODS AND SYMBOL SYSTEMS

"Sometimes," Nicole has said, "it helps to see something three different ways." The instructors in Ortho II utilized and interwove a wide range of instructional approaches to help students acquire tactile discrimination skills related to resistance. As we have seen, the instructors lectured, demonstrated, modeled, told stories from clinical practice, incorporated readings assigned for their class and others, used aids such as the skeleton, organized dyads for collaborative learning and practice, physically adjusted students' bodies and guided motion, surrounded activity with talk that focused attention, elaborated, connected, and evaluated, used metaphor, used graphics, encouraged articulation, strategically shifted—and encouraged students to shift—among senses and symbol systems (touch, sight, speech, nonlinguistic graphics, expressive motion), creating what Rogers Hall (1990) calls an ecology of representations. (Interestingly, about the only methods absent were those related to electronic technology—except for an old overhead projector used a few times—which reminds us that quite complex learning and instruction can occur in quite low-tech settings.) What is the pedagogical purpose for this range?

One reason is simply that some of these methods and orientations are part of the educational tradition of Australian manual physical therapy, developed and modified over time and place, used to help Nicole learn in Australia and, after her, Tim, who trained in this program three years before. The methods and their purposive interplay provide one way to assist the transmission of the manual techniques, their connection to concepts, and the philosophy of their use in service of clinical reasoning. Another reason for the variety was suggested to me by Tim during one of our interviews: People learn different things in different ways, so the more ways instructors have of coming at material, the more possibilities there are that one or more methods will click with all of the people in the room, who, for all their similarities—high achievers, physically oriented—are, of course, a diverse lot, as any population of 40 would be. This addresses the long-standing concern of educational psychology with individual differences.

And there is a third reason, I think, for the variety, not unrelated to the previous two: In their study of blacksmithing, Keller and Keller note that the "development of a coherent conceptual structure requires the ability to construct and move among diverse informational structures [and] the ability to translate some information from one representational mode into another" (1996:179). So to gain a rich understanding of resistance, a student may be encouraged to visualize musculoskeletal structures, verbally describe what he or she is feeling, and so on, in addition to using touch and movement. To integrate resistance, tactile discrimination, and clinical reasoning into fluid practice requires a complex and, for most of us, unfamiliar integration of sensory and epistemological domains that in our culture are usually segmented. To blur that segmentation, in fact to challenge it instructionally, seems to require, at least in this setting, a convergence of methods and a fluid play of symbol systems. One could even consider the rhetorical devices the instructors sometimes use—metaphor, synesthesia (ideas emerging from the hand), paradox (a knee is not a knee)—as contributing to this movement among ways of knowing.

The Abstract and the Concrete

For a complex host of reasons ranging from our Western philosophic tradition to the sociology and organization of work, we tend to make quick and quite consequential distinctions between mental activity that we define as abstract, theoretical, or conceptual and physical activity that we define as material, concrete, or applied. To be sure, there is some legitimacy to the distinction: In fundamental ways having to do with semiotic systems, cultural antecedents, routines of practice, and so forth, calculating a Poisson distribution is different from filling out a form at the Department of Motor Vehicles, which, in turn, is different from shaping a table leg on a lathe. Still, the ease and assurance of the distinction have led to a number of problems in the way we conceptualize intelligence, our understanding of work, and our educational practice—not to mention the invidious ways the distinction feeds into social stratification.

Sylvia Scribner, along with others who study manual work within a sociocultural tradition, emphasizes the "continual interplay between internal representations and operations and external reality throughout the course of the problem-solving process" (1986:23), thus challenging the abstract-concrete distinction. Spending time in Ortho II helps us push on it even further, for the curriculum sits astride the "academic" and the "applied." There is a body of knowledge the students learn that is essential to practice—for example, gross anatomy and biomechanical concepts like resistance—but knowing the definition of *resistance* is not very useful unless it is integrated or blended (one struggles for words here) with manual techniques. And the techniques, in turn, gain meaning as novice therapists develop the ability to derive information from them—"average feels" of different musculoskeletal structures and the data from a particular patient's structures—and form hypotheses through that information. There is an ongoing, interactive play between hand and mind that would be very hard to compartmentalize; it is hard to know, at times, how one would label the activity one observes. As noted a moment ago, this blending is evident in the language the instructors use. Take, for example, Tim's metaphors about the student therapist and her "patient" being a physical system, "links in a chain," "one circular piece of steel, rocking." Tim used language, a system of abstractions (but embodied here in Tim, his gestures, and the teacher-student relationship), to create a comparison, which is an abstraction, via metaphors that use physical objects (chain links, a band of steel). The complexity continues, for the metaphors are in the service here of the abstraction "information"—gathered, however, via the physical embodiment (therapist and patient) of the abstract notion of a system. Where does one make the abstract-concrete demarcation?

Brown, Collins, and Duguid call for a fundamental reconsideration of the "profoundly misleading theoretical separation between *knowing* and *doing*" (1988:1, emphasis in original). And activity theorists suggest that, rather than relying on the dichotomy between mind and body, we begin from the proposition that the conceptual and the physical "are not absolutely exclusive categories, but are unified by their common source in activity" (Bakhurst 1991:217). But, it seems, we need to continue to revise our theories and craft fresh vocabularies to render this "marriage of the hand and the mind" (Harper 1987:118),[3] particularly for those educators who must, finally, create the conditions for people to acquire complex kinesthetic-conceptual skills and abilities, assess when acquisition is going awry, and effectively intervene.

AUTHENTIC ACTIVITY, APPRENTICESHIP, AND COMMUNITIES OF PRACTICE

I want to be clear at the outset: I think that the last decade's worth of reformulations of cognition and learning, grouped together by Greeno (1998) as "situativity," has been very valuable in both theory building and educational practice. The situational framework has pushed us to think hard about the ways learning is narrowly conceptualized and measured. And this framework has been very helpful in thinking through the present research. But what we have seen also yields caveats about the way the situated learning literature has been advanced and interpreted in terms of educational practice. I am particularly interested here in the arguments for authentic activity (Brown et al. 1988) and the claims about communities of practice and legitimate peripheral participation (Lave 1996; Lave and Wenger 1991).

In an attempt to counter classroom instruction that is unengaging, acontextual, or detached from real-world practice, there has been a call to create educational settings that are built around practices drawn from the activity of real readers, mathematicians, scientists, city planners, and so on. Orthopedic Management II seems to be such a setting: Students are learning the very procedures and routines they will use as physical therapists, and they do so in situations that, in some ways, offer a one-to-one correspondence to actual practice. Yet it is worth considering just how much instructional intervention is involved in Ortho II — just as there is, if thought about from the perspective of a teacher, in many of the successful instructional programs that have been developed out of the situated learning perspective. To be sure, the situated learning literature notes an instructional sequence to authentic learning — whereby, as Brown, Collins, and Duguid nicely put it, there is "modeling, coaching, and fading" (1988:25) — but I am talking about much more instructional artifice than that. In the activity we have witnessed, tasks are frequently not presented in authentic wholeness but broken down and analyzed (e.g., the parts of the hand used in palpation, the steps in the palpation process); students are guided physically — held, positioned — repeatedly over time until some level of competence is attained; students are encouraged to articulate what they are doing and why and what they feel as others work on them (think of how odd this would be in most real-world settings); students appropriate mediating devices (like the movement diagrams) to assist them in acquiring techniques and concepts, devices they will not use (at least as actual graphics) as professional therapists; and so on. All this, in some ways, makes the activities the students engage in different from — though still related to — those found in authentic practice. There is a great deal of strategic instructional alteration and mediation of tasks in Ortho II; if this were not the case, the practices of physical therapy would be overwhelming and, to a degree, be kept opaque, even secret.

Let me consider, in this regard, the notion of legitimate peripheral participation, "the process by which newcomers become part of a community of practice" (Lave and Wenger 1991:29). I will begin with an anecdote drawn from my studies of skilled work. An automotive class I observed was in some ways set up as a community of practice, with kids and the instructor hanging around cars that the students themselves, family, or friends would bring in for repair. The social structure pretty well matched the description of "legitimate peripheral participation": students who were more skillful participated more fully in tuning and repairing the cars on the floor; others hung back, observing, occasionally assisting in less demanding ways; and some, over time, moved from periphery to center. But some did not. They hung out, looked on but looked around, occasionally did a few things, marked time. It was not a case of access to participation being blocked, a possibility Lave and Wenger illustrate (1991:76–79), but of there being no systematic and explicit pedagogical mechanisms to encourage, guide, and sustain involvement. To move into authentic practice does not rule out along the way a host of traditional teacherly devices, from the pep talk, to direct instruction, to the quick quiz. In fact, for some, full participation may require it; otherwise one gets a shadow involvement never leading to true participation and competence. Lave and Wenger (1991) astutely discuss the need, in a community of practice, for artifacts and activities to be "transparent" to newcomers—that is, open to inspection; I would simply suggest that pedagogic strategies not normally found in work sites and social groups could facilitate transparency and access—and without compromising the conceptual power of practice theory.

To be sure, there is within the sociocultural and situated learning literature discussion of tutor or teacher guidance and assistance (e.g., Griffin and Cole 1984; Rogoff 1995; Stone and Gutierrez 1998). How could work emerging from a Vygotskian tradition not honor the role of the more knowledgeable other? But something happens rhetorically in some of this literature that has a narrowing effect on our understanding of teaching and learning. There is a sometimes implied, sometimes explicit critique of mass education and any procedures commonly associated with it—for example, lecturing, testing, direct instruction, structured curriculum—and, in line with a long progressive education tradition, there is a contrasting validation of social process, self-direction, exploration. God knows, the progressive critique of schooling, and its newer variations, bears much truth. But the critique tends to be quickly executed, a single-hued portrait of mainstream classrooms that has the unintended effect of stripping instruction from its setting. One of the significant contributions of sociocultural and situated approaches is that they acknowledge the role of historical and cultural forces in learning, yet they sometimes fail to consider historical, political-economic, or social-psychological contexts in which particular teaching methods have merit (cf. Cazden 1992: ch. 8; Delpit 1995; Walker 1996), thus obscuring the artfulness, strategy, and variability of what good teachers do in real-world settings (Rose 1995).

In an attempt to create a synthesis of current perspectives on learning, Greeno (1998) suggests that we incorporate into the situative perspective the behaviorist focus on the instructional steps necessary to foster skill acquisition with the cognitive focus on the informational processes involved in learning. Attempts at synthesis usually leave strong proponents of particular positions unsatisfied, but I think Greeno is on to something critical here: the necessity of specific study and articulation of the way learning transpires, the way change in performance occurs, explicitly, up close, in specific domains. For even if learning is justifiably defined as participation in authentic practice, even if it is entirely describable as a social phenomenon, we still need ways to articulate in detail the processes of such participation, what goes awry when participation does not occur or occurs in inadequate ways (cf. Erickson 1996; Gutierrez et al. 1995), how a teacher can intervene, yes, to change the social organization of the classroom, but intervene on the individual level as well—for so many variables are involved in the phenomenon of participation. It seems to me that if we are to assert the rich and nuanced character of activity and of real-world practice that belies, at every turn, attempts to easily categorize it, and if we are to honor the diversity of actors, the wide variability in the histories of participants, then how can we advocate a single conceptualization of how people become proficient? Nicole was right. Sometimes it does help to see things three different ways, and some of those ways are not, at times, given their due in the sociocultural and situated learning literature.

COMPETENCE AND IDENTITY

As can be inferred by some of the vignettes in the body of this article, most students in Orthopedic Management II were developing, to varying degrees, an embodied understanding of the concept of resistance and a concomitant facility with the manual techniques to access it. They were getting a bit more adept at articulating the tactile; were applying, elaborating, focusing, and refining their "book knowledge" about anatomy and biomechanics through practice; were beginning to grasp diagnostic patterns across regions of the body; and were beginning to know with their hands. Jody and Martina, the two students who opened this article, whom I interviewed again toward the end of Ortho II, were on the path toward competence. To borrow Lave and Wenger's (1991) metaphor, they were no longer on the periphery—they were in some ways more central to the practice of physical therapy (though still with supervision and limits, experiential and legal) as they continued to develop an expertise that complicates mind and body.

There is significant literature on expertise—most of which emerges from a cognitive psychology paradigm—and, within this, a smaller literature on medical expertise (e.g., Patel and Groen 1991) which includes a handful of studies of expertise in physical therapy (e.g., Jones et al. 1994). This literature, in various ways, addresses the skills and understandings sketched in the previous paragraph. But in thinking about the students in Ortho II, I got a sense of other things going on, rarely discussed in the cognitively oriented literature on expertise but nicely captured in work of a more situated nature. As Miller and Goodnow put it, "The concept of *practice* recognizes that the acquisition of knowledge or skill is part of the construction of an identity or a person" (1995:9, emphasis in original). As expertise develops, it brings with it a socialization into the traditions and values of a community of practice, beliefs about the self, an orientation toward the world, a sense of possibility (Lave and Wenger 1991), and a motivating desire to "pursue increasing mastery of the skills, knowledge, and emotions associated with a particular social practice" (Eisenhart 1995:4).

Jody and Martina talked about noticing—outside of school—how people move, their posture, their gait. Though pressured by the rigors of their program, they spoke with excitement about pursuing orthopedics, or pediatrics, or athletic training—things seemed "wide open." They commented admiringly on the qualities and abilities displayed by Nicole, Tim, and Sydney and by the therapist who supervised their field placement, and they tentatively, hopefully, began to think that, as Martina put it, "from more experience, from hearing more people's stories—of what has happened to them and what they're going through—and . . . from hearing from other, more experienced therapists," from all this, they could project their own future competence. There was, amid the crush and frustration of their studies, desire and a sense of the future. Jody and Martina were beginning to imagine themselves as competent practitioners.[4]

I would think, and this is speculation, that before a course like Ortho II, it would be difficult to imagine expertise vividly, in detail. Before entering the graduate program, Jody, as mentioned, volunteered for three years in a physical therapy clinic, administering ultrasound, doing occasional light massage, and the like. Reflecting back on that experience, she said,

> If I had this image [of the work], it was very rough. . . . I could maybe see the big picture, but I couldn't get very detailed about it. . . . Now, I mean, I find myself [thinking,] "Oh, that person," you know, "they walk a little more this way." . . . I start noticing more things and try to cue in and try to get myself to notice the finer points.

This is a retrospective account, of course, but if Jody's characterization is even partly accurate, it suggests an outcome of Ortho II that would be missed in most evaluations and in many studies of the development of competence. Through all the pedagogical mechanisms that we saw—from direct instruction, to the mixing of symbol systems, to cooperative practice, to a field placement—students begin to develop a proficiency that particularizes imagination, with consequences for motivation and goal setting. Jody's image of competence seems to orient her toward achievement. If we tend to segment mind from body, we also miss the possible connection between the precision of technique and the driving force of imagination, though, as Eisenhart's quotation suggests, technique, knowledge, planning and goal setting, identity, and fantasy might mutually reinforce each other as people develop skill in and understanding of a complex practice like physical therapy.

ACKNOWLEDGMENTS

I owe many thanks to the students in Orthopedic Management II, the physical therapists mentioned in the article (and Lisa Vincent from the UCLA Rehab Center, as well), Julie Martinovich and Julie Scira, and the people who gave me their time to discuss or read this material: Michelle Ballif, Lauren Benjamin, Susan Florio-Ruane, Ronald Gallimore, Kris Gutierrez, Rogers Hall, Glynda Hull, Catherine Lacey, Terry Pigott, Geoffrey Saxe, James Stigler, Mavourneen Roberts, and Stephen Witte. My gratitude goes as well to Rona Pau, who typed many drafts and revisions. This research was supported by an award from the Small Grants Program of the Spencer Foundation.

NOTES

1. I use with permission the actual names of the school and the physical therapists. However, because the students still face multiple phases of testing and accreditation, I use pseudonyms for them.

2. A full treatment of the way images and understandings of the body are involved in the learning and practice of physical therapy is beyond the scope of this article. It is worth noting, though, that the cognitive-epistemological challenges facing students in regard to conceptualizing the body are formidable. They have to modify and enhance their commonsense notions of both the body and their own bodies as they use their bodies in new ways and act on other people's bodies and learn to interpret them. In addition, the different disciplines comprising their course of study — orthopedics, neurology, and so on — each has its own traditions and conceptual frameworks for understanding the body. (One could read the history of biomedicine as a history of the varied ways the body has been understood and represented.) All this, at the least, calls for significant elaboration of students' initial conceptions of the human body — theirs and others'.

3. A wonderful guide to this thinking through is the festschrift for Sylvia Scribner edited by Martin, Nelson, and Tobach (1995).

4. One of the anonymous reviewers of this article referred me to Hazel Markus and Paula Nurius's 1986 article "Possible Selves." "Possible selves," write the authors, "represent individuals' ideas of what they might become . . . and thus provide a conceptual link between cognition and motivation" (1986:954). Markus and Nurius's treatment of the role of imagined selves in behavior is as comprehensive and elaborated as mine is thin; all I would add is that particular instructional and training experiences might contribute a consequential particularity to people's conceptions of what they might become.

REFERENCES

Bakhurst, David. *Consciousness and Revolution in Soviet Philosophy: From the Bolsheviks to Evald Ilyenkov.* Cambridge: Cambridge University Press, 1991.
Bracewell, Robert J., and Stephen P. Witte. *The Implications of Activity, Practice, and Semiotic Theory for Cognitive Constructs of Writing.* Paper presented at the American Educational Research Association Conference, March, 1997. Chicago.
Brown, John Seely, Allan Collins, and Paul Duguid. *Situated Cognition and the Culture of Learning.* Report no. IRL 88-0008. Palo Alto, CA: Institute for Research on Learning, 1988.
Cazden, Courtney B. *Whole Language Plus: Essays on Literacy in the United States and New Zealand.* New York: Teachers College Press, 1992.
Cobb, Paul, and Erna Yackel. "*Constructivist, Emergent, and Sociocultural Perspectives in the Context of Developmental Research.*" *Educational Psychologist* 31(3–4) (1996):175–190.
Cole, Michael. *Cultural Psychology: A Once and Future Discipline.* Cambridge, MA: Harvard University Press, 1996.
Delpit, Lisa. *Other People's Children: Cultural Conflicts in the Classroom.* New York: New Press, 1995.
Dutton, Rebecca. *Clinical Reasoning in Physical Disabilities.* Baltimore: Williams and Wilkins, 1995.
Eisenhart, Margaret. "The Fax, the Jazz Player, and the Self-Story Teller: How *Do* People Organize Culture?" *Anthropology and Education Quarterly* 26 (1995):3–26.
Engeström, Yrjö. "Developmental Studies of Work as a Testbench of Activity Theory: The Case of Primary Care Medical Practice." In *Understanding Practice: Perspectives on Activity and Context.* Seth Chaiklin and Jean Lave, eds. Pp. 64–103. Cambridge: Cambridge University Press, 1993.
Erickson, Frederick. "Going for the Zone: The Social and Cognitive Ecology of Teacher-Student Interaction in Classroom Conversations." In *Discourse, Learning, and Schooling.* Deborah Hicks, ed. Pp. 29–62. Cambridge: Cambridge University Press, 1996.

Greeno, James G. "The Situativity of Knowing, Learning, and Research." *American Psychologist* 53(1)(1998):5–26.

Griffin, Peg, and Michael Cole. "Current Activity for the Future: The Zo-ped." In *Children's Learning in the Zone of Proximal Development*. Barbara Rogoff and James V. Wertsch, eds. Pp. 45–63. San Francisco: Jossey-Bass, 1984.

Gutierrez, Kris, Betty Rymes, and Joanne Larson. "Script, Counterscript, and Underlife in the Classroom: James Brown versus *Brown v. Board of Education*." *Harvard Educational Review* 65(3)(1995):445–471.

Hall, Rogers. *Making Mathematics on Paper: Constructing Representations of Stories about Related Linear Functions*. Ph.D. dissertation, Department of Information and Computer Science, University of California at Irvine, 1990.

Harper, Douglas. *Working Knowledge: Skill and Community in a Small Shop*. Chicago: University of Chicago Press, 1987.

Hull, Glynda, and Mike Rose. "Rethinking Remediation: Toward a Social-Cognitive Understanding of Problematic Reading and Writing." *Written Communication* 6(2)(1989):139–154.

Hull, Glynda, Mike Rose, Kay Losey Fraser, and Marisa Castellano. "Remediation as Social Construct: Perspectives from an Analysis of Classroom Discourse." *College Composition and Communication* 42(3)(1991):299–329.

Hutchins, Edwin. "Mediation and Automatization." *Quarterly Newsletter of the Laboratory of Comparative Human Cognition* 8(3)(1986):46–58.

Jones, Mark A. "Clinical Reasoning in Manual Therapy." *Physical Therapy* 72(12) (1992):875–884.

Jones, Mark A., Nicole Christensen, and Judi Carr. "Clinical Reasoning in Orthopedic Manual Therapy." In *Physical Therapy of the Cervical and Thoracic Spine* (2nd edition). Ruth Grant, ed. Pp. 89–108. New York: Churchill Livingstone, 1994.

Keller, Charles M., and Janet Dixon Keller. *Cognition and Tool Use: The Blacksmith at Work*. Cambridge: Cambridge University Press, 1996.

Lave, Jean. "Teaching, as Learning, in Practice." *Mind, Culture, and Activity* 3(3)(1996):149–164.

Lave, Jean, and Etienne Wenger. *Situated Learning: Legitimate Peripheral Participation*. Cambridge: Cambridge University Press, 1991.

Maitland, Geoffrey D. *Vertebral Manipulation* (5th edition). Oxford: Butterworth-Heinemann, 1997 [1964].

Markus, Hazel, and Paula Nurius. "Possible Selves." *American Psychologist* 41(9)(1986):954–969.

Martin, Laura M. W., Katherine Nelson, and Ethel Tobach, eds. *Sociocultural Psychology: Theory and Practice of Doing and Knowing*. Cambridge: Cambridge University Press, 1995.

Miller, Peggy J., and Jacqueline J. Goodnow. "Cultural Practices: Toward an Integration of Culture and Development." In *Cultural Practices as Contexts for Development*. Jacqueline J. Goodnow, Peggy J. Miller, and Frank Kessel, eds. Pp. 5–16. San Francisco: Jossey-Bass, 1995.

Patel, Vimla L., and Guy J. Groen. "The General and Specific Nature of Medical Expertise: A Critical Look." In *Toward a General Theory of Expertise: Prospects and Limits*. K. Anders Ericsson and Jacqui Smith, eds. Pp. 93–125. Cambridge: Cambridge University Press, 1991.

Rogoff, Barbara. "Observing Sociocultural Activity on Three Planes: Participatory Appropriation, Guided Participation, and Apprenticeship." In *Sociocultural Studies of Mind*. James V. Wertsch, Pablo del Rio, and Amelia Alvarez, eds. Pp. 139–164. Cambridge: Cambridge University Press, 1995.

Rose, Mike. *Possible Lives: The Promise of Public Education in America*. Boston: Houghton Mifflin, 1995.

Roth, Wolff-Michael, and Michelle K. McGinn. "Inscriptions: Toward a Theory of Representing as Social Practice." *Review of Educational Research* 68(1)(1998):35–59.

Scribner, Sylvia. "Thinking in Action: Some Characteristics of Practical Thought." In *Practical Intelligence: Nature and Origins of Competence in the Everyday World*. Robert J. Sternberg and Richard K. Wagner, eds. Pp. 13–30. Cambridge: Cambridge University Press, 1986.

Stone, Linda D., and Kris D. Gutierrez. *Problem Finding as Distributed Intelligence: The Role of Changing Participation in Mathematical Problem-Solving Activities in an After-School Learning Community*. Unpublished MS, University of California at Los Angeles, 1998.

Walker, Vanessa Siddle. *Their Highest Potential: An African American School Community in the Segregated South*. Chapel Hill: University of North Carolina Press, 1996.

Wertsch, James V. "The Need for Action in Sociocultural Research." In *Sociocultural Studies of Mind*. James V. Wertsch, Pablo del Rio, and Amelia Alvarez, eds. Pp. 56–74. Cambridge: Cambridge University Press, 1995.

18 *The Working Life of a Waitress*
2001

About three years into the project, I got terribly stuck. I had written the article on physical therapy and two shorter pieces for a more general education audience that drew on carpentry and plumbing. But I was having an awful time getting the focus of the book right, or, more accurately, figuring out how to sustain that focus through the different occupations I wanted to study.

And a further problem was developing with my use of the details of the work itself. Though detail was essential, how could I present it in a way that would not bog down the narrative, that would be engaging to a general audience? For a while I had been entertaining the possibility of weaving some family material into the writing, thinking, as I put it to a friend, that it might provide an "emotional engine" for the book, give it a heartbeat. But some other early readers discouraged this move, worrying that it would overly complicate the narrative.

With a lot of uncertainty, I started in on an article about my mother's work, waitressing, trying to interweave her story with scholarly analysis, not unlike in *Lives on the Boundary*. But this seemed harder, involved bigger stakes somehow. Could I do it in a way that would pass disciplinary muster? Would someone schooled in cognitive science buy it? I got myself pretty knotted up.

Then an odd thing happened. During a particularly difficult week, on a rainy day near Christmas, some friends called in midafternoon and dragged me off to see the movie *Magnolia*. It's a wonderful mess of a film, throwing in everything, even a biblical shower of frogs. The movie had nothing at all to do with what I was writing about, but its sheer inventiveness, its outrageous combinations, had a hugely freeing effect on me. A letting go or giving over. Why not write a heavily cited, footnoted, discipline-embedded account of the working life of a waitress? A cognitive biography and the use of biography to enhance a scholarly literature. This could be another test of the claims I was trying to make and a tribute, albeit an unusual one, to my mother.

This article, rewritten a bit (some of the cognitive diction smoothed out and citations removed), would become the first chapter of *The Mind at Work*.

The reader interested in the stylistic effect of this shift in audience can compare the present article with the version in the book.

One last thing to note on origins before I add a few words about the article itself. There is an interesting literature both in psychology and philosophy on the intricate interplay between cognition and emotion. (See, for a classic example, Israel Scheffler's "In Praise of the Cognitive Emotions." In a much more modest way, and with a focus on problems with composing, I discuss the issue in "Complexity, Rigor, Evolving Method, and the Puzzle of Writer's Block," p. 56.) Such interplay between feeling, conceptualizing, and analyzing is evident in both the desire to "go small" in the focus of this new project—discussed in the introduction to this part—and in the *Magnolia* incident. I would not want the reader to think that a focus on cognition necessarily means a dismissal of affect. The upcoming article pays significant attention to emotion, both in the dynamics of restaurant life and in my mother's identification with her work.

The writing of "The Working Life of a Waitress" turned out to be pivotal in the framing and continued composition of *The Mind at Work*. I have a lot of feeling for it for that reason and, of course, because it—and the whole book, really—became a testimonial to my mother.

I am especially pleased with two sections of the article.

In "On Method" I had to justify not only the combining of scholarly and personal material but also the integration of disparate research traditions. Although mixed-methods inquiry is gaining popularity in educational research, such mixing can give rise to a host of both technical and philosophical problems. I'll leave it to the reader to decide how well I handle these problems, but I feel good about my attempt to lay my cards on the table and reason through the potential difficulties in my approach.

I am also proud of the final section, "A Working Life." So many accounts of working-class life, accounts from the right or the left, tend toward the one-dimensional. I try to complicate such easy representation:

> But one of the things this project has made clear to me is how difficult it is, given our standard "story lines" for work and the constraints of our disciplinary lenses, to create a multidimensional representation of work and the complex meaning it has in the lives of people who do it every day. Let me try to tease out the layers of significance restaurant work had for my mother. They are interrelated, at times contradictory, of a piece in her experience of waitressing.

INTRODUCTION: ROSE EMILY ROSE

For a good part of her working life, my mother, like many women of her generation, waitressed in coffee shops and family-style restaurants; counters and tables; fast-paced, inexpensive food; quick turnaround; tips counted out in nickels, dimes, and quarters. My father and I would visit her at work, finding space at the counter by the cash register, or, more often, at a back booth where the waitresses ate. We would pass the time with her once the lunch or dinner rush had faded.

The hours stretched out, and since the back booth was usually near the kitchen or dishwashers, there would be the thick smell of the grill or of stale food and cigarettes, scraped and dumped. These odors hung in my mother's uniform and hair. From my own slow time, I would observe the flow of activity on the main floor, waitresses weaving in and out, warning "behind you" in a voice both impassive and urgent. I enjoyed watching things from the inside—to this day I love being in a restaurant or bar at opening or closing time—and I got a big kick out of the lingo. Tables were labeled by the number of chairs—and, thus, customers—around them: *deuces, four-tops, six-tops.* Areas of the restaurant had names: the *racetrack* was the speedy front section. Orders were abbreviated for the cook: *fry four on two,* my mother would call out as she clipped a check onto that little rotating wheel. To speak this language gave you a certain authority, signaled "know-how."

Although I am more recently coming to understand and appreciate just how much is involved in doing this work well,[1] as a youngster I certainly got a sense through my mother of its difficulty. Not at all a big woman, she could, walking full-tilt, balance seven plates on her right arm while carrying two cups of coffee in her left hand. She always seemed to know where things went: who ordered the hamburger, the fried shrimp, the steak; who wanted the cola; who requested the mayonnaise on the side. Even when she, just for a second, would flop down in the booth alongside my father—"all in," as she would say—she seemed to maintain awareness of who was finishing a meal, of who needed more coffee, of another waitress horning in on her customers. And she could be nice to mean people, cooling them down, taking guff from the cook for a returned order ("he gives you lip . . . [so] you catch hell at both ends"), keep moving and smiling, working the complaint, winning the customer over. She would comment on this especially, in quick, whispered bursts by our side.

Many years later—I am now middle-aged, and my mother, in her mid-80s, has not been able to work for a long time—I find myself reflecting with a more analytical frame of mind on those days at Norm's Restaurant or Coffee Dan's, directed by a research project of mine on the cognition involved in various kinds of work, guided by a series of interviews with my mother about the particulars of her work as a waitress.[2] Other phases of this project

From *Mind, Culture, and Activity* 8.1(2001): 3–27.

on other kinds of work (e.g., physical therapy, plumbing) have yielded fairly traditional articles and essays (Rose, 1999a; 1999b; 2000), but something different has emerged here: a desire to understand and honor a certain kind of work and its meaning for my mother through an unorthodox but, I hope, generative blending of reminiscence; life history; cognitive science; activity theory; and the sociology of work, emotion, and gender. This article reflects the blending of analysis and reflection, of genre, evidence, and mode of inquiry.

An interview with my mother, for example, about the means she used to remember all those orders—who got the hamburger and who got the shrimp—is read in terms of the cognitive science literature on expert memory and the handful of studies within that literature on the memory skill of waiters and waitresses. What I think such a reading makes possible is a heightened comprehension and appreciation of the many tasks of everyday life and, as byproduct, a testing and elaborating of disciplinary knowledge—a grounding of it in the commonplace. My mother's range of memory devices and her complex motives for developing them provide, I think, additional ways to consider that literature on expert memory. And that literature helps me, helps us, appreciate the skills of that woman laying every one of those entrees before just the right person.

This article, as well, emerges from and responds to the varied calls of so many working-class academics to devise ways to integrate the dimensions of their own sometimes bifurcated lives (Dews & Law, 1995; Ryan & Sackrey, 1984; Tokarczyk & Fay, 1993). I hope to honor both my mother's working life and the research traditions I've learned that bear on her life, using each to illuminate and investigate the other. Said another way, the article provides the occasion for me to bring together some of the things I've come to know about work and the disparate ways I've come to know them.

WORK HISTORY

Let me begin with a brief history of my mother's working life—a life initially defined by the immigrant experience, poverty, and The Great Depression. This history situates economically and emotionally the waitressing skills I analyze in this article.

Rose Emily Rose (née Meraglio) came to the United States from Southern Italy as a little girl in the early 1920s, settled with her family in Altoona, Pennsylvania where her father worked as a laborer for the Pennsylvania Railroad (and would eventually sustain a severely disabling accident), and her mother raised seven children, took in boarders, made illegal wine and beer, and did whatever else she could to enable the family to survive. Rose was taken out of school at the seventh grade to help raise her three younger brothers and to assist with the tending of the boarders: cooking, cleaning, laundering. She did this work well into her teens, eventually taking a job in a garment factory and, briefly, in a local Italian restaurant, a job that wouldn't last, for "not a soul came in there." It's important to note that this early work at home and beyond was surrounded by profound economic need; a sense of financial vulnerability would remain with my mother for the rest of her life.

The next phase of my mother's economic history came with her marriage to my father, Tommy Rose: The two opened and ran an Italian restaurant in downtown Altoona, open 24 hours a day to cater to the "round-the-clock" schedule of the Pennsylvania Railroad workers, the core of Altoona's economy. Self-described as a "raggedy" and "shy" girl, Rose developed quickly from private household labors and routinized factory work to a young woman in a public role, laden with new, often unpredictable, responsibilities: from cooking, hiring help, and ordering supplies to hostessing, waiting on and clearing tables, and tending the register. It was not uncommon for her to work 15 to 17 hours a day, for she had to remedy whatever mishaps arose. Here's a not atypical entry in a daily journal she kept during those years:

> Mrs. Benner walked out on account of Mrs. Kauffman. So here I am alone cooking. June didn't show up either. . . . I'm so tired.

But along with the accounts of exhaustion and anxiety, there is also testament to the fulfillment this new life brought:

> On this day, I'm two years in business. I love it.

For all its tribulations, the restaurant contrasted with the lonely oppressiveness of her earlier labors, provided the conditions to gain knowledge about the restaurant business through immersion in it, and enabled my mother to learn how to "be with the public."

Although financially uneven, the restaurant did well enough through the war and just after. But as the Pennsylvania Railroad — along with the railroad industry generally — began its first stage of decline, closing shops, laying people off (my mother's brothers among them), the Rose Restaurant failed, ending in bankruptcy. This was 1951. Over the next year, my parents would move to Los Angeles in search of opportunity and a warmer climate for my father, whose health was failing. They had little money and no connections whatsoever; friends and family were 2500 miles away, a lament I often heard. My father couldn't work. I was seven. This begins the phase of my mother's economic life that is the focus of this article: She went in search of the kind of work her limited formal education and her experience with the restaurant made possible, work she would continue until 1979, when illness forced her retirement at 64.

At first she waitressed in a series of coffee shops in downtown Los Angeles, the largest stretch at Coffee Dan's on heavily-trafficked Broadway. Then she moved to Norm's, a "family-style" chain, working for nearly a decade at the shop on Sunset and Vermont, by major medical facilities (Kaiser, Hollywood Presbyterian) and corporate offices, like that for Prudential; then, for her last 10 years, at the Norm's in Torrance, amid a more lower-middle class, local merchant, and retirement clientele. During her time at Coffee Dan's and Norm's Sunset, her husband would slip into grave illness and, for the last years of his life, be bedridden. I proceeded through elementary and high school. Mustering what immediate help she could, she struggled to balance work, caretaking, and childrearing. Two things should be noted here. Although my mother learned a great deal about the restaurant business in Altoona, it was in the coffee shops and chain restaurants of Los Angeles where she, by her own account, fully developed the particular physical and cognitive skills that I'll be exploring here. The second, and obvious, thing to say is that this period, from approximately 1952 to the early 1960s, was another period of severe hardship. As my mother put it simply: "Dad was ill, and you were little . . . I *had* to get work."

My father died in 1961. Eventually my mother would meet and marry a man who was a truck driver with the city, a job with stable wages and benefits. They bought a house in Torrance—a nicer house and safer area—and she began her final 10 years of waitressing at the Norm's nearby. This was a decade of economically better times. Even after she had to quit waitressing, my stepfather's employment carried them through comfortably. But my mother's inactivity during these early years of her retirement brings to the fore the centrality of physical work to her sense of who she is. For all the strain—at times to near-exhaustion—of waitressing, the work provided her with a way to feel useful, to engage her mind, and to be in the flow of things. When in the mid-1980s a neighbor got her a job as a noon aide at a local elementary school, she was revitalized. Her primary responsibility was to seat children for lunch and assist in clearing their tables. The job provided a few hours of minimum wage and, of course, no tips—it was barely a postscript to her economic life—but it held great value for her because of its mix of utility and nurturance. And it thrust her back into life's hustle. It also called on some of her waitressing skills. Although work for my mother was always driven by economic need, it was also driven by a complex of other needs: cognitive, social, existential. These needs will be evident in the discussion that follows, particularly in the final section of the article.

ON METHOD

Let me now be specific about the sources of information I used in writing this article and then say a bit more about the elements of its conceptual framework.

I conducted (and tape-recorded) three interviews with my mother during September, 1997 and March, 1998, focusing on her history in the restaurant business and, more particularly, on her work as a waitress at Coffee Dan's and Norm's. A number of my questions dealt with the physical layout of the restaurants, taking and placing orders, managing the flow of work, relations with customers and other waitresses, and tipping. During these interviews and after, I also interviewed six waitresses and two bartenders,[3] drawing from the same list of questions. (In several instances, I conducted the interviews in restaurants where the interviewees could observe with me and comment on the performance of other waitresses and bartenders.) As well, I read the small body of cognitive science research on the memory skill of waitresses, waiters, and bartenders (e.g., Beach, 1993; Ericsson & Polson, 1988; J. Stevens, 1993) and the few ethnographic studies I could find on the kind of waitressing my mother did (e.g., Paules, 1991). I would compare these interview and research findings with my mother's account, looking for points of consonance or difference. Often, there was agreement—e.g., both the other waitresses and the research literature along with my mother report the use of visual-spatial memory strategies to store and recall information about customers and orders. Points of difference led to follow-up questions for my mother and, when appropriate, a return to my other participants. In addition to conducting the interviews, I kept a record (in a notebook) of my mother's spontaneous comments about waitressing and about work in general. The notebook extends from September, 1997 to the present. From a previous project,[4] I have interviews with my mother and, individually, with four of her siblings about growing up in Altoona, about her early life there extending through the closing of Rose Restaurant in 1951. As well, my mother gave me the daily journal she kept from the early to mid-1940s, a "baby book" she started for me, and several boxes of photographs which provide not only a pictorial record of the times, but which I also used as prompts during our interviews. These materials are supplemented with local histories from the Altoona library on the city during the period of my mother's residence (e.g., Wolf, 1945)—roughly from the early 1920s to the early 1950s—and broader social histories on immigration and rust-belt economics (e.g., Bodnar, Simon, & Weber, 1983; LaSorte, 1985). In addition, I read about the growth and practice of waitressing in the 20th century (e.g., Cobble, 1991; Salisch & Palmer, 1932).

Finally, there are my own recollections of the restaurants my mother worked in from the 1950s through the late-1970s and my experience of her through those years: her demeanor at work and afterward at home; her commentary on that work; her accounts of her tips (spread out on a towel on the bed), her customers, and the other waitresses I met through her. The closeness of this experience contributes, I believe, to the felt sense I have of my mother's work and the many dimensions of meaning it had for her.

To provide analytical tools and a systematic vocabulary with which to consider these sources of information, I rely on the following research traditions and methods.

To consider my mother's memory skill, I rely on the cognitive science literature on memory, especially research on what has come to be called skilled memory (Chase & Ericsson, 1981). I also select from the cognitive science literature on attention (e.g., LaBerge, 1995), motor expertise (e.g., Starkes & Allard, 1993), and expertise in "real-world" physical task environments (e.g., Shalin, Geddes, Bertram, Szczepkowski, & DuBois, 1997) to discuss my mother's ability to attend to and navigate a hurried field of activity and make on-the-spot decisions about sequencing and coordinating her job's many emerging demands. Of particular help here—and with the analysis of memory also—is the newer literature on situated cognition, cognition within natural contexts, "environments that structure, direct, and support cognitive processes"

(Greeno, 1998; Seifert, 1999, p. 767). As well, I draw on the somewhat related conceptual frameworks of practice theory and activity theory (e.g., Cole, 1996; Engeström, 1993; Lave & Wenger, 1991), theories that elaborate the intricate relation between thought, behavior, and cultural traditions and practices—and that have generated research on the workplace, although, to my knowledge, not on work like waitressing.

As the sketch of her working life makes clear, my mother's skill at remembering orders, negotiating the flow of work, and so on was webbed in experience, values, motives, and emotion, part of a complex worldview and life history, which itself was embedded in broader early and mid-20th-century contexts. As I noted, social and economic history has helped me understand the era in which my mother came of age and conducted her working life, and understand the forces that shaped her life. And those orientations to social research that attempt to access individual lived experience (e.g., Bertaux, 1981; Lummis, 1987; Van Manen, 1990) provide a justification and method—primarily the life story interview—for eliciting people's sense of their own lives: in this case my mother's perception of the time she lived in, why she did the work she did, and how she did it.

Finally, I draw on a cluster of social psychological research on restaurant tipping (e.g., Butler & Snizek, 1976; Lynn & Grassman, 1990) and sociological research on emotion and the role of gender in the workplace (e.g., Hall, 1993; Leidner, 1991), particularly the notion of "emotional labor" (e.g., Hochschild, 1983; Tolich, 1993; Wharton, 1993), that is, the commercial use of feeling, particularly in service industries—the calling forth or suppressing of emotion as part of one's work. As my mother waited on tables, there was a fluid integration of cognition and social display, and this social-psychological and sociological literature will help me consider that display.

Let me close this section with an additional comment on method.

This article is primarily synthetic and interpretive. As mentioned earlier, it attempts a blending of research traditions not typically brought together to enable a somewhat different kind of analysis, analysis that integrates the disciplinary and the commonplace and the cognitive and the social. And, for the writer, it becomes both an act of the intellect and an expression of feeling.

In attempting such integration, I run several risks. First, there are conceptual tensions among some of the foregoing research traditions. The cognitive research on memory, for example, assumes internal mental processes—such as mental imagery—while many writers on practice theory and activity theory seek to challenge the notion of the individual information-processing self. (They would probably question the sense of subjectivity that emerges in life history research, as well.) Helpful here has been Greeno's (1998) attempt to create a synthetic situated cognition framework that subsumes cognitive and behaviorist analyses: "We propose that the situative perspective provides functional analyses of *intact activity systems* and that cognitive and behaviorist analyses characterize mechanisms that support the achievement of these functions" (p. 5). Such integrative attempts will leave some readers unsatisfied, but given the partial nature of the research on service work such as waitressing, any single approach will be inadequate to tease out the layers of complexity of that work. Yet bringing disparate approaches together may well result in the kinds of tensions just mentioned. I have tried to make these tensions explicit, and my hope is that they can be generative. Discussions of memory in cognitive science, for example, tend to be devoid of purpose and motive,[5] issues that activity theory or life history research can illuminate. Activity theory, at times, can be pretty abstract about the role of individual agency (see Engeström & Middleton, 1996; Wertsch, Tulviste, & Hagstrom, 1993) and could better conceptualize the role of feeling and emotion in activity systems. And life history research tends to underarticulate, to not detail, the role of cognitive processes in lived experience.[6]

Second, I risk violating the norms of evidence and method of particular research traditions. For example, the findings on memory in cognitive science usually issue from controlled laboratory experiments. (Though increasingly there are more descriptive attempts to render cognition in natural settings.) In the case of my mother, I rely primarily on her recollection of the memory strategies she used many years before. Although I do believe that the consonance between her recollection and the research on memory provides some support for the accuracy of her recall, I surely do not claim that interview data of this kind meet the same validity criteria as experimental findings — yet they possess validity of a different kind, as I hope becomes clear as we move through the article. I also think there can be and ought to be ways to bring data like these together analytically — the laboratory finding on memory and a person's account of memory strategies used over a long period of actual practice. To put this differently, if the research findings on memory reflect real, not artifactual, processes, then they should have value in explicating and understanding phenomena beyond the laboratory. If, to borrow Sandra Harding's (1996) phrase, "science is good to think with"[7] (p. 16), then these constructs from psychological science should be of use in helping us unpack and appreciate everyday behavior, in this case, the skill of a common working life.

Let me now consider in more detail the nature of the environments in which Rose Emily Rose demonstrated her skill.

The Restaurant

In some ways, a restaurant is a structured and predictable environment.[8] The physical layout guides movement and behavior, and the various conventions associated with dining out are well known, to customer and waitress alike. But when analyzed in terms of the interrelated physical and cognitive demands of the work itself, the environment, particularly at peak hours, becomes more complex, with a variable and ill-structured quality (see Engeström's, 1993, discussion of the inevitable tensions among the elements of workplace activity systems).

Consider the restaurant in terms of multiple streams of time and motion. Customers enter with temporal expectations: They will be seated without much delay and, once seated, a series of events will unfold along a familiar timeline, from ordering through salad, entrée, dessert, delivery of the check. Their satisfaction—physical and symbolic—is affected by the manner in which these expectations are met. But, of course, customers are entering the restaurant at different times, each with his or her own schedule, so tables (or places at the counter) proceed through meals at a different pace. This staggering of customers facilitates the flow of trade, but also increases the cognitive demands on the waitress: what she must attend to, keep in mind, prioritize, etc. This situation intensifies during peak hours, for the number of customers expected can be estimated, but not known—family-style restaurants do not take reservations—and if the numbers swell beyond capacity or an employee calls in sick, is late or quits, then, as the younger waitresses I interviewed vividly put it, you're "slammed," abruptly pushed to the limits of physical and mental performance.

Another timetable kicks in as soon as an order is placed with the cook. Different items have different prep times, and once the item is prepared, there is a limited amount of time—quite restricted for hot items—during which it can be served. As well, the serving area needs to be cleared quickly so that the cook can deliver further items. The waitress, therefore, is aware of the kitchen as she moves among her customers.

Finally, both the waitress and the management work by the clock. Profit is related to time; the quicker the turnover, the more revenue for the company, and the greater the number of tips. There can be exceptions to this principle for the waitress (but not the management); for example, the regulars who may hold a table or stool longer but tip more. Still, generally, the waitress—like her manager—is ever mindful of clearing a plate, closing out a tab, moving the process along.

Imagine these streams of time and motion as co-occurring and related but not synchronous. Any given customer may hem and haw over an order, or want a refill while the waitress is occupied, or send an item back. The cook may deliver a waitress's hot dish while she is in the middle of taking an order and is being summoned by two other customers. Tables may be full with variously contented customers while the manager feels the press of new customers gathering inside the door.

One more observation about this environment. No matter how efficiently designed the physical layout of the restaurant—for example, coffee pots, water, soft drinks, cups, glasses, and ice are all located in the same area—the waitress's motion will be punctuated by the continual but irregular demands made of her. For example, all requests for coffee do not come at the same time or in regular intervals. So one request comes during an order, and another as she's rushing back to get extra mayonnaise, and another as she's clearing a table. The waitress must learn how to move efficiently through a vibrant environment that, for all its structural regularities, is dynamically irregular. A basic goal, then, is to manage irregularity and create an economy of movement. She does this through effective use of body and mind. The work calls for strength and stamina, for memory capacity and strategy, for heightened attention, both to overall configuration and specific areas and items, for the ability to take stock, prioritize tasks, cluster them, and make decisions on the fly.

USING THE BODY

What does a waitress need to know how to do with her body? She must be able to balance and carry multiple items, using the hand, forearm, and bicep, creating stability by locking arms to torso and positioning the back. Then she moves, fast, in bursts, navigating tables, customers, other help. And since this occurs in a public space, it must be done with a certain poise. As waitress and writer Lin Rolens nicely puts it: "You learn a walk that gets you places quickly without looking like you are running. . . . This requires developing a walk that is all business from the waist down, but looks fairly relaxed from the waist up" (Elder & Rolens, 1985, pp. 19–20). With time and practice, all this becomes routine, automatic. But early in a career, the waitress will undoubtedly be conscious of various aspects of this physical performance, have to think about it, monitor herself.

My mother gets up slowly from the kitchen table where we're conducting an interview and walks over to the sink where plates are drying in a rack. She demonstrates. She turns her right hand palm up, creating a wider surface on her forearm, and begins placing plates, large and small, from biceps to fingertips, staggering, layering them so that the bottom of one plate rests on the edge of another. "You don't dare let a plate touch the food," she explains, "and it's got to be balanced, steady." Then with her left hand, she lays out two coffee cups and two saucers. She kind of pinches the saucers between her fingers and slips her index finger through the handles of the two cups. "The coffee splashes from one side to another if you're not careful. It takes practice. You just can't do it all at one time."

I ask her, then, how she learned to do it. Beginning with her own restaurant, "You watch the other waitresses, what they do." She was "cautious" at first, starting with two plates, being deliberate. Then she began adding plates, driven by the demands of the faster pace of the restaurants in Los Angeles. "Norm's was much busier. So you had to stack as many plates as you possibly could." And, with continued practice in these busy settings, you get to where "You don't even have to think about it." In a manner described in the literature on cognition and motor skill (e.g., Starkes & Allard, 1993), my mother mixed observation and practice, got some pointers from coworkers, tricks of the trade, monitored her performance, and developed competence. With mastery, her mind was cleared for other tasks.

SKILLED MEMORY

To be a good waitress, my mother says emphatically, "You have to have one hell of a good memory." Her observation is supported by a small body of laboratory and naturalistic research, and one of the things that research demonstrates is that the competent waiter and waitress have techniques that enable them to override the normal limits on human "short-term" or "working" memory. Through working memory we are able to briefly store and perform a variety of cognitive operations on both immediate sensory information and on material drawn from more durable and extensive long-term memory. Thus we are able to quickly keep track of things, to make decisions and solve problems on the fly, to make our way through the world emerging before us (Baddeley, 1986; Jonides, 1995). This conceptualization, as we see, seems nicely suited to a consideration of the cognition involved in waitressing.

Research on expert or exceptional memory—for example, of the master chess player or the mnemonist—has led to an understanding of the ways we can bypass the familiar limits on working memory, and this understanding has led some to posit the notion of "skilled memory" (Chase & Ericsson, 1981). Mnemonists use a range of techniques to give structure to an overwhelming number of items, thus reducing the load on memory. And experts in particular domains are able to draw quickly on rich stores of knowledge—a carpenter about tool use, wood, and structure, an internist about human physiology and disease—to make sense of and process new information related to their expertise.

Let me elaborate on this notion of skilled memory and relate it to my mother's work by summarizing the findings of three pertinent studies in the cognitive literature: the memory skill of a head waiter (Ericsson & Polson, 1988), of waitresses at a lunch counter (J. Stevens, 1993), and of cocktail waitresses (Bennett, 1983). Although there is variation in the results, they point to four commonalities:

1. The waiter and waitress know things about food and drink—ingredients, appearance, typical combinations—and this knowledge from long-term memory plays continually into their ability to remember orders.

2. They have developed various visual, spatial, and/or linguistic mnemonic techniques to aid memory: abbreviating items, grouping items in categories, repeating orders, utilizing customer appearance and location.

3. The routines and physical layout of the restaurant or bar contribute to remembering orders.

4. Although not strictly a characteristic of memory—as defined and studied in the psychologist's laboratory—the waiter's and waitress's memory is profoundly goal-directed: to make their work efficient and to enhance their tips.

My mother's interview exhibits each of these.

As she stood before a table, taking orders, sometimes repeating them back while writing them out, sometimes not, making small talk, my mother would "more or less make a picture in [her] mind" of the person giving her the order, what that person ordered, and where around a table (or at a counter) he or she was located. Forming mental images is a mnemonic device that goes back to the ancients (Yates, 1966), and, as we saw, is reported in the cognitive research on waiters and waitresses. Although, of course, there was undoubtedly variation in the way my mother did this, and in the different representations she formed on any given day, her picture could include dress and physical appearance: items of clothing—a red blouse, a splashy tie—and physical features like a birthmark or an unusually shaped nose. As well, there are general characteristics, broad social markers: gender, race, age, body type and weight. (My mother laughingly notes, "of course, a child's plate, you can always tell" where that will go.) My mother's beliefs and biases about these markers could play into the construction of the picture, a point I return to momentarily.

The layout of the tables (or the stools at the counter) and people's location at them enabled my mother to store and recall information about orders in a number of ways. A customer's specific position (by the window or closest to her) mattered, especially if it were somehow unusual—for example, a woman pulls a fifth chair to the edge of a four-top. Relative location also figures in, aided by other characteristics of the person or the order. My mother and I are sitting at the kitchen table, which she uses to illustrate: "The one sitting at the chair, she ordered this, *this* is what she ordered, and the next person over (my mother points to the next chair clockwise), that's [another] lady, and *that's* what she wants." Notice that my mother seems to perform some basic operations on the spatial information, something noted in the studies of waiters and waitresses. She mentions deviation, sequence, similarity—and another time-honored mnemonic device, contrast. Again, my mother points to an imaginary customer at our table: "I remember, he ordered the hamburger (she moves her gaze to the next chair), but she didn't want a hamburger, she wanted something else." So specific location as well as overall configuration matters—and other kinds of knowledge and social patterns play in.

Sometimes, it's the social expectation itself that is salient and an aid to memory. For example, cocktail waitresses make distinctions between the drinks men and women typically order (Bennett, 1983), and other waitresses I interviewed spoke of these gender distinctions as well. My mother describes a couple ordering. The man orders a T-bone steak, and the woman "would order something smaller, so naturally you're gonna remember that." And if an order violates expectation—the woman orders the steak, the man the chef's salad—that will stand out, the memorable deviation.

Some items and the routines associated with them enable the use of external memory aids. My mother describes a six-top at breakfast with orders of ham and eggs, steak and eggs, and hotcakes. As soon as she takes the order she, as a part of her route to the kitchen and back to other tables, sets a little container of syrup in front of the customer who ordered hotcakes. The aid is particularly helpful in a situation like this because "a six-top is especially hard, and sometimes you have to ask the customers who gets what." The container of syrup lightens the load by one item.

Finally, and this is not reported in the research literature, a customer's attitude, the way he or she interacts with my mother, contributes to her recall of the order. My mother comments on "how [a customer] would say something—you remember this dish is on the second table because so and so acted this way." She especially notes if "somebody [is] giving me a rough time." Of course, a particularly abrasive customer would stick in one's mind, but this raises an interesting broader issue: the way one's personal history and social position, the *feelings* related to these, play into cognition on the job.

One of the things that strikes me about my mother's report is the number of techniques it contains, the mix of strategies and processes: imagistic, spatial, verbal-propositional, affective. The research studies on waiters and waitresses report the use of multiple techniques as well, although not as many. Laboratory studies, of course, could restrict the expression of the full range — particularly the affective, which would emerge in real work situations. And my mother's recollection could compress together strategies used rarely with those used frequently. But her interviews do raise the possibility that controlled studies do not give us a full picture of the complexity of the way memory works in a setting like a busy restaurant. Such complexity might be necessary when one is hurriedly tending to seven to nine tables, with two to six people at each. As my mother put it: "Even though you're very busy, you're *extremely* busy . . . you're still, in your mind, you have a picture . . . you use all these [strategies], and one thing triggers something else." The strategies are interactive and complementary (see John-Steiner, 1995), and they enable us to get a sense of how much and what kind of work is going on in the working memory of a waitress during peak hours in a family-style restaurant.

ATTENDING TO AND REGULATING THE FLOW OF WORK

Remembering an array of orders does not, then, take place in isolation, but in a rush of activity that demands an attending to the environment, organizing and sequencing tasks that emerge in the stream of that activity, and occasional problem-solving on the fly. This context, as J. Stevens (1993) remarked in her study of the lunch counter, distinguishes waitressing from laboratory experiments on memory where material is usually "presented in uninterrupted linear sequence at controlled rates of speed," and recall "is often at the subject's pace, and is also linear and uninterrupted" (pp. 208–209). Using experimental terms to describe working memory in a restaurant, one could say that the items come in irregular sequence amid a number of distractors.

My mother's interviews contain more than 10 references to the pace and conflicting demands of waitressing. She describes a setting where an obnoxious regular is tapping the side of his coffee cup with a spoon while she is taking an order, where the cook rings her bell indicating another order is ready, where the manager has just seated two new parties at two of her tables that have just cleared, where, a moment ago, en route to the table now ordering, one customer asked to modify an order, another signaled for more coffee, and a third requested a new fork to replace one dropped on the floor. "Your mind is going so fast," she says, "thinking what to do first, where to go first . . . which is the best thing to do . . . which is the quickest." She is describing multiple demands on cognition — and it is important to remember that the challenge is not a purely cognitive one.

There is a powerful affective component to all this, one with economic consequences. The requests made of the waitress have emotional valence. Customers get grumpy, dissatisfied if they have to wait too long or if their request is muddled. The relationship with the cook is fraught with tension — orders need to be picked up quickly and returns handled diplomatically — and the manager is continually urging the movement of customers through a waitress's station. As my mother put it, you attend to your orders or "the cook will yell at you"; you try to get customers their checks quickly, "because you'll get hell from the manager." The waitress's assessment of the emotional (blended with economic) consequences of her decisions and actions plays back into the way she thinks her way through the demands of the moment.

What do we know about the cognitive processes the waitress uses to bring some control to these multiple and conflicting demands?

There is no experimental cognitive science literature on this dynamic mix of attending and immediate decision making that maps directly onto waitressing. This dimension of the work would be, I imagine, hard to simulate and study in the laboratory with any marked ecological validity. There is, however, a range of cognitive literature that applies indirectly: on attention, on motor expertise, on opportunistic planning (i.e., planning that takes "advantage of unanticipated circumstances to satisfy one's goals" (Seifert, Patalano, Hammond, & Converse, 1997, p. 102), and on expert behavior in real-world physical task environments (e.g., Shalin et al., 1997). There is, as well, a small body of research within the newer situated cognition and activity theory frameworks that examines real-world work settings, and although none of it — other than J. Stevens (1993) — deals with waitressing, some of it is pertinent here (e.g., Laufer & Glick, 1996; Scribner, 1986). Let me begin with the research on attention, much of which concerns visual information processing, for the characterization of attention drawn from that research can be applied to work like my mother's.

Attention is described in terms of its selectivity, a focusing on particular aspects of the environment; of the sustaining of that selective focus, a concentration as well as a vigilance for similar anticipated events or objects; and of the ability to control and coordinate this selective focus (e.g., LaBerge, 1995; Parasuraman, 1998). In expert performance, these processes may become more refined and automatic. Thus described, attention serves "the purpose of allowing for and maintaining goal-directed behavior in the face of multiple, competing distractions" (Parasuraman, 1998, p. 6).

There are, of course, periods in the waitress's day, lulls in activity, when she can stop and survey her station. My mother talks about a pause, standing back where she can "keep an eye on the (cash) register and all the way down (the counter)." But often the waitress is attending to things while on the move. Every waitress I interviewed commented on the necessity of attending in transit to requests, empty cups, plates moved to the edge of the table. As one waitress explained: "As you walk, every time you cross the restaurant, you're never doing just a single task. You're always looking at the big picture and picking up things along the way." This calls for a certain combination of motor skill and vigilance, captured in this passage where my mother describes her peripheral attention as she's delivering an order:

> You look straight ahead to where you're going to take your food. You can't just look completely to the side, carrying all those plates—you could lose your sense of balance. As you're going out of the kitchen, you more or less take little glances to the side.

This vigilance—from a stationary point or while in motion—is not only a matter of perceptual acuity, but also involves working memory and knowledge of the domain, knowledge of food preparation, restaurant routines, and so on. (For parallel findings in the study of motor expertise, particularly in sports, see Chamberlain & Coelho, 1993; McPherson, 1993.) My mother reveals this mix of memory, domain knowledge, and attending in her monitoring of the status of her customers' orders: "You're keeping an eye on who is not served yet. If it's (been) too long, you go check on the kitchen yourself." She recalls who ordered what and when and knows roughly how long a specific item should take to prepare, given the time of day. As she quickly checks her tables, she's attuned to a possible error in preparation.

Cognitive scientist David LaBerge (1995) used *mindfulness* as a synonym for *attention*, and although the dictionary defines mindfulness somewhat sparely as being aware or heedful, the word connotes something more, something that, I think, suits the foregoing discussion of waitressing and attention. Mindfulness, first of all, implies intelligence, a mind knowledgeable and alert. The word also connotes a heightened state and a comprehensiveness, an apprehension of the "big picture," mentioned earlier, and, as well, a cueing toward particulars, and a vigilance for aberration, as when my mother monitors those orders.

Let's return to that harried moment my mother describes where the regular is tapping his coffee cup, the cook is ringing the bell, etc. A waitress could attend to all these stimuli, and know what they mean, and yet not know what to do next. How does she decide what her next move should be?

I begin by summarizing and focusing some points made earlier. First, the waitress's response will be driven by several interrelated high-level goals: to satisfy customers (and thus boost income), to maximize efficiency and minimize effort, to manage conflict. All the waitresses I interviewed referred in some way to this cluster of goals. My mother speaks of "making every move count" and how "You think quick what you have to do first . . . in order to please people." Another waitress asks "How can I maximize my effort in that moment?" Yet another emphasizes the value of controlling fatigue by "working smart." These goals will serve to organize the waitresses' activity, providing a criterion—as Scribner (1986) found in her study of dairy warehouse workers—to accomplish the most "with the fewest steps or the least complex procedures" (p. 25).

Second, the waitress's response is shaped by various kinds of knowledge (declarative, procedural, spatial) of the domain: knowledge of the menu, of preparation times, of the layout of the restaurant, and so on. Included here is a kind of knowledge not typically mentioned in the literature on workplace cognition, but mentioned by all the waitresses I interviewed: a knowledge of emotional dynamics, both a folk psychology about dining out and the characteristics of particular customers. My mother, 20 years after retirement, can recount the quirks and traits of her regulars. As one veteran waitress puts it: "Everybody has their own personality. That's another level of learning . . . you've got to learn this way of working with people."

Third, the high-level goals and knowledge of the domain give rise to more specific action rules—waitressing rules of thumb—that, depending on the context, could aid in sequencing one's response. All the waitresses I interviewed, for example, mention the importance of attending to—even if just to acknowledge—newly-seated customers. ("The big part of this business is not to ignore anybody.") They also stress the importance of picking up orders—especially hot ones—quickly. Another rule of thumb (applicable during rush hour) is to tally and deliver checks in a timely manner. And yet another is to consider the emotional consequences of action, which calls for an ongoing assessment of character and feeling. Is the cook especially touchy today? Do you have a particularly demanding customer? My mother expresses this emotional calculus when she advises "Use your own mind and ask [of yourself] which customer will complain and which won't." Given an environment of multiple demands, these rules of thumb could guide one, for example, to attend to a new customer and serve a hot order—and forestall the circuit through the station to refill coffee. Refills would, in the moment, move lower in priority.

What is striking, however, is the degree to which the expert waitress relies on a broad strategy that makes many either–or decisions moot. And this brings us to the fourth element in the waitress's response to multiple demands. She organizes tasks by type or location. She combines and interweaves tasks in a way that greatly economizes movement, that makes activity, in my mother's words, "smooth." As one waitress put it, she is always asking "Which pieces of what I need to do fit together best?" (Again, this is reminiscent of Scribner's (1986) warehouse workers.) Although some prioritizing of tasks—guided by rules of thumb—does occur, the more common move (noted as a mark of skill by several of the waitresses) is to quickly see what tasks can be grouped and executed with least effort.

This leads to a fifth characteristic: the way restaurant routines aid in this organizing of tasks. My mother and the other waitresses I interviewed all refer in some way to a circuit through one's station that is watchful and that takes advantage of the restaurant's physical layout. As one waitress explains it:

> I always think of it as kind of a circle, because there's the tables, there's the bar, there's the coffee station, and it kind of becomes a flow of organizing what can be in one full circle, how many tasks can be accomplished, as opposed to back and forth, back and forth. I think the [waitresses] who get going back and forth are the ones who get crazy with four tables.

This description calls forth the earlier discussion of attention—the blend of anticipation, vigilance, and motor skill—but in a way that underscores the dynamic interaction of the waitress's skill and the structure and conventions of the environment.

A fascinating finding—one that emerged in all the interviews—is the observation that the expert waitress works best when the restaurant is busy. In some ways, this is counterintuitive. I would imagine that one could remember three or four orders with more accuracy than six or seven, that one could handle refills easier with a half-full station. These numbers would result in a more relaxed pace but, the waitresses claim, not in more skillful performance. (Their claim finds support in the aforementioned research literature on restaurant work and memory.) In fact, my mother insists she could never have developed her level of skill in slower restaurants. "You're not as alert . . . not thinking that quick"; you're not anticipating orders; "You're making a couple of trips" rather than a single efficient one. "In a slow place, you think slower." One waitress notes the feeling of being "like a well-oiled machine" during rush hour. Another says that "When it gets the craziest, that's when I turn on. I'm even better than when it's dead."

Of course, increased volume of trade can lead to disaster as well—if, for example, a waitress calls in sick or a critical piece of equipment fails. Every waitress tells those horror stories. But it seems that, barring the unusual mishap, the busy restaurant can lead to maximum performance. One's physiology responds—my mother talks about her "adrenaline going faster"—and there is a heightened readiness and reaction. And the increased flow of trade itself provides arrays of demands that call forth, that require the skillful response, the necessary fluid integration of attending, memory, organization of tasks, and strategic use of routine. This is not to deny the exhaustion, even the punishment, of the work, but it is telling how my mother and the other waitresses all comment on the satisfaction that they feel when they perform well under stress. Several use language similar to that of the "flow" experience "which tends to occur when confronting the highest environmental challenge with the fullest use of personal skills" (Csikszentmihalyi & Nakamura, 1999, p. 113; see Astin (1984) on the "pleasure needs" fulfilled by work). "There's a sense of accomplishment in just the mechanics of it," says one waitress, "just knowing that . . . I'm handling it all."

One traditional distinction in the literature on cognition is between information processing that is automatic versus processing that requires conscious attention and control. Although the value of automaticity is undisputed—complex behavior, from reading to baseball, would be impossible without it—there is sometimes the implication that once processing and response become automatic (in the physical task and motor skill domain especially) they hold less cognitive status. Another distinction contrasts human behavior as knowledge-driven and strategic versus behavior as shaped by properties and protocols of the environment. And, again, the resulting depiction, depending on one's philosophical outlook, can have consequences for the status granted to particular kinds of activity. Distinctions like these shape many discussions of cognition and occupation, but what strikes me as I consider the foregoing analysis of waitressing is the way they blur in practice.

When one shifts perspective to the busy floor of the restaurant itself, the basic question one asks is: What makes this work possible? The answer lies in the dynamic coherence of the automatic response and the quick thought; of a keen memory, but a memory keen in the physical moment; of the way routine contains within it multiple instantaneous decisions; of strategy and environment, each shaping the other. The key concepts here are not dichotomous but more related to coherence and rhythm, synchronicity, integration.

THE SOCIAL-ECONOMIC CONTEXT OF THOUGHT

Evident throughout this article is the fact that the waitress's thinking is situated in a complex, interlayered physical-social-economic field of activity. Her memory skill and other cognitive processes — attending, sequencing and clustering of tasks, etc. — are functional and purposive, both emerging from and structuring her work, which, in turn, is driven by and given meaning by economic incentives and, depending on personal history and psychological makeup, a host of other motives as well.

The social-emotional dynamics — and the place of economics in them — are so salient in waitressing that, of all aspects of the work, they have received the most popular and scholarly attention. I've noted them as well — the tension between cook and waitress, the potential competition among waitresses, the waitress's reading of and interaction with customers — but here I would like to discuss them a bit more fully, in order to elaborate the social and cultural context of the waitress's thinking. For purposes of space and to provide analytic focus, I concentrate on the encounter between the waitress and customer, for that is both the social and economic core of activity.[9] And it is a complex encounter indeed.

First of all, the encounter calls forth historically shaped conventions for the serving of food, associated with the house servant. In Frances Donovan's (1920) account of waitressing, *The Woman Who Waits*, published during the first stage of the feminization of food service, there is explicit treatment of the association of maid and waitress — and of the waitress's desire to distinguish her work from that of housemaid. But the association remained in waitressing (my mother's uniforms, down to the modified caps, resembled stereotyped maid's apparel), and is reflected in a number of routines of service: from modes of address, to sequence of queries about the order, to customs for serving and clearing food. ("[D]ishes are placed on the table without noise," notes a 1932 educational tract on waitressing, ". . . the hand must be trained to slip dishes into place very close to the table rather than bring them down directly from a height"; Salisch & Palmer, 1932, pp. 47–48.) Conventions and the intensity of symbolism change over time, and vary by the type of restaurant, but waitressing continues to involve the acquisition of customs of service — and one's accommodation to them. The residue of the servant's role rankles, and recent studies of waitressing reveal the number of ways waitresses resist it: from covert criticism and ridicule of haughty behavior (my mother's typical response) to direct rebuke and declaration of status. "[T]he waitress rejects the role of servant in favor of images of self," writes Greta Foff Paules (1991) in her ethnography of a family-style chain restaurant, "in which she is an active and controlling force in the service encounter" (p. 132). And one means by which the waitress expresses agency is through her use of skill and strategy to regulate the pacing and flow of work. "The customer has the illusion that they're in charge," observes one of the waitresses I interviewed, "but they're not." It's the waitress who must "get command of her tables," who is "the commander-in-chief of [her] section." This waitress still performs the customs of service, but within routines of practice that she controls.

The encounter between customer and waitress also gives rise, potentially, to a further range of emotions and social scripts, in addition to that of server and served. "Eating is the most intimate act," writes waitress Lin Rolens, "we are encouraged to perform in public" (Elder & Rolens, 1985, p. 16), and labor historian Dorothy Sue Cobble (1991) observed that waitresses "are responding to hungers of many kinds" (p. 2). On any given shift, a stream of customers enters with needs that vary from the physiological—and the emotions that attend hunger—to the desire for public intimacy. And the waitress, depending on the type of restaurant, her reading of the situation, and her own history and motives may fulfill, modulate, or limit those needs and desires. Analysis of this social–emotional dimension of waitressing, and similar occupations, has been fairly extensive over the past 2 decades, and tends toward two broad-scale findings.

First, providing service requires a good deal of "emotion management" or "emotional labor" (Hochschild, 1983). Regardless of what one actually feels, the interaction with the customer requires that the waitress display emotion that is dictated by the social and economic demands of the service encounter. My mother provides an illustration through her account of a churlish regular, a man who was always sending his steak back to the cook. "You've got to make an effort to try and please him, even though you can just kill him." Generalizing to all difficult customers, she advises: "Just try the best you can to be nice to them. Even if they're rude to you, you still smile and just go on, because that's your living."

The second finding is that the roles afforded to the waitress in the encounter with the customer play out within stereotypic gendered scripts: The waitress becomes servant, mother, daughter, friend, or sexual object. The house uniform and policy, customs of service, and other restaurant traditions contribute to this construction of gender-in-the-moment, as do broader social expectations and modes of behavior from the culture at large (Creighton, 1982; Hall, 1993; Leidner, 1991). Although I surely wouldn't have understood her behavior in these terms, I recall the clear sense I had watching my mother work that she was somehow more smiley and laughed more than when at home, a quick, not-quite-true laugh, flirtatious, with a touch on the arm or shoulder, a focused vivacity.

Good service, then, gets defined not only in terms of the skills and customs of being served, but, as well, by "smiling, deferring, and flirting" (Hall, 1993), by the enactment of various gender-specific social scripts. My mother sums it up simply but firmly: "You've got to be damned good, damned fast, and you've got to make people like you."

The social dynamics of this encounter affect the tip, a critical economic consideration, given that the base pay in most restaurants is close to minimum wage — the wage structure forces a reliance on gratuity. So the successful waitress soon learns how to play the dynamics to maximize her income. There is a fair-sized social-psychological literature on the factors that influence tipping. The shrewd waitress, for example, suggests items — appetizers, desserts, more drinks — that will increase the bill, and thus the size of her potential tip (Butler & Snizek, 1976). She can also increase her tip by smiling (Tidd & Lockard, 1978), by touching the customer on the hand or shoulder (Crusco & Wetzel, 1984; Stephen & Zweigenhaft, 1985), or by squatting or kneeling to get closer to eye level (Davis, Schrader, Richardson, Kring, & Kieffer, 1998; Lynn & Mynier, 1993). One could read this literature as an unpacking of the social skills and gestures learned in the context of restaurant work. And one can also read it, as Butler and Snizek (1976), following Goffman, suggested, as devices to control the reward structure of the service encounter.

The reward is an economic one, and is therefore affected by various economic exchange principles (see Lynn & Grassman, 1990). But it is also one fraught with symbolism — at the least, a reminder of servant status — so the reward structure includes secondary emotional elements as well. Customers, Lin Rolens observed, "tip in every spirit imaginable" (Elder & Rolens, 1985, p. 19), from a display of status, to an expression of gratitude, to an overture of friendship, to a sexualized gesture. And my mother and the waitresses I interviewed and read about express a wide range of feeling as well: from eager anticipation ("You're thinking, 'Oh boy, I'm gonna hurry up and clear that table off . . . because that's a good tipper'") and satisfaction ("It's fun to have a good night . . . all that cash in your pocket . . . it's very immediate reward") to anger ("Something that really pisses me off is when people stiff the waitress because something happened in the kitchen") and shame ("I failed today. After all I did for them, they didn't like me" from Whyte, 1948, p. 98) to a sense of injustice leading to action — Paules (1991, p. 37) wrote of a waitress who "followed two male customers out of a restaurant calling, 'Excuse me! You forgot this!' and holding up the coins they had left as a tip."

Although this field of customer–waitress emotion is, as I have discussed, shaped by the historical residue of servitude and by stereotyped gender roles, the waitress attempts to control it to her economic and emotional advantage by the way she defines this aspect of her work, by her manipulation of role and routine ("Play the people and the tips will follow," said one waitress in Elder & Rolens, 1985, p. 64), and by various mechanisms of classification that enable her to attribute a low tip to a customer's personal situation, character, or ignorance — all a part of the restaurant's folk wisdom.

The service encounter provides the tips that enable the waitress to make a living, but in addition to—or, more precisely, in concert with—the financial need, other needs of hers, depending on the waitress, can be met as well. Some waitresses gain satisfaction from contributing to a customer's enjoyment ("You supply nurturing and sustenance, the things that make life pleasurable"). Some respond to the hustle and stimulation of a busy restaurant, the sense of being in the middle of things (a big one for my mother). Some like the attention ("the spotlight's on you") and the safe flirtation. Some comment on the pleasure of the attenuated human interaction: "Though we'll never get to know each other, there's a really nice feeling that goes back and forth," notes one waitress I interviewed; another in Elder and Rolens (1985, p. 55) said, "I love taking care of people as long as I don't have to take them home with me." Some waitresses comment on the feeling of independence the job affords; Paules (1991) characterized the waitress as a private entrepreneur. And some gain satisfaction from the display of their skill ("I get to show off my memory") and, as was noted earlier, gain a feeling of competence by performing the job well.

Although perhaps obvious, it is worth stating that this array of feeling—like the cognitive processes detailed earlier—is situated in the restaurant; the various feelings are legitimized and shaped by the waitress–diner relationship. My mother developed a number of friendly relations with her regular clientele. When I asked her to perform a thought experiment and imagine how those relationships might have changed if tipping were outlawed, she gave sharp expression to the contextual nature of the restaurant friendship. "If you know they're gonna tip you, well, then you talk about your flowers, or you have a son, or you have a daughter, or whatever. But if you know they're not gonna tip, you'd be disinterested." My mother got to know some of her regulars pretty well, would talk about their problems at home, worry over them, yet, at heart, the connection to their lives was restaurant-based, for everyone involved.

In summary, the waitress–customer encounter is shaped by the historical residue of the servant role and by various cultural expectations regarding gender. It involves a good deal of economically motivated emotion management and interpersonal manipulation, all centered on the tip, which, itself, is laden with symbolism and feeling. The waitress–customer encounter also provides the occasion for the fulfillment of other needs that are not directly economic, although that fulfillment is embedded in an economic context and defined and bounded by life in the restaurant.

I'm struck by how many of our representations of a waitress's work tend to segment it. Popular accounts stress the nurturing qualities or the hardship of the work. Scholarly accounts in a few cases focus on memory skill or, more commonly, on the emotional sociology and/or gendered nature of waitressing. (This segmentation, of course, is partly determined by disciplinary orientation and partly by the space limits of scholarly journals. More comprehensive treatments can be found in Paules', 1991, book-length ethnography and Cobble's, 1991, history of waitress unions.) Yet, as I hope the foregoing demonstrates, in the complex activity system that is the restaurant, multiple cognitive processes and layers of emotion are interwoven. Memory, for example, draws on emotional material to aid in storage and recall. And customs of service and social display incorporate the cognitive, certainly in one's reading of people, one's social savvy, and one's folk knowledge of the ways of the restaurant, but also in the very particulars of routine that create the experience of service. One waitress comments on her ability to recall little details about her regulars' typical orders—that they don't like pepper or they like extra horse radish—and, as well, comments on her vigilance: "attention to detail . . . keeping water glasses full, keeping extra stuff off the table, just the little things that make it a more pleasant sensory experience . . . that's why I like it so much . . . that I'm a contributing factor in somebody having a good meal." Memory, attention, the creation of service, and a waitress's personal satisfaction are all of a piece in the busy restaurant.

Although I've just argued for a more integrated view of a waitress's work, let me now engage momentarily in my own narrowing of focus to make a further point. I think that the social and emotional aspects of being a waitress have overwhelmed our understanding of the work. And, interestingly, as waitress unions developed through this century and sought to define their occupation, they did so in terms of its social abilities, nurturing and caring (Cobble, 1991). Yet I hope the earlier sections on skilled memory and regulating the flow of work demonstrate the significant cognitive dimension of waitressing. This seems especially important, given the perception both in policy circles and in the popular mind that waitressing is among "the least skilled lower class occupations" (Montagna, 1977, p. 372) and involves little intelligence (Kwon & Farber, 1992). Skill, like intelligence, is a socially constructed notion, and one important strand of labor history and the social history of technology deals with the ways various trades and occupations have attempted to define for political and economic purposes the abilities it takes to do their work (e.g., Montgomery, 1987; E. Stevens, 1995). This is not the place to explore these dynamics in the evolution of waitressing versus other jobs in the restaurant or other blue- and pink-collar occupations. But what can be pondered is the degree to which the cognitive dimension of waitressing—and possibly other service jobs—can be lost in the more vibrant sociological story of the work. The intelligence of the work is so embedded in routines of service and social display that it largely goes undetected. Yet without the cognitive dimension, the service provided by the waitress would be impossible.

Conclusion: A Working Life

The interview for the day is completed; I turn off the tape recorder and gather up my notes. My mother rearranges a few things—paper napkins, some pill bottles—on the cluttered table. "You know," she muses, folding the napkins, "you learn a lot as a waitress. You work like hell. But you learn a lot." There's a small television set to the side, by the wall, propped up for her by my stepfather. She reaches over and turns it on, clicking through the channels: a rerun of "The Beverly Hillbillies," a basketball game ("blah"), a bass-thumping Ironman competition ("Boy, I couldn't do that"), a PBS documentary on the building of some huge suspension bridge . . . the Brooklyn Bridge. She stops at this. There are historical photographs of workers—excavating, welding, a remarkable shot of four men sitting in a net of cables high in the air. The men look Southern European, possibly Greek or Italian, look like so many of the men in the old photographs I have of Altoona. "This is interesting," she says, "they should show more things like this." She keeps watching, and we talk over the images about work and those immigrants of my grandfather's generation.

Her work in the restaurant business—and physical work in general—meant many things to my mother, and although she is now infirm, increasingly limited in what she can do with body and hand, work continues to shape her memory and desire, determine her values and identity. Many of our depictions of physical and service work—popular accounts but more than a few scholarly treatments as well—tend toward the one-dimensional. Work is ennobling or dehumanizing; work as the occasion for opportunity or exploitation; work as an arena for class consciousness and identity formation; work considered in terms of organizational structure or production systems; or of statistical indicators of occupational status, or income, or productivity, or employment trends. To be sure, each focus can have its rhetorical or analytic benefit. But one of the things this project has made clear to me is how difficult it is, given our standard "story lines" for work and the constraints of our disciplinary lenses, to create a multidimensional representation of work and the complex meaning it has in the lives of people who do it every day.[10] Let me try to tease out the layers of significance restaurant work had for my mother. They are interrelated, at times contradictory, of a piece in her experience of waitressing.

Through waitressing, my mother generated income, supported a family, kept poverty at bay. The income was low and variable, but, as she saw it, given her limited education and her early work history, she couldn't make better money elsewhere. Also, her income was somewhat under her control: By the hours she was willing to work and the effort she put forth, she could increase her tips. Although economically dependent on the generosity of others, she had developed, and could continue to develop, the physical, mental, and social skills to influence that generosity.

My mother's work was physically punishing, particularly over the long haul. She pushed herself to exhaustion; her feet were a wreck; her legs increasingly varicose; her fingers and spine, in later years, arthritic.

The work required that she tolerate rude behavior and insult, smile when hurt or angry. Although she did not see herself as a servant, she was economically beholden to others, and, in some ways—particularly in public display—had to be emotionally subservient. Yet, although she certainly could feel the sting of insult, my mother also saw "meanness" and "ignorance" as part of the work, and that provided her a degree of emotional distance. The rude or demanding customer could be observed, interpreted, described to peers, quietly cursed—and could be manipulated to financial advantage. Explaining how she would be nice to a troublesome customer, she adds: "And, then, what happens is he becomes *your* customer! Even though there are other tables that are empty, he'll wait for your booth."

Work for my mother was a highly individualistic enterprise, to be coveted and protected. She made several good friends at work, and they would visit our house, but much of my mother's interaction with other waitresses—both by my recollection and her interviews—was competitive. (Paules, 1991, depicted such competition well.) Although she considered Norm's "a good restaurant," I can't recall any expression of attachment to the company; and although much of the time she worked in Los Angeles was a period of considerable union activity, my mother was barely involved in her local. I realize now how isolated my mother must have felt: thousands of miles from family; responsible for a sick husband and a child; vigilant for incursions, even treachery, from coworkers; not connected to a union or to any civic, social, or church group; and, given her coming-of-age in the Depression and the later waning of the Pennsylvania Railroad, she was always worried about the security of her employment. A strong, even desperate, sense of self-reliance and in-her-bones belief in the value of hard work mixed inextricably with a fear that work would disappear.

An owner I know told me that the restaurant business "attracts people who want to step outside of their own lives. There aren't many professions that require you to stay so focused. You don't have time to think about anything else, and that gives you a rush, and you make money." Who knows to what degree this observation holds true across the restaurant population, but it resonates with a theme in my mother's interviews. I asked her, for example, if there was any reason, beyond the economic one, to want a full house. "When we're busy," she answered, "the time goes so fast. You're so tired, but it's better to be real busy than not busy, because then you'll have time on your hands, you'll have an idle mind." This is a somewhat different expression of the flow experience (Csikszentmihalyi & Nakamura, 1999) mentioned earlier. I suspect that the strongest protection my mother had against her pressing fear of destitution was to be consumed on the restaurant floor, attentive to cues from the environment, executing routines, her mind filled with orders, working at peak performance, the tips appearing and appearing by the empty plates, folded under cups and glasses.

Waitressing enabled my mother "to be among the public." This phrase carried a certain pride for her, as it reflected a social skill that the once-shy girl had to develop.[11] The work provided the opportunity for a low-responsibility social exchange—"I like that part. I like to be with people, associated with people"—that must have been pleasant for someone with so many cares at home. (This casual sociability has traditionally been more afforded male occupational roles.) To be among the public carried as well for my mother a sign of attainment: It was not the kind of solitary labor she had known as a girl, and it brought her into contact with a range of people whose occupations she admired.

There's a paradox here, but the logic goes like this: Yes, you are serving the doctor or the businessman, but it's *your* ability that makes everything work right; you are instrumental in creating their satisfaction. As she is fond of saying, not everyone can do that.

The restaurant, then, provided the setting for her to display a well-developed set of physical, social, and cognitive skills. It was my mother's arena of competence. Balancing all those plates on your right arm and carrying two cups of coffee in your left hand "is damned hard to do." Remembering your orders during rush hour and getting them served "gives you a feeling of satisfaction."

My mother learned everything she knew about the restaurant business through work, so there is an intimate connection between the activity of the restaurant and my mother's knowledge of it. (This kind of connection is well-documented in other studies of work, e.g., Laufer & Glick, 1996; Saxe, 1991; Scribner, 1986.) But the restaurant provided, as well, a context for other kinds of learning. Educational researchers are increasingly studying learning in non-school settings—workplace programs, social and civic clubs, etc.—but still very much unexplored is the learning that occurs in everyday, informal social exchange. Given the restrictions of my mother's formal education, her personal predilections (e.g., she did not read for pleasure), and all the demands on her life, she had limited time and means to gain information and learn new things. Yet, to this day, she possesses an alert curiosity. The educational medium available to her was the exchange with her customers, regulars particularly. Through the waitress–customer interaction, she acquired knowledge about a range of everyday activities—gardening, cooking, home remedies—and, as well, fed a curiosity that she had for as long as I can remember for topics related to medicine, psychology, and human relations. "There isn't a day that goes by [in a restaurant] that you don't learn something." Some of what she learned was a fact or a procedure (e.g., on planting roses), and some was more experiential and relational—the restaurant became a kind of informal laboratory for her to observe behavior and think through questions of psychodynamics and motivation. This aspect of waitressing engaged her; "You learn a lot, and it interests me."

Waitressing for my mother was a site of identity formation. Frances Donovan, writing in 1920, bears witness to the social transformations involving young women from the farm and from urban working-class and immigrant backgrounds, women seeking pathways out of "the restraints put upon [them] by the members of the group from which [they] came" (p. 145). Given the recent studies of waitressing, cited earlier, as an occupation embodying stereotyped gender roles, it's interesting to note that historically the work provided the occasion for a certain liberation from constraint and an opportunity for a working-class woman "to set up new standards for herself" (Donovan, 1920, p. 145). Approximately two decades later, my mother would enter the restaurant business, and, for all its hardships, it enabled her to begin to think of herself in a different way, to become relatively independent, to develop a set of skills, and to engage a wider social field than would have been possible in her mother's house or in the surrounding immigrant Italian community.

I have tried in this article to depict a commonplace working life in its complexity, to consider the physical, cognitive, social, and emotional dimensions of it, and to consider its many layers of personal meaning. And along the way, in considering such work closely, a number of broader issues were raised. The purposiveness of cognition, its embeddedness in a life world. The interaction of cognitive processes in work environments, and the way those environments both structure and are structured by cognition. The interrelation of the cognitive, social, and emotional in such environments. The possibility that the intelligence of certain kinds of work is masked by the work's social dimension. The way a work environment can be structured and routine, yet dynamic and variable. The need for a vocabulary to describe dynamic work environments that takes us beyond linearity and dichotomy and toward embeddedness, synchronicity, and complementarity. The need for layered, even contradictory, representations of the meaning of work. The role different kinds of knowledge can play in our understanding of work. The demands the study of work make on disciplinary knowledge, and the intra- and interdisciplinary tensions those demands create. The need for principled ways to address and utilize those tensions.

And, personally, the writing of this article provided an opportunity to think analytically about a kind of work that, for as long as I can remember, has been part of my life's texture, and the opportunity to more fully appreciate the hard but meaningful working life my mother created out of terrible constraint. The fact that I could pursue this analysis in concert with her, at this stage of her life, has brought me, tinged with sadness, personal and conceptual rewards — and has provided a powerful occasion for the integration of my own ways of knowing things. My hope is that the article both honors Rose Emily Rose and helps us understand a bit more about how a certain kind of work gets done.

ACKNOWLEDGMENTS

This research is supported by a Small Grant from the Spencer Foundation.

Invaluable help was provided by a host of generous informants and thoughtful readers: Alfredo Artiles, Helen Astin, Patricia Baquedano-Lopez, Deborah Brandt, Katherine Broughton, Ellen Cushman, Jane Danielewicz, Frederick Erickson, Ruth Glendinning, Kris Gutierrez, Lisa Hardimon, Sandra Harding, Celina Haro, Charles Healy, Michael Hendrickson, Deborah Hicks, Glynda Hull, Kenneth Lincoln, Julie Lindquist, Karen McClafferty, Patricia McDonough, Lisa Moore, Na'ilah Nasir, Mary Redfern, Giuliana Santini, Janelle Scott, Michael Seltzer, Richard Shavelson, Deborah Stipek, Brooke Totman, Angie Truman, Noreen Webb, Buzz Wilms, Stephen Witte.

NOTES

1. I would be remiss if I didn't acknowledge the wisdom I gleaned from Elder and Rolens (1985), Paules (1991), and J. Stevens (1993) in writing this article.

2. The restaurants my mother worked in were of a particular type, of course, and have changed in some ways since then — for example, in the technology used in placing an order — but in overall structure and practice, they have remained fairly stable, familiar. There also would be differences, although not profound dissimilarity, in some of the routines of practice between a place like Norm's and a more formal and expensive restaurant geared toward a different clientele.

3. They varied in years of experience, from 1 to 2 years to over 20 years, and worked in various types of restaurants: from a tourist-oriented bar-restaurant, to family-owned "ethnic" restaurants, to fish and steak houses, to trendy and expensive places. The interviews were 30 min to 1 hr each.

4. The project that would lead to *Lives on the boundary* (Rose, 1989).

5. There are exceptions. See, for example, the symposium "Memory Metaphors and the Real-Life/Laboratory Controversy" (Koriat & Goldsmith, 1996), particularly the contributions by Alterman (pp. 189–190), Anderson (pp. 190–191), Conway (pp. 195–196), Karn and Zelinsky (p. 198), and Neisser (pp. 203–204).

6. I thank Deborah Brandt for this observation.

7. Harding (1996) rephrased Levi-Strauss, "sex is good to think with."

8. A cognitive science treatment of the "restaurant script" is presented in Schank & Abelson (1977).

9. For a classic treatment of the tension between cook and waitress, see Whyte (1948); for illustration of the competition among waitresses, see Paules (1991).

10. An exception is Astin's (1984) sociopsychological model of career choice and work behavior.

11. Writing just after World War II, Whyte (1948) quoted a young woman: "I used to be very shy, especially coming to a big city like this. I don't know what I would have done if it wasn't for this job." He then commented: "Especially for employees who meet the public this is a very common story. The shy girl from the country comes to the city and, through her work, learns how to get along with people, makes friends, and finds her place in the city. Restaurants play an important role in adjusting rural migrants to city life" (p. 13).

REFERENCES

Astin, H. S. (1984). The meaning of work in women's lives: A sociopsychological model of career choice and work behavior. *The Counseling Psychologist, 12*, 117–126.

Baddeley, A. D. (1986). *Working memory.* Oxford, England: Oxford University Press.

Beach, K. (1993). Becoming a bartender: The role of external memory cues in a work-directed educational activity. *Applied Cognitive Psychology, 7*, 191–204.

Bennett, H. L. (1983). Remembering drink orders: The memory skills of cocktail waitresses. *Human Learning, 2*, 157–169.

Bertaux, D. (Ed.). (1981) *Biography and society: The life history approach in the social sciences.* Newbury Park, CA: Sage.

Bodnar, J., Simon, R., & Weber, M. P. (1983). *Lives of their own: Blacks, Italians, and Poles in Pittsburgh, 1900–1969.* Urbana: University of Illinois Press.

Butler, S. R., & Snizek, W. E. (1976). The waitress-diner relationship: A multimethod approach to the study of subordinate influence. *Sociology of Work and Occupations, 3*, 209–222.

Chamberlain, C. J., & Coelho, A. J. (1993). The perceptual side of action: Decision-making in sport. In J. L. Starkes & F. Allard (Eds.), *Cognitive issues in motor expertise* (pp. 135–157). Amsterdam: North Holland/Elsevier.

Chase, W. G., & Ericsson, K. A. (1981). Skilled memory. In J. R. Anderson (Ed.), *Cognitive skills and their acquisition* (pp. 141–190). Hillsdale, NJ: Lawrence Erlbaum Associates, Inc.

Cobble, D. S. (1991). *Dishing it out: Waitresses and their unions in the twentieth century.* Urbana: University of Illinois Press.

Cole, M. (1996). *Cultural psychology: A once and future discipline.* Cambridge, MA: Harvard University Press.

Creighton, H. (1982). Tied by double apron strings: Female work culture and organization in a restaurant. *The Insurgent Sociologist, 11*, 59–64.

Crusco, A. H., & Wetzel, C. G. (1984). The Midas touch: The effects of interpersonal touch on restaurant tipping. *Personality and Social Psychology Bulletin, 10*, 512–517.

Csikszentmihalyi, M., & Nakamura, J. (1999). Emerging goals and the self-regulation of behavior. In R. S. Wyer, Jr., *Perspectives on behavioral self-regulation* (pp. 107–118). Mahwah, NJ: Lawrence Erlbaum Associates, Inc.

Davis, S. F., Schrader, B., Richardson, T. R., Kring, J. P., & Kieffer, J. C. (1998). Restaurant servers influence tipping behavior. *Psychological Reports, 83*, 223–226.

Dews, C. L. B., & Law, C. L. (Eds.). (1995). *This fine place so far from home: Voices of academics from the working class.* Philadelphia: Temple University Press.

Donovan, F. (1920). *The woman who waits.* Boston: Gorham.

Elder, L., & Rolens, L. (1985). *Waitress: America's unsung heroine.* Santa Barbara, CA: Capra.

Engeström, Y. (1993). Developmental studies of work as a test bench of activity theory: The case of a primary care medical practice. In S. Chaiklin & J. Lave (Eds.), *Understanding practice: Perspectives on activity and context* (pp. 64–103). Cambridge, England: Cambridge University Press.

Engeström, Y., & Middleton, D. (1996). In Y. Engeström & D. Middleton (Eds.), *Cognition and communication at work* (pp. 1–14). Cambridge, England: Cambridge University Press.

Ericsson, K. A., & Polson, P. G. (1988). A cognitive analysis of exceptional memory for restaurant orders. In M. T. H. Chi, R. Glaser, & M. J. Farr (Eds.), *The nature of expertise* (pp. 23–70). Hillsdale, NJ: Lawrence Erlbaum Associates, Inc.

Greeno, J. G. (1998). The situativity of knowing, learning, and research. *American Psychologist, 53,* 5–26.

Hall, E. J. (1993). Smiling, deferring, and flirting: Doing gender by giving "good service." *Work and Occupations, 20,* 452–471.

Harding, S. (1996). Science is "good to think with." In A. Ross (Ed.), *Science wars* (pp. 16–28). Durham, NC: Duke University Press.

Hochschild, A. R. (1983). *The managed heart: Commercialization of human feeling.* Berkeley: University of California Press.

John-Steiner, V. (1995). Cognitive pluralism: A sociocultural approach. *Mind, Culture, and Activity, 2,* 2–11.

Jonides, J. (1995). Working memory and thinking. In E. E. Smith & D. N. Osherson (Eds.), *Thinking* (pp. 215–265). Cambridge, MA: MIT Press.

Koriat, A., & Goldsmith, M. (1996). Memory metaphors and the real-life/laboratory controversy: Correspondence versus storehouse conceptions of memory. *Behavioral and Brain Sciences, 19,* 167–228.

Kwon, Y. H., & Farber, A. (1992). Attitudes toward appropriate clothing in perception of occupational attributes. *Perceptual and Motor Skills, 74,* 163–168.

LaBerge, D. (1995). *Attentional processing: The brain's art of mindfulness.* Cambridge, MA: Harvard University Press.

LaSorte, M. (1985). *La Merica: Images of Italian greenhorn experience.* Philadelphia: Temple University Press.

Laufer, E. A., & Glick, J. (1996). Expert and novice differences in cognition and activity: A practical work activity. In Y. Engeström & D. Middleton (Eds.), *Cognition and Communication at Work* (pp. 177–198). Cambridge, England: Cambridge University Press.

Lave, J., & Wenger, E. (1991). *Situated learning: Legitimate peripheral participation.* Cambridge, England: Cambridge University Press.

Leidner, R. (1991). Serving hamburgers and selling insurance: Gender, work, and identity in interactive service jobs. *Gender and Society, 5,* 154–177.

Lummis, T. (1987). *Listening to history: The authenticity of oral evidence.* London: Hutchinson.

Lynn, M., & Grassman, A. (1990). Restaurant tipping: An examination of three "rational" explanations. *Journal of Economic Psychology, 11,* 169–181.

Lynn, M., & Mynier, K. (1993). Effects of server posture on restaurant tipping. *Journal of Applied Social Psychology, 23,* 678–685.

McPherson, S. L. (1993). Knowledge representation and decision-making in sport. In J. L. Starkes & F. Allard (Eds.), *Cognitive issues in motor expertise* (pp. 159–188). Amsterdam: North Holland/Elsevier.

Montagna, P. D. (1977). *Occupations and society: Toward a sociology of the labor market.* New York: Wiley.

Montgomery, D. (1987). *The fall of the house of labor: The workplace, the state, and American labor activism, 1865–1925.* Cambridge, England: Cambridge University Press.

Parasuraman, R. (1998). *The attentive brain.* Cambridge, MA: MIT Press.

Paules, G. F. (1991). *Dishing it out: Power and resistance among waitresses in a New Jersey restaurant.* Philadelphia: Temple University Press.

Rose, M. (1989). *Lives on the boundary: The struggles and achievements of America's underprepared.* New York: Free Press.

Rose, M. (1999a, November). On values, work, and opportunity. *Education Week, 60 & 43.*

Rose, M. (1999b). "Our hands will know": The development of tactile diagnostic skill—teaching, learning, and situated cognition in a physical therapy program. *Anthropology and Education Quarterly, 30,* 133–160.

Rose, M. (2000). Teaching tools. *Teacher Magazine, 11,* 41–44.

Ryan, J., & Sackrey, C. (Eds.). (1984). *Strangers in paradise: Academics from the working class.* Boston: South End.

Salisch, L. A., & Palmer, E. G. (1932). *An analysis of the waitress trade.* Sacramento, CA: California State Department of Education.

Saxe, G. B. (1991). *Culture and cognitive development: Studies in mathematical understanding.* Hillsdale, NJ: Lawrence Erlbaum Associates, Inc.

Schank, R. C., & Abelson R. P. (1977). *Scripts, plans, goals, and understanding.* Hillsdale, NJ: Lawrence Erlbaum Associates, Inc.

Scribner, S. (1986). Thinking in action: Some characteristics of practical thought. In R. J. Sternberg & R. K. Wagner (Eds.), *Practical intelligence: Nature and origins of competence in the everyday world* (pp. 13–30). Cambridge, England: Cambridge University Press.

Seifert, C. M. (1999). Situated cognition and learning. In R. A. Wilson & F. C. Keil (Eds.), *The MIT encyclopedia of the cognitive sciences* (pp. 767–769). Cambridge, MA: MIT Press.

Seifert, C. M., Patalano, A. L., Hammond, K. J., & Converse, T. M. (1997). Experience and expertise: The role of memory in planning for opportunities. In P. J. Feltovich, K. M. Ford, & R. R. Hoffman (Eds.), *Expertise in context: Human and machine* (pp. 101–123). Menlo Park, CA/Cambridge, MA: AAAI Press/MIT Press.

Shalin, V. L., Geddes, N. D., Bertram, D., Szczepkowski, M. A., & DuBois, D. (1997). Expertise in dynamic, physical task domains. In P. J. Feltovich, K. M. Ford, & R. R. Hoffman (Eds.), *Expertise in context: Human and machine* (pp. 195–217). Menlo Park, CA/Cambridge, MA: AAAI Press/MIT Press.

Starkes, J. L., & Allard, F. (1993). *Cognitive issues in motor expertise.* Amsterdam: North Holland/Elsevier.

Stephen, R., & Zweigenhaft, R. L. (1985). The effect on tipping of a waitress touching male and female customers. *The Journal of Social Psychology, 126,* 141–142.

Stevens, E. W., Jr. (1995). *The grammar of the machine: Technical literacy and early industrial expansion in the United States.* New Haven, CN: Yale University Press.

Stevens, J. (1993). An observational study of skilled memory in waitresses. *Applied Cognitive Psychology, 7,* 205–217.

Tidd, K. L., & Lockard, J. S. (1978). Monitary significance of the affiliative smile: A case for reciprocal altruism. *Bulletin of the Psychonomic Society, 11,* 344–346.

Tokarczyk, M. M., & Fay, E. A. (Eds.). (1993). *Working-class women in the academy: Laborers in the knowledge factory.* Amherst, MA: University of Massachusetts Press.

Tolich, M. B. (1993). Alienating and liberating emotions at work: Supermarket clerks' performance of customer service. *Journal of contemporary ethnography, 22,* 361–381.

Van Manen, M. (1990). *Researching lived experience: Human science for an action sensitive pedagogy.* Albany, NY: SUNY Press.

Wertsch, J. V., Tulviste, P., & Hagstrom, F. (1993). A sociocultural approach to agency. In E. A. Forman, N. Minick, & C. A. Stone (Eds.), *Contexts for learning: Sociocultural dynamics in children's development* (pp. 336–356). New York: Oxford University Press.

Wharton, A. (1993). The affective consequences of service work: Managing emotions on the job. *Work and Occupations, 20,* 205–232.

Whyte, W. F. (1948). *Human relations in the restaurant industry.* New York: McGraw-Hill.

Wolf, G. A. (Ed.). (1945). *Blair County's first hundred years: 1846–1946.* Altoona, PA: The Mirror Press.

Yates, F. A. (1966). *The art of memory.* Chicago: University of Chicago Press.

19   *Words in Action: Rethinking Workplace Literacy*

2003

AUTHOR'S NOTE: There is a growing body of research on the use of reading, writing, mathematics, and other symbol systems in the workplace. By the early 1980s, psychologists and public policy researchers like Larry Mikulecky and Thomas Sticht were studying literacy in a range of job settings, from factories to the armed services, and in composition studies, Lee Odell and Dixie Goswami published in 1985 an edited volume that would signal a new area of interest: *Writing in Non-Academic Settings*. Many researchers in and outside of rhetoric and composition—Glynda Hull, Rachel Spilka, and Stephen Witte, to name a few—have continued this work, revealing the rich, though not always predictable, use of language, numbers, and graphics in the flow of work.[1]

This brief essay, which is drawn from the conclusion of *The Mind at Work* but published in *Research in the Teaching of English*, falls into the preceding research tradition. Much of what it reveals is not new, but there are several things about it that I would like to highlight.

The information in it is drawn from a wider range of occupations and work sites than is found in the typical study. Also, there is an emphasis on the interaction of symbol systems in context aimed toward a job-related goal. (Steve Witte was one of the first in rhetoric and composition to get us to think in terms of multiple semiotic systems, and a lot of recent work in technology and media studies focuses on "multimodality.") Finally, given the orientation of *The Mind at Work*, there's more of a cognitive focus here than one tends to find in workplace literacy studies. This focus is important, I think, because it enables us to consider whether something substantial might be going on in rudimentary literate and numerate activity. As one pair of researchers I quote nicely put it: "Lower-order mathematics [can become] a rich source of higher-order thinking."

We live in a time of the celebration of high technology and symbolic analysis, even predictions of the end of common work, yet physical work,

From *Research in the Teaching of English* 38.1 (August 2003): 125–28.

work of body and hand, surrounds us, makes everyday life possible. For about six years now, I have been involved in a research project exploring the thought it takes to do physical work, the cognitive processes involved in various blue collar and service occupations like waitressing, hairstyling, plumbing, welding, industrial assembly, and the like. The study has led me to consider the way we categorize occupations, define intelligence, and think about learning and schooling. Of particular interest to readers of *RTE* will be my findings in the realm of literacy and numeracy. A number of people have already done important research on job-related literacy. What follows is in line with their research, though I would like to use it to help us reconsider some of the traditional ways we define and discuss written language, numbers, and graphics.

Any discussion of literacy in the workplace would need to include numeracy, for most work settings are thick with numbers. Numbers on tools and gauges, as measurements, as indicators of pressure or concentration or temperature, as guides to sequence, on ingredient labels, on lists and spreadsheets, as markers of quantity and price. Certain jobs require workers to perform calculations, to check and verify, and, at times, to collect and interpret data. A fair amount of basic math can be involved, and some workers develop a good, if informal, sense of number and pattern. As well, there is material mathematics, mathematical functions embodied in materials and actions. The cognitive demands of such math—the number of interrelated variables, the planning, the estimations—can be considerable, particularly when one is still developing competence. Another important thing to note is that a simple mathematical act can extend quickly beyond itself. Measuring, for example, can involve more than recording the dimensions of an object. I was watching a cabinetmaker measure a long strip of wood. He read a number off the tape out loud, looked back over his shoulder to the kitchen wall, turned back to his task and took another measurement, then paused for a moment in thought. He was trying to figure out a problem with the molding, and the measurement became a key element in his deliberation about structure and appearance. "Lower-order mathematics," as the authors of one recent report put it, becomes "a rich source of higher-order thinking."

The workplace is also rich in graphics. Directions, diagrams, plans, and reference books contain numerous graphic illustrations; some are fairly representational of the object in question, others, like blueprints, are more specialized in depiction and purpose, requiring training to understand them. Often, a whole array of esoteric symbols is involved, "visual jargon" for switches and receptacles, or pipe fittings, or types of welds. Workers often generate illustrations themselves, quickly, in the unfolding events of the job, illustrations meant to aid communication and forward activity. How frequently I saw someone suddenly grab a pencil—shifting the medium of representation from speech and gesture to the graphical—to sketch something, while talking, on a scrap of paper or on a piece of material itself. (Many a panel of plywood nailed into place has such a sketch drawn on its reverse side.) Those sketches can illustrate dimension, function, relation, sequence, or more, and often contain words, numbers, and specialized notations intermixed with lines, angles, and curves. This strategic blending of symbols displays a flexible disciplinary and communicative competence—the worker has to recognize the need to switch media—and signals, as surely as does a field's vocabulary, membership in a skilled occupational community.

Numbers and graphics interweave with written language, creating a complex symbolic field. Though many kinds of physical work have not required high levels of literacy, more reading than is generally thought occurs in the average workplace: from manuals and catalogues, to work orders and invoices, to lists, labels, and forms. These texts are coupled with other activities, so, for example, people read to specify a production quota or to be guided in the use of an instrument or a product. And some manufacturing and service jobs involve a good deal of "paperwork" to document and trace, integrated throughout one's work routines. The use of such texts, once mastered, becomes familiar and repetitive, not requiring much interpretation, though they may well be incorporated into an interpretive act, part of assessing a situation or solving a problem. Other kinds of texts—codes and collective bargaining agreements, for example—define work, contribute to the standardization of parts and processes and regulate social and economic relations. Such documents form a legal and organizational surround. They are typically not read in the immediate activity of work—the information in them is usually conveyed orally by peers and supervisors—but they can quickly move to the foreground of activity during labor negotiations, organizational restructuring, or the reassessment of a standard procedure.

Writing, of a limited sort, is also distributed throughout the workplace. It is used to label, to list, to record activity; it can be structured by a form or be sketchy, part of talking or thinking through a problem. It can initiate action, as in a restaurant order or a report of machine malfunction, or it can be private, as in the list hastily written as a memory aid. If the worker is in training—in the shop or in a classroom—he or she may take notes from demonstration or lecture, annotate written texts, and linguistically simplify or graphically render instructions in manuals or training materials. And in some cases, the worker—particularly in new, "restructured" industries—may need to write a lot, to record, evaluate, and make recommendations about production processes.

Traditional treatments of literacy tend to classify most of the above uses of reading and writing as basic, rudimentary: they are instrumental, repetitive, often involve limited amounts of text, infrequently call for interpretation or analysis of the text itself. There is a descriptive truth to such judgments: the uses of literacy in the common workplace do tend toward the abbreviated and routine. But I think there is also an implicit comparison here that sells workplace literacy short, comparison with literary expression or with the uses of written language in the professions or the academy. While reading and writing in many professions and, yes, even in the academy, are more routine and scripted than the comparison implies, it is surely true that, say, writing a legal brief requires significantly more literacy skill than filling out a form when a machine breaks down. Still, I've come to think we underestimate the significance of common workplace literacy.

First, our traditional categories can blinker our understanding: analytic moments can be embedded in routine, and seemingly basic reading and writing can be cognitively richer than they seem. The writing of just a single word, perhaps along with other notations, can represent much more than the word itself denotes. To the carpenter planning a roof or the paint shop foreman troubleshooting on the auto assembly line, the scribbled words "eave" or "primer" can carry with them an understanding of a structure or a process, a history of experience, and a series of options for action. Also, I'm struck by the degree to which workers shift among different symbol systems and integrate them with each other and with other cognitive and interpersonal events to make things happen. Because this occurs so frequently and in the flow of other activity — its very everydayness — I think we can miss the remarkable thing about it: the coordinated use of word, number, and line to initiate and direct action. One more thing to note. Physical work may not require high levels of literacy — and some workplaces employ many people who are marginally literate or not literate in English — but print is spread throughout the environment, and those who have trouble decoding or producing it sometimes develop a range of compensatory cognitive, linguistic, and social strategies to enable them to do their work. They engage others, read non-linguistic cues, use sight, sound, and touch to aid interpretation. Workplaces are literate environments, and people do their best to figure out how to live in them.

We know a fair amount about the cognitive and linguistic processes at play in the foregoing, but at times our analyses have been framed in the negative: what kinds of literacy and numeracy are not present, what limitations do workers reveal at the task? I surely am not calling for a romanticized portraiture here, but it would be fascinating, I think, to shift our line of sight a bit and ask what all these forms of symbolic behavior are on their own terms, in context, how they interact, what it takes to do them well, what they make happen in the world, how they might connect to other literate behaviors, in and outside of the workplace. Such understanding would lead to fuller appreciation of a whole, rich domain of symbolic activity, and would better poise us to create effective training and educational programs. So much vocational education and workplace literacy instruction is developed from a perspective of student or employee deficiency, tending toward the simplest and strictly functional of tasks. While many people in these programs have, in fact, had poor educations and do need instructional assistance, that assistance could come from a richer conceptual base, opening up curricular and pedagogical possibilities. We might, for example, rethink age-old — and largely unchanged — courses like Business Math and Business English, or, more importantly, reimagine the separation of the vocational and the academic, building from the robust cognitive processes both express. Furthermore, we would be in a better position to create fresh connection to other modes of numeracy and literacy — across institutional and class divides — to see what is different but, as well, to appreciate what might be shared as people engage their minds in the business of making a living.

NOTE

[1]Mikulecky and Sticht (1984); Odell and Goswami (1985); Hull (1997); Spilka (1993); Witte (1992).

20

"On Method" from The Mind at Work: Valuing the Intelligence of the American Worker

2004

AUTHOR'S NOTE: This is the afterword to *The Mind at Work*. As opposed to the discussion of method in "The Working Life of a Waitress," this was written for a more general audience, so the reader interested in writing for multiple audiences could compare both accounts.

Students have told me, however, that though the afterword was not written for a scholarly audience, they have found it useful in their own attempts to write about methodology. It begins by laying out the broad conceptual terrain in a straightforward way, then moves to a description of what was done and why, and then opens the lens back up to a brief overview of other related work and issues of method. When we write about methodology — and this is especially true in the social sciences I'm familiar with — the tendency is either to get dry and humdrum ("I did this, then this, then this"), listing detail with no illuminating conceptual gloss, or to lapse into highly specialized and opaque language. With a little care, it's possible to avoid both tendencies.

To place "On Method" in its own proper context, I should step back and give an overview of *The Mind at Work*, the book that resulted from the foregoing articles and the larger project investigating the cognition of everyday labor. After a framing introduction, the next six chapters cover individual kinds of blue-collar and service work. The final three chapters take a broader view, attempting a rethinking of the mental–manual, brain–hand dichotomies that shape our thinking about human activity and that manifest themselves especially in work and in school. The final chapter — from which "Words in Action" is drawn — provides a summing up and a further framing of the book's cases and concerns within democratic theory:

> To affirm our capacity as a people is not to deny the obvious variability among us. Nor is it to retreat to some softhearted notion of mind. We mistake narrowness for rigor, but actually we are not rigorous enough. To acknowledge our collective capacity is to take the concept of variability seriously. Not as slots along a simplified cognitive continuum or as a neat high-low distribution, but as a bountiful and layered field, where many processes and domains of knowledge interact. Such a model

demands more not less from those of us who teach, or who organize work, or who develop social policy. To affirm this conception of mind and work is to be vigilant for the intelligence not only in the boardroom but on the shop floor; in the laboratory and alongside the house frame; in the classroom, the garage, the busy restaurant, vibrant with desire and strategic movement. This is a model of mind that befits the democratic imagination.

And it is this model of mind, I believe, that makes necessary a strategic mix of research methods.

A concern about research methodology runs throughout my work, from the early writer's block study on down. Perhaps because my education straddles humanities and social sciences, perhaps because of my dissertation study, and perhaps because of my personal inclinations, I am drawn to the use of multiple methods, a pragmatic synthesis.

Let me illustrate with one small example, drawn from the upcoming selection:

> I find significant value . . . in combining personal material with scholarship, matching it, each providing a check on the other. For example, as I was reading historian David Montgomery's extraordinary chapter on "The Common Laborer" (in *The Fall of the House of Labor*), I kept thinking of my grandfather Tony Meraglio. As vivid as Montgomery's writing is, my knowledge of Tony — the stories I heard, the photograph on my desk — all brought a further depth of understanding to the historian's portrayal. Conversely, the context Montgomery provides, the macro view of social and economic forces, brings Tony to fuller life. He's not only a cluster of family stories but a man located in a time and a place. The table of labor statistics and the narrative of a life are, clearly, quite different ways of representing the world, but they also can complement and enhance each other.

It just seems to me that the kinds of issues we study are so complex that no single method or perspective — from historical to philosophical to quantitative — can illuminate all we need to know. As I wrote in the Introduction, there are certain core beliefs and commitments that drive my work. It has a political stance, a point of view. But I try my best to also question that point of view and the evidence I muster for it. I look for disconfirming evidence. Are there instances where the waitresses I'm studying do not cluster tasks in an efficient way? How about the times when the physical therapist doesn't reason through tactile or visual data? What do I make of these? Also, what would someone with a different disciplinary or methodological or ideological perspective think of the evidence I'm presenting and how I argue with it? There's a wonderful essay by historian David Tyack on this issue called "Ways of Seeing," in which he considers the rise of compulsory schooling in the United States through five different theoretical perspectives, and I recommend it highly. When I engage in this kind of alternative thinking, though, I tend to do it in a personalized way. I imagine particular people reading what I wrote. What would my old advisor, Rich Shavelson, say? Or my colleague Sandra Harding, the feminist philosopher? Or Janelle Scott, a former student who studies educational policy? Or my uncle, Joe Meraglio, who worked at General Motors all his life? I imagine their reactions — these competing voices in my head — and they help guide the analysis.

My experience also tells me that if we desire to address broader publics, to bring our sensibilities and knowledge to bear on social issues, we, as a group, can't restrict the techniques and appeals we use. We need, among us, to marshal a range of methods, the compelling number as well as the vivid narrative.

There is a tendency in some spheres of the humanities and social sciences to rule out of court on ideological grounds entire traditions of inquiry. The statistician who declares critical theory useless; the critical theorist who sees numbers as the devil's workshop. I'm not talking about a targeted critique of the limitations of particular methods for particular purposes. *Lives on the Boundary* contains a big dose of skepticism about the use of single-shot quantitative measures to assess language proficiency or to drive social policy. Rather, I'm concerned about wholesale dismissal, often without much knowledge of the methodology in question.

As I just noted, there are rhetorical as well as epistemological reasons for my advocacy of a pragmatic synthesis. The social challenges that face us are too multiform and intractable to be countered with a single appeal. Graphs and charts as well as horrific stories contributed to workplace protections. Statistics blended with portrait and moral argument led to Head Start.

Increasingly, people in rhetoric and composition are expressing a desire to address broader publics and influence social policy. I'll add my voice to that desire in the next part, but let me note here that I think the issue of research methodology is pertinent. The rhetorical dimension of method.

Here's a seemingly outlandish, but relatively modest, proposal: Why doesn't our field encourage (and create the conditions to make possible) a few of us to become knowledgeable — or collaborate — in both rhetoric and economics, or in statistics and feminist methods, or in teacher research and public policy analysis? I realize that there are seemingly unbridgeable philosophical differences among some of these, but that tension itself would be worthy of exploration from the inside. If nothing else, such study would provide one with more grounded arguments against, let's say, the typical models of policy analysis. A more incisive crap detector. But there is also the possibility of hybrid methodologies emerging. It's not out of the question. The mixed methods and collaborations could provide new analytic perspectives and, with those perspectives, added argumentative power in the public sphere.

There are a number of involved and contentious discussions going on these days in psychology, anthropology, and the cognitive sciences about the nature of cognition and the legitimacy of various methods of studying it. A comprehensive treatment of these discussions is beyond the scope of a book like this, but let me give a brief overview of them.

Some researchers believe that the best way to study cognition is within the structured environment of the psychologist's laboratory where conditions can be experimentally controlled. Researchers with quite different beliefs contend that naturally occurring settings — like the workplaces described in this book — provide the most accurate perspectives on the way human beings use their minds; experimental control may be sacrificed, but authenticity is gained. My own preference in doing the research for *The Mind at Work* is toward the use of naturalistic methods, though I rely on other researchers' laboratory studies (for example, of memory or attention) when they are appropriate — as in the discussion of the waitress's memory for food orders.

These questions of method intersect with further questions about the nature of cognition itself. Some scholars hold, in a tradition that goes back at least to Descartes's single and distinct *cogito*, that cognition is best modeled and studied as an individual phenomenon. The standard metaphor compares the mind to an information-processing computer. Others hold that a better metaphor is that of an ecology or an orchestra. It misleads us, they claim, to focus on that individual computer, when cognition both develops and functions in dynamic interaction with the world beyond the individual brain. Thus these scholars tend to study cognition as a system: individuals in concert with each other and with tools, symbols, and conventions delivered by the culture.

A related debate concerns the role context — the lived environment — plays in thinking. Do our mental structures and processes exist and function in some generalized way, irrespective of the particular setting we're in, or is thinking intimately dependent on the specifics of the settings we inhabit? One writer expresses the latter view this way: "The *nature* of cognitive processing is uniquely determined within its context, and . . . it cannot be studied in isolation without destroying its defining properties." Again, let us call up the waitress as an example. Are the memory strategies that she uses to remember orders supported and directed by the structure and conventions of the restaurant, and are they thus best analyzed and understood in that setting? Or are these strategies more abstract and, therefore, transferable and effective in the supermarket, the classroom, or the church social?

I've summarized and simplified the strong views of these positions, but in actual practice many scholars would locate themselves somewhere between the two. The reader interested in a fuller discussion can consult the sources

From *The Mind at Work: Valuing the Intelligence of the American Worker*. New York: Viking Books, 2004. 217–23.

I cite under "cognition" in *The Mind at Work* or, for a much briefer treatment pertinent to this book, can read the methods sections of two of my earlier articles: " 'Our Hands Will Know' "and "The Working Life of a Waitress."

I don't believe that the basic argument I'm making about cognition and common work depends, finally, on holding one of these positions rather than another. People along the continua could support it, though the laboratory-oriented psychologist would want to devise experiments to test the claims I make from more naturalistic studies.

Although I conduct studies of a particular kind, my basic orientation toward issues of cognition tends toward the eclectic and synthetic. Each theory and each methodology shines a particular kind of light on a remarkably complex cognitive and social reality, and each, I think, helps us make partial sense of the swirling whole. Particularly with a topic like the one in this book—one that is not much studied—I needed to range wide, synthesize as best as I could, trying to be mindful of and honor the tensions among these various research traditions, but seek correspondence where possible.

～

When at a job site or in a classroom, I observed people at work, writing notes on their activity and, when permissible, taking photographs of the task at hand. Once I got a sense of the rhythms of the work—its moments of less intense focus and its pauses—I would begin asking questions about what people were doing and why, trying to gain an understanding of their behavior and the thinking that directed it. As they got more familiar with me and I with them and their work, I was able to ask increasingly specific questions, probing the reasons for using one implement rather than another, for a particular positioning of the body, for the benefits of this procedure over that one. I wondered aloud how they knew what to do, given the materials and constraints of the present task, what they had in mind to do next, how they knew something was wrong. (In instructional settings, the answers to such questions sometimes emerged naturally in exchanges between student and teacher or among peers assisting one another.) Over time, the exchanges became more conversational, and frequently people on their own began explaining what they were doing and what their thinking was for doing it, a kind of modified think-aloud procedure, long used in studies of problem solving.

In some cases, I was able to conduct follow-up interviews—which I tape-recorded—after class or when the workday was over. These interviews provided the opportunity to inquire about a person's biography and work history, motives, and short- and long-term goals. These interviews also enabled me to ask further questions about the work I had observed earlier, using descriptive passages from my notes, or photographs if I had them, to ground us in specifics.

Some settings afforded additional materials that aided me in exploring practice: videotapes of a student's performance, audiotapes of a collaborative discussion of a task, CD-ROM presentations of a procedure. These provided further means for me to explore people's thinking, learning, and knowledge of a field.

Any method is subject to biases and distortions. And, of course, my presence at a site could have influenced things in all sorts of ways, just as my style as an interviewer could affect what is and isn't said. One thing I did to check myself was to have the primary participants read what I had written about them and their work. Did I get the technical details right? Did I accurately render their sense of the task?

I also sought to validate or revise my findings by seeking further perspectives and multiple sources of information on the material I observed and recorded. I would, for example, present vignettes from my notes and my photographs to other skilled practitioners—to other plumbers or hairstylists or surgeons—and invite their analysis. I did the same with psychologists or anthropologists who study cognition. And in the few cases where cognitive research had been done on the phenomena I was studying—for example, on the memory of waiters and waitresses or the mathematics used by carpenters—I was able to incorporate that research into my writing.

During the time of these studies, I was reading technical and social histories of the work in question, trying to gain an understanding of how it developed, both in its techniques and norms of practice and in the way it came to define itself and be defined by the various occupational categories our society provides. I wanted a sense of the antecedents to the work I was observing.

And there are research literatures in a range of disciplines—from biological anthropology to education—that, while not directly concerned with the kinds of work before me, were certainly relevant. Examples would include studies of the evolution of tool use; studies of attention, memory, mental imagery, problem solving, and the timing and rhythm of behavior; sociological studies of work and emotion; studies of identity development; historical studies of apprenticeship; and so on. These literatures provided rich knowledge and perspective, helping me consider more carefully and with more appreciation a novice's refinement in the swing of a hammer, or the role of emotion in remembering a customer's order, or the interrelation of manual skill and one's sense of self.

Finally, let me say a word about my use of family material. There certainly are arguments against it, arguments concerning bias and threats to objectivity. True enough. But as some feminist social scientists would argue, personal history can provide a valuable way of knowing that extends beyond one's own immediate circumstances. Given my background, I understand things about social stratification that all the reading in the world couldn't provide. Or I have a sense of the complicated and contradictory set of attitudes someone like my mother could have toward hard physical work. I find significant value, as well, in combining personal material with scholarship, matching it, each providing a check on the other. For example, as I was reading historian David Montgomery's extraordinary chapter on "The Common Laborer" (in *The Fall of the House of Labor*), I kept thinking of my grandfather Tony Meraglio. As vivid as Montgomery's writing is, my knowledge of Tony—the stories I heard, the photograph on my desk—all brought a further depth of understanding to the historian's portrayal. Conversely, the context Montgomery provides, the macro view of social and economic forces, brings Tony to fuller life. He's not only a cluster of family stories but a man located in a time and a place. The table of labor statistics and the narrative of a life are, clearly, quite different ways of representing the world, but they also can complement and enhance each other.

All of the foregoing perspectives contributed to a sharper focus on the particulars of cognition and behavior. They encouraged, as well, consideration of broader social and institutional phenomena: The way occupation gets linked to definitions of mind. The educational traditions that relegate practices typical of physical work to a curricular (and thus, career) path quite separate from the high-status course of study. The tendency of social science, segmenting human activity as it does into disciplinary domains, to reduce inadvertently the complexity of work—tool use is dealt with anthropologically or historically, skill is addressed in a few areas of psychology or, in a different way, in economics, and questions of work and identity are raised in sociology. If I have been successful, *The Mind at Work* functions as a corrective to that segmentation. Perhaps we can arrive at a synthesis whereby we consider skill, emotion, and identity on the same page. Or think about tool use and values simultaneously. Or shuttle back and forth between the close particulars of the way work gets done and larger social concerns about justice and opportunity, viewing mental and physical operations through the lens of democratic theory.

PART SIX

Public Writing: Style and Persuasion, 1989–2005

Introduction to Part Six

Most of the pieces in this final part draw on the themes of *Lives on the Boundary, Possible Lives,* and *The Mind at Work* and were written in conjunction with the hardcover or paperback publication of those books. Some are for wider but still professional audiences (*Chronicle of Higher Education, Education Week*), whereas others are for a broad readership, such as the *Los Angeles Times.* Some were written by invitation of the newspaper or periodical editor, and some I submitted following a letter of inquiry. They are framed by a current event (e.g., the inauguration of a university president, Labor Day) or a topical issue (e.g., education standards, school reform). Editorial page editors call this the "hook" to something in the news.

Some of these pieces were printed pretty much as I wrote them (e.g., "How Should We Think About Intelligence?" or *The Nation* essay). Others were heavily edited to conform to house style and/or the preferences of a particular editor (e.g., "Education Standards Must Be Reclaimed for Democratic Ends"; "Extol Brains as Well as Brawn of the Blue Collar"). It is rare in newspaper opinion pieces that the author creates the title; none of the *L.A. Times* titles are mine, and, frankly, I don't like them much. This degree (and kind) of line editing is not typically encountered in academic journal publication, so it is something each of us has to come to terms with. The key thing, obviously, is to be vigilant that changes in style don't drift into changes in meaning.

There are many forms of public writing, from broadside to poem. One reason I like the opinion or commentary piece is that it provides a good way to bring one's disciplinary knowledge—a research base, methodological rigor, a historical or comparative perspective—to bear on a current issue. And it provides a way to extend—and at times to rethink—one's own work, to test it in the public sphere and thereby broaden its influence.

But the opinion piece calls for the abandonment, or at least modulation, of many of the scholarly conventions by which we craft argument and establish authority, by which we signal membership in a discipline. This varies by the particular publication and length of the piece, but, in general, one needs to avoid specialized vocabulary, heavy allusion (and what allusions there are need to be explained), extensive data or citation. Rather, the genre calls for the dramatic statistic, fact, quotation, or metaphor, for a relatively common language, for a rhetorical appeal that has broad resonance—an appeal that might engage a reader who is relatively uninformed about the issue at hand.

The paradox here is that it is precisely one's disciplinary expertise, habits of mind, and professional experience that qualifies one to write the opinion piece—and that would be of interest to an editor—yet the writing calls for a set of conventions fairly different from those typically learned as one is socialized into a discipline.

Rhetoric and composition is deeply connected to matters of broad public interest—literacy, teaching, undergraduate education—and for a while now some within our field have been seeking public connection through service learning, courses in civic rhetoric, or involvement in workplace and community literacy projects.[1] There is talk of a "public turn" in composition studies. But the huge, clattering irony is that our field, a field that has rhetoric at its core, offers little or no graduate-level training for public writing or speaking. English and education don't either. Yet, many in rhetoric and composition (and in education) are yearning to speak to wider audiences, to insert our various bodies of knowledge and perspectives into the public record. As I write this, the Council of Writing Program Administrators and a group called Rhetoricians for Peace are beginning to do just that.

When I started working with doctoral students at UCLA, I required them to take some kind of a writing course beyond their regular curriculum. It could be an advanced exposition course, or journalism, or creative writing. We would then put our heads together to see how the lessons learned in that course might transfer to their scholarly writing. Subsequently, as I noted in Part Two, I developed two graduate-level professional writing courses within the School of Education—one focusing on academic writing and the other on the opinion piece and magazine article—so now students have a curricular space in-house to concentrate on their writing, both for their academic communities and for broader audiences. (See "A Call for the Teaching of Writing in Graduate Education," p. 162, for more detail.)

I mentioned the paradox of writing from disciplinary expertise while modifying the conventions of that disciplinary training. The paradoxical nature of all this extends a bit further. In my personal experience and the experience of my students, public writing can play back positively on one's scholarly writing. Writing the opinion piece, for example, forces precision, a honing of argument. It also helps one decide which evidence is most persuasive. And it can lead to a questioning and clarifying of assumptions. There can be, in short, a healthy play back and forth between these various genres; each accomplishes specific things for particular audiences, but each contributes to the successful execution of the other.

We academics easily develop a tin ear to the sound of our own language. We talk too much to each other, and not beyond. We risk linguistic, intellectual, and political isolation. I've been thinking a lot lately about what occurs as an associated cluster of intellectual pursuits—like rhetoric and composition—moves toward disciplinary status. Many good things come of it, of course, and I've watched our field fight for them. But with disciplinarity also comes a turn inward, a concentration on the mechanics of the profession, on internal debates and intellectual display, on a specific kind of career building—and it is all powerfully reinforced, materially and symbolically, by the academy.

There's nothing wrong with watching out for one's livelihood, of course not. And there's real value in a tradition that demands intellectual scrutiny within ranks. (A piece like "Narrowing the Mind and Page" does that.) But, as Lisa Ede smartly observed a while back, there is a tendency for disciplines, for us, to create, or at least amp up, our debates by reducing and reifying one another's positions—and then opposing them.[2] This is the academic engine, and, yes, it can contribute to more intense thinking. But it also keeps our attention focused on ourselves while all hell breaks loose in public policy and the broader public sphere.

I wonder how we might begin to turn outward as well—or maybe a better way to put it is this: to find a way outward through our disciplinary debates. How can we attend to both our field and the public domain . . . and find something generative in considering the two together?

The field of rhetoric and composition is grounded on the art of persuasion, is multidisciplinary, and has a foundational connection to teaching practice and education policy. It is the ideal place, as a number of folks have been arguing lately, to imagine a different kind of disciplinary and institutional life.[3]

We could begin in our graduate programs. Here's one small suggestion: We could offer training—through a course or some other curricular mechanism—in communicating to broader audiences, the *doing* of rhetoric. The training could include analysis of public policy and media to heighten sophistication about how they work and how one might find or create an entry point. And such training could also include rhetorical theory and history that enhances the understanding of such public intellectual work—I think here, as one example, of Jackie Royster's *Traces of a Stream*, which offers a rich account of nineteenth-century African-American women moving into and affecting public life with a rhetorically attuned public writing.

In the upcoming opinion pieces and commentaries, I try to urge a reconsideration of accepted educational practices or of standard definitions and categories, usually having to do with ability and achievement. I try to realign a standard argument or pose a different perspective on it.

There should be an element of surprise in these, something editorial page editors call the "turn," the we-usually-think-*x*-but-how-about-*y*? rhetorical move. My wish is that the surprise leads to an effective exhortation, that the reader might be persuaded to think about the issue in a new way.

If an opinion piece works, it does so, I think, because of the merits of its claim but hand-in-glove because of the rhetorical and stylistic means of offering the claim. I am taken here by a passage from George Orwell's brief essay, "Why I Write":

My starting point is always a feeling of partisanship, a sense of injustice. When I sit down to write a book, I do not say to myself, "I am going to produce a work of art." I write it because there is some lie that I want to expose, some fact to which I want to draw attention, and my initial concern is to get a hearing. But I could not do the work of writing a book, or even a long magazine article, if it were not also an aesthetic experience.

The art of persuasion comprises both the moral and the aesthetic. I hope that this collection of opinion pieces — for that matter, my work in general — either in achievement or failed attempt, honors that standard.

NOTES

[1]See, for example, Coogan (forthcoming); Cushman (1999); Peck, Flower, and Higgins (1995); George (2005); Mathieu (2005); and Wells (1996).

[2]Lisa Ede (1994).

[3]See, for example, Lunsford (2005); J. Seitz (1999); and Slevin (2001).

21   *What's Right with Remedy: A College Try*

1989

At the time of his inauguration two weeks ago, Vartan Gregorian, the new president of Brown University, assailed American schools that do not adequately prepare students for higher education.

"Everybody wants to put as much as possible on the shoulders of the university," Gregorian told an interviewer. "The first two years, colleges are expected to do remedial work for the whole nation."

"Remedial work." Correcting somebody else's mistakes. Gregorian is a bit extreme (though not alone) in viewing as remedial the first two years of college courses, but the gist of his complaint is much with us these days. Courses and programs in writing, mathematics, the sciences, learning and study skills, critical reasoning aimed at preparing students for the demands of higher learning are routinely vilified.

Many college presidents, legislators and commentators on culture talk this way about remediation: urgent, apocalyptic, angry—just anger, the anger of men at the bastions watching civilization decay.

Gregorian is Brown's 16th president. Its fourth, Francis Wayland, also an outspoken man, complained in 1841 that "students frequently enter college almost wholly unacquainted with English grammar." In 1896 the Nation ran an article entitled "The Growing Illiteracy of American Boys," which reported on a study of underpreparation at Harvard. The Harvard faculty lamented the spending of "much time, energy and money" teaching students "what they ought to have learnt already."

And so it goes. Academicians have been talking about the decline of higher education for a long time, even though colleges and universities have been growing in remarkable ways. There is a certain kind of talk, a crisis talk, serious and powerful. And troubling. It distorts the historical and social reality of American higher education, quelling rather than encouraging careful analysis of higher learning in a pluralistic democracy.

It is important to get a sense of the history of the preparatory and remedial function in American higher education, for we are not facing a new and unprecedented danger. Colleges were in the remediation business before they had yell leaders and fight songs.

From the *Los Angeles Times*, April 23, 1989, part V, pp. 1 and 3.

The history of American higher education is one of expansion: in the beginning, the sons of the elite families, later the sons of the middle class, then the daughters, the American poor, the immigrant poor, veterans with less-than-privileged educations, the racially segregated, the disenfranchised. The economic and educational environments from which these students came varied dramatically; if they were to be given access to higher education, much would have to be done to ensure their success. The remedial function, then, has been a force within the college to advance our version of democracy.

To temper any idealism sparked by this broadening of opportunity, let us also remember that the history of the American college from the early 19th century on could also be read as a history of changes in admissions, curriculum and public image in order to keep enrollments high and institutions solvent.

One reason U.S. colleges and universities increased admissions of "nontraditional" students in the early 1970s was because campuses had grown so rapidly in the '50s and '60s that, after the peak of the postwar student influx, administrators had to scramble to fill classrooms. American institutions of higher learning as we know them are made possible by robust undergraduate enrollments. And if we're going to admit people, for pure or pragmatic reasons, then we're obliged to do everything we can do to retain them.

In saying this, I am not trying to be cynical or dismissive about standards and requirements. Much work needs to be done to improve the education of school teachers, the curricula they're given and the conditions in which they teach. But university officials are shortsighted and simplistic when they brush aside responsibility for remedial courses and programs: The overlap of secondary and higher education has been, and remains, necessary in an open educational system.

Academics need, as well, to check their apocalyptic, angry, dig-in-the-heels language, for it narrows discussion of the function of higher education in American society. Let's engage this issue by sketching out some of the things a good freshman education should provide.

Young people entering college need multiple opportunities to write about what they're learning and to develop what has come to be called critical literacy: comparing, synthesizing, analyzing. They need opportunities to talk about what they're learning: to test their ideas, reveal their assumptions, talk through the places where new knowledge clashes with ingrained belief. They need a chance, too, to talk about the ways they may have felt excluded from all this in the past and may feel threatened by it in the present. They need occasion to rise above the fragmented learning encouraged by the lower-division curriculum, a place to reflect on the way particular disciplines conduct their inquiries and the way seemingly isolated disciplines can interconnect.

The fact is that one of the few places in the first year of college where a student gets a chance to do such things is *precisely* in those programs and courses labeled preparatory or remedial: tutoring centers, writing labs, remedial classes. Seen in this light, the word *remedial* tells only half the truth.

It carries the implication that colleges are correcting someone else's mistakes, are "remedying" the deficiencies and deficits of the schools or of the students themselves.

So-called remedial work, when well-applied, also helps to make up for the weaknesses in the way *higher* education is dispensed to its initiates. It enables students to do what all the current blue-ribbon reports on liberal education say they should do: engage ideas, use language, develop a sense of how intellectual work is conducted, test personal values against a tradition. Freshmen don't get much chance to do these things in their standard fare of distant lecturers, large classes and short-answer tests. Ask them.

It's clear that remedial courses help students. What we fail to see—for it is so often castigated—is that such work can also yield rich information for our colleges and universities.

Remedial courses and programs are a kind of boundary area, a transitional domain that allows us—if we are willing to look and listen—to get a keen sense of what it means to do certain kinds of intellectual work. We could gain significant knowledge, for example, about the social and cognitive processes involved in the complex literacy tasks we routinely ask our students to do: interpret literature, analyze a political or philosophical argument, synthesize a range of sources. Such knowledge would assist institutions in examining the uses of—and assumptions about—writing in the college curriculum. And everyone would benefit from that.

We need to think about our colleges and universities today in deep and generative ways. What does it mean to enter higher education in America? What *truly* is the relationship between the research and undergraduate teaching missions of the university? How is knowledge best developed and incorporated into the social structure of a pluralistic democracy?

What we hear instead are impatient, contemptuous calls to kick remediation off campus. If the hope is that such an action will straighten out secondary schools, then we have an act of either great hubris or great innocence: Pressure from the college is but one of many problems—and hardly the greatest—that schools face today. Kick remediation off campus and the primary thing you will achieve is the greater exclusion of American youth from higher education.

We need remedial programs. They are a part of our history. They are necessary if we want to further develop our democracy. They serve as a corrective to the impersonal dispensary that lower-division education has become. And, if we are wise enough to see, they can be a source of rich information.

At heart, the issue of remediation is embedded in two central questions: How is higher learning best pursued in a pluralistic democracy, and how many or how few do we want to have access to that learning? We are talking, finally, about the kind of society we want to foster.

22

School-Business Ties:
The Unexamined Paradox
of Past Performance

1990

Picture Michael Milken, junk-bond king, standing before a blackboard in an inner-city school teaching a math lesson to two African-American youngsters. His visit is part of a "principals for a day" program that brings prominent business leaders into the classrooms so they can see the good and the bad firsthand. Such field trips are becoming common as talk of school-business alliances spreads throughout the country. School districts desperate for resources and business leaders worried about the education of a future work force are trying to find common cause.

There are reasons for hope about such alliances. Many schools need dollars, materials and repairs that business can provide. School-business alliances can lead to enriched internships and various kinds of mentoring relationships between promising kids and female and minority employees who could serve as role models. Beleaguered, low-status schools would benefit from having the support of powerful community figures.

There are also reasons for skepticism. Business might want to shape curriculum and testing. Even if such influence could not be exerted directly, schools might feel pressure to apply economic and industrial models to instruction and assessment. As a result, we could see a resurgence, with a '90s spin, of the pseudoscientific, efficiency-obsessed methods of the 1910s and 1920s, when teacher effectiveness was measured by, for example, the number of arithmetic combinations that Johnny could perform in one minute. There is also the possibility that some businesses are interested in forming school alliances to sell goods rather than stimulate reform.

But of more concern are two wider-ranging issues that have to do with the complex weave of economics, culture and schooling in America.

In all the public discussions I've heard, the focus of school-business alliances is solely on the problems with the schools and what it is that business can do to help remedy those problems. The discussion never seems to include business' contributions to the conditions that have limited educational achievement. And it's here that the image of Michael Milken before the blackboard begins to take on powerful added meaning.

From the *Los Angeles Times*, April 22, 1990, p. M5.

Milken is a financial genius and a philanthropist of the first order. He also represents a trend in American business that many now agree has done more harm than good—a preoccupation with short-term interests. Although clearly not representative of all American business people, Milken brings into stark relief a fundamental contradiction in American business practice: its mix of philanthropy and short-sighted self-interest, its boardroom rapaciousness and public generosity.

Business must examine this contradiction if it wants to enter educational reform in any major way. It would be a good thing for business to give money to the schools, but the schools also need business to consider broader issues of economy and culture.

If business is to help inner-city schools and schools in depressed rural and transitional areas, it will have to understand school failure within a socioeconomic context. It will have to ask itself hard questions about the way national economic policies and local business decisions have limited the development of communities, and the effect these policies and decisions have had on schooling. Schools in a number of cities—Detroit and Flint, Mich.; Gary, Ind.—have deteriorated as decisions by major industries have devastated their local economies.

The hope of a better life has traditionally driven achievement in American schools. When children are raised in communities where economic opportunity has dramatically narrowed, where the future is bleak, sealed off, their perception of and engagement with school will be negatively affected. We must ask whether, for example, donating a slew of computers to a school will make kids see the connection between doing well in the classroom and living a decent life beyond it when all they feel is hopelessness the moment they walk out the schoolroom door. From what I can see, the business community, perhaps because some of its members so cherish a Horatio Alger mythology, has not thought deeply about the profound effect economic despair can have on school achievement.

The business community must take a hard look as well at its apparent willingness to turn out virtually any advertising campaign that will help turn a profit and at the negative influence business interests exert on entertainment and news media. So many of the commercially driven verbal and imagistic messages that surround our young people work against the development of the very qualities of mind the business community tells the schools it wants the schools to foster. The coming era, we are told, will require greater and greater numbers of people who are critically reflective and can make careful distinctions, who can troubleshoot and solve problems, who have an interpretive, analytic edge, who are willing to stop and ponder.

Yet young people grow up in an economy of glitz and thunder. The ads that shape their needs and interests champion appearance over substance, power over thought. Their entertainment, by and large, makes easy distinctions between right and wrong, the effective move and the blunder, and it trivializes intellectual work, from science to composing. The news they see highlights glamour and poise over knowledge and, now, blurs fact with "simulation." And all this—from ads to MTV to news—turns on the titillation of quick movement.

Such tactics make money in the short run, but what effects do they have on youth culture over time? The relationship of mass culture and individual habits of mind is complex, to be sure. But there is a significant disjunction between the kind of youngster business says it needs from the schools and the kind of youngster one could abstract from the youth culture that is so powerfully influenced by business interests.

If business truly wants to positively influence the education of our children, the discussion must extend beyond the immediate needs of particular schools to the economy and culture in which those schools try to do their work. Business-school alliances will not result in fundamental, long-range educational change if the terms of the alliances essentially have the powerful bestowing momentary beneficence on beleaguered classrooms. We'll need more than Michael Milken before the blackboard.

23

Education Standards Must Be Reclaimed for Democratic Ends

1991

As someone who teaches underprepared students, I find many of the policy discussions concerning these students to be less and less useful in the daily work of helping them reach their full academic potential in the classroom. The discussions are becoming polarized, intractable debates that pit equality against excellence in ways that oversimplify the complexities of teaching and learning. The issue of standards — the criteria one uses to assess competence — illustrates this polarization.

Current debates, especially as they are presented in the news media, assume two camps: One argues that calls for standards are really masked attempts to bar members of minority groups and the poor from educational advancement; the other argues that in the name of equality of opportunity and access, our educational system has abandoned excellence and the importance of holding students accountable to academic standards. But we need other ways to talk about the issue of standards if we are to forward the democratic traditions in American education, if we truly want to help students develop what educator Mina Shaughnessy calls their "incipient excellence."

To foster an alternative discussion about standards, we need to avoid the too-narrow definition of positions as either "progressive" or "conservative"; we also need to move beyond morally charged abstractions by starting from the specifics of what happens in the classroom. Although I hope that what I say applies to other domains, I will ground my discussion in the teaching of writing and begin with two classroom stories.

Vince, who recently received a Ph.D. from a prestigious psychology department, tells his story from the enviable position of one who has succeeded in the academy. Coming from working-class, Mexican-American origins, Vince learned his first English from a television set. But with his parents' encouragement, he worked hard at his second language, and by high school, he was taking college-preparatory English classes. They were designed to help students do well on achievement tests and the Scholastic Aptitude Test; the classes primarily consisted of workbook grammar exercises, although students also read some literature and wrote a few book reports. After completing high school. Vince figured he was ready for college, so he was stunned

From *The Chronicle of Higher Education*, July 3, 1991, p. A-32.

when he sat for a university English placement exam: "We were to answer a question on a reading passage—something on the use of grain—and we were supposed to argue for one position or another. 'What the hell am I supposed to write?' I thought. They wanted an argumentative paper, though I didn't know that then. . . . I knew my grammar, but applying it to that kind of writing was another story."

Vince's poor performance landed him in remedial English. As he recalls, "The teacher seemed very distant and cold. I'd get my papers back graded with a C or lower and with red marks about my style all over them." Vince couldn't figure out what the teacher wanted. "I kept trying, but I kept getting the same grades. I went through this routine for four or five weeks, becoming more withdrawn. Finally I said, 'Forget this,' and stopped going to class."

Vince took the class again two quarters later and got a teacher who gave feedback in a more useful way and was more encouraging. He started going to the campus learning center and asked for feedback from teaching assistants in other courses in which the instructors had assigned papers. He learned to write good academic prose and in graduate school was frequently complimented for his writing.

Vince's story illustrates a number of problems with how standards are used in the teaching of writing. Often, they are reduced to so-called objective measures, like multiple-choice grammar tests, and although the instruction geared toward such measures can be rigorous, it is also limited. Vince's high-school English classes had been labeled "college preparatory," so he believed they would prepare him to write in college; but they had not prepared him for even his first university writing assignment, the English placement exam. This discontinuity in requirements and the criteria used to assess performance—in this case the shift from grammatical analysis to the development of an effective argument—is common.

In his first college class, Vince faced another problem associated with standards: They often are applied to students' work in ways that shut down rather than foster learning. In Vince's case, the teacher seemed to value a literary style and rejected as inadequate Vince's more straightforward prose. Such teachers match student work against an internalized model of excellence and find the work lacking, rather than using their knowledge of genre, rhetorical strategy, and style to assess the ways a paper could be improved, given what the writer seems to be trying to do. This kind of teacher functions more like a gatekeeper than an educator.

The second, briefer story grows out of a remedial English class at an inner-city community college in Los Angeles. About 30 students are enrolled, most of them from working-class backgrounds and a variety of ethnic origins, ranging from Armenian to Salvadorian. The students have been writing educational autobiographies, and one of the interesting issues they raise involves standards. Some express anger at past teachers who didn't hold high expectations for them, who didn't explain the criteria for competence and hold students to them, who didn't help their students master the conventions of written English that they're struggling with now. Some of these teachers sound as though they were burned out, but others seemed reluctant to impose their standards for philosophical reasons or because they thought a less rigorous pedagogy was better suited to these students. One teacher, for example, is described as "hang loose," a man who created a pleasant classroom atmosphere but played down the evaluation of students' work.

This episode highlights the role that standards and high expectations play in good teaching. It also clarifies why so many minority educators and parents — though mindful of the injustices that have occurred in the name of standards — are calling for classrooms in which standards are clearly articulated and maintained. Clearly defined standards that are employed fairly facilitate learning and show students that their teachers believe in their ability to meet academic expectations.

People leery about calls for standards need to remember their benefits and reclaim them for democratic ends, despite the fact that standards and assessments in the past too often have been used to stratify students into educational tracks based more on economic and racial background than on academic ability. At the same time, the vocal champions of standards need to take a closer look at how such standards and our means of measuring them can limit, rather than advance, the academic excellence they desire.

To develop our alternative discussion about standards, we must hold Vince's story and the one from the community college simultaneously in mind, in productive tension. As we do so, some questions emerge:

- The current drive to define and insure standards by statistical measures is very strong, but what effects do such measures have on instruction? As people on both sides of the equality-excellence debate are realizing, standardized measures can limit the development of competence by becoming what Lynne Cheney, chairman of the National Endowment for the Humanities, has called "tyrannical machines" driving curricula toward the narrow demands of test preparation, instead of allowing teachers to immerse students in complex problem solving and rich use of language.

- How good are we at explaining our standards to students? Too much college teaching is like the teaching Vince encountered in his first remedial course: Teachers match a response or product against an inadequately explained criterion of excellence. To avoid such stifling imposition of standards and to encourage the emergence of students' own language, some teachers of writing refrain from applying their own criteria of effective prose. But this can be problematic as well, for many introductory-level students report that they feel cheated, and sometimes baffled, by such instruction.

- How can we reconceive standards so that they function not just as final measures of competence but as guides to improving performance? Many discussions of standards stay at the level of test scores and models of excellent performance. Instead of these static measures of attainment, our focus should shift to the dynamics of development. Such a shift, for example, would have led Vince's first teacher to make explicit the distinctions he saw between his criteria and his student's performance. He also would have tried to understand the possibilities of Vince's own style and helped Vince enhance it with some stylistic options drawn from his own repertoire.

- Are the standards we use coherent—that is, is there some level of agreement between secondary and postsecondary institutions about what constitutes competence in a given discipline? What opportunities exist—for example, through university-school alliances—that would help us articulate areas of agreement and disagreement so that students like Vince don't find themselves baffled by very different kinds of curricula and sets of expectations?

- Standards evolve through consensus, but it's an unfamiliar consensus to many of our students; so don't we need to make the historical and social processes by which standards are constructed a topic of classroom discussion? Such discussion can help us find out what students perceive our standards to be and illuminate the cultural and cognitive difficulties they might have in adopting those standards. If we are serious about the egalitarian ideals of American education, aren't we obliged to find out what lies behind the withdrawal of students like Vince?

- How reflective are we about the attitudes and assumptions that underlie our standards? How open are we to considering the provisional nature of these standards and modifying them? In writing instruction, for example, teachers sometimes judge students' work according to idealized models of composing that distort actual practice or some teachers champion the "great tradition of English prose" without considering the many ways that tradition is modified as audiences and purposes shift. What mechanisms are there within graduate training and professional life to encourage such reflection?

My hope is that addressing such questions will enable us to reframe the discussion of standards, moving it away from the either-or polarity of equality versus excellence. Perhaps such questions will help us think more fruitfully about how standards are linked to instruction and learning—and how standards can be used to truly foster competence, rather than simply judge it.

24 *What We Talk about When We Talk about School*

1996

From the summer of 1991 to just before Christmas of 1994, I traveled across the United States, visiting good public school classrooms, from preschool to 12th grade, urban and rural, Industrial Northeast to Deep South to California border town. I was trying to fashion a response to the national discussion about public schools, a discussion that, I believed, had gone terribly sour.

We have been flooded for a decade-and-a-half with alarms and bad news, with crisis talk and prescriptions for remedy. While it is surely necessary for a citizenry to assess the performance of its public institutions, this national discourse about schooling had shifted from critique to assault and dismissal, to a ready store of commonplaces about how awful our schools had become. Such talk felt dangerous to me. It was contributing to broad generalization, to retreat, to a sense of failure and fear — and it was shutting down our civic imagination. So I set out to document excellence: to fashion a kind of travelogue of good American classrooms and to use the vignettes in the journey as occasions to reflect on what public education should be in a democracy. I wanted to generate a language of educational possibility. The result was a book called *Possible Lives*.

It has been one year now since the book was published. Looking back over its reception — the reviews, the talk shows and other public events, the wide range of conversations it allowed me to have — I think I'm coming to understand a little more clearly some things about the way we talk about schools.

Let me begin with an early recognition. The book had just come out, and I was a guest on a talk-radio show in central California. The host asked me to reconcile the examples of effective schooling in the book with the widely published claims that by most any measure public schools are doing a bad job. It's a question I would continue to be asked. For me, it's a complicated one. There are many students, poor and minority in particular, who, historically, have been ill-served by our schools. And we are bedeviled by a host of ongoing problems: from school politics and funding to curricular faddism.

From *Education Week*, September 25, 1996, pp. 38, 42.

But it is also true that many of the reports of failure rely on flawed studies, statistics taken out of context, inappropriate generalizations, and so on. These limitations and misrepresentations have been well-documented by researchers at places like RAND and the Sandia National Laboratories, and recently summarized in David Berliner and Bruce Biddle's *The Manufactured Crisis*. So when asked that question about test scores and school failure, I began by admitting the problems with public education, but moved on to discuss, as well, the problems with assessing our schools through a few reductive or inaccurate measures. I suggested that we need to think in richer ways about what we want from our schools.

Four calls followed. One was from a teacher who supported my argument. But three callers weren't buying it. The disagreement wasn't surprising, but what did catch me was the vehemence of the response. It was angry, disbelieving, assured and articulate, and terribly upset. One male caller was furious. He dismissed RAND as being utterly uncredible. He said it was "patently absurd" to say the schools were doing anything right. He claimed that he "didn't know one 17-year-old who could make change."

In *Possible Lives* I write that our country is "in the grip of a nasty reactive politics," and I had tapped it. What has stayed with me from that call—for it was instructive—was the quality of the anger, the rush and the snap of it, and its sweep. It had a tremendous energy to it—it felt assaultive, a bludgeon—and it did not, in any way, invite engagement. For all its passion, it was somehow sealed off from life outside of it. It was different, for example, from the anger of community people I've known seeking to improve a local school gone to seed, an anger fueled by human connection and a vision of possibility.

David Cohen and Barbara Neufield have observed that "schools are a great theater in which we play out [the] conflicts of the culture." The anger of these callers was focused on schools, but, I kept thinking, on more than the schools: on a generation, perhaps, on public institutions, maybe, on the direction of the country. To ask for a reconsideration of its premises or architecture—of the test scores or images of schooling that comprised it—was to ask for the destabilizing of a view of the world. And that, I realized as those calls—and others like them—unfolded, would be harder than I thought to change.

But if there is among some Americans a generalized anger about the schools—and possibly much else about the social order that the schools symbolize for them—there is among others a deep, if sometimes unarticulated, dissatisfaction with the nature of our public discussion of schools, and of our other major social institutions and social problems.

As I've traveled over this last year, I've heard again and again of a weariness with the kind of assaultive language I just described—and with the equally harsh responses that assault can trigger. The result is a divisive and demonizing public discourse that seems to many like a civic dead end.

In addition, many express dissatisfaction with the very way we have come to define our big issues, a sense that our traditional discussions of race relations, the welfare state, our national identity, the public vs. private sphere, and more—that these discussions have become stale, have lost their power to capture the imagination and spark new thought. This dissatisfaction is beginning to find powerful public voice: Lani Guinier calling for a new public conversation on race; Geoffrey Canada urging a more comprehensive understanding of youth violence; Cornel West criticizing our "very limited . . . debate about multiculturalism and Eurocentrism."

Nowhere is this need for an enriched public conversation clearer than with education.

For a generation now, mainstream discourse about education has been framed in terms of decline and embattlement ("If an unfriendly foreign power had attempted to impose on America the mediocre educational performance that exists today," reads *A Nation at Risk*, "we might well have viewed it as an act of war"); economic competitiveness ("We all know that a strong and growing economy depends on an educated workforce," says IBM Chairman Louis V. Gerstner Jr.); and standards ("Standards drive excellence," observes Gov. Tommy Thompson of Wisconsin, "whether it be in business, athletics, or education"). The diction and imagery are drawn primarily from business, sports, and the military. And much of our thinking about reform is framed in such language.

It is, of course, legitimate to worry about the relation between education and the economy, and national and state goals, frameworks, and standards can play a role in improving the quality of schooling. But there is something missing here.

As I sat in those good classrooms in Los Angeles and Chicago, Missoula and Tucson, Wheelwright, Ky., and Indianola, Miss., a richer vocabulary of schooling began to shape itself. To be sure, there was concern about the economy and attempts to prepare students for it. But I also heard talk of safety and respect. A commitment to create safe public space and a respectful regard for the backgrounds and capabilities of the people in it. I saw the effect of high expectations: teachers taking students seriously as intellectual and social beings. I saw what happens when teachers distribute responsibility through a classroom, create opportunities for students to venture opinion, follow a hunch, make something new. I saw the power of bringing students together around common problems and projects—the intellectual and social energy that resulted, creating vital public space. And I saw what happens to young people, 1st graders through 12th, when they come to feel that those who represent an institution have their best interests at heart.

Safety, respect, expectation, opportunity, vitality, the intersection of heart and mind, the creation of civic space—this should be our public vocabulary of schooling—for that fact, of a number of our public institutions. By virtue of our citizenship in a democratic state, we are more than economic and corporate beings.

If we are a nation divided, we are also a nation yearning for new ways to frame old issues, for a fresh language of civic life. The last year has deepened my belief in the strength of this yearning. To generate this language for public education, we need to move a bit from the boardroom and the athletic field and closer to the good classroom—that miniature civic space—to find a more compelling language of school reform and of public education in a democracy.

25   *Saving Public Education*

1997

I have been thinking a lot lately about the way we talk about school—public school in particular. What do we hear on talk-radio, see on the evening news, read in the paper? How do education issues get shaped in legislative debates? How is school depicted in popular culture and how is it characterized in "highbrow" media, of left, right, or center persuasion? I think it's fair to say that, with some exceptions, the talk and imagery about public school tends to be negative, bleak, often cynical, at times vicious. Here are some examples that I read or heard in a two-day period: "America's schools are the least successful in the Western world"; "Face it, the public schools have failed"; "The kids in the Los Angeles School District are garbage."

God knows, there is a lot wrong with our schools—from the way we educate teachers to the often patronizing curriculums we offer our students, the tangles of school politics and the terrible things we assume about the abilities of kids from poor communities. I don't dispute that, have taught in the middle of it, have tried to write about it. And I surely don't dispute the legitimate anger of people who have been betrayed by their schools. But the scope and sweep of the negative public talk is what concerns me, for it excludes the powerful, challenging work done in schools day by day across the country, and it limits profoundly the vocabulary and imagery available to us, constrains the way we frame problems, blinkers our imagination. This kind of talk fosters neither critique nor analysis but rather a grand dismissiveness or despair. It plays into equally general and troubling—and equally unexamined—causal claims about the schools' responsibility for our economic woes and social problems. And this blend of crisis rhetoric and reductive models of causality yields equally one-dimensional proposals for single-shot magic bullets: Standards will save us, or charter schools, or computer technology, or the free market. Each of these can have merit, but careful, nuanced reflection about education gets lost in such fall-from-grace/redemption narratives.

When was the last time you heard extensive, deliberative public talk that places school failure in the context of joblessness, urban politics, a diminished tax base, unequal funding, race and class bias? Or heard a story of

From *The Nation*, February 17, 1997, pp. 20–21.

achievement that includes discussion of curiosity, reflectiveness, uncertainty, a willingness to take a chance, to blunder? How about accounts of reform that present change as alternatively difficult, exhilarating, ambiguous, promising—and that find reform not in a device, technique or structure but in the way we think about teaching and learning? And that point out how we need a language of schooling that, in addition to economy, offers a vocabulary of respect, decency, aesthetics, joy, courage, intellect, civility, heart and mind, skill and understanding? For that matter, think of how rarely we hear of a commitment to public education as the center of a free society. We need a richer public discussion than the one we have now.

Deliberation about school funding and teachers' salaries, about charter schools and national standards, about multicultural education and school-to-work programs and which method of reading instruction to adopt—all take place within a discourse of decline. This language has been with us for so long—at least since the publication of *A Nation at Risk* in 1983—that we accept it as natural and miss the ways it affects our thinking about what public schools should accomplish in a democracy and why and how they fail.

An important project for the left—and though I focus on schools, this applies to a range of social issues—will be to craft a language that is critical without being reductive, that frames this critique in nuance and possibility, that honors the work good teachers do daily and draws from it broader lessons about ability, learning, and opportunity, that scrutinizes public institutions while affirming them.

26 *Extol Brains as Well as Brawn of the Blue Collar*

2004

I am watching a carpenter install a set of sliding French doors in a tight wall space. He stands back, surveying the frame, imagining the pieces as he will assemble them.

What angle is required to create a threshold that will shed water? Where might the sliding panels catch or snag? How must the casings be remade to match the woodwork in the rest of the room? And how can he put it all together fast enough and smart enough to make his labor pay?

This isn't the usual stuff of a Labor Day tribute. Our typical tributes spotlight the economic contribution that the labor force has made to the country, the value of the work ethic. But what about the intelligence of the laborer — the thought, the creativity, the craft it takes to do work, any work, well.

Over the last six years, I've been studying the thinking involved in what is often dismissed as manual labor, exploring the way knowledge is gained and used strategically on job sites, in trade schools and in businesses such as beauty salons and restaurants, auto factories and welding shops. And I've been struck by the intellectual demands of what I saw.

Consider what a good waitress or waiter has to do in a busy restaurant. Remember orders and monitor them, attend to an ever-changing environment, juggle the flow of work, make decisions on the fly. Or the carpenter: To build a cabinet, a staircase or a pitched roof requires complex mathematical calculations, a high level of precision. The hairstylist's practice is a mix of scissors technique, knowledge of biology, aesthetic judgment and communication skills. The mechanic, electrician and plumber are trouble-shooters and problem-solvers. Even the routinized factory floor calls for working smart. Yet we persist in dividing labor into the work of the hand and the work of the mind.

Distinctions between blue collar and white collar do exist. White-collar work, for example, often requires a large investment of money and time in formal schooling. And, on average, white-collar work leads to higher occupational status and income, more autonomy and less physical risk. But these distinctions carry with them unfair assumptions about the intelligence of the people who do physical work. Those assumptions have a long history, from

---

From the *Los Angeles Times*, September 6, 2004, p. B15.

portrayals of 18th-century mechanics as illiterate and incapable of participating in government to the autoworkers I heard labeled by one supervisor as "a bunch of dummies."

Such beliefs are intensified in our high-tech era. Listen to the language we use: Work involving electronic media and symbolic analysis is "neck up," while old-style manufacturing or service work is "neck down."

If society labels whole categories of people, identified by their occupations, as less intelligent, then social separations are reinforced and divisions constrict the kind of civic life we can create or imagine: And if society ignores the intelligence behind the craft, it mistakes prejudice for fact.

Many Labor Day tributes will render the muscled arm, sleeve rolled tight. How many also will celebrate the link between hand and brain? It would be fitting, on this day especially, to have a truer, richer sense of all that is involved in the wide range of work that surrounds and sustains us. We need to honor the brains as well as the brawn of American labor.

27 How Should We Think about Intelligence?

2004

We live in a time of much talk about intelligence. Yet, we operate with a fairly restricted notion of what that term means, one identified with the verbal and quantitative measures of the schoolhouse and the IQ test. And even though scholars like Howard Gardner and Robert J. Sternberg have helped us broaden our understanding of intelligence—with concepts such as multiple intelligences and practical intelligence—we tend to undervalue, or miss entirely, the many displays of what the mind does every day, all the time, right under our noses.

I have just finished a long study of the thought it takes to do blue-collar and service work, welding to waitressing, and it has left me not only with a heightened respect for the intellectual content of such work, but also with a concern about the way we tend to judge people's intelligence by the work they do.

Consider the number of distinctions we readily make about work that carry with them powerful implications about both the work and the worker. These distinctions are usually expressed as binaries, as opposites: brain vs. hand, mental vs. manual, intellectual vs. practical, pure vs. applied, neck-up vs. neck-down. All this is intensified in our high-tech era, and, to be sure, high technology and "symbolic analysis" typically involve advanced formal education and require high levels of analytic skill. What worries me is the way we celebrate the play of mind in such work but diminish, even erase, it in other kinds of work, physical and service work, particularly. In our schools and industries as well as in our informal talk, we tend to label entire categories of work and the people associated with them in ways that generalize, erase cognitive variability, and diminish whole traditions of human activity.

One of the most unfortunate of these dichotomies, particularly in the lives of young people, has been the distinction between the academic and the vocational. This distinction characterized the high school curriculum for much of the past century and has defined entire courses of study. Though it has been the focus of significant reform over the past two decades, vocational education—and, more generally, the divide between the academic and the vocational curriculum—has been one of the most longstanding and visible

---

From *Education Week*, September 22, 2004, pp. 40–41.

institutional manifestations of our culture's beliefs about hand and brain, mind and work.

It is the academic curriculum, not the vocational, that has gotten identified as the place where intelligence is manifest. Such separation plays out on the ground, in the way school people talk, in the formal and informal terms and categories they use. Thus a language of abstraction, smarts, big ideas surrounds the academic course of study, which is symbolically, structurally, and often geographically on the other side of the campus from the domain of the manual, the concrete, the practical, the gritty.

The reforms aimed at bridging the academic-vocational divide—many spurred by the federal Perkins Act—have led to a range of solutions. Yet, any reform movement produces widely varied results. Many efforts are little more than minor adjustments to the status quo. But some efforts are ambitious, involving a cross section of a school's faculty over many months in developing a curriculum that integrates academic and vocational material. And in a few cases, a visionary faculty uses voc. ed. reform as the occasion to reimagine the very structure of high school itself and with it the academic-vocational divide.

Unfortunately, such innovation is rare. Intellectual enrichment, when it occurs, is typically achieved by beefing up the vocational side of things with traditional academic content and courses. As a practical matter, this makes sense; one of the goals of the reforms is to render more students eligible for college, so they need to have the prerequisite academic courses. But conceptually, such practice doesn't move us much beyond the narrow definitions of knowledge that separate hand from brain. These biases about mind and work—which have so influenced schooling—are infrequently raised in reform deliberations. Thus, as the education scholar Theodore Lewis puts it, vocational knowledge is not perceived as valid school knowledge. I believe that this bias will continue to limit a creative rethinking of the academic-vocational divide.

These reductive and limiting ways of thinking about intelligence also affect job training and the way work is organized, even in a time when some industries are trying to restructure and give more responsibility to front-line workers.

Consider the following example, provided by the literacy researcher Glynda Hull and her associates. They spent several years investigating the production of computer circuit boards in a high-tech workplace in California's Silicon Valley. What they found was that although the front-line assemblers were expected to be literate and analytical, the managerial structure of the factory and assumptions by managers about the mental capacity of the assemblers all contributed to a restricted development of literacy skill among the workers. Ms. Hull's cautionary tale reminds us that even at a time of much talk about occupational change—and on the part of some, a real desire for it—there remain in effect powerful beliefs about mind and work that sabotage reform and constrain human potential.

Economic and educational opportunity is typically defined in terms of slots, positions, openings, or, more generally, by the absence of structural barriers to advancement. Just so. Such definitions have been used by the courts to force opportunity where little opportunity existed. But there is another dimension to opportunity, not as obvious, less verifiable, but exceedingly important. As we just saw, it has to do with beliefs about intelligence.

I am not diminishing the kinds of ability that have increasingly formed the core of our century's conception of intelligence, for they clearly enable extraordinary achievement. Rather, I want us to consider other spaces in the picture of human cognition and the effect our partial perception has on the way we think about mind, school, and work.

How should we think about intelligence, particularly in a democratic society? Whatever the basic neurochemical mechanisms of cognition are, most psychologists would agree that the way intelligence is defined and manifested is culture-bound, affected by historical and social circumstances. So it becomes a legitimate act for a culture to ponder its ideas about intelligence: What do our ideas enable or restrict in education, in the economy, in social life? And how do our ideas map onto our foundational beliefs about the person?

As an ideal, democracy assumes the capacity of the common person to learn, to think independently, to decide thoughtfully. The emergence of this belief marks a key juncture in Western political philosophy, and such belief is central to the way we in the United States, during our best moments, define ourselves as citizens. Our major philosophical and educational thinkers—Jefferson, Horace Mann, and John Dewey—have affirmed this potential among us, our intelligence as a people.

The models and language we use have social consequences, a point worth pondering at this historical moment, as we undergo transformations in the workplace, as we struggle to provide a quality education for all. Of course, matters of the economy and of education are affected by a number of forces, but the beliefs we carry about people figure into both the development and implementation of policy. If we believe common work to be mindless, that belief will affect the work we create in the future. If we don't appreciate, if we in some ways constrict, the full range of everyday cognition, then we will develop limited educational programs and fail to make fresh and meaningful instructional connections among disparate kinds of skill and knowledge. If we think that whole categories of people—identified by class, by occupation—are not that bright, then we reinforce social separations and cripple our ability to talk across our current cultural divides.

To affirm our capacity as a people is not to deny the obvious variability among us. Nor is it to retreat to some softhearted notion of mind. We mistake narrowness for rigor, but actually we are not rigorous enough. To acknowledge our collective capacity is to take the concept of variability seriously. Not as a neat binary distinction or as slots along a simplified cognitive continuum, but as a bountiful and layered field, where many processes and domains of knowledge interact. Such a model demands more, not less, from those of us who teach, or who organize work, or who develop social policy. To affirm this conception of mind and work is to be vigilant for the intelligence not only in the boardroom but on the shop floor; in the laboratory and alongside the house frame; in the workshop and in the classroom. This is a model of mind that befits the democratic imagination.

28 Rags to Riches, Republican Style
2005

In "Ragged Dick," Horatio Alger's novel about an enterprising bootblack, one of the author's fictitious benefactors offers the following rosy observation of upward mobility in America: "In this free country poverty is no bar to a man's advancement." The belief that individual effort can override social circumstances runs deep in the national psyche. It's in Ben Franklin, in Alger's immensely popular 19th-century novels—and most recently in the official speeches and well-publicized personal stories of two of George W. Bush's Cabinet nominees, Carlos Gutierrez and Alberto Gonzales. It would have been part of Homeland Security nominee Bernard Kerik's gloss, too— he was the son of a prostitute and a high-school dropout—but other social circumstances prevailed.

Indeed, Republican strategists have long sought candidates and nominees with up-from-the-bootstraps personal histories—an observation made nearly 50 years ago by *New York Times* columnist James Reston—and in Gutierrez and Gonzales, they have two exemplars. At Gonzales' Senate confirmation hearing last Thursday, Sen. Arlen Specter even called the judge's life a "Horatio Alger story." By now, his and Gutierrez' stories are well known. Gonzales was born the son of migrant farmworkers, one of seven siblings living in a two-bedroom house with no hot water and phone. He took his first job at 12, eventually went to Harvard Law School and rose through Texas politics to become Bush's White House counsel. Gutierrez, a Cuban refugee who was 6 years old when his family fled to the States with little money, learned English from a Miami bellhop. He began his career selling Kellogg's Frosted Flakes from a van in Mexico, and nearly 25 years later ascended to CEO.

Gutierrez and Gonzales are clearly exceptional men, and their inspiring stories are served up as evidence of their character and worthiness to serve the nation. Yet Bush's selection of them for Cabinet posts, shrewd on several levels, also warrants examination as cunning political strategy. In choosing them, Bush appeals to Cuban-American and Mexican-American constituencies. And in celebrating these rags-to-riches stories, Bush offers the promise of upward mobility. When Bush named Gutierrez, he called him "a great

From Salon.com, January 10, 2005.

American success story" and "an inspiration to millions of men and women who dream of a better life." By association, the administration counters the perception that the GOP is the party of privilege, and suggests that with Republicans in charge, even people of modest means can prosper and ascend to power: Cabinet member as Everyman. This message is hugely important as the Republican Party continues to court lower- and middle-income voters.

But there is duplicity at the core of the message. Even as Bush holds out Gonzales and Gutierrez as symbols of opportunity, his administration's policies systematically erode opportunity for working people. Since Ronald Reagan's presidency, and with increased vigor under George W. Bush, the nation has witnessed a rolling back of the social protections of the welfare state, a carefully orchestrated opposition to safeguards against inequality and, with that, a widening income gap. The rich—the very rich, especially—are getting much richer, the middle stagnates, and the poor fall off the charts. Opportunity is championed while unions are threatened, workplace health and safety regulations eroded, and an increase in the minimum wage stonewalled.

And yet, one of the most striking things about rags-to-riches, Republican-style tales is that they are accounts of hardship with almost no feel of hardship to them. They reflect a kind of opportunity that exists only in a reactionary fable. (And here they differ significantly from the Horatio Alger originals.) Obstacles receive brief mention—if they're mentioned at all—and anger, doubt, or despair are virtually absent. You won't see the female cannery worker with injured hands or the guys at bitter loose ends when the factory closes. You won't see people, exhausted, shuttling between two or more jobs to make a living or the anxious scramble for minimal healthcare for their kids.

The GOP stories present a world stripped of the physical and moral insult of poverty, not just sanitized—a criticism often and legitimately made—but also distilled, a clean pencil sketch of existence without complication. These tales appear in the Republican rhetoric surrounding any issue dealing with poverty, such as public housing, entitlement programs or welfare-to-work. This erasure of poverty's afflictions makes sense. To do otherwise is to make palpable the dark side of capitalism and the injuries of social class. And conservative strategists have been working very hard, and effectively, to bleach an understanding of class from the public mind.

Along the landscape of Republican rags-to-riches stories, characters move upward, driven by self-reliance, optimism, faith, responsibility. Though there will be an occasional reference to teachers or employers who were impressed with the candidate's qualities, the explanations for the candidate's achievements rest pretty much within his or her individual spirit. The one exception is parents: They are usually mentioned as the source of virtue. Family values as the core of economic mobility.

In the Alger originals, the lucky break, the fortuitous encounter is key to the enterprising hero's ascent. There's little play of chance in the contemporary Republican version. Luck's got nothing to do with it. Nor, it seems, does raw ambition and deal making. There is not a hint of the red tooth and claw of organizational life in these tales. And you surely will not hear a whisper about legislation or social movements that may have enhanced opportunity, opened a door, or removed an obstacle. It would be hard to find a more radically individual portrait of achievement. It should be said that social and economic mobility *is* possible in the United States, more so than in many other countries. It's right to honor it. But does it happen as depicted in the Republican success stories?

In my experience, no. My parents emigrated from Southern Italy in the 1920s, came up very poor, and never finished elementary school. My father took sick when I was young, and my mother supported us as a waitress, always worrying about survival. I drifted through school, somnambulant, until my last year of high school when an English teacher encouraged me, kept after me, and managed to get me into a small college on probation. After one dicey year, I again encountered some immensely helpful teachers who started me on a winding journey that would lead eventually to my career as a college professor. Much of the journey was economically uneven, and if it were not for loans, scholarships, and a range of state and federal programs, I wouldn't have made it. Along the way, I've taught many people with backgrounds like my own. And in the last two decades I have met and interviewed many more.

The stories of mobility I have heard differ greatly from the Republican script. To be sure, there is hard work and perseverance and faith—sometimes deeply religious faith. But many people with these same characteristics don't make it out of poverty. Discrimination is intractable, or the local economy devastated to the core, or the consequences of poor education cannot be overcome, or one's health gives out, or family ties (and, often, tragedy) overwhelm.

The ones that do succeed—and their gains are typically modest—often tell stories of success mixed with setbacks, of two steps forward and one back. Such stories reveal anger and nagging worry, or compromise and ambivalence, or a bruising confrontation with one's real or imagined inadequacies—"falling down within me," as one woman in an adult literacy program put it. This is the lived experience of social class. No wonder that these stories typically give great significance to help of some kind, both private and public. A relative, a friend, or a minister lends a hand. Family and community social networks open up an opportunity. A local occupational center provides training. The government's safety net—welfare, Medicaid, public housing—shelters one from devastation.

It is the right's grand ambition, as William Greider observed several years ago, to roll back the 20th century, to take us back, in policy terms, to the McKinley era. That was a time before the protections of the New Deal and the Great Society, a time of unregulated corporate power and a Social Darwinist view of the social order. The goal is to move the nation, increasingly and on many levels, from education to healthcare to the environment, to the local over the global, the individual over the group, the private over the public. The conservatives would keep government out and let the market determine the order of things.

This is the ideological back story to the feel-good celebrations of Gonzales' and Gutierrez' rise from hardship. As the political agenda of the Bush administration is realized, more and more Americans will be stuck in poverty. Rags-to-riches stories have always been one part possibility, two parts fantasy. But in the present case, there's a bitter deceit involved. Perhaps as antidote, following Greider's lead, we should reread *The Jungle* or *The Shame of the Cities,* placing those early-20th-century accounts of industrial brutality and urban squalor alongside Republican narratives of success. People like those I grew up with and have worked with over the years will be terribly hurt in the world George W. Bush is creating, the ladder of success kicked out from under them.

BIBLIOGRAPHY

Adler-Kassner, Linda, and Susanmarie Harrington. *Basic Writing as a Political Act: Public Conversations about Writing and Literacies*. Cresskill, NJ: Hampton Press, 2002.

Anderson, James D. *The Education of Blacks in the South – 1860–1935*. Chapel Hill: University of North Carolina Press, 1988.

Applebee, Arthur N. *Writing in the Secondary School*. Urbana, IL: National Council of Teachers of English, 1981.

Bartholomae, David. "Inventing the University." *When a Writer Can't Write: Studies in Writer's Block and Other Composing Process Problems*. Ed. Mike Rose. New York: Guilford Press, 1985. 134–65.

Bartholomae, David. "The Study of Error." *College Composition and Communication* 31(3) (Oct. 1980): 253–69.

Bartholomae, David. "Teaching Basic Writing: An Alternative to Basic Skills." *Journal of Basic Writing* 2(2) (Spring-Summer 1979): 85–91.

Beech, Jennifer, "Redneck and Hillbilly Discourse in the Writing Classroom: Classifying Critical Pedagogies of Whiteness." *College English* 67(2) (Nov. 2004): 172–86.

Berliner, David C., and Bruce J. Biddle. *The Manufactured Crisis: Myths, Fraud, and the Attack on America's Public Schools*. Reading MA: Addison-Wesley, 1995.

Betancourt, Francisco, and Marianne Phinney. "Sources of Writing Block in Bilingual Writers." *Written Communication* 5(4) (1988): 461–78.

Beyer, Barry K. "Pre-Writing and Rewriting to Learn." *Social Education* (March 1979): 187–89, 197.

Bloom, Allan. *The Closing of the American Mind: How Higher Education Has Failed Democracy and Impoverished the Souls of Today's Students*. New York: Simon and Schuster, 1987.

Boyer, Ernest. *Scholarship Reconsidered: Priorities of the Professoriate*. Princeton, NJ: Carnegie Foundation for the Advancement of Teaching, 1990.

Cahnmann, Melisa. "The Craft, Practice, and Possibility of Poetry in Educational Research." *Educational Researcher* (April 2003): 29–36.

Clanchy, M. T. *From Memory to Written Record: England, 1066–1307*. Cambridge, MA: Harvard University Press, 1979.

Cohen, David K. "Loss as a Theme in Social Policy." *Harvard Educational Review* 46 (Nov. 1976): 553–71.

Cole, Michael. *Cultural Psychology: A Once and Future Discipline*. Cambridge, MA: Harvard University Press, 1996.

Connors, Robert J. "The Rhetoric of Mechanical Correctness." *Only Connect*. Ed. Thomas Newkirk. Upper Montclair, NJ: Boynton/Cook, 1986. 27–58.

Coogan, David. "Counterpublics in Public Housing: Reframing the Politics of Service Learning." *College English* (forthcoming).

Cooper, Charles R., and Lee Odell, eds. *Evaluating Writing: Describing, Measuring, Judging*. Buffalo, NY: SUNY Press, 1977.

Cushman, Ellen. "The Public Intellectual, Service Learning and Activist Research." *College English* 61(3) (1999): 328–36.

Cushman, Ellen, Eugene Kintgen, Barry Knoll, and Mike Rose, eds. *Literacy: A Critical Sourcebook*. Boston: Bedford/St. Martin's, 2001.

Dreyfus, Hubert. *What Computers Can't Do: A Critique of Artificial Reason*. New York: Harper and Row, 1972.

Durst, Russel K. *Collision Course: Conflict, Negotiation, and Learning in College Composition*. Urbana, IL: National Council of Teachers of English, 1999.

Ede, Lisa. "Reading the Writing Process." *Taking Stock: The Writing Process Movement of the 90's*. Ed. Lad Tobin and Thomas Newkirk. Portsmouth, NH: Boynton/Cook-Heinemann, 1994. 31–43.

Elbow, Peter. "The Doubting Game and the Believing Game: An Analysis of the Intellectual Enterprise." *Writing without Teachers*. New York: Oxford University Press, 1973. 147–91.

Emig, Janet. *The Composing Processes of Twelfth Graders*. Urbana, IL: National Council of Teachers of English, 1971.

Erickson, Frederick. *Talk and Social Theory: Ecologies of Speaking and Listening in Everyday Life*. Cambridge, UK: Polity Press, 2004.

Flower, Linda S., and John R. Hayes. "A Process Model of Composition." Technical Report no. 1, Document Design Project, Carnegie Mellon University, May 1979.

Flower, Linda, and John R. Hayes. "Images, Plans, and Prose: The Representation of Meaning in Writing." *Written Communication* 1(1) (1984): 120–60.

Friere, Paulo. "The Adult Literacy Process as Cultural Action for Freedom." *Harvard Educational Review* 40 (1970): 205–12.

Gardner, Howard. *The Mind's New Science: A History of the Cognitive Revolution*. New York: Basic Books, 1985.

George, Diana. "Working the Streets: Small Press Papers as Agents of Advocacy and Action." Paper presented at Conference on College Composition and Communication, San Francisco, 2005.

Gilyard, Keith, and Vorris Nunley. *Rhetoric and Ethnicity*. Portsmouth, NH: Boynton/Cook-Heinemann, 2004.

Giroux, Henry A. "Writing and Critical Thinking in the Social Studies." *Curriculum Inquiry* 8(4) (1978): 291–310.

Gould, Stephen Jay. *The Mismeasure of Man*. New York: Norton, 1981.

Graff, Harvey. "Reflections on the History of Literacy: Overview, Critique, and Proposals." *Humanities in Society* 4 (1981): 303–33.

Harris, Muriel. "Contradictory Perceptions of Rules for Writing." *College Composition and Communication* 30(2) (May 1979): 218–20.

Heath, Shirley Brice. *Ways with Words: Language, Life, and Work in Communities and Classrooms*. Cambridge, UK: Cambridge University Press, 1983.

Hirsch, E. D. "Cultural Literacy." *The American Scholar* (Spring 1983): 159–69.

Hirsch, E. D. *Cultural Literacy: What Every American Needs to Know.* Boston: Houghton Mifflin, 1987.

Holmes, David G. *Revisiting Racialized Voice: African American Ethos in Language and Literatures.* Carbondale, IL: Southern Illinois University Press, 2004.

Horner, Bruce. *Terms of Work for Composition: A Materialist Critique.* Albany, NY: SUNY Press, 2000.

Hull, Glynda, ed. *Changing Work, Changing Workers: Critical Perspectives on Language, Literacy, and Skills.* Albany, NY: SUNY Press, 1997.

Kinneavy, James L. *A Theory of Discourse.* New York: Norton, 1971.

Kintgen, Eugene, Barry Knoll, and Mike Rose, eds. *Perspectives on Literacy.* Carbondale, IL: Southern Illinois University Press, 1988.

Lanham, Richard A. *Literacy and the Survival of Humanism.* New Haven, CT: Yale University Press, 1983.

Lanham, Richard A. *Style: An Anti-Textbook.* New Haven, CT: Yale University Press, 1974.

Latour, Bruno, and Steve Woolgar. *Laboratory Life: The Social Construction of Scientific Facts.* Beverly Hills, CA: Sage, 1979.

Least Heat-Moon, William. *Blue Highways: A Journey into America.* Boston: Little, Brown, 1982.

Lee, Sy-Ying, and Stephen Krashen. "Writer's Block in a Chinese Sample." *Perceptual and Motor Skills* 97 (2003): 537–42.

Lunsford, Andrea. "Reflections on Our History and Future." Paper presented at the Conference on College Composition and Communication, San Francisco, 2005.

Maimon, Elaine P. "The NEH Institutional Development Program in Expository Writing." Unpublished workshop materials, Beaver College, 1978.

Malinowitz, Harriet. *Textual Orientations: Lesbian and Gay Students and the Making of Discourse Communities.* Portsmouth, NH: Boynton/Cook, 1995.

Mathieu, Paula. *Tactics of Hope: The Public Turn in English Composition.* Portsmouth, NH: Boynton/Cook-Heinemann, 2005.

Matsuhashi, Ann. *Producing Written Discourse: A Theory-Based Description of the Temporal Characteristics of Three Discourse Types from Four Competent Grade 12 Writers.* Ph.D. dissertation, State University of New York at Buffalo, 1979.

Mikulecky, Larry, and Thomas G. Sticht. "Job Related Basic Skills: Cases and Conclusions." *ERIC Clearinghouse on Adult, Career, and Vocational Education* No. 285 (1984).

Odell, Lee, and Dixie Goswami, eds. *Writing in Non-Academic Settings.* New York: Guilford Press, 1985.

Ohmann, Richard. *English in America.* New York: Oxford University Press, 1976.

Orwell, George. "Why I Write." *The Orwell Reader.* New York: Harcourt, Brace and Co., 1947. 390–96.

Peck, Wayne Campbell, Linda Flower, and Lorraine Higgins. "Community Literacy." *College Composition and Communication* 46(2) (1995): 199–222.

Perl, Sondra. *Five Writers Writing: Case Studies of the Composing Processes of Unskilled College Writers.* Ph.D. dissertation, New York University, 1978.

Pianko, Sharon. *The Composing Acts of College Freshman Writers: A Description.* Ph.D. dissertation, Rutgers University, 1977.

Rose, Michael Anthony. *The Cognitive Dimension of Writer's Block: An Examination of University Students.* Ph.D. dissertation, University of California at Los Angeles, 1981.

Rose, Mike. *Writer's Block: The Cognitive Dimension*. Carbondale, IL: Southern Illinois University Press, 1984.

Royster, Jacqueline Jones. *Traces of a Stream: Literacy and Social Change among African American Women*. Pittsburgh: University of Pittsburgh Press, 2000.

Rudolph, Frederick. *Curriculum: A History of the American Undergraduate Course of Study since 1636*. San Francisco: Jossey-Bass, 1978.

Russett, Cynthia Eagle. *Sexual Science: The Victorian Construction of Womanhood*. Cambridge, MA: Harvard University Press, 1989.

Salvatori, Mariolina. "Reading and Writing a Text: Correlations between Reading and Writing Patterns." *College English* 45(7) (Nov. 1983): 657–66.

Scheffler, Israel. "In Praise of the Cognitive Emotions." *Teachers College Record* 79(2) (Dec. 1977): 171–86.

Schroeder, Christopher, Helen Fox, and Patricia Bizzell, eds. *Alt Dis: Alternative Discourses and the Academy*. Portsmouth, NH: Boynton/Cook-Heinemann, 2002.

Scribner, Sylvia, and Michael Cole. "Unpackaging Literacy." *Writing: The Nature, Development, and Teaching of Written Communication*. Ed. Marcia Farr Whiteman. Hillsdale, NJ: Erlbaum, 1981. 71–87.

Seitz, David. "Making Work Visible." *College English* 67(2) (Nov. 2004): 210–21.

Seitz, James. *Motives for Metaphor: Literacy, Curriculum Reform, and the Teaching of English*. Pittsburgh: University of Pittsburgh Press, 1999.

Shaughnessy, Mina P. *Errors and Expectations*. New York: Oxford University Press, 1977.

Sheils, Merrill. "Why Johnny Can't Write." *Newsweek* (Dec. 8, 1975): 58–65.

Shor, Ira. "Our Apartheid: Writing Instruction and Inequality." *Journal of Basic Writing* 16(1) (Spring 1997): 91–104.

Slevin, James F. *Introducing English: Essays in the Intellectual Work of Composition*. Pittsburgh: University of Pittsburgh Press, 2001.

Sommers, Nancy I. *Revision in the Composing Process: A Case Study of College Freshman and Experienced Adult Writers*. Ph.D. dissertation, Boston University, 1978.

Spilka, Rachel, ed. *Writing in the Workplace: New Research Perspectives*. Carbondale, IL: Southern Illinois University Press, 1993.

Sullivan, Patricia, and James E. Porter. "On Theory, Practice, and Method: Toward a Heuristic Research Methodology for Professional Writing." *Writing in the Workplace: New Research Perspective*. Ed. Rachel Spilka. Carbondale, IL: Southern Illinois University Press, 1993. 220–37.

Szwed, John. "The Ethnography of Literacy." *Writing: The Nature, Development and Teaching of Written Communication*. Ed. Marcia Farr Whiteman. Hillsdale, NJ: Erlbaum, 1981. 13–23.

Thaiss, Christopher, and Terry Myers Zawacki. "Questioning Alternative Discourses: Reports from Across the Disciplines." *Alt Dis: Alternative Discourses and the Academy*. Ed. Christopher Schroeder, Helen Fox, and Patricia Bizzell. Portsmouth, NH: Boynton/Cook-Heinemann, 2002. 80–96.

Tyack, David B. "Ways of Seeing: An Essay on the History of Compulsory Schooling." *Harvard Educational Review* 46(3) (August 1976): 355–89.

Veysey, Laurence. *The Emergence of the American University*. Chicago: University of Chicago Press, 1965.

Wells, Susan. "Rogue Cops and Health Care: What Do We Want from Public Writing?" *College Composition and Communication* 47(3) (Oct. 1996): 325–41.

Williams, Joseph. "The Phenomenology of Error." *College Composition and Communication* 32(2) (May 1981): 152–68.

Wilms, Wellford. *Restoring Prosperity: How Workers and Managers Are Forging a New Culture of Cooperation*. New York: Times Business, 1996.

Witte, Stephen P. "Context, Text, Intertext: Toward a Constructivist Semiotic of Writing." *Written Communication* 9(2) (1992): 237–308.

Acknowledgments (continued from p. iv)

Thomas Bentz. "Wood Chuen Kwong: Canton to Chinatown." From *New Immigrants: Portraits in Passage* by Thomas Bentz. Copyright © 1981 The Pilgrim Press. Reprinted by permission.

Pamela J. Brink. Excerpt of 1.5 pages from *The Phases of Culture Shock* by Pamela J. Brink with Judith Saunders. Originally published in *Transcultural Nursing: A Book of Readings* by Pamela J. Brink, editor. Copyright © 1976. Reissued in 1990 by Waveland Press, Inc. Reprinted with permission of the author.

Peter Elbow. "Response to Glynda Hull, Mike Rose, Kay Losey Fraser, and Marisa Castellano, Remediations as Social Construct." By Peter Elbow. From *College Composition and Communication*, Volume 44, No. 4, October 1993. Copyright © 1993 by the National Council of Teachers of English. Reprinted with permission.

Garrett Hongo. "And Your Soul Shall Dance." From *Yellow Light* by Garrett Hongo. Copyright © 1982 by Garrett Hongo. Reprinted by permission of Wesleyan University Press.

Glynda Hull, Mike Rose, Kay Losey Fraser, and Marisa Castellano. "Remediation as Social Construct: Perspectives from an Analysis of Classroom Discourse." From *College Composition and Communication*, Volume 42, No. 3, October 1991. Copyright © 1991 by the National Council of Teachers of English. Reprinted with permission.

Glynda Hull, Mike Rose, Kay Losey Fraser, and Marisa Castellano. "Reply by Glynda Hull, Mike Rose, Kay Losey Fraser, and Marisa Castellano." From *College Composition and Communication*, Volume 44, No. 4, October 1993. Copyright © 1993 by the National Council of Teachers of English. Reprinted with permission.

Glynda Hull and Mike Rose. "This Wooden Shack Place: The Logic of an Unconventional Reading." From *College Composition and Communication*, Volume 41, No. 3, October 1990. Copyright © 1990 by the National Council of Teachers of English. Reprinted with permission.

Thomas Kessner and Betty Boyd Caroli. Excerpt from *Today's Immigrants* by Thomas Kessner and Betty Boyd Caroli. Copyright © 1982 by Thomas Kessner and Betty Boyd Caroli. Used by permission of Oxford University Press.

David Peck and Elizabeth Hoffman. "A Comment on 'Remedial Writing Courses.'" Response by David Peck and Elizabeth Hoffman. From *College English*. Reprinted with permission.

Mike Rose. "Afterword: On Method." From *The Mind at Work* by Mike Rose. Copyright © 2004 by Mike Rose. Used by permission of Viking Penguin, a division of Penguin Group (USA), Inc.

Mike Rose. "Case Studies of Two Students." From pp. 44–69 in *Writer's Block: The Cognitive Dimension* by Mike Rose. Copyright © 1984 by the Conference on College Composition and Communication. Reprinted with permission.

Mike Rose. "Complexity, Rigor, Evolving Method, and the Puzzle of Writer's Block: Thoughts on Composing-Process Research." From *When a Writer Can't Write: Studies in Writer's Block and Other Composing Process Problems* by Mike Rose, editor. Copyright © Mike Rose. The Guilford Press. Reprinted with permission.

Mike Rose. "Education Standards Must Be Reclaimed for Democratic Ends." From *The Chronicle of Higher Education*, July 3, 1991. Reprinted with the permission of Mike Rose.

Mike Rose. "How Should We Think about Intelligence? Bridging the Academic-Vocational Divide." From *Education Week*, Volume 24, Issue 4, September 22, 2004, pp. 40–41. Copyright © 2004, Editorial Projects in Education, Inc.

Mike Rose. "The Language of Exclusion: Writing Instruction at the University." From *College English*, Volume 47, No. 4, April 1985. Copyright © 1985 by the National Council of Teachers of English. Reprinted with permission.

INDEX

447